THE PRESENTED PAST

ONE WORLD ARCHAEOLOGY
Series Editor: P. J. Ucko

THE PRESENTED PAST

Heritage, museums and education

Edited by

Peter G. Stone
Regional Education Officer, English Heritage

Brian L. Molyneaux
Archaeology Laboratory, University of South Dakota

London and New York   In association with English Heritage

First published in 1994 by
Routledge
2 Park Square, Milton Park, Abingdon, Oxfordshire OX14 4RN

Simultaneously published in the USA and Canada
by Routledge
711 Third Avenue, New York, NY 10017

First issued in paperback 2011

© 1994 Peter G. Stone and Brian L. Molyneaux and contributors

Typeset in 10 on 12pt Bembo by Florencetype Ltd, Kewstoke, Avon

British Library Cataloguing in Publication Data.
A catalogue record for this book is available from the British Library.

Library of Congress Cataloging in Publication Data
A catalogue record for this book is available from the Library of Congress.

ISBN13: 978-0-415-09602-7 (hbk)
ISBN13: 978-0-415-51342-5 (pbk)

Contents

    US schools   443
The Native viewpoint in Native American-run museums   446
The creation of exhibits which convey multiple levels of
    information and meaning   448
The value of indigenous views of archaeology   449
Conclusion   450
References   451

32 *The benefits of multicultural education for American Indian schools:
    an anthropological perspective*   453
    J. G. Ahler

    References   459

33 *The transfer of American Indian and other minority community college
    students*   460
    M. J. Belgarde

    Introduction   460
    Community college education   460
    American Indian students   463
    Indian culture, cultural values and belief systems   464
    The conflict of values in higher education   466
        Past education   466
        Finances   467
        Lack of role models   467
        Culture conflicts   467
    The Tribal community college   470
    The success of tribally controlled community college transfer students   472
    Future problems and prospects   473
    References   475

34 *Archaeology, prehistory and the Native Learning Resources Project:
    Alberta, Canada*   478
    H. Devine

    Introduction   478
    Developmental framework   478
    Content validation   480
    Committee interaction   481
    The politics of archaeology   483
    Archaeology, museums and the world outside: a conclusion   488
    Acknowledgements   491
    Note   491
    Editors' note   492
    References   492

List of contributors

Alexis B. A. Adandé, Equipe de Recherche Archéologique, National University, Benin.

Janet Goldenstein Ahler, Center for Teaching and Learning, University of North Dakota, USA.

Ndambi Isaac Akenji, Ministry of Education, Bamenda, Cameroon.

Mary Jiron Belgarde, Turtle Mountain Community College, Belcourt, North Dakota, USA.

Shirley Blancke, Concord Museum, Massachusetts, USA.

Ruud Borman, Municipal Museum, Arnhem, Netherlands.

Lawrence E. Bradley, Department of Archaeology, University of South Dakota, Vermillion, USA.

Mike Corbishley, Education Service, English Heritage, London, UK.

Neelima Dahiya, Department of History, Maharshi Dayanand University, Rohtak, India.

Steve Dasovich, Department of Anthropology, Florida State University, Tallahassee, USA.

Ivonne Delgado Cerón, Museo del Oro, Bogotá, Colombia.

Heather Devine, Independent Researcher, Edmonton, Alberta, Canada.

Mary Engstrom, Vermillion Middle School, Vermillion, South Dakota, USA.

Pedro Paulo A. Funari, History Department, São Paulo University at Campinas, Brazil.

Emilia Moreno de Giraldo, Colegio Nueva Granada, Colombia.

Hélène Guillot, Independent Researcher, Paris, France.

Carolyn Hamilton, Department of Anthropology, University of the Witwatersrand, Johannesburg, South Africa.

John Jamieson, Fort Simpson, Northwest Territories, Canada.

David Kiyaga-Mulindwa, Department of History, University of Botswana, Gabarone, Botswana.

Carlos Eduardo López, Department of Anthropology, Universidad de Antioquia, Medellín, Colombia.

Pierre Masson, Conseil Régional d'Ile de France, Paris, France.

Aron Mazel, Department of Archaeology, Natal Museum, South Africa.

Patrick Mbunwe-Samba, Ministry of Education, Bamenda, Cameroon.

Francis P. McManamon, National Park Service, Cultural Resources, Washington D.C., USA.

Andrezej Mikołajczyk, Muzeum Archaeologiczne i Etnograficzne w Łodzi, Poland.*

Brian L. Molyneaux, Archaeology Laboratory, University of South Dakota, Vermillion, USA.

K. N. Momin, Department of Anthropology and Archaeology, University of Ibadan, Nigeria.

Clara Isabel Mz-Recaman, Museo del Oro, Bogotá, Colombia.

Matthias Livinus Niba, Independent Researcher, Bamenda, Cameroon.

Nwanna Nzewunwa, Faculty of Humanities, University of Port Harcourt, Nigeria.*

Fernando Oliva, Museo de La Plata, Argentina.

Philippe G. Planel, Independent Researcher, Die, France.

Irina Podgorny, Museo Municipal Alte, Brown, Ranelagh, Argentina.

Ajay Pratap, Scada Computer Centre, Bihar, India.

Gilbert Pwiti, Department of History, University of Zimbabwe, Harare, Zimbabwe.

Roberto Restrepo Ramírez, Museo Etnographico de Leticia, Amazonas, Colombia.

Honorio Rivera Reyes, Department of Anthropology, Universidad Nacional, Bogotá, Colombia.

Margarita Reyes, Department of Anthropology, Universidad de Antioquia, Medellín, Colombia.

Gaby Ritchie, Department of Archaeology, Natal Museum, South Africa.

Helga Seeden, Department of Archaeology, American University, Beirut, Lebanon.

Alinah Kelo Segobye, Department of History, University of Botswana, Gabarone, Botswana.

Cjigkitoonuppa John Peters Slow Turtle, Commission on Indian Affairs, Boston, Massachusetts, USA.

Peter G. Stone, Education Service, English Heritage, Bristol, UK.

Peter J. Ucko, Department of Archaeology, University of Southampton, UK.

Peter Wade, Department of Geography, University of Liverpool, UK.

Simiyu Wandibba, Institute of African Studies, Nairobi, Kenya.

Nancy Marie White, Department of Anthropology, University of South Florida, USA.

J. Raymond Williams, Department of Anthropology, University of South Florida, USA.

Leslie Witz, Department of History, University of Western Cape, Bellville, South Africa.

Irénée Zevounou, Equipe de Recherche Archéologique, National University, Benin.

Larry J. Zimmerman, Department of Anthropology, University of South Dakota, Vermillion, USA.

* Deceased

Foreword

This book is the last in the *One World Archaeology* (*OWA*) series to derive from the Second World Archaeological Congress (WAC 2), held in Barquisimeto, Venezuela, in September 1990. Despite many organizational problems (Fforde 1991, p. 6), over 600 people attended the Inaugural Session of WAC 2, with more than 450 participants from 35 countries taking part in academic sessions, and additional contributions being read on behalf of many others who were unable to attend in person.

True to the aims and spirit of WAC 1 over three-quarters of the participants came from the so-called Third and Fourth Worlds (see Fforde 1991, p. 7 for details) and the academics came not only from archaeology and anthropology but from a host of related disciplines.

WAC 2 continued the tradition of effectively addressing world archaeology in its widest sense. Central to a world archaeological approach is the investigation not only of how people lived in the past but also how and why those changes took place which resulted in the forms of society and culture which exist today. Contrary to popular belief, and the archaeology of some twenty-five years ago, world archaeology is much more than the mere recording of specific historical events, embracing as it does the study of social and cultural change in its entirety.

Several of these themes were based on the discussion of full-length papers that had been circulated previously to all those who had indicated a special interest in them, or were available to be read at the Congress. The thematic session from which this book derives was based on two volumes of precirculated papers.

The main aims of the WAC 2 Education sessions were to build on the success of WAC 1's *The Excluded Past: archaeology in education* (edited by Peter Stone & Robert MacKenzie, and now in paperback) by extending the geographic coverage of the school-based case studies, and by moving the focus more onto site and museum presentations of the past.

Perhaps the single most striking outcome of reading *The Presented Past: heritage, museums and education* is the realization that archaeology is currently at a very difficult moment in its development. The difficulty emerges particularly clearly in the context of discussions about archaeology's responsibility to the wider public, whether that public be the adult, free to enjoy a vacation and to visit museums and archaeological sites, or the captive child, forced to study and take examinations. The reader is introduced to the real nature of archaeological data, and the real problems of how its 'meaning' should be 'explained' to others. It is more difficult to attractively present the past as unknown territory, than it is to equate the material remains of the past with identifiable human groups, or datable events.

The Presented Past is exceptional in the breadth of the case studies presented, especially as it includes authors from such diverse places as the Canadian Arctic, west central Africa and several from Latin America. These case studies vividly bring to life the excitement and enjoyment experienced by children when they are taught about the past through the objects of the past, rather than as history known only to the modern world through the written texts of others. There is little doubt that a hands-on experience is attractive to both young and old. Yet until now there has been little discussion about what such 'direct' experience of the past is intended to achieve – beyond the recognition that it is a 'good' teaching experience. The student remembers more about the past through hands-on education – but more of what? Constructing one's own wooden long-house, making pots, using objects of the past as models for new artistic and technical creations, may be creating a past that is in some way 'concrete', and certainly tangible, but is it in fact creating the past, rather than merely creating a contemporary experience related to current interpretations of past processes? The people of the past were different, as they worked in very different contexts and cultural environments.

In the multidimensional aims of education, however, none of this can be seen to be bad. Indeed, hands-on experience may be essential to its aims of encouraging pride in the past, recognizing the longevity of tradition, or stressing the complexities and ingenuity of those who have gone before. Meanwhile, archaeology as a discipline has come of age, pointing out the subjectivity of much archaeological interpretation, and insisting that it must make explicit the biases (hidden agendas) of those who have accumulated archaeological data and of those who have subsequently interpreted them. Archaeologists have recently developed a self-conscious self-awareness regarding the way that archaeological evidence has often been used to 'fabricate' a (or, the) past that is the most appropriate one for those in power, for those with nationalistic aspirations, or for those seeking to establish pedigrees for their ethnic identities (see *The Politics of the Past*, edited by Peter Gathercole and David Lowenthal; *Social Construction of the Past: representation as power*, edited by George Bond and Angela Gilliam). Such self-reflective caution finds little echo in the presented 'certainties' of school-based archaeological activity in learning.

The Presented Past reveals, in fascinating detail, a range of very real problems, hitherto unrecognized except in theoretical or vague terms. The ingraining (in some cases indoctrination) of a gender-biased, peoples-specific, technologically-evaluative approach to the past begins, all over the world, as soon as children enter their first schools (though much of it may begin even earlier than this, in the home). For those countries in the happy position of having a tertiary education system which includes the teaching of archaeology, such instruction therefore needs to include the breaking down of such attitudes and, in its place, to present the past as a 'construction' in itself. In the vast majority of cases this does not happen; instead, what is presented is a firmly culture-historical approach to archaeological interpretation (all too often within a university degree in history).

This book also demonstrates some of the potential ramifications of a restrictive culture-historical approach to the presentation of the past. In the choice of what is to be presented in museum displays, highlighted in site sign-posting and tourist guides, culture-history all too often retains its domination. Educating the public about the past, in the avowed hope of preserving the physical remains of the past, often remains overtly based on appeals to pedigree, whether a pedigree of overt nationalism, regionalism or ethnic identity. Site and museum visits therefore have an inbuilt tendency to reinforce culture-historical preconceptions and stereotypes, boosted by the acontextual nature of western-based museum collecting and display, and a particular 'frozen' moment in time selected, captured and presented at, and as, an archaeological site. We seem as far away as ever (but see *Sacred Sites, Sacred Places*, edited by David Carmichael, Jane Hubert, Brian Reeves and Audhild Schanche) from being ready to present cultural landscapes unless they are characterized by human artefactual materials.

The Presented Past reveals the surprising way that, in certain contexts at least, the wider implications of such museum and site displays are often not quickly appreciated by those in authority, or may continue to suit their aims, despite apparent dramatic shifts in power. Thus, for example, 'Bushmen' culture may be seen to be both 'prehistoric' (rock paintings) and 'amusing' (songs, dance and steatopygia) whether those in charge of museums form part of an illegal white minority government or are part of a majority, non-'Bushmen', nationalist enterprise. In both, very different, instances of the use of the archaeological past by those in authority it is apparently felt necessary either to distance the physical evidence of the past from living investment, or at least make knowledge about the past inaccessible to all but the privileged. The past, in many cases, appears to be too important a commodity to allow its archaeological evidence to become the playground for all; it remains the preserve of those in positions of influence who claim to 'know' the past, to have the right to preserve aspects of it, and who deny the possibility that its on-going vitality should be allowed to result in re-interpretation, in modification of its outward characteristics – or even in its destruction.

This is not to suggest that this book is all about a static kind of archaeology. On the contrary, it is full of examples of movement, experimentation and change as the authors of its chapters explain and analyse their own attempts to counteract some of the above problems and difficulties. The overall picture is one of bold experiment, of attempts to encourage intelligent discrimination by the onlooker between alternative 'explanations' of the past, and of the remodelling of many antiquated 'sacred cows'. It is often also a picture of children involved in detective enquiry, in myth-creation and in growing self-awareness.

The Presented Past, therefore, is a lively work which demonstrates, in a highly unusual way, the actual dilemmas of current archaeological enquiry and application. The hugely curious, hungry minds of children, with their enviable capacity for invention, and for creating their own worlds, are frequently presented with interpretations of the past which – through schoolbooks, museum displays and site visits - often deliver up the past as just one more nail in the coffin of a dead, remote irrelevancy or, alternatively, as just one more building block in the evidence of a past which is recognizable and self-justifying in the interests of the identity of a particular group or people.

This book should facilitate current debate about the realities involved in the study of the past, and it should assist in relating these to the educational means available to exploit such studies. For many years, in the UK at least, academic archaeologists have paid lip service to the importance of spreading the lessons gained from archaeological endeavour to the wider public (Evans 1995). *The Presented Past* clarifies why to do so is a complex matter, raising fundamental questions about the very nature of archaeological enquiry. At the same time it points to the inherent difficulties in the assumption that it is clear what messages should be spread. Above all, perhaps, it demonstrates that, in spite of the many and varied problems involved – or even, in some respects, because they exist – education about the past is an essential aspect of human growth and endeavour.

P. J. Ucko
Southampton

References

Evans, C. 1995. Archaeology Against the State: roots of internationalism. In *Theory in Archaeology: a world perspective*, Ucko, P. J. (ed.). London: Routledge.
Fforde, C. 1991. The Second World Archaeological Congress (WAC 2). *World Archaeological Bulletin* 5, 6–10.

Preface

This book records the continuing efforts of archaeologists and educators to analyse some of the intensely complex political, social, economic and educational problems associated with the teaching of the past. Most of the chapters were first prepared for the Education theme at the Second World Archaeological Congress (WAC 2), Barquisimeto, Venezuela, in September 1990. This thematic meeting – subdivided into four sessions: 'The Wider Context of the Teaching of Archaeology'; 'The Presentation within Education of the Cultures of Indigenous and Minority Groups'; 'Archaeology in Formal Curricula'; and 'Education about Archaeology through Museums' – was organized by one of the present editors (Peter Stone) with the assistance of Shirley Blancke, Gareth Binns, Patrick Mbunwe-Samba, Iain Watson and Xavier Balbé. In order to bring such a diverse and exciting group of papers to publication Peter Stone was joined as co-editor by Brian Molyneaux.

While most of the chapters in this book were presented by their authors as part of the proceedings of the Congress in Barquisimeto, others were only available as precirculated papers or abstracts (those authors who were unable to be present in Barquisimeto were Adandé & Zevounou, Devine, Jamieson, Masson & Guillot, Momin & Pratap, Oliva and Planel). Perhaps the saddest absence was Patrick Mbunwe-Samba – stuck thousands of miles away in the Cameroon although only a matter of miles away from his waiting air ticket – for he had contributed so much to make the organization of the theme a success.

The majority of chapters in this book have been extensively revised and edited since 1990, in the light of discussions at the Congress and, frequently, after long and interesting correspondence with the editors. In some cases this has led to the combining of two original precirculated papers into one chapter. We thank those individuals concerned for their help and perseverance during this particular exercise. Borman's and Ucko's chapters were especially commissioned after the Congress for this book.

We are very sad to record that two contributors have died since WAC 2:

Andrezej Mikołajczyk and Nwanna Nzewunwa. Their chapters are reproduced here with only minor editing.

Our thanks go to contributors for their patience during the lengthy period which it has taken to get this volume to press. Peter Stone owes especial thanks to Genevieve, who sighed with reluctant understanding when he originally agreed to take on the organization of the theme for WAC 2, and then the joint editorship of this book. Brian Molyneaux offers similar thanks to Wendy. We also thank Jane Hubert for continual encouragement and for commenting on our Introductions. Most of all, we thank Peter Ucko who, as Series Editor, has guided, cajoled and inspired us to produce what we believe is an important contribution to the understanding of the modern use (and abuse) of the past.

Finally, we thank the *South African Historical Journal* for permission to reproduce the contribution by Witz & Hamilton.

Peter G. Stone
Southampton, UK

Brian L. Molyneaux
Vermillion, USA

Introduction: the represented past

Brian L. Molyneaux

The wonderful city of Jaipur was created in the eighteenth century by the philosopher maharaja Jai Singh. The pink city was built in a green wooded valley near a small lake; and it is plain that, initially, Jai Singh wanted to plan the place on the basis of the 'Vastupurusha mandala', nine squares within a square which, according to the teachings of the ancient Vedic 'shastras', was a model of the cosmos, with each square corresponding to a heavenly body. Jai Singh was forced to compromise this perfect pattern to take account of a hill and to encompass an existing village, so one of the smaller squares was detached and moved to the east.

(Anon 1992, p. 21)

Creating the past

The notion that a world culture can be created simply through improvements in technology and universal education in the sciences has lost much of its credibility in the last few years (see Friedman 1989). Science may advance, but we all move ahead through the past of our own cultures, and it is this cumulation of ideas and experience, transmitted through education and sheer daily living, that gives our thoughts meaning and our actions pattern and purpose (see Bourdieu 1977). It is not that we live in the past, but we are defined by it (cf. Lowenthal 1985, p. 185; Layton 1989, p. 3), and so the success of even the most forward-looking developments must inevitably rest on their relation to the ideas and practices of the society they are meant to serve. Science may forget its own history, but a society cannot (see, for example, the chapters in Bodley 1988, which treat issues concerning development schemes and tribal (indigenous) societies).

The need to think about advancement in social and historical terms, taking into account culturally specific ways of seeing and doing, has dramatically transformed the archaeological concept of the past and made this discipline more relevant to contemporary concerns. The 'past' was once thought to be concrete and uncontroversial, the foundation of ideologies and nations written in historical texts and stone, but recent events once again reinforce how fragile the unity created out of the past may be, as long-established nations with entrenched ideologies have been wiped off the map in virtually an instant in time, leaving some peoples in the throes of internecine strife. The problem is that the actual past is always out of reach. Even material remains, no matter how old they are, are perceived and used in the present – and so, paradoxically, they are ageless, endlessly transforming as the society around them changes. There are then two pasts: the temporal one that passes and is gone and the metaphorical 'past' that is held in the memories and traditions of a society and its surroundings. It is this diverse and ever-changing past, part of the multifarious world of ideas and personal and collective agendas of a society, that we encounter in our daily lives and through which we must work.

This book is about this important and so often tendentious idea of the 'past' and the problems related to its presentation through archaeology in the modern world. How the past is represented and communicated is the significant aspect here, as ideological and political processes at work in a society are revealed in the way they affect such knowledge resources. In a given society, for example, some versions of the past may be highly visible and even iconic, especially if they are caught up in the webs of power that suffuse social relations and structures; others may be hidden, overlooked or intentionally excluded (MacKenzie & Stone 1990) – the pasts of the marginalized, the unenfranchised, the ignored and unwanted.

Our primary concern is with 'excluded' pasts, and this for two main reasons. One is fundamentally archaeological, as the analysis of received knowledge is as vexing and critical to the analysis of the past as is the study of the material remains of an excavation site; but the most important reason is moral (see Ucko 1990, p. xx; also see Klesert & Powell 1993), as we attempt to use archaeological knowledge and techniques to remove some of the dead weight of received wisdom and tradition in the presentation of the past, to relieve an ideological burden that is felt most keenly by the oppressed. To accomplish this, we explore the rich diversity of alternative histories held and shared by people in modern societies by first considering how the past is confronted, portrayed and taught across the world (as first done in a previous volume, *The Excluded Past* (Stone & MacKenzie 1990)). Then we outline the efforts that archaeologists and teachers are making to bring together the ideologies of education with the material evidence and knowledge of the past provided by archaeology in order to counter the controlling myths of the past in their communities. All of us, editors and authors alike, hope that the approaches in this volume will help encourage others to bring the diversity visible on the streets, pathways and neighbourhoods of modern communities into their museums, classrooms and other guiding institutions so that excluded pasts will no longer exist.

Explaining the past

The integration of archaeology and education might seem to be a simple task, but as material evidence takes its meaning from its perception and use (cf. Hodder 1982 and Binford 1982), what it represents varies according to the agenda within which it is used. In spite of what may be empirically known about an object, site or prehistoric society (see Wylie 1989 for a recent discussion of the problem), the material past and the ideological past may come into conflict.

Formal education is particularly vulnerable to disputes about the interpretation of the past because of its importance as an ideological tool in society. Education in its most common sense is not the anarchy of direct and wordless encounter between individual and surroundings but a socially structured learning process, where, it is said, one learns one's place in a social group and, hence, in the world (cf. Funari Ch. 7). When experience is organized in this way, to constitute 'education', learning moves from the realm of direct experience to a world where information is created, selected and directed (via a formal curriculum or implicit agenda) to a specific audience. The distinction is important, for in the former, experience is the teacher, but in the latter, there is most often a teacher to rationalize and guide experience. Guided and organized learning is advantageous, as it gives individuals socially specific knowledge resources and abilities to help them meet the challenges in their lives. But this advantage does not come without cost: as mediated learning does not confront the world directly, it is subject to the vicissitudes of its own history, manipulated not by the chance of nature but by the activities of individuals and groups over time (cf. Vygotsky 1978 and Piaget 1962). Such guided education is therefore implicitly or explicitly bound up in the 'past' – implicitly, as it uses the vast metaphorical resources of social experience, codified and institutionalized according to a group's way of communicating ideas and other information about the world (cf. Bourdieu 1977), and explicitly, where it is formalized in subjects such as history and archaeology. And this is the problem: the past that is presented may be that of a single, dominant group in a society or, as is so common in countries now independent but with a colonial past, one that still reflects the colonialist view.

Because of the critical role of education in a society, much of the book is concerned with the young – but as defining and communicating an authoritative version of the past is one aspect of wider ideological control, there is always much to be revealed, and to promote, about the past to the public at large, and so the most important focus of the book is on the ways and means of presenting the past, whether in museums, classrooms, through the media, or in the streets. The need to develop and encourage a capacity in the public to respond critically to what they see and hear is crucial. Brookfield (1986, p. 151), for example, suggests with regard to educating adults to interpret mass media that:

the representations of political realities presented on television and in the press are often culture specific, influenced by vested interests, and reflect an unchallenged ideological orthodoxy. The mass media, sometimes deliberately but frequently unwittingly, tend to offer distorted, crudely simplistic, personalized analyses of political issues. A major task of adult education must be to remove this perceptual poison from individuals' minds and to nurture in them a healthy skepticism toward ideologically biased explanations of the world.

The chapters address some of the fundamental questions about perception and control in representations of knowledge as they pertain to 'archaeology education'. Who is doing the promoting and at what level – a national institution, such as a large museum or a universal curriculum, or, at the opposite end, a local museum installation or a school or classroom, where the interests and concerns are mainly local? And who has control over the representation of the knowledge: education or media professionals or local community people? And at the local community level, are the teachers of the same community and culture as the pupils? As the chapters in this book reveal, the answers are never simple, but the authors share the conviction that a past revealed for all its diversity is important to the future success of a world community in the midst of great transition, as old empires crumble into smaller, more homogeneous groups and new and more culturally varied unions develop.

Housing the past

The biggest problem – a conundrum, in fact – is that it is difficult, even impossible, to distinguish the past from the objects, structures and institutions that carry it today – indeed, in a sense, they are one and the same (consider here, for example, Wittgenstein's concept of the bounds of language (e.g. 1958), Bourdieu's (1977) notion of officialization, and Giddens's (1984) idea of structuration). This is clearly so with regard to ancient ruins or other sites and structures, simply because they are the material remains through which we recreate the past; but it is also the same for museums, culture houses, libraries and other repositories that have grown up as shelters for objects and records and descriptions of the past – and for educational institutions. For the self-consciously selective accumulation of material objects in museums, their conservation in heritage sites, the storage of ideas in books and in other forms of mnemonic tradition and the communication of this information through formal and informal education do not preserve 'the' past; rather, each institution provides the structure (architectural and ideological) within which much more specific pasts are conceived, structured, reinforced and promulgated.

In modern architecture, such intentions are commonly made explicitly. The design of the new Municipal Museum in Yatsushiro, Japan, for example, expresses both a commitment to international standards of museum curation and local values in the presentation of the historical artefacts it contains (Pease 1992). To accomplish this, the architect Toyo Ito adopted a radical solution: the main gallery, the largest space, is buried in an artificial hill, whereas the storage areas, metal-clad, are above ground. Ito explains (quoted in Pease 1992, p. 35):

> in contrast to the conventional museum where storage space is located out of sight, I wanted to show that a museum is the place for keeping artefacts as well as for showing them to the people. The idea of locating the storage in the air can be found in old Japanese 'Shosin' where storage space is located higher than the spaces for daily living.

Without such objects and institutions to remind and educate us (physically and intellectually) that there are ostensibly greater or more inclusive pasts than our own, our individual and social lives would be utterly different (cf. Layton 1989).

The creation of a coherent (cohesive) past (a formal history) through the institutionalization of past events and experiences and their material traces has great significance in this book, for every chapter is concerned with either renovating existing material and ideological structures, or breaking them down and building new ones. Institutions all seem designed to keep some people, ideas and practices out and some in – and so the chapters explore what (and who) the institutionalized 'past' includes and what it excludes, and they all attempt to recover and use such excluded pasts in a constructive way, in the attempt to create doors that are open to all.

The structure of the book

The book has been organized to reflect our interest in the role of the presented past in social institutions, and so it moves from overviews to particulars, covering issues associated with the interpretation of the past to the public at large, examines how such information is disseminated through museums and schools, and considers how alternative museums, displays and curricula can be developed to reflect our increasing social diversity (diversity that has come either from the increasing movement of people from place to place, or from the recognition of groups formerly unrecognized).

The concept of the public itself is as important an issue here as the concept of the past – both these terms are symbolic monoliths that obscure the actual situation in any culture. There is no single 'public' as there is no single 'past', and so, when educational programmes attempt to reach a generalized public, whether through museum displays or educational curricula, the results may be highly selective.

Sometimes this selectivity may be intentional – reflecting political agendas designed to develop or perpetuate 'national' or 'cultural' identities (sometimes with the intention either to assimilate or to ignore local diversity) (see Funari Ch. 7; Mazel & Ritchie Ch. 16; Witz & Hamilton Ch. 1; Ucko Ch. 17); and so some chapters explore ways for a society to revive or rediscover ideas and relations to the past that existed prior to invasion, occupation and exploitation by colonialist powers (e.g. Adandé & Zevounou Ch. 21; Kiyaga-Mulindwa & Segobye Ch. 2) or dominant elites (Podgorny Ch. 29; Reyes Ch. 28; Wade Ch. 30; Wandibba Ch. 24), while others struggle with the often conflicting challenges of maintaining a distinct cultural identity under fire (López & Reyes Ch. 8) or after protracted war (Seeden Ch. 5) and advocating or debating multiculturalism in education (e.g. Ahler Ch. 32; Belgarde Ch. 33; Blancke & Slow Turtle Ch. 31; Devine Ch. 34; Jamieson Ch. 35; and see Mbunwe-Samba, Niba & Akenji Ch. 22; Ucko Ch. 17).

In other instances, the general public agenda may simply reflect the relent-less inertia of ideas of history and the constructed past that are perpetuated in monuments and buildings and the heritage and education curricula designed to promote them (see Funari Ch. 7). It may not necessarily be practicable, or wise, or even possible, to replace such an infrastructure without dismantling society itself. And furthermore, trading a single self-interested group or system for a set of self-interested groups or systems may not necessarily create a healthy, 'multicultural' coalition that will further the aims of a repressed minority (or majority). The goal in many chapters is therefore not so much to deconstruct received ideologies, rigid classrooms and fusty buildings and so destroy the old, but rather to infuse already existing structures with new ideas and build diversity into them, reaching out to the public and engaging them, rather than simply expecting them to fall into place (e.g. Borman Ch. 12; Dahiya Ch. 20; McManamon Ch. 3; Momin & Pratap Ch. 19; Oliva Ch. 6; Pwiti Ch. 23; White & Williams Ch. 4). Indeed, such renovation is in the spirit of the late Andrezej Mikołajczyk (Ch. 15) and Nwanna Nzewunma (Ch. 18), who wanted to breathe life into history by taking museums outside into the streets (and see Borman Ch. 12).

The importance of this striving for encounter and participation, understand-ing monuments by living in them (however briefly and imaginatively, e.g. in Corbishley & Stone Ch. 27, Giraldo Ch. 10, Planel Ch. 14, Ramirez Ch. 11, Stone Ch. 13), and working in classrooms and museums with the materials, techniques and objects of the past (see Delgado Ceron & Mz-Recaman Ch. 9 and Masson & Guillot Ch. 26), is to re-enact part of the unspoken rhythm of life that, unlike our ideas, connects us through the fundamental comparability of our bodies and senses with the past. 'In the beginning the deed; then language comes to describe and discuss' (Ackerman 1988, p. 56).

If we are to develop a new understanding of the past, one that appreciates the complexity of its messages, then we must recognize and learn to deal with a public that is equally diverse – a confusion of individuals and groups in endless networks and levels of relations, who seem to be coherent only when joined by the circumstances of a collective task or idea. If this spirited, multitudinous history can be demonstrated through archaeology and education, then the often oppressive hold of national cultures and special interest groups, with their self-serving appeals to a general public, may be transformed into something more sensitive to the chaotic and dynamic interplay of communities, groups and individuals that actually make up a society.

Programming the past for the future

The variety of scenarios, activities and ideas found in this book show that there is no simple prescription for the study of the past, even though there are compelling reasons for giving the past back to peoples to whom it has been denied through lack of control over their own lives. Current events in our war-torn world, such as the break-up of Yugoslavia, convulsed in bitter conflict in the name of past enmities, suggest that it is naive to think that knowledge of a particular past is intrinsically good or necessary. Given that the past is a metaphorical resource (cf. Lowenthal 1985) providing information that can be drawn upon for virtually any social enterprise, some might think that many of our social problems might be eased by forgetting, rather than reinforcing the memory of past disputes and differences, crimes and glories – but the past (as experience) also teaches us lessons. What is certain is that metaphors of the past (represented as facts) were used, and probably always will be used, to justify both good and evil, depending on the situation.

This makes all those striving for historical and social identity vulnerable, as the struggle for information and rights of access to it is caught up in the dynamics of ideological control. Indeed, no amount of moralizing or legislation can identify just what level of 'past' should be supported and promulgated, as the value of the presented past to the life and well-being of an individual or group depends on whose interest is at stake (see Rowlands 1989, pp. 36–9, and see Ucko Ch. 17 for a compelling illustration of this complex issue; also consider in general the problems (in an archaeological perspective) of inequality (e.g. Miller, Rowlands & Tilley 1989) and ethnicity (e.g. Shennan 1989)).

A fundamental complication here is the clash between the commonly acknowledged need to eliminate forms of oppression based on social categories, such as race, class and gender, and the opposite struggle for individual and collective social identity, which spawns ethnicity and, hence, separateness (see Miller, Rowlands & Tilley 1989, p. 2). This issue is certainly behind the continuing controversy about ethnically or culturally specific education and multiculturalism (cf. Belgarde Ch. 33 and Ahler Ch. 32). The restoration or recreation of an 'excluded past', in the form of a more localized or specific knowledge, may possibly be disadvantageous because it fails to address the structural aspects of oppression (cf. Rowlands 1989, p. 37). The point (and the problem) is that, although an individual or group may gain identity, the notion of difference, and the system of reinforcing it, may still persist:

> A local cultural 'avant-garde' can form itself around the ethos of resistance to the status quo through the construction of as many accounts of localized pasts as there are people, or social groupings, willing to produce and act towards them. This not only frees the participants engaging in any genuinely collective project, but the idea that all pasts are essentially incomparable and unique serves to deny any verification process or assertions concerning the capacity for such different versions to account for a reality as externally constituted to them. An unintended consequence of such politics is to reinforce hierarchy, since although the subordinated and the powerless may have identity, the powerful will lay claim to science as the only means of ensuring an independent access to truth and knowledge.
>
> (Rowlands 1989, p. 38)

In spite of such risks, however, the exploration of the past at a local, community level still has the advantage of being at least potentially closer to the diversity of interests in a social group and more distant from the influence of external resources and programmes set up by outsiders, whether they are from other countries or from a dominant social group or force within the country (consider, for example, Ucko Ch. 17) – indeed, at this level, at least, it may be more possible for individual voices to be heard and acknowledged, and for pasts to be explored that are more consistent with actual social and material experience. And most clearly and resolutely, such a focus gives to the public a greater opportunity to evaluate critically what they hear, see and are taught in institutionalized settings about origins and histories and restores to them the rights to expression of their own experiences and traditions, no matter how such ideas and practices may vary with the authoritative views of archaeologists and educationalists (see Ucko Ch. 17; see Klesert & Powell 1993 for a recent discussion of the rights and privileges of archaeologists with regard to indigenous pasts).

Localizing research and education in archaeology may also be necessary simply to maintain a sense of identity within a society at large. Recent research in mass education and national curricula (Benavot, Cha, Kamens, Meyer & Wong 1991) has found a marked similarity in primary school curricula throughout the world, in spite of variations in culture (and therefore inconsistent with functionalist and historicist theories about the nature and development of national curricula (Benavot, Cha, Kamens, Meyer & Wong 1991, pp. 96–7)). Beyond the emphasis on national culture, these authors cite the influence of the modern world system as a possible factor in this standardization, as the notion of what constitutes desirable knowledge becomes oriented to global, rather than local, concerns. They note that 'the prescription of mass education is endemic, encouraged by international organizations, by professional elites, and by the dominant powers throughout the modern period' and that 'to some extent the mass curriculum is directly defined and prescribed through the influence of international organizations (e.g. the World Bank and United Nations organizations), through the models provided by dominant nation-states, and the education professionals who operate on a world-wide basis'. Such influences are not, however, simply coercive, as they 'find receptive audiences in national societies and states eager for legitimacy and progress'. Standardization is therefore – paradoxically – attached to the struggle for identity, for these authors conclude that 'national identity in the modern world-system is achieved through conformity to the institutionalized ideals' (Benavot, Cha, Kamens, Meyer & Wong 1991, pp. 97–8). The threat to diversity is therefore more than a matter of asserting local variations in the face of a national culture, as mass culture easily penetrates willing nations to reach and mould their diverse populations. Indeed, these authors unexpectedly found that national influences were relatively unimportant with regard to curriculum structure and they ask (Benavot, Cha, Kamens, Meyer & Wong 1991, p. 98): 'how much local "resistance" is there? How aware are local educators of worldwide curricular trends apart from the particular policies of their authorities?'

In recognition of the complex problems presented by institutionalization (in the study and explication of the past), the development and promulgation of mass curricula and other authoritative programming and other moral, ethical and practical issues surrounding the representation and control of the past, the book does not provide general guidelines for the use of the past in education, or a general solution to the abuse of the past (as exposed in works such as Stone & MacKenzie 1990). It does, however, attempt to show how individuals and groups in many parts of the world are attempting to deal with their own particular situations – trying to sort out the conflicting claims and goals of national and regional, collective and individual histories and relations in the attempt to better the lives of their communities.

Conclusion

The preservation of the past is important, if only to perpetuate the memories of our own lives and those of our close relations – but it also seems necessary to help define our place in a social group and community, as made abundantly clear by the archaeologists and educationalists who have contributed chapters to this book. At the same time, however, some of the problems that these authors have faced in their work suggest that the past may also be a dangerous place, part of the repertoire of dominance in a society that can, and all too frequently does, lead to open conflict. This problem, that the past is an essential, but dangerous, social need, is a conundrum that cannot be resolved here (cf. Rowlands 1989).

An important idea that emerges from the experiences outlined here is that innovation in the conception and use of the past is not necessarily accomplished by a simple change in historical 'facts' or curricula. First, there must be an appreciation of the difficulty that many individuals and groups have in competing within systems and institutions designed to preserve and perpetuate singular, officialized and authoritative pasts – most often about, or defined by, the dominant group in a community. Indeed, as I have suggested above, such pasts are an intrinsic part of the material objects selected for analysis and display and the material and intellectual structures that house and maintain them (see Mikołajczyk Ch. 15). Thus, a specific curriculum that may have a narrow focus and reach only into the shallowest historical depths may not be improved by simply adding more information, or a museum improved by adding or changing displays – the very nature of the objects and information representing the past, and the forms and structures of communication, may need to be reconsidered. Second, there must be change in the institutions that create the past, and perhaps the informational infrastructure as a whole, to be sensitive to new and diverse ways of seeing and relating to the ever-increasing information that emerges from the archaeological study of actual social interaction, past and present.

In practical terms, those involved in representing and teaching about the past must consider not only the diversity of peoples and histories within their own societies and so widen the scope of their presentations but also be aware that no past is necessarily sacrosanct, that tradition can also be a burden and a form of control.

The challenge, therefore, is to use techniques that make people aware and respectful of the past, but do not burden them so much with received traditions (with their attendant benefits and dangers) that they cannot adapt to a changing world. Otherwise, traditional monolithic national cultures may simply be exchanged for a range of similarly exclusive special-interest groups competing against one another for control (cf. Rowlands 1989).

This enlightened approach can only begin to develop, however, if those who hold responsibility for mass education accept the importance of the alternative histories within their midst. Unfortunately, gaining the favour of intellectual and political leaders may have little effect on the inertia of institutions. In some countries such histories are simply overwhelmed by the generalized concerns of national institutions and programmes, but in others, especially in former colonies, the problem is that the national infrastructure may still reflect the priorities and practices of colonialism. Although one may attempt to resolve this problem by attempting to bring together a diversity of interests under a single roof, such an approach may only create more generalities, rather than taking into account individual experience and the practical interaction of people in specific communities in specific situations (see Ucko Ch. 17). We therefore need to take the past back to the community, to provide the means for ordinary people to deal with this metaphorical world at least partly out of sight and reach of those who would control it, so that they may reflect on the past, critically, through their own social experience in their own environment.

In order to create a sympathetic environment for such a transformation, archaeologists must take advantage of the real interest shown by the general public in the past by presenting and explaining their work – but we must do this with reference to the people we are trying to reach. As Zimmerman, Dasovich, Engstrom & Bradley (Ch. 25) ask, with regard to the practical problem of bringing archaeology to schools:

> Are we attempting through our educational endeavours to bring the public into line with our goals? Is this reasonable? Teachers have different goals from archaeologists. They are concerned with a variety of issues ranging from entertaining students to maintaining discipline, from teaching critical thinking or mathematical skills to teaching factual content in subject areas. Few archaeologists go beyond simply mentioning the broader educational goals or issues. . . .
>
> Teachers are therefore forced to try to adapt our aims to their own, with little help from us.

We thus return to the fundamental issues of the nature of representations of the past and their control, and the position of archaeologists and teachers as creators, mentors and guides in the reinforcement and spread of such knowledge. The ethical issues involved in this important responsibility in a North American context are voiced by Klesert & Powell (1993, pp. 351–2) in this way:

> There is an obligation to educate the public about what archaeologists do and why it is important. This is seen by many as a way of resolving the current problem of perceptions shared by those who dislike archaeology. Goldstein and Kintigh (1990: 588) provide a reality check to this belief by pointing out that educating people as to our point of view will not make them accept it as their own. Education does, however, serve to resolve the problems accompanying ignorance (such as fear, misinformation, and intolerance), and should be pursued. It can only help, if archaeology really does provide something of value. We would add a rhetorical question: Why is this education not mutual? Are Indians the only ones who need it, or could archaeologists gain some perspective by learning, really understanding, the Indian point of view . . .?

The way forward is not therefore a choice between relativism or absolutism, or a rejection of the scientific basis for world prehistory, motivated by the desire to recognize local traditions and sensitivities, but rather to advance through transaction, by working towards mutual understanding (cf. Rowlands 1989, p. 34). As the quotations above suggest, archaeologists and teachers need to learn as they teach.

It is this spirit of engagement that best symbolizes the practical efforts of the authors here to achieve a greater measure of social justice in the study of the past in their own countries and situations. They are all motivated by the belief that, if there is going to be a shared vision of the future, there must be a recognition of the multiple pasts that have determined the present in which we stand. How this complex vision is presented in the future by archaeologists and teachers can help determine whether a society disappears into a larger entity or, if it survives, whether it will be enclosed and oppressive, or an open landscape of communities.

References

Ackerman, R. J. 1988. *Wittgenstein's City*. Amherst: University of Massachusetts Press.

Anon 1992. Mystic labyrinth. *Architectural Review* 1139, 20–6.

Benavot, A., Y.-K. Cha, D. Kamens, J. W. Meyer & S.-Y. Wong 1991. Knowledge for the masses: world models and national curricula, 1920–1986. *American Sociological Review* 56, 85–100.

Binford, L. 1982. Objectivity – explanation – archaeology 1981. In *Theory and Explanation in Archaeology*, Renfrew, C., M. J. Rowlands & B. Abbott Segraves (eds), 125–38. New York: Academic Press.

Bodley, J. H. 1988. *Tribal Peoples and Development Issues: a global overview*. Mountain View, Calif.: Mayfield Publishing Company.

Bourdieu, P. 1977. *Outline of a Theory of Practice*. Cambridge: Cambridge University Press.

Brookfield, S. 1986. Media power and the development of media literacy: an adult educational interpretation. *Harvard Educational Review* 56, 151–70.

Friedman, J. 1989. Culture, identity and world process. In *Domination and Resistance*, Miller, D., M. Rowlands & C. Tilley (eds), 246–60. London: Unwin Hyman.

Giddens, A. 1984. *The Constitution of Society*. Cambridge: Polity Press.

Goldstein, L. & K. Kintigh 1990. Ethics and the reburial controversy. *American Antiquity* 55, 585–91.

Hodder, I. 1982. Theoretical archaeology: a reactionary view. In *Symbolic and Structural Archaeology*, Hodder, I. (ed.), 1–16. Cambridge: Cambridge University Press.

Klesert, A. L. & S. Powell 1993. A perspective on ethics and the reburial controversy. *American Antiquity* 58, 348–54.

Layton, R. 1989. Introduction: who needs the past? In *Who Needs the Past? Indigenous values and archaeology*, Layton, R. (ed.), 1–20. London: Unwin Hyman; Routledge pbk 1994..

Lowenthal, D. 1985. *The Past is a Foreign Country*. Cambridge: Cambridge University Press.

MacKenzie, R. & P. Stone 1990. Introduction. In *The Excluded Past: archaeology in education*, Stone, P. & R. MacKenzie (eds), 1–14. London: Unwin Hyman; Routledge pbk 1994.

Miller, D., M. J. Rowlands & C. Tilley 1989. Introduction. In *Domination and Resistance*, Miller, D., M. J. Rowlands & C. Tilley (eds), 1–26. London: Unwin Hyman.

Pease, V. 1992. Archetypal links. *Architectural Review* 1139, 32–6.

Piaget, J. 1962. *Comments on Vygotsky's Critical Remarks concerning 'The Language and Thought of the Child', and 'Judgement and Reasoning in the Child'*. Cambridge, Mass.: MIT Press.

Rowlands, M. J. 1989. A question of complexity. In *Domination and Resistance*, Miller, D., M. J. Rowlands & C. Tilley (eds), 29–40. London: Unwin Hyman.

Shennan, S. J. 1989. Introduction: archaeological approaches to cultural identity. In *Archaeological Approaches to Cultural Identity*, Shennan, S. J. (ed.), 1–32. London: Unwin Hyman; Routledge pbk 1994.

Stone, P. & R. MacKenzie (eds) 1990. *The Excluded Past: archaeology in education*. London: Unwin Hyman; Routledge pbk 1994.

Ucko, P. J. 1990. Foreword. In *The Politics of the Past*, Gathercole, P. & D. Lowenthal (eds), ix–xxi. London: Unwin Hyman; Routledge pbk 1994.

Vygotsky, L. 1978. *Mind in Society: the development of higher psychological processes*. Cambridge, Mass.: Harvard University Press.

Wittgenstein, L. 1958. *Philosophical Transactions*. Oxford: Basil Blackwell.

Wylie, A. 1989. Matters of fact and matters of interest. In *Archaeological Approaches to Cultural Identity*, Shennan, S. J. (ed.), 94–109. London: Unwin Hyman; Routledge pbk 1994.

Introduction: a framework for discussion

PETER G. STONE

Introduction

This book is about the confluence of four approaches to the interpretation and presentation of the past: academic or theoretical archaeology; indigenous views of the past; school history; and the past as presented to the general public in museums and at 'historic sites'. All four approaches have their own priorities and agendas but, although they frequently draw on different sets of data, they have as their common thread the interpretation of past human activity. Central to all of the following chapters is a belief that the presentation of the past, in school curricula and in museum and site interpretations, will benefit from a greater understanding of how the past is interpreted by archaeologists and/or indigenous peoples.

Within academic archaeology during the past twenty or so years there has been an increase in the number of archaeologists who have argued for the extension of teaching about archaeology to an audience wider than their own students. The reasons have varied at different times and from person to person, and have included the desire to extend the understanding of the development and progress of the human species (for example, Alcock 1975, p. 2); the belief that the study of archaeology can be used as a tool to extend the 'judgement and critical power' of students of all ages (for example, Evans 1975, p. 6); and as a preparation for the study of archaeology at university (for example, Dimbleby 1977, pp. 9–10).

This interest in more extensive teaching about archaeology can also be seen as part of the much wider debate that has discussed the role and value of the past as an element of public 'heritage' (see, for example, Wright 1985; Lowenthal 1985; Hewison 1987; Cleere 1989; Layton 1989, 1990; and see Ucko Ch. 17). While many (?most) museums and historic sites seem to be concerned with the presentation of a frequently static, well-understood past that reflects the achievements of a specific period – and frequently a particular section of society – as part of a national inheritance (Hewison 1987), modern archaeology is more concerned with questioning the validity of any interpretations or presentations of the past (see, for example, Hodder 1986; Shanks & Tilley 1987), arguing, for example, that 'interpretation owes as much to the interests and prejudices of the interpreter as to the inherent properties of the data' (Renfrew 1982, p. 2).

At the same time, the study of the past in schools is predominantly the study of the past as documented by written records and, as such, is universally referred to in curricula as 'history'. This emphasis on the documentary past not only excludes much of prehistory from school curricula but has also tended to exclude the interpretation of the past through archaeological study and through indigenous (and usually oral) views of the past as well (Stone & MacKenzie 1990). Given this school view of 'the past', the contemporary archaeological suggestion that the past is 'constructed' – and is therefore open to constant reinterpretation and coexisting different interpretations – is one that does not easily equate with the way that history is taught in school curricula (see Stone & MacKenzie 1990).

This book chronicles various attempts to link together some or all of these four aspects of teaching about the past. All of the projects described in the following chapters have particular local or specific aims and objectives – for example, the introduction of 'archaeofiction' in classrooms in France (Masson & Guillot Ch. 26) or the introduction of indigenous values into local education policy (Jamieson Ch. 35) – but they all also share a common belief that an extension of the way(s) in which the past is studied and understood by students and/or members of the general public would be a 'good thing' and, if it is achieved, will enhance contemporary, and future, society as a whole. This is a belief that is frequently left largely unsubstantiated by its adherents – partly, at least, because it is almost impossible to quantify. There is, for example, no empirical evidence to prove that a greater understanding, on the part of the general public, of what can be gained from the archaeological study of a given site will ensure any greater level of protection for that site, or for any other site. However, the association between greater understanding and better protection has been accepted by many as a worthy aim to pursue (Seeden Ch. 5; Gregory 1986; Cleere 1989, pp. 8–9) and there is certainly no evidence to refute the suggested association. Equally, the argument that students have better judgement and critical awareness because they have studied the past through archaeology, as opposed to the more usual document-based study of the past, has, to my knowledge, never been systematically tested until the recent work in India reported here (Dahiya Ch.20). Dahiya's work certainly suggests that those students who studied the past through an archaeological rather than a document-based approach did learn and retain more information and, at the same time, appeared to enjoy the work more. Dahiya's work introduces a specifically educational element to the debate: from an educational point of view the success of one methodological approach over another (effectively 'hands-on', as opposed to didactic) is just as important as the fact that one group of children now has more information about the past than another, as the successful methodology may be transferable to other subjects. Until recently archaeologists have, perfectly legitimately, taught about the past in order to increase the amount of information assimilated and understood by their students about a particular period or culture. More recently, as archaeologists have seen their subject used – and abused – for political and social advantage (Layton 1989, 1990; and see Ucko Ch. 17), many of them have accepted a wider role for archaeology. This wider role is also based on the acceptance that archaeology has an educational role, in that it is a subject that requires students to work critically and carefully, without accepting any single 'true' version of the past.

This educational role of archaeology – illustrated in one instance by the methodological work of Dahiya – has yet to be accepted by those in control of teaching about the past. Also ignored is the educational role of indigenous views of the past (see, for example, Blancke & Slow Turtle Ch. 31; Jamieson Ch. 35) and any educational benefit of teaching specifically about prehistory (and see Corbishley & Stone Ch. 27).

Formal curricula

The acceptance by archaeologists of the educational importance of the wider teaching of the past – much of which has been defined as 'the excluded past' (MacKenzie & Stone 1990) – has its roots in a relatively few practical initiatives that go back little further than the mid-1970s (see, for example, Stone & MacKenzie 1990; McManamon Ch. 3; Podgorny Ch. 29; Corbishley & Stone Ch. 27). Unfortunately, there has been little or no comparable acceptance of the value of teaching about the excluded past within the world of formal education (Corbishley & Stone Ch. 27; and see Stone & MacKenzie 1990). Extolling the virtues of an 'excluded past' as an essential part of a curriculum is not the same as making it part of that curriculum. The following chapters bear continued witness to the gulf between the need for inclusion expressed by archaeologists, other academics and indigenous and minority groups, and the general failure to accept this need by those with power within the educational establishment (see, for example, López & Reyes Ch. 8; Mbunwe-Samba, Niba & Akenji Ch. 22; McManamon Ch. 3; Wandibba Ch. 24; Witz & Hamilton Ch. 1). Even where part of the excluded past is recognized – for example the existence of the past of a particular indigenous group – other significant minority groups may be overlooked (Wade Ch. 30) or dealt with unsympathetically (Podgorny Ch. 29).

It is an important point that, if the 'excluded past' is to be accepted within the curricula of formal education, its value must be couched *in educational terms*, as defined above. Zimmerman, Dasovich, Engstrom & Bradley (Ch. 25) (and see Davis 1989) suggest that most archaeologists want to teach archaeological skills and ideas in the classroom, whereas educationalists look for the means to stimulate the educational, rather than archaeological, development of children. Zimmerman, Dasovich, Engstrom & Bradley (Ch. 25) caution that continued attempts to teach archaeology in schools, without reference to the priorities of educationalists, will merely confirm the view of the latter that archaeology has no role within school curricula.

The excluded past is not always simply ignored as irrelevant, however (MacKenzie & Stone 1990, pp. 3–4). It may be kept out of the curriculum because education authority finance is controlled by those who, for political reasons, explicitly oppose its presence, as Jamieson (Ch. 35) describes in his attempts to introduce indigenous culture in a school curriculum in northern Canada. Occasionally, a pragmatic need is identified that results in the exclusion of specific archaeological information where its inclusion would destroy a consensus fundamental to the acceptance of using any archaeological information in the curriculum: Devine (Ch. 34) describes such an occurrence where the good working relationship between educators, archaeologists and Native people was threatened by a disagreement over the interpretation of some specific information. The problem was avoided by the omission of certain parts of the archaeological interpretation, which itself raised the question of control and ownership of the interpretation of the past (and see Ucko Ch. 17). In other instances, the study of archaeology and prehistory may be the victim of attitudes about their economic potential and so is denied resources. This problem is especially clear in Third World countries, as development programmes ignore the teaching of the 'excluded past' under the belief that it has little or no immediate economic value (for example, Kiyaga-Mulindwa & Segobye Ch. 2; Mbunwe-Samba, Niba & Akenji Ch. 22, although see Ucko Ch. 17; Addyman 1991; and Collett 1992 for discussion of an alternative view of the economic value of the archaeological heritage). Other developing countries regard it as a vocational subject and therefore do not include it in employment planning (Wandibba Ch. 24).

Despite these practical problems the work that archaeologists and others are now putting into producing new educational materials and courses, as described in many of the following chapters, is not only encouraging but also critical to the future of heritage education. However, convincing the educational establishment that these efforts are not merely attempts to ensure the existence of archaeological jobs is not easy, and requires co-operation among government departments, educational authorities and teachers (see, for example, Devine Ch. 34; Jamieson Ch. 35). The nurturing of such an acceptance also requires those fighting for the extension of the study of the past to develop a theoretical and educational basis for their arguments. It is, and has always been, insufficient to argue that the 'excluded past' should be taught 'because it is important' – such bland statements have almost certainly contributed to the exclusion of the prehistoric, archaeological and indigenous pasts from school curricula around the world. Some of the following chapters outline the history (if any) of such arguments (see, for example, Corbishley & Stone Ch. 27; Podgorny Ch. 29; Zimmerman, Dasovich, Engstrom & Bradley Ch. 25) and some (Dahiya Ch. 20) set out methodological arguments for teaching about the past with the help of archaeological information. A few

(Devine Ch. 34; Planel Ch. 14; and see Blancke & Slow Turtle Ch. 31; White & Williams Ch. 4) actually begin to address why and how the way the past is taught should be extended.

Informal learning

The co-operation between archaeologists and those involved in the planning and organization of formal curricula is, however, only one aspect of teaching about the past. Although success in this area may go some way towards guaranteeing that future societies will be more aware of the reasons for the preservation, study and interpretation of the historic environment, there is a pressing need to educate contemporary society, if the fragile database is not to be lost before any such enlightened future societies take on responsibility for its preservation. A number of authors refer to the continuing destruction of the historic environment and the associated illicit trade in antiquities (see, for example, McManamon Ch. 3; Pwiti Ch. 23; Ramirez Ch.11; Seeden Ch. 5; Zimmerman, Dasovich, Engstrom & Bradley Ch. 25).

The issues and events referred to in these chapters emphasize that education concerning the protection and preservation of the material past must consist of more than merely claiming that it has intrinsic value. Archaeologists need to know and, equally important, must be able to explain why such tangible evidence is vital – if they are to stop the theft of artefacts and the careless or intentional destruction of sites. If archaeologists do not explain why the physical heritage is important, they cannot blame those who, having no archaeological training or education, consciously or unconsciously destroy, or sell, parts of that heritage (see, for example, with relation to damage caused by metal detectors in the UK, Gregory 1986). Such explanations will vary from archaeologist to archaeologist and from situation to situation, but will always include the statement that archaeological evidence (as well as indigenous views of the past) can, and will, be used as a means of interpreting the past, in addition to documentary sources.

This use of archaeological evidence can enrich an individual's – or a society's – understanding of the past and, used in this way, can be regarded as beneficial. However, if access to the evidence of archaeology is not available to all, through its inclusion in formal and informal education programmes, then society runs the risk of the interpretation of archaeological evidence being biased – as it was, for example, in Germany in the 1920s and 1930s (and see Podgorny Ch. 29; MacKenzie & Stone 1990). If such a message is put across well enough, and is convincing enough, then there may be some justification in the belief that contemporary society will protect the historic environment for future generations. Time is of the essence here, as the failure to include archaeological interpretation in curricula can be argued to have contributed to the lack of understanding on the part of the general public, with regard to the archaeological-cum-educational-cum-political importance of sites. This can lead to a situation such as that found in Colombia, where so-called (by the archaeological community) 'looters' see nothing wrong in digging into burial sites – even attempting to legitimize their activities by applying to form their own trade union (Ereira 1990, p. 21). Similarly, in Lebanon, the public appear to be content to sit back and watch the wholesale destruction of archaeological sites (Seeden Ch. 5). It follows that archaeologists, and others who control the data of the past or who regard themselves as having a custodial role with regard to the historic environment, must use every means available to them – including film, television, radio, newspapers and popular publications – to reach the general public (see, for example, Frost 1983; Hoare 1983; Bender & Wilkinson 1992; Groneman 1992; Borman Ch. 12; Seeden Ch. 5; Momin & Pratap Ch. 19). There are, of course, dangers associated with this approach: media communications is an industry in its own right and responds first to business imperatives, rather than cultural or academic ones, thus creating a constant risk of distortion or sensationalizing archaeological material (Momin & Pratap Ch. 19; Witz & Hamilton Ch. 1). Indeed, as Seeden points out (Ch. 5), publicity can actually *increase* the likelihood of the destruction of archaeological sites by attracting people to them in search of 'buried treasure'. However, the potential benefits in informing society at large must surely outweigh such concerns (Andah 1990a, 1990b; Burger 1990, pp. 148–9; Ekechukwu 1990, p. 125; McManamon Ch. 3). It is essential that those already involved in this work begin to co-operate and share their successes and failures, if the present rate of destruction is to be stemmed. In addition, those archaeologists who take on this responsibility must not be penalized in their careers, as they seem to be in some parts of the world, including the United States of America, by an out-of-date peer assessment process that sees such work as less important than other aspects of an archaeological career (Bender & Wilkinson 1992). Nor must archaeologists continue to ignore the value and importance of teaching about communication within archaeology undergrad-uate courses. A number of universities offering archaeology degrees now have optional courses in heritage management, and some of these include a lecture on heritage education. Such courses, together with the study of archaeological tourism, should be included as necessary components of all archaeology degree programmes throughout the world, and should incorporate both academic and practical training (see Ekechukwu 1990).

Museum display

The traditional method of communicating with the general public has been through museum display. However, despite huge advances in the methods and technology of display, museums still reach only a tiny proportion of the population (Hooper-Greenhill 1991a). A number of contributors argue that museums are generally regarded as places for specialists or particular (usually elite) groups within society (e.g. Nzewunwa Ch. 18; Wandibba Ch. 24). This point is supported by Andah (1990b) in his assertion that African museums were created *for* the colonial population *about* the indigenous population. Andah's argument is all the more depressing when he suggests that little has changed in museum displays since the independence of African states – a point supported by Mazel & Ritchie (Ch. 16) in their discussion of Botswana and Zimbabwe and also discussed by Ucko (Ch. 17) in his analysis of the present plans for the development of the National Museums and Monuments of Zimbabwe. Further north in Africa, it is interesting (even shocking?) to note that less than 5 per cent of the visitors to the Cairo museum are Egyptians (Boylan 1991, p. 10). Andah (1990b) argues strongly that museum and cultural tourism must be aimed first and foremost at the local population, since anything else simply maintains the colonial dependency of, in his case, Africa, on the western world. Ekechukwu (1990) develops the point by emphasizing that local tourism is an essential element of the creation of a national identity, and the creation of a national museum for the national population has been identified as one of the four most vital symbols of independent nationhood perceived by newly independent governments (Boylan 1991, p. 9). Andah (1990b, p. 152) looks forward to a time when 'The museum can begin to be transformed from a reservoir of folklore for tourists thirsting for exotics, to a living image of the past, a source of culture, a crossroad for ethnic culture, a symbol of national unity'. And, in much the same way as Ucko (Ch. 17) supports the ideal of culture houses in Zimbabwe, he sees such museum centres as being designed to

> serve the function of the market place in the African past – namely an open air school; a forum for healthy debate, formal and informal on any problems of life – an institution available to all with its greenery, its gardens, local flora and fauna, aquariums and ponds, special exhibition halls (featuring both permanent and temporary exhibitions) recreational (theatre) areas, hair dressing salons, restaurants serving local dishes, craftsmen at work, craft and technology experimentation units etc.
>
> (Andah 1990b, p. 152)

The important point is that this is not a museum in the conventional western sense but rather it is an attempt to create an institution that emerges from traditional African society and custom.

Western museum structures and contents may, as Devine argues (Ch. 34), actually alienate Native peoples by presenting stereotypes of their culture – and so make such peoples museum pieces themselves (see also Hall 1991). This often unconscious stereotyping has not only adversely affected the relationship between two groups (archaeologists and Native peoples) who could be working together in the presentation of the past, but has also helped to reinforce a negative image of Native peoples among the rest of society. The insensitivity to the beliefs of Native peoples in the museum environment is testified to by Momin & Pratap (Ch. 19), who describe a scene in which some 'ethnic groups' visiting museums bow down and leave religious offerings in front of images of gods and goddesses, and are understandably upset that their sacred objects are regarded by those in authority as museum artefacts (and see Andah 1990b, p. 149; Carmichael, Hubert, Reeves & Schanche 1994). It seems obvious that Native peoples and other minority or oppressed groups should be consulted on the display and interpretation of objects related to their pasts. Indeed, such consultation should also extend to the content of formal education syllabuses referring to Native cultures (see Devine Ch. 34; Jamieson Ch. 35; Riley 1992). Unfortunately, this creative – and appropriate – approach to curriculum development does not appear to be commonplace (see Andah 1990b; Momin & Pratap Ch. 19; Ucko Ch. 17).

The International Code of Professional Ethics adopted by the International Council of Museums (ICOM) in 1986 'insists that the development of the educational and community role of the museum must be seen as a fundamental ethical responsibility' (Boylan 1991, p. 10). In order to meet this ideal – in effect to be successful in attracting people to visit museums and heritage sites and to help them to leave happy, fulfilled and somewhat the wiser – museum staff need to agree on the function of their institutions and their presentational role (Lowenthal 1993). They need to ask 'not only "who are we serving?" but, more important, "who are we not serving?" ' (Hall 1991, p. 14).

Hall (1991, p. 11) lists a set of fundamental questions asked of southern African museums at the start of such a review. They have relevance everywhere:

Why do museums educate?
Who are our audiences?
How should we educate?
When and how often should we present programmes?
Where should we present programmes?
By whom should the programme be carried out?
What are the main subjects we ought to teach?

A number of authors offer similar tentative checklists to be discussed when setting up new exhibitions (e.g. Borman Ch. 12; Delgado Ceron & Mz-Recaman Ch. 9; Giraldo Ch. 10; Nzewunwa Ch. 18). Borman (Ch. 12) argues that for too long European museums have been concentrating on how archaeologists know about the past rather than what information they have about it. He accepts that archaeological remains tend to be fragmentary records of a past culture removed from their original context that will never present a 'true' picture of what life was like in the past, but he argues that even such relatively mysterious objects can be used as an 'entrance' to the past, where visitors, having been given an introduction to the evidence by an exhibition, can be challenged to make their own personal conclusions about what life may have been like (also see Delgado Ceron & Mz-Recaman Ch. 9; Mikolajczyk Ch. 15; Stone Ch. 13). In this way visitors may begin to relate to museum displays in a

way that was impossible when one 'correct' story was disseminated through a
didactic exhibition.

These developments are a very long way from the opinion expressed in 1968
by an English professor of history (and quoted in Olofsson 1979) when he
argued:

> Let me say at once that I hate the idea of museums being used
> primarily as teaching aids of any sort. Their first job is to house
> valuable objects safely and display them attractively. . . . The
> second responsibility is to those who are already educated, to the
> student, the collector, the informed amateur. . . . A third responsi-
> bility to put above anything specifically educational is, in the case of
> certain museums, a loyalty to their own personalities.

Olofsson rejects this opinion and the chapters in her book reflect the recently
more common view of museums as educational tools. However, just as there
is at present a lack of communication between archaeologists and educationalists over the teaching of the past, so Olofsson identified 'insufficient contacts'
between museum staff and 'the school system, the main recipient of their
services' as being the major obstacle to the developed use of museums in
education (Olofsson 1979, p. 11).

While some of this lack of communication has now been resolved, at least in
western museums – especially through the hard work of many museum-based
education officers (see, for example, Hooper-Greenhill 1989) – there are still
many practical obstacles and problems to overcome before the two worlds
work in harmony. For example, in the Cameroon, Mbunwe-Samba, Niba &
Akenji (Ch. 22) note that most secondary-level history teachers never take
their students to museums nor, in fact, have many of the teachers actually been
to the museums themselves. Similarly, a recent survey in India shows only 1
per cent of history teachers using museums as part of their normal teaching
(Raina 1992; see also Dahiya Ch.20). In a recent study in England only two out
of ten museums had any liaison with the local education authorities (HMI
1990). Only when such links are made between curriculum planners and
museums can the 'abysmal gap' (Delgado Ceron & Mz-Recaman Ch. 9)
between museums and formal curricula be closed. And if this gap is not closed,
museums are 'in danger of becoming irrelevant, expensive luxuries' (Hall
1991, p. 13).

We seem to be now faced with a three- (sometimes four-)way failure of
communication (archaeologist (indigenous expert)/educator/museum curator)
that must be solved before museums will be able to take a major role in the
teaching of the past within formal education.

Archaeologists and, where they exist, museum education staff, who work
on the fringes of formal education, have helped to develop teaching programmes that extend the database that children can use to study the past. A
number of contributors describe attempts to develop museums as active rather
than passive partners in teaching children about the past (see, for example,

Dahiya Ch. 20; Delgado Ceron & Mz-Recaman Ch. 9; Giraldo Ch. 10; Mbunwe-Samba, Niba & Akenji Ch. 22; Nzewunwa Ch. 18). The unifying factor in all of these projects is the use of authentic historic artefacts as stimuli for creative work that encourages children to begin to understand the reasons why archaeologists and others value the past rather than simply to learn dates and 'facts' and visit 'treasures' behind glass cases.

Previous studies of the advantages of teaching within such a creative 'hands-on' experimental framework have in the main failed to make a direct comparison between their success and a more didactic approach (Olofsson 1979). Dahiya (Ch. 20) confronts this failure head-on and provides powerful testimony by doing so. Unfortunately, she faces enormous practical problems in convincing teachers in India to move towards a more 'hands-on' approach to teaching about the past, as over 86 per cent of Indian history teachers rely almost entirely on a 'lecture/narration method' of teaching (Raina 1992, p. 24). According to Raina, the purpose of teaching about the past in Indian schools seems to be to pass exams and 'it is a myth to think of teaching history to either "develop the skills of a historian" or to develop a proper attitude and interest in the subject' (Raina 1992, p. 26).

Such developments (as suggested in the chapters noted above) in how museums communicate and display their historic collections require the retraining of museum staff (see Adande & Zevounou Ch. 21; Mbunwe-Samba, Niba & Akenji Ch. 22; Pwiti Ch. 23; Reeve 1989; Stone 1993) and the introduction of, at least, discussion of the role of museums within undergraduate archaeology, history and education courses (Andah 1990a, p. 155; Kiyaga-Mulindwa & Segobye Ch. 2). On a more practical level, in Zimbabwe, for example, plans are presently being developed for the introduction of a Certificate in Heritage Education (Stone 1994). While this course was initially conceived as part of an internal staff development programme, other countries have expressed interest in using it as a basis for similar courses. In Kenya, annual seminars organized by the National Museum aim to reduce the gulf between museum educators and their counterparts within formal education (Karanja personal communication, and see Uzzell 1989 for a number of case studies of the training of interpreters). Such retraining must become commonplace before museums can take on their leading role in the extension of the database used in the teaching of the past.

The role of Native people in curriculum development and museum display

As part of this extension of teaching about the past, both archaeologists and educationalists must accept that there are indigenous specialists in the past who are outside the western academic and pedagogical traditions, but who nevertheless should have a central role to play in the development of teaching about their own pasts (see Ahler Ch. 32; Belgarde Ch. 33; Blancke & Slow Turtle

Ch. 31; Devine Ch. 34; Jamieson Ch. 35). Archaeologists have consistently offended the sensibilities of Native peoples by excavating burial sites and removing sacred objects and other significant cultural materials as a matter of routine, as have museums and academic institutions by studying and displaying such objects for educational and entertainment value (see Hubert 1989, 1991). Although such insensitivity is declining (at least in some areas), encouraged by legislation that often compels archaeologists and museums, among other things, to consult with Native groups and their specialists (see McManamon Ch. 3), archaeologists and museum curators still have considerable problems in interpreting and displaying the results of archaeological research to Native people – especially where, so often, the different interpretations conflict with one another (and see Carmichael, Hubert, Reeves & Schanche 1994). However, if these professionals cannot work with and appreciate the beliefs and feelings of those that they often most directly affect, then what hope is there of changing the common charge that archaeology is simply a self-indulgent pastime?

Similarly, the idea of a common curriculum across countries that contain culturally diverse groups has led to educational systems which are often insensitive to the different intellectual and social traditions of the students they are trying to reach (Belgarde Ch. 33). This is not a particularly new observation and was, for example, at the heart of Kenyatta's dislike of European education:

> We have therefore to ask ourselves whether a system of [indigenous pre-Colonial] education which proves so successful in realising its particular objectives may not have some valuable suggestion to offer or advice to give to the European whose assumed task it is in these days to provide Western education for the African.
>
> (Kenyatta 1938, p. 120)

The failure of western-style education even to take note of indigenous methods of education has resulted, in many instances, in the alienation of the majority of Native students (see Belgarde Ch. 33; Blancke & Slow Turtle Ch. 31; Devine Ch. 34). Several authors advocate new approaches to curriculum, which make use of the educational insights of traditional Native teachers, rather than simply relying on western-oriented and educated curriculum theorists (eg, Ahler Ch. 32; Devine Ch. 34; Jamieson Ch. 35). Others go even further, arguing for an integration of 'universal' and Native approaches (Blancke & Slow Turtle Ch. 31) or placing Native students in tertiary education in their own schools (Belgarde Ch. 33; also see Burger 1990, pp. 146–7). Of fundamental importance here is that most 'indigenous' systems of education have a strong foundation in the traditional beliefs of their particular group. By imposing western-style curricula on indigenous peoples educationalists have – often as a conscious decision – removed them from their own cultural heritage (see, for example, Barlow 1990; Kehoe 1990; Watson 1990).

The future

There are eight specific ways in which those committed to the teaching of the past, which includes the evidence of archaeology, and the viewpoints of indigenous groups, can help to bring about such an extension of school history and public presentation and interpretation. Wherever possible they should:

- develop professional courses in collaboration with education authorities in the presentation of archaeological evidence and indigenous viewpoints;
- stress the importance of communicating about their work in archaeology undergraduate programmes;
- educate student and practising teachers about the 'excluded past';
- publish their research in language accessible to teachers and students;
- develop contacts with the media – through television, radio, newspapers and popular publications;
- develop stronger links between traditional museum display and good educational practice;
- train museum staff in the educational value of their displays and collections;
- accept that those involved in education have their own agendas and priorities as to the role of the past in teaching.

These eight steps are not a panacea that will, overnight, change the way the past is interpreted, taught and presented. However, they do combine to form the first steps of a programme that should begin to change the way the past is taught.

References

Addyman, P. 1991. Tourism and the presentation of monuments in Zimbabwe. Draft Consultant's Report, UNDP/Unesco Project (ZI88/028).

Alcock, L. 1975. *The Discipline of Archaeology.* Glasgow: *College Courant.*

Andah, B. W. 1990a. Tourism as cultural resource: introductory comments. In *Cultural Resource Management: an African dimension,* Andah, B. W. (ed.), 116–19. Ibadan: Wisdom Publishers Ltd.

Andah, B. W. 1990b. The museum and related institutions and cultural resource management. In *Cultural Resource Management: an African dimension,* Andah, B. W. (ed.), 148–56. Ibadan: Wisdom Publishers Ltd.

Barlow, A. 1990. Still civilizing? Aborigines in Australian education. In *The Excluded Past: archaeology in education,* Stone, P. & R. MacKenzie (eds), 68–85. London: Unwin Hyman; Routledge pbk 1994.

Bender, S. & R. Wilkinson 1992. Public education and the academy. *Archaeology and Public Education* 3, 1–3.

Boylan, P. J. 1991. Museums and cultural identity. *Museum Visitor* 9–11.

Burger, J. 1990. *The Gaia Atlas of First Peoples.* London: Robertson McCarta.

Carmichael, D., J. Hubert, B. Reeves & A. Schanche (eds) 1994. *Sacred Sites, Sacred Places.* London: Routledge.

Cleere, H. F. (ed.) 1984. *Approaches to the Archaeological Heritage.* Cambridge: Cambridge University Press.

Cleere, H. F. (ed.) 1989. *Archaeological Heritage Management in the Modern World*. London: Unwin Hyman.

Collett, D. P. 1992. The archaeological heritage of Zimbabwe: a masterplan for resource conservation and development. UNDP & Unesco Project Report (Zim 88/028).

Davis, H. 1989. Is an archaeological site important to science or to the public, and is there a difference? In *Heritage Interpretation: the natural and built environment*, Uzzell, D. (ed.), 96–9. London: Belhaven.

Dimbleby, G. 1977. Training the environmental archaeologist. *Bulletin of the Institute of Archaeology* 14, 1–12.

Ekechukwu, L. C. 1990. Encouraging national development through the promotion of tourism: the place of archaeology. In *Cultural Resource Management: an African dimension*, Andah, B. W. (ed.), 120–5. Ibadan: Wisdom Publishers Ltd.

Ereira, A. 1990. *The Heart of the World*. London: Jonathan Cape.

Evans, J. 1975. *Archaeology as Education and Profession*. London: Institute of Archaeology.

Frost, J. 1983. Archaeology and the media. Unpublished BA dissertation, Department of Roman Studies, Institute of Archaeology, London.

Gathercole, P. & D. Lowenthal (eds) 1990. *The Politics of the Past*. London: Unwin Hyman; Routledge pbk 1994.

Gregory, T. 1986. Whose fault is treasure-hunting? In *Archaeology, Politics and the Public*, Dobinson, C. & R. Gilchrist (eds), 25–7. York: York University Publications.

Groneman, B. 1992. A response to Blanchard. *Archaeology and Public Education* 3, 9–10.

Hall, J. 1991. Museum education: adapting to a changing South Africa. *Journal of Education in Museums* 12, 10–14.

Her Majesty's Inspectorate 1990. *A Survey of Local Education Authorities' and Schools' Liaison with Museum Services*. London: Her Majesty's Stationery Office.

Hewison, R. 1987. *The Heritage Industry*. London: Methuen.

Hoare, R. 1983. Archaeology, the public and the media. Unpublished MA dissertation, Department of Archaeology, University of Edinburgh.

Hodder, I. 1986. *Reading the Past*. Cambridge: Cambridge University Press.

Hooper-Greenhill, E. 1989. *Initiatives in Museum Education*. Leicester: Department of Museum Studies.

Hooper-Greenhill, E. 1991a. *Museum and Gallery Education*. Leicester: Leicester University Press.

Hooper-Greenhill, E. 1991b. *Writing a Museum Education Policy*. Leicester: Department of Museum Studies.

Hubert, J. 1989. A proper place for the dead: a critical review of the 'reburial' issue. In *Conflict in the Archaeology of Living Traditions*, Layton, R. (ed.), 131–64. London: Unwin Hyman; Routledge pbk 1994.

Hubert, J. 1991. After the Vermillion Accord: developments in the 'reburial issue'. *World Archaeological Bulletin* 5, 113–18.

Kehoe, A. 1990. 'In 1492 Columbus sailed . . .': the primacy of the national myth in American schools. In *The Excluded Past: archaeology in education*, Stone, P. & R. MacKenzie (eds), 201–14. London: Unwin Hyman; Routledge pbk 1994.

Kenyatta, J. 1938. *Facing Mount Kenya*. Nairobi: Martin Secker & Warburg.

Layton, R. (ed.) 1989. *Who Needs the Past?* London: Unwin Hyman; Routledge pbk 1994.

Layton, R. (ed.) 1990. *Conflict in the Archaeology of Living Traditions*. London: Unwin Hyman; Routledge pbk 1994.

Lowenthal, D. 1985. *The Past is a Foreign Country*. Cambridge: Cambridge University Press.

Lowenthal, D. 1993. Remembering to forget. *Museums Journal* June, 20–2.

MacKenzie, R. & P. Stone 1990. Introduction. In *The Excluded Past: archaeology in education*, Stone, P. & R. MacKenzie (eds), 1–14. London: Unwin Hyman; Routledge pbk 1994.

Olofsson, U. K. (ed.) 1979. *Museums and Children*. Paris: Unesco.

Raina, V. K. 1992. Instructional strategies used by Indian history teachers. *Teaching History* April, 24–7.

Reeve, J. 1989. Training of all museum staff for educational awareness. In *Initiatives in Museum Education*, Hooper-Greenhill, E. (ed.), 30–2. Leicester: Department of Museum Studies.

Renfrew, C. 1982. *Towards an Archaeology of Mind*. Cambridge: Cambridge University Press.

Richardson, W. (ed.) 1988. Papers from Archaeology Meets Education conference. *CBA Educational Bulletin* 6.

Riley, T. J. 1992. The roots of Illinois: a teacher institute. *Archaeology and Public Education* 3, 6–7.

Shanks, M. & C. Tilley 1987. *Re-constructing Archaeology*. Cambridge: Cambridge University Press.

Stone, P. G. 1992. The Magnificent Seven: reasons for teaching about prehistory. *Teaching History* October, 13–18.

Stone, P. G. 1994. *Report on the Development of the Education Service of the National Museums and Monuments of Zimbabwe*. London: English Heritage.

Stone, P. & R. MacKenzie (eds) 1990. *The Excluded Past: archaeology in education*. London: Unwin Hyman; Routledge pbk 1994.

Uzzell, D. 1989. *Heritage Interpretation: the natural and built environment*. London: Belhaven.

Watson, L. 1990. The affirmation of indigenous values in a colonial education system. In *The Excluded Past: archaeology in education*, Stone, P. & R. MacKenzie (eds), 88–96. London: Unwin Hyman; Routledge pbk 1994.

Wright, P. 1985. *On Living in an Old Country*. Thetford: Thetford Press.

1   *Reaping the whirlwind: the Reader's Digest* Illustrated History of South Africa *and changing popular perceptions of history*[1]

LESLIE WITZ & CAROLYN HAMILTON

Introduction

In 1988 Reader's Digest pulled off what is probably the publishing coup of the decade in South Africa. Responding to the storm of popular opposition to traditional South African history that blew up in the 1980s, it produced a book that took up the challenge: *The Illustrated History of South Africa: the real story*. It sold over 85,000 copies within six months of publication and Reader's Digest has battled to keep up with the demand for the book (*Sunday Times*, 28 May 1989). It is a remarkable achievement for a history text, and one that retails in the upper-price bracket at that. In this chapter we focus on the *Illustrated History* so as to explore some of the issues raised by the public hunger for alternatives to apartheid historiography. We trace the circumstances which created the market for the *Illustrated History*, and address the question of why this particular popular text is more successful than other similar ventures (see, for example, Cameron & Spies 1989; History Workshop 1989; and Preston 1989). Finally, we question whether or not the account provided by the *Illustrated History* is indeed the 'real story'. In this context we discuss another consequence of the ongoing and heated contest over the past in South Africa: a changing popular perception of the nature of history itself and an associated shift of paradigm away from history as the story of the past towards history as an investigation of the past in the present.

South African historiography and the popular consciousness of history

With its roots in settler writings of the late nineteenth and early twentieth centuries, South African historiography was long dominated by the story of the triumph of white settlers over barbarous blacks (see, for example, Theal 1964 (1892–1919); and Walker 1928) and powerful assertions of Afrikaner nationalism (see, for example, du Toit 1897). Perhaps the most efficient conduit for the transmission of these ideas, particularly after the National Party came to power in 1948, was in the schools, where a special place was accorded to Afrikaner nationalist historiography: 'The syllabus emphasized that authority was not to be questioned, whites were superior, blacks inferior, Afrikaners have a special relationship with God, South Africa rightfully belongs to the Afrikaner' (Du Preez, quoted in Giliomee 1987, p. 3). One of the aims of the school syllabus was to inscribe apartheid and a culture of authoritarianism into student consciousness. These ideas informed both the content of what was taught and the pedagogical method used. Although changes in the history syllabus were instituted in response to limited political reforms in the early 1980s, its fundamental ideas were retained. As Van den Berg & Buckland point out, the latest syllabus, instituted in 1984, continues to reflect 'an essentially "white" perspective. . . . History from 1910 to 1970 remains very largely the saga of "white" political parties and their struggle for power.' No attempt is made to study the history of major African chiefdoms of the nineteenth century, while 'the great struggle for the land is simply relegated to statements such as "the incorporation of the independent chiefdoms"' (Van den Berg & Buckland, quoted in Giliomee 1987, p. 3).

This history syllabus is taught in schools by using an officially prescribed textbook. It is important to realize that not only do the school textbooks present a white-biased view of the past but they also do so in a manner that proclaims the text to be an unchallengeable real story of the past. Textbooks like C. J. Joubert's *History for Std 10*, published by the Nationalist-owned company, Perskor, and used by most schools in South Africa, are 'mostly descriptive rather than analytical, presenting history as a fixed body of unproblematic knowledge with little mention of original sources or the work of historians' (Walker 1990, pp. 304–5). Pupils are afforded scant space to challenge the book and debate the 'facts' which it presents.

This approach is carried into the classroom, where most pupils are required to recite and learn the facts verbatim. Crucial pedagogical devices, such as asking questions and the generation of debate, are not considered to be good practice in a generally authoritarian schoolroom. The constant monitoring of teachers and students by education officials also inhibits the introduction of innovative content and method from other sources in the classroom. Moreover, students write an external school-leaving examination based on the syllabus and are reluctant to use alternative educational materials which may be available. All these problems are further exacerbated by the lack of financial resources. Although continuing to dominate in the classrooms well into the 1980s, the apartheid version of the past was, from its inception, challenged in the public consciousness. An important form that this took was the production and dissemination of dissenting histories in certain schools, popular memory, anti-apartheid political organizations, and some of the universities.

Alternative history content was introduced into schools set up by the African National Congress during the 1954 'Bantu education boycott' (Lodge 1983). Similarly, in the Cape, in the 1950s and the 1960s, members of the

Non-European Unity Movement taught, alongside the more conventional school history, radical history at a few coloured schools. Historian Bill Nasson, who attended one of these schools, recalled how the teacher told the class: 'We are here to make sure that you aren't contaminated by the Herrenvolk poison contained in your textbook' (Nasson 1990, p. 189). What was emphasized instead was the history of the indigenous population of South Africa with specific emphasis on capitalist penetration, worker and peasant resistance and the collaboration of petty-bourgeois elements (Nasson 1990, p. 196).[2]

Members of the Unity Movement in the Cape were also producing radical texts, such as Majeke's *The Role of Missionaries in Conquest* and Mnguni's *Three Hundred Years*, which formed the basis of teaching in some schools. Both these books, published in 1952, were a direct challenge to official apartheid history. In that year there were celebrations in Cape Town commemorating the arrival of Jan van Riebeeck some 300 years earlier. Blacks in Cape Town boycotted the celebrations, as they were seen as an attempt 'to inflict a ruler's brand of history on the oppressed' (Nasson 1990, p. 205). In their histories, Mnguni and Majeke tried to show that the 300 years since Van Riebeeck's arrival were not an era of great glory but a time of 'struggle between the oppressors and the oppressed' (Nasson 1990, p. 205).

Apartheid history was also subjected to further challenges outside the schools. Some of the most resilient of these were preserved in the form of oral memories handed down across generations and recorded by early black writers like Sol Plaatje (1957), S. M. Molema (1920) and Magema Fuze (1979). Others existed only in the form of powerful oral narratives, but were largely suppressed through the assertion of the scientific accuracy of Western research over indigenous forms of the popular production of knowledge.

A more systematic and directed challenge came from a small range of Communist Party and early African nationalist history texts (see, for example, Mbeki 1964; Roux 1964; Simons & Simons 1969). These counter-histories were outlawed by draconian censorship and so-called security laws, particularly in the 1960s, but managed to continue in covert circulation.

Since the 1920s oral historians had also set about debunking the core myths on which the segregationist ideology was based. These scholars focused on the history of interaction between whites and blacks (see, for example, de Kiewiet 1941 and Macmillan 1929). In the relatively few instances where their work was produced in popular form it was aimed largely at a white middle-class audience (see, for example, Morris 1969).

It was only in the 1970s, and in particular following the 1976 schools uprising, that the history of black South Africans in their own right was investigated. This period saw a black intellectual efflorescence, strongly influenced by the ideology of Black Consciousness. A highly idealized view of the past dominated this writing. Its basic elements were an emphasis on the essential unity of the black experience and on what Sole has called 'a rediscovery of African non-exploitative relationships' (Sole 1983, p. 39). Steve Biko, the leading figure in the Black Consciousness movement, called upon blacks to rewrite their history and 'produce . . . the heroes that formed the core of our resistance to the white invaders . . . stress has to be laid on the successful nation-building attempts of men such as Shaka, Moshoeshoe and Hintsa' (Biko 1978, p. 95).

This period also saw the final retreat of colonialism on the rest of the African continent which stimulated an interest in African studies. This was rapidly infused with the materialist concerns of a new generation of left, largely expatriate South African scholars. The new radical historians investigated the processes of the emergence of capitalism and its impact on indigenous societies. They were also concerned to explore the responses of Africans to these developments. The alternative view of the past which they nurtured drew heavily on oral histories, and the culture and experiences of ordinary people for the development of a 'view from below'.[3]

The revisionist historians were not merely concerned with publishing academic treatises. They also wanted their work to have a political impact. A number of the academics concerned had been involved in trade-union education in the 1970s, using history as a basis for discussions on strategizing for the present. This involvement led them to the conclusion that the new radical history needed to be published in a suitable form for workers. The dual concerns of writing materialist South African history and producing it in accessible form coalesced in the establishment, at the University of the Witwatersrand, of the History Workshop in 1977. In its early years the History Workshop's popular forums and publications were 'aimed at a specifically working class audience, and class struggle was their central focus' (Callinicos 1990).

In sharp contrast to the marketing success of the *Illustrated History*, these endeavours, also produced in the politically heightened conditions of the 1980s, generally failed to capture widespread popular interest. Only two of the Workshop publications, *Gold and Workers* and *New Nation, New History*, managed to sell in significant numbers, although well short of the remarkable sales figures of the *Illustrated History*. Three reasons for their lack of appeal suggest themselves. The first is their failure to offer a synthesized overview of an alternative South African history. With the possible exception of *Gold and Workers*, which uses the early work of the revisionists to examine class relations in the initial stages of South Africa's industrialization, the texts produced by the History Workshop tended to focus on specific topics such as the 1921 Bulhoek massacre and the history of liquor. Even *New Nation, New History* appeared as a compendium of different topics on distinct themes. The audiences lacked the necessary framework and context in which to situate the various slices of history which were provided. Second, these publications struggled to find appropriate formats and dissemination points. Distribution outside formal networks functioned effectively to ghettoize many of these works. The major exception was *New Nation, New History*, which was widely distributed through the *New Nation* newspaper. Finally, the focus on classes and class analysis, which was at the heart of revisionist scholarship, failed to tap in successfully to many popular perceptions of oppression in South Africa. In the 1980s racial oppression remained the central focus of anti-apartheid struggles, despite their strong anti-capitalist rhetoric. While the ideas of the revisionist historians were rapidly becoming hegemonic within the academies, they enjoyed a more limited success amongst ordinary people.

By the mid-1980s countrywide school boycotts and political protest had reached a crescendo. Between 1985 and 1986, student protests involved over 900 schools and nearly 40 per cent of black school students participated in classroom stayaways (Davis 1987, p. 92). Boycott, under the slogan 'liberation now, education later', was the dominant strategy. The main demands of African education were equal access to resources and education, and elimination of racism from texts, teaching and organizations of educators. 'Virtually nothing was advanced in regard to either the methodology of teaching or the democratization of the organization of the schools, universities and other educational institutions' (Wolpe & Unterhalter 1989, p. 12).

In December 1985 the National Education Crisis Committee (NECC) was established and an attempt was made to replace the boycott strategy with a movement for the implementation of 'People's Education'. The major advances of People's Education were that it focused on establishing democratic structures at schools and sought to institute a radically revised syllabus. In terms of this latter aim, People's Education commissions were set up and the 'People's History' Commission was given priority.[4] Its aim was to correct the distortions and myths which pervade apartheid history and to enable people to develop a critical understanding of the past through analysis and collective input (Witz 1988, p. 91).

The primary text to emerge in this context was the NECC's 'history pack', *What is History?*, in 1986. Like the History Workshop's popular texts, this publication also failed to find a significant market, for some of the same reasons. Although the 'history pack' was originally conceived as more a grassroots exercise in history production, the imposition of the second state of emergency in June 1986, and the harsh crackdown on the NECC which ensued, resulted in the production of the text being left in the hands of academic historians like the ones involved in the popularization exercises discussed above. Under emergency conditions, the distribution of the 'pack' proved almost impossible. It did not feed into any context in which it could be used, except the prisons, where it was possible for small groups of detainees to meet on a regular basis and discuss the exercises. A wider circulation was not realized.

The content of the 'history pack' was even further removed from a synthesis than the topics treated by the History Workshop. Using a number of topics carefully selected for immediate relevance in the lives of the projected users of the book, the 'pack' focused on the methods of historians and on the development of critical skills by the students. It was also criticized for a lack of objectivity. Sello Rabotha, reviewing it in the *Sowetan*, went as far as saying that it was 'propaganda', not history (*Sowetan*, 17 February 1988). Although the NECC publication was a failure in terms of its outreach, the importance of the History Commission's work was that it made 'People's History' an enduring slogan.

So widespread and so deep was the movement of rejection of the existing schools history that veteran textbook writers, like A. N. Boyce, notorious for their biased texts, began to recant. Admitting that portions of his history books were apartheid-based, Boyce remarked: 'I am not proud of some of the chapters in my earlier books, but I am trying to correct the mistakes I made and I have changed some of my earlier interpretations' (*The Star*, 23 May 1985). Textbooks, like *History Alive*, from Natal's Shuter & Shooter publishers under the general editorship of Peter Kallaway, which rely heavily on revisionist historiography, started finding their way into schools. Even the Government's Minister of Education acknowledged that 'communities could hardly live and work together in peace if their education systems presented possibly one-sided, prejudiced or warped images of each other's histories'. The Minister went on to admit that the content of the history syllabus would have to be 'negotiated by historians of various orientations'.[5]

On all fronts, it was clear that apartheid history in South African schools was on the way out. The only issue was how long it would take finally to be buried, and what would replace it.

The massive challenge to apartheid history which was marshalled in the 1980s was not confined to upheavals in the schools. This period also saw the production of popular history by trade-union-oriented groups, like the Labour History Group and International Labour Research and Information Group, and community organizations, like the United Women's Organization. In 1986, *Thirty Years of the Freedom Charter* by Jeremy Cronin and Raymond Suttner was published. The book commemorated the thirtieth anniversary of the Freedom Charter, a document adopted at the Congress of the People as a programme for a future South Africa. The book, which was expressly conceived as an attempt to break the silences around the history of resistance, commences with a powerful evocation of the suppression of the voices of the people under apartheid:

> The apartheid regime has tried to wipe out all memory of the mass struggles of the 1950s. Leading political organisations of the time have been outlawed. Leaders and ordinary people have been jailed or forced into exile; others were killed. Some have been banned or listed, their words, their memories becoming unquotable. Books, pamphlets, posters, badges, flags were seized in numerous police raids, or were censored into silence. Years of campaigning, mass struggles involving millions of people, all of these the system has tried to cast into permanent oblivion.
>
> (Suttner & Cronin 1986, p. 4)

The authors themselves, both activists and academics, go on to use oral

testimonies to recreate the circumstances of the drafting of the Charter in 1955.
The importance of the recovery of this history for the democratic movement
was widely recognized. 'Terror' Lekota, publicity secretary of the United
Democratic Front, commented, 'We know that as long as we remain untu-
tored in the history of the struggle, we would repeat the mistakes of the past'
(Suttner & Cronin 1986, p. 197). The book, with its glossy appearance and the
use of the techniques of guild historians, sold well. But its appeal was largely
limited to supporters of the Congress movement, as it failed to include articles
from and interviews with people who were critical of the Charter. This meant
that the impact of these 'lessons from the past' was minimized (Innes 1986).

Popular dissatisfaction with apartheid history was not confined to black
schools and mass political organizations. Some mainstream white forums
outside the academies were affected by a wider shift of paradigm in South
African history, a movement that was in step with the reformist political
developments within the South African state. South African Broadcast
Corporation writers like John Cundill recognized that on television 'the
projection of blacks and whites interacting in situations portraying reality and
highlighting their common humanity would go far to ease the tensions of
mounting racial strife' (*The Star*, 1 October 1986). Similarly Bill Faure, the
director of the television series about the life of the nineteenth-century Zulu
chief Shaka, expressed its aims in fundamentally reformist terms: 'Shaka's life
was originally recorded by white historians who imposed upon their accounts
bigoted and sensationalist values – often labelling the Zulus as savage and
barbaric. *It is our intention with this series to change that view*' (Shaka Zulu
Souvenir Brochure 1986, p. 3 – emphasis ours).

The business community was quick to pick up on the new taste for
alternative African history. The name of a top conference facility in
Johannesburg was changed to 'Indaba', thereby invoking the traditional Zulu
concept of *indaba* as a meeting at which important matters are discussed and
resolved. The advertisement for the facility notes:

> Long, long before intrepid explorers from Europe beached their
> fragile caravels on the shores of Southern Africa, the noble Zulu
> nation had created a most useful institution. The Indaba. The
> Indaba is more than a debate, much more than a simple meeting. It
> implies a pleasurable getting together of people for a variety of
> purposes, from marriage to business. Hence the name of our
> unique hotel Indaba.
>
> (*Sunday Star*, 26 February 1989)[6]

The politics underlying the promotion of these views of African history
involve a recognition by certain white interests of the urgent need to accommodate black political aspirations and the associated views of the African past.
Powerful leaders, 'noble Zulus' and the non-conflictual *indaba* forum are
purposefully selected from the available repertoire of African history for
incorporation into a new consciousness of the past. The similarity between

these choices, and the main elements of the version of the African past promoted by conservative African nationalist politicians, are no accident. In selecting such images over others, these white interests and conservative black interests unite against radical militant popular movements and their more subversive readings of the past.

The 1980s have thus seen the routing of crude white supremacist history and the development of a popular taste, indeed a hunger, for alternative versions of the past. A number of publications, such as those produced by the History Workshop, sought to meet the public demand for a new diet but these publications, as we have seen, generally failed to satisfy the popular appetite. But one publishing house took note of the demand for alternative history and to great advantage.

Production of the Reader's Digest *Illustrated History*

The publishers who decided to meet the popular demand for a new history were the usually 'cautious and conservative', the almost 'predictably anti-communist' Reader's Digest.[7] Through a series of market surveys Reader's Digest realized that 'the faint stirrings of rebellion against the traditional view of South African history [had] grown into a whirlwind'.[8] This was particularly the case among black South Africans. When visitors to the Reader's Digest stand at the Soweto Homemaker's Festival in 1984 were asked to fill in a form stating what type of book they wanted the company to produce, the overwhelming answer was a new South African history book which 'reflected the black contribution to the nation's past' (Reader's Digest 'Bluebook'). Taking note of the trends which emerged from its surveys, Reader's Digest decided to reap the whirlwind, and publish a popular and accessible 'alternative' history of South Africa. In deciding on the content of the proposed text, Reader's Digest took into account two essential factors: the book had to be authoritative history, using the latest work of academics and their practices, and had to respond to a popular readership in order to sell the book. Although, at times, these interests coincided, at other times they were in conflict. As one respondent to a Reader's Digest market survey said, 'If you are aiming to present "a truly objective view of the past", then why are you surveying people's perspectives of South Africa's history?'[9] When the two aspects clashed, the Digest usually opted for the popular taste.

The first choice the Digest made in this regard was over who should write the book. Here it was perceived that a book written by a reputable scholar would lend the publication considerable authority. But the Digest was sceptical of the abilities of academic historians to present the text in an accessible and exciting manner, one which would appeal to readers and thus sell the product:

The standard of historical writing by most academics tends to be stuffy and poor. Apart from giving too much space to lengthy arguments, most of them fail to breathe any life into their copy. Characters are merely names instead of personalities. There is an absence of mood and atmosphere in their writing . . . many of the most popular history books are not written by academic historians, but by journalists and professional writers who have a particular interest in the subject. Alan Moorehead, Paul Johnson, Thomas Pakenham, Antonia Fraser are some of the names which spring to mind.

(Reader's Digest 'Bluebook')

Reader's Digest therefore decided to employ researchers and professional writers to make the text come alive. The necessary authority would be achieved by involving as 'advisers' historians of high standing whose role was to be 'the final arbiter of the facts' (Reader's Digest 'Bluebook'). Two prominent historians from the University of Cape Town, Christopher Saunders and Colin Bundy, were the advisers for this publication. The language, presentation and design were to be at the sole discretion of Reader's Digest.

A second way that a history text gains authority is by debating with other histories already produced, on the basis of meticulous research, usually referenced in the form of footnotes. Reader's Digest, however, wanted none of these debates among historians reflected in its text. It aimed simply to 'give the facts'. Market research had shown Reader's Digest that their audience was insistent that the book be an objective/unbiased account, and they wanted 'the facts' presented in an authoritative, definitive and entertaining way. The publishers feared that the inclusion of historical debates would turn the book into a 'mish mash . . . lack[ing] consistency and direction'. The only debates to be included were those giving points of view contemporary to an event. Moreover, historians, the Reader's Digest noted, tend to be nervous to commit themselves and therefore 'sprinkle their text with reference sources that can be used to defend their writing' (Reader's Digest 'Bluebook'). In their attempt to produce reputable history the Digest was under a lot of pressure to cite sources, yet they insisted that there be no footnotes. Although, as a compromise, an extensive bibliography was provided, the reader has very little guide of where the specific information has come from.

Finally, few academics would accept that they are presenting the real story. Today, most historians recognize that they are writing history from a particular perspective and that their evidence reflects 'witnesses to reality and not reality itself' (Kros 1987, p. 11). But the Reader's Digest survey demonstrates that the public, particularly black readers, wanted an objective history, which told the real story. In selecting the title, the publishers deliberately chose an option which would attract a black readership: *The Reader's Digest Illustrated History of South Africa: the real story*. This was against the advice of the historical advisers.

To produce the 'real story' in an interesting and accessible way, Dougie Oakes, a coloured journalist who had worked for the now defunct Cape Town black newspaper, the *Cape Herald*, was appointed project editor. His tasks were to commission writers and advisers, and to assist in editing the copy.

Chapter outlines were developed in consultation with historian Christopher Saunders and reviewed by fellow academic Colin Bundy. Bundy then gave a group of post-graduate students a list of articles to find and photocopy for the respective chapters. These photocopies were handed every week to Reader's Digest, which in turn gave them to one of a group of professional writers to write the chapters (interview with Colin Bundy, Cape Town, 20 April 1990). In this way, the historians steered the writers towards the latest and best revisionist scholarship. Good writers, capable of sticking to the concepts and deadlines which Reader's Digest wanted, had been difficult to find. In the end a lot of the writing and overwriting was done by the project editor, Dougie Oakes (interview with Dougie Oakes, Cape Town, 21 April 1990).

By the time the chapters were written Bundy was on leave and Saunders took over the role of historical adviser. Saunders played an active role as adviser, commenting on the text at various stages in the production process, from the time it was written to the time it was designed and laid out. As the final stages of production were reached, however, rigid deadlines were set, leaving the adviser little opportunity to suggest any major alterations (Christopher Saunders, pers. comm., February 1990). Finally, readers employed by the Digest checked the copy for any spelling or grammatical errors and in December 1988 the book was published and appeared on the shelves just in time to capture the Christmas market (information based on interview with Dougie Oakes, Cape Town, 21 April 1990).

Through this production process Reader's Digest achieved its two major aims of presenting an authoritative history in an exciting, accessible form. Academic authority had been lent to it by the involvement of the historians, and accessibility by the writers, editors and designers. The writers, however, were not wedded to the fundamental tenets of revisionist scholarship, and, where these tenets conflicted with the aim of producing an exciting history, they jettisoned them.

The real story?

In 500 pages the *Illustrated History* covers the history of southern Africa from earliest times to the present, i.e. 1988, when it was first published. It looks at the origins of the people of the subcontinent, the emergence of numerous precolonial African states, the complex and uneasy coexistence of African and settler societies, the onset of colonialism, contests over land and labour, the effects of the mineral discoveries, industrialization, urbanization, apartheid, resistance and reform. Picking up on key topics investigated by the revisionists, the *Illustrated History* provides a comprehensive overview that is both thorough and penetrating. Although a weighty text, the presentation of often dry scholarly insights is achieved in a fresh and colourful way. Significantly, the *Illustrated History* is the first alternative synthesis of the full sweep of South African history.

The text is enhanced by an engaging and varied layout, with lively headings and box features. A veritable treasure trove of visual material never seen before allows the past to spring to life from the pages of the book. The encyclopaedic feel, firm binding and glossy finish invest it with a resounding authority. The book also gains credibility through its claim to present the latest and best academic scholarship, that of those 'questing minds in universities both in South Africa and overseas [which] have been researching a new view of our past – the view from South Africa, not from Europe. A view that asserts that South African history did not begin with the "discovery" of the country by the Portuguese' (Oakes 1989, p. 70). This claim is strongly reinforced by the involvement of Bundy and Saunders in the production of the book. Indeed, the *Illustrated History* draws heavily on the revisionist historiography of the last two decades to challenge apartheid history. Charles van Onselen's social histories of the Witwatersrand, for instance, are used to depict the Johannesburg underworld at the turn of the century, while the work of scholars like Stanley Trapido, Shula Marks and David Yudelman is used to chart the making of the early South African state.

While the rigorous interrogation of South African history and more specific-ally the revisionist analysis of the making of the apartheid state are strongly represented, the book also attempts to cater to popular taste. The essentials of the way in which the *Illustrated History* responds to popular demand are captured in the preface. The text commences with a discussion of the 1838 Battle of Blood River and its place in South African history. The preface uses this historically and symbolically loaded moment to illustrate its aims:

> But history has many memories and many versions; one person's belief may be another's lies; today's truth may be tomorrow's fiction. A child who thrilled to the tale of stern Voortrekkers mowing down Zulu hordes may grow into an adult in search of a more balanced picture: who were the Zulu, and why did they attack so desperately and in such suicidal numbers? Why are some of them still fighting today, and why do they need to . . .?
>
> (Oakes 1989, p. 6)

In other words, the 'balance' with which the *Illustrated History* is concerned is between black and white versions of the past.

Thus, the *Illustrated History* gives the reader plenty of black history and in so doing challenges a number of the main myths of apartheid history and makes good its significant omissions. It is concerned to demonstrate that the land was not empty when the first whites arrived. It examines major black chiefdoms of precolonial times in considerable depth. The role played by blacks in the mineral revolution is balanced against the activities of whites. The book reintroduces into South African history the saga of black resistance to white domination, and looks in detail at the history of organizations like the ANC. Through the energetic explosion of some of the main myths of apartheid, black South Africans are restored to South African history in strong and positive terms. In an inversion of the hoary old stereotypes, the settler adventurer heroes of the apartheid narrative are, in turn, represented as hard, unscrupulous misfits and cold-blooded killers (Oakes 1989, pp. 98–103).

While it attempts to combine popular forms with revisionist scholarship, the *Illustrated History* is not simply the popular version of that scholarship. In fact, the *Illustrated History* is less true to that scholarship than most of the popular alternative texts already discussed. Indeed, the book is at odds with the revisionist project in three key respects. First, the book uses the classical terminology of segregation and apartheid: the classification of the precolonial African population into Southern Nguni, Northern Nguni, Northern Sotho, Southern Sotho, Western Sotho, Venda and Tsonga (Oakes 1989, pp. 64–7). One of the major interventions of radical scholarship has been to show how these divisions were a product of apartheid and, indeed, a box included in the text at the insistence of the historical adviser indicates this (Christopher Saunders, personal communication, February 1991). However, Reader's Digest decided to use the terminology 'simply because it is difficult to trace the movements and settlement patterns of the Bantu-language speakers without them' (Oakes 1989, p. 62). Second, it is, in contrast to the revisionist works, more concerned with the doings of great leaders than with the history of ordinary people. There is an attempt to show the life of ordinary people through little vignettes, but these are generally adjuncts to the main text and are used more to 'breathe life into the past'. Finally, although it does not ignore the concerns and issues raised by materialist analysis, the *Illustrated History* is oriented more towards issues of race than class. In these respects, the *Illustrated History* reflects popular taste and the concerns of its projected readership more closely than the scholarship from which it claims to draw.[10] Therefore, in its final form, the book has a strong Africanist tendency. This is despite the interventions made by Bundy and Saunders.

At the same time, however, white history remains the framing narrative of the text. The opening chapter sets the scene, getting the arrival of the whites into the first two pages. The pre-white past then follows, in 'flashback' form. Thus 1652, the date of the arrival of Jan van Riebeeck, the first 'settler', remains pivotal to the text, and the heart of the apartheid myth remains in place. In part this is because the book's stated aim of opposing apartheid history requires the central myths of the latter to be set up as its markers. The book thus fails to offer a fully reconceptualized framework of South African history.[11]

The arrival of the whites also marks a key epistemological break in the text. The pre-white past (that is, from the beginning of the Stone Age about 3 million years ago) to the first contacts with European seafarers in the 1400s, is covered in three chapters in Part I of the *Illustrated History*. The amount of space given to this section compared favourably with other histories, in which the earlier period is, at best, cursorily treated. The reasons for neglect of precolonial history in many predecessor texts are twofold. First, apartheid history relied heavily on the myth that the first blacks crossed the Limpopo river in the north at much the same time as the first whites landed in the south at the Cape. In other words, the area had no history before 1652. Once archaeological research demonstrated that the notion of the empty land was a myth, the theoretical basis of the discipline itself came under fire from anti-evolutionists. At this point, the second reason for the neglect of the pre-white past came into play for those who accepted the validity of archaeology: it was assumed that archaeological research was too complicated and insufficiently interesting for the ordinary reader.

The *Illustrated History* addresses archaeological findings directly. The strong narrative thread and continuity that is demanded of a popular text and which is absent in the known story of the archaeological past is provided instead by a focus on the activities of individual archaeologists. The story of their investigations is used as a device around which the fragmentary information provided by archaeology coheres, thus both clarifying the subject matter and adding drama and human interest to the section. In marked contrast to later sections, in which the researchers are notably absent, excluded by the editors in their search for the true story, in this, the first section, the archaeologists are even present in the photographs!

The question then arises about whether or not the first section of the *Illustrated History*, with its emphasis on the process of research and invasion, subverts the claim of the rest of the book to be 'the real story'. This does not seem to be the case. One reason is the different status accorded by the popular reader to 'history' on the one hand and 'archaeology' on the other. Whereas the former is recognized as being open to manipulation by apartheid ideologues and others, the latter is popularly invested with the objective mantle of science. While the public wants an objective history, it recognizes at the same time that it is rare. The same public has higher expectations of the science of archaeology.

History in post-apartheid South Africa

The *Illustrated History* has clearly been a success. Not only has it sold in vast quantities, but it has received rave reviews from the left and right of the political spectrum and from academics. While it is not a textbook, it is not unimaginable that, given the rapidly changing political context, the Reader's Digest history could become a feature of South African classrooms. According to the Digest's market research, most people – 72% of whites and 80% of blacks surveyed – wanted to buy the book because of its educative value, to be 'better informed about our past'.[12] With its use of parts for the revisionist historiography, its achievement of a remarkable synthesis and its appeal to popular taste, it is not improbable that the *Illustrated History* could replace Joubert.

This, clearly, is much more acceptable than old apartheid myths which were perpetuated in the classroom through Boyce and Joubert. But the one major danger of the *Illustrated History* is that it presents a history that claims to be authoritative, a real story, which is not open to dispute. It thus fits into the existing education mould and does not really move towards altering in any fundamental way the teaching of history in South Africa. Kros's point about history teaching in South Africa still holds for the *Illustrated History*:

> students are taught to regard the past and the discipline of history [in a way] which ensures that they are usually fundamentally passive recipients of so-called 'historical knowledge' and that, even when they sense that nothing is wrong, they do not know how to raise an effective challenge.
>
> (Kros 1987, p. 11)

One of the major concerns is that, when changes are made to the content of the history syllabus and the textbook, the students will continue to accept the new information passively, without question, debate or criticism. William Finnegan, in his recollections of teaching at a coloured school in the Cape in 1980, recounts that when he introduced new content many students 'readily adapted their old rote-learning methods to [the] alternative syllabus, dutifully inserting FRELIMO into their Mozambique lessons with little comprehension of the material' (Finnegan 1986, p. 47).

What mitigates the easy replacement of old versions of the past with new ones is the unprecedented recognition in South Africa today that history is open to distortion. Reader's Digest produced the *Illustrated History* because their market survey had shown that the reading public was dissatisfied with the old myths that it had been fed and wanted an objective history. What was not captured by the survey, however, was the contradiction in popular perceptions about the nature of history and whether the reading public believes that any *one* history text can provide the 'real story'. The differing and competing political agendas in force in South Africa, and the continual contests over the representation of the past, suggest that the reading public will not see any one text as providing an objective history. 'A fact is simply not a fact,' rues columnist Dries van Heerden in a review of the state of history in South Africa for the newspaper *The Sunday Times* (8 July 1990). It is as though South Africans, spurred by the sharp conflict over history production, have indicated a readiness to look not simply at 'the facts' but also at the writers and the producers of history.

In other words, the contests over the production of history in South Africa are such that people are aware of the extent to which all history is a result of the circumstances of its own production. In as much as school-children can identify the bias of Boyce and Joubert, so too the journalist from the *Sowetan* called the NECC's *What is History?* 'propaganda'. Likewise, *Thirty Years of the*

Freedom Charter was criticized for not including news of political opponents of the Charter.

The same questions must be asked about the Reader's Digest's own significant agenda beyond the financial aim of this particular project. The book was produced at a time when there was pressure on companies in the United States to divest. In this context the *Illustrated History* could be seen as an important justification for the Digest to remain in South Africa and continue selling its other publications. Moreover, by producing this key text in the particular format chosen, Reader's Digest is beginning to secure for itself sufficient political credibility to ensure the maintenance, even expansion, of its important South African market in post-apartheid times.

All of these dilemmas surrounding the *Illustrated History* point to the continued contests over the production of knowledge and the dangers of becoming too comfortable with one alternative history. South Africa has already experienced one more shift of paradigm, from that of apartheid history to an alternative, broadly liberal-left version. To a large extent the *Illustrated History* reflects this move. Another shift of paradigm now seems to be in the offing, characterized by a concern with evidence, with providing readers with enough information to be critical, i.e. evidence and the history of knowledge about the past are beginning to become part of the content of history's new narrative. The *Illustrated History* almost inadvertently touches on these things in the archaeological chapters, while in the rest of the book it systematically effaces them. The challenge for producers of history must be, within market constraints, to reflect this latest shift of paradigm and, through a focus on evidence and the process of history production, to open up the channels of contestation much further than the *Illustrated History* does. Such an approach will empower readers to read a history in its particular social and political context, and thereby contribute to the creation of a new culture of enquiry in South Africa, characterized by questioning, investigation and debate.

Notes

1 This chapter was originally published in the *South African Historical Journal*, no. 24, May 1991, and is republished here with their kind permission.
2 This infusion of some concepts from a materialist analysis with a desire to present the history of the indigenous inhabitants from their own point of view has been identified as 'radical Africanist'. See C. Saunders (1986), quoted in Rassool (1990).
3 For a more extensive discussion on the roots of revisionist scholarship see Bozzoli & Delius·1990.
4 The term 'People's History' as used in this context refers to a specific form of popular history in which the focus of the content is on the actions of ordinary people, especially the underclasses in society. People's History carries the further connotation of its own production and dissemination being controlled by the broad mass of people.
5 Report on the opening address by Dr G. Vilijoen to the Afrikaanse Studentebond Congress, *Natal Witness*, 16 July 1986.

6 Thanks to John Wright for this reference.
7 Review of *Illustrated History* in *Milwaukee Journal*, September 1989, p. 17; review by M. Plaut, BBC World Service, 15 December 1989.
8 Before the Reader's Digest publishes a book it compiles a 'Bluebook', in which it summarizes the findings of its various market surveys, sketches an outline for the envisaged book and discusses the way it intends to produce the book. Much of the information on the production process in this article relies on the 'Bluebook'.
9 Findings of Reader's Digest market survey on the *Illustrated History*.
10 One area in which the *Illustrated History* has conceded to revisionist scholarship rather than popular taste is in the use of the terms 'San' and 'Khoikhoi'. The market survey showed that most respondents (both black and white) preferred 'Bushman' and 'Hottentot'. These terms are generally not used today by historians and anthropologists, and Reader's Digest went for the general academic usage, presumably because it is 'more accurate', even though it was at odds with their market findings.
11 One recent publication which has attempted to reconceptualize South Africa's precolonial history is M. Hall, *The Changing Past* (Hall 1987). Pointedly, in a book which covers southern African history between 200 and 1860, the name Van Riebeeck is not mentioned once in the text.
12 Results of the Reader's Digest market survey.

References

Biko, S. 1978. *I Write What I Like*. San Francisco: Harper & Row.
Bozzoli, B. & P. Delius 1990. Radical history and South African society. *Radical History Review* 46/7, 13–45.
Callinicos, L. 1990. Popular history in the eighties. *Radical History Review* 46/7, 285–97.
Cameron, T. & S. B. Spies (eds) 1989. *An Illustrated History of South Africa*. Johannesburg: Jonathon Ball.
Davis, S. 1987. *Apartheid's Rebels*. New Haven: Yale University Press.
Finnegan, W. 1986. *Crossing the Line*. New York: Harper & Row.
Fuze, M. M. 1979. *The Black People and Whence They Came*. Pietermaritzburg & Durban: University of Natal Press.
Giliomee, H. 1987. The case for a pluralist South African school history. *Journal for History Teaching* 13, 2–8.
Hall, M. 1987. *The Changing Past*. Cape Town: David Philip.
History Workshop 1989. *New Nation, New History*. Johannesburg: New Nation & the History Workshop.
Innes, D. 1986. Review of *Thirty Years of the Freedom Charter*. *Weekly Mail*, 27 May–3 June.
de Kiewiet, C. W. 1941. *A History of South Africa, Social and Economic*. Oxford: Oxford University Press.
Kros, C. 1987. History for democracy. *Lengwitch* 4, 5–23.
Lodge, T. 1983. *Black Politics in South Africa since 1945*. Johannesburg: Raven Press.
Macmillan, W. M. 1929. *Bantu, Boer and Briton*. London: Faber & Gwyer.
Mbeki, G. 1964. *South Africa: the peasants' revolt*. Harmondsworth: Penguin Books.
Molema, S. M. 1920. *The Bantu Past and Present*. Edinburgh: Green.
Morris, D. 1969. *The Washing of the Spears*. London: Sphere Books.
Nasson, B. 1990. The unity movement: its historical legacy in historical consciousness. *Radical History Review* 46/7, 189–211.
Oakes, D. (ed.) 1989. *Reader's Digest Illustrated History of South Africa: the real story*. Cape Town: The Reader's Digest.
Plaatje, S. T. 1957. *Mhudi: an epic of South African native life a hundred years ago*. Alice: Lovedale Press.

Preston, A. 1989. *Pictorial History of South Africa*. Johannesburg: Magna Books.

Rassool, C. 1990. History and the 'independent' left in the 1950s: towards uncovering a Marxist intellectual tradition. Paper presented at the History Workshop Conference, Johannesburg, February 1990.

Roux, E. 1964. *Time Longer than Rope*. Madison: University of Wisconsin Press.

Saunders, C. 1986. 'Mnguni' and *Three Hundred Years* revisited. *Kronos* 11, 74–81.

Simons, H. J. & R. E. Simons 1969. *Class and Colour in South Africa*. Harmondsworth: Penguin Books.

Sole, K. 1983. Culture, politics and the black writer: a critical look at prevailing assumptions. *English in Africa* 10, 37–84.

Suttner, R. & J. Cronin 1986. *Thirty Years of the Freedom Charter*. Johannesburg: Raven Press.

Theal, G. M. 1964 (1892–1919). *History of South Africa*, 11 vols. Cape Town: Allen & Unwin.

du Toit, S. J. 1897. *Die Geskiedenis van Ons Land in die Taal van Ons Volk*. Paarl: D. F. du Toit.

Walker, E. 1928. *History of South Africa*. London: Longmans.

Walker, M. 1990. History and history teaching in apartheid South Africa. *Radical History Review* 46/7, 298–308.

Witz, L. 1988. History of the people, for the people and by the people: a brief examination of the development of People's History in South Africa, 1977–1988. *South Africa International* 19, 90–5.

Wolpe, H. & E. Unterhalter 1989. The politics of South African education, 1960–1988. Paper presented at the Research on Education in South Africa conference, Essex, March 1989.

2 Archaeology and education in Botswana

DAVID KIYAGA-MULINDWA &
ALINAH KELO SEGOBYE

Introduction

It is often argued that formal education is good in itself but for many, especially in the 'Third World', this aspect of western culture is only seen as a means to a livelihood. Parents strive so hard to send their children to school, even when their family is poor, because they see this as the only inheritance they can leave their children. Many children, too, realize early in their lives that the only way to material success is through scholastic achievement. Unfortunately, however, the demands and expectations in a formal education system are so high that informal ways of learning tend to be neglected and regarded as luxuries. This is contrary to the way that people in Botswana were traditionally taught to be good citizens and play a meaningful role in society.

The place of archaeology in both formal and informal education has been debated before at international meetings – for example, the first World Archaeological Congress (WAC) in 1986 in Southampton, England (Stone & MacKenzie 1990) – and it is generally recognized that more needs to be done to bring heritage information and issues into schools and museum programmes. Despite strong lobbies in Botswana for the place of archaeology in national education curricula, however, the subject is still not part of the system, as either a core or elective subject, except in a few private schools. Likewise, here, as in most other countries, museums have limited budgets for education, despite their valuable services in this area. This lack of progress in bringing archaeology into education in Botswana can be attributed to the conservativism of education and development philosophies typical of many countries, especially developing ones.

Most African countries adopted detailed and specific cultural policies at independence. Some even created ministries of culture to oversee the revival of indigenous culture after the colonial experience, as in Nigeria (Nzewunwa 1990a, pp. 33–6; also see Ucko 1994). Botswana did not adopt such a radical policy, however, probably because the transition from the colonial to independent status was peaceful. Yet the absence of a cultural policy has been lamented by educationalists and traditional leaders (*Dikgosi*) since independence. Participants at the 1984 Botswana Society symposium Education and Development, for example, noted that 'seventeen years after Independence there is no well articulated policy for cultural development' (Tlou & Youngman 1984, p. 6). Although policy planners were aware of the detrimental effects of colonial policies on indigenous cultures, they made little effort to radically change the imposed ideology and to re-establish a spirit of conservation and appreciation of indigenous cultures. Instead, the education system was westernized even faster as the country strove for rapid development.

Culture has been defined as the complex of distinctive spiritual, material and emotional features which characterize an individual, social group or society. It is a medium through which people can express themselves and review their achievements and shortcomings and seek new meanings and ways to overcome their limitations (Mogapi 1984, p. 187). In this spirit, cultural education has been defined as:

> the development of taste and the creation of awareness and appreciation of the national cultural heritage. Its aim is knowledge of the past for its operational value in the present, and as a source of hope for the future.
>
> (Nzewunwa 1990b, p. 189)

Botswana's national philosophy is based on the principles of unity, democracy, self-reliance and development. In principle all citizens have equal rights before the law. The Government claims commitment to social justice in all spheres of life for all Batswana. In reality, however, institutions charged with the responsibility of implementing these ideals may not succeed, as the interests of individuals and groups are so diverse. Conflicts of interest also arise when different sections of society or institutions compete for a single resource, such as government funding. The Government has in the past decade tried to ensure attainment of these principles through education, embarking on a country-wide construction of junior secondary schools to alleviate the problem of access to basic education that is especially prevalent in rural areas.

The current education policy as enshrined in the National Commission on Education report *Policy on Education for Kagisano* (Botswana Government 1977) is the most comprehensive review since independence. It instituted several major changes to improve the quality of services offered, including: a nine-year basic education programme, freely available to all Batswana children; a social studies syllabus to replace traditional subject divisions such as history, geography and other social science subjects; and a revised senior secondary O-level syllabus.

Traditional education systems in Botswana were not so competitive. In general, everyone had equal opportunity and free access to education, just as they had equal access to social and economic resources available to the community at large. This openness eliminated competition in the accumulation of material wealth. Even within such a seemingly 'free-for-all' system, of course, some individuals could achieve greater success than others. It was more the personal qualities of individuals that distinguished them, however, than the quality of formal education they received.

The traditional Setswana education used oral histories and tuition in cultural mannerisms, cultural wisdom and other social skills to teach children the norms and customs of their society. This education led up to the traditional initiation rituals of *bojale* for girls, and *bogwera* for boys, through which young people passed into adulthood (Schapera 1978). Initiation schools among most ethnic groups have been abolished at various times since the early 1900s, in most cases by kings responding to pressure from missionaries. More recently, attempts to revive them have been frowned upon by the Government and even some members of the public (see Grant 1984).

The tension between a recognition of the importance of heritage and the obvious rewards which accrue to those who excel in western education has shaped the attitudes of individuals and governments in many developing countries. Certain fields of study are now considered necessary for economic development and so have been given funding priority by many Third World governments. Studies outside these 'development' subjects must justify their existence in any institution that gets government funding. The humanities are therefore hard put to survive, as is shown by the fact that subjects such as fine arts, philosophy, anthropology and archaeology are rarely offered as major subjects in African universities.

The discussion presented here focuses on the role archaeologists and archaeology as a subject can play in the education system of a developing country like Botswana. The major influences in the character of formal and non-formal education systems in Botswana are:

1 the emphasis on Euroamerican culture in the approach to education, at the expense of indigenous cultures;
2 the dictates of national economic policies, like free-market capitalism, rapid urbanization and aid for rapid development;
3 labour migration to South Africa and, more recently, high rural to urban migration locally;
4 the low levels of household subsistence means, poverty and illiteracy in rural areas, where most people live, as compared to the conditions in urban areas; and
5 the relation of education, through western influence, to socio-economic progress, upward mobility and material success.

The history of archaeological research in Botswana

Archaeological research in Botswana is very recent and therefore is more modest than the archaeology in neighbouring countries such as Zambia,

Zimbabwe and South Africa. The earliest recorded excavations in Botswana were by Laidler (1938), who carried out limited tests at sites in eastern Botswana. Schofield (1948) followed a decade later with a regional archaeological survey of pottery. These early studies were mainly concerned with tracing regional ceramic and cultural traditions, the preoccupation of most archaeologists at that time. From then until the 1970s no serious archaeological research took place in the country, with the exception of occasional graduate student research projects. For the most part, however, the area was reduced to a backwater, as researchers in neighbouring areas considered the country inhospitable and not conducive to human settlement, especially of agropastoral communities. These false impressions were later to gain firmer ground when Afrikaner historians gave racist interpretations of the past, claiming recent arrival in the region of Bantu-speaking farmers with whom white settlers were contending for the right of occupation of land. These historians considered the area of present Botswana to be limited to the hunter-gatherer San communities.

These impressions are now being radically revised as recent archaeological research shows that very early farming communities were established in the area of present-day Botswana, dating back to the fourth century AD (Denbow 1986). In addition to agropastoralism, these communities practised metallurgy and craft production. The existence of large population groups by the ninth century is indicated by the number and size of settlement sites, some that may have had up to 20,000 inhabitants. The distribution pattern, a few large settlements surrounded by smaller ones, suggests a form of political ordering that may have provided the blueprint for the nascent state systems that were to develop in the region from the beginning of the eleventh century AD onwards (Hall 1987).

We are naturally excited about what these recent archaeological revelations signify about the past of this country, as it will have direct bearing on the way the past is conceived and communicated in schools and other educational institutions and, of course, informally to the general public.

The present state of archaeology in the country

Active archaeological research in Botswana is conducted mainly by the archaeology units of the National Museum and the University and by some foreign researchers doing graduate projects. Rescue and salvage archaeology have been done by a few archaeologists in conjunction with the National Museum. Neither the National Museum nor the University has publicized their archaeological work or developed educational programmes in the subject in public workshops or radio programmes, however, although the education department of the National Museum has recently featured programmes on oral traditions and historic monuments on its radio and newsletter programmes.

There have been lengthy debates in the United Kingdom about the inclusion of archaeology in the National Curriculum. Calls have been made by archaeological bodies and individuals for the inclusion of the subject at all levels of education as a subject in its own right and not as an appendage of other subjects like history or geography (MacKenzie & Stone 1990; Planel 1990; also see Corbishley & Stone 1994; Stone 1994). These are noble goals in an industrialized country where the practice of archaeology dates back to the last century and where it is already offered by some schools and many universities. However, the inclusion of archaeology throughout education is still a long way away in the United Kingdom; in the developing world this goal seems almost impossible to achieve. There is very little hope that archaeology as a teaching subject will be offered in schools. It may therefore be more pragmatic, for the time being, to continue seeking recognition in association with subjects currently recognized by curriculum planners as directly contributing to development.

Schools in Botswana have over the years been burdened with archaic teaching material and syllabuses from South Africa that were contaminated by the notoriously racist 'Bantu Education' philosophy. Since independence in 1966, changes have taken place, though not as fast as one would have liked. The primary-school history syllabus, for instance, had no room whatsoever for a reputable African past beyond the beginning of the benevolent missionary evangelization of the Africans in the region. Anything before that time was thought to be dark, primitive and not worth remembering. After independence a bit of local history was introduced into the syllabus. The aim, as in many other newly independent African countries in the 1960s, was to introduce an African history element but, given the lack of available information on the subject, very little success was achieved. The only information available at the time on Botswana's past was mainly based on oral traditions of Setswana-speaking peoples. In the absence of archaeological information on the country's past, such local histories could only be pushed as far back as the remembered past. The accuracy of facts transmitted through the oral medium is arguably limited by its dependence on human memory (Heinge 1974).

The secondary schools history syllabus has followed a similar course, but with better results. Many secondary schools had been offering European and/or British Commonwealth (Imperial) history to their students for the Secondary School Certificate Examinations. It was only with the coming of independence in the 1960s that the fever of African history caught on. Since then a number of authoritative works have been published on the general history of Africa as well as various national histories (e.g. Curtin et al. 1978; Clark 1982; Shaw, Sinclair, Andah & Okpoko 1993; Unesco n.d.). This has made it possible for some National Examination Boards and the Cambridge Examination Syndicate to offer papers in African history. However, the ground covered by these new history syllabuses is so extensive that archaeology appears as an introduction, covering the length and breadth of the African continent in a general way. The Cambridge History Examination paper 2160, as offered to candidates in central and southern Africa, is based on a broad African survey course. It swiftly propels the student through two topics covering the outline of the main cultural groupings: the Bantu migrations, early states and kingdoms and through to the period of European contact before it dwells at length on the colonial period. It is highly desirable to have an archaeology content within the broad coverage of these courses as this will go a long way towards dispelling the notion that archaeology is equivalent to prehistory.

Recently, however, teacher-training colleges for primary schools have begun to introduce some archaeological information in the new social studies syllabus, which offers integrated subjects in place of the traditional disciplines, such as history and geography (Botswana Government n.d.). This new syllabus aims at introducing the study of the human natural and social environment through time using an interdisciplinary thematic approach. The social studies syllabus was introduced after education reform recommendations by the 1977 National Commission on Education. The syllabus content encouraged utilization of cultural institutions and ethnographic material cultural as teaching resources. Archaeological information as cultural data was thus included in this syllabus. Its emphasis on material culture studies and society draws much from archaeological data. However, one of the main problems is the lack of both published teaching material on archaeological information and trained teachers to handle the material at primary-school level. It is noteworthy that there is still a dearth of teaching materials for this programme and teachers more often than not resort to the separate discipline approach where books are more readily available.

The nine-year programme: the social studies syllabus

The revised junior secondary schools syllabus (Botswana Government 1987) is for the last two years of the nine-year programme. It is in the last year that students take a qualifying examination to proceed to O-level. As many children fail to qualify and leave school at this level, they need to possess some skills for the job market. Teachers therefore concentrate resources on preparing the pupils for the examinations. The syllabuses of teacher-training colleges for primary and the two junior secondary-school colleges offer social studies courses based on the nine-year syllabus as outlined in the *Policy on Education for Kagisano* (Botswana Government 1977). Since neither archaeology nor anthropology is offered at these colleges, their introduction as course components within the social studies course is desirable. At present such components can be introduced by National Museum participation in conjunction with the University Archaeology Unit through workshops or modules involving prepared teaching material.

This programme of study focuses on history, culture and traditional values and customs in a family and village setting and attempts to integrate these settings into larger circles of associations and networks. Therefore, elements of

sociology, psychology, political science, economics and development studies
are integrated with history and geography in the curriculum. Formulated
through the National Department of Curriculum Development, the programme is implemented through classroom teaching. The topics are taught at
increasing levels of difficulty from when the child enters primary school to the
end of junior secondary school. Emphasis is placed on modern didactic
techniques, especially pupil-centred learning approaches.

The programme intends that pupils should:

1 show knowledge and understanding of Batswana culture, language, literature, arts, crafts and traditions;
2 realize the effects of Botswana's location and show an awareness of the
forces (climatic, ecological) and events that created the environment around
them in Africa and the world; and
3 develop the linguistic, mathematical, scientific and other practical skills that
help the student to form desired attitudes and behaviours that make for good
citizenship.

(Botswana Government 1989, pp. 1–2)

It is not until pupils are in standard 3 (8–10 years of age) that they are
introduced to topics which involve archeological information. These include
culture, the environment and society. The higher levels draw heavily on
ethnographic information and may include museum-based activities. They are
intended to introduce the students to a multicultural perspective of their social
setting in the context of world societies.

The Cambridge School Certificate history syllabus as taught in Botswana
takes the old traditional subject approach that the new Botswana junior
secondary social studies syllabus is trying to play down. A problem of
disjunction exists, therefore, when a student leaving junior secondary school
enters senior school and encounters subjects such as history and geography for
the first time as distinct subjects.

The O-level syllabus offered in Botswana is still administered by the
Cambridge Overseas School Examination Syndicate. The subject-oriented
curriculum heavily emphasizes content learning and examination. In addition,
the competition is very intense as the examination is the qualifying university
entrance. Teachers and parents therefore put great pressure on students to try
and achieve high grades. Within the O-level programme, subject streamlining
for the arts and sciences is done by most schools. Arts subjects tend to be
ranked lower than the natural sciences and technical subjects. Archaeology as a
subject is therefore highly unlikely to be offered as a core or elective subject in
the O-level programme.

Archaeologists and museums need to produce archaeological material and
literature as rapidly as possible to meet this need. This is perhaps an opportune
moment for practising archaeologists and colleagues in the museum profession. One short-term remedy would be through in-service courses in
archaeology for qualified social studies teachers. Teacher-training colleges

could then introduce some archaeology content into the existing social studies syllabus. As noted above, this step would need to be preceded by lobbying the National Curriculum Development Department.

Archaeology at the University of Botswana

The History Department at the University offers courses in both the Humanities and the Primary Education faculties. The courses with an archaeological component receive some lectures from the Archaeology Unit (operating with one staff member) that was established in 1986. These consist of the introductory lectures in the first-, second- and third-year courses in African history. The Unit also assists with some lectures and sometimes arranges museum visits for history students who go on to take the postgraduate diploma in education.

Until the academic year 1992/3, the only taught course offered by the Unit was a seminar on the prehistory of southern Africa for final-year undergraduates. This staff member also taught all the modules in history courses which had an archaeology content and teaches archaeology topics when they are covered in other departments such as Primary Education, Environmental Science (Geography) and Geology.

Students are eager to learn more about the subject and much of the teaching material on local and regional archaeology is now readily available for undergraduates. Few history students have had the opportunity to participate in fieldwork conducted by the Unit or the National Museum, however.

The archaeology in the single major BA degree programme in history is aimed mainly at catering for the personnel needs of institutions such as the National Museum and regional museums. A certificate course for museum studies has also been established to cater for the local and regional needs of trained technical personnel. In addition, the archaeology programme hopes to provide trained personnel badly needed in the government ministries such as Local Government and Lands, Home Affairs and Agriculture, which frequently encounter archaeological sites in their work. In addition, as the Government has recently recognized culture and conservation as important issues in a holistic approach to development, signalling a modification of earlier perceptions and policy, new areas of opportunity for archaeology are opening up, such as the recent inclusion of archaeological impact assessment as part of all pre-development work for the construction industry (Monuments and Relics Act 1970).

The main problem facing the teaching of archaeology within the University is the somewhat rigid structure of the Humanities BA programme. It is currently impossible to introduce archaeology as a majoring subject because the students graduating from the Humanities faculty are required by the Ministry of Education, which provides the bursaries for most university students, to major with two teaching subjects. And archaeology does not meet the criterion, as it is not taught in secondary schools. Even the few students taking a single major in history are required to take a teaching minor, that is, a subject taught at high-school level.

Until 1992 this proviso has prevented change in the structure of the history degree as offered by the Department of History. But certain developments within the University and beyond are beginning to change this picture. Indeed, the prospects for a fully-fledged archaeology course have improved with the recruiting of two archaeologists, with plans made to recruit a museum studies specialist. The Unit is now staffed to offer a fully-fledged archaeology course. For the time being, however, as in many African universities, the Unit which is charged with both teaching and research in archaeology remains subsumed under History (for a comparison of the development of the teaching of archaeology in Kenya see Wandibba 1990).

Non-formal education

Non-formal education services have improved since the 1980s with increased government support. The non-formal education serves the rural population through adult literacy programmes and other services. Most of its curricula cover subjects of particular interest to rural people such as health, farming, hunting and environmental conservation. The information is conveyed through radio programmes and village extension workers. Until 1978 non-formal education was co-ordinated by the Botswana Extension College. This was transferred to the Department of Non-Formal Education in 1978. At the University of Botswana, the Department of Adult Education was set up to train extension workers and undertake research, the production of teaching material and literature.

As a general public education service, the Non-Formal Education Department draws its teaching resources from the formal education system and from various government institutions and ministries. The radio learning programme and the extension workers' service demonstrate that the structures for public education about cultural heritage and archaeology exist. It is conceivable that when such literature has been produced it can be disseminated through these media. The environmental education projects undertaken by these departments in conjunction with the Ministry of Agriculture and Department of Wildlife have had some success to date.

Many people in Botswana, as in Africa in general, find it difficult to appreciate the value of an archaeology that has been conceived in the culture of the West. Studies of visitors to museums and heritage sites in Britain suggest that people visit places such as Stonehenge or the British Museum during leisure time. The concept of leisure time is perceived differently, however, in countries where standards of living are lower and national policies are oriented towards achieving basic services like education, health and transport. It thus becomes more complex to co-ordinate strategies for improving visitor numbers to sites and museums using the strategies developed in western countries.

If the study of archaeology is to survive and flourish in Botswana, it must be popularized and made relevant to local and regional cultural and educational contexts. Museums have successfully carried out this responsibility in many other countries. Unfortunately, the culture of museum visiting has not yet become popular in Africa, and Botswana is no exception. The majority of visits to museums in this country are of organized primary and secondary school tours and foreign residents and visitors. Ordinary Batswana rarely take time off to visit a museum. The reasons for this low turnout of local visitors are undoubtedly complex. One obvious factor, however, is that museums remain elitist and urban institutions (Nzewunwa 1990b). Indeed, MacKenzie (1990) has already pointed out the uncertainty and disagreement about the role of museums in Botswana in the absence of a well-defined museums policy (see also Grant 1990). Despite this, the National Museum and regional museums receive government funding and, through government backing, foreign aid support. Each of these museums has a vital role to play in popularizing archaeology and culture in general, therefore, and it is in the interest of archaeologists and museum curators to see to it that their subject and collections are known by as large a section of the general public as possible.

The absence of media services such as a national television service and the demands on radio time by many other services place the burden of initiating suitable strategies on archaeologists and the museum profession. The educational programme of the National Museum and Art Gallery provides a good example to follow. It has a weekly radio programme in which it informs the public about its various activities. It also publishes a free quarterly newsletter, the *Zebra's Voice*, with similar information. Perhaps most effective in the National Museum's public relations programme is its Mobile Education Service. Although it is geared towards the need of the primary schools, it also provides adult education services in rural areas. These rural visits are sometimes linked to cultural shows run under the auspices of the National Cultural Council; they are dynamic and exciting and deal with cultural issues, attracting large numbers of people in rural areas. Both the radio and mobile schools programmes reach the large population in the rural areas where most of the archaeological sites are to be found.

Archaeologists and museum curators recognize that these rural people are those who should be sensitized about the presence of these valuable cultural resources and encouraged to report them to responsible agencies for proper care and maintenance, and some new developments have taken place. The National Museum's Archaeology Department, for example, has already begun publishing information sheets for the public and the business community on archaeology in both Setswana and English. This information is distributed through schools and government offices.

The information sheets describe what archaeological sites are, how they should be treated and ways of protecting them from damage; they also encourage people to report sites to the National Museum and regional museums when they discover them. Other leaflets made for land developers and the construction industry point out the legal requirement made by the Monuments and Relics Act of 1970 which requires developers to undertake archaeological impact assessment before construction. This Act seeks to protect and preserve heritage sites all over the country from destruction either through development or sheer vandalism – such as the recent damage done to the Tsodilo hills rock paintings by both local and foreign visitors to the site.[1] The information sheet for developers (National Museum and Art Gallery n.d.) emphasizes the legal obligation which demands that all areas where developments are to be carried out, be they dams, farms or roads, are surveyed by a professional archaeologist. The archaeologist may recommend either salvage excavation, or mitigation against the projected development, if any archaeological or cultural heritage sites are encountered.

Another museum publication widely distributed in the country is the occasional journal *Lekgapho* which is produced by the Khama III Memorial Museum in Serowe. More information directed towards the public is still necessary, however, to bridge the gap between the profession and the public.

A non-governmental organization, the Botswana Society, has also done a great deal to popularize archaeology and archaeological sites in Botswana. The Society organizes research symposia, public lectures and research on various issues and arranges annual field trips to various sites of interest to its members. It also awards small research grants to researchers on Botswana and publishes an annual journal, *Botswana Notes and Records*. Symposia proceedings are also published and most have dealt with issues related to archaeology. More than fifty articles on archaeological topics alone have featured in the Society's publications since 1969 when it was founded. However, it too remains a specialized source, reaching only a fraction of the population needing information about archaeology. The Society, like other related voluntary organizations with similar objectives, is urban-based and staffed mainly by expatriate volunteers.

If the situation in popular education about archaeology is to improve, it is imperative for these societies to consider opening rural branches which can be run by local personnel who would not feel they are simply there for the small urban and expatriate or educated population (also see Ucko 1994). Devolving these societies to rural areas, as has been done by the National Wildlife Associations, would be a way to capture the interest of school-children and through them their families.

The future

Archaeologists can influence the education process of their societies at both a formal and informal level. This can be done by taking advantage of, and harnessing, already existing institutions and structures, especially those which are deemed cultural.

The objective for the future should be to direct efforts at developing a strong graduate programme offering archaeology and museum studies. The Museum Studies programme has already received good support within eastern and southern Africa for training much-needed technical staff. This is a viable proposition because it does not pose the problem of overproducing unemployable graduates. And employment opportunities still abound for trained archaeologists and museum personnel. In addition, the impetus of rescue and salvage archaeology, heritage management and environmental conservation, which Government is giving serious consideration to in the latest National Development Plan (NDP 7, pp. 1992–99), should provide employment opportunities independent of the civil service.

On a global level, the pressure for environmental conservation has grown stronger in the 1990s. The recent Rio conference on the environment is one example of the concern raised by countries and lobby organizations for better global conservation policies. Along with environmental conservation, cultural heritage preservation has been agitated for by concerned groups in the light of large-scale and rapid development. Following the National Conservation Commission in the mid-1980s, the Botswana Government has taken steps towards environmental conservation. Public and international pressure criticizing policies likely to have adverse effects has persuaded the Government to back down from some projects and engage expert assessment teams before development. This is taken as a positive indication of willingness within Government to change, and adopt policies which are desirable for conservation.

Another development with potential for archaeology is the proposed revision of the National Conservation Strategy. Although several institutions have put forward recommendations, the opportunity has not been seized by the museums and the University to put forward a case for cultural education, museum development and heritage conservation. Probably, this slow reaction can be attributed as much to a lack of co-ordination of efforts as to personal differences of approach between administrators in these institutions. Indeed, the University has only recently undertaken to form advisory boards for several departments. The History Department Advisory Board has representatives from the civil service, private and non-governmental organizations. It will be through fora like these that the urgency of issues such as heritage preservation will be dealt with and presented at the relevant ministries for planning and policy consideration. The advantage of clarified strategies for cultural education will also benefit the funding of museums and archaeology research programmes.

The few regional museums in the country have benefited substantially from donor agency funding, as has the University Archaeology Unit. These institutions would therefore do well to participate actively in public education and government lobbying to demonstrate their solidarity with respect to such an important cause. The growth of regional museums has been constrained for some time by government opposition to the establishment of independent museums. There was a tacit fear that they would promote regional or ethnic divisions and work against national unity as desired by the Government (MacKenzie 1990, p. 210; cf. Willet 1990, pp. 172–81; also see Ucko 1994). However, over the last few years a few independent museums have emerged and it is hoped that they will diversify their current ethnographic orientation to incorporate archaeology.

The relationship between culture and education was aptly summed up by the former Minister of Home Affairs when she stated that:

> our cultural heritage is what we will pass on to our children, hence, it is not right to remove from the country items of culture which are unique to our people. We should teach present generations to distinguish between that which should be preserved and that which is worthless. It is easy for people of other cultures to exploit the ignorance of culturally unsophisticated people by removing their natural heritage. The removal or destruction of a people's cultural heritage ensures lasting bondage to the people of a dominant culture. The propagation of culture is not a matter for a government ministry to tackle alone, it should be a concern for the whole nation. Culture is not just preserved in museums, libraries and archives. Not only children should be educated about the importance of culture, but their parents as well.
>
> (Disele 1984, p. 192)

We argue that cultural education is a task archaeologists cannot leave to government planners to initiate. Instead they should work together within institutions and organizations already undertaking similar work to lobby the Government to improve funding available for archaeological research and museums, conservation of sites and monuments and the integration of cultural education into the formal education system. Organizations like ICOM and Unesco already produce literature and provide back-up support for heritage management which can be used by museum professionals and archaeologists in developing countries to develop locally appropriate methods and literature.

Advances made in popularizing archaeology in countries like Britain and Nigeria offer illustrations of tasks that archaeologists in Botswana strongly need to undertake to make archaeology more relevant. Given the challenge of the value of education at both individual and public levels as a means for upward mobility and material success, museum workers and archaeologists have a daunting task to reorient these entrenched values to accommodate their subject.

Note

1 A case (as reported in the weekly newspaper *Mmegi Wa Dikgang*) was brought against a group of tourists and locals who had removed chunks of painted rock and written their names on the rock face. The case is still with police awaiting prosecution.

References

Botswana Government 1977. *Policy on Education Education for Kagisano*. Report of the National Commission on Education. Gaborone: Ministry of Education.

Botswana Government 1987. *Social Studies Revised Junior Secondary Syllabus*. Gaborone: Ministry of Education.

Botswana Government 1989. *Nine Years Social Studies Syllabus: standards one to nine*. Gaborone: Ministry of Education.

Botswana Government n.d. *Social Studies Syllabus for the Primary Teacher Training Colleges in Botswana*. Gaborone: Ministry of Education PTTC Social Studies Panel.

Clark, J. D. 1982. *The Cambridge History of Africa* vol. I. Cambridge: Cambridge University Press.

Corbishley, M. & P. G. Stone 1994. The teaching of the past in formal school curricula in England. In *The Presented Past: heritage, museums and education*, Stone, P. G. & B. L. Molyneaux (eds), 383–97. London: Routledge.

Curtin, P. *et al.* 1978. *African History*. London: Heinemann.

Denbow, J. 1986. A new look at the later prehistory of the Kalahari. *Journal of African History* 27, 3–28.

Disele, K. Hon. 1984. Culture and education are synonymous. In *Education and Development in Botswana*, Crowder M. (ed.), 191–3. Gaborone: The Botswana Society.

Grant, S. 1984. The revival of *bogwera* in Kgatleng – Tswana culture or rampant tribalism? A description of the 1982 *bogwera*. *Botswana Notes and Records* 16, 7–17.

Grant, S. 1990. A past abandoned? Some experiences of a regional museum in Botswana. In *The Politics of the Past*, Gathercole, P. & D. Lowenthal (eds), 214–23. London: Unwin Hyman; Routledge pbk 1994.

Hall, M. 1987. *The Changing Past: farmers, kings and traders in southern Africa 200–1860*. Cape Town: David Philip.

Heinge D. 1974. *The Chronology of Oral Tradition: quest for a chimera*. Oxford: Clarendon Press.

Laidler, P. W. 1938. *South African Native Ceramics: their characteristics and classification*. Transvaal: Royal Society of South Africa.

MacKenzie, R. 1990. The development of museums in Botswana: dilemmas and tensions in a frontline state. In *The Politics of the Past*, Gathercole, P. & D. Lowenthal (eds), 203–13. London: Unwin Hyman; Routledge pbk 1994.

MacKenzie, R. & P. Stone 1990. Introduction. In *The Excluded Past: archaeology in education*, Stone, P. & R. MacKenzie (eds), 1–14. London: Unwin Hyman; Routledge pbk 1994.

Mogapi, K. 1984. Education and cultural identity. In *Education and Development in Botswana*, Crowder M. (ed.), 187–90. Gaborone: The Botswana Society.

National Museum and Art Gallery n.d. *Are You Planning any Construction Work?* Gaborone: National Museum, Monuments and Art Gallery.

Nzewunwa, N. 1990a. Archaeology in Nigeria. In *The Excluded Past: archaeology in education*, Stone, P. & R. MacKenzie (eds), 33–42. London: Unwin Hyman; Routledge pbk 1994.

Nzewunwa, N. 1990b. Cultural education in west Africa: archaeological perspectives.

In *The Politics of the Past*, Gathercole, P. & D. Lowenthal (eds), 189–202. London: Unwin Hyman; Routledge pbk 1994.

Planel, P. 1990. New Archaeology, New History – when will they meet? Archaeology in English secondary schools. In *The Excluded Past: archaeology in education*, Stone, P. & R. MacKenzie (eds), 271–81. London: Unwin Hyman; Routledge pbk 1994.

Schapera, I. 1978. *Bogwera Kgatla Initiation*. Cape Town.

Schofield, F. J. 1948. *Primitive Pottery*. Cape Town: South African Archaeological Society.

Shaw, T., P. Sinclair, B. Andah & A. Okpoko (eds) 1993. *The Archaeology of Africa*. London: Routledge; pbk 1994.

Stone, P. G. 1994. The re-display of the Alexander Keiller Museum, Avebury, and the National Curriculum in England. In *The Presented Past: heritage, museums and education*, Stone, P. G. & B. L. Molyneaux (eds), 190–205. London: Routledge.

Stone, P. & R. MacKenzie (eds) 1990. *The Excluded Past: archaeology in education*. London: Unwin Hyman; Routledge pbk 1994.

Tlou, T. & F. Youngman 1984. Introduction: an agenda for the 1980s and beyond. In *Education and Development in Botswana*, Crowder M. (ed.), 1–8. Gaborone: The Botswana Society.

Ucko, P. J. 1994. Museums and sites: cultures of the past within education – Zimbabwe, some ten years on. In *The Presented Past: heritage, museums and education*, Stone, P. G. & B. L. Molyneaux (eds), 237–82. London: Routledge.

The Unesco General History of Africa n.d. London: James Currey.

Wandibba, S. 1990. Archaeology and education in Kenya. In *The Excluded Past: archaeology in education*, Stone, P. & R. MacKenzie (eds), 43–9. London: Unwin Hyman; Routledge pbk 1994.

Willett, F. 1990. Museums: two case studies of reaction to colonialism. In *The Politics of the Past*, Gathercole, P. & D. Lowenthal (eds), 172–83. London: Unwin Hyman; Routledge pbk 1994.

3 Presenting archaeology to the public in the USA

FRANCIS P. MCMANAMON

Introduction

Recognition of the need for more and better public education about archaeology is a worldwide phenomenon that also has many proponents in the United States, led by national archaeological organizations and public agencies with archaeological programmes (see DiCicco 1988; Cleere 1989, p. 9; Rogge & Montgomery 1989; Stone & MacKenzie 1990; Knoll 1990, 1992; Potter 1990; McManamon 1991a; Milanich 1991; Smith & McManamon 1991).

The Society for American Archaeology (SAA) and the Society for Historical Archaeology (SHA) have active committees on public education. Public education and outreach to the general public were identified in a survey of SAA members as one of the highest priorities of the Society (Fairbanks Associates 1988). Recent annual meetings of the SHA have included several symposia on public education and outreach. The importance of such activities was further emphasized by the results of the 'Save the Future for the Past' project (e.g. Lerner 1989; Neumann & Reinburg 1989; Judge 1991; Reinburg 1991), a co-operative project by the SAA and a variety of public agencies and private organizations. The action plan developed to implement recommendations from this project calls for a series of public education activities, including both formal and informal education, volunteer programmes and public outreach of many sorts (Society for American Archaeology 1990, pp. 15–17). The Archaeological Institute of America (AIA) has recently revitalized its Committee on American Archaeology and has long recognized the importance of public education through its popular magazine, *Archaeology*. In a recent issue (January/February 1991) *Archaeology* ran a special section devoted to public education programmes throughout the United States. In addition, AIA's St Louis chapter has had for many years an active public education programme co-ordinated with the local public school system (*Archaeology* 1991, p. 40).

A great deal of educational material related to archaeology is being distributed to the public in outreach programmes in the United States. Two recent listings of archaeological activities and products aimed at the public include over 1500 examples (Knoll 1990, 1992). These listings are summaries of the national clearing-house, the Listing of Education in Archaeological Programs (LEAP), supported by public and private agencies and individual archaeologists or educators who send in information for listing; it is maintained by the Archaeological Assistance Program of the National Park Service. The listings include examples of adult education programmes, popular articles, audiotapes, brochures, exhibits, classroom presentations, films, newspaper articles, posters, press releases, school curricula, public service announcements, slide presentations, television programmes, videotapes and other kinds of outreach programmes or products.

Public officials throughout the Federal Government promote public education in a variety of ways. The Secretary for the Interior (1991), the Federal official in the United States responsible for national leadership and co-ordination in archaeological and historic preservation programmes, has made improving public education opportunities a principal focus of his strategy for government archaeology in the United States. The 1988 amendments to the Archaeological Resources Protection Act included a provision that required Federal land-managing agencies (Federal agencies manage about one-third of the land in the USA) to establish public education programmes to inform the public about the value and importance of archaeological resources and their preservation and so reduce, and ultimately eliminate, archaeological vandalism and looting (see McManamon 1991b, pp. 266–7). It is a worthy, and very long-term, objective.

Several government agencies involved in archaeology have developed publicly oriented programmes. The Bureau of Land Management has a nationwide programme entitled 'Adventures in the Past' (Brook 1992). The Forest Service has for several years provided opportunities for the public to visit or take part in professionally run archaeological investigations through its national programme, 'Passports in Time' (Osborn & Peters 1991). The National Park Service has provided public interpretations at its archaeological units for many of its seventy-five years. Other national, State, Tribal and local agencies are making similar efforts to educate the public (e.g. Butler 1992).

Why is public education important?

In the United States, and many other places as well, most archaeological investigation is paid for by public funds. A conservative estimate of the amount spent by Federal agencies in the USA on their archaeological programmes is $75–100 million (see Smith, McManamon, Anzalone, Hand & Maxon 1988; Keel, McManamon & Smith 1989; McManamon, Knoll, Knudson, Smith & Waldbauer 1992). Other funding is provided by State and local governments to archaeologists in State agencies, university systems and public museums, and such organizations, and the private sector, also spend money to meet Federal requirements related to archaeological preservation.

With public funds at all levels of government in the USA shrinking, it is important that the public continue to support spending on archaeology, through the elected and appointed officials who make such financial decisions. The public reasonably expects some direct return for its support from government programmes, and so archaeologists in government agencies have taken a more direct interest in public interpretation, to help maintain a constituency that will support these activities and even extend them.

The second major reason for public education programmes is that individuals often determine whether archaeological sites are preserved or destroyed. Law-abiding and conscientious citizens will not vandalize or loot sites if they can be convinced that these actions may be illegal and will certainly diminish the heritage left to all people. As Fagan, an archaeologist both prolific and successful in educating the public, has noted, archaeology is almost unique among the sciences in having an interested public following. In this time of eroding archaeological records, wholesale looting, vandalism and social condoning of pot-hunting, good press relations are therefore a basic responsibility of the archaeologist (Fagan 1991, p. 18). An interested public is one of the most effective means of protecting sites in local development schemes and land-use plans, as people can serve as the eyes and ears of local, State, or even national officials who are responsible for site preservation. Certainly, there are not enough officials or even trained archaeologists in the United States to serve such a widespread monitoring function, nor will there ever be. Such interested people may help to monitor the condition of archaeological sites, providing regular observations and reports to preservation authorities (e.g. Hoffman 1991).

An active, informed public, supportive of archaeology and archaeological preservation, can serve as an invaluable source of political, voluntary and economic backing. If archaeological sites are to be preserved for the very long term, and if archaeological administration, planning, investigations, reporting and curation are to be supported for the long term, more and better public education must become an actively pursued and highly regarded part of the discipline of archaeology.

What is the message?

Archaeology does not seem to lack enthusiasts among the public, as it is both attractive and compelling. Public events often draw significant numbers of interested local citizens, and even tourists (see Peters, Comer & Kelly 1987, p. 1; Potter & Leone 1987; Bense 1991). Archaeologists will fail, however, if they rely on this built-in interest in their subject. An interest in archaeology most often results from romanticism or a longing for adventure (see Fagan 1984, pp. 177–8; DeCicco 1988, p. 841). Archaeologists must turn this predisposition towards what can be learned by means of modern archaeology without snuffing out the excitement that attracts people in the first place. This is not an easy translation, but with careful planning, forethought and skilful execution it can be achieved. There are growing numbers of successful public education and outreach programmes from which to draw advice and recom- mendations. One requirement that is consistent among all of these successful programmes is detailed planning of logistics and careful consideration of the message(s) that the programme aims to project (see Peters, Comer & Kelly 1987; Potter & Leone 1987; Hoffman & Lerner 1988; Potter 1990).

Within the disciplines linked most closely to cultural resource management in the United States, anthropology, archaeology, curation, history and histori- cal architecture, public agencies, rather than academic institutions, have devoted more time to public education. This may seem ironic, but it is not surprising; formal training in archaeology rarely includes lessons in public communication. On the contrary, academic success usually depends on the mastery of a very specialized vocabulary and abstract concepts. Such special- ization is necessary, but we should recognize that effective translation for the general public is also an important and legitimate professional activity. This latter message, in fact, is being heard with increasing frequency in academia (e.g. Redman 1989; Milanich 1991).

All the support and activity in the public education area is encouraging to those who see such education as a critical need. As public education becomes a more common concern, we want it also to be as effective and efficient as possible. We must come to know our audience better, to focus our message on the audience at hand, and to use appropriate means of communication.

Potter (1990, pp. 610–12), in his insightful comment on public education, remarks that there is no single message that archaeologists should be aiming at the public. 'The most significant and meaningful messages are not "one size fits all". Instead, they are local. Different communities have different pasts and need to know specific things about those pasts' (Potter 1990, p. 610). This key realization is echoed and pressed by others (DeCicco 1988; Fagan 1991):

> Few archaeologists will ever find a pharaoh's tomb or buried gold
> . . . most finds are of purely local, or perhaps regional, importance,
> even sometimes, frankly dull. But the information that comes from
> them is of more than passing local significance and educational
> value. This is where archaeologists can work miracles with public
> relations, provided they develop close links with the local media.
>
>   (Fagan 1991, p. 18)

Some messages, therefore, must be of local interest and sufficiently interest- ing to attract individuals with no special archaeological training, showing how people lived in an area at some point in the past, an unexpected event or an unusual kind of feature or artefact found locally. Potter (1990, p. 610) urges that archaeologists who want to construct interesting, even useful, messages seek out what members of the public know, think about, or use from the past.

Such outreach and reflection upon the context in which archaeology is being done is, to some theorists, essential (e.g. Leone, Potter & Shackel 1987). Certainly, from a practical perspective in public education this is also good advice and, again, it is emphasized by others in their own work and experience from working with local media (Peters, Comer & Kelly 1987; DeCicco 1988; Fagan 1991, p. 19).

Although local, community-specific messages are essential to successful public education, they should directly or indirectly make general points related to the value of archaeological resources, the care that must be used when studying these resources, and the non-renewable, often fragile, nature of archaeological remains. General points such as these have been suggested for use in educational, volunteer and other public outreach programmes designed to work over the long term on the prevention of archaeological looting and vandalism (Lerner 1991, p. 103). Such general messages are the ultimate goal of public education, to create a public that believes that:

1 interesting and useful knowledge can be learned from archaeological remains if properly studied;
2 the proper study of archaeological remains is careful, painstaking work that includes fieldwork, lab work, report preparation and distribution, and the curation of collections and records; and
3 archaeological remains are often fragile, always non-renewable, and ought not to be destroyed wantonly.

A public so informed would abhor site destruction and support archaeological activities and preservation, but unfortunately only a small percentage of people hold these beliefs at this point. Working to increase that percentage therefore seems a worthwhile goal.

Even now we can distinguish several special 'publics' that should be learning about archaeology. We can begin to identify the range of means of delivery appropriate for these different audiences. In the remainder of this chapter three different publics are considered. These publics are not mutually exclusive, nor are they of the same size, but each is important and merits attention. We should recognize that for our educational goals to be realized our messages to these different publics must be geared to their levels and kinds of interests.

Wooing and educating the general public

It seems sensible to subdivide the general public so that messages and means of delivery may be focused on smaller sections of this large and varied group (Shields 1991). Focused messages are likely to have the most positive and lasting effect. Unfortunately, we do not have detailed survey data that can be used to divide the general public according to their knowledge of or interests in archaeology. We need to engage experts in marketing, advertising and public relations to help us stratify the general public in a rational, effective way.

There are, however, important subgroups within the general public that are predisposed to appreciate archaeology, actively support archaeological projects, and even volunteer time and services in a variety of ways. Boy Scouts, Girl Scouts, community public-service organizations, natural resource conservation organizations such as the Audubon Society, the Sierra Club, the Nature Conservancy and so on, and retired persons organizations can be mobilized for archaeology (Lerner 1989, 1991). We should be considering how this can be done effectively and efficiently, and identifying projects and programmes for such groups. There also is a special role for journalists, reporters and editorialists in efforts to reach the general public (Fagan 1991). The educational potential of professionals in print media is recognized in DeCicco's primer (1988), which guides archaeologists in contacting and cultivating print media outlets. The articles in Peters, Comer & Kelly (1987) focus much of their attention on the means of seeking out and managing electronic media.

Beyond such special subgroups there lies a vast general public awaiting attention and outreach. Some specific information is beginning to appear about this public's interest in and knowledge about archaeology. Pokotylo & Mason (1991), for example, present survey results from 550 households in Vancouver, British Columbia, that show the need for better information and more effective means of communication about archaeology. Over half the respondents included 'fossils, such as dinosaurs' among objects studied by archaeologists. More encouraging was the high degree of interest, or potential interest, in archaeology expressed by the respondents. Ninety-three per cent had visited a museum with archaeological exhibits and 61% had visited a historic or archaeological site. Eighty-four per cent responded that archaeology was relevant to modern society and 67% thought that more information about archaeology should be made available to the public. The Pokotylo & Mason results compare favourably with recent surveys in Great Britain and the United States concerning interest and 'literacy' in science (Culliton 1988; Hively 1988; Durant, Evans & Thomas 1989). The results of these surveys suggest that only about 5% of Americans are truly scientifically literate, about 25% are informed or interested in science, and the remaining 70% are more or less uninterested in scientific topics, although this majority has a positive view of science and is generally supportive of scientific endeavours. Feder (1984, p. 536), in an earlier survey involving 186 students at Central Connecticut State University, recorded similar misunderstanding and uncertainty about archaeological information among his respondents, but he also discovered that they would be quite interested to learn more about the subject. If these survey results are reasonable reflections of public knowledge and interest, they suggest fertile ground for effective public education.

To further public knowledge of archaeology, more mass-media education projects and programmes need to be developed. Positive, short presentations for the mass audience, such as television and radio public service announcements concerning archaeological preservation or more general public resource preservation campaigns, are being produced and distributed with greater frequency and often use celebrities such as Harrison Ford (a.k.a. Indiana Jones), Clint Eastwood, Lou Gossett, Jr, Ted Danson and Jean Auel. Other kinds of popular presentations include widely distributed brochures, messages printed on supermarket shopping-bags, posters and bookmarks. These devices are often used effectively in conjunction with annual 'archaeology week' celebrations in a growing number of States.

There are other examples and an even larger number of possibilities for making a positive impression on the mass audience. Most archaeologists are novices in this area; we need to seek help and continue our efforts at knowing our general public better and communicating with these people more effectively.

Ways for the general public to participate in archaeology

Positive mass media messages may also awaken interest in the study of archaeology, and such interest may be served in a variety of different ways and at different levels. People can read books or newspapers or journal articles about archaeological sites, excavations, or other archaeological subjects. They can visit museums or public sites or parks with archaeological collections on display and archaeological interpretations. If they are especially interested, and willing to spend some of their time, and possibly money, they can take part in professionally supervised archaeological projects, such as excavations or site surveys, or they may be able to work in laboratories with artefacts.

There are a number of accessible books about archaeology aimed at the interested public and several popular and readily available magazines regularly publish well-researched and well-written articles about archaeology. *Archaeology*, published bimonthly, is devoted entirely to articles, book and film reviews, travel and exhibition news and regular columns on archaeological topics. Other magazines regularly publish articles on archaeological topics: *National Geographic* (published monthly), *Natural History* (published bimonthly), *Scientific American* (published monthly) and *Smithsonian* (published monthly). These magazines are available from booksellers and at local libraries throughout the United States. A large number of more specialized journals also publish articles about archaeology. For example, in most of the United States there are State-wide archaeological organizations whose members are particularly interested in the archaeology of their area. Members include both those interested in archaeology as an avocation or hobby and full-time professional archaeologists. Typically, these organizations publish a quarterly journal about archaeological investigations and research results within the State.

For especially interested individuals there are a number of specialized regional and national journals that publish articles, book reviews, comments and opinions about archaeology.[1] The coverage is often detailed and technical, but these publications provide interested readers with a general up-to-date view of the American archaeology scene. While these more technical journals will not be found in every local library, they are typically found in university libraries or other large public libraries and are usually available through interlibrary loan programmes.

Television programmes and videotapes can also provide accurate and interesting information to individuals who want to learn more about archaeology. Nearly everyone in the United States has seen one of the 'Indiana Jones' movies, and so 'archaeology' is now a household word. The adventure in modern archaeology is not the sort of rough-and-tumble adventure of the 'Indiana Jones' films, however. The real adventures of discovery and time travel in modern archaeology are often portrayed in videos and television programmes. Many of these can be seen regularly on public broadcasting stations, such as the *Nova* series sponsored by the Public Broadcasting System (PBS), which regularly has shows on archaeological topics. Other series or individual programmes can also be found each month on PBS stations. Increasingly television programmes, as well as other films not produced for television, can be obtained for rent or purchase through video rental stores or film distributors. The Learning Channel, a commercial cable channel, has recently begun broadcasting a weekly series on archaeology. Those interested in finding more videos about archaeology can consult the comprehensive list in *Archaeology on Film*, compiled and edited by Allen & Lazio (1983). Videos that have appeared since the publication of this book in 1983 may have been reviewed in *Archaeology* magazine, which publishes such reviews as a regular feature.

For those interested in visiting sites or museums, there are thousands of archaeological sites with interpretation programmes and museums that interpret archaeological remains throughout the United States and in other countries. In the United States, sites and museums are operated by Federal, State, Tribal, local and private organizations. *Archaeology* magazine publishes in each issue a listing of current archaeological exhibitions at museums throughout the country. *Archaeology* also publishes two travel guides each year: the March–April issue lists sites in the Old World that can be visited or at which individuals can volunteer time to excavate; and a listing in the May–June issue provides information about similar opportunities in North, Central and South America.

The most complete listing of archaeological sites and museums in America north of Mexico that welcome visitors is found in *America's Ancient Treasures* (Folsom & Folsom 1983). This book is a guide to hundreds of archaeological sites and museums that can be visited in the United States and Canada. Many entries have very detailed descriptions of the exhibits and archaeological remains at the sites. The October 1991 issue of *National Geographic* magazine also provides a national directory of sites or museums to visit, but is much less detailed. Archaeological guidebooks are also available for different regions of the country, especially the Southwest (e.g. Lister & Lister 1983; Noble 1991).

As for participatory experiences in archaeology, such as volunteer activities, open houses and tours, opportunities are increasing (e.g. Potter & Leone 1987; Hays 1989; Redman 1989; Smith & McManamon 1991). Such programmes should always include a clear and definite message that independently collecting artefacts from the surface or digging are not appropriate or constructive ways to participate in archaeology. Unauthorized collecting or digging for artefacts is illegal on Federal land and many other kinds of public land, as well as on private land without permission. More importantly, doing archaeology without the proper training and professional support destroys potentially important archaeological information about the context in which artefacts and structures are found.

Until recently, the only way for most people to become involved directly in a professional archaeological study was to enrol in a college field school. Normal work schedules and college semesters being what they are, it was difficult for many people to take advantage of these opportunities, although they are regularly available (Archaeological Institute of America 1992; American Anthropological Association 1992). Now people have the opportunity to participate in professionally supervised archaeological investigations if they are willing to contribute time and, usually, money. The travel guides published annually in *Archaeology* magazine list opportunities to volunteer and participate in excavations, surveys, or lab work. Several private organizations also conduct such programmes.

Increasingly, public agencies at all levels use volunteer help in archaeology, overseen by professional archaeologists (e.g. Cressey 1987; Bense 1991; Hoffman 1991). The Bureau of Land Management and the Forest Service have nationwide programmes to inform interested individuals about volunteer opportunities to participate in archaeological and historic preservation projects (Osborn & Peters 1991; Brook 1992).

It is frequently possible to involve the public in a variety of ways in a specific archaeological project. Bense (1991) provides such an example in a project in Pensacola, Florida, that aimed to develop and focus public support for the preservation of local archaeological sites. The project was highlighted by the development and marketing of a colonial archaeology trail that publicized the archaeological remnants of Pensacola's colonial town heritage. The programme involved many sectors of the public as volunteers and ran regular field trips for public school classes to local sites (Bense 1991, p. 11).

Reaching out to students and teachers

Students and teachers are a section of the general public that deserves special attention because they present special opportunities (Selig 1989). Many archaeologists already make periodic presentations before school groups. We can also focus mass-media promotions on students, through, for example, bookmarks for school libraries, poster contests in schools, or other activities. This publicity can have far-reaching consequences, as children's ideas and attitudes can have a strong effect on the behaviour of their parents and grandparents. Teachers should become a focus as well, for they may be particularly able to instil an appreciation of archaeology and archaeological resources in their students.

How can teachers be reached effectively and efficiently? The experience of the Archaeology for the Schools Committee of the Arizona Archaeological Council (ACC) illustrates the realities of attempting to integrate archaeology into public school systems in the United States. There is no national school curriculum or specific requirements for students in US public schools; State governments control some aspects of school programmes, such as teacher certification, pupil attendance and general curriculum guides, but most of the control and specific requirements for classroom instruction are developed and imposed at the local school district level (Rogge & Bell 1989, pp. 2–3). This means that not a single office at the national or State level could, assuming those in charge wished to, mandate the inclusion of archaeology within a widely used curriculum. Nor is there much time available within the typical tightly packed school curriculum for archaeology to be squeezed in as a separate subject.

The ACC found, after at least one false start, that establishing a teacher accreditation workshop was an effective way to reach teachers (Rogge & Bell 1989). They learned that personal contact with teachers was an important step in getting them to incorporate archaeology in their classrooms. An initial mailing was done to virtually every school in Arizona (there are about 910 schools in the 210 school districts of the State) but the committee received responses from only a dozen teachers. As they learned more about the way school systems operate, the committee members realized that their mailing probably hadn't reached many teachers:

> we learned that media specialists and librarians in every school probably receive several mass mailings a week, and we suspect most of our cherished packets probably never emerged from the bottom of the stack to be hung on bulletin boards or to be routed to the teachers themselves. Without some personal contact, even our bright multihued packets were probably read by few teachers.
>
>   (Rogge & Bell 1989, p. 3)

Using the lessons of their experience, the committee has since taken a different approach, one that recognizes both the limited availability of time in the existing curriculum and the need to contact teachers directly.

> We are currently promoting archaeology as supplemental [lessons] that can be implemented without overloading teachers who feel stressed by the materials they are already expected to cover.

Supplemental activities can range from a 45-minute exercise that presents a realistic perspective on prehistoric Indians (in conjunction with Columbus Day or Thanksgiving) to a several week unit involving a mock dig. Or, it could simply include arithmetic story problems about the average number of sherds per broken pot or an art project modelling a prehistoric pit house or pueblo.

(Rogge & Bell 1989, p. 3)

It is fortunate that archaeology provides examples for teaching in a wide variety of subjects, because it opens up the potential for developing new educational applications. This is among the attractive qualities identified by others (e.g. Higgens & Holm 1986) that archaeology has for teachers and students. These characteristics also include:

1 its compatibility with hands-on activities and exercises;
2 its easy combination with work outside the formal classroom, including outdoor activities, visits to museums and working with nearby archaeological sites, laboratories or exhibits; [and]
3 its compatibility with exercises thought to develop thinking skills in general and scientific reasoning in particular.

(Selig 1991, p. 3)

In many States, approaches to teachers are under way involving curricula development, 'in-service' workshops, archaeological summer courses or field schools for teachers (e.g. Green 1988; Hawkins 1988; Charles & Walden 1989; Williams 1989; Ellick 1991; Selig 1991).

However, even the attractive attributes of archaeology do not ensure teachers' interest in using it in their classrooms. A number of organizations have identified teachers as a group to target for public education projects. The American Anthropological Association has a Task Force on the Teaching of Anthropology. The National Trust for Historic Preservation is forming a National Center for Heritage Education (National Trust for Historic Preservation 1989; Patrick 1989; Hunter 1990). The National Park Service is developing a series of lesson plans, based upon historic properties listed in the National Register of Historic Places, for history and social studies teachers (Shull & Hunter 1992). Many of these 'Teaching with Historic Places' lesson plans include archaeological aspects of historic properties and some of the historic properties are primarily archaeological sites – for example, Knife River Indian Villages in North Dakota (Metcalf 1992). The Public Education Committees of both the Society for Historical Archaeology and the Society for American Archaeology have identified elementary- and secondary-school teachers as especially important audiences.

There is, in fact, intense competition for teachers' attention and interest. Geographers, backed by the substantial resources of the National Geographic Society, and historians have major initiatives under way for improving the teaching of their disciplines in secondary and elementary schools (e.g. Bradley

Commission on History in Schools 1988; Gagnon 1989). Science education is also a topic of recent concern and attention. Again teachers, along with the design or redesign of elementary and secondary curricula, are receiving a great deal of attention (e.g. American Association for the Advancement of Science 1989).

All of this focus on teachers, teacher training and curriculum development makes it even less likely that courses devoted exclusively to archaeology will become standard in elementary or secondary schools in the United States. Yet, as recognized by many, the wide range of disciplines that archaeology is related to in the humanities and the social, biological, mathematical and physical sciences provides many opportunities for using archaeological examples, lessons, techniques and concepts in a variety of courses at all educational levels.

Devising effective means of reaching teachers and effective materials and ideas for them to use are two of the major immediate challenges in educating this important subset of the public. Throughout the United States, archaeologists have begun to work with educators on materials for use in a variety of classroom settings.

Another major challenge is expanding and servicing a network of teachers interested in using archaeology as an instructional tool and at least three newsletters, with teachers as their principal audience, attempt to address this challenge.[2]

The challenge of Native American outreach

It is ironic that the segment of the public most directly connected to the past societies that most American archaeologists study, modern American Indians, has not been a primary audience for archaeological public education and outreach. In 1985, following discussions among archaeologists, Native American representatives and their advocates, this general lack of outreach was noted as a serious problem:

> archaeologists and physical anthropologists have failed to communicate their research goals effectively. Few benefits from such research are perceived by the [Native Americans] themselves. There is, moreover, a strong suspicion in some quarters that the research is undertaken for motives of personal advancement of the researcher, without intent to benefit the subjects.
>
> (Dincauze 1985, p. 1)

Although there are some notable and promising exceptions to this lack of attention and concern about sharing archaeological information with Indians (e.g. Kaupp 1988; Bishop, Canouts, DeAtley, Masayesva & Qoyauayma 1989; Blancke & Slow Turtle 1990; Ravesloot 1990), such works are still in the minority.

Those concerned with the preservation of archaeological collections linked to modern Native American groups may pay a severe price for this inattention. Increasingly, Indian groups and tribes insist on the repatriation of all or parts of such collections. Legislation passed by Congress in 1989 and 1990 directs the Smithsonian Institution, Federal agencies and museums receiving Federal funds to work with Tribes and other Indian groups on the repatriation of some portions of the collections they currently hold (see e.g. McManamon & Nordby 1992). Archaeologists must move swiftly to recognize the legitimate concerns of these Tribes and other organizations and to work with them to provide more information about the past that they recognize as relevant (e.g. Klesert 1992; Ravesloot & Chiago 1992).

Archaeologists must take note of the challenge that this sets for them. Reid (1992a) has identified two aspects of this challenge after reflecting upon a recent attempt at dialogue between Native Americans and archaeologists. He noted that Native Americans involved in the discussions

> raised objections to their oral traditions being labelled myths and legends by archaeologists. They preferred to reference them as 'stories' and probably would not object to 'oral history'. . . . Archaeological accounts of the past, especially the past of a particular Native American people, are perceived by them to present a threat to traditional Native American accounts of that same past. The perceived threat is that the archaeological account eventually would replace the traditionally constructed past and erode, once again, another piece of their culture. . . . After two full days of listening to academic papers, the all-Indian panel voiced the opinion that archaeologists appeared not to reach conclusions, which I take to certify their powers of observation. More disturbing, however, was their assertion that the archaeology of the Southwest had no relevance for southwestern Indians. . . . Do Native American oral histories and scientific accounts of prehistory complement one another, like traditional and modern medicine, or is one destined to be subsumed by the other? These are issues that archaeologists must discuss among themselves and with Native Americans.
>
> (Reid 1992a, p. 195)

There is no doubt about the importance of cultural history information to Native Americans (see Parker 1990, 1991). Response by Tribes and other Native American organizations to the National Park Service Tribal Historic Preservation programme has been widespread and intense. The call for grant applications by Tribes to improve Tribal historic preservation programmes through an appropriation by Congress generated several hundred proposals. An advertisement in *Indian News* of the availability of bookmarks promoting archaeological preservation generated forty replies from Indian primary- and secondary-school programmes, libraries and Tribal governments requesting at least 20,000 bookmarks, mainly for distribution to students. One requester described a Tribal traditional children's society and how the bookmarks would 'make excellent educational treats and make parents aware of the importance of preserving our historical sites'.

Some Indian Tribes and other Native American organizations, such as the Makah, Navajo and Zuni Tribes, have had cultural preservation programmes for many years (see articles in Klesert & Downer 1990; Begay 1991). And in recent years there has been widespread interest by Native Americans in cultural centres, language retention programmes and other activities related to Tribal historic and cultural preservation (Fuller 1991; Sadongei 1991; Warren 1991). Native Americans increasingly seek training and technical information and themselves serve as instructors in course work on protection and preservation of archaeological and ethnographic resources. National Park Service courses in curation, interpretation, archaeological protection and ethnography have benefited from Native Americans' participation as instructors as well as students. Concern about the contents and care of objects in archaeological collections has fostered an interest by Native Americans in museum methods and techniques as well as sources for training in museology.

Most archaeologists working in the USA on prehistoric or historic archaeological sites related to Indians cannot ignore Tribal concerns legally (see Carmichael, Hubert, Reeves & Schanche 1994). Archaeological investigations on Federal land (about one-third of the United States) must be preceded by consultation with Indian Tribes that are likely to have an interest in, or to be culturally affiliated with, the archaeological sites that will be investigated. Such consultations have been required by the regulations implementing the Archaeological Resources Protection Act since 1984. The enactment of the Native American Graves Protection and Repatriation Act in 1990 requires Federal agencies to consult with Indian Tribes likely to have some connection with a range of 'cultural items', specifically, Native American human remains, funerary objects, sacred objects, and objects of cultural patrimony that may be found in archaeological sites, whenever such sites are to be excavated or when they are inadvertently discovered or exposed. The consultation is intended to provide the concerned Tribes with an opportunity to discuss with the Federal agency officials how these Native American human remains and cultural items should be handled, described and analysed. Furthermore, after whatever removal, description and analysis the Federal agency officials determine to be appropriate are completed, any Native American human remains and cultural items are to be repatriated to the most closely culturally affiliated Indian Tribe, if that Tribe requests their repatriation.

Certainly, archaeologists must pay more attention to Indian concerns and interests in the treatment and disposition of remains and objects that most archaeologists have thought of as their own. This has caused much concern within the discipline, not only in the United States, but also in other countries where aboriginal peoples have asserted their rights.

Over the past two decades tribal Indians have gone from being wards of a paternalistic federal agency – the Bureau of Indian Affairs – to asserting authority and power in the best traditions of American self-interest. And, indeed, the entrance of new, powerful participants in any field of endeavor creates a wrenching of traditional structures with attendant discomfort for many.

(Reid 1992b)

This includes archaeologists, and others, for the new power of Indian Tribes in these matters also affects physical anthropologists, museum collection managers and curators. All these professionals must take up the challenge and step towards Indians, offering the benefits of archaeology, but with an awareness that other ways of knowing about the past will also be espoused by those with whom they are attempting to establish new relationships.

An archaeologist who has conducted scientific archaeology with and for American Indians for a number of years offers this advice:

If archaeologists expect Indians to respect their scientific perspective, and if they wish to be allowed continued access to Native American remains in order to pursue this particular perception of the world, they must in return be willing to concede the equal validity of Native American wishes concerning those same remains. They must be willing to conduct such research in a manner that does not violate basic anthropological ethics concerning the welfare of those cultures being studied. This effort does not imply capitulation to anti-scientific radicals . . . it simply requires an adherence to tenets of anthropological relativism . . . a willingness to learn and understand the Native American world view and to eschew arrogance in the education of Native Americans as to the anthropological view of things. The two points of view (anthropological and Native American) are not mutually exclusive.

(Klesert 1992, p. 21)

Conclusion

Public education is not *terra incognita* for archaeologists. Fascination with and writing about the ancient past or archaeological remains is evident from at least the time of Herodotus, who recorded the antiquities of Egypt and legends about them. In England, the *Illustrated London News* and other popular publications provided the general reading public regularly with stories of archaeological discoveries and excavations from at least the middle of the nineteenth century onwards (Bacon 1976). More recently in the USA, news weeklies, *National Geographic* (and see Gero & Root 1990) and *Archaeology* magazines, and other magazines and media outlets report regularly about certain aspects of archaeology. Public interpretation in National Parks and other public lands and at many national, regional and local museums frequently include presentations of archaeological information to the public.

However, attention to public education by many professional archaeologists is minimal. To continue in this way is folly; it will make archaeology less accessible and less important to the American public that, in one way or another, pays for most of the archaeological investigations done in the United States (Keel, McManamon & Smith 1989, pp. 13–25, 50–2). It seems especially foolish not to take advantage of existing interest in archaeology and use it to support legitimate archaeological activities and preservation.

Archaeologists in academic institutions must rely on the general public's interest in archaeology to fill their course offerings so that their departments remain strong or continue to grow. Archaeologists involved with public archaeology rely on lay people to support Federal, State, Tribal and local archaeological resource preservation activities and programmes. All archaeologists depend on individual members of the public to protect archaeological resources that they find on their land, in their jobs, on their vacations or in other situations.

Public education and outreach meet a public need, as is shown by the large numbers of people that enjoy them during State archaeology weeks, open houses held at scientific excavations, and the increasing number of programmes offering non-archaeologists opportunities to participate in professionally supervised investigations. Public programmes help preserve resources by reducing the looting and vandalism of sites and providing volunteers to help with site monitoring, stabilization, retrieval and preservation activities. Educational programmes stimulate students, offering practical and intellectually challenging activities and leaving positive impressions about archaeology and the need to preserve archaeological resources on audiences ranging from preschoolers to senior citizens. Such public programmes and efforts might even provide a way to revive synthetic interpretation within American archaeology, a process made increasingly difficult within academic institutions by rampant overspecialization. Public education and outreach in archaeology need to continue to grow. What archaeologists have learned in this arena over the past years should be widely shared with other archaeologists, educators and public administrators. Archaeologists should also make use of the positive aspects of popular culture, such as the Indiana Jones movies, and the works of Agatha Christie, Jean Auel, James Michener and other novelists who use archaeology or archaeological information in their plots, to explain the differences between these uses of archaeology and the real thing. But, and here is the real challenge, we need to do so without losing the appreciation of and interest in archaeology that Indiana Jones and his like have aroused.

Acknowledgements

The summary report of the Listing of Education in Archaeological Programs (LEAP) would have been impossible without the diligence and extra effort of Patsy Knoll, Jean Alexander, Val Canouts, Larry Karr, Ruthann Knudson and Juliette Tahar. Robin Coates, LaTia Adams and Lori Hawkins each contributed to the updating and expansion of the original manuscript. Dick Waldbauer and Patsy Knoll provided comments and additional ideas for the section on Native Americans. Carol Pierce has provided practical and theoretical advice related to education in the classroom, and Adalie and Kate constantly reveal the students' perspective on these matters. I appreciate the comments, efforts and suggestions that I have received and hope those who have assisted me agree with the points made in this chapter.

Notes

1 There are about a dozen regional journals, such as *Arctic Anthropology, Man in the Northeast, Southeastern Archaeology, Plains Anthropologist, The Midcontinental Journal of Archaeology, Kiva* and others. The national specialized archaeological journals that devote much of their space to the United States include: *American Antiquity, Historical Archaeology, Journal of Anthropological Archaeology, Journal of Field Archaeology, Latin American Antiquity* and *North American Archaeologist*. International journals also regularly publish articles on American archaeology, including: *Antiquity, Canadian Journal of Anthropology, Journal of World Prehistory* and *World Archaeology*.

2 *Anthro Notes*, published by the Department of Anthropology, Museum of Natural History, Smithsonian Institution; *Archaeology and Public Education*, published by the Public Education Committee of the Society for American Archaeology; and *Teaching Anthropology Newsletter*, published by the Department of Anthropology, St Mary's University, Halifax, Nova Scotia, Canada. A related journal is *Remnants*, published by the Education Service of English Heritage. It focuses on the cultural resources of England, but includes much information about lesson plans, classroom activities and other aspects of teaching that can be adapted to American situations.

References

Allen, P. S. & C. Lazio 1983. *Archaeology on Film*. Boston: Archaeological Institute of America.

American Anthropological Association 1992. Summer Field School List. Washington: American Anthropological Association.

American Association for the Advancement of Science 1989. *Science for All Americans: a project 2061 report on literacy goals in science, mathematics, and technology*. Washington: American Association for the Advancement of Science.

Archaeological Institute of America 1992. *Archaeological Fieldwork Opportunities Bulletin*. Boston: Archaeological Institute of America.

Archaeology 1991. A sampling of creative initiatives. *Archaeology* 44, 40–3.

Bacon, E. 1976. *The Great Archaeologists and their Discoveries as Originally Reported in the Pages of the* Illustrated London News. New York: Bobbs–Merrill.

78   F. P. McMANAMON

Begay, D. R. 1991. Navajo preservation: the success of the Navajo Nation Historic Preservation Department. *CRM* 14, 1–4.

Bense, J. A. 1991. The Pensacola model of public archaeology. In *Archaeology and Education: the classroom and beyond*, Smith, K. C. & F. P. McManamon (eds), 9–12. Washington: National Park Service.

Bishop, R. L., V. Canouts, S. P. DeAtley, V. Masayesva & A. Qoyauayma 1989. An American Indian Outreach Program: discovering a partnership between high tech research and traditional knowledge in the Hopi classroom. Paper presented at the 1989 Western Museums Conference, Phoenix, Arizona.

Blancke, S. & Cjigkitoonuppa J. P. Slow Turtle 1990. The teaching of the past of the Native peoples of North America in US schools. In *The Excluded Past: archaeology in education*, Stone, P. & R. Mackenzie (eds), 109–33. London: Unwin Hyman; Routledge pbk 1994.

Bradley Commission on History in Schools 1988. *Building a History Curriculum: guidelines for teaching history in schools*. Washington: Education Excellence Network.

Brook, R. A. 1992. Adventures in the past. *Federal Archaeology Report* 5, 1–4.

Butler, W. B. (ed.) 1992. *State Archaeological Education Programs*. Denver: Rocky Mountain Regional Office, National Park Service.

Carmichael, D., J. Hubert, B. Reeves and A. Schanche (eds) 1994. *Sacred Sites, Sacred Places*. London: Routledge.

Charles, T. & M. B. Walden 1989. *Can You Dig It? A classroom guide to South Carolina archaeology*. Columbia: South Carolina Department of Education.

Cleere, H. 1989. Introduction: the rationale of archaeological heritage management. In *Archaeological Heritage Management in the Modern World*, Cleere, H. (ed.), 1–19. London: Unwin Hyman.

Cressey, P. J. 1987. Community archaeology in Alexandria, Virginia. *Conserve Neighborhoods* no. 69. Washington: National Trust for Historic Preservation.

Culliton, B. J. 1988. The dismal state of scientific literacy. *Science* 243, 600.

Davis, H. A. 1991. Avocational archaeology groups: a secret weapon for site protection. In *Protecting the Past*, Smith, G. S. & J. E. Ehrenhard (eds), 175–80. Boca Raton, Fla.: CRC Press.

DeCicco, G. 1988. A public relations primer. *American Antiquity* 53, 840–56.

Dincauze, D. F. 1985. Report on the Conference on Reburial Issues. *Bulletin of the Society for American Archaeology* 3, 1–3.

Durant, J. R., G. A. Evans & G. P. Thomas 1989. The public understanding of science. *Nature* 340, 11–14.

Ellick, C. 1991. Archeology is more than a dig: educating children about the past saves sites for the future. In *Archaeology and Education: the classroom and beyond*, Smith, K. C. & F. P. McManamon (eds), 27–32. Washington: National Park Service.

Fagan, B. M. 1984. Archaeology and the wider audience. In *Ethics and Values in Archaeology*, Green, E. L. (ed.), 175–83. New York: The Free Press.

Fagan, B. M. 1991. The past as news. *CRM* 14, 17–19.

Fairbanks Associates 1988. Management study of short-range and long-range needs for organization and operations. Prepared for the Society for American Archaeology, Washington, D.C.

Feder, K. L. 1984. Irrationality and popular archaeology. *American Antiquity* 49, 525–41.

Folsom, F. & M. E. Folsom 1983. *America's Ancient Treasures*. Albuquerque: University of New Mexico Press.

Fuller, N. 1991. Ak-Chin Him Dak – a new model for community heritage management opens to public. *CRM* 14, 36–7.

Gagnon, P. A. 1989. *The Future of the Past: the plight of history in American education*. New York: Macmillan.

Gero, J. & D. Root 1990. Public presentations and private concerns: archaeology in the pages of *National Geographic*. In *The Politics of the Past*, Gathercole, P. & D. Lowenthal (eds), 19–37. London: Unwin Hyman; Routledge pbk 1994.

Green, W. 1988. *Iowa's P.A.S.T. (Programming Archaeology for School Teachers)*. Iowa City: Office of the State Archaeologist, University of Iowa.

Hawkins, N. W. 1988. *Classroom Archaeology: a curriculum guide for teachers*. Baton Rouge: Division of Archaeology, Department of Culture, Recreation and Tourism.

Hays, K. 1989. Men, women and dirt: Earthwatch volunteers and the Homol'ovi Research Program. In *Fighting Indiana Jones in Arizona: Society for Conservation Archaeology, 1988 Proceedings*, Rogge, A. E. & J. Montgomery (eds), 9–12. Portales, N.Mex.: American Society for Conservation Archaeology.

Higgens, P. J. & K. A. Holm 1986. Archaeology and precollege education. *Practicing Anthropology* 8, 24–8.

Hively, W. 1988. Science observer: how much science does the public understand? *American Scientist* 76, 439–44.

Hoffman, T. L. 1991. Stewards of the past: preserving Arizona's archaeological resources through positive public involvement. In *Protecting the Past*, Smith, G. C. & J. E. Ehrenhard (eds), 253–9. Boca Raton, Fla.: CRC Press.

Hunter, K. 1990. A national center for heritage education. *Cultural Resource Management Bulletin* 13(3).

Judge, W. J. 1991. Saving the past for ourselves. In *Protecting the Past*, Smith, G. S. & J. E. Ehrenhard (eds), 277–82. Boca Raton, Fla.: CRC Press.

Kaupp, A. 1988. The Hopi–Smithsonian Project: bridging a gap. *Anthro Notes* 10, 11–14.

Keel, B. C., F. P. McManamon & G. C. Smith 1989. *Federal Archaeology: the current program*. Washington: National Park Service.

Klesert, A. L. 1992. A view from Navajoland on the reconciliation of anthropologists and Native Americans. *Human Organization* 51, 17–22.

Klesert, A. L. & A. S. Downer (eds) 1990. *Preservation on the Reservation: Native Americans, Native American lands and archaeology*. Navajo Nation Papers in Anthropology no. 26. Shiprock, Ariz.: Navajo Nation Archaeology Department, Navajo Nation Historic Preservation Department.

Knoll, P. C. (ed.) 1990. *Listing of Education in Archaeological Programs: the LEAP clearinghouse, 1987–1989 summary report*. Washington: National Park Service.

Knoll, P. C. (ed.) 1992. *Listing of Education in Archaeological Programs: the LEAP clearinghouse, 1991–1992 summary report*. Washington: National Park Service.

Leone, M. P., P. B. Potter, Jr & P. A. Shackel 1987. Toward a critical archaeology. *Current Anthropology* 28, 283–302.

Lerner, S. 1989. Preventing the problem. *Bulletin of the Society for American Archaeology* 7(5), 6.

Lerner, S. 1991. Saving sites: preservation and education. In *Protecting the Past*, Smith, G. S. & J. E. Ehrenhard (eds), 103–8. Boca Raton, Fla.: CRC Press.

Lister, R. & F. Lister 1983. *Those Who Came Before*. Tucson: University of Arizona Press.

McManamon, F. P. 1991a. The many publics for archaeology. *American Antiquity* 56, 121–30.

McManamon, F. P. 1991b. The Federal government's report response to archaeological looting. In *Protecting the Past*, Smith, G. S. & J. E. Ehrenhard (eds), 261–70. Boca Raton, Fla.: CRC Press.

McManamon, F. P., P. C. Knoll, R. Knudson, G. S. Smith & R. C. Waldbauer 1992. *Current Federal Archaeological Programs*. Washington: National Park Service.

McManamon, F. P. & L. Nordby 1992. Implementing the Native American Graves Protection and Repatriation Act. *Arizona State Law Journal* 24, 217–52.

Metcalf, F. 1992. Knife River: early village life on the plains. A 'Teaching with Historic Places' supplement. *Social Education* 56, following p. 312.

Milanich, J. T. 1991. Archaeology in the sunshine: grass roots education through the media and public involvement. In *Protecting the Past*, Smith, G. S. & J. E. Ehrenhard (eds), 109–16. Boca Raton, Fla.: CRC Press.

National Trust for Historic Preservation 1989. *Heritage Education: opportunities for partnership*. Washington: Program Council, National Trust for Historic Preservation.

Neumann, L. & K. Reinburg (eds) 1989. Save the past for the future: special report. *Bulletin of the Society for American Archaeology* 7, 3–10.

Noble, D. G. 1991. *Ancient Ruins of the Southwest: an archaeological guide*. Flagstaff, Ariz.: Northland Publishing.

Osborn, J. A. & G. Peters 1991. Passport in time. *Federal Archaeology Report* 4, 1–6.

Parker, P. 1990. *Keepers of the Treasures*. Washington: Interagency Resources Division, National Park Service.

Parker, P. 1991. America's Tribal cultures – a renaissance in the 1990s. *CRM* 14, 1–3.

Patrick, J. J. 1989. Heritage education in the school curriculum. Paper presented at the Planning Forum for the National Center for Heritage Education, sponsored by the National Trust for Historic Preservation and the Waterford Foundation, Waterford, Va., 16–19 November 1989.

Peters, K. S., E. A. Comer & R. Kelly 1987. *Captivating the Public through the Media while Digging the Past*. Technical Series no. 1. Baltimore: Baltimore Center for Urban Archaeology.

Pokotylo, D. L. & A. R. Mason 1991. Public attitudes towards archaeological resources and their management. In *Protecting the Past*, Smith, G. S. & J. E. Ehrenhard (eds), 9–18. Boca Raton, Fla.: CRC Press.

Potter, P. B., Jr 1990. The 'what' and 'why' of public relations for archaeology: a postscript to DeCicco's public relations primer. *American Antiquity* 55, 608–13.

Potter, P. B., Jr & M. P. Leone 1987. Archaeology in public in Annapolis: four seasons, six sites, seven tours, and 32,000 visitors. *American Archaeology* 6, 51–61.

Ravesloot, J. C. 1990. On the treatment and reburial of human remains: the San Xavior Bridge Project. *The American Indian Quarterly* 4.

Ravesloot, J. C. & C. M. Chiago 1992. Working together to understand the prehistory and history of the Gila River Pima, Arizona. Paper presented at the 1992 Annual Meeting of the Society for American Archaeology, Pittsburgh, Pa.

Redman, C. L. 1989. Revitalizing archaeology through public outreach. In *Fighting Indiana Jones in Arizona: American Society for Conservation Archaeology, 1988 Proceedings*, Rogge, A. E. & J. Montgomery (eds), 25–7. Portales, N.Mex.: American Society for Conservation Archaeology.

Reid, J. J. 1992a. Editor's corner: recent findings on North American prehistory. *American Antiquity* 57, 195–6.

Reid, J. J. 1992b. Editor's corner: quincentennial truths and consequences. *American Antiquity* 57, 583.

Reinberg, K. M. 1991. Save the past for the future: a partnership to protect our past. In *Protecting the Past*, Smith, G. S. & J. E. Ehrenhard (eds), 271–6. Boca Raton, Fla.: CRC Press.

Rogge, A. E. & P. Bell 1989. *Archaeology in the Classroom: case study from Arizona*. Archaeological Assistance Program Technical Brief no. 4. Washington: National Park Service.

Rogge, A. E. & J. Montgomery (eds) 1989. *Fighting Indiana Jones in Arizona: American Society for Conservation Archaeology, 1988 Proceedings*. Portales, N.Mex.: American Society for Conservation Archaeology.

Sadongei, A. 1991. New training opportunities for American Indians at the Smithsonian Institution – the American Indian Studies Program. *CRM* 14, 11–12.

Secretary for the Interior 1991. *A Strategy for Federal Archaeology*. Washington: Office of the Secretary, Department of the Interior.

Selig, R 1989. Anthropology in public schools: why should we care? *Anthropology Newsletter* February, 28.

Selig, R. 1991. Teacher training programs in anthropology: the multiplier effect in the classroom. In *Archaeology and Education: the classroom and beyond*, Smith, K. C. & F. P. McManamon (eds), 3–8. Washington: National Park Service.

Shields, H. M. 1991. Marketing archaeological resource protection. In *Protecting the Past*, Smith, G. S. & J. E. Ehrenhard (eds), 167–73. Boca Raton, Fla.: CRC Press.

Shull, C. D. & K. Hunter 1992. Teaching with historic places. *Social Education* 56, 312.

Smith, G. S., F. P. McManamon, R. A. Anzalone, J. W. Hand & J. C. Maxon (compilers) 1988. Archaeology and the Federal Government. *CRM Bulletin* 11, 1–36.

Smith, K. C. & F. P. McManamon (eds) 1991. *Archaeology and Education: the classroom and beyond*. Archaeological Assistance Series no. 2, Departmental Consulting Archaeologist, Archaeological Assistance Division, National Park Service, Washington, D.C.

Society for American Archaeology 1990. *Save the Past for the Future: actions for the '90s*. Washington: Society for American Archaeology, Office of Governmental Relations.

Stone, P. & R. MacKenzie (eds) 1990. *The Excluded Past: archaeology in education*. London: Unwin Hyman; Routledge pbk 1994.

Warren, W. 1991. A model cultural center at Pojoaque Pueblo. *CRM* 14, 4–6.

Williams, J. A. 1989. *Illinois Archaeological Resource Materials with Annotated Bibliography for Teachers*. Springfield: Illinois Historic Preservation Agency.

4 Public education and archaeology in Florida, USA: an overview and case study

NANCY MARIE WHITE & J. RAYMOND WILLIAMS

Introduction

Florida's cultural record is heavily affected by geography and history. The state is growing explosively; it has a higher population density than California, is the fourth most populous in the USA and predicted to be the third most populous by AD 2000. Since the land development and tourist boom early in this century, this phenomenal growth has meant massive clearing of forests and wetlands and the draining and filling of swamps and coastlines, all for construction of retirement and vacation homes, office buildings, mobile home parks, and theme/amusement parks. The relentless drive to cover the state with concrete and condominiums continues unabated. However, Florida's tourism also means that it spends more by far than any other state; this year about $12 million on historic preservation. It is now nearly impossible to do archaeology in Florida that is not in some way public.

Archaeology in Florida is complex and interesting because of the State's natural environment, its geographic location and geology, and its historical situation as the first area of the USA to be contacted by Europeans. Florida is a long peninsula jutting southward between the Gulf of Mexico and the Atlantic and Caribbean, attached to the rest of the continent by a long east–west 'panhandle' (Fig. 4.1). These two parts roughly separate two contrasting modern cultures: the urban, tourist-oriented peninsula and the rural panhandle. Together they make up an unexpectedly large state – 1200 km from Pensacola to Miami.

Prehistoric Floridans had different kinds of adaptations, from the largely coastal peninsular environments to the rich farmland of the northwest panhandle. Preservation of material culture is widely varied. Though based upon limestone bedrock, Florida's sandy soils tend to be too acidic for the survival of organic material. But deep springs in the peninsula have yielded organic Palaeo-Indian and Archaic period remains, such as wood and other plant materials, bone and ivory tools and human skeletons, some with preserved brain tissue.

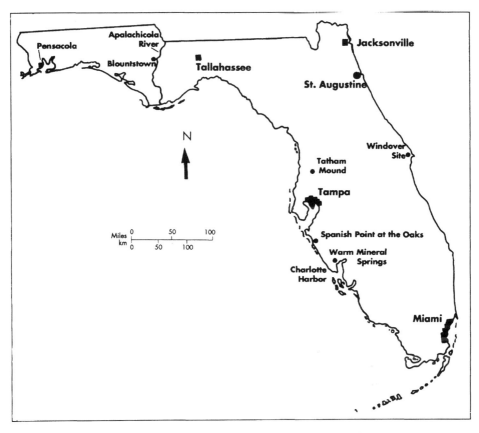

Figure 4.1 The State of Florida, showing archaeological sites and areas mentioned in the text.

During the last two millennia before contact (the Woodland and Mississippian cultural periods), the contrast between panhandle and peninsula becomes more apparent. More fertile northwest Florida may have seen early experimentation with cultivated plants. During later prehistory densely populated hierarchical chiefdoms developed here, supported by intensive maize–beans–squash agriculture and temple-mound ceremonial centres. The more sparsely occupied peninsula saw the development of some less materially spectacular cultural adaptations, with little or no agriculture. However, in the southern peninsula there were complex tributary chiefdoms apparently based totally upon the gathering of wild resources. Later south Florida cultures had linguistic and cultural connections with Caribbean, Central and South American cultures.

When the Spanish arrived in the early sixteenth century, Florida was quickly affected by Old World microbes and weapons. There was rapid culture change among aboriginal groups, especially when the Spanish established their missions. Later, British, French, Americans and Creek Indians from the north came into the region. All these contacts have given anthropologists much material to explore the interaction of different cultural traditions and resulting new forms. The most significant of these new societies was the Seminoles, a seventeenth-century tribal amalgam of the survivors of several aboriginal ethnic groups, all influenced by European, African and American cultures and genetics. Many Seminoles fled the length of the state to south Florida to develop a new and different form of social and environmental adaptation (Weisman 1989). They have been quite successful, at first in resisting the American military, later in profiting from tourism, and recently in establishing a very profitable bingo industry.

One way in which archaeologists have got support for protecting or investigating cultural resources is by getting the public involved. This chapter is a brief report of the kinds of archaeology going on in Florida today with the participation of local people who are learning to cherish the cultural heritage of their land.

Archaeological research, cultural resource management, the State and the public

Florida's Department of State is committed to historic preservation and archaeological research. A showcase example is the site of San Luis de Talimali, once the principal Spanish mission among the Apalachee Indians. This mission is located in Tallahassee, Florida's modern capital. It was founded in the 1630s at a major native village, and lasted until its destruction by the British in 1704. It included a fort, church, cemetery, Native and Spanish village areas, and Native council house (Shapiro 1987). In 1983 the Department of State acquired the 20 ha site with a dual aim: to investigate the past and to bring the excitement of archaeology to the public, whose tax dollars support the work.

Excavations, research, displays and tours continue year-round. Annually there is a huge 'rediscovery' day that includes actors in authentic costumes portraying the different ethnic roles, historic foods, displays of artefact manufacturing processes, and lectures attracting thousands of people. Each year, as more is learned about the scientific discoveries concerning early historic cultural interaction between Natives and Europeans, more of the general public is educated in Florida's cultural heritage.

On a smaller scale, at our own State university in Tampa (the University of South Florida), we convinced administrators that they should not disturb the land before checking for archaeological and historic sites. A partial survey of the 660 ha campus in Tampa was funded. One site was located and further excavations supported when construction was planned at this site (Williams & Estabrook 1988). Besides students studying how to excavate, local people and members of the local archaeology society get involved in the University's digs.

More Americans now recognize that constant destruction of cultural re-sources seriously affects the quality of life and of education about the past. Historic preservation laws at the Federal, State and local levels enjoy much popular support, but they do not go far enough and are not well understood. Some legislation is at a grass-roots level, not dependent upon Federal leader-ship or funding. Hillsborough County, where the University is located, recently used the money from the sale of bonds to purchase lands for develop-ment into parks, based on criteria such as sensitive ecological settings. There was also an interest in prehistoric and early historic sites, so the county had surveys done (e.g. Grange & Williams 1977). Site preservation was often possible, but, if it was not, rescue excavations were done in the path of roads or other facilities. Interpretive centres including archaeological displays were also built to give the public tangible results.

The State has a similar, larger programme known as CARL (Conservation and Recreation Lands), for which up to $40 million per year may be set aside from taxes on oil, gas, phosphate or solid mineral leases to purchase tracts of land to protect them from development. One major criterion for land purchase is archaeological and historical value. Since 1979 over $50 million have been used to buy more than 50,000 ha. The San Luis Mission was a CARL purchase costing over $1 million. Two other properties, The Grove in Tallahassee and the Deering Hammock in Miami, cost over $22 million. These sites have many important qualities, but the major features were historic structures requiring preservation. The public visits them daily.

A well-funded project is the underwater archaeology excavation at Warm Mineral Springs in southwest Florida (Cockrell & Murphy 1978; Skow 1986). Dated at 12,000 years BP, it is one of the oldest sites in the southeast. Human skeletons and other organic remains were found 13 m below the surface of the spring on a ledge that was probably dry land during the Pleistocene. Amateur archaeologists first brought out skeletons, including crania said to have had brain tissue intact. By the 1970s professionals began research there. Public interest and extensive news coverage helped secure over $1 million from the Florida legislature and other sources over several years. A State senator in this district who likes to dive with the archaeologists helped obtain the funds.

In a similar fashion, a State senator who chaired the Senate Appropriations Committee secured funds for archaeological, historic and architectural work at Spanish Point at the Oaks, in southwest Florida. This site has prehistoric occupational remains and late nineteenth-century structures – early for that part of Florida (which was only admitted to US statehood in 1845). Funds totalling nearly $1 million to date have supported research, excavation and restoration (Almy & Luer 1987). The funding was possible because of the efforts of an influential resident and lay historian who lobbied for legislative support. As with Warm Mineral Springs, this project's success is a testimony to the influence of a few local residents interested enough in the past to push in the right direction. The site will soon be a well-preserved tourist attraction.

Diverse American social groups help to channel State support of archaeology, as at Fort Mose, in northeast Florida near historic St Augustine. Kathleen Deagan, of the Florida Museum of Natural History (FMNH), is known for her research at St Augustine, the oldest permanent non-Native settlement in the United States. She is now excavating at Fort Mose, considered to have been the first free African-American community in the country. The fort was established in 1737 by the Spanish Crown for escaped slaves from more northerly British colonies (*The Florida Catholic*, 20 March 1987). Charles V decreed in 1693 that any slaves who fled the British would be given freedom in La Florida, but this was not completely an altruistic move, since the slaves had first to become Catholic and to settle at Fort Mose. The fort site was chosen where the inhabitants could be self-sufficient and also act as a fortified buffer between the English and Spanish to the south. Support for investigations here was obtained by a black State representative, who asked for $100,000 from the legislature. Public interest is high in historical questions being investigated here, such as attitudes and living conditions of freed slaves and other little-known aspects of their lives in colonial times. *The Florida Preservation News* (published by the Florida Trust for Historic Preservation and the State's Bureau of Historic Preservation) notes in the July–August 1991 issue that this project is inspiring a push to include more African-American history in school textbooks.

Archaeological research and public education in Florida has also been accomplished with support by private individuals and organizations only. One good example involves people who are members of the Florida Anthropological Society (FAS), which has over 600 members, including about 60 professionals. Amateurs in several FAS chapters often co-operate with professionals to salvage sites threatened with destruction. A recent case in St Augustine, for example, was the salvage excavation and analysis of two sites, with the co-operation of the landowners, developers and local news media generating publicity to draw volunteer diggers from among local residents (Tesar 1986).

Some cultural resource management (CRM) projects begin with State-required private money, but generate more lasting results when the public get interested. At the far northwestern end of the state, local volunteers and private funding have enabled archaeologists to excavate endangered sites in the city of Pensacola and make the city enact a historic preservation ordinance covering any planned development. The city of Tampa also requires archaeological survey and adverse impact mitigation prior to construction projects downtown. In 1980, excavations for a parking garage uncovered portions of Fort Brooke, from the Seminole War periods from the 1820s to the 1850s (Piper & Piper 1982, 1987). Burials were given to the Seminole Tribe for reinterment on a new parcel of land, where today stands their interesting combination of cultural centre, craft store, new burial ground and giant bingo hall.

In Miami, Dade County archaeologist Robert Carr found the Cutler fossil site during a CRM survey. It contains Pleistocene fossil species and human cultural and skeletal remains (though their association is still uncertain – see

Carr 1986). When a Miami newspaper described the site, the story was picked up by the national news. The publicity spurred local palaeontological and archaeological enthusiasts to action. The landowner, who was planning development, would have been required to finance some excavation. But he donated about $150,000, far more than would have been necessary, to a new south Florida non-profit organization known as the Archaeological and Historical Conservancy, for work at the site. Dade County contributed $35,000. The landowner, it turned out, had studied archaeology as a student and had participated in excavations, and still maintained an interest. The assistance was possible because of the excitement generated by newspaper, radio and television coverage. It must be accepted, however, that, in such cases, the project director must spend an enormous amount of time away from the research dealing with the public.

Near Cape Canaveral, the now famous Windover site was discovered when drainage work for a housing development turned up well-preserved human skeletons containing brain tissue (Doran & Dickel 1988; Levathes 1987). Other organic remains included wooden stakes used to hold down the 7500-year-old burials in the pond, bone and wood artefacts, ecofacts, including the earliest US bottle gourd fragments, and woven matting covering the burials, which was impregnated with what was determined to be 'gelatinous body fluids'. The huge public interest and international news coverage of the discovery helped obtain $800,000 from the State legislature, $5000 from the National Geographic Society (for analysis and preservation of the textiles), $3000 from IBM, $5000 from the Ford Foundation, $2000 from visitors to the site, $24,000 from a private educational fund, and about $50,000 from the landowning company. Technical problems in the excavations were massive. The pond had to be drained and continually pumped. Landowner Jack Eckerd, a well-known Florida businessman, contributed much of the construction and pumping equipment and underwater engineering through his company. He was recognized by the National Park Service through the Southeast Preservation Award, and by the Florida Archaeological Council with a Stewards of Heritage Conservation Award. During the five months of the two-year period that it was open, 18,000 people visited the site. A full-time public relations co-ordinator became necessary.

Another project funded almost exclusively with private dollars took place at Amelia Island, on the northeast coast just above Jacksonville. This was the site of the seventeenth-century Spanish Franciscan mission of Santa Maria. The landowners uncovered human remains during land clearing, and called Piper Archaeological Research, Inc., of St Petersburg, a private archaeological contract firm. Piper and later FMNH's Jerald Milanich conducted extensive excavations with funding from the landowners ($75,000) and a small amount from the Department of State ($5000). These landowners were later given a Heritage Conservation award. As with others mentioned here, they were private donors who went beyond merely securing a tax deduction for their money; they took a real interest in the past.

Near Charlotte Harbor, on the southwest coast of Florida, FMNH archaeologist William Marquardt obtained private donations of nearly $60,000, as well as housing, food and other assistance, for investigations of prehistoric and later sites of the Calusa Indians. The work has produced remains of complex societies that were based not on agricultural economies but on the gathering of wild resources in rich estuarine environments. To date, Marquardt has secured two large Special Category Historic Preservation grants from the state, totalling nearly $420,000. His team includes many local resident volunteers, from students to retired folks. The latter are numerous in this part of the state, and have time, money and useful skills of great benefit to the project. All are recognized in a regular newsletter put out by the project.

For the 450th anniversary of the Hernando de Soto expedition in Florida (in 1989) the Department of Parks and Recreation wanted to mark with interpretive signs the explorer's exact route. FMNH's Milanich began both field and archival research to pinpoint the route and explore cultural questions about the impact of the expedition. As part of this project the Tatham mound north of Tampa was excavated (Mitchem & Hutchinson 1986; Mitchem 1989), providing evidence of a very early historic mass burial of aboriginals with some Spanish artefacts and signs of trauma (such as a sword cut on a skeleton). The work was aided by amateur diggers, and supported by a donation of $59,000 from a famous American science-fiction author who lives nearby and wanted to write a historical novel based on the excavation's findings (Anthony 1991).

It is often said that historic and archaeological site preservation in the USA is more difficult than in the rest of the New World or in the Old World because the people of today have no connection with those of the past, and few are descended from the prehistoric indigenous people. Native American populations here were smaller than in Central and South America, and British policies tended more towards driving out and obliterating them, unlike the Spanish, who needed them alive for labour. In fact, a mass guilt over the tragic fates of most Native American cultures seems to characterize many American feelings today. There is lately more of a fascination for the past, for science, and for preserving all aspects of the environment that have something to teach us. These projects demonstrate how the public's interest in archaeology and history can be used to secure support, which ultimately benefits the community through education, tourism, local pride, and preservation of local and even national heritage. Research support can be sought from specific public-interest groups, and the wider public benefits emphasized. Even when descendants of the original indigenous peoples in the area no longer exist, other Indian cultural groups, as well as the local people in general, can be of enormous help as their interest grows.

A case study in public education and archaeology: northwest Florida

For several years the University of South Florida has conducted a programme of archaeological survey and excavation along the Apalachicola river valley in northwest Florida. Funded by State and Federal grants, this work has resulted in the discovery of hundreds of prehistoric sites of all time periods, the construction of a regional chronology, and the first explorations of a number of research questions on topics ranging from coastal–inland comparative adaptations to the origins of socio-political complexity in late prehistory (White 1986). This is the largest Florida river, flowing out of the Chattahoochee river, which originates far to the north in the Georgia mountains. It was a major prehistoric population centre, but the area is now rural, agricultural and relatively remote.

Many Apalachicola valley residents today are hunters, fishers and collectors. The bays in the delta region are a major oyster- and shrimp-producing area for the nation, and the Gulf of Mexico here is known for sport-fishing. Catfish and bass, wild turkey and quail abound, and deer are larger than in the rest of Florida. Many people still utilize wild resources not just for sport but for subsistence. In addition, much of the land is in planted forest, and many residents are employed as foresters, loggers and rangers. There are countless individuals with information to share on the habitats and behaviours of and means of obtaining wild species.

Working outdoors so often, nearly everyone collects 'arrowheads' or prehistoric pottery. Thirteen years ago we introduced an excellent technique for locating new sites: the public 'archaeology day', at which residents are invited to bring in their collections to be identified and to share their site locations. The people always delight in demonstrating how much more impressive are their artefacts than the modest specimens displayed by the professionals. One old gentleman who had collected for sixty years once brought his most unusual artefacts (huge 'fishtailed' Palaeo-Indian projectile points), which he keeps in a bank vault. Much of his collection has made possible a revision of the record for this area, where ten years ago archaeologists thought there was no Palaeo-Indian presence at all (Milanich & Fairbanks 1980).

For 1990 support was obtained from the Florida Endowment for the Humanities (FEH) for archaeological test excavations at two Woodland period sites in the Apalachicola valley. Research goals centred around questions of subsistence at these riverine shell middens, and ceramic chronology within the sites' estimated 500-year range of occupation (c. AD 400–900). But the project was originated not by the archaeologist but by the local people. The Civic Center director in the city of Blountstown, having once asked FEH for funding for a Shakespeare programme, successfully approached them again for support for a huge public archaeology project. She interested local librarians and family historians, representatives of the newly re-formed Tribal group of Creek Indians, and residents from housewives to school-children to retirees, in participating in a professional operation in both the field and the laboratory.

Figure 4.2 Public archaeology project in the Apalachicola valley of northwest Florida near Blountstown: University of South Florida student supervises young local volunteer in recovering artefacts and animal bone from the waterscreen at a riverbank shell midden site of the early Woodland period, dating to AD 400. Photo: Nancy Marie White.

She also secured matching funds through private donations. The local land and timber company allowed work on its property along the river, thus gaining much-needed good publicity. The news media, from local to State, picked up the story of the project and generated interest as far away as neighbouring states. And the scope of the project could be widely expanded because so much more labour was available than just field school students from USF.

There are always problems and dangers with such a project involving public participation. Parents want to bring their children too, down to 6 years of age. Self-proclaimed experts want to tell the professionals the truth about how stone tools were used, or other aspects of life in prehistory (doubtless sometimes they are correct!). Some people want to keep any artefacts they find, or walk away disappointed when each shovelful of soil does not contain projectile points.

The large number of people made it necessary to use much co-ordination. Students were first trained for a week by themselves, then taught to handle the public (for urban college students this was an ethnographic experience in itself). One student was appointed PR person each day and did nothing but meet visitors and explain the project. Others were spread out to supervise the volunteers and judge what tasks each could handle (Fig. 4.2). The availability of lab work made it possible for disabled people also to participate, and night and weekend labs allowed people with day jobs to join us too.

The work was constant and intense for the students and graduate supervisors. We seldom got a chance to rest after a hard day's digging, because someone would usually drive up to the camp with a truckload of artefacts from some local site, not understanding why we could not come and dig it up right away. Many local participants expressed no greater interest than they would in just collecting anything. But others came to realize the importance of the past to them personally, perhaps because they are so close to the land themselves, and because stronger family ties and historic connections in this region may foster a greater reverence for the past.

FEH is interested in bringing scholars to the people. Though they want to support the humanities, not science, we persuaded them that many rural children had never seen a microscope, for example, so this must be included (plus it allowed for volunteers to sort materials recovered from flotation of soil samples). They also agreed to radiocarbon dating, ethnobotanical and zoo-archaeological analyses, which we contracted out to specialists. In this region people are already sophisticated enough from years of artefact-collecting experience to know that archaeology does not involve dinosaurs. Now they were able to learn on a day-to-day basis how scientists work.

The highlight of the project was a large-scale archaeology day. There was a picnic, slide programme and social gathering. Collectors from three States brought their artefacts to display (Fig. 4.3). We insisted on promoting ethical behaviour and not permitting sales of anything except display cases. Professional and amateur flint-knappers, a potter, and Creek Indian craft-workers demonstrated their techniques and wares. The project ethnobotanist

Figure 4.3 Archaeology Day at Blountstown; local collectors bring their cases of artefacts to display and learn about, exchanging information with the professionals. Photo: Nancy Marie White.

demonstrated native plant use and served aboriginal-style dishes. An archaeological conservation specialist spoke on caring for and restoring artefacts before and after removal from the ground. Children and adults practised throwing a spear with an atlatl and working with clay. We as professionals gained knowledge of new site locations and artefact types, but more important, everyone gained a greater respect for the cultural resources for what they are and what they can tell us about ourselves, not only about all those who came before. In 1991 the Civic Center director won a Heritage Conservation award for this small but meaningful project.

In 1992, a popular booklet on the area's archaeology was completed (White, Simpson & McMillan 1992) and distributed to local residents, children and all who participated in the project, as well as agencies connected with land management.

Conclusion

These examples show how Florida's professionals have found it important to educate the public at the local level, with broader motives than just to support scientific investigations. However, combining good research with good public archaeology is a difficult task. Our public archaeology graduate programme at USF requires students to develop both research expertise and the communications and public relations skills they will need as professionals. They learn that members of the public are more important than just to provide funding; they need to be involved both to help protect the resource and to learn to appreciate the cultural heritage of the land they live on today.

References

Almy, M. & G. Luer 1987. *Spanish Point: a guide to prehistory.* Osprey, Fla.: Gulf Coast Heritage Association.

Anthony, P. 1991. *Tatham Mound.* New York: William Morrow & Co.

Carr, R. 1986. Preliminary report on excavations at the Cutler fossil site (8Da2001) in southern Florida. *Florida Anthropologist* 39, 231–2.

Cockrell, W. A. & L. Murphy 1978. Pleistocene man in Florida. *Archaeology of Eastern North America* 6, 1–13.

Doran, G. H. & D. N. Dickel 1988. Multidisciplinary investigations at the Windover site. In *Wet Site Archaeology,* Purdy, B. (ed.), 263–89. Caldwell, N.J.: Telford Press.

Grange, R. T., Jr & J. R. Williams 1977. An archaeological survey of the proposed Alderman's Fort Park in Hillsborough County, Florida. Tampa: Department of Anthropology, University of South Florida.

Levathes, L. E. 1987. Mysteries of the bog. *National Geographic* 171, 397–420.

Milanich, J. T. & C. H. Fairbanks 1980. *Florida Archaeology.* New York: Academic Press.

Mitchem, J. 1989. Redefining Safety Harbor: late prehistoric/protohistoric archaeology in west peninsular Florida. Doctoral thesis, Department of Anthropology, University of Florida, Gainesville.

Mitchem, J. & D. L. Hutchinson 1986. *Interim Report on Excavations at the Tatham Mound, Citrus County, Florida: season II.* Florida State Museum, Department of Anthropology, Miscellaneous Project Report Series, no. 28. Gainesville: Florida State Museum.

Piper, H. M. & J. G. Piper 1982. Archaeological investigations at the Quad Block site, 8H1998, located at the site of the old Fort Brooke municipal parking garage, Tampa, Florida. St Petersburg: Piper Archaeological Research.

Piper, H. M. & J. G. Piper 1987. Urban archaeology in Florida: the search for pattern in Tampa's historic core. *Florida Anthropologist* 40, 260–5.

Shapiro, G. 1987. *Archaeology at San Luis: broad-scale testing, 1984–1985.* Florida Archaeology, no. 3. Tallahassee: Florida Bureau of Archaeological Research.

Skow, J. 1986. This Florida spa holds a surprising lode of prehistory. *Smithsonian Magazine* 17, 72–83.

Tesar, L. 1986. Cooperative archaeology: St Augustine example. *Florida Anthropologist* 37, 156–64.

Weisman, B. R. 1989. *Like Beads on a String: a culture history of the Seminole Indians in north peninsular Florida.* Tuscaloosa: University of Alabama Press.

White, N. M. 1986. Prehistoric cultural chronology in the Apalachicola valley: the evolution of Native chiefdoms in northwest Florida. In *Threads of Tradition and Culture along the Gulf Coast*, Evans, R. V. (ed.), 194–215. Pensacola: Gulf Coast History and Humanities Conference.

White, N., T. Simpson & S. McMillan 1992. *Apalachicola Valley Archaeology*. Blountstown, Fla.: W. T. Neal Civic Center.

Williams, J. R. & R. W. Estabrook. 1988. *Archaeological Investigations at the USF Village Site (8Hi2187), Hillsborough County, Florida*. University of South Florida Department of Anthropology Archaeological Report, no. 16. Tampa: University of South Florida.

5 Archaeology and the public in Lebanon: developments since 1986

HELGA SEEDEN

Introduction

Cultural heritage cannot be saved and preserved without public support and participation. People are naturally curious about past cultures but the development of interest in heritage preservation depends largely on the current context and information about it. 'In Lebanon today the past is widely viewed in terms of metal detectors and export commodities: archaeological expertise is deployed not to develop or cherish cultural identity but to sell it off' (Gathercole & Lowenthal 1990, p. 92). For a decade and a half, however, Lebanon has suffered intermittent warfare, increasing fragmentation of communities, prolonged economic and cultural deprivation and declining educational facilities. Its complex situation may therefore be used to illustrate the important link between information available to the public and the treatment, destructive or otherwise, that cultural material receives.

Since the end of military action and the reopening of most areas of Lebanon in the early 1990s, everyone has begun to move around eagerly. Young people and children now visit the ancient ruins at Baalbek, Tyre, Tripoli, Beiteddin and Byblos, some for the first time. In the absence of any government heritage management policies in Lebanon, however, prolonged political and educational isolation of whole communities has produced separate and sometimes irreconcilable views of the past. People's interest in their heritage has not vanished, but they tell different 'stories'. While keen to understand and passionate about 'wanting their past back', therefore, this generation's interest in archaeological sites often produces imaginary and parochial explanations, influenced by intercommunity fears and prejudices.

The realization that such parochial interpretations are incompatible and possibly due to past isolation and misinformation will be slow and difficult. Without appropriate heritage information, this young public will fail to develop a cultural identity, and some will continue to sell its fragments off. Two main obstacles stand in the way of appropriate heritage management education, however: the economic attraction of the 'treasure hunt', fuelled by demands from the local and international antiquities market and glamourized by the tabloid press and television; and the pseudo-scientific misinterpretation of culture history. A survey of the local Lebanese treasure-hunt scene shows that these people have little awareness of the contextual value of cultural material or of whose heritage is being destroyed and so provide nothing in the promotion of their discoveries to help improve cultural education in post-war Lebanon. And the fact that most archaeological research in Lebanon has been conducted by foreign specialists who tend to speak to their own specialist audience, rather than to the communities in the country of origin of their research, is a further obstacle to the redevelopment of heritage interest in our war-torn country. Despite these problems, however, public demand for information about the country's past has survived and, in fact, greatly increased as a result of the reopening of the various regions and the hope for peace. This burgeoning interest is clear in the immediate public response whenever and wherever relevant appropriate information is made available.

The treasure hunt: epidemic and addiction

Archaeology in Lebanon is popularly identified with the age-old idea of the 'treasure hunt', the search for rare and valuable objects in temples, tombs and other ancient sites. The looting of sites and illegal trafficking in antiquities has taken on epidemic proportions, not only in Lebanon, but in Asia, Africa and South America (Fforde 1991; Joukowsky 1992a, 1992b).

Illicit trade in cultural material is in many ways similar to drug trafficking. First, the majority of clandestine diggers of artefacts – like coca planters – earn little and would easily shift to more regular jobs with an income if these were available. The money – and big money – is made by the dealers, particularly those with international connections. It is the dealers who supply the antiques market, and as demand increases, so do prices. Second, antiques collectors tend to want original objects, even though it is possible to obtain modern copies that cannot be easily distinguished from the originals, as shown by museums that exhibit first-class duplicates of their most valuable art treasures.

The bulk of illegal exports from Lebanon goes to Europe, the USA and Japan, to meet a growing demand in these countries for ancient works of art. This alarming trend has contributed greatly to the unabated destruction of evidence from the Near Eastern past.

The local scene: the story of two sites

A decade of continued absence of general government control in Lebanon, coupled with rising foreign demands for antiques, has resulted in a dramatic increase in clandestine excavations (Hakimian 1989). Further destruction, and some archaeological 'discoveries', have resulted from a hectic and uncontrolled building industry and associated indiscriminate bulldozing. Today, illegal excavations mark the entire countryside (Fisk 1992) and whole settlements have fallen to the bulldozer.

In this chaotic situation anything goes! Someone finds a gold ring and an entire village sets out in a frenzy to pockmark the surrounding countryside. These villagers generally have no idea about the significance of their actions beyond the desperate hope of one day hitting upon 'real treasure'. Such people come daily to the archaeological museum and department offices at the American University of Beirut with questions concerning the identity and value of finds and often leave disappointed.

The story of Kamid el-Loz in the Biqa' (see Marfoe 1978) and a discussion of the present state of the ancient city of Tyre reveal the historical, economic and political trends in the treatment of the cultural landscape during this difficult period.

From 1963 to 1981, the site of Kamid el-Loz was rigorously excavated by the University of the Saar (Hachmann 1989). Unfortunately, the foreign archaeologists as well as the local Department of Antiquities failed to make Kamid's story known to people in Lebanon. The University of the Saar produced a voluminous and learned series of publications in Germany, but these works are accessible only to western scholars who also read German. Not until 1991 did a comprehensive report of these excavations appear in Beirut and when it did, it was in English (Hachmann 1991; see this work also for bibliography). Most significantly, no Arabic version of work done at Kamid el-Loz exists. This situation prompted one Beirut newspaper to accuse the Department of Antiquities of having allowed foreign excavators to take away important archaeological material from Lebanon and publish it abroad (As-Safir 1991).

The publicity surrounding this excavation, and the years of conflict, had tragic consequences, however. In nineteen years of careful excavation, the professional archaeologists found a small 'treasure' of a gold necklace and other artefacts associated with a young girl in her tomb. This material is on official loan in Germany for safe-keeping and formed the basis of a successful travelling exhibition there (Hachmann 1983). After the Israeli invasion of Lebanon in 1982, however, the excavations at Kamid could not be resumed, and so the site was left open to looters. Spurred on by news of the discovery and subsequent story of this gold 'treasure' in the Lebanese press, bulldozers have turned the site upside-down in a frantic search for more riches, destroying fragile architectural evidence and the fine-grained stratification of the remains of earlier millennia in the town's history.

The fact that the looters found very little to satisfy their own expectations compounds a tragic irony: after the promising beginning of scientific investigation at this important bronze age settlement and the first efforts to inform the Lebanese public, it was largely destroyed and its ancient history completely eradicated (Seeden 1991). We have now lost the chance to study the rise and fate of one of the earliest urban centres in this rich agricultural plain.

Figure 5.1 High-rise apartment blocks invade the excavations in Tyre (in 1991), while schoolboys play football in the Roman-period hippodrome, the goal marked by two columns.

Another, almost legendary site in Lebanon is Tyre (Seeden 1992a). Tyre was declared a 'World Heritage Site' in 1979 but nothing has been done to rescue the archaeological site from what is now a booming, bustling, sprawling town. In fact, the old town of Tyre has been eclipsed. The standing columns of classical Tyre seem like mere matchsticks today, as unfinished high-rise apartment blocks loom above areas excavated by the Department of Antiquities (Fig. 5.1). These excavations, which remained largely unpublished (Salame-Sarkis 1988), are in a state of grave neglect. Anyone can enter them, since the gates are down or open. And because of this lack of protection the ancient city has suffered. In late spring of 1989, for example, one of the few chiselled stone sarcophagi – standing close to a one-storey museum (Fig. 5.2) which is scheduled to house a collection of local antiquities – was blown up so that broken sculpture chunks could be carried to the market-place. The sarcophagus might have been safer inside the museum, but no museum could hold Tyre's nearby, stone-built hippodrome, where schoolboys play football, the goalposts marked by two columns. In fact, football fields are very popular on archaeological sites today. The Islamic site of 'Anjar has one just between the partially reconstructed Umayyad 'palace' and the ruined building said to be a mosque.

Figure 5.2   The site museum of Tyre, built during the last war years, still empty and closed.

The international antiques market, archaeology and the media

Gold from Baalbek

The complete absence of popular information about Lebanon's surviving heritage and its meaning has left a vacuum which is only too easily filled by almost daily 'treasure stories' in the local and international news media. In Baalbek last spring, Lebanese gendarmes arrested a worker who was reported to have found gold while building his house. He said he had received a cash payment in US dollars for the hoard, and then handed the left-overs to a representative from the Department of Antiquities: two Roman-period earrings and a few gold foil leaves of a laurel wreath. Meanwhile a member of a well-known and well-to-do Baalbek family is said to have sold the 'treasure' for at least fifteen times the original price to a dealer. The treasure has since 'disappeared'. The worker was taken to prison, the Department representative wrote a report about his uninteresting catch and its estimated monetary value, and this is where the story ended. Will the arrested man renew his clandestine digging in the future?

The Sevso silver scandal

Since February 1990 news media have copiously reported this multi-million dollar scandal (e.g. 'Marquess Hopes £40M Silver Hoard will Stay Intact after Sale', in the *Guardian* (Manchester and London) and 'Ancient Roman Silver to be Sold', in the *New York Times*, both on 10 February 1990). The treasure, purported by the auction house Sotheby's to be fitted out with legal Lebanese export papers, is Roman in date and eastern European in manufacture. It consists of 14 pieces of splendidly decorated silver table-ware, 4 plates, 5 ewers, a basin, a vase and a casket. The treasure's magnificence fits the grandiose Roman-period temple complex at Baalbek, so it was said to have come from there. Sotheby's are reported to have offered it for sale in New York for an initial price near $100 million, as described in colourful accounts in a number of local newspapers and magazines (e.g. the Beirut daily newspaper *Al-Diyar*, 16 March 1990, p. 5; the Beirut daily newspaper *As-Safir*, 11 April 1991, p. 7; and the magazine *Assayad*, no. 2365, pp. 24–7) (Fig. 5.3), and even on Lebanese prime-time television. The story was therefore seen by a wide Lebanese audience, in town and country.

Like 'Indiana Jones' and other similar Hollywood fantasies, this story fired everyone's imagination (also see McManamon 1994; White & Williams 1994). For weeks on end students came to archaeology classes waving newspaper cuttings with another sequel to the treasure saga and Lebanese children began to ask their parents for shovels and pickaxes of material more resistant than plastic.

Unfortunately, as the emphasis of all this coverage was limited to the glamorous treasure and its stunning, spiralling price, all local and many foreign reports ignored the initial robbery and subsequent fraud in this scandal. Serious investigation had revealed that the silver hoard was not only manufactured in eastern Europe but also probably originated there, in the region of the former state of Yugoslavia. The treasure had been illegally exported to Switzerland long before any Lebanese involvement in it.

To date, the sale in New York has been stopped for investigation, and the Lebanese Government has paid dearly for its part in this investigation (the fees of New York lawyers) – more than one regional museum in Lebanon could have been set up with these funds! And the local effect of this international controversy between 'antiques barons', in their strongholds in western European capitals, was a fantastic incentive for continued and increased looting in the ancient towns of Lebanon. Sales of metal detectors have risen sharply in this country ever since this story was carried into people's houses.

To whom does the material belong?

In Lebanon today, therefore, there is much to be regretted about the way the past is conceived and used by the general public. Where does the blame lie? Who is responsible for informing the Lebanese or any public about their heritage? These are questions of world-wide import.

Local administrative chaos and geographical fragmentation have combined with a tragic ignorance on the part of the indigenous population concerning their own past and archaeological heritage. Both factors have increased drastically over the past decade, so that with every new generation of pupils and students the level of knowledge of the past falls, while general insecurity and

Figure 5.3 The Sevso silver treasure story appeared in colourful sequences in local magazines and newspapers (*Assayad* 1990, title-page).

hopelessness raise the gambling spirit in many a mind. Total ignorance of, and hence lack of concern for, the intrinsic value of their heritage is replaced by the consumption of glorified strike-it-rich tales from the popular media. The criminal offences of the local and international antiques business involved in perpetrating these events are irresponsibly withheld.

Another and perhaps most important threat to local archaeology comes from the misuse of information by professional archaeologists. Research on Near Eastern archaeological subjects is often done in the West, at places considered by some to be 'at the fountainhead of science' (W. Röllig, personal communication, 1989), but such institutions are isolated from the social and historical realities of the Lebanon and its cultures and so may fail to understand the significance of the material they recover.

A paradox exists, for example, in 'orientalist' studies: on the one hand, some of the finest Islamic art has been collected and elegantly displayed in western museums; on the other, there are qualified specialists who show a derisive lack of interest, if not downright ignorance, of the present culture of the Middle East. The combination of contempt for contemporary Near Eastern culture and narrow specialist interest in 'oriental' art can only be fuelled when racist attitudes (explicit or implicit) are brought into analysis, encouraging irrational arguments, sometimes defended in scientifically presented publications.

In this vein, Sir Mortimer Wheeler could write on the Roman-period temples in Baalbek:

> Balbeck remains one of the very great monuments of European architecture; a position for which geographically it only just quali-fies, for beyond the hills of Anti-Lebanon which rise above it to the east begin the sands of Asia and an essentially alien mind.
>
> (quoted in Harding 1963, p. 65)

Such cultural chauvinism often has clear political connotations. Despite well-researched evidence to the contrary (Gras, Rouillard & Teixidor 1989, pp. 170–97), one-sided accounts of 'Phoenician child sacrifice' (Brown 1991) and the 'worship of the golden calf' continue to appear in publications. And while material in some places is at the mercy of looters, with little or no local scientific know-how available to investigate or publish it, elsewhere foreign scientific arrogance continues to parade its own prejudices in the popular and not so popular press.

For example, while very few practising archaeologists are left in Lebanon today (see Seeden 1989), Harvard experts can present material excavated at the Canaanite and Philistine site of Ashkalon with little reference to the cultural context of animal power considered sacred (Stager 1991). A small metal figurine of a bull, complete with its clay shrine, dating to the second millen-nium BC, was described in the *International Herald Tribune* (26 July 1990, pp. 1–2) and the science section of the international version of *Time* magazine (6 August 1990, p. 7) as a 'totally unexpected find', 'the only one of its kind ever found', and 'providing important [but unspecified] evidence to help explain religious development in the region'. The implicit reference to degenerate bull-worship and unspeakable orgies is made explicit by the picture of a girl prostrate under a huge golden(?) bull, coming from no better source than Cecil B. De Mille's 1956 film *The Ten Commandments*! And the only reference to the societal and religious context of the object in question is derived from the Old Testament of the Bible.

In reality, small figurines of sheep and bulls, many in bronze and innumerable ones in clay, are among the most common finds of Near Eastern agricultural societies. Literally thousands have been found all over the Near East, and clay shrines are not rare either (Hachmann 1983, p. 160). Nor are the figurines limited to the Bronze Age (third and second millennia BC): by the time the Ashkalon bull figure was made in the sixteenth century BC, this craft was already thousands of years old. To this day village children make and play with such figures (Ochsenschlager 1974, pp. 170, 174), the equivalent of toy cars in an average middle-class household in the industrialized world.

To whom does the archaeological heritage belong?

Is Lebanon's cultural heritage the property of:

- the treasure-hunters here in Lebanon who behave as if the material under ground is theirs to loot and sell, destroying all archaeological evidence in the process;
- the collectors addicted to the possession of original treasures from the past, knowing full well that removal of artefacts from the context of their use in a specific place and situation destroys their cultural information forever;
- or the scientists, when among them there are a number who misrepresent and misinterpret archaeological material, as in the cases cited above?

The archaeological heritage belongs to none of the above. It belongs to the people who occupy the land and are surrounded by a visible and hidden legacy in the archaeological remains of the activities, lives and creativity of its past. Lebanon's heritage has to be saved, cherished and protected, if Lebanon and the Lebanese are going to preserve their culture. No one can live without a memory which forms their identity.

Problems in education in post-war Lebanon

The difficulties in reaching a wider public at school level in Lebanon today are evident in population figures. In 1985, with roughly 85,000 inhabitants, Baalbek, for example, had the second-best educational system in the Biqa'. It had 27 schools, 9 public and 18 private, catering to 13,059 pupils, with 38 per cent in public schools. It also sported an Association for Young University Graduates and five youth clubs (Rifai 1986, pp. 85–91). Since 1985 rural migration and refugees have more than doubled the population figures, although the number of children per family has gone from an average of twelve, in the 1950s, to four today (Rifai 1986, p. 63). One-half of the population is below 20 and in need of schooling.

These rising population figures show clearly in the sprawling popular quarters of Beirut and other major towns and villages in the country. Some communities, like the ones at Tyre, have invaded large parts of archaeological sites.

Unfortunately, the population boom has been accompanied by a decline in the general level of education, on account of the sixteen years of war. In the first year of general peace, this decline appears in catastrophic public examination results. In 1991, the baccalaureate examination was administered for the first time since 1986: over 75 per cent of the students failed! Teachers were stupefied by these results, but several contributing factors can be isolated. Almost two decades of irregular schooling and lack of upkeep, damage and outright destruction of schools have prevented the educational system from responding to the rising population in need of schooling. And teachers' salaries have been reduced to a pittance because of inflation.

Public demand for and popular information about the past

Where does teaching and learning about the past fit into this bleak context?

It may appear that there is no hope for Lebanon's past, at present or in the future. The western world is more seriously disturbed by problems resulting from drug trafficking than it is by the illegal trade in antiquities. Cures for the evils concerning the Lebanon must come from within the region, however, from within our local communities. And indeed despite, or perhaps because of, the hopeless situation reported above, there are some promising movements and events taking shape in Lebanon.

Archaeology students conducted a survey of the attitudes to the past among a sample of urban and rural inhabitants; their results confirmed that a large number of people of all ages have a genuine, if uninformed, concern about their past. They most often expressed a fear that something irretrievable was being broken, stolen, or lost. A sizeable percentage of people interviewed, particularly in the villages, said that they would feel much happier if 'things' in and above ground were kept, preserved or, better still, 'put safely into museums'. Children easily rallied around the idea of open-air exhibition parks with information conveyed through stories. They are today's children, bright and modern; they ask questions and want information.

As children grow older, the 'scientific truth' of the information offered becomes more important to them. To respond to this interest, a limited village press information service was begun in *Sawa*, Unicef's magazine for children (first issue 1989) – often read by parents, too. The story of Kamid el-Loz, 'How a treasure was found and lost', was told in one issue, another described ancient Byblos and still another covered Baalbek's imposing Roman-period and Islamic buildings, the best known and most impressive in Lebanon.

The Qal'a or fortress of Baalbek and the temples there are prime examples of a continued love affair between the people of the region and their archaeological sites. These sites are overrun at weekends with hundreds of local visitors from the towns and villages of the Biqa', and from all over Lebanon and the region. Indeed, most Lebanese would defend Baalbek against serious and clandestine destruction. This attraction is one asset which will help spread concern for the less impressive and more fragile sites in the landscape, places that can only be protected through co-operation with the people who live there.

Walid Jounblat, while he was Minister of Public Works, initiated a series of positive measures, beginning in his own area of influence. A sixth-century Byzantine church, found near the harbour of Jiyyeh during sand-mining operations, was rescue-excavated. The particularly well-preserved mosaics, dated by inscriptions, were removed and reset in the gardens and stables of the eighteenth-century palace of the emirs of Mount Lebanon at Beiteddin. An illustrated guidebook (Seeden, Attar, Atallah & Jounblat 1989) was produced, providing a brief history of the palace and its context, and of the mosaic-makers along the Lebanese coast. The book is based on original sources in word and illustration, and was conceived in Arabic for the local reader; it also contains English and French translations. A similar book presenting the story of Baalbek from prehistoric to recent times will follow (Seeden, Amhaz, Rifai & Attar Forthcoming).

Most visitors to Baalbek will be eager to visit the site museum there. The Mamluk tower on the steps of the so-called Bacchus Temple has been restored for that purpose, with cases and floors made ready for exhibits, but unfortunately all work has stopped. An unprepossessing miniature fountain preserved from one of the medieval houses in the Arab castle daily fills over a dozen large plastic water containers and hence provides drinking-water for several Baalbek households. Now it is a centre of attraction, especially for children in summer. How much more exciting will be the arrows-slits, crenellations and steep stairways into mysterious cross-vaults and chambers of the medieval tower, when they are brought back to life with period artefacts and activities!

Our own present pilot rescue project at the American University of Beirut is to save information from Tyre's first known child cemetery, already illegally excavated. It was undertaken with two specific goals: to preserve this important material in and for Lebanon; and to make the information available at once to the public at large so that it can help raise awareness of the value of the country's cultural heritage (Seeden & Sader 1991). A small exhibition was planned with the help of a team of architects and archaeology students from the American University of Beirut and set up first in a Beirut bank. Most Lebanese were surprised to find an archaeological exhibition at a bank, but it had nearly 3000 visitors during two summer months! The display was accompanied by public lectures in Beirut and Tyre, in both Arabic and English. Its general impact among students and public was good and far-reaching: newspapers, television and radio stations covered the event over a

Figure 5.4 Tyre 1991: rescue project saving the first Phoenician child cemetery, part of a reconstruction exhibition in Beirut. Students and archaeologists of the American University of Beirut co-operated in setting up this exhibition with funds from a Beirut bank and several interested individuals.

one month period. The exhibition (Fig. 5.4) has now moved to the Bank of Lebanon, where it will remain until the regional museum at Tyre is opened (Seeden 1992b).

In the local social and educational context, it is obvious that such museums will not house specialists' exhibits. The negative attitude towards specialist interests and approaches was clearly evident during a museum workshop in May 1990, attended by local and foreign specialists, museum custodians, representatives of the Ministry of Education and students of Yarmouk University. It was repeatedly stated by participants that specialists, if left to their own devices, can be the 'death' of a museum, as they will not take local interests and attitudes into account (also see Ucko 1994). Because of this attitude, the role of the specialist/scientist in future museum development was restricted to that of making sure that the information offered was correct. In addition, there was a common understanding that the lighthearted and imaginative forms of information intended for children, in exhibitions and literature, are also enjoyed by adults – sometimes secretly – and so are a potent form of communication for all ages.

One of the highly successful museums recently established in the area is the Museum of Jordanian Heritage (founded in 1988) which is now the oasis-like centre of the 30,000 student Yarmouk University in northern Jordan. Small, manageable and sensitive, it joins the living ethnographic present with the clearly defined past of a society in its environment through the ages (see Mershen & Amman 1988). This museum has already become a model for the region.

Conclusion

Active museum and site protection programmes, coupled with public information campaigns, therefore hold the best promise for improving the local situation of a cultural heritage threatened and ignored. The regional museum of Beiteddin in Lebanon has been the first to prove this point. It received around 10,000 visitors per week in the summer of 1991. Together with future museum information centres at Baalbek, Tyre and elsewhere, it can help break the isolation of the people from their cultural heritage.

There is even one useful result in mass-media distortion of the Lebanese heritage: the polarization of treasure and information. Although some children do want to 'dig for gold', they will soon tire of it when they realize that they are only building castles in the sand. By contrast, increasing numbers of Lebanese youngsters want instruction in archaeology, even though they know full well that there are no regular jobs in this profession in the country. They come in quest of knowledge, despairing over their own ignorance and that of their community about the past. Several hundred young Lebanese were eager to take courses in archaeology at the Lebanese University last autumn, despite the lack of an adequate Arabic textbook covering archaeology, either its theory or practice.

Lebanon is not alone in its predicament, and the peculiar situation of this country's archaeological heritage can be resolved. One of the main problems behind the continuing destruction of heritage in Lebanon, and elsewhere, is the criminal trafficking in antiquities and the misinterpretation or misuse of archaeological material in the media. Newspapers and magazines, television and radio, must help to create local awareness of the cultural value of the past and help to meet the popular demand for information that such publicity creates, by replacing the crude sensationalism of so much of present-day coverage with the archaeological information that the public clearly wants. Only then will local sites find a measure of protection, and Lebanon's past survive into the future.

References

Brown, S. 1991. *Late Carthaginian Child Sacrifice and Sacrificial Monuments in their Mediterranean Context*. Sheffield: University Press for American Schools of Oriental Research.

Fforde, C. 1991. The preservation of cultural property. *World Archaeological Bulletin* 5, 30–3.

Fisk, R. 1992. The biggest supermarket in Lebanon: a journalist investigates the plundering of the country's cultural heritage. *Berytus* 39, 243–52.

Gathercole, P. & D. Lowenthal 1990. Introduction to the rulers and the ruled. In *The Politics of the Past*, Gathercole, P. & D. Lowenthal (eds), 91–3. London: Unwin Hyman; Routledge pbk 1994.

Gras, M., P. Rouillard & J. Teixidor 1989. *L'Univers phénicien*. Paris: Arthaud.

Hachmann, R. 1983. *Frühe Phöniker im Libanon*. Mainz: Ph. von Zabern.

Hachmann, R. 1989. Kamid el-Loz 1963–1981: German excavations in Lebanon I. *Berytus* 37.

Hakimian, S. 1989. Une archéologie parallèle: les découvertes clandestines et fortuites au Liban. *Berytus* 35, 199–209.

Harding, G. L. 1963. *Baalbek*. Beirut: Khayats.

Joukowsky, M. S. 1992a. Ethics in archaeology: an American perspective. *Berytus* 39, 11–20.

Joukowsky, M. S. 1992b. An update on Tyre: what is being done? In *The Heritage of Tyre: essays on the history, archaeology, and preservation of Tyre*, Joukowsky, M. S. (ed.), 115–19. Dubuque, Iowa: Kendall/Hunt.

McManamon, F. P. 1994. Presenting archaeology to the public in the USA. In *The Presented Past: heritage, museums and education*, Stone, P. G. & B. L. Molyneaux (eds), 61–81. London: Routledge.

Marfoe, L. 1978. Between Qadesh and Kumidi: a history of frontier settlement and land use in the Biqa', Lebanon. Unpublished PhD dissertation, University of Chicago.

Mershen, B. & I. M. Amman (eds) 1988. *The Museum of Jordanian Heritage*. Irbid, Jordan: Al Kutba.

Ochsenschlager, E. 1974. Mud objects from al-Hiba: a study of ancient and modern technology. *Archaeology* 27, 162–74.

Rifai, M. T. 1986. Sauvegarde du patrimoine architectural des ruines de Baalbek face au développement de la ville. Unpublished PhD thesis, Sorbonne University, Paris, France.

Salame-Sarkis, H. 1988. La nécropole de Tyr: à propos de publications récentes. *Berytus* 34, 193–205.

Seeden, H. 1989. Lebanon's past today. *Berytus* 35, 5–12.

Seeden, H. 1990. Search for the missing link: archaeology and the public in Lebanon. In *The Politics of the Past*, Gathercole, P. & D. Lowenthal (eds), 141–59. London: Unwin Hyman; Routledge pbk 1994.

Seeden, H. 1991. Bulldozers destroy what scientific archaeology exposed. *Berytus* 37, 3.

Seeden, H. 1992a. Tyre summer 1990: an eyewitness report. In *The Heritage of Tyre: essays on the history, archaeology, and preservation of Tyre*, Joukowsky, M. S. (ed.), 127–30. Dubuque, Iowa: Kendall/Hunt.

Seeden, H. 1992b. A *tophet* at Tyre? The story of a discovery and an exhibition. *Berytus* 39, 39–51.

Seeden, H., K. Amhaz, M. Rifai & M. Attar (eds) Forthcoming. Baalbek between past and future. Beirut.

Seeden, H., M. Attar, M. Atallah & F. Jounblat (eds) 1989. *Beiteddin Past and Present*. Beirut: Beirut International Press.

Seeden, H. & H. Sader 1991. *Sur 1991* (Exhibition brochure). Beirut: Beirut Catholic Press.

Stager, L. E. 1991. Ashkalon discovered: from Canaanites and Philistines to Romans and Moslems. *Journal of the Washington D.C. Biblical Archaeological Society*, pp. 2–7.

Ucko, P. J. 1994. Museums and sites: cultures of the past within education – Zimbabwe, some ten years on. In *The Presented Past: heritage, museums and education*, Stone, P. G. & B. L. Molyneaux (eds), 237–82. London: Routledge.

White, N. M. & J. R. Williams 1994. Public education and archaeology in Florida, USA: an overview and case study. In *The Presented Past: heritage, museums and education*, Stone, P. G. & B. L. Molyneaux (eds), 82–94. London: Routledge.

6 Education as a means of protection of the archaeological heritage in the districts of Buenos Aires Province, Argentina

FERNANDO OLIVA

Introduction

Archaeology is well advanced in the Province of Buenos Aires, bringing to light important evidence of the past 10,000 years of history in the region. Little attention has been paid, however, to the transfer of this knowledge to the education system and to the community at large. The indifference of modern scholars to the outside world is shown by the content of the textbooks used to teach primary-school children about prehistory. These books contain ethnocentric and deprecatory concepts of the first inhabitants of Bonaerense (i.e. Buenos Aires) territory (Estrada 1981a).

Anthropologists in Buenos Aires Province have recently begun to improve the situation, however, holding informal conferences and courses for teachers, taking students to archaeological sites, making presentations in classrooms and so on. These activities have often developed with the help of directors of museums and other cultural institutions, with regional museums acting as the means of contact with the community. Likewise, the central government of Buenos Aires Province has conducted anthropological and archaeological field trips since 1990 for the training of their employees involved in work with the public. Together with various anthropologists, they have developed a wide range of topics including cultural ethnocentrism, the peopling of the Americas and our own region, the local indigenous people, and the archaeological record, and they have discussed how these facts and ideas are seen within, and relate to, the community. These programmes are a landmark in Argentine education, as they represent the first action towards improving cultural education by a provincial state in the Argentine.

Problems in the transmission of knowledge about cultural heritage to the educational community in Buenos Aires Province

Population and geography

The first archaeological research in the Pampas was done at the end of the last century by Florentino Ameghino (1910, 1911), who identified ancient stone-tool industries and placed them within an evolutionary framework. Following the work of Ameghino, however, research became influenced by the nationalism that accompanied the consolidation of the national state of the Argentinian Republic. In archaeology, an interest in the origin and evolution of humanity was replaced by the search for indigenous national traditions (Politis 1992).

In 1948 archaeology was given new life by the arrival in the Argentine of an Austrian scholar, Osvaldo Menghin. He revised the archaeological collections held in Buenos Aires Province and initiated stratigraphic excavations in various sites (Menghin & Bormida 1950). Since then, archaeological research in the region has greatly improved, with a number of systematic studies of Pampean archaeology appearing in the 1970s and more localized studies in the province in the 1980s. In fact, recently obtained dates in the Pampean Region have called into question existing chronologies and the archaeologists involved have proposed new patterns of cultural development (e.g. Beron & Migale 1991; González de Bonaveri & Senatore 1991; Madrid & Salemme 1991; and Oliva 1991).

All this archaeological effort has shown us that a large part of the territory of Buenos Aires has been widely occupied by hunting and gathering peoples for at least 10,000 years. But similar efforts have not been made to spread this knowledge within the region. The majority of the people have a poor perception of the prehistoric past of their territory, limited to the vague idea that at the arrival of the Spaniards in Río de la Plata there were some 'savage Indians'. This situation of abundant scientific production, but scarce diffusion among the general public, also happens in other parts of the world and perhaps especially in the Third World.

This problem is particularly critical in countries where there is a population of indigenous and other groups who are politically and economically disadvantaged, and so have no influence or control over their education or access to information about their heritage. In Argentina, such marginalized populations exist in both the cities and rural areas, posing complex problems for any general approach to heritage education.

In Buenos Aires Province, for example, the population consists of a very few descendants of the aboriginal population and a mass of descendants of European immigrants (mainly Spaniards and Italians) who are unaware of the prehispanic past of the territory.

This population is distributed in two clear sectors. The first is the small but densely populated *conurbano* (conurbation) represented chiefly by the city of

Buenos Aires, the second, the interior, comprises most of the Province and consists of a much less densely distributed population scattered in smaller cities, towns and hamlets. The economic organization of the population is much less clear, however. Large concentrations of economically and socially marginal groups are simply not registered, especially in the *conurbano*. This is illustrated by a comparison of population levels and primary public schools in the urban centres and interior: the *conurbano*, with 62% of the population, has only 29% of the primary schools while the interior, with 38% of the population, has 71% of the primary schools. This unequal distribution of resources to the marginalized population is a primary factor to consider if policies of protection and education about the national heritage are to be set up.

The socio-political situation of the last two decades

During the 1970s Argentina, along with most other Latin American countries, experienced political problems, and these affected the nature and development of archaeology. At the beginning of this decade almost all of Latin America was ruled by governments of democratic origin. At the same time, however, many national economies underwent considerable problems and a variety of groups established guerrilla war as a method of implementing their ideals. These problems were the excuse for powerful economic interests to support the establishment of military governments, guided by right-wing-oriented political movements, such as that of Pinochet in Chile and Videla in Argentina. In the mid-1970s, a military coup took place in Argentina, bringing with it a socio-economic plan, known as 'plan Martinez de Hoz' after its creator, the Minister of the Economy during the first phase of the military government. As this economic plan was being implemented, 30,000 people 'disappeared' at the hands of paramilitary and police groups clearly identifiable with the Argentinian Government. In addition, leaders, politicians and other people who did not agree with the government were classified by the central power as 'subversive', and suffered varying degrees of persecution. The need for power of the groups that represented the military ultimately led to a war with Great Britain for possession of the Islas Malvinas (called the Falkland Islands by the British). For Argentina, this war represented more than 1000 dead, economic losses of great importance, and the persecution of anyone who objected to the war.

In this period of 'order' established by the military, 1976–83, universities were a focus of persecution, causing some archaeologists to emigrate to different parts of the world, and several prominent investigators were fired from their posts (see Politis 1992).

At the beginning of the 1980s nearly all of Argentina fought for the installation of democracy and it was finally reinstituted in 1983. The respect for individual rights and the restoration of parliament quickly created an atmosphere of free expression, in which new ideas could be voiced and tested. Coincidentally, archaeology began to thrive. Anthropology and archaeology departments, which had been closed during the military government, were reopened. In Olavarria, a city in the Province of Buenos Aires, a new Department of Anthropology was created: la Facultad de Ciencias-Sociales de la Universidad Nacional del Centro, Olivarria, Buenos Aires (see Politis 1992). A new funding body was set up, the Concejo de Investigaciónes Científicas y Tecnológicas (CONICET), which provided subsidies to numerous archaeological groups for fieldwork and the modernization of equipment. And scholars and researchers excluded from their work during the military governments took up their posts again.

In spite of a long tradition of archaeological investigations in the Pampas, therefore, the diffusion of archaeological knowledge to the community has been greatly limited by historical, socio-economic and political problems and has only recently begun to increase.

New actions to preserve the heritage in the Province of Buenos Aires

At the beginning of the 1980s, the vast majority of the archaeologists in Argentina were young professionals. This situation helped the introduction of a new perspective, with numerous themes that were ignored in earlier times – especially the relationship between archaeologists and local people and the preservation of cultural heritage. Since then, contact between archaeologists and their communities has increased slightly, as archaeologists have become involved in a variety of formal and informal activities.

Numerous lectures, conferences, meetings and workshops have been held in the last few years that bring together a wide variety of people concerned with heritage issues: politicians and bureaucrats, museologists, archaeologists and anthropologists, educators and their students, and members of the general public.

In 1987 the First National Meeting of Anthropologists took place, giving scientists, archaeologists and educationalists an opportunity to examine and develop their relationships (Caracoche, Haber, Olmo, Queiroz & Ratto 1987). In 1988, educational policies were discussed further at the inaugural meeting of anthropologists in Buenos Aires Province while their second meeting, in 1989, discussed a plan of action concerning the politics of archaeological resources and community education.

This plan aimed to carry out actions tending to promote the protection and diffusion of the archaeological heritage. Its three main objectives were:

1 the inclusion of archaeological knowledge in the educational system;
2 the organization of regional meetings with the different sectors interested in themes relating to the archaeological heritage (archaeologists, museum experts, politicians, etc.);
3 the creation of a database recording the archaeological projects, collections and regional museums of the province.

(Oliva, Cinquini & Data 1989)

Informal communication with teachers, students and the general public was given special emphasis, and so public lectures, conferences and discussion groups devoted to regional archaeology were planned – principally in those districts where the archaeological work is done (i.e. Tres Arroyos, González Chávez, Puan, Tornquist, Coronel Pringles and Saavedra). The first regional archaeological meeting was held in the town of Pigue, with teachers, museum staff and the general public in attendance. It marked a significant development in protection and conservation in the region, because the organization was done jointly with the Dirección de Museos Monumentos y Sitios Históricos and the city governments. The participants discussed ways of establishing links between archaeologists and the community and how archaeological information could be disseminated to the public, and they considered how archaeologists and the different public institutions could work together on various heritage issues, such as education, protection and tourism. In addition, a series of talks was given on the theme of education (García, Castells, Colangelo, Domenico, Jiménez & Paladino 1991; Oliva, Salinas & Zopi 1991) and a provincial Member of Parliament proposed a bill to protect painted cave sites in the Sistema de Ventania in the Province of Buenos Aires and an important stratified settlement site, Arroyo Seco 2 (Frayssinet 1991).

The second regional archaeological meeting, held in 1991 in the city of Chascomus, was attended by over 200 people and had representatives from 30 per cent of the districts in Buenos Aires Province. Such attendance is only surpassed in Argentina by national archaeology congresses, and so reflects the interest generated by these new archaeological initiatives amongst museum staff, students, politicians and teachers.

These and similar efforts resulted in a variety of educational outreach programmes. In 1989, for example, city council members and the Director of the Coronel Pringles Museum brought together teachers, students and archaeologists working in the district for a series of activities (Madrid & Salemme 1989). In the small village of Chasico (in the district of Tornquist), pupils from the primary school participated in fieldwork, with the help of the regional museum of Chasico and the local government (Oliva, Cinquini & Data 1989). And other archaeologists have helped teachers to develop courses in archaeology for local schools, introduced students to archaeology through conferences and visits to museums, and publicized their research to local communities.

A particularly successful project was an interdisciplinary one involving a geologist, biologist and archaeologist (the author) that was developed for the Ecology and Environment Commission of Saavedra district. For eight weekends, groups of about thirty students from two middle and secondary schools camped near a variety of archaeological sites under investigation and learned about the way of life of the people who had lived there. The students had to carry out tasks related to each of the disciplines, for which they had prepared in advance in the classroom. The archaeological fieldwork varied with the site: a cave with rock art, a surface site, stratified sites, and so on. The students helped survey, dig test-pits, and record rock art. At the end of this work, a reunion was held in the city of Pigue, where they had the opportunity to share their experiences (Oliva, Silva & Ustua 1991).

Provincial initiatives

The new movement among young professionals in Buenos Aires Province to change the traditions of anthropological research and spread archaeological knowledge throughout the whole community will only be successful if the Province provides the means to integrate the various educational activities described above into a co-ordinated programme.

As part of this process, the Dirección General de Escuelas y Cultura de la Provincia de Buenos Aires and his department co-ordinated a set of studies on the various heritage issues – protection, diffusion, education and heritage legislation – with the goal of organizing them into a coherent system (Oliva 1990).

In the field of archaeology, the protection of the archaeological heritage was examined in three main areas: (a) technical and scientific research; (b) legislation; and (c) education. A range of tasks was undertaken: archaeological sites and collections of the Buenos Aires Province were checked, advice was given to several municipalities, museums and cultural associations which required scientific support, and ordinances and national and provincial laws were analysed, in order to co-ordinate joint policies between the three levels of jurisdiction (Oliva & Sempe 1992). But the most important aspect of this initiative was the development of long-term educational programmes.

Primary education was the priority target, as primary-school children represent the society of the future. In order to determine the present condition of education about the past at this level, the syllabuses and educational textbooks currently in use were analysed. Then a training programme for primary-school teachers, but also open to other teachers and to the general public, was conducted through the Jornadas de Capacitación en Arqueología y Antropología of Buenos Aires Province.

Analysis of the textbooks

The textbooks are used by a large number of teachers as resource guides, against the advice of the Dirección General de Escuelas y Cultura, who think that they only superficially follow the syllabuses. The syllabuses themselves, it should be noted, only refer to the aborigines who inhabited the Pampas at the time of the Spanish conquest (Dirección General de Escuelas y Cultura 1986; Estudios Sociales n.d.; Ordenamiento Primer Ciclo 1986).

We decided to analyse the content of twelve textbooks published at different times and chosen for their continuing popularity. They represent all the textbook titles available in La Plata public libraries.

Some of the perceptions of the past contained in these books are:

1 The textbooks mention the indigenous people of Buenos Aires Province, but in the majority, the time depth of Pampean culture has not been developed. The exception is an older textbook in which it was stated: 'We can't subtract from our blood and spirit the ancestral voice of the aborigines which for millennia have populated our land' (J. Perón in Peuser Edition 1950).
2 In every textbook there are errors and omissions in historic and ethnographic accounts, as the authors have ignored published archaeological information. Eight of the textbooks also have errors in the sequence of events.
3 With regard to the social groups in the Pampas, we found that six texts treated them neutrally, whereas the other six treated them negatively.

These are some of the typical comments:

- This place was found to be occupied by aboriginal peoples, that is to say, they were born here. These people lived in primitive conditions. They were grouped in tribes and answered to a chief or cacique. Different groups had different degrees of culture. There were very advanced peoples who worked the land, and other peoples who were completely savage.

(Passadori, Astolfi, Fesquet, Veronelli,
Fresquet & Chan 1978, pp. 5–7)

- When the Spanish conquerors arrived in this land, they found aboriginal peoples who lived in savage conditions.

(Equipo Didactico 1978, p. 2)

- In Buenos Aires Province there were savage Indians.

(Estrada 1981a)

It is clear from these quotes that some of the textbook authors have extremely ethnocentric views, treating the aboriginal people superficially and misrepresenting their cultures. This problem has been recognized in at least one textbook, which has been recently corrected and improved (Santillana 1988), but as for the others, there is no justification for their continuing to convey such errors and omissions. There are specialized bibliographies that provide enough information to deal with the topic in a different and more informed way (e.g. Austral 1971; Madrazo 1973; Politis 1984).

Sessions on training and participation in archaeology and anthropology in the Province of Buenos Aires

From 1990 to 1992, sessions on training and participation in archaeology and anthropology were held in various cities in several districts in the Province of Buenos Aires; the instruction was given by archaeologists working in the area and the courses followed the guidelines of the Department of Primary Education. The goals of these sessions were:

1 to bring an anthropological view of culture into education;
2 to offer help to teachers by providing specialized information about the aboriginal people of Buenos Aires Province;
3 to incorporate the notion of the time depth of bonaerense cultural development within a wider American context;
4 to obtain a basic idea of the forms of access by the public to knowledge of the archaeological past;
5 to offer a panorama of information about the cultural past of the Pampas in order to help reconstruct and revalorize the social and historic identity of the community; and
6 to create a consciousness in people about the importance of knowledge and the protection of the archaeological heritage.

The themes developed included: culture as a concept, cultural relativism, the peopling of the Americas and archaeological investigations in the Pampas, the time of hispanic–indigenous contact, archaeological research in the local community, the relation between archaeology and the community, the role of education in protection of cultural heritage and current problems faced by indigenous people in Buenos Aires Province. A book was written to develop further the points of the programme (Oliva In Press). The people who attended these sessions were given a copy of the first version of the book.

As the programme used the hands-on approach – workshop courses and actual teaching – to establish an exchange of knowledge between researchers and future academics, an effective transfer of knowledge was achieved.

Conclusions

Buenos Aires Province presents certain difficulties for the archaeologists who are attempting to update knowledge of the past and make it available for use in education. The different problems in the urban and rural areas make any general approach to cultural research difficult because of the different social and economic priorities.

The climate is now beneficial in many ways, as democracy means that there are no ideological prosecutions, missing people or politically motivated killings. And, indeed, in the last years, some official sectors have indicated some interest in the subject. But unfortunately, there is no unified category, from a legislative point of view, within which archaeological heritage can be placed (see Oliva & Sempe 1992). And academics continue to leave the country as they did in the 1970s because of scarce funding and low salaries. Unless the actual socio-economic situation in the country changes, therefore, the situation is not likely to improve.

A key to the future success of archaeology in Argentina is education.

Change is urgently needed in the way that the past is taught, as indicated by the state of the textbooks commonly used in schools. Such success can only come about, however, if efforts are made at the local level to make people aware that heritage preservation is an important goal. Local populations are the best keepers of their own heritage, and they are also able to develop it most efficiently. The training and participation sessions in archaeology and anthropology in the Province of Buenos Aires between 1990 and 1992 were limited in time and scope, but they represent an important step in the development of future long-term educational policies.

The continuing lack of co-ordination at the different levels of government (national, provincial and local), the lack of research funding and the low salaries for researchers are problems still to be resolved, but they will be eased as the general education of the population about their past improves. This is the challenge for present and future generations of archaeologists working in the Province of Buenos Aires.

Acknowledgements

I am grateful to G. Politis, P. Madrid and M. Saghessi who provided constructive comments for the first draft of this paper. Moreover, the critical remarks by B. L. Molyneaux were taken into account and became an important influence in the final paper. I must also thank S. Fuentes, G. Politis (UNLP), E. Pons Carden-Jones, L. Price and C. Carreras (University of Southampton) for translating the Spanish text into English, and T. Sly and N. Bradford (University of Southampton), who assisted me with illustrations. I alone am responsible for the ideas expressed in the text.

References

Ameghino, F. 1910. *La industria de la piedra quebrada en el Mioceno Superior de Monte Hermoso*. Buenos Aires: Congreso Científico Internacional.
Ameghino, F. 1911. *Une Nouvelle Industrie lithique: l'industrie de la pierre fendue dans le Tertiaire de la región littorale du sud de Mar del Plata*. Buenos Aires: Anales del Museo de Buenos Aires.
Astolfi, J., A. Fesquet, H. Fesquet & L. Chan 1982. *Manual del alumno bonaerense* 4. Buenos Aires: Kapelusz.
Austral, A. 1971. El yacimiento arqueológico vallejo en el noroeste de la Provincia de La Pampa: contribución a la sistematización de la prehistoria y arqueología de la Región Pampeana. *Relaciones* 5.
Babino, E., J. Orero, V. Santarone, M. Malasteta, P. Inera, I. De Calvo, C. Campobassi, P. Zarur & J. Salgado 1965. *Manual Peuser de la nueva escuela 5to. grado*. Buenos Aires: Peuser.
Beron, M. & L. Migale 1991. Control de recursos y movilidad en el sur pampeano: el sitio Tapera Moreira–Provincia de la Pampa. *Boletín del Centro* 3, 40–51.
Caracoche, S., A. Haber, D. Olmo, P. Queiroz & N. Ratto 1987. Proyecto para la

reconstrucción de la identidad de la Provincia de Buenos Aires: el aporte de la arqueología para la comprensión e interpretación del proceso historico. Primer Encuentro de Antropólogos. Buenos Aires.

Codex 1962. *Manual práctico de materias 3er. grado*. Buenos Aires: Codex.

Dirección General de Escuelas y Cultura 1986. *Educación B sica 2 primaria: lineamientos curriculares*. Buenos Aires: Dirección General de Escuelas y Cultura de la Provincia de Buenos Aires.

Equipo Didactico Editorial Kapelusz 1978. *Conocimientos en acción: estudios sociales bonaerense 6*. Buenos Aires: Kapelusz.

Estrada, A. 1981a. *Manual estrada 5to. bonaerense*. Buenos Aires: Estrada.

Estrada, A. 1981b. *Manual estrada 4to. bonaerense*. Buenos Aires: Estrada.

Estudios Sociales n.d. *Planeamientos curriculares bonaerense 4 a 7 grados*. Buenos Aires: Dirección General de Escuelas y Cultura de la Provincia de Buenos Aires.

Frayssinet, C. 1991. Proyecto de ley: protección de diversos sitios arqueológicos de la Provincia de Buenos Aires. *Boletín del Centro* 1, 21–4.

Garcia, E., F. Castells, A. Colangelo, M. Domenico, A. Jimenez & M. Paladino 1991. La tarea es encontrar el tronco que nos une. *Boletín del Centro* 1, 10–11.

Gonzalez de Bonaveri, M. & M. Senatore 1991. Procesos de formación en el sitio San Ramon 4 Chascomu's. *Boletín del Centro* 2, 65–77.

Edition Gram 1966. *Manual Graf 2*. Buenos Aires: Graf.

Edition Kapelusz 1966. *Conocimientos en acción: ciencias sociales*. Buenos Aires: Kapelusz.

Edition Peuser 1950. *La nación argentina justa, libre y soberana: ano del libertador San Martin*. Buenos Aires: Peuser.

Edition Santillana 1986. *Area de las ciencias sociales*. Buenos Aires: Santillana.

Madrazo, G. 1973. Sintesis de arqueología pampeana. *Etnia* 7.

Madrid, P. & M. Salemme 1991. La ocupación tardia del sitio 1 de la laguna Tres Reyes, Adolfo González Chaves, Provincia de Buenos Aires. *Boletín del Centro* 3, 165–79.

Menghin, O. & M. Bormida 1950. Investigaciones prehistoricas en cuevas de Tandilia (Provincia de Buenos Aires). *Runa* 3.

Oliva, F. 1990. *Reflexiones y aportes para la inserción de la arqueología en la enseñanza primaria en la Provincia de Buenos Aires*. Buenos Aires: Dirección General de Escuelas y Cultura de la Provincia de Buenos Aires.

Oliva, F. 1991. Investigaciones arqueológicas desarrolladas en el sector occidental del Sistema de Vetania y la llanura adyacente 1987–1989. *Boletín del Centro* 1, 39–41.

Oliva, F. (ed.) In Press. *Jornadas de Capacitación en Arqueología y Antropología de la Provincia de Buenos Aires*. Buenos Aires: Dirección General de Escuelas y Cultura de la Provincia de Buenos Aires.

Oliva, F., N. Cinquini & M. Data 1989. Experiencia educativa en un sitio arqueológico, Chasico. Paper presented to a meeting on 'The Use of the Past', Universidad Nacional de La Plata.

Oliva, F., L. Salinas & C. Zopi 1991. Seis posters y cuadernillos para alumnos de escuelas primarias de la Provincia de Buenos Aires: proyecto. *Boletín del Centro* 1, 41.

Oliva, F. & C. Sempe 1992. Una nueva alternativa en la protección del patrimonio arqueológico en la Provincia de Buenos Aires. Paper presented to a meeting on 'The Use of the Past', Universidad Nacional de La Plata.

Oliva, F., D. Silva & J. Ustua 1991. Experiencias educativas en el campo con alumnos de niveles secundario y terciario en los partidos de Puan y Saavedra. *Boletín del Centro* 1, 16.

Ordenamiento Primer Ciclo 1986. *Planeamiento curricular bonaerenser*. Buenos Aires: Dirección General de Escuelas y Cultura de la Provincia de Buenos Aires.

Passadori, J., J. Astolfi, A. Fesquet, A. Veronelli & L. Chan 1982. *Manual del alumno bonaerense 5to*. Buenos Aires: Kapelusz.

Passadori, J., J. Astolfi, A. Fesquet, A. Veronelli, H. Fesquet & L. Chan. 1978. *Manual del alumno bonaerense 6to*. Buenos Aires: Kapeluz.

Politis, G 1984. Investigaciones arqueológicas en el área interserrana bonaerense. *Etnía* 32, 7–52.

Politis, G. 1992. Política nacional, arqueología y universidad en Argentina. In *Arqueología en America Latina hoy*, G. Politis (ed.), 70–88. Bogotá: Fondo de Promoción de la Cultura.

7   *Rescuing ordinary people's culture: museums, material culture and education in Brazil*

PEDRO PAULO A. FUNARI

Introduction

Bourdieu (1992, p. 113) stressed recently that we have spoken too much about consciousness, too much in terms of representation. The social world does not work in terms of consciousness, it works in terms of practices, mechanisms and so forth. It is beyond dispute that people conform to or dissent from established views much more through practices than theories, through material than immaterial influences.

Growing up, therefore, has much less to do with scholarly knowledge learnt 'by heart' than with real, material life. Possibly most of us would agree with Bates that 'it was not, indeed, until I left the school that my education began' (Bates 1985, p. 25). And according to Graham Greene,

> The child will pick up all he needs to know in the fields or in the streets; because so much of his time is free, and his speculation endless, he will soon know as much as his elders who are confined to their desks.
>
> (Greene 1985, p. 236)

This is not to deny the value of formal education, but to imply that the success of education depends on the relation of its learning programmes to the down-to-earth ordinary activity that defines our humanly constituted world (Funari 1990, p. 9). The problem is that education does not tend to reflect the interests of common people; it is often just a means of transferring elite culture to the masses (Brando 1984, p. 18). In Brazil, the domination of the elite in education persists in a society that still feels the effects of the long period of army rule (1964–85), still plagued by murder squads (Kiernan 1990, p. 93) and widespread arbitrariness inside and outside the learning world.

The Brazilian school system and its auxiliary pedagogical departments in museums were traditionally defined as important tools for the reproduction of social relations, strengthening the ideological hierarchies and reproducing social and cultural inequalities (Singer 1986, p. 52).

This was a hidden agenda in formal syllabuses (*curriculum oculto*, cf. Tedesco 1985, p. 46) that made knowledge seem worthless in practical terms, as it was diffused through segmentation into distinct subjects, like chronological history and physical geography (Martins 1982, p. 26). And museums have also served by and large to distance and disenfranchise people from their past. The past becomes a succession of pre-interpreted, securely named and labelled objects, anaestheticized by means of the museum display (Shanks & Tilley 1987, p. 93; Tilley 1989, p. 113; cf. Vargas & Sanoja 1990, p. 53).

An effect of this form of education is the transformation of naturally independent-minded children and youngsters – and indeed, the public at large – into passive conformists (see Fletner 1956, p. 157; cf. Freire 1971, p. 103). As Freire (1983b, p. 68) has stressed, the more pupils try to store the information they receive, the less they will be able to develop the critical consciousness that they can receive from direct experience. This idea reflects the main feature of traditional pedagogy: the passivity produced hinders the development of democratic freedom (*unsere Schule kann deshalb heute keine Schule der Demokratie sein*: Wagenschein 1956, p. 52).

An alternative educational approach suggests that 'education only could make sense as critical self-reflection' (Adorno 1969, p. 87) – thereby challenging learning manipulation (Hoernle 1969, p. 118). Pedagogy should not conceal social contradictions but rather enable students to understand and so expose them (Gadotti 1978, p. 13; Franco 1983, p. 31). Such an approach aims at transforming learners into creative beings, through a notion of 'praxis, authentic dialogue between the teacher and the taught', in which the student assumes 'an awareness and capacity as a human to transform the world' (Jenks 1977, p. 266).

This alternative therefore challenges the traditional, imitative education by directing study to the world of daily life, so that the learner may confront, and eventually understand, the materiality of social relations and their historical roots.

There is a significant role for archaeology in such an education. Archaeology is not the mere collection of artefacts (Cabrera 1988, p. 289) or the manipulation of the past (Leone 1982, p. 754). As its primary source of information is the material production of a society, and as understanding the world is a material process (Shanks & Tilley 1989, p. 44), of reading through material culture the mental structure, world-view and general culture of a people (Leone 1988, p. 336), archaeology works directly with ordinary people's culture and so may be an important tool in the consciousness-raising of a society (MacKenzie 1990, p. 3).

Yet archaeology cannot separate itself from its historical and social roots; and so Brazil must overcome the social and historical legacy of oppression within which archaeology has been practised in the past several decades. For this reason, the main goal of archaeology in contemporary Brazil, as it is in many other parts of the world, is to rescue ordinary people's culture, through education about the past in museums and schools.

Brazilian archaeology, museums and society

Laura da Veiga (1985, p. 193), describing the twenty-one-year dictatorship period in Brazil (1964–85), stressed that 'military administrations, among other things, tried always to control the civilian population, first and foremost the large masses of people excluded from the regime's profits, using both repressive and demobilizing tactics'. Not only did police and military authorities carry out repressive actions, clamping down civilian opposition, but there was an upsurge in executions by death squad. In 1973, for example, 'conservative sources estimated the number of their victims at 1,300 in Southern Brazil alone' (Pike 1982, p. 85). This violence against ordinary people is explained by a social exclusion model which put some 85 per cent of the population outside the market economy, in absolute or relative poverty (Andrade 1987, p. 12). Millions of children live today in streets, thousands of them being killed by death squads each year (Cardoso 1991).

One of the first actions undertaken by military plotters in the aftermath of the 1964 coup was to draw up a blacklist of thousands of their political opponents (Pike 1982, p. 119). Humanist archaeologists, like other liberal-minded people, would be subject to persecution and expulsion. Suppressing humanist archaeology at its roots, it would be possible to introduce archaeology as a 'weapon of oppression', in Lumbreras's (1981, p. 6) words, through the training of a generation of practitioners within the ideological framework of the dictatorship.

With regard to museums, Jacobus (1991) recently studied the evidence relating to the management of the Museu Arqueólogico do Rio Grande do Sul (MARSUL) during military rule and produced a frightening description of what he described as the destruction of archaeological assets with the connivance of the public authorities. This was possible thanks to what he called the feudal treatment of a public institution (Jacobus 1991, p. 6), as the military authorities reinforced and renewed patronage practices in public administration. These feudal or mafia-like structures were established in museums thanks to the repression of humanist management, the worst case being the expulsion of the Director of the Pre-History Institute (IPH-USP), the humanist Paulo Duarte (Funari 1991).

It is no surprise, however, that this period could still, as late as 1988, be considered by some proud fieldworkers to have been the golden age:

> In the 1960s Brazilian archaeology went through a very dynamic phase, with extensive fieldwork. Archaeologists from overseas grew in number, in turn creating national Brazilian projects based on foreign funding. Such activity had a profound effect on Brazilian fieldwork methods, influencing the whole generation of researchers who are now active.
>
> (Lima 1988, p. 25)

In the wake of this 'dynamic phase' of Brazilian life, as Rodrigues has observed: 'the traditional pattern of conciliation broke down. There would be no more conciliation: adversaries were no longer adversaries but mortal enemies, a Brazilian could no longer profess a different view without being considered as an external enemy' (in Wirth 1984, p. 226; cf. Dassin 1986; Ames 1988, p. 169).

And this archaeological tradition continues today, maintained through 'university teaching, control of research funding, personal and political relationships' and so forth (Kristiansen 1983, p. 73; cf. Durrans 1989, p. 67).

In this political climate, it is only too natural that material culture studies have been not so much at the centre of professional archaeologists' attention, as this archaeological approach attempts 'to promote a constant reflection on human and societal conditions and bring this to present-day social criticism' (Nordblach 1989, p. 28). People are becoming increasingly aware, however, that material culture (and thus archaeology) 'provides the raw data for the teaching of those subjects concerned with the social world' (MacKenzie & Stone 1990, p. 5). And indeed, Brazil is very rich in historical assets, from countless buildings, squares and monuments scattered throughout the country, to whole colonial towns, like Ouro Preto, and the planned capital city of Brasilia.

In this context we must consider the role archaeology has been playing recently and the perspectives open to its development in the country in these two important directions: heritage management and museum public education, and within the school system. Outside formal school education, the main pedagogical use of archaeological assets is to be found in the large national or state museums, as they have educational staff to deal specifically with issues of material culture, with a Pedagogical Service addressed to school-children and the general public.

Historical assets and public displays

Following a general trend (cf. Uruguay's case in Toscano 1990, p. 2) from the nineteenth century, the idea of a national museum has been to build an upper-class European identity (Hale 1989, p. 225), opposing the European/civilized/upper-class culture to the indigenous/black and ordinary people's 'primitive and natural' one. More recently, however, thanks to the loosening of political bonds in the country, there have been some attempts to represent a more accurate view of society in museum displays and exhibitions, and with these innovations, the development of museum hands-on activities.

The most striking example is the Pre-History Institute at the University of São Paulo, which vindicated the memory of the persecuted humanist and prehistorian Paulo Duarte, expelled in 1968 at the height of military hysteria, through the renaming of its museum as Paulo Duarte's Museum (Bruno & Mello Vasconcellos 1989, p. 185).

Even though such developments are positive, one cannot say, however, that ordinary people's culture, aims and aspirations are reflected in Brazilian museums in general. The ideal role of a museum in society may be expressed in the words of Vargas & Sanoja:

> Museums should encourage the development of human thought, pointing out peculiarities, dissimilarities, similarities, and connections between the historical processes of different peoples. They should be didactic tools enabling people to connect facts, objects and pictures to real life. They should provide incentives for reflection and for the private study of history.
>
> (Vargas & Sanoja 1990, p. 53)

But the reality is that museums tend to be huge rhetorical constructions, usually displaying artefacts of the upper class, reflecting elite ideology and aiming at the naturalization of social relations as inevitable and eternal (Shanks & Tilley 1987, p. 93). Indeed, besides the direct, repressive role museums played during the most difficult period of army rule, there is a more subtle and pervasive aspect of the relationship between museums and the public which goes beyond the boundaries of the military period: its inner disciplinary function (Foucault 1979). This concept of discipline is not in the sense of a military enforcement but is a symbolic domination that is a subtle, and because of this, more brutal, means of oppression (Bourdieu 1992, p. 115). Such symbolic violence means that the museum manipulates relations, suppressing contradiction, fixing the past as a reflection of the appearance of the present. The present recognizes itself and is justified. The museum as an ideological institution of this kind therefore suppresses difference and heterogeneity in society through its carefully structured depiction of the artefactual past. Material displays carry implicit and biased messages about the past: people obey, collude or positively accept their own inferior social position, oppression or exploitation, and ultimately become oblivious to their own subordination (Miller, Rowlands & Tilley 1988, p. 15).

If, during the military rule, it was easy to say that directors in charge, as successors to expelled scholars, were not representative of the general population, today it is not difficult to understand the continuity of the same managers in the same or different museums claiming this kind of legitimacy. For people in power, especially people controlling museums, it may be fashionable to talk about a society's appropriation of the past through memory, about the importance of a group's feeling of belonging to something (Meneses 1987, p. 188); but at the same time such talk avoids the issues of the control of the past, of social interests involved in material culture and, ultimately, of the lives of ordinary people (and students and scholars).

Paulista Museum with its strong national appeal is a case in point. Built in the late nineteenth century as a huge memorial monument celebrating the country's independence, it is used to reinforce in the popular mind a mystic and imaginary history that justifies social inequalities and social exclusions.

From 'patriotic educational visits' to the museum to official catalogues, there is no trace of a critical approach to its function. Instead of 'demystifying archaeology, teaching about how a past is constructed, and discovering how the past was used' (Leone, Potter & Schakel 1987, p. 285) the Paulista Museum has as its overt purpose the reinforcing of its function as a 'civic cathedral':

> the memorial monument (i.e. Paulista Museum) is not only an architectural monument, but the figured reincarnation of a nation-building act (i.e. the Imperial Independence proclamation by Peter the First in 1822). . . . This true civic cathedral is still a worshipping place for many 'pilgrims'.
>
> (Meneses 1991, p. 5)

Paulista Museum: material identity and elite designs

The Museu Paulista da Universidade de São Paulo (known as Museu do Ipiranga) was made up of private collections offered to the São Paulo State Government on 28 August 1892. The Museu do Estado (State Museum) changed its name to Paulista Museum and was moved to a huge independence memorial building. On 7 September 1895, commemorating the 63rd anniversary of the proclamation of Independence, the museum was officially inaugurated. The main building was designed by the Italian Thomaso Gaudenzio Bezzi in Italian Renaissance style. The history section is composed of more than 6000 artefacts (pictures, furniture, coaches, clothing, religious objects, stoneware and so forth). From its inception, the Paulista Museum was planned as a huge São Paulo State eulogy to the elite and as a material discourse on the State's pretensions to dominate the country as a whole.

The birth of the independent Brazilian nation is located at São Paulo (Ipiranga) and, as a consequence, histories of Brazil always focus on the area. The colonial period in Brazil is interpreted as a brave adventure of Paulista founding fathers discovering the backlands (*sertão*), settling throughout the Portuguese colony and conquering the huge areas beyond the reach of Portuguese law. Brazil as a whole was therefore not a Portuguese colony but rather a huge country conquered by Bandeirantes, as the people from São Paulo were known. This conquest was carried out through fighting not only against Indians in the west but also against Spaniards (towards the south and west) and against rebelling blacks in the north (Moura 1981). There was no other unifying principle in the colony: without Bandeirantes there would not have been a Brazil. Portuguese settlements could, after all, have developed as in Spanish America as a series of independent regional countries, and so if there is any Brazilian identity, which contrasts clearly with Spanish-speaking Latin America, it is the result of a Bandeirante project.

This is the colonial Brazil as interpreted by the Paulista elite, a historical interpretation which became standard from the late nineteenth century, thanks to the economic development of São Paulo State which led to its political hegemony. In fact, Paulista Museum as a building was planned as a direct challenge to Rio de Janeiro's ambition to continue to dominate the political life of the country after the proclamation of the Republic in 1889, in particular, as a direct response to the National Museum at Rio de Janeiro, transferred to the Quinta da Boa Vista, the former São Cristóuão Palace, the official Imperial family mansion (1892).

Affonso de Escragnolle Taunay, Director of the Paulista Museum from 1917, preparing the 1922 Independence centenary, supplied the material basis for the São Paulo political slogan: *non ducor, duco*. Bandeirante destiny was to rule, not to be ruled (Mota 1990, p. 22).

Taunay tried to set up a full collection of artefacts on Bandeirante activities. Two pictures are particularly revealing: the foundation of São Vicente and the departure of *The Monsoon*. São Vicente was the first town founded in Brazil (at São Paulo) in 1532 and the real beginning of the country could not have been anywhere else: the first Brazilian town was a Bandeirante achievement. The oil painting by Benedito Calixto (Fig 7.1) shows the founding of the village at the moment when settlement transformed the whole landscape, as the Portuguese became Bandeirante and the Indians became ordinary servants of Bandeirantes. Ideologically, Indians are represented converting to Catholicism, thanks to a priest, and the Bandeirante destiny is portrayed in the image of a backlands settlement in the background and the core of dignitaries at the centre of the picture looking at the continent as if figuring out a way to conquer it.

The picture of *The Monsoon*'s departure by Almeida Júnior (Fig 7.2) deals with another symbolic Bandeirante activity: the departure of settlers from Araritaguaba harbour (nowadays Porto Feliz) in the Tietê river in the direction of the Cuiaba' mines. The painting shows the brave Bandeirantes being blessed by a Catholic priest and served by ordinary subordinates, particularly a black slave who is shown carrying a trunk. Once again, the elite Bandeirante are represented as conquerors while the ordinary people are represented as passive servants.

The famous painting by Pedro Américo (Fig 7.3), *Independence or death*, sits in the main room (salão nobre) of the museum. It was painted in Europe in 1888. Following a scheme by Meissonier in his *Friedland battle* (1807), Peter is shown proclaiming Independence, followed by his party. As in Almeida Júnior's picture, the river, this time the Ipiranga, is a Bandeirante reference, and the ordinary servants are both the passers-by at the left of the picture and all the observers of the painting, all of us, servants to this important elite act: independence from above, independence in São Paulo and under the aegis of Bandeirantes.

All three pictures, as with the other artefacts in the museum, reflect clearly São Paulo elite ideology. Bandeirante elite 'was relatively impenetrable to women, non-whites, and immigrants and was narrowly recruited among a small pool of highly educated men who, more often than not, were property owners' (Love & Barickman 1986, p. 764).

Figure 7.1 Painting by Benedito Calixto (1853–1927) showing the foundation of São Vicente. Museu Paulista da USP, São Paulo.

Figure 7.2 Painting by Almeida Júnior (1850–99) showing the departure of settlers from Monção. Museu Paulista da USP, São Paulo.

Figure 7.3 Painting by Pedro Américo (1843–1905): *Independence or death*. Museu Paulista da USP, São Paulo.

Love & Barickman (1986, p. 765) noted that 'the economic leadership, phasing into dominance, that São Paulo established in the period [1889–1930] still persists today'. The Paulista Museum has continued to play a special ideological role in maintaining this Bandeirante mythology. Directors are politically appointed and they have established a whole administrative network to maintain this 'civic cathedral'. It is interesting to note that fascist ideology and policies, always concerned with the cult of the elites, were imported to São Paulo; just as the elite hegemony in Italy was identified with the ancient Roman military dictatorship, so in Brazil the Bandeirante men were known as 'our Roman soldiers'. During military rule (1964–1985), Paulista Museum continued to play this ideological role unchallenged. And since then, despite the emergence of counter-discourses and freedom in the country, Paulista Museum has continued to be managed by people appointed according to their political beliefs.

Its main task therefore continues to be to protect elite tradition. Although the 1990 catalogue commemorating its centenary includes statements asking for a less partial and conservative reading of the past, with the inclusion of displays countering the conventional wisdom (notably Mota 1990, p. 22), its rooms, artefacts and permanent displays continue as before. After all, 'the allegory set up by this civic cathedral is still effective' (Meneses 1990, p. 21) – effective in masking relations, in glorifying elite ideology and in maintaining people in power (including museum management).

For the 'pilgrims', the ordinary people, however, there is no place for their identity, for their culture, for their past. The problem is not only, not even mainly, related to factual misrepresentations and masking tactics, although this is not an irrelevant aspect. Pedro Américo's picture of Peter I and his party at the moment of the so-called 'proclamation of Independence', all riding horses – instead of the actual mules used on that occasion (Zanettini 1991, p. 5) – is a misrendering which should not be concealed from the public eye; it should rather be compared to real archaeological evidence relating to both the Imperial party and ordinary people's lives at that time. Poor people, native inhabitants and black slaves, the vast majority excluded from this official past, should not be left out if, as Trigger (1990, p. 785) says, 'archaeologists must strive to transcend their own colonial heritage by sponsoring a vigorous programme of affirmative action' in relation to Native peoples. In this effort, it is important to remember that the cultural diversity of the whole society must be addressed. Indeed, if archaeologists are 'to help create a more humane social order', they must also attempt to valorize the 'culture of resistance' of the other large exploited and unrepresented people, the Africans (Epperson 1990, p. 36).

It would not be very difficult to bring ordinary people to museums. This could be carried out through the introduction of political content into conventional displays, taking artefacts out of their traditional chronological narrative (Shanks & Tilley 1987, p. 98) and stressing ordinary people's culture, as part of an attempt 'to construct a different history – one of resistance against domination' (Rubertone 1988, p. 37). But unfortunately, the persistence of ideological control by the Brazilian upper class and its bias in favour of social exclusion, as reflected in the main museum displays, suggests that extensive change will be long in coming. Long ago Manuel Gamio (1916, 1922) tried to integrate archaeology with Native arts and culture, but archaeological museum management in Brazil is still backward in relation to other parts of Latin America (Funari 1990, p. 10) – reflecting the fact that museum innovation is a political and ethical problem relating to competing issues of national identity and social reality.

Archaeology within the school system

While museums have been slow to change from their high ideological purposes, educationalists and ordinary teachers have been using the day-to-day experiences of students as a main learning tool in schools. The study of the mundane (Giddens 1987, p. 218), present and past daily material life (Carvalho, Hate, Antonacci, Aquino, Reis & Nicolau 1986, p. 6), helps school-children to understand how power relations within society are expressed in the world around them. In Brazil, the classroom, with its student benches, blackboard, teacher's chair and raised platform arrangement is clearly designed to convince students that knowledge and power are equated and exercised through the manipulation of material things (Tragtemberg 1985, p. 43).

Awareness and self-reflection (Freire 1983a, p. 18) resulting from this pedagogical approach have been not only preached by leading thinkers but actually carried out by ordinary teachers (e.g. Alves 1991). Such teachers have been able to shape a creative and critical strategy aiming at instilling a human-izing approach to social life.

My own experience in this began in the late 1980s when, as a scientific adviser, I was first given responsibility for dealing with material culture in a new history syllabus proposal to be introduced in São Paulo State primary and secondary schools. Most recently, I have been working with vocational schools in the development of a critical syllabus.

Vocational students, with their potentially emancipating working-class background (Foracchi 1964, p. 147), are particularly likely to understand that 'the will to change springs up from working, from fighting, from social practices, from organized action' (Gadotti 1983, p. 142). For them, material culture study and archaeology are not 'just a youthful pastime' (Podgorny 1990, p. 189) but truly a consciousness-raising process.

Vocational high schools attached to the Paula Souza São Paulo State Technic Education Centre (CEETEPS) and associated with the São Paulo State University (UNESP) introduced a new history syllabus centred on 'the work-ing world and popular culture'. An important aspect of this new approach is the study of the pervasive African culture in Brazilian society. African culture is often dismissed by ordinary people as having mean and contemptible traits, rejected equally by blacks, mulattos and Europeans as 'barbaric' (also see Wade 1994). It was to counter this estrangement, invisible and inaudible (Friede-mann 1988), and to challenge widespread racist rationalizations (Moura 1988, p. 17) that African culture was chosen to be at the centre of the students' work.

Slavery and black culture are studied as challenging 'current popular belief, that slaves had their culture destroyed by slavery and that they were mindless dupes of the system' (Orser 1991, p. 40). Rather, students are shown that 'slaves resisted their bound condition and expressed their anger through both long-term, non-violent acts and short-term, violent confrontations' (Orser 1991, p. 40).

Archaeology is important in this work, because as Brown & Cooper have pointed out, 'Africans and African-Americans may often be "invisible" in written history, but through carefully constructed archaeological research, they do not have to remain that way' (Brown & Cooper 1990, p. 19).

The archaeology of race and class identifies the material elements of domi-nation, power and ideology revealing that enslaved Africans and their de-scendants nurtured and sustained traditions in spite of the oppressive, dehumanizing conditions of slavery (Singleton 1990, pp. 73–4; cf. Scott 1988, p. 424). As material culture not merely reflects social relations but participates actively in their creation, operation and maintenance (Howson 1990, p. 88), African-related spatial organization and artefactual grammars (Slenes 1989, p. 18) may be studied in order to change common-sense preconceived misjudge-ments in relation to black customs. Research into slave musical instruments and African prototypes (Blassingame 1979, figs 13–14) will foster in the students the awareness that samba actually is of African origin and that black people are at the root of this national symbol, thus disputing the picture of the European upper-class music background painted by official discourse. But perhaps the most effective subjects relate to Afro-Brazilian architecture, enabling ordinary students to understand black architectural heritage. For example, Camdomble temples, which are known directly and indirectly by the students themselves, constitute an interesting starting-point for understanding black material culture. Using temple ground plans, students realize that the central post, at first glance an architectural feature, has a clear symbolic rather that functional role. It has nothing to do with ceiling support (Bastide 1973, pp. 328–33), being absent in private buildings and not always reaching the temple ceiling. The temple central post plays a symbolic role, being at the same time the world axis and a phallic fertility symbol. This African religious trait therefore helps students to understand that, far from being crude, barbaric and foreign, African-Brazilian heritage is at the very root of ordinary people's culture.

Conclusion

There are always limits to dominance (Miller 1988). Excluded pasts (MacKenzie & Stone 1990) and a critical approach to them enable us to challenge current educational practices.

Indigenous/minority oppressed groups can rescue their own memory with the help of a critical archaeology and a social engagement by people, especially teachers and other educationalists, dealing with material culture, archaeologists and museum management alike. As knowledge does not exist in a social vacuum (Champion 1991, p. 144), only this ethical commitment to the ordinary people will enable us to challenge present ideology, which is made to seem timeless and matter-of-fact, and to examine how the past is constructed and used by others (Handsman & Leone 1989, pp. 119, 134). Considering the political importance of museums and their management, this ethical approach is always difficult, and especially so in Latin America (cf. Vargas & Sanoja 1990, p. 53), where humanism has often been the victim of open repression, thanks to its defence of basic human rights.

People challenging current ideas as presented by authorities and ruling elites are usually attacked by those in power as 'paranoiac'. Those in power tend to regard the exclusion of Blacks, Indians and ordinary people from a national identity scheme as a natural, given fact – and if threatened, elite ideology will try to destroy the challenge, sometimes literally, as the Paulo Duarte example shows beyond dispute, and sometimes through the isolation of critical and creative approaches (Williams 1965, p. 19) as radical, unscientific or auto-biographical.

In Brazil, ministers, secretaries, museum directors and other bureaucratic intellectuals continue to think that the country is made up of 20 million citizens and 130 million inhabitants (non-citizens). This radical exclusion of ordinary people from official identity explains why Paulista Museum continues to be as exclusive and elite-oriented as a century ago, and explains why Brazilian identity, as forged by the elite, continues to be a Bandeirante one. Brazilian identity is still an elite Bandeirante project. The task of challenging this one-sided identity is just beginning. Even though it is not easy to challenge conventional material discourses about the past as presented in our museums and schools, it is nevertheless a task ordinary people are imposing on us, and one we must take up willingly.

Archaeologists and teachers face the same challenges in trying to overcome the more general dehumanizing aspects of our societies (Zamora 1990, pp. 56–8). Many teachers imbued with humanist ideals (Kern 1985, p. 10) aim at producing a citizenry aware of the actual diversity and vitality of the society at large. And there is a growing understanding that 'the specifics of curricula are ultimately of much less relevance than the exercise in mental agility . . . how well they learn to read, how sharp they learn to think, and how adventurously they imagine' (Berman 1989, p. 120). There is also a growing acknowledgement that we must rethink the traditional equation of upper-class/erudite with the right culture and the characterization of ordinary people/popular with the wrong.

Reform is no easy task, as the Brazilian writer Machado de Assis stressed as early as 1878, and it is necessary for all of us to understand and, if necessary, confront tradition (Pereira 1991, p. 88): 'no reform is useful and long-standing without enduring the resistance from tradition, the combination of routine, laziness and incompetence. This is the baptism of new ideas and at the same time their purgatory.'

Acknowledgements

I owe thanks to the following friends and colleagues who forwarded papers (sometimes unpublished ones), exchanged ideas and helped me in different ways: Júlia A. Alves, Leonel Cabrera, Arno A. Kern, Mark P. Leone, Mário Maestri, Clóvis Moura, Charles E. Orser Jr, Gustavo Politis, Michael Rowlands, Michael Shanks, Robert Slenes, Maria de Fátima S. de Souza, Christopher Tilley, A. H. Toscano, Bruce G. Trigger and Paulo E. Zanettini. The ideas expressed here are my own, for which I alone am therefore responsible. This research was possible thanks to the following institutions: Brazilian National Research Council (CNPq), Centre for the Improvement of Brazilian Lecturers and Professors (CAPES), São Paulo State University (UNESP), Paula Souza Vocational Educational Centre (CEETEPS) and the São Paulo State Pedagogical Studies and Rules Centre (CENP-SP). Only the patience and aid of my wife Raquel enabled me to complete this research.

References

Adorno, T. W. 1969. *Stichworte*. Frankfurt: Suhrkamp.

Alves, J. A. 1991. Plano de ensino. Unpublished ms, Escola Técnica Estadual, São Paulo.

Ames, B. 1988. Military and society in Latin America. *Latin American Research Review* 23, 157–69.

Andrade, M. C. 1987. *Abolição e reforma agrária*. São Paulo: Ática.

Bastide, R. 1973. *Estudos Afro-Brasileiros*. São Paulo: Perspectiva.

Bates, H. E. 1985. Grammar School, Kettering. In *The Old School*, Greene, G. (ed.), 227–36. Oxford: Oxford University Press.

Berman, R. A. 1989. Perestroika for the university. *Telos* 81, 115–21.

Blassingame, I. W. 1979. *The Slave Community: plantation life in the Antebellum South*. New York: Oxford University Press.

Bourdieu, P. 1992. Doxa and common life. *New Left Review* 191, 111–21.

Brandão, C. R. 1984. *Saber e ensinar*. Campinas: Papirus.

Brown, K. L. & D. C. Cooper 1990. Structural continuity in African-American slave and tenant community. *Historical Archaeology* 24, 7–19.

Bruno, M. C. O. & C. Mello Vasconcellos 1989. A proposta educativa do Museu de Pré-História Paulo Duarte. *Revista de Pré-História* 7, 165–86.

Cabrera, L. 1988. *Panorama retrospectivo y situación actual de la arqueología uruguaya*. Montevideo: Universidad de la Republica.

Cardoso, J. 1991. Rua sem saída, o assassínio de dois menores marginalizados em São Paulo revela una guerra de exterminio no país. *Istoé-Senhor* 1144, 42–6.

Carvalho, A. M. M., C. H. Hate, M. A. M. Antonacci, M. A. Aquino, M. C. D. Reis & S. Nicolau 1986. *Proposta curricular para o ensino de história*. São Paulo: CENP.

Champion, T. 1991. Theoretical archaeology in Britain. In *Archaeological Theory in Europe*, Hodder, I. (ed.), 129–60. London: Routledge.

Dassin, J. 1986. *Torture in Brazil: a shocking report on the pervasive use of torture by Brazilian military government, 1964–1979, secretly prepared by the Archdiocese of São Paulo*. New York: Random House.

Durrans, B. 1989. Theory, profession and the political role of archaeology. In *Archaeological Approaches to Cultural Identity*, Shennan, S. J. (ed.), 66–75. London: Unwin Hyman; Routledge pbk 1994.

Epperson, T. W. 1990. Race and the disciplines of the plantation. *Historical Archaeology* 24, 29–36.

Fletner, W. 1956. Die Erziehung und das Leben. In *Erziehung wozu?* 149–63. Stuttgart: Kroener.

Foracchi, M. 1964. *O estudante e a transformaçao da sociedade brasileira*. Unpublished PhD dissertation, University of São Paulo.

Foucault, M. 1979. *Discipline and Punish: the birth of the prison*. Harmondsworth: Penguin Books.

Franco, M. L. P. B. 1983. O ensino de segundo grau: democratização ou nem uma coisa nem outra? *Cadernos de Pesquisa* 47, 18–31.

Freire, P. 1971. *Educação como prática de liberdade*. Rio de Janeiro: Paz e Terra.

Freire, P. 1983a. *Educação e mudança*. Rio de Janeiro: Paz e Terra.

Freire, P. 1983b. *Pedagogia do oprimido*. Rio de Janeiro: Paz e Terra.

Friedemann, N. S. de 1988. *Cabildos negros: refugios de Africanía en Colombia*. Caracas: Universidad Católica Andrés Bello.

Funari, P. P. A. 1990. Education through archaeology in Brazil: a bumpy but exciting road. *Archaeology and Education* 1, 9–11.

Funari, P. P. A. 1991. Archaeology in Brazil: politics and scholarship at a crossroads. *World Archaeological Bulletin* 5, 122–32.

134   PEDRO PAULO A. FUNARI

Gadotti, M. 1978. Revisão crítica do papel do pedagogo na atual sociedade brasileira. *Educação e Sociedade* 1, 5–16.
Gadotti, M. 1983. *Educação e poder: introdução a pedagogía do conflito*. São Paulo: Cortez.
Gamio, M. 1916. *Forjando patria*. Mexico City: Editorial de la Universidad Nacional Autónoma de México.
Gamio, M. 1922. *La población del valle de Teotihuacán*. Mexico City: Editorial de la Universidad Nacional Autónoma de México.
Giddens, A. 1987. *Social Theory and Modern Sociology*. Cambridge: Polity Press.
Greene, G. 1985. The last word, Berkhamsted. In *The Old School*, Greene, G. (ed.), 227–36. Oxford: Oxford University Press.
Hale, C. A. 1989. Political and social ideas. In *Latin America Economy and Society 1870–1930*, Bethel, L. (ed.), 225–300. Cambridge: Cambridge University Press.
Handsman, R. G. & M. P. Leone 1989. Living history and critical archaeology in the reconstruction of the past. In *Critical Tradition in Contemporary Archaeology*, Pinsky, V. A. & A. Wylie (eds), 117–35. Cambridge: Cambridge University Press.
Hoernle, E. 1969. *Grundlagen proletarischer Erziehung*. Frankfurt: Suhrkamp.
Howson, J. E. 1990. Social relations and material culture: a critique of the archaeology of plantation society. *Historical Archaeology* 24, 78–91.
Jacobus, A. L. 1991. Destruição do património arqueológico com a conivência do poder público. Unpublished manuscript, Porto Alegre.
Jenks, C. 1977. Powers of knowledge and forms of the mind. In *Rationality, Education and the Social Organization of Knowledge*, C. Jenks (ed.), 23–38. London: Routledge.
Kern, A. A. 1985. A importância da pesquisa arquaeológica na universidade. *Revista do CEPA* 12, 5–11.
Kiernan, V. 1990. Modern captialism and its shepherds. *New Left Review* 183, 75–94.
Kristiansen, K. 1983. Ideology and material culture: an archaeological perspective. In *Marxist Perspectives in Archaeology*, M. Spriggs (ed.), 72–100. Cambridge: Cambridge University Press.
Leone, M. P. 1982. Some opinions about recovering mind. *American Antiquity* 47, 742–60.
Leone, M.P. 1988. The Georgian order as the order of merchant capitalism in Annapolis, Maryland. In *Recovering Meaning*, Leone, M. P. & P. B. Potter (eds), 330–45. Washington: Smithsonian Institution.
Leone, M. P., P. B. Potter & P. A. Schackel 1987. Toward a critical archaeology. *Current Anthropology* 18, 283–302.
Lima, T. A. 1988. Patrimônio arqueológico, ideología e poder. *Revista de Arqueología* 5, 19–28.
Love, J. & D. J. Barickman 1986. Rulers and owners, a Brazilian case study in comparative perspective. *Hisz* 66, 743–65.
Lumbreras, L. G. 1981. *La arqueología como ciencia social*. Lima: Peisa.
MacKenzie, R. 1990. The recovery of Africa's past. *Archaeology and Education* 1, 1–5.
MacKenzie, R. & P. Stone 1994. Introduction: the concept of the excluded past. In *The Excluded Past: archaeology in education*, Stone, P. & R. MacKenzie (eds), 1–14. London: Unwin Hyman; Routledge pbk 1994.
Martins, J. S. 1982. *Sobre o modo capitalista de pensar*. São Paulo: Hucitec.
Meneses, U. T. B. 1987. Identidade cultural e arqueología. In *Cultura brasileira, temas e situações*, Bosi, A. (ed.), 182–90. São Paulo: Atica.
Meneses, U. T. B. 1990. O salão nobre do Museu Paulista e o teatro da história. In *Às margens do Ipiranga*, Meneses, U. T. B. (ed.), 20–1. São Paulo: Museu Paulista.
Meneses, U. T. B. 1991. Às margens do Ipiranga: museu e tempo da história. *D. O. Leitura* 8, 1–6.
Miller, D. 1988. The limits of dominance. In *Domination and Resistance*, Miller, D., M. J. Rowlands & C. Tilley (eds), 63–79. London: Unwin Hyman; Routledge pbk 1995.
Miller, D., M. J. Rowlands & C. Tilley 1988. Introduction. In *Domination and Resistance*,

Miller, D , M J. Rowlands & C. Tilley (eds), 1–28. London: Unwin Hyman; Routledge pbk 1995.

Mota, C. G. 1990. O Museu Paulista e o panteão da Independência. In *Às margens do Ipiranga*, Meneses, U. T. B. (ed.), 22. São Paulo: Museu Paulista.

Moura, C. 1981. *Rebelições da Senzala: quilombos, insurreições, guerrilhas*. São Paulo: Ciências Humanas.

Moura, C. 1988. *Sociologia do negro brasileiro*. São Paulo: Ática.

Nordblach, J. 1989. Comments on archaeology into the 1990s. *Norwegian Archaeological Review* 22, 24–8.

Orser, C. E. 1991. The continued pattern of dominance: landlord and tenant on the postbellum cotton plantation. In *The Archaeology of Inequality*, MacGuire, R. H. & R. Paynter (eds), 40–54. Oxford: Blackwell.

Pereira, A. 1991. *Machado de Assis: ensaios e apontamentos avulsos*. Belo Horizonte: Oficina de Livros.

Pike, D. W. 1982. *Latin America in Nixon's Second Term*. Paris: American College in Paris.

Podgorny, I. 1990. The excluded present: archaeology and education in Argentina. In *The Excluded Past: archaeology in education*, Stone, P. & R. MacKenzie (eds), 183–9. London: Unwin Hyman; Routledge pbk 1994.

Rubertone, P. 1988. Archaeology, colonialism and seventeenth century Native–America: towards an alternative interpretation. In *Conflict in the Archaeology of Living Traditions*, Layton, R. (ed.), 32–45. London: Unwin Hyman; Routledge pbk 1994.

Scott, R. J. 1988. Exploring of freedom: post-emancipation societies in comparative perspective. *Hispanic American Historical Review* 68, 407–28.

Shanks, M. & C. Tilley 1987. *Re-constructing Archaeology*. Cambridge: Cambridge University Press.

Shanks, M. & C. Tilley 1989. Questions rather than answers: reply to comments on 'Archaeology in the 1990s'. *Norwegian Archaeological Review* 22, 42–54.

Singer, P. 1986. Diploma, profissão e estrutura social. In *Universidade, escola e formação de professores*, Catani, D. B., H. T. Miranda, L. C. Menezes & R. Fischmann (eds), 51–67. São Paulo: Brasiliense.

Singleton, T. A. 1990. The archaeology of the plantation south: a review of approaches and goals. *Historical Archaeology* 24, 70–7.

Slenes, R. W. 1989. Na sezala uma flor: as esperanças e as recordações na formação da família escrava. Unpublished MS, Campinas.

Tedesco. J. C. 1985. Reproductivismo educativo y sectores populares en América Latina. In *Educaçao na América Latina os métodos teóricos e a realidade social*, Madeira, F. R. & G. N. de Mello (eds), 33–79. São Paulo: Cortez.

Tilley, C. 1989. Archaeology as socio–political action in the present. In *Critical Traditions in Contemporary Archaeology*, Pinsky, V. & A. Wylie (eds), 104–16. Cambridge: Cambridge University Press.

Toscano, A. H. 1990. Pasado y presente de la arqueología uruguaya (1876–1990). consideraciones teóricas e institucionales. Unpublished MS, Montevideo.

Tragtemberg, M. 1985. Relação de poder na escola. *Educação e Sociedade* 20, 40–5.

Trigger, B. G. 1990. *A History of Archaeological Thought*. Cambridge: Cambridge University Press.

Vargas, I. & M. Sanoja 1990. Education and the political manipulation of history in Venezuela. In *The Excluded Past: archaeology in education*, Stone, P. & R. MacKenzie (eds), 50–60. London: Unwin Hyman; Routledge pbk 1994.

Veiga, L. da 1985. Educação movimentos populares e a pesquisa participante: algumas condideraçoes. In *Educação na América Latina métodos teóricos e realidade social*, Madeira, F. R. & G. N. de Mello (eds), 187–201. São Paulo: Cortez.

Visser, R. 1992. Facist doctrine and the cult of the Romanità. In *Journal of Contemporary History* 27, 5–22.

Wade, P. 1994. Blacks, Indians and the state in Colombia. In *The Presented Past: heritage, museums and education*, Stone, P. G. & B. L. Molyneaux (eds), 418–37. London: Routledge.

Wagenschein, M. 1956. Wesen und unwesen der Schule. In *Erziehung wozu?*, Wagenschein, M. (ed.), 49–61. Stuttgart: Kroener.

Williams, R. 1965. The creative mind. In *The Long Revolution*, 19–56. Harmondsworth: Penguin Books.

Wirth, J. D. 1984. An interview with José Honório Rodrigues. *Hispanic American Historical Review* 64, 217–32.

Zamora, O. M. F. 1990. A arqueología como história. *Dédalo* 28, 39–62.

Zanettini, P. 1991. Indiana Jones deve morrer. *Jornal da Tarde, Caderno de Sábado*, 18 May, 4–5.

8 The role of archaeology in marginalized areas of social conflict: research in the Middle Magdalena region, Colombia

CARLOS EDUARDO LÓPEZ & MARGARITA REYES

(translated by Carlos David Londoño)*

To the memory of Josue Vargas, Miguel Angel Barajas and Saúl Castañeda, peasants of Carare region

Introduction

Archaeological research in Colombia has thrived in the past four decades, as shown by the wide regional and temporal coverage it has achieved and the continuous flow of publications from the region (also see Delgado Ceron & Mz-Recaman 1994; Ramírez 1994; Reyes 1994). And new theories and methodologies are constantly being applied to the ever-increasing data from our surveys. Nevertheless, there are areas of the country distant from large economic centres or dangerous to work in because of social disorder that have received little attention in research programmes. Such places cannot simply be ignored, however, as they are just as important to an understanding of Colombian history and prehistory as the more accessible areas.

One very important research area that is, at present, marginalized by social conflict is the inter-Andean region of the middle basin of the Magdalena river, central Colombia. For decades, this region has been a focus of complex social struggles between governments and right- and left-wing groups, making research there truly difficult. An archaeological initiative in Cimitarra that involved the local community in an ambitious heritage project was tragically cut off by the murder of three community leaders in 1990 (Medina 1990; López Castaño 1991). But then new impetus was given to research by the construction of an oil pipeline and a major powerline, and the rescue archaeology that was done has yielded important information about the region's prehispanic history.

These results are significant to the scientific community, but most of all, they provide a new source of hope for the local communities, as they are becoming increasingly interested in their heritage and so gaining a clearer understanding of their place in the world.

* Departamento de Antropología, Universidad de Antioquía, Medellín, Colombia

There has been a long-standing concern with the education of the inhabitants in the Magdalena River region and a common belief among archaeologists that the dissemination of their research within the region would be beneficial. Given the opportunity provided by the pipeline construction, we were able to work with the people of some small settlements that were traditionally outside the government's scope of influence and beset by social problems, creating in them an interest in education and culture through participation in archaeological research.

The Magdalena River region

One salient characteristic of Colombia is its varied relief, due to the threefold division of the Andean cordillera and its diverse ecological environments. There are dense tropical jungles, wide savannas, and mountain ranges with highland and snowy peaks.

The long valley of the Magdalena river, which runs northward between the Cordillera Central and Cordillera Oriental, is particularly remarkable within Colombia's complex ecological mosaic. The climate of the river's middle basin is hot, and its natural landscape is covered by humid forests which are quickly losing ground to pastureland.

The archaeological work described below has been carried out in the departments of Santander and Antioquía, at Cimitarra and Puerto Berrío. The area is lower than 200 m above sea-level, with a mean temperature above 25° C and an annual precipitation between 2000 and 4000 mm (Fig. 8.1).

Historical background

The first European *conquistadores* to go inland on the continent did so by following the Magdalena valley upriver towards the south. Sixteenth- and seventeenth-century chronicles describe populations with different cultural adaptations to various environments. The native population was decimated during the conquest and the colonial periods of the fifteenth and sixteenth centuries, leaving the forested space of the middle basin of the Magdalena river uninhabited until early in the twentieth century. The present occupants of the region are therefore not descendants of ancient indigenous populations, but migrant peasants from other parts of the country who arrived there in the mid-twentieth century.

Historically, socio-political unrest in Colombia has had multiple causes, the most important of which are related to landholding patterns, which preserve the *latifundio* (large expanse of land owned by one person), and to discontent associated with oil exploitation by foreign companies. In the 1960s and 1970s, the Magdalena Medio region was home to left-wing guerrilla groups; in the 1980s they were vigorously repressed by the army and extreme right-wing paramilitary groups.

Scientific investigation in this unstable context was indeed difficult. There were few previous references to show the archaeological importance of the region: the Reichel-Dolmatoffs (1944) wrote an article about the distribution of burial urns along the Magdalena river; that same year, Félix Mejia Arango described pottery and lithics found in a prehistoric tomb at Cimitarra (Mejía Arango 1944). It was only in 1974 that a new investigation took place in the region; archaeologist Gonzalo Correal Urrego, taking the valley as a possible route for the early peopling of the continent, surveyed its banks in the search for preceramic sites (Correal Urrego 1977). In 1976, Herrera de Turbay & Londoño (1977) excavated a tomb in Puerto Serviez; they found sixty-three burial urns, with anthropomorphic and zoomorphic lids. The most thorough study of the zone, however, was that done by Carlo Castaño Uribe and Carmen Lucía Dávila (1984). They undertook a thorough survey and were able to locate several habitation and burial sites, as well as workshops and cultivated fields. They obtained C14 dates that place the making of the urns between the eighth and twelfth centuries AD.

Archaeological research in Cimitarra

The Magdalena research began when peasants discovered nearly thirty Indian tombs in the *municipio* of Cimitarra. A group of community leaders informed the Department of Anthropology of the Universidad Nacional in Bogotá of the finds, thus giving rise to a series of archaeological projects between 1987 and 1990 in which the community participated actively. Local interest not only speeded up the progress of the archeological survey, excavation and conservation; it also stimulated a desire in the participants to work together to create programmes to recover the local prehispanic history and to educate the people.

Several community organizations (Junta de Acción Comunal, Asociación de Trabajadores Campesinos del Carare), as well as civil authorities and schools, were very interested in building a House of Culture–Library–Museum (Casa de la Cultura–Biblioteca–Museo). The intention was to exhibit pieces donated by peasants or recovered by archaeologists, but more important still, to create a 'living museum' of the inhabitants' culture (also see Ucko 1994).

Survey and excavation were successful because of the constant help of peasants who were familiar with the territory and had knowledge of what it looked like before the removal of the primary forest. With this expertise it was possible to comb the zone in detail and to locate and recover archaeological remains, all of which were recorded in field and laboratory reports. Twenty-five sites with evidence of prehispanic occupation were clearly identified; three of these were excavated and corroborated earlier evidence that the region was occupied between the tenth and fourteenth centuries AD by related Karib-speaking groups. The association among these peoples was made by the common practice of burying the dead in burial urns. A book and several

Figure 8.1 The Middle Magdalena region.

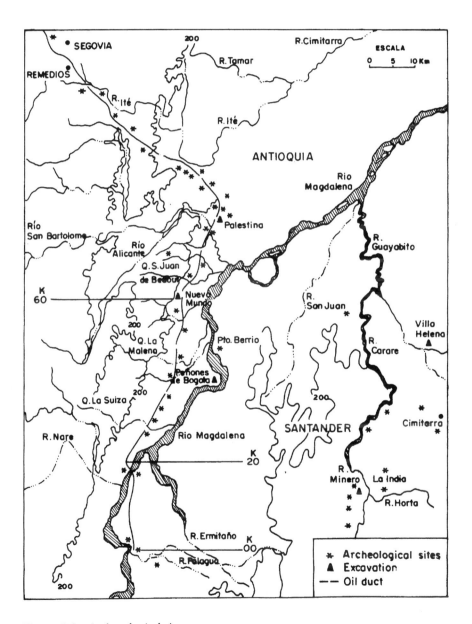

Figure 8.2 Archaeological sites.

articles resulted from this research (Castaño Uribe & Dávila 1984; López Castaño 1988a, 1988b, 1991).

The murder of the three local leaders during political tension early in 1990, however, spelled the end of the project. The House of Culture–Library–Museum building, already started, was left unfinished, as were plans to train local teachers in prehispanic history.

Rescue archaeology: another chance for heritage development in the Magdalena Medio region

Investigations were renewed in mid-1990 on the opposite bank of the Magdalena river, in the department of Antioquía, because of the construction of the Vasconia–Coveñas oil pipeline. This construction permitted detailed coverage of a long segment parallel to the river (Fig. 8.1).

The contributions of this investigation to Colombian archaeology were of fundamental importance, since a series of lowland preceramic sites were located, and contexts were found for tools previously rare in Colombia, such as bifacial projectile points and scrapers retouched using the pressure technique.

Three C14 dates obtained corroborated human presence in the Magdalena river valley around the eleventh millennium before the present, which complemented, with new data, older evidence of Paleo-Indian occupations in Colombia. New evidence of later groups was also recovered (López Castaño 1989; Oleoducto de Colombia 1991).

The salvage archaeology projects had better logistical support, since they took place in the context of a massive construction project in which enormous capital was invested. The research was therefore largely finished, although violence impeded work in some places. A second phase of investigation took place in 1991 in the *municipio* of Puerto Berrío, with financial backing from the Fundación de Investigacione Arqueológicas Nacionales. New evidence of early human populations was found; reports of the investigations are being produced, and step by step the results are being disclosed.

Archaeology and education

Our experiences in the two projects showed the social and intellectual value in community involvement. Although the salvage research was successful in terms of its archaeology, it was not as beneficial in a social sense as the initial work on the other side of the river, for the working methodology did not initially require or include direct participation of the community, and so there was no direct help from peasants from the area, which had contributed greatly to the earlier investigation in Cimitarra. Nevertheless, the results were made public in the schools and House of Culture of the *municipios* of Puerto Berrío and Remedios as the investigation proceeded.

The stimulation provided by this interaction with the community made us realize the social nature of archaeology and revealed a persistent problem in archaeological research: notwithstanding the different degrees of contact with local communities in projects, all too often the investigators are immersed in their scientific pursuits, and so do not acknowledge or give credit to the community – in some cases not even following basic norms of decency. This situation keeps repeating itself, distancing and breaking liaisons between popular and intellectual modes of knowledge, both of which are equally valid and relevant. This is truly a loss, since by working together with a community, archaeologists may improve science's understanding of reality (and see Ucko 1994).

Carrying out investigations in a marginalized region of social conflict, with the active participation of the community, therefore generated a number of questions concerning Colombian education and values, and information transmitted through means that range from school texts to mass media (also see Delgado Cerón & Mz-Recaman 1994; Ramírez 1994; Reyes 1994).

School texts used in present-day Colombia (see also Reyes 1994) do not give enough importance to prehispanic cultures, focusing attention on only those aboriginal groups described by Spaniards in the sixteenth century. Students are not made to understand that the history of Colombia is a process that has gone on for thousands of years during which humans adapted in different ways to various environments. On the other hand, throughout its short history in Colombia, and as far as prehispanic history is concerned, archaeology has moved mostly within scientific and academic environments; most of the research reports and published works are written for a small number of specialists.

It is important to emphasize that archaeology is not solely associated with the past for, as Binford (1983, p. 23) notes, 'The archaeological record . . . is a contemporary phemomenon and observations we make about it are not "historical" statements.' This concept is fundamental, since alternative interpretations and results have to be proposed during work with a community, not only in relation to the past of the community, but well rooted in its present and with projections for its future. It was, and still is, important in our work to show communities how they can enhance their lives by recovering their own past.

It is also important to improve the training of teachers in matters concerned with local history, as this aspect of education is particularly inadequate in rural areas. In this context, the archaeologist's job, as part of fieldwork, should also include the general disclosure of the details of a project to the public, and more informative talks with teachers and community leaders about the goals and wider importance of the research. In addition, local people need to be included as participants in survey and excavation, for local students or workers, once instructed in archaeological techniques, become the most efficient assistants, because of their greater knowledge of the area.

Conversations with teachers and students have shown that most of the educational information – including historical information – is assimilated with little or no questioning; there is also a tendency to value the culture of 'progress and technology' more than traditional cultural ways. It is for this reason that the social sciences, and especially our discipline, should become more socially committed, and accept part of the responsibility in the search for ways to empower people to recognize and assert their own identity, and to understand their own reality. This would be very useful, on the one hand, to bring popular knowledge out of anonymity, showing that it is valid and can be in its own way scientific; on the other hand, it would teach the community to value, rescue and demand respect for its roots.

Community leaders with foresight as to the value of mutual experience in the quest for cultural heritage have helped to achieve these goals in the Magdalena Medio. There has been a continuous effort to apply experience in terms of what is known as 'investigation–participative action' (Investigación–Acción–Participativa). The idea is to restate the relationship between the participants in research – subjects and objects – questioning and breaking down the differences between them in terms of education, science, culture and social relations.

It is most important to share the knowledge acquired with the community. According to Orlando Borda (Borda & Brandao 1987), the 'systematic devolution' of research is successful to the degree that regional support groups assume and express their practical interests. Therein lies the importance of planning research with the 'object' community prior to its execution. Unfortunately, as Lleras observes, archaeological investigations with current social applications are rare:

> One could say, with little fear of being proven wrong, that only one out of any fifty investigations carried out has any practical application; the rest merely constitute a mass of historical and cultural data, so far largely unutilized.
>
> (Lleras Pérez 1988, p. 26)

In the case of Cimitarra the project was presented to the Communal Action Committee (Junta de Acción Comunal), with whom the project's objective and potential were discussed. Owing to the rather delicate public-order situation, it was also presented to the military and civic authorities. Conferences and workshops were given throughout the project, usually in schools in the area – but unfortunately, the murders caused the work to be suspended.[1] In Puerto Berrío and Remedios, however, the full reporting of the research was accomplished, and besides the conferences, a pamphlet outlining the work was edited and distributed (Oleoducto de Colombia 1991).

The past: a road to a better future

Unfortunately, in many places in Colombia, governmental presence is visible in the form of military equipment and installations, rather than in health, education, or training programmes. Extremist activities from left- and right-wing groups do not help in the search for practical alternatives for a more dignified future.

In view of their marginality, inhabitants of these regions tend to be enthusiastic about proposals of research that will shed light on their heritage. Peasants who know every square metre of the terrains that they have prepared and cultivated also come to appreciate the value of lithic and ceramic remains, once they understand the importance of these remains to their own history. The oldest remains of human habitation in Colombia were found in the highlands of the Sabana de Bogotá, and were dated at 12,500 years BP (Correal Urrego 1986). It is probably true, however, that the entry route of the first inhabitants of not only Colombia, but of all South America, may well have been the Magdalena river valley. The ancient spearpoints, painstakingly carved out of chert, are therefore of great historical value, something which the inhabitants of the region have begun to understand and appreciate. For these people, it is vital that their locale be noteworthy for reasons other than violence; they want other people to pay attention to their values, one of which is respect for their past, and for its relevance in the nation's cultural formation.

A preliminary analysis of the investigations in which the communities were active participants shows that significant results have been achieved. As far as archeology is concerned, it is clear that it would be valuable to increase the number of participative investigations, thereby showing that by recovering our ancestors' legacy, we will enhance the search for our own identity. These investigations have also shed new light on the role of adaptation of hunting-gathering groups to jungle environments; it can therefore be said that the investigations were fertile conceptually, as well as materially.

The Magdalena Medio region is an area of great scientific interest, and despite the different manifestations of conflict – guerrilla, right-wing paramilitary groups and drug trafficking – it is vital to promote permanent research programmes. It is a difficult and dangerous job, but it is critical that these studies continue unabated. The results would be the creation of a regional perspective which could help explain the socio-cultural changes that have occurred throughout Colombian history. Archaeology's insertion into the community as an educating force can also help investigators themselves, since people who know the value and role of archaeology will protect that which forms part of their own lives: their heritage. The people of presently marginalized areas, whose ancestors have contributed so much to the present culture and society of Colombia, await the chance to play a role.

Note

1 The project designed to spread archaeological information to the community in Cimitarra was later successfully carried out in the *municipio* of Curiti, Santander (Reyes 1991, 1992).

References

Binford, L. 1983. *In Pursuit of the Past*. London: Thames & Hudson.
Borda, O. & R. Brandao 1987. *Investigación participativa*. Bogotá: Ediciones de la Bande Oriental SRL.
Castaño Uribe, C. & C. L. Dávila 1984. *Investigaciones arqueológicas en el Magdalena Medio: sitios colorados y mayaca*. Bogotá: Fundación de Investigaciones Arqueológicas Nacionales, Banco de la República.
Correal Urrego, G. 1977. Investigación arqueológica en la Costa Atlántica y el valle del Magdalena: sitios precerámicos y tipologías líticas. *Caldasia* 11, 35–111.
Correal Urrego, G. 1986. Apuntes sobre el medio ambiente pleistocénico y el hombre prehistórico en Colombia. In *New Evidence for the Pleistocene Peopling of the Americas*, Bryan, A. (ed.), 115–31. Orono, Maine: Center for the Study of Early Man, University of Maine.
Delgado Cerón, I. & C. I. Mz-Recaman 1994. The museum comes to school: teaching packages as a method of learning in Colombia. In *The Presented Past: heritage, museums and education*, Stone, P. G. & B. L. Molyneaux (eds), 148–58. London: Routledge.
Herrera de Turbay, L. & M. Londoño 1977. Reseña de un sitio arqueológico en el Magdalena Medio. *Revista Colombiana de Antropología* 19.
Lleras Perez, R. 1988. Historia prehispánica y permanencias culturales. In *Historia y culturas populares*, 25–40. Tunja: Instituto de Cultura y Bellas Artes de Boyacá.
López Castaño, C. E. 1988a. Exploración arqueológica en Cimitarra (Santander) Sitio Villa Helena 1. *Boletín de Arqueología* 2, 11–25.
López Castaño, C. E. 1988b. Exploración arqueológica en Cimitarra (Santander). *Arqueología* 5, 47–60.
López Castaño, C. E. 1989. Evidencias precerámicas en los municipios de Puerto Berrío, Yondó y Remedios, Antioquia. *Boletín de Arqueología* 4, 3–24.
López Castaño, C. E. 1991. *Investigaciones arqueológicas en el Magdalena Medio, cuenca del río Carare*. Bogotá: Fundación de Investigaciones Arqueológicas Nacionales.
Medina, C. 1990. *Autodefensa, paramilitares y narcotrafico en Colombia*. Bogotá: Editorial Documentos Periodisticos.
Mejia Arango, F. 1944. Cementerio indígena de la Cimitarra. *Boletín de Arqueología* 1, 113–20.
Oleoducto de Colombia 1991. *Proyecto arqueológico oleoducto Vasconia–Coveñas*. Bogotá: Instituto Colombiano de Antropología–Oleoducto de Colombia S.A.
Ramirez, R. R. 1994. Creative Workshops: a teaching method in Colombian museums. In *The Presented Past: heritage, museums and education*, Stone, P. G. & B. L. Molyneaux (eds), 172–8. London: Routledge.
Reichel-Dolmatoff, G. & A. Reichel-Dolmatoff 1944. Urnas funerarias de la cuenca del Magdalena. *Revista del Instituto Etnológico Nacional* 1, 73.
Reyes, H. R. 1994. Ethnic representation in Colombian textbooks. In *The Presented Past: heritage, museums and education*, Stone, P. G. & B. L. Molyneaux (eds), 398–407. London: Routledge.
Reyes, M. 1991. Hacia una propuesta de educación y difusión de la historia prehispanica a nivel escolar y popular (Curiti, Santander). Unpublished dissertation, Universidad Nacional, Bogotá.

Reyes, M. 1992. La noche de un dia muy largo. Serie Ninos de Colombia 4. Instituto Colombiano de Antropología, Colcultura, Santa Fé de Bogotá.

Ucko, P. J. 1994. Museums and sites: cultures of the past within education – Zimbabwe, some ten years on. In *The Presented Past: heritage, museums and education*, Stone, P. G. & B. L. Molyneaux (eds), 237–82. London: Routledge.

9 The museum comes to school in Colombia: teaching packages as a method of learning

IVONNE DELGADO CERÓN &
CLARA ISABEL MZ-RECAMAN

Introduction

It is no longer realistic to think that museums were created simply for the purpose of rescuing and preserving objects from the past. They must turn into institutions with the capacity to face the problems of modern society and to propose new possibilities of change, rather than remain as passive collectors of material culture. This is a cultural role: museums must work within an educational system which is undergoing profound changes.

The teaching of the social sciences is in crisis. Following endless years of constantly repeating names, dates and events, students reach the end of their secondary education lacking even a minimum comprehension of the society in which they have lived and studied (also see Ramírez 1994). It is clear that teachers have instructed without social awareness, as they tend to limit themselves to providing students with factual knowledge and teaching in a merely informative manner. For this reason, students have to rely on memory, without reflection or analysis, and thus turn into passive beings who retain information only until the day of the examination.

Education therefore must no longer be seen simply as a means of transferring culture, but as an integral part of a process of social emancipation. Museums must try to become places of freedom and democracy, in which children and adults can recover lost or forgotten cultural values and traditions and, through this process of discovery, learn to develop their capacity for independent decision-making in society. The principal task of a museum, therefore, is to preserve objects from the past for the purposes of education and communication for the future.

Education in museums

One teaches history not to give children a knowledge of the past, but to make them aware that the past is all around them. This can only be accomplished if the traditional emphasis on the learning of facts and events is replaced with activities that enable children to learn about their environment directly. The acquisition of practical knowledge is as important as cognitive development, for education is a social activity:

> It is not the storing of a set of prefabricated ideas, images, feelings or beliefs, etc., but learning to look, listen, think, feel, imagine, believe, understand, choose and desire . . . it implies learning to recognise oneself as a human being . . . and acquiring the ability to give back to the world one's own version of a living, active being, who is at the same time a self-manifestation and a self-realisation.
>
> (Peters & Dearden 1985, p. 38)

To study a culture is therefore not an end in itself, but the opportunity to strengthen the capacities and aptitudes of children, and to develop their practical skills.

The study of a community can encourage students to adopt a critical and reflexive attitude to it, so that they come to understand how the past has influenced present-day society. Churches, town squares, museums and the other historical features of a community need to be used by the teacher and integrated into a strategy for the teaching of social sciences. Indeed, it has been proved that classes outside school increase educational potential through the diversity of situations they provide for teaching. Equally, contact with the environment allows the child to progress from facts to ideas, and from observation to explanation. Thus the environment becomes a teaching method in itself (Luc 1981, pp. 73–80).

The role of activity in social learning implies that any programme carried out by a museum should emphasize self-discovery rather than instruction, as it helps people to learn to take up a critical attitude towards life and the world around them, rather than simply being receptacles filled with facts.

A more dynamic approach to the use of museum collections in education is possible because, although museum collections are a record of the transformations which have come about as a result of past interaction between people and nature, this information is not limited to the organization of knowledge: all material culture presupposes the development of attitudes, values and skills.

Exhibitions, and other programmes, should therefore be directed towards achieving certain specific objectives: to create enthusiasm, to excite curiosity, to teach basic techniques or skills, to promote active learning, to clarify methods and processes, and to provide information and stimulate awareness. The goal is not that of turning visitors into specialists in a particular field, but of encouraging them, individually or collectively, to develop the capacity to use the knowledge they acquire in new contexts. Specialization in a particular field is the objective of later, higher education (Hansen 1984, p. 180).

The Museo del Oro

The Museo del Oro (Gold Museum), like all historical museums, is a primary source for the study of the social sciences. This is why the museum supports formal education, while at the same time offering alternative methods of teaching and analysis. Indeed, it is important that the museum rescues the new concept of history, which emphasizes that the description of data must give way to the development of a critical and interpretative study of history. The reason is not simply that one turns to the past for an explanation of the present, as well as a projection into the future – it is a matter of rescuing the collective history of the entire community, turning away from the traditional emphasis on heroic individuals and events, and so allowing all individuals to recognise themselves as historical beings, participants in the making of local history.

In order to accomplish these goals, the mystery needs to be removed from the objects in a museum, so that children relate to the world that they and their ancestors have actually lived in. Proposals for innovative teaching should therefore encourage the close observation of objects, of awakening the imagination, of developing the capacity to create and the spirit of criticism.

Working with pre-Columbian materials, for example, may help both students and teachers to close the abysmal gap between museums and schools, as these objects will become the starting-point for enquiries into the indigenous history of our society, and will also lay the foundations for the development of a historical and scientific method.

The 'Museum Comes to Your School' project

The Museo del Oro has prepared a programme for schools of teaching packages on pre-Columbian society, based on its archaeological collections, (also see Giraldo 1994). This pioneering project, known as 'The Museum Comes to Your School', was begun in 1986 and, following a year of experimentation and an investigation of educational projects in museums in Europe and North America, it was officially launched in Colombia in 1987. It was an innovation for our museums, as the only activity they were customarily involved in was guided tours, and it has become a priority project of the Educational Services Office and of the Bank of the Republic's regional museums.

The project was developed by the Museo del Oro's Educational Services team, along with teachers and anthropologists. Three general themes related to the different gold-working cultures of the indigenous inhabitants of the Colombian territory were developed ('A Look at our Ancient History', 'The Muiscas and their Pottery' and 'The Muiscas and their Stone Tools') and tested with students in Bogotá. With this experience, the packages were modified and more were added ('Trading among the Pasto Indians' and 'The Chief of the Pasto Indians'). Following the success of the tests in Bogotá, the museum decided to introduce the programme to a wider public, and so in 1988, it was officially launched in Bogotá and in the regional museums located in Cartagena, Santa Marta, Pasto, Ipiales, Pereira, Manizales, Armenia, Leticia and Cali. Additional themes have been developed since ('Barter among the Zenú Indians', 'The Great Tairona Builders', 'The Quimbaya Indians' and 'Animals in the World of the Calima Indians').

The project goals

The use of teaching packages is an efficient method of conveying information and involving students in learning activities. The packages are designed not only to communicate facts and ideas, but also to give students experience in following scientific methods, thereby enhancing their research skills. As the students work in groups, the packages aim to develop co-operative attitudes and habits, and establish new ways of understanding responsible participation in society, so that students will be more aware of the indigenous world, and the potential contribution of indigenous values in modern society.

Within this general philosophy, our purpose in developing these packages has been:

(a) to provide incentives for scientific research and criticism, observation, reading, the use of sources of information, analysis, the assessment and testing of hypotheses and for learning how to synthesize ideas, on the part of both educators and students;

(b) to update knowledge of pre-Columbian cultures, by placing them in their own time and context;

(c) to develop and strengthen a cultural identity in children, teachers and in the community as part of a concept of education for change and social development, allowing students and teachers to acquire information and form opinions of the pre-Columbian cultures, and exposing the myths of the 'Indian' concept;

(d) to provide a programme for use as a support tool in formal education, giving teachers the opportunity of learning about other teaching methods and permitting the renewal of knowledge and innovation in the classroom;

(e) to stimulate students to reflect so that they themselves may establish a link, through their own interpretations, between the past and the present, and understand that they too form part of history;

(f) to contribute to the improvement of the content of school curricula in the area of social sciences; and

(g) to motivate municipalities and schools to undertake to create their own museums, illustrating the reality of their communities.

The programme is aimed in particular at groups from the fourth to sixth grades, but it can be used in early primary education courses and at higher levels. Experiments have been done, for example, with groups of university students, with excellent results: by working with the teaching pack, students of education and social sciences have been exposed to a different way of teaching in the social sciences, one emphasizing the active participation of the learner; design students have been able to learn more about the social context of design by working from the objects to their interpretation; and students of conservation and heritage preservation have used the information in the pack to help them in their approach to regional heritage issues.

A critical part of our task has been to educate teachers, in an effort to draw them away from the outdated teaching methods in which they were caught, and turn them into carriers of cultural values and guides to others. The programme encourages them to exercise their creativity in the classroom in order to generate enthusiasm and good learning habits.

The teaching pack

Each package consists of samples of original prehistoric objects, an explanatory booklet, posters and suggestions for activities, games and other pastimes.

Figure 9.1   Teaching pack: case, objects and posters.

Objects

The packages bring into the classroom samples of prehistoric objects and trade goods, including axes, knives, graters, millstones, necklaces, pendants, nose ornaments, ear ornaments, and zoomorphic and anthropomorphic representations (Fig. 9.2). They are of a variety of materials including bone, pottery, stone, shell, gold and other metals. Among the objects, for example, is a votive figure in copper with the representation of a snake on it, that comes from the Muisca archaeological region. The Muisca people lived in this area between AD 900 and AD 1500. For the Muisca the snake was a sacred animal related to their mythology. From the Quimbaya archaeological region, dated to the period AD 1000 to AD 1500, there is a spindle whorl used to make cotton threads. It is made of ceramic with incised decoration. This piece is an original. Also from the same region there is a cylinder stamp (original) used for textile- and body-painting. From the Zenú archaeological region we have several fragments of figurines that represent a man and a woman made of ceramic, dating from the period AD 400 to AD 1500. These figurines were part of the decoration of very big vessels used in rituals and funerary ceremonies. And from the same area we have included stone net-weights.

The inclusion of some original pieces lends authenticity to the collection and attracts the children towards pre-Columbian culture and, as the study of artefacts is a way of reaching those who made them, to prehispanic people.

The students can not only handle these objects, they can also use the packing boxes as bases to mount small displays. A display may be expanded with other elements, such as maps or models made by the students themselves, or with items that they bring to class.

Booklet

The booklet that comes with the artefacts puts them into context and shows the child that there is a wider range of information about artefacts than meets the eye. The information describes the objects, and conveys something of their meaning and function through myths, legends and other stories that cover a number of themes interesting to children, such as the creation of the world, the animals, the stars and other natural phenomena, and more specifically, the creation of the Tairona culture and the story of the birth of the river Sinu. The booklet guides the teacher in a simple and concise way through the techniques, ideas and goals of modern research. This aspect is critical because the teacher will later act as an intermediary between the museum and students, integrating the work of the museum in a valid and lasting way into the activities of the class.

At the end of the booklet, a number of suggestions have been made for the teacher to continue work in the classroom. These activities are aimed at achieving the active participation of the students and so stimulating their creativity. Reading and writing are important skills which may be developed in this way. It is hoped that, through reading the stories and legends in the

Figure 9.2 Display of objects.

booklet, students will make reading a daily habit. By being encouraged to write stories related to the objects and themes in the package, the children are able to recreate the world through their own imaginations. If they create something personal within the context of this programme, it will help them to develop innovative attitudes in general – and this will contribute greatly to their intellectual development. Indeed, free personal expression can give one the courage to take risks, a valuable skill when studying other creative subjects, such as languages, art and literature.

Posters

All the packages include posters which stimulate the ability of the child to perceive and select visual information – an important first step in learning. In addition, some of the posters are game boards (see below).

Activities

The activities outlined in the booklet enable the student to act as an historian, comparing customs of the present day with those of earlier times and so discovering gradually that the modern world is founded in the past.

The activities are designed to be carried out by groups of four to six students. The artefacts are shared out among them for observation and handling. This last aspect is vital, bearing in mind an essential characteristic of all children that teachers often forget and which should be exploited: children are 'born investigators' and therefore constantly present problems and ask questions to which they want to find the answer.

Once the objects have been examined by each student, the group discusses each one, debating such aspects as how the object was made and what it consists of, what its meaning and function might have been, and whether it had any relation to some aspect of the life of the individual student. Afterwards, with the guidance of the teacher, the children will discover more about the objects in their cultural situation and they will be encouraged to make comparisons with their own experience.

For example, a student could be asked to compare a Tairona village to a modern city, answering questions such as: What do they have in common? How are they different? Where would you prefer to live? Why? Or the teacher might ask the group to compare the laws of the Muisca people with those of today and ask: Which do you find most agreeable? What would you change? What would you add?

The use of comparisons is an effective learning strategy because it helps students to see relations between things. A most important goal in this is to get the children to appreciate that people in different times and places have solved common problems in different ways, and that such creative differences are therefore an essential part of human co-operation. The more they practise together, the more they will become good problem-solvers.

It is also important to include the artefacts in these activities because objects are in some ways much more significant than words as a basis for the formation of knowledge. An object can awaken the interest and curiosity of the child and stimulate research (Durbin, Morris & Wilkinson 1990, p. 4). Research has also suggested that the observation of images and the experiences they provide are more easily remembered than orally transmitted information (also see Dahiya 1994). And since most of the objects in the teaching packages are actual artefacts, they have the potential to motivate the students even more. There is nothing truer than Ernesto Sabato's dictum: 'It is certain that nothing of importance can be taught if one has not the ability first to cause amazement' (quoted in Muñoz, Landazábal & Landazábal 1984).

All artefacts have the potential to shed light on a human group and give an impression of relationships which would otherwise be difficult to understand. This is perhaps because each person possesses the capacity to perceive the meaning of an object within a broad context. The collection therefore becomes a tool leading to the understanding of social phenomena, a point of departure for comments which are aimed not only at informing, but at spiritual formation, at thinking, deducing, comparing and reaching conclusions, at broadening emotional capacity and at stimulating curiosity.

Games and other pastimes

Finally, activities are complemented by games and other amusing pastimes which, in addition to diversion and entertainment, provide an agreeable way of learning (Fig. 9.3). Some of the games are didactic. These games represent an important, fundamental aid in the teaching–learning process:

Figure 9.3   Boys playing with one of the games included in the teaching package.

Playing games is a complex activity which stimulates the emotions, motor activity, cognitive faculties, fantasy, inventiveness and, at the same time, it feeds on continuity and change, which are alternately dominant, and this is what makes them interesting and attractive.

(Rohrs 1990, p. 65)

In one game, for example, the children learn about the role of animals in the world of the Calima Indians. The game encourages students to identify the animals of the region, learn about their habits and discover something of their importance and symbolic meaning to the Calima people. In this way students become more sympathetic with Calima traditions and values.

It is hoped that such games will provide ways of developing inventiveness, intelligence and skill. Through these activities, the children help themselves to explore problems and form their own opinions, and so the games aid in the process of intellectual development, through an emphasis on testing and self-knowledge.

Project coverage and evaluation

In a country where traditional education is still prevalent, it has been a long and difficult task to implement this project; there is still a lack of commitment by most teachers to a change of attitude in the routine running of their social sciences classes. However, it has been noted with great satisfaction that some educators have begun to search for new teaching alternatives, and they have learned to discuss change and work differently in the classroom.

At present the Teaching Packages Programme is functioning in ten cities. To date, more than 200,000 children and some 1000 educational groups have benefited from them. The following are data for Bogotá.

In order to measure the response to the project, questionnaires were filled in by teachers and students. When these were analysed, it became clear that our original objectives had been achieved. Respondents particularly commented on the project: reinforcing earlier learning; imbuing the children with an appreciation and respect for indigenous objects and, through them, indigenous culture; linking with other curricula; and interesting children who, for socio-economic reasons, are not able to visit museums.

The evaluation of the students produced interesting data regarding the impact of this new material. Of all the activities which were carried out with the packages, the study of the objects and the games were what most held attention and interest. Most of the children agreed that the package made the class different and more interesting: 'We learned while playing.' As they had the opportunity to handle the objects, the children acted as anticipated, with curiosity, interest and respect for them. And many of the students said that they would like their teacher to bring more teaching packages to class.

158   I. DELGADO CERÓN & C. I. MZ-RECAMAN

Apart from this brief evaluation, assessments of use of the packages in classroom situations have also been carried out, allowing us to correct any problems in the implementation of the programme, such as the clarity of the booklet and of the games.

Conclusion

Allowing students to work in activities involving artefacts, rather than simply learning from school texts, helps to impart in them the inquisitiveness of a researcher, developing analytical skills and ideas and generating more informed attitudes and values about the past as knowledge increases (Durbin, Morris & Wilkinson 1990, pp. 3–13).

Although the use of artefacts in teaching can increase learning potential, the success of such a programme depends to a large extent on the responsibility and interest with which the teachers develop it. Teachers should try to make their students learn to be critical individuals in all aspects of their lives. They must be guides, who lead activities, rather than instructors. The aim is to give both teachers and students an historical spirit based on the study of the past in an effort to comprehend the present.

References

Dahiya, N. 1994. A case for archaeology in formal school curricula in India. In *The Presented Past: heritage, museums and education*, Stone, P. G. & B. L. Molyneaux (eds), 299–314. London: Routledge.
Durbin, G., S. Morris & S. Wilkinson 1990. *A Teacher's Guide to Learning from Objects*. London: English Heritage.
Giraldo, E. M. de 1994. The Colegio Nueva Granada Archaeological Museum, Colombia: a proposal for the development of educational museums in schools. In *The Presented Past: heritage, museums and education*, Stone, P. G. & B. L. Molyneaux (eds), 159–71. London: Routledge.
Hansen, T. H. 1984. El Museo como Educador. *Museum* 36, 176–83.
Luc, J.-N. 1981. *La enseñanza de la historia a través del medio*. Madrid: Cincel.
Muñoz, M., J. A. Landazábal & J. I. Landazábal 1984. Acerca de la educación de la infancia. *Educación y Cultura* 2, 71–6.
Peters, R. S. & R. F. Dearden 1985. *La educación como proceso de desarrollo de la razón y del pensamiento crítico*. Madrid: Narcea.
Ramirez, R. R. 1994. Creative workshops: a teaching method in Colombian museums. In *The Presented Past: heritage, museums and education*, Stone, P. G. & B. L. Molyneaux (eds), 172–8. London: Routledge.
Rohrs, H. 1990. La importancia del juego desde la perspectiva de la investigación pedagógica. *Universitas* 28, 555–66.

10 The Colegio Nueva Granada Archaeological Museum, Colombia: a proposal for the development of educational museums in schools

EMILIA MORENO DE GIRALDO

Introduction

The study of archaeology has become engrossing, attractive and of lasting importance to students at the Colegio Nueva Granada in Colombia. The inspiration for this interest is the Archaeological Museum established by the school to motivate students and stimulate their interest in their cultural heritage.

The idea for the museum came during the 1983–4 school year, when I used a sabbatical leave from the school to develop a curriculum for teaching Colombian folklore. For twelve years I had studied this subject and had used folklore and other anthropological information as part of the enrichment activities I organized each year for my ninth-grade students in Spanish; my interest in expanding this programme was intensified in this particular year when I organized a cultural programme for all students in the high school when we celebrated the awarding of the Nobel Prize to Colombian writer Gabriel García Márquez. Because of my belief in the significance of the past to the present, I decided to go deeper and explore the fascinating world of our ancestors by taking courses in pre-Columbian and modern Indian cultures.

During this time I was approached by the Parent–Teachers Association (PTA) to help in the purchase of a collection of thirty pre-Columbian vessels, made by the Narino Indians, for the school. I was delighted at this opportunity because folklore and archaeology are two key areas in anthropology and they could be used to complement the presentation of these artefacts in classes.

The creation of a school museum

After the purchase of this great collection, I proposed that an exhibition devoted to the culture of the Narino be set up. The plan was to involve the school community – students, teachers and parents – in the creation of the display, and by working with cultural material from one of the societies that contributed to the foundation of modern Colombian society, help us all come closer to our ethnic roots. I stressed in the plan that it was especially important to bring out important social values in this experience, such as solidarity, a sense of honour, pride in one's heritage and ethnic culture, and pleasure in giving without expecting return – values that seem to fade from the minds of young people under the pressures of contemporary life.

One by one, these ideas were approved by the school administration and the PTA and an archaeologist and museologist were brought into the project to transform this modest plan and its small collection into a museum.

In early 1985 work began with eighteen students from my ninth-grade Spanish class. Students from other grades also joined the group as well as one student's mother who was a painter. After walking round the school, we decided that the best place for the museum was in the Administration Building, in a lounge for teachers on the second floor. The space was not really ideal for our needs, but it was secure, furnished around a fireplace, and had a very pleasant atmosphere, with good natural light. Views through its windows of trees and mountains added to its attractions. We emptied it during a single weekend and moved everything down to the first floor. The following Monday we went as a group to inform the Director of our chosen site. We could say, because of this, that we had a 'squatters' museum'.

The work was divided according to the knowledge, skills and preferences of the participants. Each person was responsible for a specific task and, in addition, became a collaborator in support of other work groups. With the team in place, we created a museum logo and began to produce the display, making maps, watercolour illustrations, graphs, screen stencils, a mock-up of an Indian dwelling, a ceramic plaque illustrating ceramic decoration techniques, a vessel with roller-stamped designs and a burial chamber. And as our museum would have no physical boundaries, we produced stencilled designs, using pre-Columbian images, to create a decorative border.

Our normal free time on Wednesday afternoons and weekends was forgotten, as we worked hard to meet the exacting standards of our scientific director. In spite of the frustrations and the scepticism of many observers, our group nourished itself with idealism and patriotic pride; it became an honour to work on the project even though there was no academic reward for it. All of this effort culminated with the inauguration of the Colegio Nueva Granada Archaeological Museum and the awarding of our membership credentials in the Colombian Museum Association on 12 June 1985.

The nature and goals of the museum

The Archaeological Museum is the first and only museum in the country to be developed and interpreted by children. It was created by donations from the PTA, from students, and from other benefactors. It is a museum for children and adults, Colombians and foreigners. In order to make it accessible to all types of people, the explanatory texts were written so as to avoid vocabulary only comprehensible to specialists in the field.

The museum has no defined physical space. The lounge, designed for teachers, was barely large enough for our first exhibition and, indeed, proved to be too small for a subsequent one, which spilled out into an adjoining corridor. We compensated for this lack of space by putting displays over the windows and creating the effect of spaciousness by means of mirrors.

The museum has no staff. Guides for exhibitions are students who participate in the projects. The museum director guides regular visits. There are no guards. Up to now nobody has damaged or stolen any of the exhibited materials, many of which have been in full view of the public outside their showcases. There is a voluntary director. Scientific and technical direction is in the hands of a voluntary curator, who provides guidance in designing and setting up exhibitions.

The museum integrates a variety of interests and activities in the school community: different disciplines, such as art, social studies, Spanish and literature; and the different groups that make up our community. The school and the PTA collaborate financially; and high-school students, alumni and other volunteers create the educational material for exhibitions. Personnel of the General Services Department also give assistance, especially with electrical installations and carpentry.

The objectives of the museum are:

1 to become active agents in our own history;
2 to reaffirm national identity by learning about our culture and our country in order to develop love and respect for them;
3 to reaffirm our self-esteem in order to project our identity and become citizens of the world;
4 to carry out the work of cultural dissemination by utilizing the presence of representatives of thirty-four different nationalities who make up our school community;
5 to provide teachers and students of different instructional areas with a worthwhile teaching resource;
6 to connect the past and the present by making the study of the former an active process and integrating it with national life;
7 to take advantage of the years devoted to schooling to nourish students' minds with all kinds of vital experiences which contribute to forming a moral conscience, sincere devotion to duty, and patriotism and hope in the country's future;
8 to develop creativity and stimulate in students the desire to pursue research; and
9 to work together with professionals who can guide us and with other museums and cultural institutions that can support us and make our achievements possible.

Elementary-school programmes in the museum

Once the museum opened it became a site for enrichment activities for the 'History of Colombia' course taught at the fourth grade level, in particular for a unit on aboriginal peoples that focused on the Muiscas and Caribs. The goal of the museum visit was to integrate the history of Colombia with archaeology in a novel way for students: by taking them out of the classroom and showing them images and objects from other cultures, rather than simply telling them about such things. We hoped that this experience would generate interest in and respect for museums at the same time as it generated pride in and admiration for our ancestors.

Each visit begins with a discussion of the idea of a museum. What is a museum? Why is it important? What activities can we engage in there? How should we stand so as to see the objects well, and how close should we get to the glass cases? What tone of voice must we use when talking to others and asking questions? The object of these first few minutes is to generate a positive attitude, respect and curiosity in the children. This discussion is followed by brief recounting of the history of the museum, emphasizing the role of the school community in its creation and of the school as curator, housing and protecting the museum as part of our Colombian cultural heritage.

During this guided visit, the values that characterized our ancestors are highlighted by the illustrations and pieces in the collection and by the information given. For example, when the children examine the ceramic vessels, we conclude that our ancestors were practical and had a simple, efficient technology: their cooking-pots had tripodal bases so they did not turn over in campfires, for example, and they buried another form of vessel in the ground, to keep liquids cool. Baskets are used to show the role of women in the culture: we tell the children that women discovered how plants germinate and, consequently, were responsible for establishing the basis of agriculture, and we remind them that discoveries by women occurred while they remained at home caring for their children. And when we examine a ceramic coca flask, we reflect on the differences in the uses of the coca leaf between these cultural ancestors and our contemporary society, and the irreparable damage being caused us today.

The children clearly enjoy this hour in which they travel back several centuries in time and space and learn about the culture of an important ancestral group – and that there are in fact other cultural groups in the country which they could study in future years in school. Time is short because there are always questions and contributions from the students. When a recess period follows the visit, some will prefer to stay on for a while, examining details in silence. Others will return later, bringing friends along or classmates or family members. Their fascination is recorded in the comments and evaluations they make about the experience in the visitors' book.

These students also use the teaching packages designed by the Museo del Oro, Bogotá (see Delgado Ceron & Mz-Recaman 1994), and they usually have a field trip to the National Museum and to the Museo del Oro. But these activities do not take the place of a school museum, as only in such a place can the work of the students be properly integrated with heritage education and such learning be a continuous process through the school years. Indeed, in the 1989–90 school year, when we had to live through a period of social and political insecurity, field trips to the large museums were suspended, and so the only contact the students had with their cultural heritage was our small school collection.

Learning about culture through ceramics

In 1987, two of the educational activities proposed in the initial plan were implemented: a ceramics workshop, and, subsequently, an exhibition of pieces produced by the students. These students already have some knowledge of pre-Columbian art, as it is presented as part of the sixth-, seventh- and eighth-grade art curricula. The goal of this workshop is to understand pre-Columbian art and the Colombian societies of these times more directly, by having the students experiment with the different techniques that pre-Columbian potters used to fashion and decorate clay objects.

The hall is decorated with pre-Columbian objects such as coca flasks, axe heads, Tairona necklaces, masks and baskets. Posters showed a number of archaeological sites, including San Agustín and Buritaca 2000. The students are allowed to handle all the objects, putting on the necklaces, for example. They are also provided with as many books on the art of the period as can be found.

First, the nature of pre-Columbian art is explored: its general characteristics, historical period, and the main prehistoric cultures that produced it in Colombia. During the next two sessions, audiovisuals on pre-Columbian art are shown. These include some 300 slides with a recorded cassette commentary. The material was purchased by the school from the Bank of the Republic's Museo del Oro. Then the techniques involved in creating ceramics and producing jewellery are explained: stencil rollers, direct modelling, hammering, lost-wax moulding, false soldering, filigree, etc. All these concepts are illustrated with audio-visual materials.

The next two classes are devoted to learning the decoration techniques: excision, incision and stencilling. The students first participate in a conceptual exercise to stimulate their creativity: they think about a region where the Indians lived, like Buritaca or Pueblito in the Sierra Nevada of Santa Marta; they imagine that they were the artists responsible for creating a piece to be used in an important ceremony; and they imagine what this piece would have been like. Through this process, the students begin to create their own designs on paper. Then they study some original pre-Columbian ceramic pieces and try to copy these designs on paper using stencil rollers – they are always amazed at how well these tools work. And finally, when the students try to

Figure 10.1 Children painting and decorating ceramics based on photographs of archaeological specimens.

create the designs themselves, they discover that it is actually very difficult and that pre-Columbian ceramicists were truly artists (Figs 10.1 and 10.2).

The students also learn how to take notes describing the objects in a museum: they make a sketch of the object, note its size and shape and the colour of the clay, describe the type of decoration applied and the decorative style, discuss the object's probable function and its cultural affiliation.

The children then visit the school museum. The teacher shows them two ceramic pieces and the pupils copy the designs and make notes about them. This step prepares them for a visit to one of the larger museums in the city, such as the Museo del Oro and the Archaeological Museum of La Casa del Marqués de San Jorge.

When the students return to the art room they are enriched by field trips and by observing a great variety of works, and this experience helps them plan the kind of ceramic piece they will actually make. They also have access to photographs and to the pre-Columbian objects in the collection to help them in their design. Copying is quite acceptable, because a main goal of this unit is that all the students experience success, even those who are not artistically talented. They can create such simple objects as scrapers, for example.

Then the actual production begins, with the class atmosphere enhanced by Indian music. As the clay burns to a creamy colour, red, black, or other darker colours are daubed on the pots to give them the desired shade and tone.

Figure 10.2 Children's work based on photographs of archaeological specimens.

Throughout this process, the students keep their pieces damp, storing them in plastic bags at the end of each class period. When all the pieces are prepared, some are fired in the classroom kiln so that the students may see the pre-Columbian technique. The remainder are fired later in an electric oven. Finally, the students apply their chosen stencil designs with the roller – designs already tested on cloth, or their arms and faces! And when the ceramic pieces are done, the class sets up an exhibition for the school and the parents.

The success of this workshop is shown by the fact that an exhibition of a selection of ceramics made by the children will soon be going to the Policemen's Museum of Bogotá, to inaugurate a hall dedicated especially to Colombian children.

The Narino culture exhibition

In 1988, we organized a large-scale anthropological project for tenth-grade Colombian history students called 'Narino: 1200 Years of History'. Using collections from the museum to complement activities planned by the school, we demonstrated what had been the region's culture from its earliest settlement *c*. AD 700 and traced developments up to 1988, examining the lives, work, dreams and folklore of the area's inhabitants throughout their history.

The opening day of the exhibition was an anthropology day at the school. A wide variety of activities took place: a lecture on the Indians of today, a presentation of their music and oral traditions, a handicrafts exhibit, a video show of native culture, a luncheon of typical Narino foods and, finally, a guided tour of the museum exhibition.

The exhibition consisted of three-dimensional posters, maps and objects of Narino society, its economy and material culture. The posters included water-colour illustrations, colour photographs and handicrafts, musical instruments, and costumes, and they were decorated with stencils created by some of the students. There was also a display of different varieties of grains and potatoes, fruits and vegetables and the regional flora and another of some typical Napanga costumes from Pasto and Pasto crafts, such as their distinctive varnish-work, wood-carving, palm-weaving, textiles, hats and basketry.

The methodology used to develop this second exhibition at the museum was essentially scientific. The students did the background research on Narino culture, wrote the texts and prepared the displays. Great attention was paid to detail: the two girls responsible for the dressing of the mannequin in traditional costume, for example, were taken to the Museum of Regional Costume so that they could learn this skill from an expert. And the students acted as guides for their own project and interpreted the exhibits to visitors.

Unfortunately, as we lacked physical space and had to use the corridor adjacent to the museum to set up the exhibits, we had to close the exhibition after two months. As a result, we could not maintain the tie between past and present which emphasized the values of those creative and sensitive people who live in the province of Narino in the southwest corner of Colombia. The fact that we were able to involve outside institutions in the exhibition, how-ever, created some positive repercussions. For example, through contacts with the Botanical Garden, which provided the specimens of native flora, a pro-posal for an ecological project emerged, one that would involve the entire school community, as well as cultural organizations, to protect the school's natural resources. The proposal was to recover eroded land, to cut down trees of exotic species which were unsuitable for the terrain and the buildings, and to plant new trees of ornamental native species.

Senior independent study projects

Twelfth-grade students pursue an independent study project as an internal requirement for obtaining their degrees from Colegio Nueva Granada. The project lasts three weeks. During this time they do not come to school and must often travel outside the city as part of their research. Archaeology has been selected on occasions for such research, with projects on Muisca metal-working, for example.

Most recently, a student (Alejandro Dever) was assisted by the museum in his study of the columns of Ramiriqui, Bayueta and Tunja in the province of

Figure 10.3 Children trying out their models of goldwork based on photographs of archaeological objects.

Boyaca and their pre-Columbian social context. He was motivated by the fact that, although the sites have been known for at least a hundred years, the area is still largely unexplored. The existing research suggests that the prehistoric inhabitants were so advanced that they could trace the movements of the stars, sun and moon; this idea is supported by the evidence of the site of El Infiernito, doubtless an astronomical observatory and the Chibcha's most important religious temple.

As part of his research, Alejandro travelled along the route taken by Bochica – master of the Chibchas according to Indian mythology – as he travelled through the different villages in what today are Cundinamarca, Boyaca and Santander. The end-products of his research were a paper and a video, which he filmed and edited. He used a computer to digitize the images in the photographs he took, turned them into colour positives and in this way included them in the video.

As in the case of the ceramics workshop, this project had an effect outside this particular student's programme. Anecdotes of the voyage and the achievements of this priest to the sun, extracted from Alejandro's diary of his field trip to Boyaca, are being used to enrich the studies by fourth-grade students of Chibcha culture.

Extra-curricular activities

Art classes are offered for students in the Elementary School as part of the
activities programme organized by the PTA. For the students, the educational
ideal is consistent with the general goals of the school: to develop a knowledge
of, and a love for, pre-Columbian art and culture, to use the museum as an
educational resource, reaffirm national identity and, for foreign students, to
offer positive familiarization with Colombian culture. The museum, on the
other hand, obtains funds that, it is hoped, will allow it to begin financing its
own activities.

The children may choose to work with clay to make ceramics, or work with
plaster to make sculptures in the style of the San Agustin culture, create pieces
inspired by pre-Columbian metal- and goldwork (Figs 10.3–10.6) in papier
mâché, or create petroglyphs in plaster from designs inspired by mythological
traditions.

These courses have been a great success. At the end of each, an exhibition is
organized. We have had great support from parents and they are always
delighted by the excellent quality of the pieces produced. Everyone is pleased
with the positive atmosphere and enrichment stimulated by the classes.

Figure 10.4 Making and painting an armlet based on an archaeological gold example.

Figure 10.5   Constructing a papier mâché figure based on archaeological designs.

Conclusion

The programmes and activities described above, part of a continuing educational process at the Colegio Nueva Granada's Archaeological Museum, show that the museum has been truly a generator of innovative ideas and change.

From this experience, we may suggest that success in implementing educational museums requires several important elements.

1 There must be a harmonious combination of archaeology and other educational areas at the three basic levels of education, elementary, middle school and secondary, so that students are motivated throughout their school careers to appreciate the vitality of their cultural heritage and its role in modern achievements.

2 The educational programme must be directed by educators who have direct contact with students and thus are able to establish levels of expectancy.

3 Adminstration must be handled by professionals in order to maximize the use of human and economic resources in an institution.

4 The sponsors and participants in such projects must have absolute confidence in the benefits of such a project.

5 Museum guides must have special sensitivity when showing museums to children. The information guides transmit must be spiced with enthusiasm, excitement, patience and deep understanding of the importance of what they

Figure 10.6 The proud owner wearing the result of a copy of an archaeological design.

are doing. Guides must show pride in their culture. When children become guides for their own projects, their enthusiasm is easily passed on to any kind of public, motivating their classmates to create similar works or awakening interest in adults.

6 In museum development, it is necessary to consider the relative convenience of nearby cultural centres. A system must be designed with all urgency that will facilitate museum loans to educational institutions.

7 Parent–teacher associations need to be strong and active. We believe that the PTA of Colegio Nueva Granada is a model of such a group, contributing co-operation, creativity, effort and determination. The PTA organizes sports, social and cultural events with the goal of generating funding to finance enrichment programmes for the community as a whole.

In spite of our past and current successes, important decisions have yet to be made about our museum's future. The administration of Colegio Nueva

Granada, together with the PTA, will have to decide whether they wish to continue with this Educational Museum Project. If they agree, it will be necessary to build a permanent facility and, indeed, a site is under consideration, on the terrace on the roof of the Administration Building.

It would be ideal in fact to establish an anthropology department that would function jointly with teachers in other academic areas. This development would help promote interdisciplinary studies at all grade levels. Human beings perceive the world as a whole; therefore, why fragment education? With an integrated cultural programme, the activities of archaeology, museology, anthropology and folklore could be brought together, and this would help in the continuing effort to reveal and publicize the contributions of all the founding peoples of the country to our modern society.

Reference

Delgado Cerón, I. & C. I. Mz-Recaman 1994. The museum comes to school in Colombia: teaching packages as a method of learning. In *The Presented Past: heritage, museums and education*, Stone, P.G. & B. L. Molyneaux (eds), 148–58. London Routledge.

11 Creative workshops: a teaching method in Colombian museums

ROBERTO RESTREPO RAMÍREZ

Teaching in museums

Museums today are necessary tools in education. They are visited by people who are educated in a variety of formal and non-formal ways, in schools, the workplace and the community (see Borrero 1984, p. 38). And museums are also concerned with teachers and the way they talk about the past.

Teaching archaeology in museums is difficult, however, because students in our primary-school system are almost completely uninterested in social studies – a result of boring curricula of names and dates and historiographies, of 'irrefutable' facts given to passive children. Indeed, Restrepo has pointed out that this type of education is unaware of its subjectivity; it 'demands of the student a standard performance, without the possibility of obtaining knowledge by any means other than following the pre-established path' (Restrepo 1989, p. 164).

In addition, guided visits in archaeological museums for primary-school students tend to follow the rigid script of museologists, with negative results.

This approach needs to be changed; whoever works in a museum should not accept the traditional methods but should create a place whose doors are open, so that children visiting the museum can freely participate and express themselves. In this way we can create a more humanized education, because it will allow the child to use the creative thoughts that have been lost in the mass of dates, names, data and events that is thought of as social studies (Zubiría & Zubiría 1987, p. 68).

Through quiet but constant work, the Museo del Oro (Gold Museum), Bogotá, Colombia (also see Delgado Cerón & Mz-Recaman 1994), has become an active part of the process of building our national identity. In the past fifty years this institution has contributed to the preservation of the most representative collection of archaeological treasures from all regions of the country and it contributes to scientific research into the cultures that produced them through archaeological fieldwork funded by the Fundación de Investigaciones Arqueológicas del Banco de la República.

During the 1980s the Museo del Oro expanded its activities to a wider community by opening regional museums in different Colombian cities, displaying the achievements of pre-Columbian cultures (Delgado Cerón & Mz-Recaman 1994).

A good example of how to integrate archaeology teaching in a museum for young people is provided by the Museo Quimbaya (Museum of Quimbaya Gold) in the city of Armenia, capital of the Quindio department, in the central Andes region of Colombia.

The Museo Quimbaya

The Museo Quimbaya, one of the three museums with regional themes in the region of the Old Caldas, which includes the departments of Caldas, Risaralda and Quindio, displays goldwork of the Quimbaya archaeological region. The term Quimbaya is given to an artefact inventory that is found mainly in graves, in the foothills and mountains along the middle Cauca river valley, settlement areas of many indigenous people (Labbé 1988, p. 97).

During the conquest, the name Quimbayas referred to just one of the groups living on the western slopes of the Central Cordillera in the middle reaches of the Cauca valley. This is the most densely populated region of Colombia today, and covers the three capitals of the Old Caldas and many of the minor towns (Friede 1978, p. 13). The Quimbayas shared their rich territory in the middle Cauca valley, fertilized by volcanic ash, with neighbouring groups named in the Spanish chronicles as *quindos*, *bugas*, *carrapas*, *gorrones* and *irras*, among others (Friede 1978, pp. 13–14).

The lack of dates and exact knowledge of the context and location of the pieces of the collection, as of the archaeological region as a whole, is due to the looting of Indian graves. Looting, or *guaquería*, as it is known in the popular media, began in the Quindio in 1540, when the Spaniards took enormous amounts of gold from graves, and it has increased ever since. In fact, looting during the colonial period was minimal compared with what has been taken out since the middle nineteenth century (Valencia Llano 1989, p. 64).

Since the founding of the Museo Quimbaya in 1986, the challenge has been to set up teaching and publishing programmes in a community with a long tradition of grave-robbing and a complete ignorance of the value of the indigenous culture, in spite of the obviously intricate technology used by these goldsmiths and the beauty of their depictions of the human figure.

The first step was to produce museum guides, containing accurate archaeological information. Along with the Spanish chronicles, we used museum documents and a few scattered excavation reports, such as the study of ceramics from the Cauca river valley by Bruhns (1971), the classification of gold objects by Plazas (1980), and the regional classification of archaeological pottery of the Quimbaya region by Duque Gómez (1970, pp. 113–31).

After the experience of using these teaching aids with schoolchildren, however, it became clear that something had to be done to make the information more interesting. We had to try to break the barrier of the curriculum, the glass cases that do not allow the child to touch, manipulate and know the physical essence of the Quimbaya artefacts. If this cultural knowledge was to be useful, it was necessary to enable the children to use all their faculties, and therefore we proposed to develop activity-based workshops.

The museum workshops

Workshops, used in many museum educational services around the world, are guided by the idea that an interested and active child will better appreciate the contents of the museum and have a better and more lasting memory of the experience. They allow the student to go beyond the formal knowledge of the artefacts on display and the traditional guided visit, to be active, rather than passive, learners.

The museum workshop emphasizes the natural curiosity of children, the individual process of discovering and knowing the world, by allowing them to work with raw materials, such as clay, from which pieces of the museum collection were made. This direct experience reinforces the contrast with the traditional static display of untouchable objects and shows the children that by their very nature such objects ask to be touched and explored (Cameron 1970, p. 26).

The area and setting of the space for these workshops is important to their success. The Museo Quimbaya is fortunate in having a large room set aside for the purpose that is close to the collections. The workshop leader is a trained teacher, whose job is to create the appropriate educational environment so that the children will learn comfortably.

The workshop begins with games, activities that condense thought and action – important elements in learning. One of the advantages of the large size of the Museo Quimbaya, with its corridors and gardens, is that it invites children to run, jump and play. This helps them to break through the formal atmosphere that exists in traditional museums.

The information for the workshops is taken from the existing guides, but it is constantly being updated as the results of ongoing archaeological research are made available in the Quimbaya region and in neighbouring areas such as the Calima region (Cardale, Bray & Herrera 1989), the sites of the Guabas and Buga cultures (Rodríguez 1989), and the Magdalena valley (Castaño Uribe 1988).

Gradually, through the workshops, archaeological knowledge from these excavations is introduced to the children so that they will begin to understand something about their own past, the cultural life in the Quimbaya region after the tenth century AD, and the cultural interchange between these people and their neighbours along the Magdalena and Cauca rivers.

To explain better the characteristics of the workshops, I refer to three that have been included in the education programming of the Museo Quimbaya.

The pottery workshop

The goals of this workshop are: to reinforce the importance of pottery, as a museum object and as part of the daily and ritual life of its makers; to give the children the opportunity to discover meanings in some of the pottery pieces, as suggested by the variety of anthropomorphic, zoomorphic, and other representations on them; to teach the children to see the variety in Quimbaya pottery; and to reinforce the instruction received in museum tours about the decoration and manufacturing techniques of prehispanic pottery.

In the first session, the children handle the clay while the instructor explains its origin and describes its physical characteristics, its regional names, and the ways that the indigenous people get the material. After this, a video on pottery is shown and in the workshop room the participants play a game with a set of illustrated tokens. At the end of the game, they begin to form the clay into coils and gradually build these up into simple pots or cups. Some of these objects are stored in moist conditions so that they can be worked on in the next session, while others are allowed to dry. A week later, the children take out their pots and decorate them. They decorate the pots that are still workable with incisions and appliqué, using various wooden gravers, and paint the ones allowed to dry with paint and bees wax. They are also shown a negative painting technique. In the last two workshops, modelling techniques are practised and special pots, called *alcarrazas*, are made; these were very common in the prehispanic ceramic complex of the Colombian southwest.

The 'Let's bring back to life the picturesque jungle of the Quimbaya' workshop

The goals of this workshop are to reinforce instruction received in the museum about the ecology of the region, including the importance of the *guadua* (*Bambusa guadua*) and its relationship with the natural forest; the environmental management skills of the Quindio peoples throughout time; the characteristics of the native flora and fauna, in relation to the information of the chronicles; and a formal study of the pottery and goldwork.

This programme is intended to develop an ecological conscience in the children. It is necessary therefore to complement these workshop activities with one or two outings to a rural area, where the children are in contact with a nature that in prehispanic times was bountiful; here they learn about certain plant and tree species that are already scarce in the area, like the *guadua* and wax palm. There is also an emphasis on textual sources for descriptive information, so that the children will be motivated to read more about the Quimbayas.

In the first two sessions, the children make clay sheets, representing a landscape, and fashion small huts on them, using splinters of bamboo for the walls. Then they simulate with different materials the *guaduales* and bridges and some of the animals that live in such surroundings. In the third session the children are able to read about the flora and fauna mentioned by the Spanish chronicles in the museum guides. They are then invited to draw the scenes described in these texts and are also encouraged to write their own stories.

What this workshop accomplishes is to allow the children to weigh the human impact on the environment and the changes since pre-Columbian times. As Hansen (1984, p. 182) has observed, museums contribute to the development processes in a region and so must be aware of these ecological problems.

The 'Let's remember the pre-Columbian goldsmith techniques' workshop

Because of the tremendous curiosity amongst the visitors about the use, function and techniques of manufacture of the gold pieces, we developed a workshop showing 'lost wax' casting, and hammering and embossing techniques. The goal of this workshop is to supplement museum instruction about the development of these techniques and to emphasize and reinforce the extent of the technological sophistication of the goldsmiths. The information came from earlier work done by the Educational Services of the Gold Museum in Bogotá years ago and from research identified in an excellent bibliography on technological studies of Colombian prehispanic gold pieces (Plazas & Falchetti 1983). The interest among the participants of this workshop about the meaning of the gold pieces also prompted us to discuss the social role of this metal in prehispanic times, particularly its ceremonial character.

This workshop activates the curiosity of the children and other young people towards the ideas represented by the artefacts displayed in the museum and so enriches their appreciation of prehispanic art and culture as a whole. As stated by Sergeewich (1984, p. 201), art provides the teacher with a way of reaching children's minds and therefore constitutes an ideal environment within which they may form their vision of the world.

In the first session, after a guided tour of the museum and detailed observation of the gold pieces, the teacher brings together the group and talks about various aspects of these objects, from their manufacture, using creole beeswax in the 'lost wax' casting method, to the Quimbaya beliefs in the sacred character of the metal and the ceremonial context in which it was smelted. Then the participants heat various pieces of beeswax in a pottery crucible with a Bunsen burner; the wax melts and each person uses it to make a number of objects similar to the artefacts observed, as well as a wax funnel. When these objects are dry and solid they are placed in liquid clay (*barrotilla*). While this dries, the group make other figures in wax. After some minutes, and as the final phase, the wax objects are covered with the clay, containing sand temper, and the funnel is placed on top, with its mouth left open. These moulds are then left in a closed place to dry. A week later, in a second session, the participants get their moulds, hold them with tongs and expose them to the heat of a fire. The wax inside the moulds melts and the contents are poured out. Then the teacher prepares a plaster cement mixture, diluted in water, and instructs each participant to pour this thick liquid through the funnel until the space inside the mould is filled, as it was first filled with wax. When the cement is dry, the clay moulds are broken, exposing pieces of plaster in exactly the same shape and with the same details as the wax originals. These objects can then be decorated. In the third session, the children glue together various pieces of foil or golden metallic paper, place these on a soft surface and press into them with a wooden burin to make figures in relief. This activity is meant to introduce the subject of the hammering and embossing techniques used on real gold.

Conclusion

Museum workshops offer heritage education that limits the use of recorded information about the archaeological or geographical milieu and dull chronologies of historical data, instead engaging their participants through physical and intellectual activity that brings ideas and values from the past into the life of the present. Any museum that adopts the pedagogic workshop's methodology will find that their educational impact on young people improves greatly.

The whole spirit behind these museum workshops is the need to make children and other young people aware of their own cultural roots, and in the long term create in them a sensitivity about the archaeological past in their region. The workshops also strengthen in the participants a concern for the conservation of the cultural resources of the museum. This important aspect of cultural study used to be of interest only to museum professionals, but conservation is the responsibility of us all, and so the public as a whole should be able to obtain as much information as possible about it (Guichen 1984, pp. 232–3). Certainly, the handling of actual raw materials, and prehistoric artefacts, in the workshops lets children appreciate the fragility of the collections and the best ways to handle and keep them. When young people are allowed to take part in a dynamic relationship with the past through such workshop activities, therefore, the experience of a regional museum becomes an enriching one that gives them a clear idea of their own cultural heritage and how to appreciate and protect it.

References

Borrero, A. 1984. *La educación no formal o permanente*. Bogotá: ASCUN-ICFES.
Bruhns, K. O. 1971. Stylistic affinities between the Quimbaya gold style and little-known ceramic styles of the middle Cauca valley, Colombia. *Ñawpa Pacha* 7–8, 17–24.
Cameron, D. F. 1970. Nuevos museos para nuestra época. *El Correo* 23.
Cardale, M., W. Bray & L. Herrera 1989. Reconstruyendo el pasado en Calima: resultados recientes. *Boletín del Museo del Oro* 24, 3–33.
Castaño Uribe, C. 1988. Reporte de un yacimiento arqueológico Quimbaya Clásico en el valle del Magdalena: contribución al conocimiento de un contexto regional. *Boletín del Museo del Oro* 20, 3–11.

Delgado Cerón, I. & C. I. Mz-Recaman 1994. The museum comes to school in Colombia: teaching packages as a method of learning. In *The Presented Past: heritage, museums and education*, Stone, P. G. & B. L. Molyneaux (eds), 148–58. London: Routledge.

Duque Gómez, L. 1970. *Los Quimbayas, reseña etnohistórica y arqueológica*. Bogotá: Imprenta Nacional.

Friede, J. 1978. *Los Quimbayas bajo la dominación española*. Bogotá: Carlos Valencia Editores.

Guichen, G. de 1984. Enseñar a conocer el patrimonio. *Revista Museum* 36 (144). Paris: Unesco.

Hansen, H. 1984. El museo como educador. *Revista Museum* 36, 176–89. Paris: Unesco.

Labbé, A. J. 1988. *Colombia antes de Colóm*. Bogotá: Carlos Valencia Editores.

Plazas, C. 1980. Clasificación de objetos de orfebrería precolombina según su uso. *Boletín del Museo del Oro* 3, 1–27.

Plazas, C. & A. M. Falchetti 1983. *La orfebrería prehispánica de Colombia*. Bogotá: Museo del Oro.

Restrepo, L. C. 1989. *La trampa de la razón*. Bogotá: Arango Editores.

Rodríguez, C. A. 1989. La población prehispánica del valle medio del Río Cauca entre los siglos VII–XVI D.C. (Culturas Guabas y Buga). *Boletín del Museo del Oro* 24, 73–89.

Sergeewich, K. 1984. Un centro de creación infantil en Eriván. *Revista Museum* 36. Paris: Unesco.

Valencia Llano, A. 1989. La guaquería en el viejo Caldas. *Boletín del Museo del Oro* 23, 61–75.

Zubiría, M. de & J. de Zubiría 1987. *Fundamentos de pedagogía conceptual*. Bogotá: Plaza & Jamés.

12 'The Fascinating World of Stonehenge': an exhibition and its aftermath

RUUD BORMAN

Introduction

An exhibition called 'The Fascinating World of Stonehenge' was held in the Municipal Museum of Arnhem, Netherlands, from 26 November 1988 until 29 January 1989. It was the highlight of ten years of archaeological displays that were intended to popularize archaeology in general, as well as in the province of Gelderland in the Netherlands. The exhibition attracted over 50,000 visitors and received an enormous amount of publicity; it was later put on in a reduced version in the Goois Museum in Hilversum and in the Museactron in Maaseik (Belgium).

But why should an exhibition about megalithic monuments be organized in a municipal museum in Arnhem? And why should that famous stone monument on Salisbury Plain in southern England be a central part of an exhibition in the Netherlands? Many people were puzzled, especially during the efforts to plan and finance the exhibition. Arnhem has no such monuments, and there are none in Gelderland, of which Arnhem is the capital. In fact, the nearest megalithic monument is more than 100 km away, just over the German border. It is one of the so-called *Hunebedden* (hunebeds, i.e. northern European megalithic burial monuments), at the spot named the *Duwelsteene* (stones of the devil) which, like identical monuments in the northern province of Drenthe and in northern Germany, were believed to have been built by *Huns* (giants).

One reason why the name of this famous prehistoric monument was used in the exhibition's title was to draw public attention to the whole phenomenon of megalithic monuments. Stonehenge served as an introduction to a period when, over much of Europe, enormous stones were moved to special places and erected as ceremonial centres and burial sites, all as part of the wider spread of goods, ideas and other aspects of culture. Indeed, members of the public were astonished to learn how widely the tradition of building huge stone monuments and practising a common burial rite with similar grave goods spread. Most visitors still supposed that prehistoric people seldom went beyond their own village.

There was also an important link between the Gelderland region and the less famous, but equally interesting, hunebeds. The people of Gelderland did not put up large stone monuments, but it was people with a similar material culture that were the builders of such megaliths. Pottery found in the hunebeds is similar to pottery found in the settlements on the Veluwe river in Gelderland. Many stone axes found in Gelderland can also be attributed to the hunebed builders; and the Veluwe is also a rich place for burial finds associated with the later Bell Beaker burial rite, evidence of which has also been found in other parts of the Netherlands. This link allowed the Municipal Museum in Arnhem to show off its assortment of artefacts of the hunebed builders as well as a marvellous collection of grave goods of the Bell Beaker tradition.

The most important aspect of the exhibition, however, was an attempt to change the way the public thinks about prehistory. For a long time people in the Netherlands believed that artefacts represented only the past of the particular site where they were found. The average visitor pictured a primitive group living in a very limited space. This attitude is puzzling, however, because in almost all prehistoric periods, similar forms of material culture were widespread. Even in the smallest local history museum an interested outsider soon discovers objects that are almost identical to those seen in other museums, sometimes very far away.

Archaeologists have been aware of this cultural spread for a long time, but as they seem to dislike the popularization of their profession, and as teachers teach prehistory only as an incidental subject, innovations in archaeological content and ideas have not really penetrated general education. As a result, popular attitudes have been burdened with the old images and outmoded insights and opinions of a tired system.

In the past few decades, however, archaeological thinking in the Netherlands has begun to change, as part of the general shift from the old culture-history approach, where the goal is to attempt to write the story of the progress of culture through the ages, to the modern interest in how individual social groups adapt to their particular environments through time. The burgeoning interest in the social aspects of prehistory have also transformed the way that archaeologists look at their own society – the context in which their ideas, attitudes and methods are formed. As part of a growing awareness of social responsibility, they have become less reluctant to popularize their results and reconstructions and have been interested in exploring new possibilities for presenting them to the public.

Creating new ways of attracting the public is, however, not straightforward. Traditionally, archaeology is hidden away in cellars and attics and is presented in large, boring rows and ranks of objects – you could almost imagine yourself in a prehistoric surgery! And for a long time a favourite topic in archaeological displays has been a concern with the conduct of the profession itself, with its methods and techniques. Such subjects are interesting and important, but their significance is difficult to communicate to the viewer, who is primarily interested in the prehistoric remains that are the actual object of archaeological research.

Given the spirit of change in archaeological thinking, an exhibition about megaliths seemed a good way to get people to think about archaeology in a broader theoretical context, presenting not only information about the meaning and function of the monuments but also aspects such as the history of their interpretation and their preservation. These goals demanded experimentation with new display techniques, with special attention to the way the information was presented.

The museum decided that the exhibit should take a regional approach, and so the coverage extended to megalithic sites across northwest Europe, including Ireland, Great Britain, the Netherlands, Belgium, northwest France and northeast Germany. And Stonehenge was picked for its international recognition as a symbol of the past.

The preparations

From the beginning we aimed at an exhibition for a broad group of spectators; we intended to make it attractive to look at, with clear and concise information. It was to have the following themes:

1 General introduction: information about the phenomenon of megalithic monuments, their age and distribution;
2 The history of the way in which these monuments were perceived: the first written reports concerning these monuments, the attitude and ways the church dealt with these (the heresy of pagan remains, christianization, demolition-parties), the first 'scientific' essays, destruction for building material, archaeological investigation and care of monuments, the attention of sculptors, painters and writers, and the use of megaliths as means of publicity;
3 A regional survey: (a) Ireland, (b) Scotland, (c) south England and Wales, (d) northern Netherlands and northwest Germany, (e) eastern Belgium, (f) Brittany; types of megaliths present, their age and distribution, and discussions of the major regional sites (New Grange, Maes Howe, Callanish, Stonehenge, Avebury, Carnac, etc.).

A working group was set up, involving specialists in several disciplines, and many long discussions were held. Although a real megalithic monument could not be included in the exhibition, we wanted to impress upon the public the scale of these constructions, what enormous stones the people of the past transported and raised. We therefore decided to try and convey this sense of monumentality through photographs and measurements of the size and weight of individual stones, hoping that if the pictures were large enough, we would approach reality, albeit on a modest scale.

Figure 12.1 The large model of Stonehenge built specifically for the exhibition. Photo: Foto Gemeentearchief Arnhem.

Several exciting and elaborate schemes were proposed for the display of the rest of the information, but financial restrictions and practicality meant that it was necessary to use traditional exhibition means and methods: archaeological objects, photos, maps, models, slide presentations and connecting texts.

Museums and sites were visited throughout the area covered by the exhibition in order to organize loans, and to prepare a slide presentation, for the exhibition. The slide presentation was to be an audiovisual spectacle, using twelve projectors to show the history of the megaliths on an enormous screen. Most of the photographs were taken on location, by the writer.

Two large models of Stonehenge (Fig 12.1) and New Grange (Fig 12.2) were built, each about 4 m by 4 m. The Stonehenge model was placed in the first part of the exhibition. It represented the monument in both its original and final shapes. A specially designed illumination made it possible for visitors to see the effect, on a small scale, of the sunrise on 21 June, the summer solstice.

All available literature on the subject of megalithic monuments was collected and summarized by the working group. A total of over 15,000 pages of text were read and distilled into a few dozen pages; these were used for the text of the exhibition, information sheets, slide presentation, lessons and information for the media.

After a year and a half, everything was ready. As the exhibition was being

Figure 12.2 The large model of New Grange built specifically for the exhibition.
Photo: Foto Gemeentearchief Arnhem.

completed, a huge publicity campaign was launched. Press releases were sent
out throughout Europe, appropriate lesson plans were sent to schools in the
district (within a 50 km range) and posters were put up in countless museums
and at all important railway stations in the Netherlands. And every visitor to
the museum in Arnhem who wanted more information could consult a
permanently staffed information desk with the relevant literature.

The exhibition

Photographs, maps, ground-plans and drawings were fixed on high, narrow
panels in a stone-grey colour, presenting the idea of standing stones. Three
different types of text were used: headline texts designed to isolate subjects,
explanatory texts, and captions for the objects and illustrations.

The main way through the exhibition was clearly indicated, but it was
possible for visitors to follow their own route, as each section also stood on its
own.

During the preparations we realized that the public would have questions
about the megalithic monuments: their meaning and purpose, their age, how
they were built, and so on. If possible, an answer was given in the explanatory
texts, but to us it was most important to point out that in prehistoric Europe

different agricultural communities had erected such monuments (not everywhere at the same time or in the same way) and that such groups had regular
contact over large distances – as shown by the distribution of tools and ritual
objects and the presence of imported objects.

From the reactions of visitors and the media it was clear that this approach
was a success. The visitors' book contained the following examples: 'A great,
impressive, fascinating, educative, intriguing, magnificent, fine, well-prepared
and conveniently arranged exhibition'; and 'Very informative, beautiful
models, artistic slide-presentation and great collection'.

The exhibition was covered 76 times in daily and weekly papers, 12 of them
with nationwide coverage. In 18 magazines of various kinds, articles appeared
about 'The Fascinating World of Stonehenge'. The Belgian paper *De Standaard*
(3/4 December 1988), for example, said: 'The Fascinating World of
Stonehenge is a prestigious collection . . . a scoop for the continent, the first
survey of the megalithic culture in pre-Christian Northern and Western
Europe' and the paper *Eindhovens Dagblad* (6 December 1988) commented that:
'Photos and maps give a great impression of the geographical spread of such
monuments. . . . Beautiful models are shown. . . . Also the great variety in
construction of the monuments comes out clearly in the many photos.'

This area of study, long since familiar to archaeologists, was suddenly
accessible to a large public. Over 700 people attended the opening – a surprisingly large crowd for a Dutch audience. People were constantly astonished by
what they saw and read and the exhibit inspired a number of visitors to
investigate the subject further. And long after the exhibition, and even today,
the archaeological division of the museum is regularly bombarded with questions about megalithic monuments.

The lessons developed by the schools to complement the exhibition were
also a great success: enthusiastic pupils formed a large proportion of the
visitors.

As an exhibition and educative experiment 'The Fascinating World of
Stonehenge' was a great success.

The aftermath: searching for new forms of display

We did not want to follow up the success of the megalith exhibition by simply
copying the display techniques for use with other material. We saw this as a
chance to reassess traditional types of display and to question why it had taken
so long to change our approach. Recently (too) much attention has been given
to the way archaeological material has been recovered, and more attention
must be paid to making the displays of material culture interesting.

Some of the obstacles to more interesting presentations have to do with the
nature of artefacts. Archaeological finds are on the whole difficult to display.
Most objects of interest to archaeologists are fragmentary, sometimes because
they are the by-products of activities such as tool-making or because they are

fragile, like ceramics. In addition, many objects need special conditions of temperature or humidity for their preservation. And, most problematically, archaeological finds are removed by excavation from the context of their origin and use.

Further problems are caused by poor exhibition areas (often the attic or cellar of a museum) and sometimes there is not enough money to finance a well-presented exhibition. This usually leads to dull displays of rows of pottery and tools.

Many of the museums in the Netherlands developed from private collections made prior to the twentieth century. Artefacts were traditionally displayed in sound, old-fashioned showcases and arranged in rows, like surgical instruments, accompanied by a text giving the location of the find and its approximate age. In reality, however, there was not much more to tell. Archaeology was still in its infancy. The antiquarian dug, collected and saved, and showed what he thought was worth showing.

In the twentieth century, however, many museums changed the way they collected and displayed cultural material. Interest grew in modern art and other fields of collecting, and so archaeological finds gradually disappeared into cellars and attics. Archaeologists were generally powerless to stop this trend: only a few were associated with museums, and most of them were usually in the field.

As archaeological research progressed, the past became much clearer, but museums maintained their static displays and minimal information. The results of current archaeological research were not included, so the visitors had to make do with hopelessly outdated information. Nothing, or nearly nothing, was included in school curricula.

After the Second World War the output of archaeology grew enormously, with many, often large-scale, excavations taking place all over the country. In addition, amateur archaeology made its mark. Sensational finds were made, and this fuelled publicity and made archaeology popular with the public. This increase in public interest caused a reaction in museums; they paid increasing attention to the quality of the permanent displays and held a growing number of thematic exhibitions.

Urban archaeology has aroused interest in the more recent past (late Middle Ages, seventeenth and eighteenth centuries). Beginning in the 1970s, a great many scientific publications were issued for the general public, and these brought archaeology to countless readers.

Responding to all these social and academic developments, museums now tend to give more information than ever before and many are experimenting with new types of display. Indeed, the traditional display techniques, dating from the 1950s, are all but dead; museums had concentrated on creating beautiful exhibits, but these techniques did not allow the visitor to see objects in their environment. Materials like glass, synthetics or aluminium keep the past at a distance. However beautiful, panels with pictures or text are no compensation. New methods of display and interpretation must be found that address the problems of inappropriate display space; the use of unsympathetic materials in exhibition design; and the overuse of textual explanations that are too detailed and long for the majority of visitors. Amongst these initiatives and developments will certainly be the employment of more audio-visual aids; more interactive displays; more use of models and reconstructions; and greater reliance on experimental archaeology as means of educating and interesting visitors.

The aftermath: archaeology and education

During our assessment of the problems and prospects for future exhibitions following 'The Fascinating World of Stonehenge', the most urgent need for innovation was clearly in the basic education of the public about the past.

Little of the new archaeological information and techniques that have emerged in the past few decades has found its way easily into schools. In primary and secondary schools prehistory is still a marginal subject and is poorly taught, usually consisting of talk about out-of-date theories. For example, children were long taught that the Batavians were the first real inhabitants of Holland and before this time the past was grey and misty. Now it was recognized that someone had built the hunebeds, round barrows and urnfields of earlier times, but hardly anything sensible could be said about them.

Indeed, communication of archaeological research to schools and the public at large has been the most difficult problem facing heritage educators. It is very rare that the public can see the tangible results of an excavation; the finds must be thoroughly analysed for scientific reporting and until then they are inaccessible to the public. And when results are reported, field archaeologists tend to use scientific reports; such archaeologists are usually not interested in popularizing their work or are too busy to do it. At best, they talk to the press or produce a pamphlet, but that is all.

The interest of the media is short-lived, however. Curious or sensational finds occasionally attract general attention, but the public interest is never sustained; such discoveries are too far apart in time.

Since the onset of the 1980s, however, some archaeologists have published books accessible to the general public and so have achieved a breakthrough. They pictured the past in national, regional and local perspectives and used contemporary research methods and information. As a result, the idea that before the coming of the Batavians only wild, primitive and insignificant peoples lived in this region was finally demolished.

Although the amount of information available about the past has increased dramatically, the use of educational specialists in archaeology is still in its infancy. Until recently, not a single institution in the Netherlands that conducted excavations had someone available to take care of education or publicity. The 'missing link' is a person who takes care of this problem, one who deals with the public or keeps the press informed. This person has barely emerged in the archaeological world, however. In some places, educational specialists are found working in museums, with minimal finances, fighting against a whole world of misunderstanding. 'What do we have to do with all those heaps of sherds?' is often heard. It takes room, money, labour and a clear idea of what the effort is all for.

Even if an institution has an educational specialist, however, the limitations of museum display sustain the age-old problem. As artefacts are often poorly displayed, limiting the possibility of interpreting them to the public in an interesting way, the response of visitors is often equally stilted. This all leads to the conclusion that there is no interest in archaeology. It is a vicious circle that is impossible to break through. Indeed, one is confronted with the paradox that those who have the power to change the situation, the public and the politicians, are also those who have created and sustain it, and yet do nothing, in spite of the fact that they are clearly not thrilled by a showcase full of artefacts.

Who can resolve this problem? Amateur archaeologists, who work away at their research industriously, but without support? Museum archaeologists, who are often only able to keep on fighting for the importance of their collection and an acceptable presentation of it because they refuse to set aside their ideals? Managers of museums who prefer contemporary arts when they have more than one department to care for? Archaeologists must accept responsibility for the decades of non-publicity and non-education.

It is time to take another route. In some countries, ways have been found – confront the public with their past, take the visitors back in time, give them surroundings that provide an opportunity for them to relive the past. The Archaeological Park in Xanten (Germany) and the Jorvik Viking Centre in York attract a great number of visitors exactly for this reason.

Museum visitors and expectation patterns

Since the success of 'The Fascinating World of Stonehenge' as an exhibition and educative experiment, we have been working continuously on improving the display of archaeological objects – creating a more visitor-friendly presentation.

In developing an archaeological display there are three essential issues:

1 the aim of the museum (e.g. general display of information, education);
2 the part of the public it is trying to reach; and
3 what this public should expect to see.

With regard to the aims of a museum, the nature of the display depends on the nature of the collections and research programmes. In a region rich in archaeological finds the vastness of a collection, and not just its quality, may be brought into the picture. Furthermore, one should think about what information should be included and how it should be presented. Usually a chrono-logical story and information about the age and location of the objects is all that is given. Some attention is usually also paid to the excavation. If one really wants to show and make the public experience the past, however, one should choose another design.

With regard to the museum audience, it must be stressed that 'the public' does not exist. One may speak about kinds of visitors, but not about the average visitor. There are, for example:

1 The professionals, who often want to see things they do not know from their own observation, such as special objects which they know from publications, or are interested in other people's exhibition techniques. They are not so interested in the objects themselves.
2 Amateur archaeologists and historians, who may follow their interests in the past through an organization or alone, have similar concerns to the pro-fessionals but may be more interested in the objects.
3 Visitors, adults and children, who are interested in the past but not actively involved in studying it and who want to see as well as to learn.
4 Visitors who only occasionally enter museums and more or less expect to find something old.

The first two groups are relatively small and are especially interested in recent results of excavations or thematic exhibitions. The same applies to the third category, but these people tend to be also interested in the past in general, especially of their own community and surroundings. In the last category people are only superficially or incidentally interested.

Each of these different kinds of visitor expects to see finds and information about them in an archaeological display, but what they would prefer in terms of presentation is not so obvious. Visitors to museums are used to the idea that archaeology is displayed in dull formations in showcases and this is what they expect.

Conclusion

Education is critical to stimulating and activating interest in the past. We believe that readers, listeners and spectators are in principle interested in archaeology. The same applies to people who visit museums. But somewhere along the way, that interest subsides. It should have been created by parents, teachers, or other people surrounding a growing child, through stories and books. Indeed, good teachers are often identified by professionals as the main reason for becoming archaeologists in the first place. Often the first contact with the past at school seems to have been decisive: the inspirational teacher can create a lifelong interest; the dull teacher, only taking into consideration facts and dates, may poison the minds of many regarding history and archae-ology. It is not so important that teachers' knowledge is up-to-date if they have the ability to carry children away into the past and bring it alive.

Story-telling, no matter how vivid, is not enough to sustain interest in a museum, however, if the past is simply translated into rows of objects which kill the imagination or sustain it only by artefacts made special by their age or uniqueness. We must continue to create new ways of communicating about the past, using the whole museum environment, as it is at once a storehouse for the fragile remnants of our past, a source of scientific research and education materials, and an intriguing landscape for the visitor. With this effort, we can ensure an increasing public interest and understanding of our regional heritage.

13 The re-display of the Alexander Keiller Museum, Avebury, and the National Curriculum in England

PETER G. STONE

Background

The Avebury sites

The World Heritage Site of Stonehenge and Avebury is made up of two distinctive and separate parts – the first comprising Stonehenge and its surrounding prehistoric landscape, the second, about 25 km to the north, comprising the area around the prehistoric henge monument of Avebury. The latter area includes six prehistoric sites presently under the management of English Heritage, the national organization charged with the statutory protection of the historic environment in England (Fig. 13.1). These sites are: (1) the huge bank and ditch of a neolithic henge monument enclosing the substantially re-erected remains of a number of circles of undressed standing stones and enclosing much of the modern village of Avebury; (2) the remains of the causewayed enclosure of Windmill Hill; (3) the largely re-erected section of part of the West Kennet Avenue of stones that seems to link the henge monument at Avebury to (4) the site of another stone circle known as the Sanctuary; (5) the excavated and rebuilt remains of the Long Barrow funerary monument of West Kennet; and (6) Silbury Hill, the largest artificial structure in northern Europe (see, for example, Coupland 1988). In addition to these monuments, this part of the World Heritage Site also contains the remains of numerous other prehistoric structures. All of the sites lie within an easy two-hour drive of a series of major urban centres including London.

There has been extensive interest in the Avebury area since (at least) the seventeenth century, for example the work of antiquarians John Aubrey and William Stukeley (see Ucko, Hunter, Clark & David 1991), and more recently a whole plethora of popular books has been produced to satisfy the demands of the interested lay public (for example, Burl 1979; Pitts 1986; Malone 1989). Four of the English Heritage-managed sites (the main henge, West Kennet Long Barrow, West Kennet Avenue, and the Sanctuary) were extensively restored in the early and middle part of this century after archaeological investigation (Ucko, Hunter, Clark & David 1991).

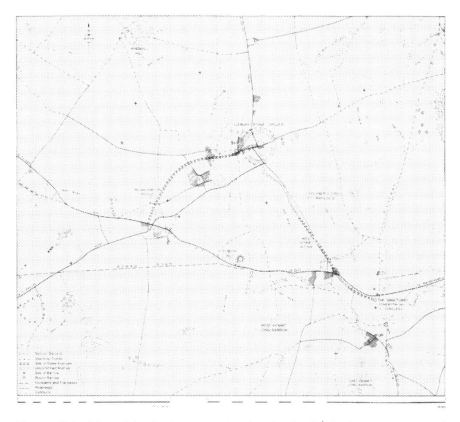

Figure 13.1 Map of the Avebury area showing the six sites in the management of English Heritage. By courtesy of English Heritage.

The museum in Avebury is named after the millionaire archaeologist Alexander Keiller, who worked in the area in the early part of this century, and is housed in a building itself protected by law for its historic value as the stable block of a largely extant sixteenth-century manor-house. The main holding of the museum is the Keiller bequest – collected by Keiller over a number of seasons of excavation in the 1920s and 1930s at Windmill Hill and Avebury and embellished by artefacts he collected and bought from abroad. The museum also holds most of the finds and archive of more recent excavations at West Kennet Long Barrow and Silbury Hill (Piggott 1962; Atkinson 1967, 1968, 1969, 1970) and is the official repository for all archaeological finds from the local area.

School visits to the Avebury region

For the past twenty or more years Avebury has been a popular location for school visits, with over 11,000 school-children visiting the museum annually. It is estimated that at least a further 10–15,000 school-children annually visit one or more of the sites without visiting the museum. Until recently, the majority of these children have been in the 7 to 11 age range – the time at school where prehistory is most commonly taught (although see below). Most of these visits were supported by materials produced in school by teachers, although two specific handbooks for teachers on the Avebury sites have been produced (Coupland 1988; Stone 1990a).

However, this situation is in the process of changing. All school-children in England now have to follow a prescribed National Curriculum that leaves little time for teaching about the prehistoric past (DES 1989; Stone 1992; and see Corbishley & Stone 1994). The history curriculum (DES 1991) is made up of a core of compulsory units of work covering topics such as 'Tudor and Stuart Times' and 'Victorian Britain' supplemented by a series of optional courses such as 'Ships and Seafarers' and 'Writing and Printing'. There are no core units that cover any prehistoric period. Because of the huge amount of historical material included in the curriculum, most teachers try to combine core and optional units – for example by teaching about ships and seafarers in Tudor and Stuart England. Teachers, therefore, have very little opportunity to introduce their own ideas or content into this curriculum. Moreover, the new curriculum has been introduced very quickly with, initially, few new resources for a large number of (especially primary) teachers who have never had to teach history before.

Despite this somewhat gloomy picture, opportunities do exist for teaching about prehistory within the new curriculum (Stone 1990b, 1992) and for using museums in particular (NCC 1990; Stone 1993). One of the optional units for 11- to 14-year-olds has to cover 'An episode or turning point in European history before 1914' and in its advice to teachers on the history curriculum the National Curriculum Council (NCC), an advisory body to Government, has suggested studying the 'Neolithic Revolution' for this unit (NCC 1991). Teachers can also use museums and prehistoric sites while working on optional 'local history' units or data from prehistory when working on op- tional units such as 'Houses and Places of Worship' or 'Food and Farming'.

The re-display

For a number of years the English Heritage Regional Team (that has collective accountability for the monuments and museum at Avebury) has been aware that the exhibition in the Keiller Museum, originally set up in the 1960s, was in dire need of re-display (Fig. 13.2). Limited funds for this work were made available for the financial year 1990/1. The team included the Ancient Monuments Archaeological Inspector for the sites, representatives from the

Figure 13.2 The Alexander Keiller Museum, Avebury, before the re-display. Photo: English Heritage.

English Heritage Museums Group, an in-house Design and Interpretative Manager and me, the Regional Education Officer. At various times during the year this core group was assisted by architectural, mechanical and engineering and works staff.

A more extensive project to develop a Visitor Orientation Point in a building in the central car-park at Avebury at the same time as the refurbishment of the museum, was put aside until longer-term plans for the presentation of the whole of this part of the World Heritage Site have been finalized. This delay meant (and means) that the new exhibition in the museum was to be (and will be for the foreseeable future) the only point of interpretation (other than brief interpretation panels for individual sites) for the prehistory of the area.

It was my prime concern that the re-displayed museum would relate as closely as possible to the constraints, attitudes and opportunities imposed and offered by the new National Curriculum. This especially meant focusing on the nature of historical (archaeological) evidence and the subjectivity of interpretation based on such evidence (see below). However, the education policy developed for the museum (see, for example, Hooper-Greenhill 1991) was based on the re-display being interesting and, we hope, informative, for the general visitor as well as for education groups. Educational requirements were to have a high profile in the work of the project team but once the re-display was complete, education groups would have to compete for gallery space with all other visitors and would have no special area or handling collection set aside for them within the museum. (There is, however, a classroom-sized study base available for education groups to book within the village but away from the museum.)

The constraints

As mentioned above, the museum collection is housed in a protected building that cannot be extended or altered. This gave maximum internal dimensions for exhibition space of just under 50 square metres. We also only had one year in which to carry out the project – from initial plans to completed re-display. If we went over the financial year-end the money would disappear. Finally, the budget was very small – £30,000 to cover the cost not only of actually re-displaying the museum but also of script writer, external designer, new sales counter and facilities, associated building work and exhibition-related electrical modifications.

Given the timescale for the project, the limitations of space and especially the extremely tight budget, it was clear from the start that we were not going to be able to introduce the latest examples of interactive museum display techniques, nor were we going to be able to replace, for example, all of the old display cabinets. The new exhibition was going to have to rely substantially upon graphics and revised text rather than any major renewal of presentation hardware and this in itself was a major and stimulating challenge.

What to present?

Our first real problem was to decide what type of exhibition we wanted to put on in the museum. What particular message(s) – if any – did we want to give to our visitors? In this we were somewhat constrained by the Keiller bequest that partially directed us as to what should be displayed. However, within these limitations we still had the opportunity to focus on, for example, the entire World Heritage Site, or the six monuments under our management, or the Neolithic of southern England more generally, or a little of all three. We were very conscious that the museum was, and still is, the only place where a display focusing on the prehistory of the area is really possible or appropriate.

Before making any final plans as to the content of the re-display we discussed our plans with a number of archaeologists who were specialists in the Neolithic, or who had worked on the Avebury sites in particular. Not surprisingly, after consulting six different people we had six very different views! However, through this exercise we gathered a host of relevant and interesting ideas – many of which were finally welded into the overall framework with which we attempted to underpin the exhibition (see below, p. 196). I also carefully went through all of the National Curriculum subject documents – especially history, science, technology, English, mathematics and art – to identify where teachers and children might be able to use the material available in the museum collection to develop their work.

We also looked carefully at the visitor profile for the museum. It has been estimated (Cobham Resource Consultants 1990) – that about half a million people visit Avebury every year. Of these, only about 40,000 visit the museum. About 15,000 of these visitors gain free access as members of either English Heritage or the National Trust (a nation-wide charity whose members support the conservation of the historic and natural environment) and a further 11,000+ receive free access as formal educational groups (mainly schools but also including university and college groups and some adult education parties). This leaves only 14,000 or so visitors out of the original half a million who were willing to pay for access to the present museum at the door. Leaving aside the complex issue of charging for heritage attractions and museums, the figures were depressing. Obviously the museum was not attracting a complete cross-section of the population. Visitors in the UK expect to have to pay for access to most sites and most museums and, practical problems apart (visitors have to be particularly persistent to find the museum building, located as it is away from the main tourist route through the site), we had to assume that part of this reluctance to visit was due to the type and content of museum display (museum staff had commented that a quite a lot of people peeked in through the door and then left without paying to look around the museum). Because they are usually expected to pay, visitors have become increasingly demanding of the quality of exhibitions and displays. The Keiller Museum was obviously not fulfilling visitor expectations and they were staying away.

As educational groups make up over a quarter of the visitors, I arranged for a number of schools to ask their pupils what they would want a new museum display to tell them about the people who built the Avebury monuments. All of the children involved were from first, primary or junior schools (with an overall age range of 5–14). We combined the children's responses and drew up a table of the twenty things the children most wanted to know. The results are shown in the Appendix (p. 205) and paint a salutary picture for archaeologists. Nearly all the questions refer to those areas that archaeology cannot reveal with any level of certainty. They wanted to know about social, religious and practical things that are central to their own world – and would have been central to the world of those people living in the Avebury area in the Neolithic – but which have left little or no evidence in the archaeological record. They had presented us with quite a task! We also discussed the most appropriate types of display for older children with a few secondary-level teachers and Education Authority advisors.[1] Time constraints made it impossible for us to survey undergraduate and other students in higher education as to their thoughts on the most useful type of display for them. We therefore had to assume that many of the points raised by those university-based archaeologists we had already approached would have covered what they wanted their students to get out of the museum.

Earlier general surveys (for example, Hodder, Parker Pearson, Peck & Stone n.d.; Stone 1986) had already given some ideas as to the relevant interests of the general public, and further information about this group, including the questions most frequently asked at the museum and comments made about the 1960s display, was forthcoming from the museum staff. From these sources we inferred that many general visitors would be interested in many of the questions raised by the school survey. Museum staff also indicated that visitors had expressed interest in those antiquarians and archaeologists who have studied Avebury and its monuments over the centuries – the story of the re-emergence of Avebury – and that people would be especially interested to be able to see some of the actual tools and instruments used by Keiller and his workforce during the early twentieth-century excavations.

Armed with this background information we decided on our own particular approach. We argued that the great strength of the museum was its unique collection of artefacts from a range of neolithic sites. However, we suggested that only a few (usually archaeologically specialized) visitors would be interested in the artefacts for their own sake. We therefore agreed that the re-display would concentrate on the strengths of the collection and would be object-led, using artefacts found during excavation of the six sites under our management. However, we were also convinced that there should be a running theme behind the displays that would place the objects in a more general context and which, we hoped, would begin to address many of the questions raised by the children – a theme that would almost certainly provoke more questions than it would ever be capable of answering. This idea was finally formulated in an internal memo:

> The key concept is that of 'prehistoric cosmology'. The monuments in the Avebury landscape were theatres for rites and ceremonies which both reflected and supported prehistoric ideas of world order, the place of people within that order, the relationship of people and gods, and the nature and transmission of authority (whether spiritual, educational or political). Over a period of about a thousand years these separate theatres became linked into one huge theatrical landscape. The monuments are thus the collapsed and grass-cloaked clues to an integrated system of religious, social and political beliefs which may well have been quite as complex as (though different from) our own. . . . As regards Avebury, unfortunately we do not know what the cosmology was! So we have to use the monuments (and their contents) to try to build a picture of that crucial motivation for their construction and use.

Our theme was to show how archaeologists interpret such fragmentary, 'grass-cloaked' evidence from the past and that, while the data of archaeology may in themselves be regarded as a collection of 'objective' artefacts, any interpretation of these data is necessarily subjective and always open to question and modification. We were, however, conscious that we had to balance this view of our understanding of the interpretation of the past with the desire on the part of many of our visitors to be told in a more didactic way 'what it was like'.

The new display

One of our fundamental decisions, taken early on in the project, was that we would drastically reduce the number of artefacts on display. We argued that a display of twenty similar arrowheads may be extremely interesting to a specialist but would tend to alienate and bore the majority of our visitors – especially if it nestled between displays of twenty similar flint scrapers and twenty similar pieces of handaxe! The whole collection would, of course, have to be available to those who wanted to study it, but our duty in the re-display of the museum was to non-specialist visitors. This decision freed some space in display cases to add more illustrative material and generally to lessen the density of display. It also meant that we were able to remove some display cabinets entirely. One set of cases had always been a problem as they were too high for children to see into. Their removal provided a far better visitor circulation pattern, generally created more space in the museum, and gave us space to display some of Keiller's tools and instruments and to introduce a small 'hands-on' section where visitors can feel the weight of a hafted axe and handle (modern) antler picks.

The central feature of the re-display is a chronological tour of the six sites. Each display is object-led but also has a newly commissioned artist's illustration, in colour, of the site in the Neolithic. Objects in the display are, wherever possible, seen in context in the illustration. Each case also boasts a new air photograph of the site as it is today. Throughout, we attempted to address our theme of the subjectivity of archaeological interpretation by continually thinking back to the children's questions. Our lack of ability to answer them satisfactorily kept us constantly aware that what we were trying to interpret were the intangibles of the past rather than any concept of a past well understood and definitive in nature.

We decided to dot around the new display a series of 'clipboards' that could be used to raise questions in visitors' minds about the various sites and their particular functions and locations. They also describe what can be seen from the various sites. The text on the clipboards is easily changed so if new questions come up – a site that might be affected by nearby development, for example – they can be updated relatively easily. We also hope the clipboards will encourage visitors to the museum to go out into the landscape and visit the other sites. The last clipboard, which is much larger than the others and is, in fact, the last major display in the museum, raises the contemporary issues of conservation and preservation and gives the visitor a brief idea of the work of English Heritage and its role as regards these issues.

The practicalities

Our first major problem was a disagreement within the project team as to whether or not the new display should include a full-size 'neolithic figure'. The debate concentrated on the contradiction between the desirability of having a figure to draw in visitors and to give them a strong message about the people in the Neolithic and the well-rehearsed arguments about lack of detailed (any?) knowledge about people's appearance. If we were to have a figure, what clothes would he (or she?) wear? Trousers? Kilts? Cloaks? Jackets? What would they be made from? Would they be dyed with rich colours or plain? What footwear should we give the figure? Would the figure be tattooed? What about body-painting? Jewellery? If male, would the figure be clean-shaven or bearded; long-haired or crew-cut? The questions were endless and answers were in short supply. The only thing we could agree on was that no figure should be produced which could possibly support the 'dinosaur-hunting grunter-groaner' image of prehistory (Richardson 1987, p. 76).

We eventually agreed to use our own disagreement to re-emphasize our major theme – illustrating the limitations of archaeological evidence and the subjectivity of display. Our figure was to be schizophrenic, full-size but presented in two halves: one side showing a fully dressed yet ragged individual, coping with existence – but only just; the other side illustrating an individual from a society more interested in its presentation and, perhaps, rather more 'sophisticated' – painted, tattooed, with well-made clothes and bedecked with jewellery (Fig. 13.3 and cover). Neither side has any attributes that were not potentially available to anyone living in southern England in the Neolithic. Below our character a caption suggests to visitors that, because of the nature of archaeological evidence, 'the experts' are unsure about what people really looked like in the Neolithic and that the two options shown in the figure are two extreme views and – importantly – what do they, the visitors, think? Next to the caption sits a cartoon firmly dispelling the image of the 'grunter-groaner'.

We also guessed (steered by the results of the general surveys mentioned above) that most visitors would, perhaps subconsciously, be more at home with the less sophisticated view of the model. We therefore agreed to angle the figure so that this was the image visitors would see on their arrival at the museum – the more sophisticated side would only be revealed as visitors moved around the display. This angling has quite a dramatic effect as visitors are suddenly confronted by the figure's 'sophisticated' side. We hoped that this would cause them to pause for a moment to question their own preconceived views of what people in the Neolithic may have been like, and initial comments from museum staff indicate that many visitors really do confront the issue and discuss the relative values of the two sides of our figure as they learn more about neolithic technology and life from the rest of the museum display.

We decided to continue this 'schizophrenic' theme in some of the newly commissioned artwork for the re-display. In one instance the same scene is presented in two illustrations with individuals sitting and standing in the same places but dressed differently in the two illustrations (Figs 13.4 and 13.5) – in much the same way as the two sides of our figure. We also have the figures doing slightly different things in the two illustrations in an attempt to get visitors to think about what they are looking at and about what life would have been like in the Neolithic.

Figure 13.3 The symbolic presentation of 'fact' versus 'imagination' through the use of a divided image. Photo: English Heritage.

Figure 13.4 The symbolic presentation of 'fact' versus 'imagination' – illustration assuming 'sophistication'.

As a team we were very aware of the complex debate now in progress with regard to the use of human remains in archaeological exhibitions (for an overview of issues and history of the debate see Hubert 1988, 1991). Interestingly, museum staff had informed us that a child skeleton was the most popular exhibit of the old display with young and old visitors alike. Despite this, we agreed that we were content for human remains to be on display only given that (a) no group claims that the remains are those of their group's ancestors and prefers the remains not to be on display and (b) there is a valid reason for the display of the remains. We were not content for human remains to be exhibited for sensationalism or just for the sake of it.

To our knowledge no group has, to date, attempted to lay claim to any prehistoric human remains from England. However, our second concern was equally important. In the end it was decided to keep the child skeleton as a justified and relevant part of the re-display as it provided a further example of the subjectivity of interpretation and acted as an emotional handle to help bridge the gap of 5000 years between the builders of the monuments and the modern museum visitor.

Figure 13.5   The symbolic presentation of 'fact' versus 'imagination' – illustration assuming lack of 'sophistication'.

The panel above the skeleton now reads:

Charlie/Charlotte?

This may be the closest we shall ever get to someone from the neolithic world. Known to custodians and visitors as 'Charlie', this skeleton of a child has been in the museum for nearly fifty years. Yet we are not even sure whether it was a boy or a girl.

The bones are lying just as they were found in the 1920s in the outer ditch at Windmill Hill. The child was buried about 5,000 years ago, with the head facing the rising sun. The curled-up position resembles sleep: perhaps the child was expected to 'wake' again after death.

Charlie was about three or four years old. The shape of the head is odd, and some experts have suggested the child died of hydro-cephalus ('water on the brain'). However, the deformity may have been caused after death by weight of soil in the grave.

Who was 'Charlie'? And what would Charlie think of us, if we could meet?

202 P. G. STONE

The display of human remains is an extremely complex issue. However, it seems that the display of Charlie has been justified by the positive response it has provoked. To our knowledge there have been no complaints over the display of the child's remains and teachers frequently comment on the beneficial impact the remains have had on their children – turning the past from something studied in textbooks to something that really happened. The remains have also been used by teachers as a stimulus to introduce the topics of what museums should display and who controls the presentation of the past.

All new exhibitions need a period of assessment and review where the visitors put designers' ideas to the test. This review is central to any re-display and we are in the process of such a review at present. What we have tried to do in the new exhibition is to create an atmosphere where questions are raised not only about the Neolithic but also about our own understanding and presentation of the period, its objects and people. The review and clipboards should give us the opportunity to react with relative ease to the constantly changing questions that are raised by new interpretations of the Neolithic period in general and of the Avebury sites in particular.

The re-display and the National Curriculum

In National Curriculum history the content of the history study units taught to children is tested against three 'Attainment Targets' that are regarded as being the fundamental attributes of a good historian. Each Attainment Target has ten levels of attainment with only the brightest child being expected to reach level 10 at the end of their school career. These Attainment Targets are:

1 *Knowledge and understanding of history*
   The development of the ability to describe and explain historical change, and analyse different features of historical situations.
2 *Interpretations of history*
   The development of the ability to understand interpretations of history.
3 *The use of historical sources*
   The development of pupils' ability to acquire evidence from historical sources, and form judgements about their reliability and value.

(DES 1991)

With the emphasis in the re-display as described above on the subjectivity of archaeological interpretation the new museum is especially suited to the development of an understanding of the last two Attainment Targets. Specially prepared notes for teachers on how to use the museum display as a tool to develop these skills have been produced and are sent out to teachers on request. These, together with other articles in the educational literature (for example, Stone 1992) and some general DES guidelines that, for example, stress that all children 'should have opportunities to learn about the past from a range of historical sources' that include 'artifacts and buildings and sites'

(DES 1991, p. 13), begin to question the wideranging misunderstanding that there is no place for the teaching of the prehistoric past within the National Curriculum.

Given this support material, and the NCC guidelines mentioned above, it can be seen that the National Curriculum does offer a limited but potentially secure position for the teaching of at least one period of prehistory. However, the point to emphasize is that many teachers who now have the opportunity to teach about prehistory do not know enough about the subject. They need help. Museum archaeologists are in a unique position to give that help. The NCC has already published a guide to the National Curriculum for museum and site staff (NCC 1990). It cannot be emphasized too strongly that museum and site staff need to get to know the National Curriculum well and quickly. If we, as museum educators, can show teachers how they can approach a range of subject areas through visiting our museums, then they will build visits into their timetables. If we do not make these contacts, a golden opportunity will have been lost and timetables will have been filled with other work.

Conclusion

We have attempted to re-display the Alexander Keiller Museum in a way that is interesting, educational and fun. We have tried to explain some of the techniques of modern archaeology and of those antiquarians and archaeologists who have studied the monuments before us: techniques and a history that underline our contemporary understanding of the Neolithic and of these monuments in particular. We have tried to explain what we know – and to point out what we do not know – about the Avebury sites and the Neolithic. We hope we have achieved an environment that is more welcoming to visitors – be they specialist academics, general visitors, or educational groups. The museum is intended, especially for the latter, to serve as an example of how the evidence of prehistory can be accommodated within the constraints of the prescribed National Curriculum. Time alone will tell whether we have been successful.

Acknowledgements

My thanks go to Brian Davison, Tim Johnston and Patrick Adam of the project team and to Liz Hollinshead and Peter Ucko for reading and commenting on an early draft of this chapter.

Note

1 We tried to get older pupils to answer the questionnaire but unfortunately curriculum constraints (most older children tend to visit the museum later in the year) and our own timescale did not allow this to happen.

References

Atkinson, R. 1967. Interim report on excavations at Silbury Hill. *Antiquity* 41, 256–62.
Atkinson, R. 1968. Note on excavations at Silbury Hill. *Antiquity* 42, 299.
Atkinson, R. 1969. Note on excavations at Silbury Hill. *Antiquity* 43, 216.
Atkinson, R. 1970. Note on excavations at Silbury Hill. *Antiquity* 44, 313–14.
Burl, A. 1979. *Prehistoric Avebury*. New Haven: Yale University Press.
Cobham Resource Consultants 1990. Interim report on Avebury visitor survey. Unpublished.
Corbishley, M. & P. G. Stone 1994. The teaching of the past in formal school curricula in England. In *The Presented Past: heritage, museums and education*, Stone, P. G. & B. L. Molyneaux (eds), 383–97. London: Routledge.
Coupland, L. 1988. *The Avebury Monuments: a study pack for teachers*. London: English Heritage.
DES 1989. *National Curriculum: from policy to practice*. London: Department of Education & Science.
DES 1991. *History in the National Curriculum*. London: Department of Education & Science.
Hodder, I., M. Parker Pearson, N. Peck & P. G. Stone n.d. Archaeology knowledge and society. Unpublished survey material.
Hooper-Greenhill, E. 1991. *Writing a Museum Education Policy*. Leicester: Department of Museum Studies, University of Leicester.
Hubert, J. 1988. The disposition of the dead. *World Archaeological Bulletin* 2, 12–39.
Hubert, J. 1991. After the Vermilion Accord: developments in the 'reburial issue'. *World Archaeological Bulletin* 5, 113–18.
Malone, C. 1989. *The English Heritage Book for Avebury*. London: English Heritage.
NCC 1990. *Guide for Staff of Museums, Galleries, Historic Houses and Sites*. York: National Curriculum Council.
NCC 1991. *History Non-statutory Guidance*. York: National Curriculum Council.
Piggott, S. 1962. *The West Kennet Long Barrow*. London: HMSO.
Pitts, M. 1986. *Footprints through Avebury*. Avebury: Avebury Press.
Richardson, W. 1987. Isn't it all about dinosaurs? An experiment in a junior school. In *Degree Digging Dole: our future*, S. Joyce et al. (eds), 66–77. Southampton: Department of Archaeology, University of Southampton.
Stone, P. G. 1986. Are the public really interested? In *Archaeology, Politics and the Public*, C. Dobinson & R. Gilchrist (eds), 14–21. York: Department of Archaeology, University of York.
Stone, P. G. 1990a. *The First Farmers*. Southampton: Department of Archaeology, University of Southampton.
Stone, P. G. 1990b. Teaching the past, with special reference to prehistory, in English primary education. Unpublished PhD thesis, University of Southampton.
Stone, P. G. 1992. The Magnificent Seven: reasons for teaching about prehistory. *Teaching History* 69, 13–19.
Stone, P. G. 1993. Life beyond the gallery: education, archaeology and the new millennium. In Southworth E. (ed.) 'Ready for the new millennium?' Futures for museums archaeology. *The Museum Archaeologist* 17, 53–6.
Ucko, P. J., M. Hunter, A. Clark & A. David 1991. *Avebury Reconsidered from the 1660s to the 1990s*. London: Unwin Hyman.

Appendix: The twenty most common questions asked about prehistory

(In no particular order but ★ = probably the most common questions asked)

1★ Where did they go to the toilet? – How did they get rid of it?

2★ What clothes did they wear? – What were they made of? – How did they make them? – Were they really tatty? – What did they wear on their feet? – Did they have jewellery?

3★ How did they die? – How old were they when they died? – Where did they go when they died (means both how were they buried and did they go to 'heaven')?

4★ What were their houses like? – Did they have an upstairs? – What were houses made from? – Where did they sleep? – Separate rooms or all together?

5   What did they use for light?

6★ What did they wash with? – Did they wash? – Did they have brushes and combs? – Did they have make-up? – Did they cut their hair? – Did they shave?

7   What language did they speak?

8   Did they have wives? – How many?

9   What did they eat? – What animals did they hunt?

10★ Did children have to go to school?

11   How did they get around? – Did they have any kind of transport – especially when they were old and could not walk?

12   Were there any old people? – Were they looked after well?

13★ Did they have Christmas/birthdays? – Did they have parties?

14   Did they draw/do art? – What did they draw?

15   Did they have shops? – Did they have any nice things?

16★ What toys/games did they have?

17   What did they think about the world?

18★ What were their weapons like? – What were they made of?

19★ What animals did they have? – What animals didn't they have that we have now?

20   Were there any physical differences between them and us?

14 Privacy and community through medieval material culture

PHILIPPE G. PLANEL

Introduction

A gulf exists between modern children and the medieval past that is presented to them as their heritage. With regard to our view of past cultures in general, the attitude to the medieval at first glance seems paradoxical. Whereas ancient peoples, non-western cultures and even our own immediate ancestors are often seen as different from us, medieval people are commonly held to be similar. A cultural continuity does exist between us and medieval times in many aspects of our life: institutions, settlement, literature and art are rooted in this epoch. Yet our understanding of the otherness of the medieval period is impeded if we assume that medieval people were 'just like us'. On the contrary, medieval people were undoubtedly very different from us in some respects, as they had their own unique set of relations to the material and social worlds. Unfortunately, the notion of similarity between medieval times and our own is common in the teaching material prepared for schools and this has led to an inaccurate view of medieval life.

An analysis of medieval attitudes to community and privacy, as reflected in material culture, will show some of the unique aspects of medieval society and point to ways of changing the educational approach to this challenging period. It is argued that medieval material remains should be presented thematically, situated within a continuum, and interpreted across cultures as well as across time.

Current approaches to medieval times

There is a sharp contrast between the quality of recent interpretations of the material remains of prehistory and corresponding interpretations of the material remains of the medieval period. On the one hand prehistorians, in their attempts to give meaning to the archaeological record, have used methods and ideas from a wide range of disciplines, such as anthropology, psychology and geography, to discover the people and society behind the sites and artefacts. Translated into the classroom and the school visit this has meant that stone-age man is at last being rescued from 'grunter-groaner' status. On the other hand, historians and archaeologists of the medieval period have been less concerned with diversifying their interpretative methods, with the result, it seems, that the mass of medieval people have still to be rescued from caricature.

There may be many reasons for this state of affairs, but perhaps those who study the European medieval period think that documentary sources already provide an insight into medieval life that the prehistorian will never have; there is also an opinion that medieval people were very much part of western civilization and that an ethnographic approach is not appropriate in this area of study. The result is clear, however: thousands of children now visit medieval sites as part of school programmes, but the interpretative framework used to present information about the period does not help them understand medieval people, as the profound differences of life in another place and time – so obvious in the material culture – are not emphasized.

There is of course much that is right about the current approach towards interpreting medieval sites to children. Typically, on a visit to a medieval site, relationships are established between the wealth of a family or a dynasty and the way this wealth is expressed, in innovations and refinements in building techniques and architectural features made in line with changing needs. Chimneys, fireplaces, garderobes (lavatories), larger window openings, door-stops and other features all demonstrate advances away from the bleak Norman keep with its purely military imperatives. The children may also be shown the many activities that were carried out in a medieval castle or manor-house and will study these places as centres of power and local government.

This approach does not, however, sufficiently contrast medieval times with our own; medieval people are often reduced to caricature or, worse, they are portrayed as just like us, except that they dressed and ate differently and lived in different kinds of houses.

Documentary sources can rescue a number of individuals from caricature, since documentary sources were written by real medieval people, and these sources can be used by children. However, documentary sources tend to reflect the preoccupations of the tiny literate class in medieval society and can only rarely be identified directly with sites that school parties currently visit. Some sites visited by children are described in very few documentary sources, not one of which can be attributed to anyone who was directly connected with the site.

Current approaches, then, tend to be literal and task-orientated. It is true that children are encouraged to walk around castles and find out answers for themselves, a discovery method of learning, but usually they discover fact and function rather than symbol and process.

A more imaginative interpretative framework is therefore necessary in presenting these remains. The answer does not lie in a more academic approach; it is not suggested that school-children study the development of the Romanesque arch in the hope of reconstructing medieval metaphors of life. We need to show children, with their enormous gift for imagination, the extent to which behaviour in the past may be compared with modern behaviour. There is little point in taking children from the classroom to a medieval site merely to catalogue and measure architectural features, and perhaps to populate it with a few colourful medieval personages. The aim of a site visit ought to be to enrich present lives by examining past lives. The question is: how can we use material remains to fulfil these aims?

Privacy and community

One way to use material culture in teaching may be to take a theme, such as 'privacy and community', and contrast present attitudes and practices with those of the past, as exemplified by the spatial relationships of buildings from the past compared with the spatial relationship of buildings of the present. For children this means starting with their own experience of privacy and community, in their own homes, and moving backwards and outwards – outwards because, if children understand the past better, they will perhaps be able to understand contemporary peoples with different ways of life.

When children draw plans of their own houses and compare them with those of their classmates, they realize that amidst variety there is regularity. In English houses built this century they are unlikely to find bedrooms that can only be reached by going through other bedrooms. Also, rooms for sleeping, eating and entertaining will probably be differentiated. However, for some children living in slightly older terraced houses in England this may not always be so. The back bedroom, for example, may only be reached through another bedroom. In this way, houses standing and lived in today can be shown to mark observable transitions in a continuum stretching back hundreds of years.

As well as contrasting present and past attitudes towards privacy and community, some common threads may also be sought out. The social sciences provide broad general statements about privacy, statements which may see obvious, but which have the merit of having been tested. As Adler & Rodman (1982, p. 124) observe, for example, we generally grant more personal territory and greater privacy to people with higher status. In medieval times, however, it was only at the very apex of society that people enjoyed the sort of privacy and personal space that today most people have come to take for granted; this observation may be verified by visits to medieval castles and houses. Documentary sources can be used to show that, even in the upper levels of society, bedrooms were also reception rooms, even dining-rooms, and this lack of a division between sleeping and living continued to exist until comparatively recently.

We know very little about the houses of the poorest people, but enough is known of the arrangements of houses of those of average and above-average wealth for us to say that throughout medieval society there was a very different understanding of personal space and privacy than exists today. Even a rich fourteenth-century London grocer had to find room for four beds and a cradle in his chamber (Platt 1979, p. 91). Indeed, despite huge differences in wealth and status in medieval times, there may have been more of a consensus between the medieval nobleman and 'the poor man at his gate' on this subject than that which would exist between the same medieval nobleman and the owner of a luxury house today. Life was very public in medieval times: death, dishonour, punishment and reward were all public events.

Much of medieval castle life revolved around the hall, the key public building, and there is no doubt that status and position were closely reflected in the way the hall was used. How can the most be made of this? To prompt children's imagination, teachers and educators perhaps need to have their own imaginations stirred. An ethnographic example (Jones 1981, p. 157) shows how space may be demarcated in a public building:

> The class, affiliation, rank and status of individuals is both ac-knowledged and re-affirmed on each occasion that a mixed group of individuals gather in a Waigali *atrozan* house. This is because the *ama*, the main room of the house, is regarded by them as being divided into different areas, each of which has a special quality. . . .
> The space just inside the door, between the door and the first pair of columns, is low status, the back wall opposite the door is high status. The space in between is graded so that as one walks across the room away from the door, each step takes us into an area of higher status.

Okehampton Castle, Devon, is visited by large numbers of school children. The hall of Okehampton Castle only exists as a ruined shell, yet it too carries messages as to status demarcation in its use of space (Higham 1984, p. 4):

> The horizontal edge low down in the wall plaster of the north wall reflects the upper edge of a stone bench, the base of which was recovered in excavation. The lightly built wall running across the east end of the hall represents the front edge of a raised dais. In front can be seen the remains of a large open hearth.

The hall was probably also used to transact business with tenants, tradesmen and others, who would enter by a door in the east wall from an antechamber. If children can bring to these tantalizing physical remains an understanding of the basic divisions and roles in castle life – the lord, guests, stewards, servants and other inhabitants – then the potential for constructive role-play exists on-site. However, we need not stop there. The role-play evolved by the children can then be compared with some of the known principles of social interaction, thus investing the exercise with more meaning. For example, if children act out the lord's banquet, do the seating arrangements they have chosen reflect the following statement (Porteous 1977, p. 41)? 'Much research has been performed on the spatial aspects of social dominance in small groups. Several studies have shown that persons generally regarded as leaders claim certain seating positions, notably end seats at rectangular tables.'

In fact, Okehampton, like many sites, is itself an example of several stages in a continuum. On the old motte sits the original keep, where there was practically no differentiation between public and private, whilst below lies the fourteenth-century castle where elegant south-facing lodgings looked out over the deer park. The hall was beginning its evolution towards a servants' hall.

Even luxurious fourteenth-century lodgings were semi-public bed-sitting rooms (Young 1984, p. 5) rather than bedrooms, however. When great fourteenth-century lords ate in their lodgings, it was still true that 'It is not seemly that a lord should eat alone' (Burke 1978, p. 33).

Among the most notable features of the shells of the lodgings at Okehampton, besides the garderobes, are the fireplaces. These latter features limit how much each room could be subdivided by less durable timber or wattle and daub partitions. If we allot several rooms in Okehampton Castle to its owners, the Courtenay family, and their guests, then it becomes clear that the rest of the household had to share accommodation. Late medieval households were very large, with over 130 people living at Okehampton Castle (Higham 1984, p. 2).

In a community such as Okehampton Castle, life would be lived in public. Most of the domains which we regard as private, events such as childbirth, procreation and death, and emotions such as joy, anger and grief, would be publicly known events and public emotions. Even in the better documented eighteenth-century, where witnesses in adultery trials were usually servants, 'prying curiosity clearly made sexual privacy almost impossible for anyone of standing who wished to conduct a discreet affair' (Stone 1979, p. 170).

Dressing up as medieval people is currently a popular activity on sites visited by school-children, but putting on the outward apparel of medieval people will not, of itself, help us get 'under the skin' of our predecessors. It is also appropriate to study foreign cultures to understand the foreign nature of behaviour in the past, namely cultures where the private domain is much less clearly defined than in our own culture and where private concerns are expressed publicly.

For any inhabitants of a medieval castle, some of whom would sleep 'on benches along the walls [of the hall] upon filled palliases, or simply on a carpet of rushes and herbs on the floor' (Burke 1978, p. 33), there was no privacy in the way we understand the term; personal space was not delimited by physical barriers. Does this mean that no privacy or personal space existed? This is not a question that the documentary historian is necessarily best placed to answer. As Altman (1981, p. 42) observes:

> If one examines carefully a culture with seemingly little privacy, privacy mechanisms will eventually be uncovered. . . . Some cultures may appear to have little privacy, but this is probably due to a

traditional view of privacy as solely a physical environment process and not a complex behavioural system that draws on many levels of functioning.

Ethnographic examples and other sources from the social sciences do not serve as parallels, but they remind us that in medieval culture, dress, language, attitude and 'body language' may have granted non-physical privacy: 'The Yagua of the Amazon live in a large open house and achieve "privacy" through a social convention which allows someone to become "absent" and, in effect, invisible, by turning away from the centre of the house' (Rapaport 1969, p. 66).

The ethnographic evidence also opens up other dimensions. For example, studies of villages in Brazil where there is little physical privacy in the immediate living environment reveal sheltered places outside the village where private acts and associations could be carried out (Altman 1981, p. 12). Such evidence allows us to be more imaginative in our understanding of the relationship of a castle to its immediate surroundings. We tend only to think of known archaeological and historical entities such as deer parks, fields and forests. Studies of communities where the physical environment cannot be used to give basic privacy demonstrate a certain amount of ribaldry and teasing about bodily functions (Altman 1981, p. 38). A reading of Chaucer confirms that this was indeed a dimension of medieval life. It has been argued that it was only gradually, with the spread of Renaissance 'civility', that we find 'the physical withdrawal of the individual body and its waste products from others' (Stone 1979, p. 171).

Uses and abuses of a multidisciplinary approach

Anthropology and history have run separate courses since the eighteenth century, yet, as Cohn observes (1987, p. 19), the two disciplines are united by a number of factors: 'Historians and anthropologists have a common subject matter, "otherness"; one field constructs otherness in space, the other in time. . . . Both forms of knowledge entail the act of translation.'

A late medieval lord and his establishment lived a life so different from ours that the translating skills of both the historian and the archaeologist are necessary. According to Young (1984, p. 5):

> The life of a great lord was lived to a complicated ritual designed to emphasize his position and importance. Every aspect of his life from getting up in the morning to going to bed at night would be surrounded by this ritual of which the peak would be attained at meal times, when the lord's food was served in a complicated ceremonial culminating in a magnificent procession from the kitchen to his chamber.

There are of course limitations to the use of ethnographic examples; many are taken from non-stratified societies where the concept and experience of privacy are usually more uniform. For a highly stratified community such as a medieval castle, where behaviour was enforced from above, it may be more relevant to examine sociological studies such as those of Goffman (1961) on 'total institutions', where inmates, like the lower ranks of castle servants, perhaps, are so rigidly controlled as to allow no 'role separation', no privacy, in their lives.

Anthropologists and ethnographers are also hampered by the lack of any temporal dimension. Cultural stereotypes become social facts fixed in time. For example, English reserve and reticence are contrasted with Mediterranean or Arabic traits, the latter being 'highly sensory, with people interacting at very close quarters' (Altman 1981, p. 62). Medieval English traits may well have been highly sensory too!

Filling in the gaps in the continuum

In northern Europe we are not fully aware of the extent to which our cultural preconceptions about privacy and community stem from comparatively recent, late nineteenth-century improvements in housing across most of the social scale. Differentiation in room use is therefore a relatively recent phenomenon. We are perhaps not surprised to read that 'The great houses of the fifteenth and sixteenth centuries had been constructed of interlocking suites of rooms without corridors, so that the only way of moving about was by passing through other people's chambers' (Stone 1979, p. 169).

However, more surprisingly, as Muthesius notes:

> Most historians of working-class housing categorically deplore the lack of privacy in this early period [the early nineteenth century], seemingly unaware that the notion of privacy was relatively new even in better-class housing. . . .
>
> Even in the later 18th century we find grand terraced houses where not even all the best rooms were separately accessible.
>
> (1982, pp. 138, 144)

Artefacts and privacy

The continuity of daily life and living space which characterized medieval castles, villages and towns should not be confused with a community of interests. Another element of material culture, an artefact rather than a building, can be used to demonstrate this point.

Keys were widely used in medieval society; the extent of their use can be seen in the 'Drainage Collection' in Salisbury Museum. This collection features dozens of keys dredged from the medieval waterways of Salisbury in the nineteenth century. Today we, and 'we' includes children, use keys to protect personal space and to protect property. We use a key both to lock ourselves into our rooms and to lock things up in our rooms. The existence of keys on a medieval archaeological site is evidence of social differentiation, because their use, for the protection of both space and property, was confined to the upper echelons of the social pyramid. The medieval castle may well have resembled a 'total institution' in this respect; those who held the keys and those who did not had a very different set of interests.

A wider view

The physical boundaries of castles and small defended settlements define a communal living space more akin to courtyards in Moslem countries than the built environment of modern Europe. The buildings in modern streets face outwards, whereas the outer bailey of a castle and the outer wall of a Moslem courtyard are relatively featureless and face inwards, with repercussions for the people, and sense of community, inside. Walls serve to define a community, to mark it off from nature or from other communities, and it is useful to consider the extent to which supposedly defensive walls serve this function.

The medieval walls of Southampton are termed defensive, but perhaps this is not the whole story. If Southampton's town walls were built to keep people out, why were the most vulnerable parts in the circuit, the quays, undefended? French raiders were able to disembark and walk into the town in 1338 (Planel 1986, pp. 21–2). Carelessness? Or were walls and castles as much about status and demarcation as safety and defence? Were churches and cathedrals as much about communal pride and display as buildings to pray in?

Prehistorians ponder on the symbolic role of Stonehenge and prehistoric art, yet interpreters of the medieval past are rarely willing to consider buildings, features and artefacts as metaphors. We attribute our rationality to those who lived in the medieval past, a 'foreign country' in which, in all probability, we would only just be able to make ourselves understood. In any case medieval people were non-rational, they were haunted with hopes and fears: we need look no further than the medieval eschatology of death or notions of medicine. The medieval system of belief was to a great extent based on superstition. We should not seek total rationality in the material remains of such a culture.

Conclusion

'Privacy and community' is only one of the themes through which the material remains of the medieval period can reveal differences between ourselves and inhabitants of the past. Others themes could be 'subsistence', 'power and control' and 'belief'. One of the problems with interpreting any particular period without reference to a continuum is that these periods become frozen in time. In reality periods in the past are like geological strata; they represent stages in a process that continues today. History is also non-linear. Open-plan offices, open-plan homes, and mixed wards in hospitals are now standing nineteenth- and early twentieth-century notions of privacy on their heads.

In practical terms there is a need for agencies such as English Heritage to present heritage as a continuous and continuing process. There is little in Okehampton Castle that average school-children will immediately recognize as their own heritage. In fact the word 'heritage', like the French word *patrimoine*, seems to be used most often when there is actually a discontinuity with the past. However, if the past is treated thematically, rather than as a number of hermetically sealed time capsules which we can from time to time open, then children can not only see where they came from, but how they got where they are.

As to the theme of 'community and privacy', children should be able to see some of the steps in the journey between Okehampton Castle and their modern homes. And they need to stop off at other stages in the continuum, for example in a block of industrial 'back-to-back' houses in the north of England where people had achieved a degree of privacy in their homes and yet had to walk past other houses to get to the toilet blocks. In fact English Heritage does consider 'back-to-back' houses as heritage and also helps councils and other bodies buy, restore and maintain such properties, but these elements have yet to form part of a thematic whole in presentation, particularly where interpreting these aspects of material culture to children is concerned (although see Corbishley & Stone 1994).

History teaching in all English and Welsh schools is now directed by the National Curriculum. Whilst the National Curriculum for history provides scope for a thematic approach in some areas, it does not do so for settlement and the built environment. This past, for the present, will have to wait.

References

Adler, R. B. & G. Rodman 1982. *Understanding Human Communication*. New York: Holt, Rinehart & Winston.

Altman, I. 1981. *The Environment and Social Behaviour*. Monterey, Calif.: Brooks-Cole.

Burke, J. 1978. *Life in the Castle in Medieval England*. Totowa, N.J.: Rowman & Littlefield.

Cohn, B. S. 1987. *An Anthropologist among the Historians*. Oxford: Oxford University Press.

Corbishley, M. & P. G. Stone 1994. The teaching of the past in formal school curricula in England. In *The Presented Past: heritage, museums and education*, Stone, P. G. & B. L. Molyneaux (eds), 383–97. London: Routledge.

Goffman, E. 1961. *Asylums*. New York: Anchor Books.

Higham, R. A. 1984. *Okehampton Castle*. London: English Heritage.

Jones, S. 1981. Institutionalised inequalities in Nuristan. In *Social Inequality*, Berreman, G. D. (ed.), 151–62. New York: Academic Press.

Muthesius, S. 1982. *The English Terraced House*. New Haven: Yale University Press.
Planel, P. 1986. *Southampton Town Walls*. Southampton: Southampton Teachers' Centre.
Platt, C. 1979. *The English Medieval Town*. London: Secker & Warburg.
Porteous, J. D. 1977. *Environment and Behaviour: planning and everyday urban life*. Reading, Mass.: Addison-Wesley.
Rapaport, A. 1969. *House Form and Culture*. Englewood Cliffs, N.J.: Prentice-Hall.
Stone, L. 1979. *The Family: sex and marriage in England 1500–1800*. London: Penguin Books.
Young, C. J. 1984. The history and planning of Minster Lovell Hall. Lecture to Oxfordshire County Council in-service training course.

15 What is the public's perception of museum visiting in Poland?

ANDREZEJ MIKOŁAJCZYK

Informing the public

Museums in Poland have been in serious crisis in recent years (Mikołajczjk 1990), in contrast to the situation in many other countries, where museums have thrived. The problems have emerged from the many years of unfavourable operating conditions, especially after the economic troubles following the imposition of martial law in December 1981 (Fig. 15.1) by the falling Communist regime. The changes that are now taking place in Poland, however, present both a challenge and an opportunity for museums, as they need to attract new audiences to survive. This is not an easy goal. The acquisition, conservation and storage of objects, the conducting of research, and the exhibition of collections can all be achieved directly; investing the collections with a value and conveying their meanings and those of archaeological sites and monuments to the public, however, must be achieved through indirect means.

Measuring public response is a problem, since the influence of a museum on the consciousness of individuals and groups is overwhelmed by the impact of newspapers and the broadcasting media, and the activities of pressure groups and propaganda.

Because the public needs to be informed, museums are now being shaken from their long-standing complacency and are being galvanized into action. Traditional museum practice is now being questioned both from within the museum field and from without. What is a museum for, and how does it relate to other institutions in society? If it is claimed that a museum is a place where objects are investigated, collected, documented and exhibited for the benefit of people, what is it that people want or need? And how can museologists best serve the interests of their communities, now and in the future?

The need for museums to be successful may be illusory and perhaps one should ask whether the primary reasons for their existence are becoming outmoded, and whether there is now a conflict of purpose between provider and customer. It is hoped that most people have a positive image of museums,

Figure 15.1 Armoured vehicles moving against Solidarity in December 1981 as seen through a window of the Archaeological and Ethnographical Museum in Łódź. Photo: T. Karpinski & W. Pohorecki.

however, even if they do not often visit them, and so perhaps there is still a readiness in the public to be persuaded that museums have something to offer. The important goal is to determine what the public's perception of museum visiting is.

The museum environment

Polish museums are poorly designed, frequently outdated and schematic on the one hand, and limited by a lack of funds on the other. The exhibition rooms, like the buildings as a whole, are not properly fitted for modern displays. In Łódź, for example, the Archaeological and Ethnographical Museum (founded in 1931), one of 545 museums in Poland, was regarded as one among 44 museums of special significance for the national heritage. The archaeological and ethnographic research conducted in Poland, along with the activities of the numismatic department, have created a collection of about 200,000 items. The collections are carefully studied, treated in conservation workshops, published in the museum's journal *Prace i Materiały Muzeum Archaeolgicznego i Etnograficzenego w Łódźi*, and exhibited. In contrast to its extensive research programmes, however, the exhibition room is small, a bottleneck blocking any reasonable access to the objects themselves as well as the information explaining the cultural and historical context of the exhibits.

Here the Polish museums recall a sad story of the entire post-war period, when no new museum buildings (with perhaps one or two exceptions) were constructed; in their place, a number of old buildings were more or less efficently adapted as museums. In a country that devotes so much attention to architectural heritage protection, the lack of a museum building programme seems to be an unbelievable paradox. The old manors, towers, castles, palaces, town halls, and other exceptional and ordinary buildings that were adapted as museums have many functional problems: small rooms, bad lighting, lack of security systems and inadequate staircases are the everyday features faced by museum staff and visitors.

It was the building investments policy of the Government in the last decades that suspended construction in favour of restoration, and they encouraged restoration no matter how expensive it was. The museum people were told that they should feel happy that any work was to be done at all. And now it is very difficult to make our visitors feel that way when they visit a museum.

Museums and community: the Archaeological and Ethnographical Museum at Łódź

In spite of these problems, the museums try to be community-oriented institutions. For example, when it comes to facilities, many museums with the right attitudes and enough space, such as the Archaeological and Ethnographical Museum in Łódź, do encourage local societies with relevant interests to make use of them for meetings.

The Łódź Museum closely co-operates with the Polish Archaeological and Numismatic Society and with the recently founded Scientific Association of Polish Archaeologists. In the past thirty years the members of the Archaeological and Numismatic Society have met twice a month in the museum, attending lectures and arranging temporary exhibitions of coins and medals, some of which were quite popular. Particularly in the last decade the society arranged regular archaeological conferences and exhibitions, reporting on recent excavations carried out by different institutions.

During the troubles of the last few years the museum was regarded as the base for the integration of the archaeological community in central Poland. The coin collectors, in particular, were strongly influenced by the museum. The Numismatic Department is excellently run and has its own exhibitions and publications, and it has a policy of giving assistance to collectors. And as the museum is a seat of the Committee of Numismatic Collections, part of the Polish National Committee of ICOM, it is held in high esteem by the

Numismatic Society members. Thus visiting the museum is a special kind of social event for them, at once private and public, formal and informal. This spirit of co-operation contributed greatly to a better understanding of the museum's task in protecting the cultural heritage, including coin hoards and stray finds, and this has led to the donation of many coins by the public.

The development of numismatics is a good example of why the role of a museum in the community is so important, as it can grow in strength and stature if it takes the needs of the public into account.

School education at the Łódź Museum

Given the size and extent of the Łódź Museum's holdings, the public's perception of museum visiting is a serious issue, as the institution has a considerable potential for education.

The educational goals of museum staff in contact with young people should be to help them appreciate the museum as a learning resource available throughout their lives. If this is not done, museums may run the risk of appearing too closely associated with school visits, and hence being set aside as young people mature.

In Łódź, the school curriculum had numerous gaps in its coverage of the past, and so the museum was inspired to develop educational links with local primary and secondary schools. School-teachers and other educationalists were encouraged to use the museum for teaching, especially for history and geography, and a series of conferences was held to attract teachers who had initial hesitations.

The museum supported this educational project by creating permanent exhibitions on central Poland's prehistory and the early Middle Ages, subjects which correspond to the themes and events covered in the textbooks. It also produced films about archaeology, ethnography and ancient history. The films are quite popular among school-children, so they often tell us. The interest of teachers and children is also engaged by activities and competitions sponsored by the museum; in late 1989, competitions devoted to the Greeks and their ancient civilization and to Christmas-tree decorations attracted many hundreds of pupils, from almost fifty primary schools.

Needless to say, a curriculum transformed into exhibitions helped teachers present both prehistory and history in a comprehensive way for primary-school children, but what is ideal for these students is not accepted in the same positive way by older children and adults. Visitors come with widely differing interests and propensities to learn, but adults should not simply be offered information at the same level as the children. However, the museum caters to school-children, since they are the majority of visitors, and so the interests of older groups are not satisfied. In any event, the resources of the museum educational officer are largely taken up with this primary education programme. Since the archaeological displays on central Poland's prehistory and

Figure 15.2 Fashion show to attract the public. Photo: T. Karpinski & W. Pohorecki.

early Middle Ages suited the expectations of the school system, therefore, they have remained in place for a long time, in spite of growing criticism.

The unspoken pressure to maintain the current programme continues, since the museum has been discovered by schools to be a useful and inspiring resource. In fact, when another local museum reduced its educational programme, the Archaeological and Ethnographical Museum almost immediately inherited its clientele.

The museum and the public

The limited space available for other permanent exhibitions has led to a choice of one topic, the folk-art of the traditional Polish village, while the rest of the vast domain of ethnographic cultures is represented in a sequence of temporary displays. Temporary exhibitions are best in a city as polluted as Łódź; dust falls everywhere and penetrates the closed windows and display cases, destroying the beauty of any exhibit over time. It is an unexpected environmental impact on the visitors' perception of the museum. Because of this problem the museum once held an archaeological exhibition of prehistoric costume, reconstructed according to excavated evidence, outside museum walls. It was in the form of a fashion show and attracted large crowds (Fig. 15.2).

Although the permanent exhibitions remained so long that many visitors objected, the museum took special care in developing the temporary displays. The idea of portraying the vast range of human cultures, past and present, was to provide much scope for creativity and flexibility, drawing on the strengths of the museum – its humanistic purpose, the quality of the collection, and its technical and economic facilities. As usual, the latter are the Achilles heel, which can reduce even the brightest idea to a dark or grey reality.

As a most important first step, we consulted the public to find out what they wanted in an exhibit that they were not able to get from the permanent exhibitions. Taking into account advice given both by the museum staff and visitors (from interviews, remarks written in the visitors' book, phone calls and other contacts with students, school-teachers and our colleagues from other museums), we complemented the permanent exhibitions with subjects that reflected public interest and were intended to lift up people's spirits in the troubled 1980s. Public opinion was reflected in a series of exhibitions related to aspects of Polish culture in the past.

'Polish Folk-dress' presented a panorama of regional, traditional costumes from the first half of the twentieth century (Fig. 15.3); 'Bread is Made' showed the ethics of labour in the countryside, centred on the making of bread as the basic food and the symbol of survival of the Polish people, with all its cultural implications (Fig. 15.4); 'The Archaeological Pedigree of Manors' showed the evolution of the gentry's residences in Poland from the fourteenth to late eighteenth century; and 'Polish Folk-art' and 'Polish Folk-sculpture' were formal displays of peasants' art of the late nineteenth and twentieth century.

Several exhibitions from Hungary, Russia, Sweden and Czechoslovakia have related to the prehistory, ethnography and coinage of our neighbours. Numismatic exhibitions such as 'Early Medieval hoards of Silver in Poland' and 'Currencies of the Wars from the Eighteenth to Twentieth Century' emphasized the value of the coins as witnesses to history, and not only as items for collecting. Other exhibitions, such as 'Polish Historical Commemorative Medals', appealed to national and independent tradition. 'Polish Christmas', devoted to the most respected and celebrated holiday in the life of Polish family and community and related to the feelings and aspirations of the people, opened in spite of obstacles put in the way by higher authorities. The exhibit was warmly received and appreciated by the visitors, clearly demonstrating the links between the museum and community.

In response to visitors' suggestions, the museum also sets up displays of recent acquisitions: the results of each archaeological season as well as the ethnographic and numismatic additions to the collections. These are an important instrument in public relations for the museum, as they show the public the current interests and research activities.

The museum cinema, which offers free access on Sundays, has focused its repertoire on films of prehistoric, historic and ethnographic sites and monuments. Unfortunately, the regular audience is small. The visitors prefer the films devoted to ancient Mediterranean civilizations, but the availability of such pictures is rather limited in Poland. Every two years a festival of

Figure 15.3 Polish folk costumes exhibited temporarily in the Archaeological and Ethnographical Museum in Łódź as well as in other Polish and foreign museums. Photo: T. Karpinski & W. Pohorecki.

ethnographic films is also held. Videos produced in Poland and occasionally received free from foreign institutions have also been introduced, and this has enlarged the cinema repertoire considerably.

Museums and the family

Museums tend to have aims, principles and curricula intended to develop educational links beyond schools. But what about the kindergartens and the early primary-school grades? The issue is a serious one. Łódź has a large textile industry employing thousands of women who work in large factories in the three-shift system; the problem of taking care of young children is therefore of great social and educational importance. What can serious museums do for such children? Łódź had a long tradition of concern about this problem and in 1980 found a solution – puppet shows, produced by a new department entirely devoted to this popular traditional art. As they originate from folk-customs, the puppet shows transmit both the folklore of traditional culture and universal values, such as the struggle between good and evil. This new venture was immediately supported by Polish puppet theatres as it finally provided a way for the museum to stimulate a child's aesthetic sensibility and popularize folk-traditions.

Figure 15.4 'Before bread can be made the harvested rye must be threshed in a barn' – reconstruction at the temporary exhibition appeals more to the visitor's imagination. Photo: T. Karpinski & W. Pohorecki.

When museum doors begin to open for the youngest people, they help to instil in them the value of museum visiting. The first exhibitions were received enthusiastically by both children and their parents.

When the public are given direct access to objects in handling sessions, museum educators can offer them the possibility of taking the first step in interpreting a part of the world, a way of enabling them to be in control of their own learning process that is restorative and leads to self-respect. Learning from real things and real places is the method that has been used for many years by the educational officers of the Archaeological and Ethnographical Museum in Łódź. School-children who show a special interest in archaeology or ethnography are invited to join the Inter-School Circle of the Lovers of Archaeology and Ethnography. Attending monthly meetings in the museum they advance their knowledge and interest through direct contact with museum archaeologists, ethnographers and with the excavated objects.

One of the frequent questions asked by these young people is how archaeological sites are excavated; the only answer is to take them to the excavations. During the summer holidays, young people are able to join the excavations, spending two weeks at different sites. From the mid-1980s this programme has been arranged with the necessary support of the educational authorities. The young people are thrilled by this trip into the countryside – so important, as they live in an industrial centre – and it reflects the idea of a museum as an institution where informal learning takes place. Perhaps this programme reveals, in some sense, the strength of the museum: the institution to some extent controls its own framework and can reinterpret objects, and, at the same time, can offer people the opportunity to make their own meanings and interpretations.

Museums should develop clear policies and both long- and short-term objectives in relation to their public, as they can help the people through difficult times in their political, social and economic life, such as they have experienced in Poland over the last decade.

Reference

Mikołajczyk, A. 1990. Children and the past in Poland: archaeology and prehistory in primary schools and museums. In *The Excluded Past: archaeology in education*, Stone, P. and R. MacKenzie (eds), 252–61. London: Unwin Hyman; Routledge pbk 1994.

16 Museums and their messages: the display of the pre- and early colonial past in the museums of South Africa, Botswana and Zimbabwe

ARON MAZEL & GABY RITCHIE

Introduction

South Africa is on the threshold of major change. Indeed, one of the most commonly used political clichés in South Africa today is 'the new South Africa'. What does this cliché imply and what is the 'new South Africa' going to herald? Is it simply going to mean a change in power-holders, leaving many of the relations of domination intact, or will there be fundamental changes affecting the entire fabric of society?

The struggle for the 'new South Africa' has been fought on many different terrains and with varying intensities. Political struggles will always involve rival claims to knowledge. On the education front, battles have been fought on the streets and in the classrooms. But education is not only about teachers, children and students and what happens in classrooms and lecture theatres. Rather there exists a battery of social institutions that provide public education in one form or another. Museums are among these institutions. In addressing perceptions and understandings, we need to examine ideas being perpetuated through educational institutions and, specific to this chapter, how museums have served to entrench particular notions.

One of the key roles that museums play is to present information about what happened in the past. As Lumley (1988a, p. 2) commented: 'Museums, precisely because their function has been to present ideas to a wider public in three-dimensional and accessible forms, have been an important vehicle for representing the past.' History, we argue, is not simply a 'set of facts' about the past but rather a set of ideas about the past held in the present. From this it follows that, museums with history displays, in whatever form, are not, and cannot claim to be, neutral institutions. On the contrary, it is now becoming widely accepted that museums as social institutions embody and reflect the dominant values, norms, beliefs and ideas of the societies in which they are situated. It follows then that, because museums are mostly controlled by dominant groups, they are institutions in which dominant interpretations and versions of the past are popularized and presented through display.

Museums give physical expression to particular ideas. Whether audio-visual, artefactual or textual, all presentations are ideologically loaded. This does not mean that museum displays in themselves create public understanding, as education takes place in numerous contexts and through many different media. But museum displays can certainly be said to influence public perceptions, particularly of history. Museums attempt to make history 'come alive' through the presentation of objects (the more 'authentic' the objects available for display, the better), through the presentation of realistic 'reconstructions' in the form of period rooms, dioramas, living history museums and so on.

If we are to bring about fundamental change in the education sphere, and particularly in museums, it is necessary for us to be clear about the nature and content of messages communicated through the presentation of history. It is acknowledged that in the museum context, ideology is reflected not only in the displays but in all spheres of the institution, such as the education and research programmes, and in the formulation of collecting policies. For example, it is a specific understanding of 'our world' that informs collections policy and strategy in museums, which then to a large degree influences the content of what is made available and accessible to the public in the form of displays. In this chapter, however, we have a specific focus – the presentation of pre- and early colonial history in, first, the museums of Natal and KwaZulu (which, although having a definite regional character, do in many ways reflect the portrayal of relations of domination to be found in South African museums) and, second, in the museums of Zimbabwe and Botswana.

In order to gain a better understanding of museum presentations of early and precolonial history in South Africa, it is necessary to examine a host of other issues. The first question that comes to mind is 'To what extent are South African presentations simply apartheid-based?' Is it not too simplistic to see the problems within the South African museums (racist presentations, exclusions, bias and the dominant themes of white history) as exclusively the problems of legislated apartheid? If apartheid and its associated racism are the informing principles behind displays of precolonial history in South Africa, then the displays in Zimbabwe and Botswana, countries no longer bridled by the political yoke of colonial control, should be fundamentally different. One of the methods that can be used to assess this is to examine the presentation of gatherer-hunter and herder history in the museums of Zimbabwe and Botswana. The main object of this study, therefore, was to ascertain the extent to which the problematic presentations in South Africa were only apartheid-derived phenomena, and to what extent they were based on more deep-rooted perceptions, attitudes and practices.

The two case studies that follow differ in that the study of museums in Natal and KwaZulu present the finds of an extensive survey of close on thirty museums whilst the Zimbabwe and Botswana study concentrates on two displays. These studies are nevertheless complementary as they are both informed by the same theoretical positions and are both concerned with the critical examination of museum displays of pre- and early colonial history.

History in the museums of Natal and KwaZulu

The aim of the project to be reported here was to investigate how pre- and early colonial history was portrayed in the museums of Natal and KwaZulu. The latter is a nominally independent homeland situated primarily within the province of Natal. This survey was conducted by one of us (AM) and John Wright in 1987 and the following case study draws heavily on their published reports (Wright & Mazel 1987, 1991). While some of the displays may have changed and new ones been mounted, the patterning reflected in Table 16.1 essentially still characterizes the museums of Natal and KwaZulu. When we initiated the study we did not anticipate finding much relating to early history, but we did expect to find sufficient material to enable us to discern some patterning in the displays. However, we found less than expected. The project was then expanded to focus not only on the presences but also on the absences.

Concerning the museums of Natal, it is evident from Table 16.1 that the displays in these museums are completely dominated by European settler history until the 1920s, with few displays relating to early colonial and precolonial history. The displays that do exist on the latter are generally of poor quality, out of date and do not convey any sense of history. There are no displays on evolution and the Stone Age displays are mostly small and uninformative. At the time of our 1987 survey there were no rock-painting displays which even attempted to interpret the paintings. Displays consisted entirely of painted stones that have been removed from rock shelters and/or copies and pictures of paintings. Since then the Himeville Museum has erected a small interpretive display which introduces new explanatory concepts about rock-paintings. Displays on the African farming communities occur at only two museums. One of the museums (Greytown) had a mix of dated pottery on display while the other (Spioenkop) is a stone-walled archaeological site which had been excavated and converted into a site-museum. More prevalent in these museums are static ethnic displays which deal with the 'Bushmen' or the 'Zulu'.

Different emphases are evident in the museums of KwaZulu (Table 16.1). Here the focus is on the nineteenth-century Zulu Kingdom and in particular the Zulu Royal House and its associates, and to a lesser extent on 'traditional Zulu' material culture and iron age archaeology. In the KwaZulu Cultural Museum in Ulundi there are small exhibits on the Stone Age and rock-paintings, and the only reference to human evolution is on an A4 sheet of paper.

To contextualize the previous discussion, it is necessary to elaborate briefly on what is known about the early and precolonial past of the areas under consideration. Extensive archaeological research has been done in this region over the last two decades. There have been several excavation projects that cover the last 100,000 years of gatherer-hunter history, and especially the last 10,000 years. Rock-paintings have also been extensively researched over the last three decades. This research has taken place mostly in the Natal

Table 16.1 Themes displayed and themes omitted in the museums of Natal and KwaZulu. The museums in Ulundi fall under the KwaZulu Monuments Council while the rest fall under the white-controlled state, provincial and municipal authorities (after Wright & Mazel 1987, 1991).

	Evolution of human species	'Stone Age'	Rock paintings	'Bushman Ethnic' display	'Iron Age'	Zulu kingdom	'Zulu Ethnic' display	Precolonial African–European contacts	European settler history
Colenso	–	–	–	–	–	–	–	–	×
Dundee	–	–	×	–	–	–	×	–	×
Durban									
Killie Campbell	–	–	–	–	–	–	×	–	×
Local history	–	–	–	–	–	–	–	×	×
Natural history	–	–	×	×	–	–	×	–	–
Eshowe	–	–	–	–	–	–	×	–	×
Estcourt	–	–	–	–	–	–	–	–	×
Giants Castle	–	×	×	×	–	–	–	–	×
Greytown	–	×	–	×	×	–	–	–	×
Himeville	–	–	×	–	–	–	×	–	×
Kokstad	–	–	×	–	–	–	–	–	–
Ladysmith	–	–	–	–	–	–	–	–	×
Mngungundlovu									
Dinganstat	–	×	–	–	–	–	×	–	×
Mngungundlovu site	–	–	–	–	–	×	–	–	–
Newcastle	–	–	–	–	–	–	–	–	×
Pietermaritzburg									
Macrorie House	–	–	–	–	–	–	–	–	×
Natal Museum	–	–	×	×	–	–	×	–	×
Voortrekker Museum	–	–	–	–	–	–	–	–	×
Pinetown	–	–	–	–	–	–	–	–	×
Richmond	–	–	–	–	–	–	–	–	×
Spioenkop	–	–	–	–	×	–	–	–	×
Stanger									
Shaka Monument	–	–	–	–	–	×	×	–	–
Stanger Museum	–	–	–	–	–	×	×	–	×
Ulundi									
KwaZulu Cultural Museum	×	×	×	–	×	×	×	–	–
Nodwengu	–	–	–	–	–	×	–	–	–
Ondini site museum	–	–	–	–	×	×	×	–	–
Vryheid	–	–	–	–	–	–	–	–	×
Weenen	–	–	–	–	–	–	–	–	×

Drakensberg, probably the most comprehensively recorded rock-painting area in South Africa. Paintings from the Natal Drakensberg have been extensively used in the development of the most recent interpretations of rock-paintings. The history of the African farming communities that have occupied Natal from around AD 250 has also been the focus of several large research projects. Much of this research has concentrated on the period before AD 1000 but sufficient is known about aspects of the later period to mount displays on them. Numerous aspects of eighteenth- and nineteenth-century history of the region have been extensively researched. Thus, there exists a considerable amount of information on the early history of the region under consideration here.

How then do we account for this overwhelming neglect of pre- and early colonial history in the museums displays of Natal and KwaZulu and how do we account for the evident biases? Why is it that the majority of displays on African people in the museums of Natal are in the form of static ethnic displays? What are the reasons for the displays in the KwaZulu museums having such a strong emphasis on the nineteenth-century Zulu Royal House and the relationship of the current KwaZulu leadership to that period? Why are there not more displays which deal with the history of the gatherer-hunters and African farming communities? We shall first concentrate on the museums in Natal.

Many museum personnel would argue that the reason for exclusions is simply because there is insufficient display material. But this is not the case, because for the precolonial period the range of surviving original objects is greater than commonly thought. Moreover, displays do not have to be object-orientated, and can be mounted using a variety of techniques such as photographs, maps and line drawings. In the museums examined, such techniques were put to good use in many of the displays on European settler history and can be used effectively for the earlier periods.

A greater problem has been the slowness with which academics have made available the information they have generated. In addition many museum personnel have not sought out current research findings. This, however, can only be used as a partial explanation for the biases and omissions that exist in the displays. Of more significance is the influence, however subtly and unconsciously it manifests itself, of the ideologies of Natal's dominant groups in the shaping of the 'official' and public attitudes to the past, and hence of museum display policies and practices. As Wright & Mazel (1991, p. 65) have argued:

> Whatever the overt or immediate motives behind the mounting of displays, their primary ideological function is starkly clear. They register white settler occupation of land assumed to be empty of inhabitants. They serve to legitimise private ownership of that land by a small group of families. They serve to make the history of white settler communities synonymous with the history of

'progress', and thus to justify continued white domination of blacks. They shut out the history of an African 'peasant' class and of an African working class, and serve to deny the claims of African people in the present to more land and to a greater share in the products of their own labour.

By ignoring the history of the African population and at the same time highlighting the period which saw the rise in, and entrenchment of power by, the white landed gentry and merchants, these displays make a profound political statement. It must be emphasized that by the 1920s the 'success story' was complete and that there are no displays for the subsequent period. From the 1920s onwards we begin to enter into the period from which there are still people living today who would be able to dispute claims made in museums.

If there is no place for African people in Natal's colonial history, then there can be no acknowledgement that the region has a precolonial past. For this reason it is best to deny this past, for to declare it would raise a host of sensitive and uncomfortable questions. For example, the decimation of Natal's gatherer-hunter population between the 1840s and 1880s would have to be dealt with. But, clearly, while one can deny the African population a history, their *existence* cannot be denied. The most convenient way to deal with this problem is to relegate them into separate, static, ethnic displays which deal with people in a fixed and standardized way, and which by their very nature promote ethnic separatism. The beliefs which such displays represent can be traced back, first, to the British tradition of Africanist anthropology that played a significant part in formulating the divide-and-rule policies of successive colonial administrations, and second, to apartheid ideology which has been the cornerstone of South Africa's race policies.

While the museums of Natal serve to emphasize white settler history and *their* domination of this region, the KwaZulu museums serve to promote the ideological requirements of the current KwaZulu leadership. As mentioned earlier, while the displays in these museums cover various aspects of the archaeology of the areas that constitute KwaZulu, the emphasis is on nineteenth-century and present Zulu royalty and those associated with them.

The legitimacy of the present KwaZulu leadership is asserted in two ways in the displays. First, it is asserted by portraying the Zulu Royal House as deriving its authority unproblematically from its hereditary position rather than from the decree of the South African state. There is no recognition, for example, that after the overthrow of the Zulu monarchy in 1879 successive kings were not recognized as such by the colonial authorities. Even then kings were only recognized when it was convenient to do so in terms of the implementation of apartheid policy and the development of homelands. Giving expression to such factors would undermine the impression being officially promoted at present that the royalty and the KwaZulu leadership derive their power from their heritage and not from powers devolved by the apartheid state. Second, another aim of many of the displays is to portray the

Chief Minister of KwaZulu, Chief Mangosuthu Buthelezi, as one of the 'natural' leaders of the 'Zulu' people by virtue of his close relationship with, and genealogical relationship to, the Royal House. Not only are there numerous pictures depicting Chief Buthelezi at official functions – sometimes alone and at other times with the King – but his name is commonly enshrined on plaques and inscriptions detailing how he led fundraising campaigns or unveiled gravestones.

The 'absences' in the museums of KwaZulu include, among other things, there being no mention of civil wars and disputes within the Zulu Royal House and tensions between the leadership and the underclasses in the nineteenth and twentieth centuries. Mention of these would threaten the myth of past and present Zulu unity that is strongly advocated by the current leadership. The emphasis on, and the need to maintain, this unity can only be fully comprehended in the context of the political struggles that have raged in Natal and KwaZulu over the last ten to fifteen years. In essence, it relates to Chief Buthelezi fighting to maintain and consolidate his support base in this region at a time when there have been unprecedented challenges to his leadership. This has occurred with the rapid growth of the independent trade union movement in the 1980s, the formation of the United Democratic Front in 1983, and the increasing popularity of the African National Congress. These struggles have come sharply into focus in the last couple of years as thousands of people have lost their lives in political fighting. In terms of such political struggles, it becomes evident that historical interpretation and presentation, and popular understanding of the past, play a central role in how groups of people perceive themselves and others.

Pre- and early colonial history displays in Zimbabwe and Botswana

The examination of museum displays in Zimbabwe and Botswana, done by Ritchie (1990), was not intended to be a comprehensive study, but had a specific focus on looking at displays on gatherer-hunters and herders. The objective was to gain an understanding of the manner in which objects (including casts of people) have been assembled into particular configurations.

Apart from structural and administrative changes, museums in Zimbabwe have changed little since independence in 1980 (Nduka, personal communication, 1989; although see Ucko 1994). After independence it was stated that national priorities were resettlement, education and health. Further, it was even suggested by some that museums should close (Nduka, personal communication, 1989). Thus, for the last decade museums have been competing for funds with, for example, unemployment projects and rural development programmes (Collett, personal communication, 1989). As Nduka (personal communication, 1989) commented: 'It's not that the government doesn't appreciate museums, but there are other priorities.'

In both Zimbabwe and Botswana funding problems have clearly placed severe limits on museum activities (also see Kiyaga-Mulindwa and Segobye 1994; Ucko 1994). With regard to Zimbabwe in particular, this factor has to be taken into consideration when the limited changes in display content and message since independence are being examined (also see Collett 1992).

The first example is at the Museum of Human Sciences in Harare (and see Ucko 1983). One of the first displays that visitors see on entering this museum is a display on the 'Stone Age'. This display contains a graphic illustration of the sequence between 2 million to 80,000 years ago. The physiological development of humans is illustrated next to this sequence, displayed to fit graphically into the same sequential time-scale. The skull used to illustrate *Homo sapiens* is specified as a 'Bushman' skull, and the text on *Homo sapiens* reads:

> Thinking Man, early Homo Sapiens began a steady development of culture and social organisation.

The connection between the earliest 'Thinking Man' and the skull of a 'Bushman' holds a number of implications – the main implication being that 'Bushmen' are the earliest type of humans, just learning to think. 'Bushmen' are thus at the bottom end of the steady 'development towards culture and social organisation', and are therefore a perfect example of 'man in his most primitive state'.

This display leads on to a display about 'The Bushman'. The central signboard reads:

> THE BUSHMEN
>
> People of the past . . .
>
> Still survive today.

From this sign an arrow points to a map of Africa, which surrounds an illustration of a male figure, equipped with quiver and bow and clothed in leather skins. The text about the 'Bushmen' being our 'living link with the Stone Age' includes a physical description. Opposite this display stands a manners-and-customs display of photographs and objects, entitled 'How the Bushmen Live Now'. The text reads: 'The Bushmen are a cheerful people who express themselves through dancing and singing.'

A most revealing method of assessing visitor responses is listening to comments made by visitors to the galleries. One of the comments heard in the Harare Museum was made in response to the 'How the Bushmen Live Now' exhibit. The visitor commented: 'When you go and look for those people in the bush where they live, they just run away.'

It is a useful comment, in that it reveals the extent to which the displays perpetuate the public perception that 'Bushmen' are people who not only still live in skins, but who can be sought out, or who *should* be sought out, in the bush 'where they live'. Another comment overheard in response to these displays was made with reference to a 'Bushman' cave scene. This scene displays a standing male figure, painting on the side of the cave. Next to the man a woman squats at the hearth, while a child plays in the foreground. A young visitor commented: 'See how the man paints the house while the woman cooks the food.'

Information has been compacted into this display in such a manner that the male figure paints images on the wall of the cave while the female figure engages in 'traditional' domestic labour – in the same space and time. The way the past is used to legitimize the present, however unintentionally constructed, is clear from this display. If the 'Bushmen', 'who can only just think', operate in this way – with men engaged in tasks such as painting, with women engaged in food preparation – then this must be natural and instinctual. Thus the gender roles displayed give the impression of being immutable.

At the National Museum and Art Gallery in Gaborone, Botswana, there is very little display space assigned to either gathering and hunting or to herding. On entering the galleries, visitors can read an information board about the arrival of farmers in southern Africa, which makes the following reference to gatherer–hunters (the San): 'they entered a land where the only inhabitants, the San or Sarwa (better known as the Bushmen), lived by hunting wild animals and collecting plants and insects.'

Further on in the galleries a board informs visitors that 'the earliest farmers came from different areas . . . in Botswana they traded with and married the earlier inhabitants, the San and Khoe (Sarwa and Kgothu)'. The River San are also referred to in a display on the 'Peoples of the Okavango Delta'.

When questioned about the limited mention of gatherer–hunter and herder communities, a museum staff member explained that there are no displays on the San in the Gaborone museum because the 'first gallery' has not been completed. The galleries in this museum are designed to work in a series that visitors would move through, in order to gain a full and integrated understanding of Botswana, its position internationally today, and its position in the long history of human existence. The 'first gallery' displays are planned to begin at 90 million years ago, in order to convey to visitors the age of the earth. Displays on the early, middle and later Stone Ages will follow, in order to position Botswana in the context of southern and eastern Africa. This display will try to link gatherer–hunters and herders to, respectively, the Stone Age and the introduction of domestic stock (Campbell, personal communication, 1989).

It is clear from a description of these displays that until now postcolonial Zimbabwe and Botswana museums have had little success in moving away from presentations of different groups of people based on colonial discourse. There appears to be little difference between the rhetoric governing the construction and communication of displays in the museums in Zimbabwe, Botswana and South Africa. While funding obviously places severe restrictions on the extent of changes that can be made, this factor does not fully explain the nature of constructions about the past, nor does it take into account the manner in which museum knowledge is produced and presented.

Discussion and conclusion

The messages communicated by museums are dependent on communicator and context. Museum personnel communicate a particular message through museum rhetoric. The displays communicate another message, often intended by museum personnel, and necessarily influenced by the meaning brought to displays by viewers. This chapter attempts to expose another message communicated by museums – a message founded upon the politics of the production and presentation of knowledge, and on the uses of the past, in the southern African colonial context. This is a context in which museums even in the politically postcolonial countries of Zimbabwe and Botswana to some extent still find themselves enmeshed.

Simply expressed, the messages in the museums included above are about power and control. Our major concern, and the reason for conducting this research, is to examine the extent to which museums are likely to change in the 'new South Africa'. At the time this research was done funding restrictions had prevented Zimbabwean museums from making changes beyond the relettering of display labels, and the inclusion of material which, under the white-controlled Rhodesian regime, was excluded. What has happened in effect, though, is that much of the same colonial discourse is still ingrained in the language of display. South African museums are, without doubt, going to be subjected to similar financial constraints, given the pending redistribution of funds within education and elsewhere.

The question that South African educationalists and museologists need to be asking, therefore, is whether it will be satisfactory simply to include material on issues, topics and areas of history that have until now been excluded. Or is a fundamental restructuring of museums as a concept, as display space, as educative forum and as 'preserver of national heritage' going to be required? Names and content can be changed but this will not alter the European colonial construction of the production and presentation of museum-derived knowledge. If museums are to serve adequately South Africa's people generally, and progressive education specifically (taking into account the problems of illiteracy, enormous school groups, English as a second or third language), it ought to be clear that simple inclusions will not be sufficient to change the way in which museums are used.

Museums, as institutions with distinctly European origins, exist as the material embodiment of the cultural memory of a nation or state. The history we learn in schools is usually the same type of history which a museum remembers, and museum-type knowledge is embedded in the politics of colonialism. For this reason it is not surprising that the museum ethos and aesthetic in postcolonial countries have not altered much. Display content, in terms of the ratio of black and white history, may have changed, thus illustrating the shift in the black–white relations of power in postcolonial countries, but there has been no fundamental change in the discourse of museums.

It will only be with a deep understanding of all the notions associated with museums (for example, knowledge, learning, display, objects, history, authentic, preserve, heritage) that we will be in any position to address the root problems of the biased, narrow and didactic nature of museum presentation. Apart from the messages communicated through the 'presences' and 'absences' in display content, there are a host of other subliminal messages communicated by museums that have a critical effect on the way that interpretations presented in museums are understood by the public. These are, for example:

1 the authority with which museum knowledge is presented;
2 the manner in which objects are ordered and constructed into displays; and
3 display techniques, particularly the boundaries reinforced by glass cases.

We have not dealt directly with these issues but they will have to become part of museum discourse if we are to achieve a better understanding of the ways museums operate and the messages they communicate.

Museums are one of the main types of institution (besides formal education, school textbooks, newspapers and television) that present history to the public. In this chapter we have tried to give a brief analysis of the current state of museums in South Africa relative to museums elsewhere in the subcontinent. While southern African museums embody and reflect peculiarities of a colonial historical discourse, and South African museums specifically embody the workings of separateness or apartheid, it is clear from the international literature that many of the issues facing the presentation of history and culture in South Africa are also pertinent elsewhere (Lumley 1988b). A research trip to Zimbabwe and Botswana (by G R) revealed that the 'colonial bias', so evident in our South African museums, is still in part embodied in the museums of postcolonial, liberated countries. The problem with South African state-dominated presentations of the past is therefore, at root, apartheid – but only in that apartheid is the most extreme form in which the presentation of different cultures as separate, wholly independent groups has found expression.

It will take more than an inclusion of previously excluded material to change the presentation of relations of power expressed in the entire structure of museums – men over women, colonizer over colonized, powerful over powerless. Indeed it is not simply the content of museum displays that needs to be addressed, but the structure of museums, the message of museums as a whole, and the way that 'cultural heritage' is defined, collected and presented (see Ucko 1994).

References

Collett, D. P. 1992. *The Archaeological Heritage of Zimbabwe: a master plan for resource conservation and development.* UNDP & Unesco Project Report (Zim 88/028).
Kiyaga-Mulindwa, D. & A. K. Segobye 1994. Archaeology and education in

Botswana. In *The Presented Past: heritage, museums and education*, Stone, P. G. & B. L. Molyneaux (eds), 46–60. London: Routledge.

Lumley, R. 1988a. Introduction. In *The Time-Machine*, Lumley, R. (ed.), 1–23. London: Routledge.

Lumley, R. (ed.) 1988b. *The Museum Time-Machine*. London: Routledge.

Ritchie, G. 1990. Dig the herders/display the Hottentots: the production and presentation of knowledge about the past. Unpublished MA thesis, University of Cape Town.

Ucko, P. J. 1983. The politics of the indigenous minority. *Journal of Biosocial Science* Suppl. 8, 25–40.

Ucko, P. J. 1994. Museums and sites: cultures of the past within education – Zimbabwe, some ten years on. In *The Presented Past: heritage, museums and education*, Stone, P. G. & B. L. Molyneaux (eds), 237–82. London: Routledge.

Wright, J. & A. D. Mazel 1987. Bastions of ideology: the depiction of precolonial history in the museums of Natal and KwaZulu. *Southern African Museums Association Bulletin* 17, 301–10.

Wright, J. & A. D. Mazel 1991. Controlling the past in the museums of Natal and KwaZulu. *Critical Arts* 5, 59–78.

17 Museums and sites: cultures of the past within education – Zimbabwe, some ten years on

PETER J. UCKO

Introduction

This chapter investigates questions surrounding education about the past in what, to some, may appear to be an unusual way. It starts from the work of an outstandingly gifted group of people – Zimbabwean archaeologists and administrators as well as foreign consultants – working for, or with, the National Museums and Monuments Service of Zimbabwe (hereafter, NMMZ). This group is currently concerned with the protection of Zimbabwe's archaeological past, and the facilitation of education about that past.

The chapter investigates whether the frame of reference adopted by the group is essentially counter-productive to desirable long-term aims of education about the past and to the long-term future well-being of the discipline of archaeology in a country such as Zimbabwe. The analysis contains a case study of the history and development of an alternative, albeit little-developed, Zimbabwean 'culture house' approach to the past, and it makes frequent references to apparently somewhat similar developments in a far distant country, Papua New Guinea (hereafter, PNG). Both examples demonstrate the difficulty of drawing anything but an unsatisfactory and artificial hard-and-fast line between what is to be considered archaeological and what is to be classed as other (non-archaeological) evidence about the past. Once the arbitrariness of such a division is recognized, the implications for an effective educational policy about the past in any country are seen to be both multifarious and complex.

The following analysis rejects any notion that archaeology is, or should be, restricted to the study of only a 'remote' past (in time or place) – in what follows, archaeological concerns are explicitly taken to incorporate the 'ethnographic', the 'oral historical', the literary, as well as the 'archaeological' past. In rejecting any assumption of a qualitative difference between the nature of material cultures from recent, as opposed to more distant, pasts, the approach adopted here is in tune with the Zimbabwean concept of a multifaceted and dynamic 'past' safely housed under local control as such a concept emerged from numerous discussions in 1981 (Ucko 1981). This approach is, however, in conflict with several of the structural and organizational divides that were inherited by the newly independent nation of Zimbabwe in 1980.

Examination of the reasons why such bureaucratic divides have continued into the Zimbabwe of the 1990s takes analysis into the much more general areas of ethnogenesis, ethnic diversification and ethnic continuity. Whereas educational policy about national and ethnic identities is, naturally, of concern to central governments everywhere, these are particularly sensitive areas of enquiry in new nations such as Zimbabwe or PNG. The complex interplay of the various factors involved in the detailed local case studies examined here are, in reality, of much wider significance than only to the Zimbabwe of 1994.

To isolate a remote past investigated by archaeology from the more recent past (to which archaeology is not considered relevant) may be useful for government and the elite of a country, but it runs the risk of either leaving the study of archaeology where it so often is – outside public consciousness – or of disenfranchising the more distant past from any living reality or contemporary relevance. In all this, the role of education, and a country's educational policy, are clearly of central and crucial concern.

ZIMBABWE: A CASE STUDY

Zimbabwe's National Museums and Monuments Service: to 1981

On 1 October 1972 the National Museum of Rhodesia and the Historical Monuments Commission were amalgamated (National Museums and Monuments of Rhodesia Act (Chapter 313), and National Museums and Monuments of Rhodesia Amendment Act 1976, and various by-laws). The resulting service was a typically European system, combining museums and site recording and preservation under a newly created Board of Trustees. The amalgamation did little to alter the basic nature of the structures of the organization concerned, responsibility for sites and museums deriving from the 1930s. With regard to the former, members of the controlling Monuments Commission were originally clearly envisaged as coming from the white community, since, although they 'have been appointed from all walks of life, . . . all have studied, in one aspect or another, the subjects [of] History, Prehistory, Geology or the preservation of Fauna and Flora' (Cooke n.d., p. 4). With regard to the latter, the Board of Trustees of the National Museums of Rhodesia were 'individuals [who were] usually outstanding national or local professional business personalities, and have made a success of their own careers' (Smithers 1967, p. 464).

In 1981, one year after Independence, nothing had really changed: as one senior member said (G. Bond, pers. comm., 16.1.81), 'Running a museum service is like running a business and what we are looking for on the Board are people like accountants, successful businessmen, lawyers and people of influence such as doctors.'

Museums

In 1981 there were five national museums. The Queen Victoria Museum in Harare had been designated the national museum for the human sciences, entitled the 'Museum of Man' (now to become the 'Zimbabwe Museum of Human Sciences'). By and large, at that time, its ethnographic collections were poor; for example, there were only about fifty baskets, mainly unprovenanced, and cataloguing activities were unsystematized and incomplete. No clear policy regarding the purchase and acquisition of new specimens seemed to exist; it was apparent, for example, that the museum had no plans to buy examples of those basket types not represented in its collections but still being made in rural areas (and see Ravenhill 1987). At that time, the museum at Mutare retained a display of human sciences material, including several interesting ethnographic items, which had not been altered since 1962. No one on the staff specialized in the human sciences and information on provenances was not forthcoming. The museum at Bulawayo ('The National Museum') contained a large display – unchanged for some twenty years (Garlake 1982c, p. 32) – of human science materials but no detailed information about the collection was available there. At Great Zimbabwe only the first gallery of the site museum had been established by 1981, and it included some excellent specimens – but it made no mention of Great Zimbabwe's indigenous origin (Garlake 1982c, pp. 31–2). The museum at Gweru contained neither ethnographic nor archaeological material, being entirely devoted to the display of European-derived weaponry – a non-interpretative exhibition which was nothing 'but obscene' (Garlake 1982c, p. 32) – though it was at that time also to become the National Costume Museum.

Zimbabwe in 1981 had inherited a national museum service in which any interest of local groups in their own heritage was being stifled by a museum policy of removing the whole country's research and reserve collections of local cultural materials to the Queen Victoria Museum in Harare. As a result of this policy the museums at Bulawayo and Mutare had no specialized curatorial staff to answer questions about the human sciences material on display. This bad museology (and see Ravenhill 1987) was officially justified (Jackson 1980, pp. 5–6) on the grounds of alleged financial advantages, and privately (H. D. Jackson, pers. comm., 1981) as an attempt to facilitate research work by international scholars,[1] aims that were considered more important than presenting the majority population with the possibility of handling comprehensive collections of relevance to its own heritages. For the majority of Zimbabweans in 1981, museums therefore seemed to have little point – many (see Ucko 1981) considered that the whole museum service should be disbanded, on the grounds that the concept of a museum was European and exaggerated the static nature of collections. As Garlake (1982c, p. 31) wrote (and see Ames 1992, pp. 3–4):

> The role of museums in a colonial or neo-colonial society has
> always been to entertain the tiny leisured elite of colonist,
> Comprador and foreign tourist. The people's culture is both
> pillaged and denigrated. Objects torn from their social environ-
> ment are carefully isolated and displayed as strange and exotic,
> sometimes valuable and artistic, but always devoid of any social
> and historical significance, and unrelated to the life of a people.

About this 1981 situation, Garlake's explanation (1982c, p. 32) was that 'Many
of those entrenched in power in Zimbabwe prior to Independence do not
readily accept the desirability or necessity for change; nor indeed can they
envisage a role for museums different to their colonial role.'

Monuments

Under the 1972 legislation the status of monuments was defined: 'on the
recommendation of the Board, the Minister may . . . declare any monument
to be a national monument'; 'no person shall excavate any ancient monument
or national monument' nor 'make any alteration to, destroy or damage, or
remove from its original site or export from [the country] any national
monument, ancient monument or relic or any part thereof'.

In order 'to provide for the preservation of monuments, relics and other
objects of historical or scientific value or interest' and 'to compile and complete
a register of all national monuments and of any relics that it has acquired or
that have been brought to its notice', the Commission was empowered to
employ Inspectors of Monuments and 'wardens' (very few of which were ever
appointed). After the Independence war, in several parts of the country, it took
several years for many sites to be made safe for visits by the very small number
of NMMZ Inspectors in employment, and several of the sites had become
totally overgrown, with walls destroyed by cattle and pathways untraceable.

Whatever the official position regarding sites and public education (Chipoka
1992), in 1981 no effective use of archaeological sites in teaching existed; for
example, the ruins at Chibvumani, whose existence was announced by a
permanent signpost on the main road, had never been used for a class visit by
the teacher in the nearby school.

In 1981, about two-thirds of all the Declared National Monuments were of
black African cultural derivation; half of these were ancient monuments, such
as Great Zimbabwe and Khami, and the other half, paintings made some time
earlier by 'Bushmen' peoples. Although the powers of the Act allowed the
Board to acquire '(a) a national monument or relic; [or] (b) any land in
connection with a national monument; [or] (c) any right over any land in the
vicinity of a national monument', in almost no case had the Act been invoked
to protect sites of major significance to living Zimbabweans of African descent. There was nothing in the early 1980s to demonstrate any less of an elitist
and cavalier attitude to the past, and the public's potential interest in it, than
had been shown some thirty years earlier: thus, for example, one of the

country's most influential archaeologists of the 1950s (who, as Garlake (1982b, p. 4) says, not only emphasized the scientific nature of archaeology but also its 'mystery' in order to deliberately and considerably increase the alienation of archaeology from the rest of society) entitled his book *Inyanga, Prehistoric Settlements in Southern Rhodesia* and wrote: 'Like so many names in the district, "Inyanga" is misspelled and should be Nyanga. However, it is now so well established in its Europeanized form that it would be mere pedantry to spell it otherwise' (Summers 1958, p. 6). In the face of persisting attitudes such as these, as well as the cynical enforced movements of whole groups of people in the name of expatriate definitions – and redefinitions – of what characterizes 'traditional heritage' (Ranger 1989a), it is hardly surprising that the majority of Zimbabweans had no reason then or in the 1980s to share in the aims and activities of the NMMZ, since their interests were virtually ignored.

Zimbabwe's National Museums and Monuments Service: 1991+

Currently, more than ten years after Independence, there *have been* changes – but perhaps fewer, and less striking ones than some may have expected, or indeed hoped for.

Museums

Although postcolonial Zimbabwe is now involved in disseminating knowledge of the past (deriving from studies of material culture) through its formal schools education system at the national level of curriculum and syllabus (see Pwiti 1994), and although teachers are seconded from the Education Ministry to the NMMZ (the latter being situated in the Home Affairs Ministry), these five Education Officers are given no archaeological training; and they have no career structures within the NMMZ (Stone 1994). In the rural context, even though it is official policy to make museum education available to the rural public, in practice – as stressed by Pwiti (1994) and others (e.g. Mabvadya 1990, pp. 11, 25–6; *Report 1992*, p. 14; Stone 1994) – such educative services currently remain of an extremely limited kind, without the requisite background training or access to even minimally adequate financial or vehicular support, and these services have, in any case, no reason to place any particular emphasis on the value and significance of the study of the past.

In the same vein, museum displays continue, with regard to the indigenous cultures of Zimbabwe, to present a public face today which, at least in some important respects, is not appreciably different from its former colonial one: they remain authoritarian and unimaginative, particularly in captions and labelling which are often biased, dated and stereotypic (see Ucko 1983a, pp. 30–1; Mazel & Ritchie 1994) – and this *despite* formal objections lodged with the relevant museum curators about the use of terms such as 'Negro', the negative caricaturing of 'Bushmen' peoples and culture, and displays apparently suggesting a direct evolutionary development from *Australopithecus* to *Homo erectus* to *Homo neanderthalensis* to 'Bushmen' (and see Anon 1975).

Such possibly fundamental aspects of a western-derived archaeological/ museum professional 'insensitivity' are perhaps all the more curious given that the Board's personnel now includes prominent Zimbabwean archaeologists and others – of undoubted ability and commitment to NMMZ affairs – who have, over recent years, successfully initiated two new temporary displays in Harare, have redesigned and re-captioned the museum display at Great Zimbabwe (in 1992, in order to present and interpret the archaeological material in several Zimbabwean languages and to use less esoteric and specialist archaeological terminology – W. Ndoro, pers. comm., 3.2.93) and have assured a display of artefacts at Gweru. It appears that some of the more fundamental problems still have to be acknowledged and openly confronted; thus, it appears that the previous Zimbabwean policy of centralization of all human sciences material culture in Harare has, in practice, been quietly dropped, although the official policy does not seem to have been officially reversed. Despite Independence, and the improvements in museums such as that at Great Zimbabwe, most national museums continue to appear to be remote from the actualities and major concerns of the living. For example, in the capital's museum there are stored boxes full of (unresearched) Shona skeletons uncovered during building developments – skeletal remains for which there is no museum policy and whose mere discovery was sufficient to make the newspaper front pages (Mabvadya 1990, p. 15). This static extracultural 'safe-keeping' has the potential to fuel any negative public perception of archaeologists and (physical) anthropologists as no more than what some Native Americans call 'bone lickers' (Ucko 1987, p. 167) (and see below, p. 272).

The recent words of the Director of the National Museum of PNG about the qualities needed by museums if they are to survive as institutions in the so-called Third World, summarize the challenge to Zimbabwean museums in the 1990s and highlight the necessity for them to change their ways:

> The view that museum collections are little more than odd assortments of exotic curios remains, unfortunately, a common notion today. . . . at the end of the day they are really no more than odds-and-ends, the unimportant relics of almost forgotten cultures. . . .
>
> The . . . former Assistant Director-General of Unesco for Culture once described museums as immature transplants from the elitist cultural milieux of nineteenth-century Europe. He went on to note that, 'despite the fact that the museums are already staffed by indigenous specialists, the attitude of the latter is largely that of their European mentors of yesterday, a closed professional group, elitist in the sense that the museum exists mainly for their own scholarly pursuits'.
>
> . . . To dispel notions that museums are nothing but 'houses of

the dead' which exist solely to serve close-knit patronage, museums must change, that is, if they are to survive into the next century.

(Eoe 1991a, pp. 1–2)

Monuments

The situation with regard to the management of archaeological sites has undoubtedly improved, since, by 1991, all five regions have been allocated archaeological Inspectors. However, many of these Inspectors have had trouble getting adequate budgets to carry out inspections of all the sites within their regions. Dissatisfaction with their actual positions has led to current demands that the service's preservation of monuments work should be separated from the service's museum work (Collett 1992, pp. 58–9). Ironically, ten years after Independence, the service is active not in declaring more sites of indigenous importance (Mabvadya 1990, p. 13) but in de-scheduling sites of European derivation (Cooke 1972). Regional archaeological Inspectors within the NMMZ are, not surprisingly, far from reassured by mere assurances from the Executive that this one-way activity will soon change.

Matters in Zimbabwe are very far from static. The signs are that the later years of the 1990s will show a burst of activity. Thus, for example, some of the archaeological monuments have been provided with new site museums (see below, p. 262) and are currently the subject of intense interest as the possible source of increased national and international tourism, thereby also providing the country with badly needed foreign currency. Indeed, if one were asked to judge from the draft title of Addyman's (1991) report commissioned by the United Nations Development Program and supported by the NMMZ, 'A strategy for the presentation of ancient monuments and the maximisation of their potential as economic touristic educational and recreational resources', there would be little, if anything, to distinguish Zimbabwean strategy from, for example, many UK approaches in the 1990s to its own past. It appears that the NMMZ – through staging, in July 1992, a Donors' Conference to recommend and endorse a Master Plan 'for the development of Zimbabwe's archaeological and historical heritage' (*Report 1992*, p. 2) – has decided on a heritage tourism development strategy[2] which contains considerable inherent dangers. The NMMZ has chosen to ignore Addyman's own clear warning that its

> disadvantages are obvious: inevitable commercialization of an at present miraculously preserved natural environment; pressure of visitor numbers leading to conservation problems; the anti-social effects on the community of mass tourism; and a tendency for outside interests to cream off the benefits.
>
> (Addyman 1991, p. 28; and see Ndoro 1993)

If successful, the result at some sites will be education about the past in the form of theme-park entertainment based on a combination of static displays (e.g. reconstructed house types) and actors (demonstrating how things had

been done in the past) (Collett 1992, p. 23). Alongside these proposals goes the
new claim (D. Munjeri, pers. comm., 11.11.91) that 'promotion of tourism to
[archaeological and historical sites in rural areas] would result in rural development and uplifting of the living standards of the people residing around such
sites' – presumably a reference to the proposed development of curio markets
and site staff wearing traditional dress in association with some of the main
archaeological tourist centres (Collett 1992, pp. 23, 80, 83; and see Masona
1992). In the words of the Donors' Conference report, there is a 'need for the
NMMZ to generate funds by way of curio sales, entry fees, and opening of
lodges at such places as Great Zimbabwe' (Report 1992, p. 11).

As far as site education is concerned, the current situation appears to be
more or less unchanged from that of the 1980s (Mabvadya 1990, pp. 9–11, 24;
Addyman 1991, pp. 10 (3.5), 46 (10.2); Chipoka 1992). However, improvement is planned not only through such traditional recipes as the improvement
of facilities for children visiting the sites, but also through the revolutionary
proposal that responsibility for the care of at least some archaeological and
historic sites should be vested in suitably located large schools (Collett 1992,
pp. 14, 21, 26, 35–6, 39, 87; and see Stone 1994).

Twenty years of the NMMZ: a summary

In concentrating on the formal education system and on tourist-driven forms
of cultural heritage management to give instruction about the past, Zimbabwe
in the 1990s appears to have turned its back on what was, in the 1980s, a plan
to involve the wider Zimbabwean people in their local heritages through the
creation of 'culture houses'. Analysis of how and why certain decisions were
taken about the creation of culture houses sheds light on who controls and
thereby 'owns' the past (McBryde 1985; Layton 1989a; Stone & MacKenzie
1990). Despite a growing theoretical literature on the role of the past in the
creation and maintenance of identity (see below, pp. 258–60), this detailed case
study provides unusual insights into how the nature of archaeological attitudes
and practice play a role in negotiations of identity. It also raises important
questions about the complex relationships between nationalism and local
enthusiasms in a Third World independent country, even ten years after
Independence.

Culture houses

Zimbabwe

In 1980, the at that time new Division of Culture of the Ministry of Education
and Culture had prepared a short 'discussion paper' about 'culture houses' in
connection with a budgetary request to the Treasury. The document proposed
establishing one culture house in each of the then 55 local districts in the first
year, with a further 55 houses built by the third year (i.e. two culture houses
per administrative district). It also recommended that such centres be built

largely by the communities themselves with local materials, to ensure 'maxi-mum local participation'. The Government would supply only the 'skeletal steel structure and roofing materials'. These culture houses were to 'provide a focal point for library, Museum, arts and multi-functional facilities'.

It is possible that at least some part of this concept of a culture house derived from practices in Mozambique, particularly the aptly termed 'bear [sic] foot archaeologists' who, it was proposed in the discussion paper, would gather material of local interest so that 'in this way the people will become the custodians of their historical and traditional heritage'. The concept tried to encapsulate the past, as well as the continuing and the future nature of culture(s), in local centres under the effective control of local/district groups. Such living centres of cultural activity were conceived of as recognizing the worth of traditional practices at the same time as being visible statements of confidence about the future. In part at least the idea of culture houses may have been a response to the perceived deficiencies of existing nationally run museums: under local control there would surely be respect for secret and sacred materials (and see Eoe & Swadling 1991, pp. 270, 273 for PNG and the Pacific), 'elders' would be given respect and would be recognized as appropri-ate teachers for all kinds of knowledge, 'natural history' would be displayed and explained according to non-western perceptions and, above all, such centres would be both genuine and alive – without any need for dressing up or pretence that culture had died away (Ucko 1981).

Culture houses/cultural centres in a wider context
The success or otherwise of ventures dealing with local cultural expressions can of course be judged by many different criteria. Ventures can be evaluated in terms of their success in fulfilling local cultural and educational aspirations, although much research remains to be done on the complex interrelationships between such local aspirations and national identity (see below, p. 259). Another way in which local cultural ventures can be assessed is in terms of their financial viability. In many areas of the world local cultural centres have become enmeshed in tourism activities.

In the USA (and see Blancke & Slow Turtle 1994), for example, the Gila Indian Center in Arizona, 'a tribal non-profit corporation', consisting of the Gila Heritage Park (with village settings from five cultures), the Historical Museum (with traditional static displays of 'the rich and ancient life of the Gila River Indian Community'), a restaurant, and a shop selling authentic crafts, is a complex exclusively aimed at the tourist travelling between Phoenix and Tucson. The displays are informative, with a printed guide (Anon n.d.b) and news sheet of Pima/Maricopa legends, and the Center represents a rare collaborative effort between members of several Indian communities, the Arizona State Museum and the staffs of several university anthropology departments. However, it does not seem to be the focus of local indigenous cultural activities. The delightful Navajo Tribal Museum at Window Rock, Arizona, USA, with its tasteful displays and free catalogue (Hartman &

Kadoyama n.d.) covering cultural activity from prehistory to the present, is
another example of collaboration between State museums and Indian people:
'Navajo medicine men and a professional Navajo linguist worked closely with
the museum staff to ensure that the story told was both correct and appropriate' (Doyel n.d.). Apparently designed and created 'as an educational facility
through which [the Navajo] can learn, teach their children, and show the rest
of the world their proud heritage', the museum again appears to derive its
vitality from the 'many wonderful items on display and for purchase by those
wishing to take something with them [from] the Navajo Arts and Crafts
Enterprise, owned and operated by the Navajo Tribe' (Doyel n.d.).

In another part of the world, PNG, many of the local cultural centres appear
to have been spin-offs from individual expatriate initiatives (Blacking 1984,
pp. 9ff.; 1990; Mawe 1991; several other chapters in Eoe & Swadling 1991; and
see Jamieson 1994). However, at least some were independent of European
influence (e.g. Kombea 1991), resulting from actions by local leaders who feel
that their culture is threatened by the encroaching national culture and by
young people moving away from traditional behaviour (J. Mangi, pers.
comm., 6.9.86; Ucko 1986a). In PNG the concept of local cultural centres was
supported by the Australian Government and later, after Independence, by
both central and provincial governments, the former operating through The
National Cultural Council – with responsibility for the construction of a
cultural centre in each province – and the latter through direct grants to the
centres. With a few notable exceptions (e.g. Burton 1991), almost all had some
touristic ambitions, usually also involving the sale of artefacts, and some of
these were even conceived as buttresses against the negative impact of *major*
tourism (e.g. Namuno 1991; see also Marenge & Normu 1986). The vast
majority of these PNG cultural centres appear not to have survived after the
initial receipt of Unesco or governmental grants. Nevertheless, the concept
continues to flourish, with many groups continuing to express their cultural
and educational dreams through plans for failed or for projected cultural
centres (see many chapters in Eoe & Swadling 1991).

The concept of cultural centres or houses can thus be seen in various
countries of the world (and see Ames (1992, p. xv) for further examples),
especially in areas where individual cultures are threatened by imposed values,
whether colonialist or nationalist.

The Murewa Culture House
Whatever the original Zimbabwean derivation of the concept of a culture
house,[3] fieldwork (Ucko 1981) served to flesh out the possible functions of
Zimbabwean culture houses and to establish that support for such a concept
was overwhelming in all except one region.[4] The ideal culture house, as it
developed during consultations, would probably comprise at least one lock-
able room for sacred and profane objects of particular value to the community;
another room for books, articles and manuscripts relevant to the language and
history of the group(s) concerned; a room devoted to oral histories and

autobiographies; another for arts and crafts, including direct sales; and a place for mobile displays. Closely associated with each culture house would be a physical area prepared and maintained for song and dance.

The actual form and details of culture houses would obviously vary from area to area, with local groups – as the report stressed – being given the responsibility of determining the specific nature of their own culture houses: 'It is evident that the concept of a culture house as a "nerve centre" representing not only past traditions but also "living culture" is a complex one which will require enormous qualities of flexibility' (Ucko 1981: 21.6.81, Bikita group meeting). That Zimbabwean culture houses might therefore be potentially troublesome was clear from the realization that their development should be dynamic, sometimes no doubt resulting in disputes about the number and localities of particular houses. In some localities and areas disputes could be accepted as signs of success, demonstrating genuine involvement in the development of culture houses and concern with the very essence of contemporary cultural activity.

The whole culture-house concept as it emerged through consultation accorded amazingly well with Devalle's later (1992, p. 17) theoretical assessment of cultural processes in the context of developing countries in general: 'the efforts at reconquering their own history, at reinventing it if badly destroyed on the basis of whatever collective memory has kept. . . . [Such] reconquered history is opposed to official history, which is never sympathetic to the subaltern sectors.'

Through its culture-house plans in the early 1980s, independent Zimbabwe appeared to be set on a course which included the establishment of a past meaningful to its local populations, through the creation of a system of linked cultural centres. This project would be capable of gaining respect at home and abroad by giving visible evidence of the Zimbabwean Government's care and concern for the country's constituent cultures. Culture houses would be the creation of the local people themselves (including responsibility for the appointment of the culture-house custodians) and their continuation and vitality would depend on the degree of significance the people attributed to them, how they functioned in practice, and the position they would attain within the society at large.

The opportunity appeared to have been taken, for in January 1986 the Murewa Culture House (Fig. 17.1) was opened officially by the then Prime Minister, Robert Mugabe, who argued:

> Nationhood means a people has a soul and selfhood [whose] key elements are music, dance, sculpture, painting, pottery, drama, various forms of oral and written literature and social wisdom. . . .
> There is need to rediscover our cultural heritage, to polish up and refine what we have acquired; and to pass on the legacy to the young generation so that these precious things are not allowed to die with passing generations.

Figure 17.1 Commemorative Opening plaque of the Murewa Culture House. Photo: P. Stone.

However, despite some incipient moves to acquire land or buildings in two or three other areas,[5] Murewa remains, in 1994, the only culture house in Zimbabwe, and it has been deemed a failure (McCartney 1985) because it was not created under the 'right' conditions, i.e. it was imposed by Government and lacked local involvement.

According to this version of events, a Cultural Officer had been resident at Murewa since December 1983 in impressive but more-or-less empty buildings lacking electricity, without a budget to acquire objects or hire technicians to mount displays. McCartney (1985, p. 10) suggested that local people did not consider the cultural house theirs and that consultation with the local population had been inadequate:

> Who 'owns' the culture house? Who *controls* it? The former Minister referred to the people as the 'targets of cultural development'. It is an uneasy metaphor; Murewa has certainly been 'hit', but with what, and to what end? As a mechanism for strengthening community culture, the centre may yet prove its worth, especially by providing a venue for performances, but local responses to the place are hesitant. Even if the members of the community evinced pride in their new acquisitions, it would be pride in the bounty of government, and perhaps in their good fortune, rather than in their own achievement. There is little sign of pride. There is antici-

pation, there is bemusement, there is indifference, there is – surprisingly, in view of the size of the investment, and the ambitions which preceded it – a measure of ignorance. There is, in short, no evidence of the centre having been given birth by community enthusiasm.

However, such was not the perception of a UK visitor a few years later (J. Clutton-Brock, pers. comm., 11.1.87) who reported that the culture house now had a library full of books, arts (e.g. Fig. 17.2) and crafts were on sale, an art gallery section had modern carvings, and dancers practised outside for a public performance. And there were four full-time employees including an enthusiastic caretaker. So, similarly, said *The Herald* (25.9.87):

> The culture house, the first of its kind in Zimbabwe, now seems to be set to combat the old preconception that the most important cultural happenings take place in the towns and cities.
>
> The house has been operating for three years now, and it has spread its net far and wide to bring all sorts of products and activities under one roof.
>
> 'We try to cater for all aspects of our culture, not only those concerning Murewa. Since Zimbabwe has cultural agreements with several countries, visiting diplomats are invited here to see what we have to offer,' Cde Mutasa said. The house has a gallery

Figure 17.2 Arts on sale at Murewa Culture House at a special exhibition in 1992. Photo: P. G. Stone.

displaying drawings by school pupils and works of art by local artists.

Next to the gallery is a museum housing a collection of contemporary and traditional art and crafts from Murewa district and other centres. There are photographs depicting Zimbabwe's cultural heritage.

The museum houses *mbira*, cattle yokes, axes, animal skins, earthenware pots and other traditional items, and artefacts are being added to the collection all the time.

Weekend film shows are held at the house, as well as seminars for the private and public sector.

A permanent theatre group, Murewa Theatrical Works, has been formed.

The Zimbabwe National Dance Company is booked to perform two shows at the complex.

'We are in the process of building up a district dance company which will be a baby of the National Dance Company. People in Murewa need to be exposed to such dances as *mbakumba*, *zangoma*, *mhande* and *isichekiche*,' he said.

Other projects in the pipeline include a music competition, a screen printing workshop, and a public speaking workshop.

Thus, by 1988, there appeared to be evidence of community culture as well as a significant educational role for this culture house. Headmasters of primary and secondary schools had been invited there to an orientation seminar for discussions which included the role of the national archives, the role of museums in Zimbabwe, the role of the National Gallery of Arts and Crafts in the development of a people's culture, as well as the role and function of culture houses. An Inter-schools Public Speaking Competition was also about to be held.

Today, therefore, the Murewa Culture House is clearly a national success in at least some of its aspects. It is an impressive building structure, set in beautifully curated flower-beds and lawns (Fig. 17.3), with sufficient Zimbabwean content to impress the important visitor to the country – often the guest of Government – who is whisked to this prestige cultural centre under the control of its Education Ministry and then whisked away later on a short visit to the site of Great Zimbabwe under the control of another of its Ministries, that of Home Affairs.

Despite this, all was clearly not well. In late 1989 the Research Department of the (then) Ministry of Youth, Sports and Culture was directed to undertake an evaluation of Murewa Culture House; part of

the rationale behind the evaluation was (2.4) to examine if there is any need for changing or adding to the Physical Structure of the Culture House and to bring the Culture House more in line with

Figure 17.3 The impressive Murewa Culture House building set in well-maintained surroundings. Photo: J. Hubert.

the original aims for which it was built [, and] (2.6) to make Murewa Culture House more effective in its work.

(Report on the Evaluation of Murewa
Culture House 1989, pp. 1–2)

Problems with culture houses

Subjected to critical analysis, Murewa Culture House reveals a further set of considerations. It is closed for most of the weekends – perhaps the most likely times for locals (adults and children) to be able to make use of it. Its library holdings depend on a minuscule purchasing budget and, more significantly, most of its books are multiple presentation copies donated as propaganda from several (then Communist) foreign embassies (Fig. 17.4) – the result being that almost nothing can be found on African or Zimbabwean matters and very little of relevance to Zimbabwean school curricula. The two round structures (Fig. 17.5) intended for respectively male and female craft production are used solely for storage and, partly owing to lack of vehicles, the influence of the Culture House does not extend effectively into the surrounding rural areas.

All this can be linked to the fact that Murewa Culture House is an arm of central Government. This national function is one, if not *the*, reason for the choice of its location at Murewa, a location never mooted in any of the initial surveys or reports, but which allows quick and easy access from Harare.[6] Major government finance was available for *its* construction. Unfortunately,

Figure 17.4 Murewa Culture House library. Photo: J. Hubert.

Figure 17.5 Murewa Culture House craft production centres now used for storage. Photo: J. Hubert.

in terms of the original essential concept of local control of culture-house affairs, its local and financial basis also allows for direct administration, and budgetary control, from Harare, rather than from the District.

The early history of the Murewa Culture House includes innumerable struggles between local District, local Provincial and central Government regarding recruitment of culture-house staff (Report 1989). One unexpected consequence of central administration has been the imposition of public-service regulations, including such encumbrances as the requirement to pay for any overtime work at weekends. Being so near to Harare has also resulted in a poor selection of artefacts for sale in Murewa Culture House, since it is clearly more profitable for local craftspeople to take their own wares by bus to Harare and to gain immediate financial reward, rather than to lodge their works in the Culture House to await a potential buyer's visit there, with payment sometimes coming several months, or even years, later.

Hidden beneath this major locational influence on affairs lies one of the tensions originally anticipated in discussions about the culture-house concept (Ucko 1981), but clearly not resolved at Murewa: a clash between the old and the young – the former considering the sale of artefacts as diminishing the spiritual importance of the Culture House, and the young welcoming a potential new market outlet.

The Culture House museum is also in trouble (Fig. 17.6). Not very long after the official opening of the Culture House, local 'donors' were complaining both at the paucity of visitors and that they should have been paid for their works now being displayed anonymously there (and see below, p. 261). In addition, all spirit-medium accoutrements have been removed from the museum.

By 1991 Murewa Culture House was clearly no more the genuine focus of local indigenous cultural activities than is the Gila Center mentioned above. Yet, according to all accounts, initially – despite its origins – it had been an enormous cultural and local community success. In purely local terms, one of the most damaging decisions taken had been to forbid the sale of alcohol within the Culture House grounds, many locals therefore preferring to remain in town in the bars. The other most damaging decision was to have forced the exclusion of spirit mediums (and their followers) from Culture House affairs. The *banya* (spirit medium's hut) (Fig. 17.7), initially in active use, was subsequently ordered to be a symbolic and not functional construction, despite the fact that the actual specific site location of the Culture House within Murewa had originally been determined in consultation with the ancestral spirits through the mediums.

*N'anga*s were also banned, this action deriving from the central public service decision to second an ordained Christian priest from Manicaland to be the Director of the Murewa Culture House. It was he who, it appears (D. Mutasa, pers. comm., 8.5.91), requested permission from Harare to exclude from the Culture House all living religious rituals except Christian church activities and services. Mutasa's argument rested on three main points: first,

Figure 17.6 Murewa Culture House museum objects. Photo: J. Hubert.

that there were at least three 'rival' *n'anga*s within Murewa District and competition between them to be allowed to practise within the Culture House would inevitably cause trouble; second, that any *n'anga* living within the Culture House grounds would demand security for his hut and objects; and third, that if *n'anga*s were allowed a place within the Culture House, Christians and others would have nothing to do with the Culture House.

Figure 17.7   The decaying spirit medium's hut close to the location of the Murewa Culture House. Photo: J. Hubert.

Such tensions – and their resolutions – were, as seen above, always envisaged as part and parcel of a successful culture-house development, but, here in Murewa, the cultural groups were not allowed to determine their own 'cultural' way forward. It is alleged (Report 1989, p. 11 (really 10)) that many groups of Murewa locals reacted to the authoritarian refusal to allow *n'anga* involvement at Murewa Culture House affairs by boycotting it, and claimed that such actions reflected a desire to impose an outside culture (governmental and/or Christian) on their local culture(s).

At another analytical level (Cheater 1991, p. 15; 1992), the displacement of *n'angas* from the realms of government-supported cultural affairs can be seen as part of the continuing vacillations in the attitude of Independent Zimbabwean politicians towards 'traditional' positions of authority and power (such as chiefs, headmen, *n'angas*, spirit mediums). It is certainly true that rumours abound that the opening of the Murewa Culture House by the (now) President had been a disaster in the eyes of local traditional people. It is alleged that the government minister who was host to Mugabe disallowed any role for the local politicians, and prevented local *n'angas* from even meeting him. It is claimed that the opening ceremony alienated both of the groups – spiritual and political – whose local support was essential for a meaningful culture-house infrastructure in the District.

At a different level the Murewa Culture House is undoubtedly fulfilling a nationally perceived need – that of an organized centre for educational seminars, workshops and training. Even in this role it needs more financial support, for example to be able to fence off its area from animals, and to provide adequate toilets, kitchens and accommodation for residential courses and for staff. All in all, however, the Murewa Culture House can no longer be seen as part of a development plan for the support of local culture and local education.

Control of the past

It is difficult to envisage how a constructive cultural initiative with regard to culture houses will ever be possible as, from the inception of the NMMZ, there have been structural and bureaucratic divides within Zimbabwean bureaucracy. 'Culture' has been something of a political football in Zimbabwe as it has been in many other countries (for the Pacific, see Eoe & Swadling 1991, p. 268). Indeed, whether or not 'culture' should be the prerogative of a new ministry at all was the subject of intense debate in Zimbabwe in 1981, as was the question of whether it should be linked to education. The Ministries of 'Information', of 'Tourism', and of 'Youth, Sports and Recreation' all considered culture to be within their domains. Having inherited a European system of classification, Zimbabwe had also inherited the concomitant difficulty of distinguishing between Culture, Science and Arts, and the problem of whether or not Culture should be a separate Ministry, a Sectional part of a Ministry, or some sort of ministerial appendage. As the British Council stated (letter, 15.5.81) 'the matter of whether the Ministry of Education and Culture or the Ministry of Home Affairs will have responsibility [for Local Culture Houses] is still in the melting pot'. By 1987 there were still no government policy guidelines on culture, these being 'left to civil servants whose concept of culture is Western oriented' (T. Mudariki, pers. comm., 29.1.87). Meanwhile, responsibility for culture houses was shifted from Ministry to Ministry; by 1991 it had returned to the Ministry of Education and Culture while NMMZ had continued to hold tight (as a 'parastatal') to its place within the Ministry of Home Affairs.[7]

In 1981 several senior museum staff in Harare had been worried by the possibility of a transfer of the NMMZ to the then Ministry of Education. In general there was little awareness of the functions or nature of the new Cultural Division of the Ministry; nearly everyone connected with the NMMZ in Harare at that time was highly sceptical about the feasibility, or even desirability, of the proposals set out in the Division of Culture's discussion paper. I had suggested in my 1981 report (Ucko 1981, recommendation 22) that the development of culture houses should take place *within* NMMZ in order to make explicit that this development was accepted by Government as a *national* concern and obligation (and, only incidentally, that NMMZ should therefore become a statutory body within the Ministry of Education and Culture) (Ucko 1981, recommendation 1). Some of the officials concerned thought that the NMMZ on no account would wish to be associated with culture houses. However, others considered that they might be a good idea, if the Government made available extra finance and staffing and if the proposed developments were put under the control of the existing regional NMMZ organization and if adequate conservation facilities were made available.

Already at this stage in the 1980s, therefore, it was not clear to what extent it was bureaucracy and political relations which were causing difficulties or, alternatively, how far the various Zimbabwean concepts of a static archaeological past, the role of education, or the nature of the national heritage were determinants of decision-making. In the 1990s the situation is, if anything, more rigid and power bases more entrenched: 'It would be well-nigh impossible for National Museums and Monuments of Zimbabwe to consider offering the "official support" for the "culture house" concept because such support can only be provided by the relevant Ministry', i.e. Ministry of Education and Culture (F. P. Matipano, pers. comm., 6.6.91). Indeed, there is already evidence of non-cooperation between the two heritage education-related ministerial enterprises, the Home Affairs' NMMZ having apparently refused to loan even temporary exhibitions to the Education Ministry's one existing culture house, or to train its staff in such skills as conservation (D. Mutasa, pers. comm., 8.5.91). Likewise, Education sees no priority in increasing the number of Education Officers to be based in NMMZ and, yet, future co-operation between the two Ministries is clearly essential for several foreshadowed educational developments with regard to NMMZ (Stone 1994). Furthermore, there is now another contender as the *alma mater* of Zimbabwean culture and education – the National Arts Council – which is attempting to formulate 'the National Cultural Policy of Zimbabwe' (*The Herald*, 21.9.91; and see Cheater 1992). Not surprisingly, therefore, entrenched political infighting continues between individuals, Ministries and various other organs of Government (*The Herald*, 5.7.91; Anon 1991, pp. 17, 40). This National Arts Council draft cultural policy document is at pains to define Government's role within culture, as it does for languages, *promoting* Shona and Ndebele, while only *allowing* other 'minority languages' to 'develop' as part of the heritage. Whereas theatre, music, dance, crafts and literature are to be *promoted*, 'Zimbabwe antiquities will be preserved and protected from destruction, theft or illegal exportation. Where they were taken away every effort will be made to recover them.' The draft concludes, 'it is essential that all Zimbabweans participate actively in the creation of a culture that is responsive to their needs and aspirations'. Neither archaeology nor culture houses are explicitly mentioned anywhere in this draft policy document.

At the bottom of this seemingly bureaucratic power struggle are two national interest groups. One, a 'parastatal' based in Home Affairs, relatively well-financed and with trained personnel, concentrates on the museum- and site-based evidence of the past but in financial competition with other interests such as the police; the other, based in Education, is more poorly staffed and responsible for local cultural initiatives but in financial competition also with sporting activities (and see also, for Micronesia, Eperiam 1991, pp. 178–9). In the current Zimbabwean context this is all the more unfortunate as it is quite possible that some of the site museums established by the NMMZ over the past few years could become the focus of the previously proposed culture houses in some Districts. In addition, any future culture houses can be expected to wish to display loan collections deriving from existing museums, as well as to feature in their local context (whether on a temporary or permanent basis) those local items of material culture (from the archaeological or recent past) which are currently housed within national museums in towns. Much the same sentiment has recently been expressed about the situation in PNG (Eoe & Swadling 1991, p. 269) with conference participants stressing the necessity for close co-operation between national museums and provincial cultural centres.

At one level of analysis, it is possible to see such bureaucratic and political conflicts, as does Cheater (1992), as part of a larger incompatibility between some aspects of Zimbabwe's early avowed 'socialist' agenda and some of its nationalist ones. In this situation, she argues, there is an irreconcilable tension between the nature and variety of 'rural' traditions and the national policy of black Zimbabwean politicians. She isolates, as particularly symptomatic, the anti-traditional situation of the black urban 'westernized' youth of Zimbabwe (Cheater 1991, pp. 7–8, 11–14; 1992), exactly that 'outcast' group which, in PNG, is seen to be causing so many problems and whom Eoe has earmarked as being particularly appropriate as a target for a new 'people-oriented' museum role (Eoe 1991a, pp. 2–3). At the same time as exhorting such groups to 'find culture', the Zimbabwean nationalists find it politically essential to make negative qualitative evaluations about some of the elements of rural 'cultural activities: large burial payments to relatives, the marriage of very young girls to older men, widow inheritance, the sororate', and so on (Cheater 1991, pp. 15–16). To such a list the draft (1991) National Cultural Policy of Zimbabwe adds the 'negative traditional practice [of] witchcraft [which] will be discouraged' (11.22 'traditional Medicine').

Such potential conflict between future national identity in a way dominated by the West, with a sanitized set of 'traditional' practices from the past, can also be greatly affected by external funding agencies which can have a pro-found influence on internal events, since they almost invariably follow the policies of those in power in the host country, a point which Addyman (1991) does not discuss for Zimbabwe. Thus, as Cheater (1991, 1992) points out, the area of 'rural culture' to be promoted by nationalist politicians in Zimbabwe is the 'performing arts', supposedly 'traditional' and easily promotable by visits to foreign countries and by presentation to visiting dignitaries, as well as being lucrative via visiting foreign tourists. So we find major international funding bodies, such as the Ford Foundation, currently withdrawing from the internal problems of Zimbabwean cultural diversity to concentrate instead on what are considered to be the positive aspects of the 'interface' inherent in the

Ethnomusicology Program at the Zimbabwe College of Music and the Dance Foundations Course at the National Ballet (P. Fry, pers. comm.).

> The former, [it is claimed, is] concerned with 'traditional' as well as 'contemporary' music, so while it collects and collates 'ethnic' musical traditions from around the country, it is also interested in the musical forms that emerge in cities as part of the process of the formation of 'national' musical forms.
>
> (Fry 1991, p. 10)

The latter

> is an attempt to bring together the many dance traditions of Zimbabwe by training a multi-racial dance company . . . it brings white and black people and traditions together in a courageous attempt to express, through dance, the various ethnic traditions of the country *and* their inter-relationships.
>
> (Fry 1991, p. 10)

Whilst such projects have the potential to accommodate the dynamic and multifaceted character of Zimbabwean culture, the emphasis has clearly shifted completely away from any attempt to support the distinctively local. More generally, however, such exercises in 'filtering' local cultural activity – not least through bureaucratic agencies, whether internal or from overseas – must be recognized for the political exercises that they are. It is through such negotiations about acceptable areas of culture – often to form the basis of educative support activities – that the nature of 'culture' is redefined, thus affording the means by which dominant groups may appropriate parts of local cultural activity to themselves (Merlan 1989, pp. 106–7, 114–5).

> To maintain [the] conception of the nation-state it is necessary constantly to stress the existence of only *one* cultural model, *one* history, *one* language, *one* social project. At the most, diversity can be 'tolerated' by the state but not fully accepted. . . . On the one hand, cultural plurality is underplayed in the name of 'national integration'. On the other, differences based on 'racial', ethnic or cultural grounds are reinforced to cover the contradictions arising out of domination, class relations and conflicts.
>
> (Devalle 1992, p. 20)

Thus, 'the culture and history of the different populations composing the nation-state are censored: ethnicity is codified and made immutable in response to the needs of the codifiers acting as self-styled "true" spokesmen of their societies' (Devalle 1992, p. 21).

Cheater (1991, p. 9) takes the history of the Zimbabwean culture-house experiment as an example of the consequences of the overall situation as she has isolated and analysed it, an experiment which failed ostensibly for lack of finance but really as a result of its inherent contradictory position *vis-à-vis* the more powerful agenda of Zimbabwean national politics. As we have seen above, the actual detailed events surrounding the creation and development of the Murewa Culture House do, in part at least (e.g. the clash between 'old' and 'new' authority), complement Cheater's analysis, but they also reflect a host of other considerations about the way that the past may be handled by a (new) nation.

The idea of a museum

One such consideration takes us back to the perceived notions of museums, and their role in the field of culture. There is a considerable literature (e.g. Akenji 1991; Ames 1992; Adande & Zevounou 1994; Funari 1994; Nzewunwa 1994), deriving from many parts of the world, questioning whether the western European concept of a museum is apposite to non-European interests and traditions. 'Exhibitions, and museums themselves, have come to be criticized as hegemonic devices of cultural elites or states. They distort and hence mask the oppression of the cultures they supposedly represent' (Durrans 1992, p. 11). More concretely, for example, in the Pacific, there are numerous warnings (e.g. Fusitu'a 1991, p. 198, for Tonga) against the notion of a museum separated from the true repositories of cultural property – Tonga private homes – and many expressions of disquiet about the potential of museums (and museum collecting) to introduce an element of financial gain and financial self-sufficiency into the sphere of culture, where such interests are totally inappropriate (e.g. Silau 1991, p. 90, for PNG). Indeed, there are both attempts to establish a non-European historical epistemology for 'museums' of the past, for example the Cook Islands' 'houses of esoteric knowledge', 'entertainment house where the art of warfare was taught', 'Are-Korero where history was taught and the Pia-Atua [which] highlighted religion' (Tutai 1991, p. 201), as well as attempts to incorporate the museum phenomenon within 'traditional' systems via nomenclature – 'Haus Tamboran', for example, to apply not only to the National Museum but also to local cultural centres in PNG (J. Golson, pers. comm.). Generalizing in the context of PNG, Blacking (1984, pp. 22–3) stresses that:

> Cultural Centres must be more than museums that preserve and recall the provincial heritage, shops that sell craft goods, and venues for entertainment. They must be places for continuing education about the present and future, as well as the past, and spiritual centres whose work ensures that each member of the community can participate in the processes of achieving modernization without losing the richness of regional diversity. . . .
>
> [T]he organizers of provincial centres may wish at first to develop their existing regional strengths in carving, craft-production, drama, or whatever. But if they can also have a vision of the 'ideal'

cultural centre, they may be encouraged to try something new. . . .
The task of a cultural centre is to harness and coordinate all these
and other resources in such a way that none feels excluded from
using them.

Nowadays, even in the western world, there is movement away from the
static and 'artificially contextualized' (Ames 1992, p. 52) display, and this
movement incorporates the evidence derived from archaeological enquiry, just
as much as the ethnographic; more and more it is becoming clear to some
western archaeologists (e.g. Addyman 1990) that their isolation of the archaeological past into static protected sites, or even areas, and static museum
collections has been a recipe for disaster, leading variously either to public
apathy on the one hand (e.g. Shanks & Tilley 1987; Layton 1989a, 1989b;
Hodder 1991a; Fowler 1992, pp. 102–5), or even to civil disobedience on the
other (e.g. Bender & Edmonds 1992). Indeed, the relevant role of archaeology
and the living vitality of the evidence of the past in another African country,
Nigeria – both with regard to museum displays and site protection – can be
held up as a positive icon for the future (Champion & Ucko In Press). To do
otherwise, and to relegate 'cultural diversity . . . presented as a museum
exhibit ("exoticism", "culture for tourists") isolated from social reality and
thus innocuous', creates a situation whereby the state 'appropriate(s) for itself
the expressions of culture of the subordinate sector and . . . attempt(s) to
integrate these expressions in a modified form into its discourse of national
unity' (Devalle 1992, p. 21).

The NMMZ is apparently committed to a course of opting out of any
concept of a living past, and of archaeology in the present.

Indeed, in Harare, an unpopular static 'Shona Village' is currently on display
in the museum (P. Garlake, pers. comm., 1981; Ucko 1981, p. 9; Mabvadya
1990, p. 27), while tourists buy artefacts from the National Gallery or witness
'performance' and (since 1985) buy art outside Harare at the *commercially* run
'Chapungu Village [which also houses] a reproduction of a nineteenth-century
Shona village, comprising five huts, one of which houses the *n'anga* (traditional healer and soothsayer) who is available for consultation at no extra cost'
(*A Tourist Paradise*, June 1991, p. 11). Having adopted a static museum
approach, it is perhaps not surprising that NMMZ seems unwilling to recognize 'traditional'[8] Zimbabwean attachments to material culture objects, and
thus has no place for such ongoing cultural concerns amongst the public.
Museums, if they are not to remain isolated in their conception of an archaeological, exclusively static, past need to be flexible. In the early years of
Murewa Culture House an old woman had donated a carved walking-stick to
its museum, only to request it back when her dead brother's spirit caused her
bad dreams and objected to the walking-stick being left there. At Great
Zimbabwe requests for the return of previously donated pottery, 'knife and
sheath, brass work and some of the old objects used in ancestral rituals'
followed the departure of a trusted curator when the local people no longer

Figure 17.8 Site museum under construction in the shadow of the Nyanga mountains. Photo: J. Hubert.

thought of the village as a 'good place to keep old treasured things in' (L. Hodges, pers. comm., 1981). Such attitudes towards 'heirlooms' do not appear to have any place in the plans of NMMZ, which takes such objects into permanent custody for static display.

Nor is this approach confined to urban museums, since at some sites Norwegian 'aid' has been accepted, in the form of large, currently empty and standardized museum structures (Fig. 17.8). Here the implications are even more widespread than for treasured heirlooms, for these site museums, which currently act only as eyesores and potential embarrassments to the integrity of the painted rock shelters of the Matopo Hills or the towering dominance of the Nyanga mountains of Ziwa and Nyahokwe, are in areas of intense significance to the living. No one is sure what is to be displayed in these Norwegian-funded site museums, but what is clear is that Addyman's recommendation (1991, 1.37 (7.5)) that 'Ziwa and Nyahokwe should be managed, marketed and interpreted as a pair, aspects of the same remarkable archaeological landscape' is a far cry from the culture-house ideal which would vest control in the local people of the area who continue today to see these (*three*) mountains as living significant sites of very special importance. Similarly, Addyman's (1991, 9.5.1) statement about the Matopo Hills, that 'the conjunction of a beautiful, well-run and much loved National Park and a series of prehistoric art sites of international importance makes [them] an obvious candidate for the development of archaeology-based tourism', reduces the sites to 'prehistory' (and see Ucko 1983a, p. 34), and totally disregards the complex attitudes of the majority population towards the whole area and its rock shelters (Ranger 1989a).

By divorcing the archaeological museum-based static past from current living involvement in the past (as *we* define it), in placing other priorities above the correction of stereotypical and misleading museum captions, and in making its priority the preservation of monuments and sites of the past for cultural tourism, NMMZ is about to make the traditional western approach to the past its own. It is striking that the current Master Plan (Collett 1992) relegates discussion of sites that are 'symbolically' or 'culturally significant' to less than one page, merely noting that the existence of such sites 'may, on occasion, conflict with the official aims of governments in developing countries' – i.e. local control and limitation of access to sites in order to define and manifest subgroup identity *versus* open tourist access to all sites for the benefit of a unified nation (Collett 1992, p. 48). As the then Executive Director of the NMMZ Service said (F. P. Matipano, pers. comm., 6.6.91): 'our development Plan though envisaging a programme of site museums, the reasons, aims and objectives of these are not necessarily the same as [culture houses]'. Indeed they are not, since they are driven by government policy which requires NMMZ – which itself has taken the decision to separate the archaeological past from all other evidence – to be 'self-sustaining' (*Report 1992*, p. 4), even though this 'will lead to conflicts with other values associated with the heritage, e.g. educational and cultural values' (Collett 1992, p. 7).[9]

Creating a 'preserved and protected' national culture

Why should 'relevant' museums, the concept of 'living sites', and culture houses, be receiving such a hard passage in Zimbabwe? Can it be simply and satisfactorily explained solely in terms of government financial policy and ministerial power-base allegiances? Surely not.

Can it then be adequately understood in the context of the struggle against an oppressive white minority government? There are, of course, good arguments at such times against focusing on so-called 'tribal' cultural differences, since any division of an oppressed majority might serve to weaken the main aim, the successful acquisition of majority government. But, since 1981, Government has officially acknowledged the differing cultures of the country, and the people in the rural areas undoubtedly have a very strong desire to be allowed to express themselves within their various cultural or ethnic idioms, while at the same time identifying with the Zimbabwe nation. Indeed, in many cases, what used to be called a tribal or linguistic or ethnic culture is no longer coterminous (if it ever was – see Garlake 1982b, p. 8; Ranger 1989b) with a local culture. Cultural change is, and always has been, omnipresent and inevitable. On the face of it, therefore, the Zimbabwean culture-house concept embodied none of the features which could have explained the perceived fears by those in authority, for it took as a given that 'ethnicity' is often not the same as 'tribalism', and explicitly recognized that neither of them is necessarily coterminous with district 'cultural identity' in the Zimbabwe of 1981 or of today. There is, indeed, no inevitable one-to-one correlation between the languages and the cultures or tribes of the country. In this context, therefore, it would appear that those in authority in the new Zimbabwe went too far in their attacks during 1980 and 1981 on the multicultural background of their country. Thus, the President (*The Herald*, 15.6.81), in an article under the heading 'Out with laziness', says:

> All tribal or regional self-interest, and the cardinal evil of nepotism must never be allowed to rear their ugly heads in Zimbabwe, for these make for the erosion of talent and the crowning of corrup-tion. . . . Putting aside the fetishes of race, culture or tribe and the evils of apathy and laziness. . . . We must lose our ethnic identities in order to find our true selves within the context of Zimbabwean identity.

Similarly, the Deputy Minister of Education and Culture wrote (*The Sunday Mail*, 5.7.81): 'By the time our children leave secondary school, they should simply regard themselves as Zimbabweans irrespective of their tribal, regional and racial origins.'

Could such stress on monoculturalism be directly accounted for by the then impending clashes between 'tribal' followers of Mugabe and Nkomo? Perhaps such public utterances needed to be made in preference to reassurances regard-ing the qualitative worth of local cultures. In the Zimbabwean situation, however, apart from Shona and Ndebele – and unlike the Botswanan situation as described by MacKenzie (1990) and Grant (1990) – we are talking about such small minority groups (e.g. Tonga 1 per cent, Venda 1 per cent, Ndau 3 per cent) that suspected insurrection of these smaller groups surely cannot have been the sole answer.[10] Yet, still in 1986, Prime Minister (now President) Mugabe (as reported in the *Guardian*, 12.5.86), felt it worth denigrating cultural differences: 'ZANU . . . is sensitive about any suggestion of friction [even] between the three sub-groups, or clans, of the majority Shona tribe that dominates both the ruling party and the Government' (and see Ranger 1989b, pp. 118–19).

Can the monocultural emphasis have derived from suspicion of the prior colonial classification? The histories and ethnographies of Zimbabwe, what-ever their mainly colonial origins and their shortcomings (see Garlake 1982b, pp. 7–10, 14–15), make it clear that different cultural groups came into the country on numerous occasions, sometimes settling in large numbers (e.g. International African Institute 1955). There is little doubt that the history of the country is immensely complex, and that intercultural exchanges and admixtures have frequently occurred at least over relatively recent years (Garlake 1982b, pp. 14–15; Ranger 1989b). In any case it can be assumed that many of the cultures of today are not exactly the same as those of 100 or 200 (let alone 1000 or 2000) years ago. Academic ascriptions, by outside observers, of 'tribal' or other labels – together with assumptions about unchanging cultural continuity – can indeed be dangerous. After all, until very recently in South Africa, tribal studies were used as a basis of efforts to divide the majority (Hall 1984), and to demonstrate peoples' previous 'inadequacies' (Ucko 1983b, 1985; Hall 1984). In white-dominated Rhodesia (as in South Africa) academics and others had carried out 'delineation studies' between 1964 and 1967 which are still the basis of fear and distrust regarding any government interest or action which appears to necessitate enquiry into the cultural/ethnic/tribal composition of the country (and see Ranger 1989b, pp. 119–20 for renewed reference to such studies in the late 1970s). Nevertheless, such fears are more likely to be endemic in the rural population rather than to be effective checks on any agreed government action.

Of course, multicultural policies have not only been problematical for the national government of Zimbabwe. PNG perhaps affords the clearest example that any bland assumption that acceptance of cultural diversity will easily give added support to the unity of national governments is likely to be simplistic. After all, the preamble to the PNG Constitution explicitly states that:

> We the People of PNG pay homage and respect to the memory of our ancestors; We the People of PNG acknowledge the worthy customs and traditional wisdom of our people . . .

and the fifth national goal directs:

> the fostering of a respect for and appreciation of traditional ways of life and culture, including languages in all their richness and variety.

Yet, as we have already seen above, few (if any) of the cultural centres in PNG have survived expatriate interest, or the termination of outside financial grants. The national government has not thought it worth while continuing such support. In addition, in practice, when culture houses *have* come into being, the results are not always as were ideally envisaged (whether for PNG or Zimbabwe (Ucko 1981)), since the local emphasis may lead to culture houses remaining exclusively inward-looking; thus, in one area of PNG:

> At present there is little local interest in exhibits from outside the Province. However, once students look into their own traditions, their interest in exhibits from other cultures in P.N.G. and other countries of the world might grow. At the moment there is little, if any, exchange of exhibits between Cultural Centres in P.N.G. The Enga Museum would be prepared to send out exhibits although it may be some time before there will be an interested population to receive them.
>
> (Tumu & Kyakas 1991, p. 61)

In other individual circumstances, such as in the Solomon Islands, a cultural centre may become the only locus 'to act as a catalyst for the renewal of interest in indigenous values and systems and their reincorporation into twentieth century life' (Totu & Roe 1991, p. 121). In other words, in the context of the nationalism of a newly independent country – and perhaps in particular in the context of a nation (or regions within a nation) which has suffered profound change in the past through colonial interference – support for local cultural activity may result in mere localized and introverted revivalism. There is a clear risk to national government in either process. Nor can it be simply assumed that claims to individual (or ethnic) identity based on oral history will disappear once a country has escaped from colonialism (Garlake 1982b, p. 15).

The current problems of the culture centre initiative in PNG are in sharp contrast to the continuing hopes for such locally based initiatives; thus, Blacking (1984, p. 9) described the ideal for a multicultural nation as: 'a national culture that combines but does not suppress the distinctiveness of many, apparently different regional cultures' (and see Blacking 1990, p. 169), while a recent conference concluded:

> cultural heritage institutions, such as museums and cultural centres, by actively promoting and strengthening local customs, traditions and languages, serve as an aid to government in the maintenance of law and order and the reduction of anti-social behaviour during a period of great social change. When successfully carrying out this role, museums and cultural centres become dynamic and interesting places and in this way serve their community and visitors. By and large such (often expatriate) visions get nowhere: for many new nations, 'politically the past is inconvenient, often troublesome and therefore expendable'.
>
> (Groube 1985, p. 54)

There is a growing and recent body of international literature which suggests that adequate analysis of the apparently somewhat heterogeneous material and information which has been discussed above will depend on an understanding of the nature, role and process of the phenomenon currently often referred to as ethnicity (e.g. Eriksen 1991), particularly in relation to nation-states (e.g. Weaver 1984). Some of the literature should serve to link the level of analysis adopted for the case of Zimbabwe by Cheater (see above, pp. 255, 258) to a wider context of the resistance to Zimbabwean culture houses, and to modern approaches to the nature of archaeological evidence.

When Zimbabweans say, 'What is language without culture? What is culture without language? What are people without culture? What are people without identity?' and, in 1981 at least (Ucko 1981), go on to stress that such local cultural concerns do not vitiate larger national concerns – nor national pride – perhaps the sincerity of such beliefs camouflages hidden dangers. Certainly there is literature which stresses the intimate family and friendship contexts of identity-formation, and suggests that this intimacy is the basis of 'why ethnicity can be fashioned into such a powerful political force' (Eriksen 1991, p. 139).[11] Elsewhere it is claimed that 'ethnicity as a metaphor for opposition becomes "subversive" in the eyes of the state and the ruling classes' (Devalle 1992, pp. 16–17). Assuming that such analyses have point to them, it is the use of languages which is felt to be especially significant. For example, Devalle (1992, p. 17) has stated that:

> the languages of . . . ethnic minorities are marginalized or their existence is denied, while the language of those in power is imposed as the official one. . . . The power-holders [then classify ethnic languages, or their users] as 'folklore', 'dialects' and 'tradition' [, reflecting] the great potential language has for practical political purposes and for maintaining a people's identity.

And this comment finds a close echo in the results of the 1981 survey (Ucko 1981), which revealed that many groups in Zimbabwe felt aggrieved that no government, including the current one, had ever recognized their distinct cultural qualities. For many years they had expressed their anxiety and disquiet by complaining to Government that their languages were no longer taught in schools (and see Murphree 1988). When the people spoke of their 'language' they used the word to include all their cultural activities. According to analysts such as Devalle (1992, p. 19) such apparently unthreatening sentiments fundamentally challenge 'the nation-state [which is to be] portrayed as an all-embracing inter-class collectivity, a supercommunity with no internal contradictions' – an entity which is potentially at risk challenged by any 'regional and ethno-national movements'.

Ethnic identities are not static, whatever the members may claim at any particular moment. Their terms of reference may change according to context (in PNG, from village to language group to province to nation (Groube 1985, p. 57)), and their reference points – often located somewhere in a past – may, or may not, coincide with the evidence of chronologically situated material culture (Roosens 1989, p. 12; Eriksen 1991, pp. 129–49). Such change occurs in all areas of cultural activity, no less in language, 'styles' of behaviour, kinship, religious beliefs, or economics than in art works or material culture (Devalle 1992, p. 16). To claim to be a member of a visible group is arguably more a decision about contemporary affairs and political decision-making about maintaining cultural difference than it is about continuity from an archaeologically uncovered past (Eriksen 1991, p. 129; Devalle 1992).

Nor, today, can one continue to claim that the details of such an archaeologically derived past are any more 'factual' than any other social constructs. As is now well demonstrated, despite the tangible nature of most archaeological remains, this leaves the interpretation of the significance of such material culture as much a matter of changing opinions and changing assumptions as it is in other areas of social enquiry. In PNG, for example, models of archaeological interpretation should have changed drastically as a result of absolute dating methods, but the old models of migrations and racial superiority cling on among the writings of some archaeologists as well as in the views of the 'taught' local populations (Groube 1985, pp. 61, 64, 66–7, 69–70). Such a changing nature of interpretation applies just as much to all the 'real' archaeology of Zimbabwe – all that material (e.g. Sinclair, Pikirayi, Pwiti & Soper 1993) about which few living Zimbabweans (so far?) claim either knowledge or sentiment – as it does to the materials which are the basis of understanding about the more recent past. It was, after all, to safeguard this supposedly acultural material that NMMZ was primarily created and around which its activities mainly revolve.

Creating the past

It is here that several ironies regarding the treatment of the past can be seen most clearly. In adopting a static reconstructional approach to archaeological evidence of the past, and attempting to implement this approach to the highest possible international standards (including the training overseas of key members of staff, the employment of outside consultants and the adoption of the most up-to-date conservation and scientific techniques), NMMZ has now been forced to attempt to attract and educate via a strategy of site presentation equating the past with entertainment through theme park reconstructions. It can, of course, be, and indeed often is, argued that there is nothing inherently wrong with such an approach to teaching or, more specifically, to education about the past (Addyman 1990, pp. 261–2; Fowler 1992, pp. 116–17; Stone 1992). Nevertheless, Durrans's (1992, p. 12) distinction between educationally oriented museums, which try to fill visitors' minds, and theme parks, which try to empty their pockets, remains essentially apt.

In the Zimbabwean context, however, there is a clear initial risk in such a strategy. As has been shown elsewhere (Ucko 1981), British and Rhodesian colonialism both had as one of their aims the denigration of most aspects of indigenous Zimbabwean cultural activity. One result is that, whilst many traditional values remained alive in Zimbabwe, they remained hidden beneath the surface of free public expression (Ucko 1981). The NMMZ is currently involved with some sites (e.g. the Matopo Hills, Ziwa and Nyahokwe) and material culture (e.g. Shona axes) of genuine concern to living Zimbabweans, but is ignoring (or is ignorant of) their current significance; it also refrains from highlighting in its displays typological and other evidence of some kind of cultural continuity, albeit associated with dynamic changes in functions over time and in different contexts (e.g. Dewey 1985), and is assuming that all are acultural prehistoric remains. That this is clearly not the case is shown by the fact that, recently, authorized survey at the archaeological site of Mutota included an invitation to local school-children and the public in general to come and witness what was going on. To the archaeologists' surprise, the local spirit medium forbade any plans for excavation at this 'sacred' site (G. Pwiti, pers. comm.). Once archaeology loses the respect or trust of the people, the NMMZ's job of public education about the past becomes even more difficult (and see Condori (1989) for a striking parallel with events in Bolivia).

Nevertheless, apart from such misunderstandings about the continuing significance to living groups of some objects and of some significant sites, the vast majority of archaeological evidence – the different ceramic types and styles, the worked bones and flints, and the vague scatter of past artefactual activity – is (presumably) material which the average citizen does not even recognize, let alone appreciate as having any worth for the documentation and understanding of their own, and their nation's, past. As Kennedy (1991, p. 149) has put it regarding PNG, much, if not most, archaeological material concerns 'a past often far beyond the reach of any oral or written source'. It is in this context that NMMZ's site museums and its national museums' educational outreach programmes are seen by the service as vital instruments in the battle to involve the general public, and to educate as many as possible to an appreciation of the Zimbabwean heritage – such education to result in improved protection of the heritage and more effective implementation of existing legislation. Laudable as such aims clearly are, they sit uneasily with a static approach to the archaeological past, since 'the past' (see next page) has an 'unfortunate' propensity to being appropriated by the living from the moment that its potential importance is recognized. As membership of ethnic groups changes, and as such groups reorientate themselves *vis-à-vis* others, so the potential significance of complexes of material culture will be differentially assessed and their potential as symbols of past group identity differently evaluated. As Weaver (1984, p. 184) has pointed out, what she calls 'private' ethnicity may derive its validity of practice *either* from 'knowledge that their behaviour approximates traditional forms' *or*, simply, from the knowledge 'that it is distinct from surrounding non-aboriginal lifestyles'. That material culture can be part of such group identity flagging is made clear by Roosens (1989, p. 12): 'Cultural traits that are postulated as external emblems (cloth, language, etc.) or even as fundamental values (e.g. faithfulness in friendship) can . . . be taken from one's own tradition or from other people's or simply may be created.' Certainly, claims to, and for, ethnic identity almost always make reference 'to a common past and usually to a territory' (Devalle 1992, p. 19), such 'invented traditions (being) concerned with establishing a legitimating continuity with the past, not with understanding historical discontinuities and the evolution of social contradictions' (Devalle 1992, p. 21). Therefore, in this sense at least, NMMZ will have succeeded in its educational aims only when its own, dated, approach to the nature of the archaeological evidence of the past is clearly adjudged to be deficient by the public's claims, and counterclaims, to ownership.

There is still a further point to be considered in this regard, namely (as seen at the beginning of this chapter) the claim by western archaeologists – as also, according to Garlake (1982b, p. 2), by all the Rhodesian archaeologists for the first sixty years after colonization – that the information deriving from material culture which is uncovered *archaeologically* is somehow of a different, more objective, kind than *other* evidence of the past (for example historical records or information derived from oral history – and see Muriuki 1990). The use of archaeology and archaeological discoveries in affording a link to a past with which they can identify or, conversely, cutting a people off from such a past – with the assumed consequence of making it more difficult for them to act as a coherent group – has only relatively recently begun to receive serious attention in the literature (e.g. Ucko 1983a, 1985; Hall 1984; Olsen 1986; Layton 1989a, 1989b). In the context of ethnic identity formation, the symbols of identity, or the charters from a suggested traditional past, are continually being reformulated – often by the nation-state concerned. Legitimation of ethnic identity rests in the hands of the nation-state, which may, on occasion, 'incorporate some of the symbols of aboriginal demands in their definitions. . . . Over time, it [such a limited ethnic identity] can become institutionalized, significantly affecting the perceptions of the minorities, both their own and those of the society-at-large' (Weaver 1984, pp. 184–5). Or, in other words, 'the state appropriates for itself the expression of culture of the subordinate sections and attempts to integrate these expressions in a modified form into its discourse of national unity' (Devalle 1992, p. 21). From this perspective there is no justification for archaeologists attempting a convenient separation of the oral history or ethnographic evidence about the recent past from their own archaeological discoveries about a more remote past. Archaeological evidence from rock art in Australia, whether in Western Australia or Queensland and from whatever remote date, can suddenly become a gender symbol or a defining icon of current group identity (e.g. Mowaljarlie, Vinnicombe, Ward & Chippindale 1988; Layton 1992, p. 248), just as can the Igbo Ukwu 'bronzes' from eastern Nigeria (Champion & Ucko In Press). Nor is there any justification for the western tendency – at least until the recent events in eastern 'Europe' – to think of problems of cultural and ethnic identification as being a particularly Third World malaise. This is a western conceit, for such questions of identity are equally pertinent everywhere and, as recent events in the former USSR and Yugoslavia have demonstrated, can rear up with fervent emotional ferocity in what have been considered to be the most unexpected places.

The crisis of interpretation

The fact is that results of studies of the past (including those of archaeology) have often become primary fodder for political usage (e.g. Ucko 1983b, 1989a, pp. xv–xix). No doubt this will always be so with such a 'scarce resource' as 'the past', but it is particularly the case with archaeological interpretation, which is essentially non-scientific and subjective (see also Olsen 1986; Shanks & Tilley 1987; Olivier & Coudart 1992). The apparent irony is that archaeological data are often seen to be essential for political 'justification' of proposed actions, whereas archaeological interpretation is in reality particularly poor in its methodology when it tries to confront exactly such questions as those of cultural continuity or discontinuity that might make it relevant to the analysis of those processes of culture change so often at the basis of political debate and conflict (Garlake 1982b, pp. 11–13; Shennan 1989). In the context of archaeology in Zimbabwe, Garlake (1982b, p. 3) has shown that 'the settler paradigm [of assumed Bantu and other major invasions within "an unchanging tribal Africa" (Garlake 1982b, p. 6)] has . . . governed all protohistoric research in Zimbabwe even though archaeologists all recognized the absurdity of the settler view on the origins of Great Zimbabwe'. He continues (Garlake 1982b, p. 14) by stressing that only when archaeology ceases its 'esoteric process of description and classification of artefacts and share[s] in analysis of processes of change . . . [will] it become increasingly comprehensible and significant to people outside the discipline'.

Not surprisingly, the new approaches to archaeological interpretation in Zimbabwe which have very recently begun to develop (e.g. Sinclair, Pikirayi, Pwiti & Soper 1993) have not, so far, had a chance to be reflected either in museum displays or within site presentations. Garlake's superb popular publications of the early 1980s (e.g. first editions: 1982a, 1983) remain highly exceptional works of interpretation and skilful presentation for children and adults alike. Archaeology has also now found a place within school history textbooks (see Pwiti 1994). Nevertheless, for the wider adult public the overall picture presented by Garlake about the 1980s (see above, pp. 239–41) remains true in the 1990s.

As a discipline, archaeology since at least the 1950s has everywhere become wedded to western-based assumptions about the primary interest and importance of linear chronology (and with it, the importance of scientific dating techniques). In its development archaeology has now become even more entwined with the heritage industry (and with it, the need for conservation and reconstruction of particular kinds of very visible monuments to suit the convenience of tourism). Such preoccupations therefore make its pronouncements appear irrelevant at least to other cultural traditions which concentrate instead on different forms of chronological schemata (Layton 1989a; Ucko 1989b, p. xiv) or where, as in PNG, 'the past is private, individual, and secret, not public property or the object of curiosity by outsiders' (Groube 1985, p. 53). In the Zimbabwean context, for example, the collapse of ancient walls at least at some sites is seen to be the intentional acts of relevant ancestors (Mabvadya 1990). Whether or not the heritage and touristic developments affecting archaeology are to be welcomed, they have little to do with what we now recognize about the use of the archaeological evidence of the past. As Hodder (1991a, p. 70) has put it:

> The reading of an event is . . . never finished. Particularly in the case of long-lived monuments in the past, we must assume that they were continually open to new interpretations and to new meanings, as they are today. The context in which an event is read is continually changing. There is therefore always something specific and particular to any full interpretation of an event.

In this context it is disturbing to find that the numerous commissioned technical reports on how to preserve Great Zimbabwe (e.g. Rodrigues & Manuelshagen 1987) have been concerned exclusively with method and technique, apparently based on the assumption that it is self-evident which particular moment in the (highly damaged and often reconstructed) past of that monument should be preserved. Similarly, perhaps, it is a striking feature of the current plans for tourism in Zimbabwe that education about the value of the past (through Education Officers and by the inclusion of heritage matters within school curricula) is assumed to be an easy, almost automatic, matter leading inevitably to improved 'awareness' of the heritage amongst the public (Collett 1992, pp. 16–17, 85–6) – as if, indeed, there is only one version of the past to be understood or appreciated. Here the lesson from PNG may be apt and timely for, if Groube (1985, p. 60) is to be believed, despite the words of the PNG Constitution and the all-embracing legislation (see above, p. 265), 'the immediate past is already dim . . . [and] the past is irrelevant', with PNG students showing actual antipathy towards it.

Apparently, in contrast to PNG, almost every Zimbabwean considers himself or herself an expert on the country and its peoples, and many have a genuine interest in learning more about their ancestors, even through excavation and site recording programmes by archaeologists (G. Pwiti, pers. comm.). Any assumption by NMMZ about the automatic consequences of formal education regarding the preservation of archaeological sites may, however, be naive and even dangerously counter-productive. After all, Zimbabweans have very varied interests and backgrounds, and some of them assume that archaeology equates with disturbance of the dead (Mabvadya 1990, p. 16). In addition, existing traditional rural involvement and concern with the monuments of the past has not yet led to extensive visiting of 'archaeological' sites or museums. Thus, there is little to suggest that Collett's reports of interviews in English with a 'grab sample' of Zimbabwean visitors to Great Zimbabwe over the four-day Easter holiday in 1987 – requesting that restoration of collapsing walls should be carried out as authentically as possible (Collett 1992, pp. 12, 89–92) – are more representative (or should be considered more important) than the beliefs of a few rural Zimbabweans, interviewed by Mabvadya in 1990, who take such wall collapses to be 'the spirits destroying their own sites with the intention of making a shift of their home just as living people will do when they want to move to a new area. . . . these spirits may use anybody or wild animals to do it' (Mabvadya 1990, pp. 13–14, 22). Simply to recognize baboons as one of the exogenous causes of Great Zimbabwe's or Khami's wall collapses (Sassoon 1982; Rodrigues & Manuelshagen 1987) and imposing various western 'solutions' (including shooting) to prevent them from continuing to do so may be culturally counter-productive.[12]

Conclusions: whose 'house' is it to be?

Current archaeological interpretation focuses on attempting to understand the archaeological evidence in its past cultural and social context; current heritage management must focus on the understanding of the past in its modern context. Given a combination of these two interests, archaeology clearly has the potential to be of interest to everyone. Great Zimbabwe, rather than becoming an international tourist theme park entertainment, could become, in Garlake's (1982c, p. 32) words, the opportunity 'to teach the contemporary citizens of Zimbabwe: lessons about living together in societies which transcend tribe, and about exploiting the Zimbabwean rural environment in ways that can support a city, using the most elementary agricultural technology' – all messages deriving from archaeological investigation and archaeological evidence.

As has been seen above in the discussion of culture houses, and the Zimbabwean attitude to heirlooms, there is nothing inherent in the nature of archaeological evidence to make it aseptic and moribund – this only comes about through the attitudes of those who promote the kind of archaeological interpretation which serves their own interests and those of the elite of society and interests of the day. Garlake (1982c, p. 5) correctly warns against a real perceived danger for the future, namely that it could be indigenous archaeologists themselves who, to maintain themselves as an elite, choose to 'again retreat . . . further into the purity of their own discipline'.

There is some evidence that Garlake's warning has not been heeded and that Zimbabwean archaeology has not yet changed its (western) ways. In Ranger's (1982/3) view, the new orientations of archaeological enquiry and interpretation since the 1970s should have opened vistas on the past of Zimbabwean ordinary persons for the education of the ordinary Zimbabwean citizen of today, but he thinks that this has not happened: a 'people's history' can only be found in archaeological interpretations of the Stone and Early Iron Ages, while those of later periods continue to focus on a chief's and king's history. Indeed, there is also evidence of another kind to suggest that archaeology in Zimbabwe is retreating even further from the chance of popular participation; Ndoro (1993) stresses the alienation of the local rural community at places like Great Zimbabwe, where its potential involvement in traditional skills for the conservation of the site has been rejected in favour of 'expensive imported high technology'.

At first sight there is, of course, nothing wrong in having chosen Zimbabwe as the name of the nation – on the contrary (Addyman 1992). However, at least in the context of the present analysis of Zimbabwe's approach to teaching about the past, it is necessary to recognize that this adoption of the past of Great Zimbabwe as the nation's symbol (and, at least in part (Garlake 1982c, p. 31) correcting past archaeological misinterpretations of that site) has been accompanied by the nation-state's accepting only two current Zimbabwean languages as suitable ethnic markers (see above, p. 242, and Murphree 1988, pp. 126–7). It is possible to see this situation as reflecting a government's hesitancy to acknowledge fully its own variety of contemporary traditions – which themselves, of course, derive from the past – a tactic 'that makes it possible for the national government at times to ignore the existence of diversity at the local level' (Jones & Hill-Burnett 1982, p. 238). In choosing to represent its ideals through a symbol of dynastic power – a static (bird) symbol of the past, a castrated elitist dominant moment in past time (Kuklick 1991, pp. 135–7) – the Government's tactic can be seen further to allow it 'at [most] other times to use [the created ethnic elite] as a mechanism to manipulate the elite structure' (Jones & Hill-Burnett 1982, p. 238).

Of course all this is a real challenge to the NMMZ. Should its role be to support the view of the nationally symbolic site of Great Zimbabwe as an impressive static mass of cemented and reconstructed walls,[13] 'its ruinous state conjuring up romantic and picturesque images' (Ndoro 1993), or should it dare to admit that it is aware that the living focus of local attention is Great Zimbabwe's sacred cave(s) – and not especially the walls (which provide useful stones for the fields) at all? Should its new educational programme set out to represent Great Zimbabwe as the tangible material result of an organized past modification of the physical and cultural landscape of the modern country of Zimbabwe? As such it could be shown to represent one, or more accurately many, activities of unique importance in the record of past human behaviour. Equally, other facets of a potential Great Zimbabwe symbolism could be stressed and presented for public discussion: whatever its ethnic pedigree – and Garlake (1982d) stresses the cultural *dis*continuity between those cultural groups which were responsible for its original construction and those cultural groups which later tried to protect the monument from white settler inter-ference – Great Zimbabwe has been vested, no doubt from a heterogeneous variety of sources (D. Collett, pers. comm.), with all kinds of meanings, including its having been, from ancient times, the seat, or location of power, of spirit mediums living at the Eastern Enclosure of the Hill (Garlake 1982d, pp. 27–8). More recently it has been the host to local *n'angas* and to major spirit mediums, as well as being the focus of battles against the colonial regime in its last years. Thus, Great Zimbabwe is far more than a remote ancient archaeolo-gical site. In addition, it embodies a unique set of symbolic messages about indigenous African cultural continuity, of irresistible fascination and signifi-cance to, at least, every Zimbabwean. Sophia Tsvatayi Muchini was not only a spirit medium of extreme importance to the revolutionary anti-imperialist movement who was based (from 1974) within the 'archaeological' site of Great Zimbabwe – and whose tragic arrest at the instigation of NMMZ in 1981 even hit the British newspapers – but she was seen by many to be the reincarnation of the indomitable leader of 1896/7, Ambuya Nehanda, symbol of a glorious past and the hope for a glorious future (Lan 1985, pp. 5–8, 217–19, 222). Sophia herself also claimed to be a vehicle for Chaminuka, commonly accepted as a sixteenth- or seventeenth-century Shona spirit medium (Lan 1985, p. 6; and see Beach 1980, pp. 104–5), and she extended her lineage to Eve, seeing Great Zimbabwe as 'God's place' (Beach 1980; *The Times* 30.3.81; Bourdillon 1982, pp. 191–2; Garlake 1982b, pp. 16–17).

If the untenable dichotomy between a remote archaeological past and a more accessible non-archaeological one continues to be fostered by the NMMZ – as opposed to vesting effective control of all kinds and aspects of the past in some kind of living culture-house concept – then archaeology will continue to be isolated as a practice of interest and relevance to only a small elite. The old inherited assumptions and preconceptions about the nature of the past – as well as the European-derived orthodoxy of the nature and status of the discipline of archaeology – will only have become Zimbabwean when it would not be possible for NMMZ even to conceive of not including some aspects of such a uniquely Zimbabwean symbolism in the message to be transmitted by it as part of NMMZ museum and site educational programmes. Unfortunately, as has been seen, not all the signs are positive: it may be symptomatic of the overall situation that even the 'Master Plan' which is the 'blueprint for strategy' (*Report 1992*, p. 4) and the current driving force behind NMMZ seems, by referring to Great Zimbabwe as a '*medieval*' (my italics) ancient structure (Collett 1992, p. 27), determined to continue to ascribe to this African site of such potential symbolic significance, a traditional European pedigree.

Acknowledgements

I have given thanks for assistance with my work in Zimbabwe in 1981 elsewhere (Ucko 1983a). Later I received information about the culture house development from Juliet Clutton-Brock, Taka Mudariki and Dawson Munjeri. I am grateful to Peter Gathercole for his editorial comments on a previous version of this chapter written at that time (Ucko 1986b). I owe an enormous debt to many people in Zimbabwe who, in 1991 – some of them for a second time – discussed culture houses with me: John Mapondera, Michael Gandidze, Fay Chung, Gilbert Pwiti, D. Mutasa, Dawson Munjeri, C. Musiwa.

I have benefited from comments on various drafts of this chapter by Angela Cheater, Dave Collett, Jack Golson, Olivia Harris, Gwilym Hughes, Sian Jones, Brian Molyneaux, Webber Ndoro, Gilbert Pwiti, Terence Ranger, Thurstan Shaw, Stephen Shennan and Peter Stone. I am particularly grateful to Jane Hubert for having helped in the preparation of the previous version of this chapter, for having shared Zimbabwe with me in 1991, and for having criticized this manuscript.

Notes

1 Ironically, perhaps, it was also a policy which upset those like Robinson who had retired to Bulawayo and could no longer get access to research materials and who became isolated from their archaeological colleagues (Phillipson 1991, p. 4).
2 Not for the first time. In the early 1980s a several million dollar development plan for Great Zimbabwe was clearly also aimed at the foreign tourist (Garlake 1982c, p. 32).
3 As it turned out, the culture house principle was not new to Zimbabwe. In pre-

Zimbabwe Rhodesia a virtual culture house existed, albeit, as in several of the above examples, firmly embedded (at least in its origins) in expatriate initiative, and tourism (Anon n.d.a). The Karanga village, near the ruins of Great Zimbabwe, was intended to be an authentic reconstruction of a nineteenth-century Shona village (except for the chicken house, which was moved away from its traditional frontal position 'because of its smell'!). When the curator of the future village (under the Inspectorate of Monuments) went to live at Great Zimbabwe, people began to bring objects to her (L. Hodges, pers. comm., 23.6.81). In fact, she received more material than she could fit into the site museum display area, which added to the reasons why a village needed to be constructed, since it would be an appropriate place to house the objects. The Karanga village was built with the help of local old people and prisoners and guards from the local gaol. Everyone joined in with enjoyment, including a woman who painted chequered designs on house walls, using white clay from faraway traditional sources. The museums service paid two full-time salaries, for a female potter and for a well-respected *n'anga* (in this case a diviner and herbalist), who received medical enquiries from all over Africa. Tourists would thus be able to see the two at work, and also buy their wares. At this stage the village became significant to the local population since, when the tourists were not present, the two 'employees' lived in traditional ways, and local people began to use the village, carrying out certain rituals, and, before entering, making the right obeisances (L. Hodges, pers. comm., 1981). The 'Karanga Village' was totally destroyed by fire before Independence.

There are contradictory statements about the 'Shona Village' which again exists within Great Zimbabwe (the 'Great Zimbabwe Traditional Village') (Fig. 17.9). According to A. Vines (pers. comm., 5.6.93), it is the main focus of interest for Zimbabwean visitors to Great Zimbabwe whatever the ostensible reasons for their visits (e.g. even on 'Open Days' meant to stimulate appreciation of the archaeological remains). However, according to Collett (1992, p. 23), it is not a success, having few, if any, of the qualities of the earlier 'living village'. Criticisms include the paucity of activities being undertaken and the dubious authenticity of *n'anga* practices. Current plans (Collett 1992, pp. 22–4, 34–5, 68, 80–1) are explicitly designed to create a theme park – whose emphasis should be on profitability – and thereby to destroy any relevance to the concept of a living heritage. In its place, a nineteenth-century frozen act would be created (and see Ranger (1989a, p. 246) for the history and political context of planned traditional structures in the Matopo Hills) – with the 'actors' accordingly dressed in long-abandoned forms of clothing – at a site which will be physically relocated to enable it to be closely associated with a new curio market.

4 According to the Report on the Evaluation of Murewa Culture House (1989, p. 5 (really 4)), there was only one objector, Matabeleland South: 'Matabeleland South local authorities associated "Culture Houses" with similar institutions in Australia meant for Aborigines. (This was considered racial and insulting by authorities.)'
5 Apparently seventeen culture houses were planned for 1981/2 for which sites had been identified and maps produced. Even when finances were frozen by the Ministry of Economic Planning and Development (11.1.82), many of the initiatives continued, with demarcation and site plans being drawn up (Report on the Evaluation of Murewa Culture House 1989, p. 66 (really p. 4)).
6 There are strong rumours (both in Harare and in Murewa) that Murewa was chosen as the location for a very visible and prestigious cultural centre as a reward for previous political activity by an influential person who derived from Murewa.
7 There are some signs that this whole matter may not yet be a dead issue. Thus (although not reported in *Report 1992*), in his speech on the last day of the Donors' Conference of July 1992, Mr Dusan Dragic of UNDP (the Donor Agency) made it clear that he considered that NMMZ should be placed either within the Ministry of

Figure 17.9   The 'Great Zimbabwe traditional village' in 1992. Photo: P. Stone.

Education and Culture or should, in some other way, be separated from the Ministry of Home Affairs. In closing the Donors' Conference, the Minister of Home Affairs, the Hon. Mr Dumiso Dabengwa (MP), is reputed to have said (but not remarked in *Report 1992*) that he himself had never understood the logic of the NMMZ being located within his Ministry rather than within Education!

8 Although unlikely, it is possible that such 'traditional' attitudes are of relatively recent derivation. In PNG it is reported that at first the Abelam

> found it easy to part with objects that had basically fulfilled their religious functions. But in recent times, perhaps because of the government's new emphasis on culture and traditions, the Abelam have begun to hold on to their most important carvings. In many villages where carvings are for sale, the best and oldest pieces are now retained.
>
> (Beier 1991, p. 81)

9 However, it is striking that Masona (1992) envisages the 'ideal' theme park as being a 'living museum' with almost all the features and qualities of the culture house!

10 However, it is possible to argue that, as all three groups had relatives in neighbouring states their potential threat was greater than might appear at first sight (D. Collett, pers. comm.; and see Murphree 1988); in particular the Ndau tended to support ZANU Ndoga and, thereby, Renamo (Vines 1991a, pp. 84–5).

11 Certainly, at least in a 'Fourth World' context, Jones & Hill-Burnett (1982, p. 239) claim that a nation cannot afford to 'allow an ethnic elite to develop and spread an ideology that might smack of a splinter "nation" '.

12 This is not to suggest either that baboons are the major cause of wall collapses (W. Ndoro, pers. comm.), or that baboons are not often themselves considered to be sacred (W. Ndoro, pers. comm.).

13 Vines (1991b, p. 15) has drawn attention to the way that Home Affairs' policy has

vacillated over the image to be presented by the site: 'the label "ruin" has been removed from its official designation. It has now been renamed "monument".'

References

Adandé, A. B. A. & I. Zevounou 1994. Education and heritage: an example of new work in the schools of Benin. In *The Presented Past: heritage, museums and education*, Stone, P. G. & B. L. Molyneaux (eds), 315–25. London: Routledge.

Addyman, P. V. 1990. Reconstruction as interpretation: the example of the Jorvik Viking Centre, York. In *The Politics of the Past*, Gathercole, P. & D. Lowenthal (eds), 257–64. London: Unwin Hyman; Routledge pbk 1994.

Addyman, P. V. 1991. Tourism and the presentation of monuments in Zimbabwe. Draft Consultant's Report, UNDP/Unesco Project (ZI88/028).

Addyman, P. V. 1992. The archaeological heritage of Zimbabwe. Unpublished paper delivered to the Donors' Conference, Harare, July 1992.

Akenji, N. I. 1991. What African museums should contain. *Kaberry Research Centre Bulletin*, 25–9.

Ames, M. M. 1992. *Cannibal Tours and Glass Boxes: the anthropology of museums*. Vancouver: University of British Columbia Press.

Anon 1975. *Tribes of Rhodesia. Queen Victoria Museum, visitor's companion*. Salisbury: National Museums and Monuments of Rhodesia.

Anon 1991. Backstage 'conspiracy' rocks Arts Council. *Horizon* 17 September, 40.

Anon n.d.a *The Karanga Village*. Salisbury: National Museums and Monuments of Rhodesia.

Anon n.d.b *Gila Heritage Park*. PO Box 457, Sacaton, Arizona 85247, USA.

Beach, D. N. 1980. *The Shona and Zimbabwe 900–1850*. London: Heinemann.

Beier, U. 1991. The Maprik Cultural Centre, East Sepik, Papua New Guinea. In *Museums and Cultural Centres in the Pacific*, Eoe, S. M. & P. Swadling (eds), 79–85. Port Moresby: Papua New Guinea National Museum.

Bender, B. & M. Edmonds 1992. Stonehenge and the politics of the past. *British Archaeological News* 7, 64.

Blacking, J. 1984. *Papua New Guinea: cultural development*. Paris: Unesco Assignment Report, serial no. FMR/CLT/CD/84/15.

Blacking, J. 1990. Culture houses in Papua New Guinea. In *The Excluded Past: archaeology in education*, Stone, P. & R. MacKenzie (eds), 160–72. London: Unwin Hyman; Routledge pbk 1994.

Blancke, S. & C. J. P. Slow Turtle 1994. Traditional American Indian education as a palliative to Western education. In *The Presented Past: heritage, museums and education*, Stone P. G. & B. L. Molyneaux (eds), 438–52. London: Routledge.

Bourdillon, M. F. C. 1982. Freedom and constraint among Shona spirit mediums. In *Religious Organisation and Religious Experience*, J. Davis (ed.), 180–94. London: Academic Press.

Burton, J. 1991. The Romunga Haus Tumbuna, Western Highlands Province, Papua New Guinea. In *Museums and Cultural Centres in the Pacific*, Eoe, S. M. & P. Swadling (eds), 66–9. Port Moresby: Papua New Guinea National Museum.

Champion, T. C. & P. J. Ucko In Press. An enforced reminiscence. In *Africa: the challenge of archaeology. Essays in honour of Thurstan Shaw*, Andah, B. (ed.). Lagos: Heinemann.

Cheater, A. 1991. O tempora! O mores! Ambiguities and contradictions in the political management of culture in Zimbabwe's attempted transition to socialism. Unpublished paper delivered to Association of Social Anthropologists' Conference.

Cheater, A. 1992. Ambiguities and contradictions in the political management of culturism in Zimbabwe's reverse transition to socialism. In *Socialism: ideals, ideologies and local practice*, C. Hann (ed.), 102–16. London: Routledge.

Chipoka, J. H. 1992. Education and cultural resource management. Unpublished paper delivered to the Donors' Conference: Harare, July 1992.

Collett, D. P. 1992. *The Archaeological Heritage of Zimbabwe: a masterplan for resource conservation and development*. UNDP & Unesco Project Report (ZIM 88/028).

Condori, C. M. 1989. History and prehistory in Bolivia: what about the Indians? In *Conflict in the Archaeology of Living Traditions*, Layton, R. (ed.), 46–59. London: Unwin Hyman; Routledge pbk 1994.

Cooke, C. K. 1972. *A Guide to the Historic and Pre-Historic Monuments of Rhodesia*. Bulawayo: Bulawayo Historical Monuments Commission.

Cooke, C. K. n.d. *Our Heritage – the Past*. Bulawayo: Commission for the Preservation of National and Historic Monuments and Relics.

Devalle, S. B. C. 1992. *Discourses of Ethnicity: culture and protest in Jharkhand*. New Delhi: Sage Publications.

Dewey, W. J. 1985. Shona ritual axes. *Insight* 85, 1–5.

Doyel, D. E. n.d. Foreword. In *The Land, the People: an exhibit presented by the Navajo Tribal Museum*. Window Rock, Arizona: Navajo Tribal Museum.

Durrans, B. 1992. Behind the scenes: museums and selective criticism. *Anthropology Today* 8, 11–15.

Eoe, S. M. 1991a. The role of museums in the Pacific: change or die. In *Museums and Cultural Centres in the Pacific*, Eoe, S. M. & P. Swadling (eds), 1–4. Port Moresby: Papua New Guinea National Museum.

Eoe, S. M. 1991b. Conclusion. In *Museums and Cultural Centres in the Pacific*, Eoe, S. M. & P. Swadling (eds), 275. Port Moresby: Papua New Guinea National Museum.

Eoe, S. M. & P. Swadling (eds) 1991. *Museums and Cultural Centres in the Pacific*. Port Moresby: Papua New Guinea National Museum.

Eperiam, E. 1991. The Pohnpei Museum, Federated States of Micronesia. In *Museums and Cultural Centres in the Pacific*, Eoe, S. M. & P. Swadling (eds), 178–83. Port Moresby: Papua New Guinea National Museum.

Eriksen, T. H. 1991. The cultural contexts of ethnic differences. *Man* 26, 127–44.

Fowler, P. J. 1992. *The Past in Contemporary Society: then, now*. London: Routledge.

Fry, P. 1991. Ethnic, and national identities and the role of cultural activities: a proposal for a modest cultural program in Zimbabwe and Mozambique. Unpublished Report to the Ford Foundation.

Funari, P. P. A. 1994. Rescuing ordinary people's culture: museums, material culture and education in Brazil. In *The Presented Past: heritage, museums and education*, Stone, P. G. & B. L. Molyneaux (eds), 120–36. London: Routledge.

Fusitu'a, E. 1991. The preservation of cultural property in Tonga. In *Museums and Cultural Centres in the Pacific*, Eoe, S. M. & P. Swadling (eds), 195–9. Port Moresby: Papua New Guinea National Museum.

Garlake, P. 1982a. *Life at Great Zimbabwe*. Gweru: Mambo Press.

Garlake, P. 1982b. Prehistory and ideology in Zimbabwe. *Africa* 52, 1–19.

Garlake, P. 1982c. Museums remain rooted in the past. *Moto* July, 31–2.

Garlake, P. 1982d. *Great Zimbabwe Described and Explained*. Harare: Zimbabwe Publishing House.

Garlake, P. 1983. *Early Zimbabwe: from the Matopos to Inyanga*. Gweru: Mambo Press.

Grant, S. 1990. A past abandoned? Some experiences of a regional museum in Botswana. In *The Politics of the Past*, Gathercole, P. & D. Lowenthal (eds), 214–23. London: Unwin Hyman; Routledge pbk 1994.

Groube, L. 1985. The ownership of diversity: the problem of establishing a national history in a land of nine hundred ethnic groups. In *Who Owns the Past?*, McBryde, I. (ed.), 49–73. Melbourne: Oxford University Press.

Hall, M. 1984. The burden of tribalism: the social context of southern African Iron Age studies. *American Antiquity* 49, 455–67.

Hartman, R. P. & M. M. Kadoyama n.d. *The Land, the People: an exhibit presented by the Navajo Tribal Museum*. Window Rock, Ariz.: Navajo Tribal Museum.

Hodder, I. 1991a. Post-modernism, post-structuralism and post-processual archaeology. In *The Meanings of Things*, Hodder, I. (ed.), 64–78. London: HarperCollins Academic.

Hodder, I. 1991b. *Reading the Past*. Cambridge: Cambridge University Press.

International African Institute 1955. *Ethnographic Survey of Africa. Southern Africa Part IV: the Shona and Ndebele of Southern Rhodesia*. London: International African Institute.

Jackson, H. D. 1980. National museums and monuments. In *The Annual Report of the National Museums and Monuments for the Year Ended 30th June 1980*, 4–7.

Jamieson, J. 1994. One view of Native education in the Northwest Territories, Canada. In *The Presented Past: heritage, museums and education*, Stone, P. G. & B. L. Molyneaux (eds), 495–510. London: Routledge.

Jones, D. J. & J. Hill-Burnett 1982. The political context of ethnogenesis: an Australian example. In *Aboriginal Power in Australian Society*, Howard, M. C. (ed.), 214–46. St Lucia: University of Queensland Press.

Kennedy, J. 1991. Who should protect Papua New Guinea's archaeological heritage? In *Museums and Cultural Centres in the Pacific*, Eoe, S. M. & P. Swadling (eds), 148–51. Port Moresby: Papua New Guinea National Museum.

Kombea, P. 1991. Ialibu Cultural Centre and Museum, Southern Highlands Province, Papua New Guinea. In *Museums and Cultural Centres in the Pacific*, Eoe, S. M. & P. Swadling (eds), 50–2. Port Moresby: Papua New Guinea National Museum.

Kuklick, H. 1991. Contested monuments: the politics of archaeology in southern Africa. In *Colonial Situations: essays on the contextualisation of ethnographic knowledge*, G. W. Stocking (ed.), 135–69. Madison: University of Wisconsin Press.

Lan, D. 1985. *Guns and Rain: guerrillas and spirit mediums in Zimbabwe*. London: J. Currey.

Layton, R. (ed.) 1989a. *Who Needs the Past?* London: Unwin Hyman; Routledge pbk 1994.

Layton, R. (ed.) 1989b. *Conflict in the Archaeology of Living Traditions*. London: Unwin Hyman; Routledge pbk 1994.

Layton, R. 1992. *Australian Rock Art: a new synthesis*. Cambridge: Cambridge University Press.

Mabvadya, E. 1990. Cultural resource management. Unpublished BA, final year dissertation, Department of History, University of Zimbabwe.

McBryde, I. (ed.) 1985. *Who Owns the Past? Papers from the annual symposium of the Australian Academy of the Humanities*. Melbourne: Oxford University Press.

McCartney, M. 1985. Culture – a house with many rooms. *Insight* 85, 8–10.

MacKenzie, R. 1990. The development of museums in Botswana: dilemmas and tensions in a front-line state. In *The Politics of the Past*, Gathercole, P. & D. Lowenthal (eds), 203–13. London: Unwin Hyman; Routledge pbk 1994.

Marenge, A. & J. Normu 1986. History of the West New Britain Cultural Centre. Precirculated paper, in *Archaeological 'Objectivity' in Interpretation*, World Archaeological Congress vol. 2 (mimeo). London: Allen & Unwin.

Masona, T. 1992. Marketing and the heritage industry. Unpublished paper presented to the Donors' Conference, Harare, July 1992.

Mawe, T. 1991. The establishment and management of provincial cultural centres in Papua New Guinea with special reference to the Southern Highlands, Papua New Guinea. In *Museums and Cultural Centres in the Pacific*, Eoe, S. M. & P. Swadling (eds), 37–49. Port Moresby: Papua New Guinea National Museum.

Mazel, A. & G. Ritchie 1994. Museums and their messages: the display of the pre- and early colonial past in the museums of South Africa, Botswana and Zimbabwe. In *The Presented Past: heritage, museums and education*, Stone, P. G. & B. L. Molyneaux (eds), 225–36. London: Routledge.

Merlan, F. 1989. The objectification of 'culture': an aspect of current political process in Aboriginal affairs. *Anthropological Forum* 6, 105–16.

Mowaljarlie, D., P. Vinnicombe, G. K. Ward & C. Chippindale 1988. Repainting of images on rock in Australia and the maintenance of Aboriginal culture. *Antiquity* 62, 690–6.

Muriuki, G. 1990. The reconstruction of African history through historical, ethnographic and oral sources. In *The Excluded Past: archaeology and education*, Stone, P. & R. MacKenzie (eds), 173–82. London: Unwin Hyman; Routledge pbk 1994.

Murphree, M. W. 1988. The salience of ethnicity in African states: a Zimbabwean case study. *Ethnic and Racial Studies* 11, 119–38.

Namuno, J. 1991. The West New Britain Cultural Centre, Papua New Guinea. In *Museums and Cultural Centres in the Pacific*, Eoe, S. M. & P. Swadling (eds), 92–100. Port Moresby: Papua New Guinea National Museum.

Ndoro, W. 1993. The conservation and presentation of prehistoric urban sites: Great Zimbabwe ruins. Unpublished paper presented to WAC Inter-Congress on Urban Origins, Mombasa, Kenya.

Nzewunwa, N. 1994. The Nigerian teacher and museum culture. In *The Presented Past: heritage, museums and education*, Stone, P. G. & B. L. Molyneaux (eds), 283–9. London: Routledge.

Olivier, L. & A. Coudart 1992. An Old World tradition of theoretical and archaeological research from the French point of view. Unpublished paper presented to EuroTAG, Southampton.

Olsen, B. 1986. Norwegian archaeology and the people without (pre-)history: or how to create a myth of a uniform past. *Archaeological Review from Cambridge* 5, 25–42.

Phillipson, D. W. 1991. Keith Robinson and iron age archaeology. *Zimbabwea* 3, 1–4.

Pwiti, G. 1994. Prehistory, archaeology and education in Zimbabwe. In *The Presented Past: heritage, museums and education*, Stone, P. G. & B. L. Molyneaux (eds), 338–48. London: Routledge.

Ranger, T. 1982/3. Revolutions in the wheel of Zimbabwean history. *Moto* December/January, 41–5.

Ranger, T. 1989a. Whose heritage? The case of the Matobo National Park. *Journal of Southern African Studies* 15, 217–49.

Ranger, T. 1989b. Missionaries, migrants and the Manyika: the invention of ethnicity in Zimbabwe. In *The Creation of Tribalism in Southern Africa*, L. Vail (ed.), 118–50. London: J. Currey.

Ravenhill, P. 1987. The past and the future of museology in sub-Saharan Africa. *ICCROM Newsletter* 13, 34–6.

Report 1989. Report on the evaluation of Murewa Culture House, September–December, 1989.

Report on the Conference on Heritage Resource Conservation and Development, 27–31 July 1992. National Museums and Monuments of Zimbabwe.

Rodrigues, J. D. & L. Manuelshagen 1987. *Preservation of Great Zimbabwe and the Khami Ruins*. UNDP Project Report (ZIM/85/008).

Roosens, E. E. 1989. *Creating Ethnicity: the process of ethnogenesis*. London: Sage Publications.

Sassoon, H. 1982. *The Preservation of Great Zimbabwe*. Paris: Unesco Restricted Technical Report, serial no. FMR/CLT/CH/82/156.

Shanks, M. & C. Tilley 1987. *Re-constructing Archaeology*. Cambridge: Cambridge University Press.

Shennan, S. J. (ed.) 1989. *Archaeological Approaches to Cultural Identity*. London: Unwin Hyman; Routledge pbk 1994.

Silau, T. 1991. The Madang Museum and Cultural Centre, Papua New Guinea. In *Museums and Cultural Centres in the Pacific*, Eoe, S. M. & P. Swadling (eds), 86–91. Port Moresby: Papua New Guinea National Museum.

Sinclair, P. J. J., I. Pikirayi, G. Pwiti & R. Soper 1993. Urban trajectories on the Zimbabwean plain. In *The Archaeology of Africa: food, metals and towns*, Shaw, T., P. J. J. Sinclair, B. Andah & A. Okpoko (eds), 705–31. London: Routledge; Routledge pbk 1994.

Smithers, R. H. N. 1967. The duties and responsibilities of museum trustees. *SAMAB* 8, 464–6.

Stone, P. 1992. The Magnificent Seven: reasons for teaching about prehistory. *Teaching History*. October, 13–18.

Stone, P. 1994. Report on the development of the Education Service of the National Museums and Monuments of Zimbabwe. Unpublished MS.

Stone, P. & R. MacKenzie (eds) 1990. *The Excluded Past: archaeology and education*. London: Unwin Hyman; Routledge pbk 1994.

Summers, R. 1958. *Inyanga, Prehistoric Settlements in Southern Rhodesia*. Cambridge: Cambridge University Press.

Totu, V. & D. Roe 1991. The Guadacanal Cultural Centre, Solomon Islands: keeping custom in the 1980s. In *Museums and Cultural Centres in the Pacific*, Eoe, S. M. & P. Swadling (eds), 113–21. Port Moresby: Papua New Guinea National Museum.

Tumu, A. & A. K. Kyakas 1991. The Enga Cultural Centre, Wabag, Papua New Guinea. In *Museums and Cultural Centres in the Pacific*, Eoe, S. M. & P. Swadling (eds), 53–63. Port Moresby: Papua New Guinea National Museum.

Tutai, V. 1991. The Cook Islands Museum. In *Museums and Cultural Centres in the Pacific*, Eoe, S. M. & P. Swadling (eds), 201–4. Port Moresby: Papua New Guinea National Museum.

Ucko, P. J. 1981. Report on a proposal to initiate 'Culture Houses' in Zimbabwe. Unpublished Report to the Government of Zimbabwe.

Ucko, P.J. 1983a. The politics of the indigenous minority. *Journal of Biosocial Science* Suppl. 8, 25–40.

Ucko, P.J. 1983b. Australian academic archaeology: Aboriginal transformation of its aims and practices. *Australian Archaeology* 16, 11–26.

Ucko, P. J. 1985. Australian Aborigines and academic social anthropology. In *The Future of Former Foragers in Australia and Southern Africa*, Schrire, C. & R. Gordon (eds), 63–73. Cambridge, Mass.: Cultural Survival, Inc.

Ucko, P.J. 1986a. External Consultant Report: Department of Anthropology and Sociology (Archaeology). Unpublished MS, University of Papua New Guinea.

Ucko, P. J. 1986b. Another case of irreconcilable issues?: the fate of 'culture houses' in Zimbabwe, in *Final Papers, Volume 4* World Archaeological Congress (mimeo). London: Allen & Unwin.

Ucko, P. J. 1987. *Academic Freedom and Apartheid: the story of the World Archaeological Congress*. London: Duckworth.

Ucko, P. J. 1989a. Foreword. In *Archaeological Approaches to Cultural Identity*, S. J. Shennan (ed.), ix–xx. London: Unwin Hyman; Routledge pbk 1994.

Ucko, P.J. 1989b. Foreword. In *Who Needs the Past?*, R. Layton (ed.), ix–xv. London: Unwin Hyman; Routledge pbk 1994.

Vines, A. 1991a. *RENAMO: terrorism in Mozambique*. London: J. Currey.

Vines, A. 1991b. Digging deep. *Southern African Review of Books* May/June, 14–15.

Weaver, S. M. 1984. Struggles of the nation-state to define Aboriginal ethnicity: Canada and Australia. In *Minorities and Mother Country Imagery*, Gold, G. L. (ed.), 182–210. Newfoundland: Institute of Social and Economic Research.

18   The Nigerian teacher and museum culture

NWANNA NZEWUNWA

Introduction

The need to foster a close relationship between museums and education is most pressing in Nigeria today. The emphasis in our educational system has shifted to science and technology, with a stress on practical activity and the production of visible and concrete results. However, most Nigerian teachers have not been exposed to the implications of the museum as a multi-purpose institution for presenting the past – and even the present – to modern generations. Largely because the earlier educational systems did not appreciate this role, with many people regarding the museum as an obsolete concept, museum development has been slow, and its potential contribution to the Nigerian education system has not been generally recognized. The lack of exposure of teachers to the idea of using museums as cultural resource centres, in other words the idea of a museum culture, has meant that museums have not been established in places where they could be accessible to most of the people, particularly the rural people, who constitute the bulk of the population.

Creating a museum culture for the Nigerian teacher is an important step in continuing to strengthen our culture as a whole. The idea behind it all is to encourage schools – teachers and learners, particularly youngsters – to meet the past first hand. Since the cultural material on display in a museum was created by means of science and technology, we believe that a museum culture will fire the younger generations with a desire to be creative and thus help achieve a new technological era in Nigeria. There is, therefore, a genuine role for museums and the past in our country.

The new cultural education philosophy

Since gaining their independence, African countries have stressed the need to revive and maintain their national cultural identities, submerged, marginalized or completely obliterated by colonialism. They have at the same time realized that paradoxical problems exist in their attempt to achieve this, since they get more and more drawn away from their roots by the attractions of western living standards and the unpredictable trappings of their plunge into the economic whirlwind of capitalism in the developed world. Such attractions are reinforced in the constant bombardments of the external mass media.

The colonial educational system inherited by African countries produced candidates for white-collar jobs. This proved to be detrimental to some of the traditional educational values because it subdued indigenous cultural heritage and halted local artistic and technological development. For as long as these traditional values were allowed or forced to wilt and decay African countries came to depend more and more on the factories in the industrialized world for even the simplest domestic items such as kitchen knives and farming implements which they had hitherto produced locally. This trend reached a ridiculous point in Nigeria in the 1970s, when unprecedented wealth was created as crude oil lifted the economic base. There was no attempt to stand back, reconsider the situation and reverse the modernizing trend by going back to the roots of the culture and taking what was good from the past as an incentive towards the future. This destructive drift was possible because we did not take refuge in history, in our traditional values, and were thus tossed about by every wave and set adrift by every tide.

Education is the key to rediscovering these values. In its traditional setting education was involved in everyday life: the farm, home factory, the field, the kitchen, market and wrestling ground were all 'schools'. This made traditional education a continuous process, one in which the older generation passes on the essence of society to the younger generation. It is therefore a useful instrument in facilitating the integration of the young with the old and in creating in individuals an awareness of their potential as creative and critical human beings.

The new Education Policy in theory recognizes the central place of cultural studies in the upbringing of the Nigerian child. Unfortunately, popular thinking in Nigeria is that the museum is useful only to the historian or material culture-bound scholar or the artist. The real truth, however, is that it is a storehouse of knowledge that preserves, protects and displays our cultural heritage and therefore serves both the human and physical scientist, the rural and urban, the child and the adult, indeed humanity in its widest definition.

The Government recently published its Cultural Policy and set up a new, separate Ministry of Culture. However, the Ministry – and policy – are far removed from educational policies and infrastructure. Until and unless cultural and educational ministries learn to work together, the new policy and Ministry will have no positive impact on cultural education.

The question that arises therefore is how and when the Government translates intent into action or practice. It is common knowledge that museums as conceived by governments are elaborate, prestige institutions which are expensive outfits that are usually few and far between. This further under-mines the use of museums as centres of cultural education.

The curriculum approved by the Government of Nigeria for primary and secondary schools tacks cultural education on to social studies, an omnibus that carries no serious cultural heritage components. The curriculum does not give the teacher enough scope to utilize museums for projecting the past as a continuing aspect of the present and the future. To this extent therefore the curriculum is a failure.

Museums in cultural life

In order to develop a museum culture it is necessary to understand the place of museums in today's society, to determine how the message about their importance to society can be disseminated, and to demonstrate how the public can realize the full benefits of museums.

The contribution of museums to cultural life has been seen in a variety of ways. In addressing the fourth General Conference of the International Council for Museums (ICOM) and the International Council for Monuments and Sites (ICOMOS) in Owerri in 1981, Onunaka Mbakwe, then Governor of Imo State in Nigeria, described a museum as 'an institution designed to preserve the past of the future, and to present the past to the contemporary period for the enrichment of knowledge'. In its orthodox sense, derived from the Greek, the museum conveys the impression of awe, relaxation, display or exhibition, seriousness, enquiry and learning (Bazin 1967; Ucko 1994). Some people criticize the museum, however, calling it 'alien', 'thoroughly imported', and an 'elitist, urban-based cultural institution' which serves colonial interests, concepts and orientation. The reason is that museums often have no direct relevance to Africans, who are largely rural dwellers but who all the same are the makers of the material culture on display in African museums.

Because of this range of conflicting views, museum professionals have been developing a new museums philosophy that takes the public more fully into account. The National Seminar on Museology in Nigeria, held in Zaria in March 1976, concluded that museums had four principal roles: conservation, exhibition, research and education. Effah-Gyamfi (1982) also identifies four roles for museums: (a) demonstrating the cultural richness of their owners and thereby their contribution to the environment of world culture; (b) providing recreation, entertainment and relaxation for the public at large and thereby informally educating them; (c) serving as a cultural resource centre for schools, from primary to tertiary levels; and (d) undertaking research and providing results to enhance knowledge in general. Nzewunwa has seen the museum in Nigeria as a public institution established for 'public education without stric-tures, normally collecting, conserving, researching, entertaining, stimulating national interest, protecting the resources for the reconstruction of the nation's

past and providing the cultural historical link between Nigerian peoples'
(Nzewunwa 1984, p. 106).

In view of these varying roles, the museum may be appropriately regarded
as a public affair. An important task in the new approach therefore is to take
into account public habits and opinions in developing exhibitions, to present
what visitors might want to see. If members of the public are to realize the
maximum benefits of a museum, however, they must first develop an awareness of what museums can provide. Such education is most effectively carried
out with children, and so the teacher is seen as the key to the development of a
museum culture.

Gifted teachers with initiative may create small museums in their classrooms
or schools which will capture the attention and fire the imagination of students
and pupils. However, such initiative is expensive and no ordinary public
school in Nigeria today can afford such a luxury. The expensive enterprise
which education has become recently drives further away the hopes that
cultural education will grow in Nigeria.

Museums development and education

It is sad therefore that the Nigerian museum establishment has not yet
reached an understanding of its important educational objective. As a cultural resource centre, the museum contains objects or material that can
be referred to simply as cultural documents which speak about our technology, our arts and crafts. These documents have embedded in them stories about aspects of our past economy, politics, religion, health and social
and cultural behaviour.

The aim of displaying these materials should not simply be to show them off
as aesthetic objects or as cultural achievements; they should also tell a more
comprehensive story of humankind. In other words, the central philosophy
behind a museum exhibition should be to convey a clearer understanding of
human societies. Because these societies are dynamic and not static and because
taste has changed over time, museum exhibitions in Nigeria need to move
away from the drab stereotypes of rows of objects in glass cases to more
functional and practical exhibitions in which stories are told through the
exhibits, their arrangement and their explanatory notes.

A museum exhibition should progress in stages as would a story. In each
stage the teacher should be able to explain to the child or pupil the subject
matter, the how and why of each stage; an exhibition on the development of
metallurgy, for example, should illustrate stages in the mining of ore, smelting, smithing and production of materials.

The humble beginnings of a more enlightened policy in establishing generalized museums with permanent or temporary exhibits depicting technology,
warfare, government, economy and business are now in evidence. One successful example in Nigeria is the Museum of Colonial History in Aba, which is

a pictorial museum that tells the story of the colonial phase of Nigeria in pictures.

The idea of mobile exhibitions or mobile museums as an alternative or supplement to the traditional Nigerian experience of highly localized museums has also been mooted. It had been suggested as appropriate for reaching more people, especially in areas that are located far away from the nearest conventional museum (Nzewunwa 1990, p. 195). The mobile museum has its disadvantages, however: its display space is limited and valuable and fragile objects cannot be shown because of the risks of damage or theft in transport.

There is greater merit in moving individuals (students, pupils) from their schools to the museum. Here the student may see more of the process through which an object passes to reach the exhibition case, for the exhibited objects are more at home in a well-prepared setting. The interaction with museum staff also helps to create a more relaxed atmosphere and there is more room to move around, more people to meet and new relationships to explore among other visitors outside the circle of one's schoolmates.

The teacher and the museum

The inevitable question is: how does the teacher develop the relationship between museum and education?

The teacher guides the students to the museum and may entrust them to the better care of a member of the museum staff, who takes over as a 'teacher'. This gives an opportunity for the teacher, the children and students to benefit from the knowledge of others beyond their classroom situation. This no doubt creates curiosity, and greater attentiveness and responsiveness on their part. Such a successful and exciting trip leaves a new set of impressions in the minds of the students. They will be inspired to visit the museum again, to explore more, to consolidate the gains of the first visit. Such an experience will also make students aware that leisure and relaxation with friends and visitors from far and near may be taken up at the museum complex. This attractive atmosphere therefore beckons them again and again.

The teacher's role in creating this awareness in students cannot be underestimated, but unfortunately at times the teacher may have little or no experience of a museum (also see Mbunwe-Samba, Niba & Akenji 1994). The Museum Education Unit of the National Commission for Museums and Monuments therefore offers educational programmes for children, in crafts and art, during vacations. These activities allow children to do something creative in the museum environment, to pursue something exciting, something challenging, and to produce something tangible. This has proved a popular programme for children in Lagos, Jos, Oron, Aba, Kadun and Calabar where the unit operates.

If students can develop a museum culture, they may very well avoid the boredom that often infects students when they study the past. For example, a history class on human origins or the technology of early man or even a study of early currencies in Nigeria may benefit greatly from an excursion to a museum. A trip out of the formal classroom enlivens learning, taking advantage of the many informal aspects of education that one experiences in daily life, through personal discovery and social interaction.

According to Aggarawal (1983, p. 151):

> the quality of student participation depends on the depth of knowledge, the quality and quantum of interaction which the teacher brings forth during the learning process. . . . The teacher must keep in view that discovery and enquiry are inseparable, this is the realization of new relationships.

The present and the future

In 1989 the National Commission for Museums and Monuments of Nigeria revived its education programmes by using the opportunity offered by the 60th Anniversary of the Women's Riot of 1929 in Aba (the Aba Riot) to move out of Lagos and mount a workshop for over one hundred history and social studies teachers in and around Aba. This was an attempt to bring the museum to those who will take it to the children. By exposing the teachers to a supplementary or alternative resource to the textbook, it was hoped that they would in turn bring their experience to their school-children.

But this was a rare opportunity. Nigeria is enormous, the teachers numerous and the school population large. It is not therefore likely that a museum programme would reach an appreciable number of teachers in even one state of the federation in a short time. But perhaps that is not the saddest note. Emphasis is shifting fast in Nigeria. With dwindling economic fortunes and the reordering of government priorities the prospects for cultural projects are no longer bright. This will further slow down the pace of cultural education. Herein lies the crisis! Only if teachers and the nation adopt the maxim of 'Catch them young' and expose the public to museum culture much earlier in their lives will we realize a better cultural harvest.

References

Aggarawal, J. C. 1983. *Teaching of History*. New Delhi: Vikas Publishing House.
Bazin, G. 1967. *The Museum Age*. Brussels.
Effah–Gyamfi, K. 1982. Towards the decolonisation of museums in Africa. Paper given to the Fourth Annual Conference of the Archaeological Association of Nigeria, Zaria.
Mbunwe-Samba, P., M. L. Niba & N. I. Akenji 1994. Archaeology in the schools and museums of Cameroon. In *The Presented Past: heritage, museums and education*, Stone, P. G. & B. L. Molyneaux (eds), 326–37. London: Routledge.
Nzewunwa, N. 1984. Nigeria. In *Approaches to the Archaeological Heritage*, Cleere, H. (ed.), 101–8. Cambridge: Cambridge University Press.

Nzewunwa, N. 1990. Cultural education in West Africa: archaeological perspectives. In *The Politics of the Past*, Gathercole, P. & D. Lowenthal (eds), 189–202. London: Unwin Hyman; Routledge pbk 1994.

Ucko, P. J. 1994. Museums and sites: cultures of the past within education – Zimbabwe, some ten years on. In *The Presented Past: heritage, museums and education*, Stone, P. G. & B. L. Molyneaux (eds), 237–82. London: Routledge.

19 Indian museums and the public

K. N. MOMIN & AJAY PRATAP

Introduction

Indian museums have played an increasingly important role as information storehouses meant to serve the needs of the public. The enterprise is extremely complex, however, a product of the size and ethnic diversity of the Indian people, their languages, and the varying histories of different parts of India. There has been an increasing diversity in the size and types of museums and collections in the country since the eighteenth century.

The general, museum-going public in India can best be distinguished, perhaps, in terms of literacy, for the main issues surrounding the development and use of museums concern their representation and dissemination of information. The vast number of semi- or non-literate peoples, by far the larger group, poses interesting problems for museum curators, as they must design their displays to communicate to a diverse set of minds. The conceptual difference between the generally scientific goals of museum display and indigenous perceptions is well exemplified in the popular terms for museums in the past: Jadughar (House of Magic), Murdaghar (House of the Dead) and Ajayabghar (House of Strange Things). According to Verma (1947) people would visit the local museum 'on their way home after a dip in the holy river Ganges . . . to have a darshan of [to bow to] so many gods and goddesses housed in the building' (Verma 1947, p. 6). Indeed, Markham & Hargreaves (1936) noted that, while annual attendance in some museums exceeded a million visitors a year, Madras Museum had an astounding swell of visitors on two festive days, Dwadeshi and Kannupongal, when crowds would total between 63,000 and 130,000 each day. With its vast collections of rare, valuable and sacred objects, a museum is clearly an attraction that many people might compare to visiting a great temple or seeing one of the highly popular circuses, and in fact transcending almost all other cultural spectacles big or small. In Baroda Museum and Picture Gallery, in Baroda, Gujarat State, for example, some of the ethnic groups who visit the museum will still bow down before the images of gods and goddesses and sometimes offer flowers and coins.

Unfortunately, however, some other groups of people today find museum displays largely incomprehensible. There is seldom a visible public demand, whether from literate or non-literate sections, for the reorganization of displays or changes in museum information services. There is also a general lack of archaeological information of a scientific nature about indigenous culture for the public. All this indicates that the degree of effectiveness of the existing system for the management of cultural information is questionable. A proper consideration of the contribution of Indian museums and their goals and aims must also include, therefore, their historical development and their situation within the wider network of cultural information resources in India.

The nature and development of museums and other cultural institutions

Indian museums date to the early part of the nineteenth century (for example, the Indian Museum, Calcutta), but most were founded later in the century, mainly to house the antiquities acquired by the Government of India and the Provincial governments. As Chandra has noted, 'the archaeological excavations were yielding rich crops of antiquities and therefore most of our museums became crammed with images, inscriptions, terracottas and pottery and other minor antiquities' (Chandra 1945, p. 14). Since that time, there has been a steady growth in museums. From twelve in 1857 the number increased to a hundred in 1936 (Markham & Hargreaves 1936), still a very small number for such a vast and heavily populated country. At the time of independence in 1947, however, there was a great public demand for a national museum as a necessary step towards national reconstruction, and after the founding of the National Museum, India made remarkable progress in museum development.

The traditional local rulers in India made generous donations of their private collections to museums and many of their palaces have been converted into museums, controlled by governments. The National Gallery of Modern Art in New Delhi was founded in 1954 in Jaipur House, a large mansion belonging to a ruling family. Most of the other palaces are now State museums, including the Salar Jung Museum in Hyderabad (now in a modern building), the Mysore Palace Museum, Karnataka State and the Baroda Museum and Picture Gallery in Vadodra, Gujarat State. In Vadodra there are two more museums known as the Palace Museums: one of them houses foreign paintings and artefacts, the other, traditional weapons of war and costumes.

The public awareness of and support for cultural heritage in India can be seen in several private museums. The outstanding example is the Prince of Wales Museum, Bombay, established in the 1920s; it was the first Indian museum to be started by a museum society. The Calico Museum of Textiles in Ahmedabad, Gujarat State, is owned by textile industrialists.

And in Ahmedabad there are two private museums administered by charitable foundations, the Vishala Vessels Museum, housing a great variety of traditional vessels and household objects, and the Shreyas Museum of Gujarat Folk Arts, with a rich ethnological collection. On the other hand, the Raja Dinkar Kelkar Museum, Pune, in Maharashtra State, started as a private museum of folk arts and crafts and is now a State institution.

Today, the latest addition, the National Museum of Natural History, New Delhi, brings the total to 360 museums.

The emergence of independent cultural institutions such as the Delhi-based Indian National Trust for Art and Cultural Heritage (INTACH) is recent although precedents may be found in the Indian Heritage Society and the Bombay Natural History Society and earlier societies like the Asiatic Society of Bengal and the Bihar and Orissa Research Society. INTACH fills a most important role as a non-governmental body that monitors heritage issues and provides crucial support for heritage interest among the general public, as it and the other societies are much more accessible to amateur researchers and others interested in their local heritage than government bodies involved in cultural research. INTACH's programme for raising public awareness about heritage issues is pursued by local chapters around the country, where activity is organized by local concerned groups of citizens. Most recently, for example, INTACH has organized a museum of Christian culture in the former Portuguese colony of Goa, which provides a fascinating mix of Indian and European culture. Independent research is further supported by INTACH's network of local chapters, as they provide for an all-India network of resource personnel, and by some smaller scale independent institutions which have undertaken to document folk traditions and create databanks, along with private collectors who continue to hold on to their valuable collections of art.

The Archaeological Survey of India and the State Departments of Archaeology also have a major portion of the responsibility for the management of monuments and site museums (see Momin 1968) in rural as well as urban areas, and the excavation and preservation of archaeological sites of national importance – the tourist attractions where people of all categories visualize the glory India had.

The Anthropological Survey of India is also a major source of information regarding the large number of aboriginal and semi-aboriginal peoples of India. The survey developed the People of India project to manage this information; it consists of a computerized database of facts and figures relating to the many ethnic groups, for public and official use. The file on each group, emulating the Human Relations Area Files, consists of a textual report, cultural data in numerical form, maps, photographs, and demographic information such as on migrations and present occupations. The survey is also preparing an atlas of biological, linguistic and cultural data on the Indian peoples and an ecological map of India, this in collaboration with the Centre of Ecological Sciences, at the Indian Institute of Science, in Bangalore. The People of India Project is also planning other collaborative texts and monographs to be written by scholars outside the Anthropological Survey (see Anthropological Survey of India 1991, 1992). These institutions also handle museums of their own, adding to the total number of cultural exhibits available in the country.

Problems with the dissemination of cultural information

Museums and the other cultural institutions in India provide a wealth of cultural resources for display to the public and to support research, but their main purpose is to educate the masses to appreciate and feel proud of their cultural heritage. Museums can no longer afford to cater only for a handful of scholars. They have to come out of their four walls and approach the masses to justify their existence, to make themselves relevant to modern society. Indeed, museums in India have special responsibilities to the people, as they must contribute to the socio-economic revolution that is taking place today. As the museums stand for all classes of people, the responsibilities of the museum authorities are to communicate with people of all categories. It is the duty of modern museums therefore to highlight the changes and the new ideas in Indian society and the socio-economic goals that go with them, so that they can be understood and implemented more effectively.

On the practical level, it is most essential to have properly researched background information and thoughtful and creative display. Indian culture is a living culture and there are themes and myths, religion and philosophy behind all the objects in a museum; unfortunately, there is no tradition of consulting ethnic groups prior to setting up displays on them or for them. The ethnographic dioramas in the Indian Museum at Calcutta are a typical example.

These dioramas, also a familiar display technique in natural history museums at New Delhi and Bombay, contain life-size clay replicas of aboriginal groups and their dwellings. The gallery at the Indian Museum at Calcutta contains perhaps two dozen of them. In themselves, these might be seen as good craftsmanship but in conjunction with the rest of the museum, in which the 'great tradition' of Hindu culture is displayed on regular shelves and open displays, the aboriginal dioramas seem like glorified fish-tanks. That they may be compared with similar glass cases housing stuffed wild Indian fauna is less than incidental, a very revealing clue as to the museum curators' actual view of the status and nature of aboriginal society. The situation is therefore most unfortunate since it creates a very incorrect impression on visitors to the museum who may not have the information, or the means to get it, to see through the implicit and erroneous assumptions in such dioramas.

As most of the established museums and many others are in old buildings and palaces with large collections and congested halls, modern innovation is difficult. And these days Indian museums are more inclined towards western museological principles, stressing the presentation of only a few objects in one single big hall. But are such selective and spare displays justified in a country like India which has such a vast treasure of antiquities and remains and such a great variety of different ethnic groups and religions, material culture styles and techniques? In addition, objects of arts and crafts always have some relationship with daily or ceremonial life, with the beliefs, customs and myths of the people. So Indian museums should try to display their artefacts in a traditional environment to make them more meaningful to the visiting public rather than blindly following western methods.

The Calico Textile Museum, Ahmedabad, is the best example of an institution that has displays more suitable to Indian artefacts and life styles. Its collection represents Indian textiles of every kind, including tents, canopies, carpets, temple hangings, tapestries, saris, patkas, costumes and horse trappings from the sixteenth to the twentieth centuries, housed in a wooden two-storied building brought from a historical town, Patan, in North Gujarat. The walls and floors are plastered with mud mixed with cowdung and there are no modern showcases or other such devices. Another noteworthy example of traditional display is the Vishala Vessels Museum at Ahmedabad. Its great variety of brass, copper and iron vessels and household objects is displayed using natural village settings with typical houses in the form of dioramas. The objects are not mounted on pedestals to make them seem precious or showcases to isolate them from the viewer, but rather in huts and on platforms with thatched roofs made of bamboo and grass, and plastered with cowdung and clay.

Museums and other cultural institutions should also actively reach out to all the levels of the community in exhibit planning. Educational and cultural programmes for local communities must not only be based on the collections but closely related to the history, archaeology and art of the region concerned. Local legends, rites and traditional festivals can provide themes for the involvement of the public, as can the memories of heroic deeds and other achievements of a community's ancestors. With such common ground the local public can associate themselves directly with the museum programmes. The Salar Jung Museum, for example, holds temporary exhibitions on various themes of socio-religious significance at the time of various festivals, such as the 'Lord Krishna in Indian Art' exhibit, shown on Janamastami Day (Birthday of Lord Krishna) and themes such as Christianity and art, at the time of Christmas, and the Islamic contribution to Indian Art. Such activities may encourage people to visit museums and create more interest in the cultural heritage of the country.

It is critical that cultural institutions preserve, promote and protect cultural life itself, especially as it is continuously threatened by technological and social change. The rapid disappearance of ancient arts and crafts is a matter of common concern to all Indian museums. In the Craft Museum in New Delhi, devoted to traditional arts and crafts, objects of daily life are displayed to re-create their cultural context and the craftsmen actually demonstrate the traditional techniques of making the objects in traditional workshops. When children are exposed to the traditional cultural heritage of India through interaction with traditional craftspeople, they not only become acquainted with their techniques and materials but they also see creativity first hand. This experience has created a new awareness of and admiration for India's ancient cultural heritage and symbolizes the urgency of preserving rural technology and traditional aesthetic values in the face of rapid change.

Similarly, the Salar Jung Museum organizes practical training courses on the ancient arts, with the idea of bringing these rural skills into urban areas. The courses include bronze-casting, lapidary work, woodwork, Bidri artwork and courses for women on tribal embroidery. The holding of such training programmes by the museum for its community not only helps to keep the old indigenous arts and crafts alive but also opens up new opportunities for self-employment.

Teaching archaeology in Indian museums and schools

Effective utilization of museum services means as well that there must be a bridge between the museums and the rural masses who form the majority of the population. All the leading museums in India are located in urban centres, particularly in the prominent cities, and so the rural population rarely benefits from museums. In addition, most of the cultural information itself is designed to inform the urban public about the rest of the country; very little is intended to inform the rural population, also most often the semi- and non-literate public, about urban Indian history and society. This is unfortunate, because although urban society has its good aspects, rural people need to be informed that in most ways they are better off. If urban history was brought into rural communities in local museums and schools, it would be at least possible that potential migrants to cities would discover what really awaits them in respect of housing, jobs, and the rather less salubrious environment they would have to live in.

In view of the vast geographical area of India and its complex social mosaic, museums have developed teaching programmes and other extension services in order to reach the community. Such programmes attempt to take into account the variety of interests and needs in the population, reaching them through the loan of display material and travelling exhibitions. Even then, however, the main consumers of this information are urban people. A much more diverse population, however, is contacted through mobile exhibitions. These are used by the major art, archaeology and ethnography institutions and by science museums, as the developing country has an urgent need to educate the rural and urban communities in the field of science and technology.

Suggestions for the extension services to establish contacts with schools (Sarkar 1977–9) and teacher-training colleges are already being implemented. A successful experiment was carried out to train apprentice teachers at the Museum and Art Gallery at Chandigarh in Haryana State and now it is a common practice at Chandigarh Museum. The Archaeology

Museum at Baroda University organizes temporary exhibitions after every excavation, inviting trainee teachers and upper-year students. And Birla Industrial and Technology Museum in Calcutta and Visveshriya Industrial and Technology Museum in Banglore organize short-term training courses for school-teachers in science and technology in the museum and through museobuses reach out to the rural areas.

These outreach programmes are critically important, as there is little emphasis on archaeology below undergraduate level in formal education. In fact, with the exception of Allahabad, Lucknow, Baroda and Calcutta universities, there is no undergraduate teaching of archaeology in India. At a regional level the curricula have only a vague smattering of Indian history, with no formal study of the regional histories for which there is an increasing demand.

In a country as culturally diverse as India with, according to the People of India Project, 4403 communities, there is clearly a need for historical research for each ethnic group and community. The traditional focus on 'great' historical figures and events is academically dead, but until alternative histories are written and widely circulated, the old ideas will prevail. Why, for instance, should an aboriginal student be expected to be familiar with the great Hindu tradition, while a Hindu student in the same school can remain ignorant about the equally great and culturally fascinating and diverse aboriginal history of the country?

Reaching the wider public

Some large cultural centres have been established to bring the many uses of cultural heritage under one roof. Such centres emulate the Smithsonian Institution in the United States, combining archives, galleries for display, operas and theatres, and act as repositories of cultural information with links to similar institutions within and outside the country.

In theory, such centres are attractive as they increase public choice as to the nature and variety of information they desire. Yet, since these are in metropolitan areas where there is already a plethora of cultural information, there seems little justification for even more resources directed to an already well-informed urban population, when the information needs of the non-urban public and the non-literate section of the urban and rural public are so great.

Mass media, especially radio and television, and information technology are commonly seen as the best solution to the problem of bringing the vast and varied public in greater contact with heritage resources. Programmes about archaeology have appeared on television and radio but only a few are systematic, well planned or researched, suggesting that research centres do not have well-developed links with the media. The one exception to this rule – the university-based Audio Visual Research Centres – produce programmes that are broadcast on the national television as part of the Open University. Another newly emerged factor is the appearance in India of international networks like the BBC, CNN and STAR TV which have overnight added to the volume of information available to the domestic public. As these networks also provide alternative views of the Indian situation, they offer competition to the national network, Doordarshan, in the area of cultural reporting, and so the viewer stands to gain in terms of choice and quality.

It is not sufficient to be merely enthusiastic about newer technologies of information processing and dissemination; it is necessary to think systematically about their fit within Indian society. Television, for instance, is still a high-priced commodity and although much of the country is theoretically covered in terms of broadcast radius and frequencies, a much smaller area is actually covered because TV sets do not exist in most of the rural areas. In addition, the level of programming required for these areas poses further problems. The overall implications of the arrival of the so-called global networks in India, a country of over 850 million people, are profound, as Indian peoples become more familiar with far-flung cultures. It is also troubling that the programmes on these new networks tend to be urban in focus. And yet, if these networks are to respond to the needs of the rural population, what will their programming be like? More 'agricultural news', as on the Doordarshan network? Soap operas?

The real issue here is that technology itself will not solve the problems of managing India's massive cultural infrastructure; if all cultural data could be dumped on computer disks and then by some mechanism transmitted around the country for public and private use, it would certainly not solve the problem of a proper cultural management system – a majority of Indians would have no use for cultural data conceived and presented in this form. A re-examination of the whole cultural information system is therefore called for, to reveal the bottlenecks in its operation and to expose the wasteful replication of functions and so encourage an integrated output of information for the benefit of the public and its decision-makers.

The vexing question of how to mix modern technology with a rural society such as India continues to be a problem as the gulf here is clearly the one defined by literacy. Under these circumstances, information technology cannot easily accomplish its full potential for improving access to cultural heritage in Indian society without the help of the traditional educational institutions, schools and museums. The time is gone, therefore, for museums to play their roles in isolation, as they now face competition from these other sources of cultural information for the attention of the public. If these institutions are going to succeed, however, they must not only keep abreast of modern developments, but must also become more sensitive to the realities of local situations and so help to give voice to the concerns of the diverse public they are supposed to serve.

Acknowledgements

Parts of this chapter are based on the experience gained by one of the authors (Anjay Pratap) while working at the Indira Ghandi National Centre for the Arts, New Delhi, from February 1988 until July 1991.

References

Anthropological Survey of India 1991. *Annual Report, 1990–1*. Calcutta: Anthropological Survey of India.

Anthropological Survey of India 1992. *Annual Report, 1991–2*. Calcutta: Anthropological Survey of India.

Chandra, M. 1945. National reconstruction and museums. *The Journal of Indian Museums*, 1, 13–25.

Markham, S. F. & H. Hargreaves 1936. *The Museums of India*. London: The Museums Association.

Momin, K. N. 1968. Site museums in India. Unpublished research project MS, Department of Museology, University of Baroda.

Sarkar, S. R. 1977–9. Scope of communicating museum activities in the rural belt. *Studies in Museology* 13/14.

Verma, B. 1947. Inaugural address to the Museums Association of India. *The Journal of Indian Museums* 3, 6–8.

20   A case for archaeology in formal school curricula in India

NEELIMA DAHIYA

The importance of archaeology in history

History is one of the core subjects in the curriculum of Indian secondary and senior secondary schools, as it is in other countries. It is intended to equip students with a knowledge of the human past, including that of their own ancestors and society. Pupils of secondary and senior secondary schools in India, however, commonly consider history boring, uninteresting and mind-boggling. The reason for this distaste is that most history teachers stress the rote learning of bare facts, dates and names. This problem may be related to the fact that the history taught in Indian schools tends to be the record of dynasties of kings and their wars (see Sankalia 1965, p. 2).

If such studies include archaeology, however, this elitist and lopsided view of society may be corrected. The aim of archaeology in India should be not simply to depict the story of kings, queens and their paraphernalia and the wars fought, won and lost by them, but to record the occurrence of particular events and processes and their implications for the society as a whole. Thus, the past is primarily the story of common people and their strivings through the ages. If it were not for archaeology, most of the past contribution and heritage of the common people and the non-literate societies which still abound in a large part of the globe would have remained unrecognized. Archaeology is in fact the most potent means for students to develop a rational and scientific outlook in tradition-bound societies such as India. The teachers of Indian national history should therefore give more recognition to archae-ology because it makes a specific contribution to social solidarity and the national and emotional integration which are the most avowed objectives of history in Indian schools.

India, being a multilingual, multireligious and pluralistic society, is con-stantly faced with the danger of conflict among its different groups. Archaeological material may be used to create a sense of sharing of common traditions and belonging to the same past among persons of different communities and groups. The similarities found in archaeological objects produced in different cultures at different times easily bring home to the pupil the point that in the past all societies passed through certain similar kinds of technological development, though the time of their use of a similar technology may not have been the same and they may have skipped some forms of technology altogether. Since socio-cultural development is generalizable in this way over different places, it helps to check the tendency to look for, and exaggerate, differences among societies in their political, social and economic systems and instead encourages pupils to look for affinities and similarities between peoples, thus building an attitude of universal kinship.

In recent years, the role of archaeology in making the teaching of the history of the remote past more comprehensive, authentic and scientific has been taken into account in curriculum development in India. The secondary and senior secondary school curricula recently prepared by CBSE (Central Board of Secondary Education 1989a, 1989b) for Delhi and all Indian examinations prescribe the teaching of history of ancient and medieval periods in classes IX and XI (c.14 years old and c.17 years old). For teaching prehistory and protohistory, archaeology constitutes the exclusive source, while for the teaching of recorded history, archaeology is secondary, but still important.

The National Council for Educational Research and Training (NCERT) has published textbooks of Indian history that are prescribed by the CBSE for teaching history to the children of the schools affiliated with that body. These textbooks include illustrations of artefacts along with the description of the life and activities of the people who made them. This is a step forward in using archaeology as a teaching aid, but illustrations are still a poor substitute for actual objects. Material objects can be seen, touched and talked about, they bring the past alive in concrete form for the students, thus making the teaching–learning process highly interesting, lively, scientific and, above all, easy to grasp.

Archaeology has a problematic role in India, but this should not be misconstrued to mean that Indian historians, authors of textbooks or teachers see no value in its teaching; an overwhelming majority of the teachers agree, in principle at least, that there is a strong case for the inclusion of archaeology in the formal school curriculum. It is simply that most of them do not put this principle into action.

The teaching survey

I conducted a survey amongst history teachers in selected schools in the State of Haryana and the Union Territory of Delhi about the use and importance of archaeology in teaching secondary-school students about the ancient and medieval periods. One hundred and ten teachers took part from CBSE-affiliated secondary and senior secondary schools in Delhi, Rohtak, Gurgaon,

Sonepat, Kurukshetra and Hissar Districts of Haryana that also followed the history syllabus and textbooks prepared by NCERT. These teachers were given a comprehensive questionnaire (see Appendix 1) especially concerned with their methods of teaching and the teaching aids, including archaeological material, which they used. Their response to various questions yielded the following information.

An overwhelming majority of the teachers (105) admitted that the chief method of teaching they use is the lecture and that the most popular teaching aids are historical maps and printed charts (used often by 82 teachers and on a few occasions by 10). As to the use of illustrations of archaeological objects printed in textbooks, 93 respondents said that they do not refer to them at all. Five replied that they point them out while teaching about the life and activities of the contemporary people but do not explain their details. The remaining 12 teachers said that they use these pictures as best they can to help students understand the material culture of contemporary society.

As to the comparative importance of various teaching aids, all except three of the respondents assigned greatest importance to archaeological finds and second greatest to their replicas. Charts and maps were assigned third and fourth ranks by 58 and 43 teachers respectively. The number of teachers assigning other ranks to these two aids was still lower. Other teaching aids were put at lower ranks.

The teachers who assigned most importance to archaeological finds were also asked why they considered archaeology the most important aid for teaching history. A majority of them (97) replied that no other method makes the achievements of the people of the remote past look as real and credible to the pupils as does archaeology. Other teachers gave no specific reason for their response.

It was also found that most of the sampled teachers (96) were strongly in favour of the principle of including archaeology in the secondary-school curriculum. However, to another question which sought to find out how much archaeology teachers included in teaching about the life and activities of ancient peoples, almost all of them admitted that they make no use of archaeological finds at all except charts of material objects representing such cultures. The following reasons were advanced in this regard:

absence of archaeological display in the school (102);
overcrowded curriculum (difficult to cover within given time) (97);
lack of expertise in archaeology (78);
involves more waste of time with less gain (63);
institution's head is opposed to this method (27);
absence of provision of even minimum educational facilities and teaching aids (54);
teachers of other subjects are opposed to this approach (19);
useless from examination point of view (22); and
parents consider it a waste of time (13).

As to the practice of visiting historical places, only eight teachers in Delhi and none in Haryana stated that they arranged such visits occasionally. And unfortunately, these few regarded the advantage of visits to historical sites as quite negligible, calling them sightseeing trips (see also Corbishley & Stone 1994; Stone 1994).

Regarding the sufficiency of time given for teaching history, it was found that teachers' opinions were equally divided: half of them thought it to be adequate whereas the other half pleaded for more time for this discipline. At present, classes IX and X (14- and 15-year-olds) allot 4 out of a total of 45 periods of 40 minutes each per week devoted to instructional work to history. For classes XI and XII (16- and 17-year-olds), history is given 8 out of 48 periods.

The last question in the survey asked whether teachers were satisfied that the teaching methods available to them for history fulfilled the aims and objectives of this subject. Sixty-two of them replied in the negative, whereas 23 gave a positive answer. The remaining 25 teachers supplied no response.

The survey revealed four major facts with regard to teaching about the past in India. First, teachers of history in secondary schools in India are, in general, not happy with the way they teach history. Second, these teachers perceive archaeology as the most effective aid to teaching as it adds elements of reality and completeness to the teaching–learning process. Third, they feel strongly that archaeology needs to be included in the formal curriculum at secondary and senior secondary level. And fourth, they reveal a number of impediments that prevent the replacement of lecture-dominated teaching with more partici-patory methods using archaeological information.

In order to determine how effective a more dynamic approach to teaching history (including the use of archaeological material) might be as compared to the traditional lecture approach, a field study was conducted with XIth-grade students. The method and some of the findings of that study are reported below.

The field study

The study was conducted with XIth-grade students from two large senior secondary schools (Bijwasan and Najafgarh) situated in semi-urban areas of the Union Territory of Delhi. The course prescribed by CBSE for this grade is Ancient Indian History.

The students of each school were randomly placed into two groups, A and B. In this way, it was hoped, the two groups would be roughly similar in such variables as intelligence, motivation, previous achievement and home back-ground. By not combining the post-experiment performance of pupils of both schools, school and teacher factors were also controlled.

Group A in each school was taught by the experimental method, that is, the method in which archaeology was used. This method included teaching with

Table 20.1 Results of achievement of two groups from two schools

School	Group	N	Σx	$/x$	Σ^x	SD	t	Significance level
I	A	83	5180	62.40	4706.0	7.53	3.50	.01
	B	83	4848	58.40	4295.25	7.19		
II	A	68	4033	59.30	7193.36	10.28		
	B	68	3706	54.50	8523.0	11.19	2.608	.02

the help of charts, pictures printed in textbooks, replicas and models, visits to museums to study cultural material such as artefacts, dress, weapons, pottery, coins and figurines of the time and visits to historical sites and monuments. Group B was taught by the traditional method, which included narration and verbal explanation of the subject matter, blackboard writing, reading from the prescribed textbook, and reference to historical maps and charts.

The time devoted to each group was fixed as 6 hours and 40 minutes (10 periods, each period of 40 minutes' duration) for teaching the topic entitled 'Rise and Growth of the Gupta Empire'. The same teacher taught both the A and B groups in a school.

Group A spent a day at the archaeological museum in Delhi to study the development of material and aesthetic culture and then went to Mahrauli (Qutab) to see the famous iron pillar and so get first-hand and authentic knowledge about the level of technological advancement achieved by artisans in forging, alloying and casting metal. Pupils' understanding of life during the Gupta period was further deepened by being shown pictures of Buddha Ajanta paintings, Gupta coins, temples and pillars in textbooks and charts and by having their social implications explained. Unfortunately, neither of the two schools had replicas or models of archaeological materials nor any videos of objects found in excavations of sites of the Gupta period. Maps showing the Gupta Empire and excavated sites were also used.

Group B was taught by means of the chalk-and-talk method. Teachers also occasionally used textbooks and maps to explain difficult points. On the day that Group A visited the museum and historical sites, Group B revised the contents of the topic in hand, spending as much time for this work as group A spent on their field trip.

The achievement of the pupils of the two groups was tested by a multiple choice test (see Appendix 2). A study of these results is summarized in Table 20.1.

A study of these results shows that there was a statistically significant difference in performance between the group A students and the group B students (based on the 't' values test (see Garrett & Woodworth 1969, pp. 215, 461) used to measure the significance of the difference between the means of scores obtained by the two groups). This result suggests that there is a real difference in the performance of students in group A and those in group B, and so clearly establishes the superiority of the method involving the active study of archaeology over the conventional method of teaching history.

Concluding observations and suggestions

India correctly claims that it possesses a rich and proud heritage; but how can the validity of this assertion be actually demonstrated without the support of its material culture? Given the general state of history teaching in India, there is an urgent need to make the ancient history of India really meaningful to students. The best way to do this is to make archaeology part of the secondary-school curriculum.

At first, archaeology should be used by the history teacher, rather than taught as an independent subject, as a way of creating a better comprehension of history – as recommended in the workshop organized by the University Grants Commission (UGC) on 'History Teaching in India'.

Since teaching about the development of humanity with the help of archae-ology requires greater effort as well as a higher level of skill than teaching based on mere narration and lecture, a change in attitude, as well as the acquisition of an appropriate level of skill, is needed. The authorities must organize seminars, conferences and refresher courses to train teachers to use archaeological materials in a creative way, as archaeological finds cannot speak for themselves. It is most important that teachers develop both historical and social perspectives, so that events and processes can be taken into account.

Because of problems in the distribution of modern technology and the current socio-economic conditions in India it is not yet possible to use ad-vanced computer methods of presenting archaeological information (Reilly & Rahtz 1992). Nevertheless, the replicas and models of archaeological remains in school museums and galleries can still be a useful and important medium through which to teach ancient and medieval history. In fact, the school museum is a good alternative to state and central museums, as these formal institutions are generally located too far from most secondary schools and so visits to them tend to be time-consuming and expensive. Replicas and models require only the cost of their production, an expenditure that the Indian State Governments must be prepared to make in the interest of quality education. These objects must be supplied free of charge to all secondary schools and the teachers of history advised to make fullest use of them.

In addition to the setting up of school museums it is also suggested that slides and videos of material remains should be prepared for use in schools. The Government must provide mobile vans for this purpose so that all schools may benefit. The exhibitions will help pupils picture the growth and develop-ment of Indian society in its totality in a concrete and easily assimilable way.

For a proper understanding of human history, it is also essential that teachers work from both local and general perspectives. Such an approach will help to demolish the wall of racial separatism which is polluting the minds of many people, remove superstitions and irrational beliefs and broaden vision so that the students look for common features in the diversity of regional societies.

And, as has been shown by the statistical study of experimental and traditional teaching methods, it is also very important that students visit excavated sites and places of historical significance if they are to understand better the development of human society. These visits give pupils a taste for learning through direct experience and, in particular, contact with the real objects about which they are being taught. It is therefore recommended that, in the syllabus prescribed for history, excursions and visits to excavated sites or places of historical significance be made compulsory, and exercises relating to these visits be incorporated into student assessment (see also Stone 1994).

It is also essential that pupils be educated about the importance of archaeological sources for knowing about the growth of human society. A study of this topic would also be helpful in inculcating in the pupils a feeling of appreciation for our old monuments, buildings and other objects symbolizing our cultural heritage and a consciousness of the need for their proper preservation, conservation and maintenance.

Lastly, the teacher education programme currently in vogue in Indian colleges of education should also be recast. At present, archaeology is not given the place it deserves, being rather perfunctorily dealt with in an outline of methods. One chapter should be added which deals exclusively with the importance and use of archaeology as a means of teaching history.

If the teachers of history make full use of all the cultural material related to India's complex history, they will expand their pupils' awareness and understanding and therefore help to eliminate narrow loyalties in favour of broader concerns when the situation so demands. Archaeology in particular can provide a safeguard against distortions in historical data caused by personal biases, inclinations and false perceptions. It promotes belief in the ultimate unity of the human race and in the idea that 'the whole universe is my family' – an ideal so lovingly cherished in Indian culture, ethos and thought.

References

Central Board of Secondary Education 1989a. *Secondary School Curriculum*. New Delhi: Government of India.

Central Board of Secondary Education 1989b. *Senior School Curriculum*. New Delhi: Government of India.

Corbishley, M. & P. G. Stone 1994. The teaching of the past in formal school curricula in England. In *The Presented Past: heritage, museums and education*, Stone, P. G. & B. L. Molyneaux (eds), 383–97. London: Routledge.

Garret, H. E. & R. S. Woodsworth 1969. *Statistics in Psychology and Education*. Bombay: Vakils & Simons.

Reilly, P. & Rahtz, S. (eds) 1992. *Archaeology and the Information Age: a global perspective*. London: Routledge.

Sankalia, H. D. 1965. *An Introduction to Archaeology*. Poone: Deccan College.

Stone, P. G. 1994. The re-display of the Alexander Keiller Museum, Avebury, and the National Curriculum in England. In *The Presented Past: heritage. museums and education*, Stone, P. G. & B. L. Molyneaux (eds), 190–205. London: Routledge.

Appendix 1

Questionnaire for history teachers of Indian secondary and senior secondary schools

Dear History Teachers,

The present questionnaire contains twenty questions which are designed to seek information about the methods of teaching history currently in use in our secondary and senior secondary schools with special reference to the use of methods based on archaeology. Some of the questions also seek teachers' opinion regarding the difficulties experienced in using archaeological evidence for better comprehension of contemporary history.

It is needless to say that the validity of the proposed study would depend upon the nature of the respondents' answers. You are, therefore, requested to please respond to these questions in a manner that represents your genuine views.

Questionnaire

Name

School

Class taught

Qualifications

Teaching experience

1 Which method of teaching history is mostly used by you?
2 Do you use archaeological evidence, when needed, for explaining:
   (a) the chronology of historical events;
   (b) interaction among different societies;
   (c) the socio-economic and cultural development of human society;
   (d) the role of archaeology in completing historical gaps?
3 How frequently do you use the following teaching aids to facilitate the comprehension of the subject matter? (often, sometimes, or never)
   (a) archaeological remains
   (b) replicas/models
   (c) maps/charts
   (d) visits to historical places, excavation sites
   (e) electronic & mechanical devices (TV, video, radio, slide projectors, etc.)
4 Rank the following teaching aids in order of their importance for making the material culture of the contemporary period easy to understand:
   (a) early archaeological remains
   (b) replicas/models
   (c) charts
   (d) maps

(e) visits to historical sites/excavation sites

(f) electronic and mechanical devices (radio, TV, video, film strips, etc.)

5 For those who assigned first rank to archaeological finds/replicas in the last question: give your reason.

6 Do you think that archaeology should be made a part of the formal school curriculum for teaching history?

7 Should archaeology be introduced as an independent discipline like other teaching subjects or as a tool discipline for better understanding of history?

8 What are the difficulties in using archaeology as a source for teaching history? List the problems in order of their relative seriousness.

9 How often in each session do you take your students on excursions and visits to sites of historical importance? (several times, once or twice, never)

10 How far is the nearest historical museum located from your school? (1 to 10 km, 11 to 20 km, more than 20 km)

11 How many periods are allotted in your school for instructional work in a week?

12 How many periods in a week are allotted for teaching history?

13 Do you feel satisfied with the method of teaching history used by you at present?

14 Do you think that the abilities, skills and attitudes sought to be developed in pupils through history are developed in them in most of the Indian schools?

15 What use do you make of the illustrations and pictures of cultural material of a given period of history printed in textbooks used by you?

(a) only refer them to the pupils

(b) explain the details of the illustrative material and their role in understanding the life of the contemporary society

(c) make no use

16 What methods of teaching history through the application of archaeology would you suggest for Indian schools in the present context?

17 What facilities would you need for using archaeology for the teaching of history to the classes you teach?

18 Do you think that for the application of archaeology in the teaching of history an additional paper on archaeology should be introduced in teacher-training colleges?

19 How important is the role of modern communications media such as TV, radio, video, and computers etc. in facilitating the understanding of this subject by the pupils? (very important, important, negligible)

20 Do you think that a topic concerning methods of teaching history involving the application of archaeology should be added in the syllabus of teachers' colleges?

Appendix 2

Achievement test in history
Topic: Rise and growth of the Gupta Empire

Time: 20 minutes

Note: Each question is followed by 4 possible answers. Only one is correct.
Each correct response carries 2 marks.

1 On the ruins of the Kushan Empire rose a new empire that established its
   sway over a good part of the former dominions of both the Kushanas and
   the Satvahanas. What was that empire?
   (a) Sakas
   (b) Mauryas
   (c) Guptas
   (d) Chalukyas
2 In which part of India have early Gupta inscriptions been found?
   (a) Uttar Pradesh
   (b) Bihar
   (c) Punjab
   (d) Madhya Pradesh
3 Why did Chandra Gupta II marry his daughter Prabhavati to a Vakatka
   prince, a Brahmna by caste?
   (a) He did so to protect himself from being attacked by Vakatka kings.
   (b) Prabhavati was deeply in love with the Vakatka prince.
   (c) The Vakatka prince eloped with Prabhavati.
   (d) Chandra Gupta II got indirect control of the Vakatka Kingdom
        through his daughter.
4 The coin depicting Samumdra Gupta with a Veena in hand shows that:
   (a) He was a great lover of art and culture.
   (b) Samumdra Gupta indulged in song and dance at the cost of his royal
        duties.
   (c) Samumdra Gupta passed his time in such activities because the admin-
        istration of his empire was taken over by the powerful queen.
   (d) He wanted to present himself as a man of peace and cover his aggress-
        ive nature.
5 The Lichchvi princess whom Chandra Gupta I married belonged to:
   (a) Gujrat
   (b) Malwa
   (c) Bengal
   (d) Nepal
6 What was the second capital city of Chandra Gupta II?
   (a) Prayag
   (b) Kasi

   (c) Ujjain
   (d) Patliputra
7 In which State of India is the city of Ujjain situated?
   (a) Madhya Pradesh
   (b) Uttar Pradesh
   (c) Orissa
   (d) Karnataka
8 What was the period of Fa-hien's visit to India?
   (a) AD 410–425
   (b) AD 405–420
   (c) AD 399–414
   (d) AD 395–410
9 Which of the Gupta kings adopted the title of Vikramaditya?
   (a) Chandra Gupta I
   (b) Chandra Gupta II
   (c) Samumdra Gupta
   (d) Sakanda Gupta
10 What was the cause of prosperity of Malwa during the reign of Chandra Gupta?
   (a) Chandra Gupta's conquest of western Gujarat
   (b) His control over Vakatka Kingdom
   (c) The heavy tax levied on farmers
   (d) Malwa traders' silk trade with China
11 In which State did the rulers of Vallabhi establish their independent authority due to the weakness of the successors of the Guptas?
   (a) Bihar
   (b) Uttar Pradesh
   (c) Madhya Pradesh
   (d) Gujrat
12 The inscriptions of Gupta kings show that they adopted such pompous titles as 'Paramesvara', 'Mahrajadhiraja' and 'Maha Bhattarka'. What do you infer from this?
   (a) They were boastful kings.
   (b) They ruled over lesser kings in their empire.
   (c) Such titles frightened the feudatories and dissuaded them from rising in revolt.
   (d) They induced a sense of discipline in their army and administrative machinery.
13 The image of Goddess Laxmi found invariably on one side of the Gupta coins signifies that:
   (a) Gupta kings whose images are depicted on the other side of the coins presented themselves as incarnations of the god Vishnu;
   (b) Gupta kings were fanatic Hindus;
   (c) they thought that Laxmi being a goddess of wealth would bring prosperity to their empire;

(d) they accorded a place of great honour to females?

14 Why did horse archery become prominent in military tactics during the Gupta period?
   (a) because the archer would take a better aim at his enemy on horseback;
   (b) because chariots were more costly;
   (c) because horses did not flee from battleground in time of danger;
   (d) because horses increased mobility and speed of the army.

15 It is known that during the Gupta period posts acquired a hereditary nature. What could be its implication for the power of the king?
   (a) It weakened the king's power.
   (b) It did not have any effect on it.
   (c) It relieved the king from several onerous duties allowing him more time for more important work.
   (d) Administration became more efficient which increased the king's popularity among his subjects.

16 The division of the Gupta Empire into 'Bhuktis' and these into 'Vishayas' was similar to the present division of:
   (a) Tehsils into Paragnas and Villages
   (b) Districts into Tehsils and Paragnas
   (c) States into Districts and Tehsils
   (d) Country into States and Districts

17 Affairs of the towns during the Gupta period were carried on by corporate bodies consisting of professional groups of:
   (a) merchants and bankers
   (b) scribes
   (c) artisans
   (d) all the above jointly

18 At Bhita and Vaisali there existed guilds of:
   (a) silk-weavers
   (b) oil-pressers
   (c) numerous types, such as artisans and traders
   (d) bankers

19 What does the abundance of gold coins issued during the early Gupta period suggest?
   (a) Gold was the only metal known to the people.
   (b) More attractive coins could be made of gold than any other metal.
   (c) Gold coins were needed to pay salary of high officers in cash.
   (d) Gupta kings were opposed to their images being made on cheaper metals.

20 Gupta administration did not need as elaborate administrative machinery as was required by the Mauryas because:
   (a) their empire was mostly managed by feudatories;
   (b) the territory under them was not as large as it was under the Mauryas' rule;

(c) their administrative machinery was more efficient than that of the Mauryas;

(d) the subjects of their empire were more civilized and law-abiding than those of the Maurya kings.

21 The development of the feudal system during the Gupta period is mainly due to the fact that:

(a) the rulers subjugated by the Guptas, especially by Samumdra Gupta, were not dispossessed of their kingdoms but turned into tribute-paying vassals;

(b) many state officials had grabbed land from the peasants and begun to manage it themselves;

(c) the Gupta kings were not so strong as to prevent the growth of feudal lords;

(d) they had no money to pay to the state officials so allowed them to occupy and rule over a part of the territory put under their charge.

22 What was the position of the priestly class (Brahmans) during the Gupta period?

(a) Gupta kings were indifferent towards the priestly class.

(b) Being followers of Buddhism, Guptas hated Brahmans.

(c) Relationship between Gupta kings and Brahmans was cordial though not very close.

(d) Brahmans were under royal patronage and got land grants on a large scale.

23 Idol worship in the temples became a common feature during the Gupta period. What was its reason?

(a) Gupta kings made laws that required the people to bow before the idols in the temples.

(b) The priestly class installed idols in the temples in an effort to convert the people into idol worshippers.

(c) Idol worship by people was a source of income to the priests, so they encouraged it.

(d) Since Gupta kings worshipped idols, the people also turned into idol worshippers.

24 Which one of the following factors resulted in the proliferation of the caste system during the Gupta period?

(a) prohibition of 'Anulom' and 'Pratilom' marriages

(b) assimilation of foreigners into society

(c) a check on the absorption of tribal people in society

(d) the custom of marriage in one's own caste

25 The recovery of a 2-metre-high bronze image of Buddha from Sultan Ganj near Bhagalpur and Fa-hein's mention of having seen a copper image of Buddha as high as 25 metres and a Buddha image recovered from Sarnath suggest that:

(a) Gupta kings were tolerant towards Buddhism;

(b) they gave more importance to Buddhism than Hinduism;

(c) they accorded equal respect to both Buddhism and Hinduism;

(d) they changed their religious faith and became followers of Buddhism.

26 What do you think about the state of art and craft and metal technology during the Gupta period from the picture illustrations of Buddha's images, the iron pillar of Delhi and the Ajanta painting given in your textbook?

(a) The Gupta period gave much impetus to metal technology but not so much to the art of painting.

(b) It saw much development in the art of painting and the artistic aspect of images but not so much in metal technology.

(c) The Gupta period gave no boost either to art and culture or to technology.

(d) During that period both art and culture as well as science and technology were given a great boost.

27 Which works of art and craft and literature show that the nature of art and craft and literature produced during the Gupta period was mainly religious?

(a) the final compilation of the Ramayana and the Mahabharata and the image of Buddha

(b) Arya Bhatia and Romaka Siddhanta

(c) Amarkosha

(d) Abbijnanasakuntalam and Megha Dutam

28 What was the main type of play written during the Gupta period?

(a) tragedy

(b) comedy

(c) mixed type with almost even distribution between the two types

(d) mixed type but with more tragedies

29 Which aspect of the life of the people experienced a decline during the Gupta period, the so-called golden age of ancient India?

(a) scientific and technological

(b) artistic and literary

(c) trade and economics

(d) the status of shudras and women

30 The painting of Apsara (Ajanta painting) produced in your textbook is marked by:

(a) beauty, brilliance and the non-fading quality of its colours;

(b) unattractive features and an ugly face;

(c) disproportion in various parts of the body;

(d) absence of ornaments and headgear.

31 Buddha images of Gupta period recovered from various sites have been shown in:

(a) sitting posture;

(b) standing posture;

(c) different postures depicting various events in Buddha's life;

(d) preaching posture.

32 What do the panels of images, the big one in the middle of panel and other smaller ones on both its sides found at some excavated places of Gupta period, show?
   (a) that Gupta kings believed in more than one god and goddesses;
   (b) that these panels had no such implication; they only represented crafts-men's preference from an aesthetic point of view;
   (c) that the Guptas ruled over smaller vassals;
   (d) that no meaning can be read in them; they were made to just occupy the empty space on the panel.

33 Why did the silk-traders of the Gupta period give up that trade?
   (a) The demand for their products increased so much that they could not cope up with it and so gave up the trade.
   (b) The lack of skilled workers forced them to do so.
   (c) The demand for Indian silk declined in foreign markets.
   (d) The Gupta kings discouraged trade in silk.

34 What was the source of much of the wealth of the Gupta kings?
   (a) very heavy land tax
   (b) heavy levy on traders and merchants
   (c) the looting of treasures of kings subjugated by them
   (d) no definitely known source

35 Which of the two Gupta kings extended the limits of their empire more?
   (a) Samumdra Gupta and Skanda Gupta
   (b) Chandra Gupta I and II
   (c) Samumdra Gupta and Chandra Gupta I
   (d) Samumdra Gupta and Chandra Gupta II

21 Education and heritage: an example of new work in the schools of Benin

ALEXIS B. A. ADANDÉ & IRÉNÉE ZEVOUNOU

The authors dedicate their contribution to the memory of Mary Hagihara Kujawski Roberts, Director of the Museum of Art of the University of Iowa, who died on 2 September 1990. This homage is given to a colleague who always believed that cultural action and liveliness in museums would be of particular benefit to young people.

Introduction

Cultural affairs became part of development policies in Benin during the decade of development that began in 1969 under the sponsorship of Unesco. Here, as in many other African states, important economic projects had previously been set up without taking any account of the socio-cultural environment of the people affected by the changes that would result.

The price of ignoring the cultural domain has been high. The first cadres of the emergent African nations had western educations; they formed local elites deeply contaminated with an ideology characterized by a disdain for indigenous cultural values. As a result of this residue of colonialism, thirty years later, and despite the rehabilitation of cultural heritage in official speeches and the greater emphasis given to African history, a hiatus still exists between the content of education programmes and the heritage of traditional culture. Most seriously, the unique features of African civilizations have hardly been taken into account in the organization of formal education.

In order to understand this paradoxical situation, we will examine a modern educational environment which continues to produce 'intellectuals' who are ill-equipped to deal with the real needs of their society, and yet are those who are recruited to perpetuate colonialist development policies which obstruct the progress of Africa today. In addition, we also consider the solutions advanced by some African researchers in tackling the problem and reversing ongoing cultural attitudes. As an example of these new approaches we will consider several cases from the Benin school system based on the cognitive and pedagogical implications of using the resources of cultural heritage – in the main, museum and archaeological collections – in education. Finally, with the broadening of current initiatives in mind, we will take account of the need to integrate cultural heritage systematically into the education of young people and into continuing education.

Integrating cultural heritage with the Republic of Benin's education system

In common with most African states, the Republic of Benin (formerly Dahomey) embarked on a series of educational reforms, the principles of which date to 1967, formulated for the member states of the Organisation Commune Africaine et Malgache (OCAM). Reforms specific to Benin were put in place in 1977.

The first reform (1967) focused in particular on history and geography syllabuses in secondary education. The aim was to standardize the contents and methods of teaching in history amongst the French-speaking African countries; the subject matter related much more to Africa, unlike previous syllabuses, which were thinly disguised copies of French syllabuses.

The second reform (1977) was intended to deal with the more obvious lacunae in the OCAM syllabuses which had emerged from a rigorous appraisal of the results and errors of ten years' experience. Unfortunately, the new Benin school syllabuses were launched with inadequate funding and poor planning for their dissemination, with evidence of neither common sense nor any grounding in educational theory. As a result, ten years later, another impasse was reached.

Although these reforms failed, they had addressed the specific problem of the legacy of colonial education, that is, the inappropriate nature of formal education when set beside both the real needs and the aspirations of African peoples, in the hope of coming to terms with the hiatus between modern education and cultural heritage. The 1967 reform had restored dignity to the continent of Africa as a subject fit for study. The 1977 reforms attempted to take into account the social, cultural and natural environment by introducing the study of the local area in primary education. These initiatives in teaching therefore allowed reform-minded educationalists to make use of information relevant to the lives of young people and generally accessible to the population as a whole.

Some examples of the use of cultural heritage in the Benin education system

The 'haut-fourneau' of Bensékou

A pioneering initiative in the study of local communities was the work done by the pupils of the state school on the iron-ore smelting furnace of Bensékou, a little village in the Borgou in the northeast of Benin. The village owed its name to this now defunct industry (Gbesseh-Kou, 'iron ore exists', corrupted by the French colonialists into the present form, Bensékou) and the furnace still survives, surrounded by an imposing slag heap.

Practical study of this traditional village activity was set up in the village school by a creative teacher named Osséni Rouga. Together with his pupils he visited the furnace, about 2 km from the village, examined the remains, and recorded an oral tradition about the site and the history of the village (Adandé 1981, pp. 81–2).

The fact that this village had both an archaeological feature and an extant oral tradition about it shows the potential educational value of cultural resources in the local environment. If this programme was repeated through-out the country, new data might even emerge for professional researchers, especially from areas that have not been extensively investigated by archaeologists.

From school to museum: Gelede masks at the Porto-Novo Museum

It is believed in Benin that museums today are legacies of the colonial past, and must therefore tailor their aims to suit the needs of the Benin people in order to survive. Because of this principle, efforts have been made to transform these institutions into learning centres.

In 1987, for example, a team of researchers from the Direction des Musées, Monuments et Sites (DMMS) and concerned teachers from Cotonou school, in association with researchers from the University of Michigan (Roberts & Roberts 1987) and sponsored by the ethnographic museum of Porto-Novo, developed a primary-school learning experience around an exhibit of Gelede masks.

Gelede masks are a significant feature of everyday life in this part of the country. Along with their historical significance, these masks possess aesthetic qualities which make them appealing to older children (between 9 and 12) and also play an important social role in the settling of local disputes (Ayari de Souza & Brathier-Scailteur 1987, p. 30).

The working group brought teachers and other educators from a number of different teaching establishments to the museum in order to plan the special exhibition for the children. Many of the teachers had never visited a museum, as they had previously regarded museums as institutions devoted to the tourist industry and of no concern of theirs.

When the exhibition was set up, school-children were brought to the museum and divided into small groups led by museum guides and teachers. In front of each mask there was a question-and-answer session (Fig. 21.1) and at the end of the tour, lasting an average of forty minutes, the children freely expressed their impressions of the experience through drawing, colouring or poetry (Figs 21.2 and 21.3).

The spontaneous reactions by these children to the masks indicated the great value of museum artefacts for young people in general, as these objects provoked a wide variety of questions and impressions – showing teachers that artefacts can be used in the teaching of social values, history, geography, biology and other aspects of cultural life.

The experience also showed the kind of material and logistical problems involved if such a programme were to be implemented: display hardware would have to be adapted to young people, transport arranged, and teaching material produced. Consequently, the working group recommended that the project should be turned on its head, 'bringing the museum to the school' and by this means reaching schools distant from the city.

First steps in archaeology and the preservation of the cultural heritage

The Equipe de Recherche Archéologique Béninoise de l'Université Nationale du Bénin, in conjunction with researchers in the fields of science and education, developed a project whose main aim was to kindle in both young and old a greater interest in archaeology and the preservation of the cultural heritage, and to bring the cultural heritage and the education system closer together.

As part of this initiative, the Department of History and Archaeology organized an exhibition of archaeological collections on the university campus at Abomey-Calavi in 1988 to celebrate ten years of archaeological research in Benin. When this exhibition was transferred to the royal palace at Porto-Novo, it was a great success, as over 3000 young people visited it (Table 21.1). Many pupils, and also teachers, discovered for the first time what archaeology was about, its methods as well as collections of archaeological artefacts. The palace has since acquired the status of a museum.

Teaching material was also developed, linked to a project dealing with the historical sources of the Kingdom of Allada, and featuring a component entitled 'Archaeology in the classroom: the excavations at Allada and Togudo' (Adandé & Garnier n.d.). The information was put on a set of cards, some produced to give background information to teachers and teaching suggestions and some designed for the children, and photographs and maps were provided. This teaching pack was first tested in a simulation exercise with college students and in the classroom.

This project was a first attempt to resolve the problem of a lack of teaching resources, using information from archaeological work in Benin. It led to the development of a systematic collection of teaching aids – pictures, sounds and documents – to be used as resources where access to the material remains, the monuments, or living witnesses was not possible. The documents may be used in the classroom by teams or groups of children, or they may act as a

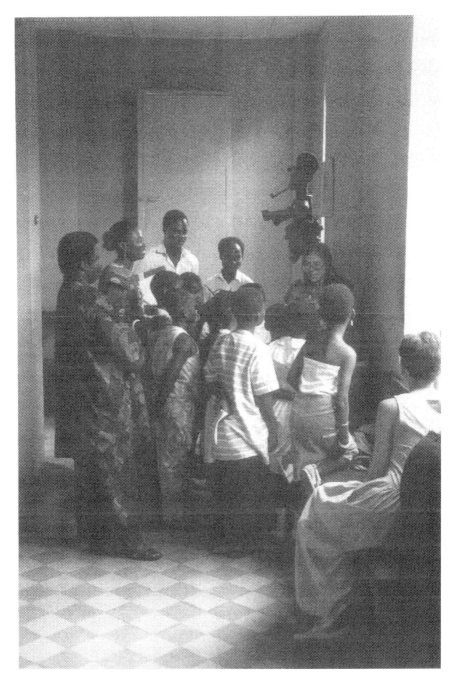

Figure 21.1 A group of students and teachers in front of a museum guide.

Figure 21.2 Students in the free expression session (drawing, colouring, writing poetry).

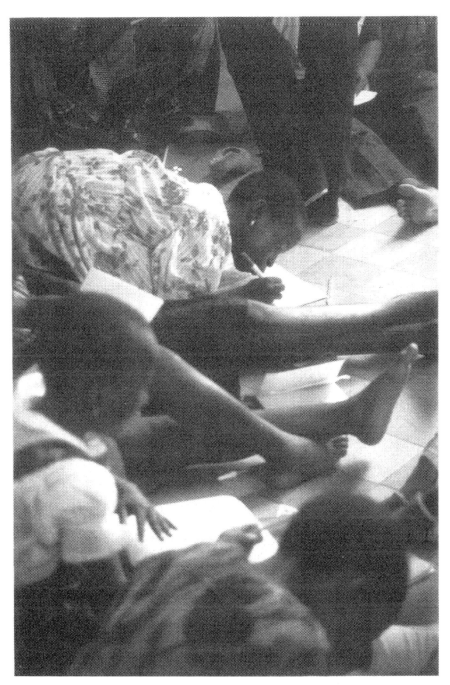

Figure 21.3 A close-up of students writing in their notebooks during the free expression session.

Table 21.1 Statistics of visitors at the first archaeological exhibition at Porto-Novo

	Total visitors	Total student population in Porto-Novo	Percentage
Primary school	2431	31,866	7.62
Secondary school	938	11,860	7.9
Total	3369	43,726	7.7

Source: Musée Honmè – Palais royal de Porto-Novo

point of departure to search out the vestiges of the past in the immediate vicinity of a school or college. It is hoped that these materials will ultimately encourage more extensive research into the rich resource base of local history.

Because of this educational initiative, it will be easier to establish excavation schools in archaeology or involvement in the restoration of historical monuments, when conditions allow it, because the public will be more knowledgeable. Indeed, such involvement presupposes a considerable awareness of archaeology and the need to protect and restore the material remains of heritage, and the existence of adequate financial support. In the immediate future, however, it is most important to prepare the necessary resources for the widespread introduction of cultural heritage in teaching programmes.

Reasons for choosing schools as centres for cultural heritage research

Several reasons may be advanced to justify the choice of educational institutions as the recipient of heritage research projects.

First, there was the political will, as exemplified by African leaders in official speeches which stressed the re-evaluation of cultural heritage and its integration with the education process. For example, the Intergovernmental Conference on Cultural Politics in Africa (AFRICACULT), held at Accra (Ghana) in 1975, recommended that education should be embedded in the reality of peoples and that systems should be reoriented towards integrating cultural values with the civilizations of Africa. Similarly the Conference of African Ministers of Education (MINEDAF) meeting in Lagos (Nigeria) in 1976 highlighted the need for education to produce individuals embedded in the cultural traditions of Africa and within the environment of the continent, conscious of their political and civic responsibilities (Bureau Régional de l'Unesco pour l'Afrique [BREDA]/Unesco 1981, p. 3).

Second, schools are an ideal place for putting such principles into practice. Early on, eminent researchers and well-known teachers from west Africa made concrete proposals for an integration of cultural heritage with teaching (Afigbo 1976; Andah 1982). The most important target populations for these initiatives were children of school age, as they tend to be open to new ideas and receptive to innovations which match their aspirations. Indeed, the experience of 'the school goes to the museum' project demonstrated the receptiveness of young pupils and their ability 'to acquire a new framework for assessing museums and artefacts from cultural heritage' (Brathier & Roberts 1987, p. 5). In addition, children may pass on to their families and relations new, positive ideas and attitudes acquired at school about cultural resources, their promotion and preservation.

Finally, the introduction of research initiatives in the school system served as a point of departure for the elaboration of new teaching methods.

Some problems were encountered by these initiatives. There was sometimes a politico-administrative hostility to classes going beyond the confines of the school. But most often the difficulties were related to the secondary position allotted to research in the theory of education and more generally to the status conferred on scientific research in African countries – particularly in the Republic of Benin. This reticence about educational innovation may be the result of limitations in the teacher-training sector, as there is a general unwillingness to change certain outmoded methods in teaching.

Towards a co-ordinated approach in treating cultural heritage as an educational resource

The psychological and historical factors alluded to above help to explain why so far teaching programmes and methods make so little use of the cultural resources of the African people. The gulf between traditional methods of instruction and cultural heritage and the system of formal education in Africa has not, however, been researched to any great extent. If obstacles in the way of educational change are to be overcome, strategies have to be developed which will take into account the integration of old and new, the retraining of teachers and other educationalists and the development of new teaching methods and materials.

Innovating always means to some extent coming into conflict with the prevailing system. As a result, it is important to envisage a preparatory stage of information and consciousness-raising for teachers, followed by a harmonizing process whereby the innovation will not be seen as a new constraint or a 'foreign body'.

Developing human resources is a crucial issue in the spread of innovations, concerning both teachers and the museum staff who are involved in working with schools, and the researchers – archaeologists, linguists, anthropologists and other specialists – who wish to see educational benefits in their research. School and college teachers in particular need to understand the changes in the system as they arise, and so they need to receive the appropriate training.

A seminar on making use of cultural heritage in education, held at Freetown (Sierra Leone) in 1980, highlighted the need to encourage and develop basic research on the subject in universities and other institutions. The Freetown seminar encouraged African states to support teacher-training in this area, to widen the field of experience of teachers and give them, amongst other things, a command of the national languages, the very vehicle for the transmission of cultural values, as well as an understanding of indigenous thought processes (BREDA/Unesco 1981, pp. 4–13).

For museum staff and researchers, the problem is rather more delicate because, to our knowledge, there are no appropriate training facilities on the African continent. The success of the 'school in the museum' programme, however, has resulted in the evaluation of this form of education by the Direction des Musées, Monuments et Sites en République du Benin and elsewhere in Africa, such as Zimbabwe (Unesco 1986, p. 15). As a general rule education officers, where they exist in African museums, emerge from the school system, and so it should be considered whether there should be specialized training in the interpretation of museum artefacts to the public – in other words, *museum education*.

Conclusion

We have tried to use the practical experience of learning programmes outside schools to meet one of the greatest challenges that black Africa faces: that of ensuring the future of the past. The area chosen for this study has been the school system of Benin where several new departures in education encourage a greater emphasis on cultural heritage in the education of young people.

The prospect is that these ground-breaking schemes will flourish, but before this wider development can be contemplated, educational research must be encouraged and teaching and museum staff trained, and money must be found for the financing of such programmes. Indeed, although some elements of heritage can be introduced directly or can be adapted, especially in the plastic arts, music and drama, oral history and technology, there are resources and teaching aids to prepare: syllabuses must be designed, textbooks written, work cards and teaching packs, posters, photographs or engravings, slides, tapes and videos produced. Finally, evaluation procedures must be set up which take into account cognitive, psychological and sociological developments, all generally closely linked into the interdisciplinary approach appropriate to bringing cultural heritage into education.

An awareness of other cultures, and other approaches to the teaching of cultural heritage, may be fostered through an exchange of ideas between specialists, teachers and museum education staff, both regionally and internationally. In this process historical and ethnographic museums, at national and local levels, will also play a key role (Adandé 1985, 1990). It would not perhaps be out of the question to organize an exchange of teaching materials and bulletins between museum education services in North America and Europe, especially those with important African collections, and national museums of Africa. Publications on these generally inaccessible parts of African cultural heritage would be very useful for the school-children of Africa (Caraway

1985). In western Europe and North America, the problem of spreading information about cultural heritage is now being addressed through such journals as *Archaeology and Education* (see, for example, Shaw 1989 and Stone 1989).

We are at the very beginning of a long-term programme of research and action which, together with an increase in human, financial and material resources, will ultimately involve the whole country in a process of continuing education. This is a stage where creativity and a good deal of imagination are required. Hearts and minds must be moved in support of innovations that lead to a rehabilitation of indigenous cultural values, an affirmation of national identity and restoration of the element of historical continuity in the minds of young African school-children.

References

Adandé, A. 1981. Un exemple de recherche archéologique. *Recherche Pédagogie et Culture* 55, 81–2.

Adandé, A. 1985. Pour un musée local des arts et métiers traditionnels. Paper given at the séminaire régional sur les musées locaux et régionaux en Afrique de l'Ouest, Lomé, May 1985. West African Museums Project I. A. I.

Adandé, A. 1990. Cultural heritage, archaeology and education. In *Cultural Resource Management: an African dimension*, Andah, B. W. (ed.), 102–3. Ibadan Owerri: Wisdom Publishers.

Adandé, A. & Ph. Garnier n.d. Les sources de l'histoire du Royaume d'Allada 1 – Archéologie en classe: les fouilles à Allada et Togudo. *Images et documents: archéologie et histoire*. Porto-Novo: Institut National pour la Formation et la Recherche en Education.

Afigbo, A. E. 1976. History, archaeology and schools in Nigeria. *West African Journal of Education* 20, 407–17.

Andah, B. W. 1982. *African Development in Cultural Perspective (with special reference to Nigeria)*. Ibadan: B. W. Andah.

Ayari de Souza, R. & M. Brathier-Scailteur 1987. L'école au musée. *Bénin-Magazine* 7–8, 29–31.

Brathier, L. & A. Roberts 1987. Expérience pilote d'animation muséale pour enfants: l'école au musée. *Ehuzu* 2966, 5.

BREDA/Unesco 1981. Subregional seminar on the use of cultural heritage in education, Freetown, 29 September – 3 October 1980. Final Report ED/CC/BREDA/80/SCM/CRE/8.

Caraway, Caren 1985. *African Designs of the Guinea Coast*. Maryland: International Design Library & Stemmer House Publishers.

Roberts, M. Kujawski & A. Roberts 1987. Rapport sur l'élaboration d'un project d'animation au musée ethnographique de Porto-Novo 12 mai – 13 juin 1987. Direction des Musées, Monuments et Sites en République du Bénin – Minstère de la Culture, de la Jeunesse et des Sports. Porto-Novo: cyclo.

Shaw, Rachel 1989. Combining archaeology and education – an example from England. *Archaeology and Education* 1, 5–9.

Stone, Peter 1989. Editorial: a long and winding road. *Archaeology and Education* 1, 1–5.

Unesco 1986. Seminar 'Musée et éducation', Guadalajara, Jalisco, Mexico, 3–7 March. Final Report ED-88/WS-6.

22 Archaeology in the schools and museums of Cameroon

PATRICK MBUNWE-SAMBA, MATTHIAS LIVINUS NIBA & NDAMBI ISAAC AKENJI

Introduction

Cameroon has had three different colonial masters: it was a German territory from 1884 to 1914 and then was divided into two parts after the defeat of Germany in the First World War, one part, a fifth of the country and population, administered by Britain and the rest by France. Today, this influence persists as Cameroon is officially a bilingual and bicultural country. Unfortunately, this complex situation has profoundly affected the teaching of Cameroonian history, as each group has competing interests depending on their attachment to the colonial heritage. This is especially so in education about the past and the role of archaeology in its study.

The general public in Cameroon have a lot of misgivings as to what archaeology is and what it does. In fact, many people believe that archaeology is simply a white man's science that involves the unnecessary digging up of graves, with the result that ghosts of the dead are released to torment the living (pers. comm. Akenji with some traditional rulers and government personnel in Bamenda, 1987). Such people are not aware of the potential value of archaeology to provide information about the past ways and systems of life of our ancestors and as a means of building a stable nation (see Andah 1985; Ndambi 1987).

Such attitudes are not generally countered by the formal education system, however, for education has tended to follow the subjects and structures of the colonialist system before it, ignoring the diversity of language dialects and ethnic groups in Cameroon and therefore leaving little place for an understanding of their distinctive pasts.

All formal education in Cameroon is state-controlled and although the state gives permission to mission bodies (voluntary agencies) and to individuals (lay private) to run schools, the curricula, syllabuses, timetables, examinations and certification, as well as the general supervision of instructional programmes, are the prerogative of the state. Because of this control, those who do not conform to the many texts and decrees regulating education are sanctioned sometimes by the closure of the establishments or by the withdrawal of subventions.

Like the public administration of the country, Cameroon's formal educational system and practices are very highly centralized. Whatever is taught at any level is decreed by the Government. Of the ten administrative provinces in the country two are English-speaking. The anglophone provinces run a 7:5:2-year system respectively of primary, secondary and high-school courses and the francophone sector runs a 6:4:3-year system. There is no difference in university education, although the only university is very French-oriented. Both sectors have a two-year pre-school system called the nursery school, but this is available only for those living in the cities. The examination system is still different in the anglophone and francophone systems and attempts have been made since 1960 to harmonize the school syllabuses without much success.

Education is not compulsory: many children in the rural areas therefore do not attend school.

The multicultural heritage of our curricula is considered by some people in authority as a weakness rather than a strength and because of well-founded suspicion, attempts at subtle assimilation by the francophone majority are being resisted by the anglophone minority even where the reforms are for the better. French is taught in the English middle schools beginning in class 4 (ages 8 and 9) and English is used as a language of instruction for all subjects from the age of 4 while French is a language of instruction in the francophone sector and English is taught from the age 4.

In the bilingual secondary schools – there is at least one in most provinces – instruction is given in either language beginning in the third year, depending on whether the teacher is anglophone or francophone. The idea behind the creation of these bilingual secondary schools was very good because they were intended to be centres where national unity was to be emphasized but, in time, their programmes have become unwieldy and since the first ones were established shortly after Independence in 1960, no evaluation has been done on them. In fact, the same programmes have remained in place for thirty years after Independence!

It is against this background of educational problems and uneasy cultural relations that the place of archaeology in the schools and museums of Cameroon must be considered.

The place of archaeology in the school curricula

Archaeology, as a discipline, is not taught at any level in the entire educational system save at the University of Yaounde where students take a history degree or a postgraduate qualification with a 'specialization' in archaeology

(Mbunwe-Samba 1990). It is only at this level that a few history students come in contact with, and gain some smattering of knowledge about, archaeology.

Though a student may earn a Bachelor's degree with work in archaeology, the number of such students is small and few actually end up using their knowledge for the promotion of the subject, either in the classroom or elsewhere. There is no motivation, no material to work with and no scholarships for further study, since archaeology is not on the Government's so-called 'priority list' and is not considered of any utilitarian value in development in the same way as are agriculture, medicine, engineering, economics, English and French.

The result is that the total number of trained archaeologists is about half a dozen. But even among these specialists there are no materials with which to work and so there is no encouragement for others to enter the profession. Of the qualified ones, a few teach in the University and one or two work as researchers in the Institute of Human Sciences, an institution within the Ministry of Higher Education, Computer Sciences and Scientific Research. The other non-specialists (those with first degrees) are earning their living as either history or language teachers in secondary schools. At that level, there is no opportunity to bring archaeology into the system as teachers have to follow the prescribed syllabus.

In the primary and secondary schools, however, a considerable part of the syllabus is spent on intensive studies of the past. Primary-school pupils in class 5 (9–10-year-olds) study prehistory, early civilizations (Egypt, Mesopotamia, China, Hebrews, Phoenicians), Greek and Roman civilizations, the Dark and Middle Ages, Islam and the Crusades. Class 6 primary pupils (10–11 years) study the Renaissance, the Age of Discovery, the Reformation, empires of the Western Sudan (Ghana, the Aimoravides, Songhai, the Kotoko), early migrations in west Africa, the slave trade and industrial revolution among other topics. Pupils in the last year of the primary school begin from the scramble for Africa to the present day and an interesting topic with some archaeological flavour, 'West Cameroon Antiquities – Buildings and Monuments', is slipped in for this class in anglophone Cameroon. In the end-of-course examination this syllabus is examined under general knowledge (social studies) at the primary level.

At the secondary-school level the same syllabus introduced in the fifth year of primary school is repeated in depth in the first three years of the secondary school. The last two years are devoted to the final examination in which English and European history are taught and examined.

The nature of the history at this level is a survey of the evolution and development of humanity up to the present in its social, political and economic aspects. In forms 1 to 3, for example, the history syllabus is as follows: time periods in human development (palaeolithic and neolithic man); early man; neolithic man (progress in the use of fire, agriculture); other cultural revolutions (copper and bronze age); neolithic Africa, the Iron Age etc.; introduction to early civilizations (Egypt, Nubian, Berber, etc.); and neolithic Africa,

Mesopotamia, Persia, India and China. Although these subjects in the last three years of primary school and the first three years of secondary school are archaeological topics, no teachers treat them as such at any of these levels. It is, in fact, not out of place to describe archaeology in Cameroonian schools as the 'handmaiden of history' (Wilding 1986). Despite the presence of archaeology in the history syllabus and despite its recognition as a veritable source of history, archaeology is never mentioned beyond the introductory history lessons. In other words, pupils are never introduced to the aims, scope and methods of archaeology in the same way they are introduced to the concepts and methods of mathematics, physical and natural sciences (also see Corbishley & Stone 1994). Why is it so?

An obvious reason is that in the teacher-training system archaeology is never mentioned as a discipline let alone taught to the students. Even history is given short shrift in the colleges which train primary- and secondary-school teachers. In the lone Advanced Teachers College (for secondary-school teachers), history is paired up with geography. Worst of all, the intake into the History/Geography Department is the lowest because of a quota system. As the word 'archaeology' is only mentioned in introductory lessons in these training colleges, it is not surprising that teachers have no idea of archaeology.

It is no wonder then that, even though history teachers teach about the Palaeolithic and Neolithic periods, their explanations at best end at the definition of these terms. And archaeology education is not helped by the fact that some of the textbooks used by the students are unadapted and those produced by Cameroonians are copied from obsolete texts produced many years ago by the European colonizers without cognizance of the vocabulary or level of the student.

The lack of support for education about the past has created a general malaise in history teaching. There have been many complaints in Cameroon schools that, unlike English, mathematics, geography and French, where new methods of teaching have been introduced and seminars are being organized regularly to improve the methods of teaching these subjects, history teaching has remained the same. History lessons are said to be boring, students are said to rely on cramming from copious notes dictated to them by teachers at primary and secondary levels and perhaps even at the University some of them copy word for word from outdated history books.

The most fundamental reason may come, however, from the colonialist legacy itself. The entire syllabus aims broadly at giving the children the stages of human cultural evolution from its humble beginnings to the complexity of the modern world. Unfortunately, this is done only from the European perspective, which at its best is biased and racialist. From that perspective the role of Africa and the African in human cultural advance is mostly passive. Africans are not shown as having originated anything; rather they are consumers of initiatives from outside the continent.

This approach to the study of the past is what has been bequeathed to us by the colonial rulers. This colonial syllabus is jealously guarded and is still religiously followed save for minor modifications three decades after Independence. Constitutionally, Cameroon is termed a bilingual and bicultural country. What is ignored, however, is that, as in any other African country, beneath this façade of European heritage there is a multiplicity of indigenous cultures, manifested in over 200 ethnic groups each with its own dialect and traditions.

Perhaps the introduction of archaeology even as an adjunct to history will be useful because it may help create interest in local and regional origins and development, and so engage the general public in an appreciation of their own past. In addition, the teaching of archaeological methods in schools would help train the young in the scientific analysis of events and the interpretation of material culture, rather than simply filling them with historical 'facts'. This scientific approach will give students the opportunity to find out things for themselves and so help them to draw reasonable conclusions about the issues and events of life.

Tests of attitudes to archaeology

In order to test the attitudes of history teachers to the past, and so help to determine how best to promote archaeology in the educational system, one of us (Mbunwe-Samba) conducted a survey among history teachers at secondary-school level.

Although only 17 out of 70 (23%) history teachers returned their questionnaire in time for this analysis, the answers had some quite revealing trends. All the 17 respondents except one were graduates and 8 had postgraduate qualifications; the length of time they have been teaching history ranged from one year to 18 years, with 8 of them having from 10 to 18 years' experience.

The vast majority of these teachers had little actual contact with the remains of the past: 41% of them had never been to a museum; 35% of them did not know and had not visited a historical site; 65% of them did not know and had not been to an archaeological site; 65% of them had no formal training in archaeology; 53% of them had never found any archaeological objects in their environments; 76% of them had not been to a site excavated for archaeological finds; 71% of them had not taken part in any excavation; and 65% of them had not read any book on archaeology and two others did not know any titles or authors.

Surprisingly, however, an astonishing 82% of them thought that archaeology should be taught in the secondary schools as a subject and yet the same proportion had never taken their students to a museum of any kind!

When asked what possibilites (facilities) exist in their institution for the teaching of this subject if it were introduced, 71% said there were no facilities, but of the two who thought some facilities existed, one said there was a small laboratory and the other said they have a bus to carry students to sites.

If the above sample reflects the situation in secondary schools across the country (and there is no reason to suggest it does not), the situation in primary schools will almost certainly be as bad, if not worse, as none of the teachers will have received any further training in ancient history or archaeology than what they themselves received in their own primary and secondary education.

What to do about the problem

The multiplicity of problems which face archaeological research and practice in Cameroon are aptly summarized by Ndambi (Ndambi 1987, p. 3) in his suggestion that education needs to:

1 balance the past and the present by enlightening the general public on the norms and values of Cameroonian material culture or cultural property and traditional institutions, through archaeological publication;
2 establish a Department of Archaeology and Anthropology in the University of Yaounde;
3 build modern and well-equipped provincial museums as repositories for the preservation of Cameroonian cultural property;
4 include archaeology and anthropology in the so-called 'priority subjects' so as to enable Cameroonians studying these subjects abroad to have government scholarships;
5 institute a better Cameroon Antiquities Ordinance similar to that of the Nigerian Antiquities ACT of 1953;
6 establish an archaeological laboratory unit for the sole purpose of processing and analysing archaeological materials;
7 budget adequate government finance for planned regional excavations in Cameroon with the collaboration of the international research funding programmes of some advanced countries;
8 train appropriate personnel in the Department of Museum Management and to retrain museum attendants.

If all these recommendations were implemented, the introduction of archaeology in schools, whether as a discipline in itself or even as part of history, would be an easy affair.

Bringing archaeology into the schools

Afigbo (1986) argues that the introduction of archaeological methods into history teaching in the Nigerian situation will make history more practical and relevant to pupils. The same argument can be made for the Cameroon. For three decades history has been taught from the same Eurocentric perspective which is now totally outdated for the present generation of Cameroonian children. Thus more and more pupils are losing interest in history. They consider it irrelevant in their present world. In Nigeria and the Cameroon history is being gradually replaced by social studies and in the latter drastic cuts are already being made in the intake of student teachers into the History/ Geography Department of the Advanced Teachers' College. History can only be saved if archaeology is injected into it.

In studying prehistory, pupils should be introduced to the techniques and methodology of archaeology, as well as visiting examples of palaeolithic and neolithic sites in order to see the evidence of the past directly. Interest in prehistoric sites could then be easily transferred to historical monuments such as buildings, tombs and statues, and through the experiences gained in visits to archaeological sites, the children can be taught to read and interpret these sites for themselves rather than being glued to their books in the classroom.

The introduction of the subject right from the primary level of education would be a useful addition to the proper understanding of culture and society. And the scientific basis of archaeology is very stimulating and more immediate and objective than the chronological and topical facts of history. As Shaw has observed:

> even if archaeological methods may be unable to resurrect the names of kings or give details of political events in the way that history can, this absence of political and personal detail is often a positive advantage: it makes clearer the general social and economic picture, which in historical writings is sometimes obscured and overlaid by the more superficial political happenings and for which indeed the historical evidence is sometimes scanty or lacking.
>
> (Shaw 1975, p. 12)

A non-political, non-sectarian and non-racial past portrayed by a modern approach to archaeology should imbue children with a more balanced outlook on the world around them. Such study should go some way to reduce the bigotry which is the bane of the modern world.

An archaeology syllabus in Cameroon should start with local material and move outwards to the wider world. Pupils should first be acquainted with their own environments, and then gradually introduced to archaeological sites in their province and Cameroon as a whole. Pupils would then study African and finally world archaeology.

To realize such a syllabus, teachers must be trained not only in archaeological methods but in the skills to teach the subject to young people. Teachers already in the field without such training will have to take refresher courses to orientate them to teach archaeology. The training courses should cover simple ways of interpreting artefacts, and include visits to museums and historical sites and seminars with archaeologists and museum professionals.

To make this training possible, the Government must make money available. A department of archaeology must be created at the University with the necessary staff, both teaching and supporting, trained to run it. Field trips for excavation must be undertaken. Apart from university academic training, provision must be made at the Advanced Teachers' College for the training of archaeology teachers.

In addition, it is necessary for the recently established National Museum to begin its archaeological programme without delay, with the necessary equipment and a duly appointed curator, for archaeology education will not be possible without the influence on the general public provided by museums.

Archaeology and museums

Museums in Cameroon perform what Ndumbi (1982) describes as the 'hidden curriculum' of archaeology, as the artefacts present signs and symbols related to such powerful social forces as ideology and power. Such implicit ideas are especially evident in the palace museums of the traditional rulers of Cameroon, popularly called *Fons* in the Bamenda Grassfields. These museums collect, store, preserve, conserve and present for educational studies a wide variety of cultural materials, including portraits of the royal lineage, their artefacts, moveable antiquities (e.g. talking drums and weapons), skeletons and skins of sacred animals associated with traditional rulers, inscriptions and engravings found on door-posts/pillars, stools, headgear, warshields and traditional costumes. A typical palace museum rich in cultural property is the palace of the Njoyas in Foumbam, established in 1889 and reorganized in 1935 (Ndumbi 1982). It contains a large collection of the material culture of the Bamoum people and it is therefore a classic place for archaeological education to start in Cameroon.

There are also anthropological museums in Cameroon, devoted to collecting and preserving anthropological and archaeological documents and other cultural materials. The museums at Douala, Maroua, Yaounde, Buea and Bamenda, for example, have photographs, films and tapes of interviews conducted with local rural non-literate groups on their lifeways, including religious worship, marriages, death and birth ceremonies, economic activities, and interpretations of festival masks and ritual apparatus. A particularly important centre for ethnographic research is located in Bamenda at the Kaberry Research Centre. The major objective of this institution is to carry out educational research on the socio-cultural systems of the Bamenda Grassfields of Cameroon (see the *Kaberry Research Centre Bulletin* 1, May 1989) and disseminate the results of this research for the education of the general population.

Although there are some positive developments in the museums system in Cameroon, there are also many serious problems in all parts of the infrastructure, involving organization, staffing, funding, artefact conservation, research, training, commercialization and security.

Political appointments at the highest levels of museum organization mean that these institutions are run by people with no knowledge of museum science, and has led to a very acute shortage of trained curators, especially in the Bamenda and Yaounde museums. This has led to a general lack of conservation of artefacts. In addition, the government allocation for the funding of the museums is always discouraging and is too little for the purchase of new equipment. And because of the lack of trained personnel, the museums cannot provide adequate information or support for research or interpretation of the collections to the general public.

Security is also a serious problem: most public museums have had cases where cultural objects have been stolen and sold in the antiquities market: for example, the theft of 'Afo-A Kom' (a wooden carved statue of a man and his two wives, of the Kom Kingdom of the Bamenda Grassfields) in 1974 and its sale to American tourists who took it to add to the American Museum in Washington D.C. (*Cameroon Tribune*, 9 January 1986).

Because of these problems a number of measures must be taken if the museum culture of Cameroon is to be developed:

1 The organization of publicly owned museums in the Cameroon should be one of the priorities of the Government and the appointment of staff should be based on expertise.
2 A comprehensive museum collection policy should be introduced and laws proclaimed against illegal trading in antiquities.
3 Government funds for training curators, conservators museum interpreters, and managers need to be provided.
4 Active encouragement should be given to the ideal and establishment of local authority or community museums, for it is at such local and community levels that the objects collected by museums have the greatest popular appeal and archaeological significance.
5 Museums should be adequately equipped with materials for conservation of their collections.

Other solutions

Some people have argued that perhaps our salvation and the changes of our fortunes in the recognition of archaeology in Cameroon do not lie wholly in the creation of a department of archaeology in the University, the expansion and improvement of museums or on the total reliance on professional archaeologists who are in very short supply anyway. In the words of Afigbo (1986, p. 4) talking about the teaching of archaeology in Nigerian schools:

It thus becomes necessary to borrow a leaf from Britain where Archaeology began largely as an affair of amateurs who have continued to play a recognized role in the work of locating and uncovering the archaeological wealth of Britain with the cooperation and encouragement of specialists.

At present, there are very few informed amateurs in Cameroon, given the fact that the Government's scarce and meagre resources are being competed for by more immediate needs which may not include free education and where the majority of the population are still struggling to satisfy basic survival needs. As a new Ministry of Tourism has been created, however, the solution to some of the basic problems (creation of museums, training personnel, curators and museum attendants, the use of mass media to sensitize the population, the institution of the Cameroon Antiquities Ordinance, etc.) may be resolved. This Ministry can then request the expertise of the half-dozen or so archaeologists in the country to improve the important cultural sites and so stimulate the tourist industry which, in many African countries, such as Kenya and Tanzania, is a good foreign exchange earner (although see Ucko 1994). Thereafter the need for maintaining the structures set up by this Ministry will force Government to introduce archaeology into the school system – something that has not happened because the present curriculum is crowded and a new subject cannot be allowed when the survival of many long-established ones is seriously threatened. In this case necessity will dictate the pace of reforms.

Conclusion

It will take a long time indeed to convince people that archaeology, as a discipline, has any utilitarian value but the time will come when we will realize that archaeology has something new to offer in the reconstruction of our past and that the reconstruction of the experiences of human society in the distant past will continue to have relevance to the life of our extant populations. Even if, because of our state of development and our economic standing, we have some needs more immediate than archaeology, we must still continue to keep aspects of this important subject alive (teaching it as a branch of history at least) and thus using its rigorous scientific methods and techniques of investigations, its terminology and reasoning processes and at the same time keeping up the basic training of personnel to maintain our rich material cultural heritage for the benefit of posterity.

We should realize that if our museums, monuments and culture houses are well organized, this could help boost the Cameroon tourist industry and show the western-educated elite in our country that our native lifeways are different from but not inferior to the white or colonial culture to which these accultur-ated people cling so tenaciously. At the same time a wider understanding of the value of archaeology among the general population in the understanding and transmission of our cultural heritage should begin to curtail the illicit trade in cultural artefacts.

However, it is when considering the predicament of a people facing over-whelming odds that one tends to agree with an old man who told Mbunwe-Samba rather earnestly during an interview that it was hard to relax in a museum observing a skeleton, or in a game park observing animals, or in a botanical garden looking at the different species of trees, when you are not sure where your next meal is coming from. This declaration may sound pessimistic but it is reality and it is honest talk coming from one who needs our attention. Cultural heritage does not put food in one's mouth, but it can provide the social foundation for a new self-confidence, one that can help make life in our developing nation more bearable for the silent majority who have been the victims of our complex colonial past.

References

Afigbo, A. E. 1986. Archaeology and the schools. *West African Journal of Archaeology* 16, 155–64.

Andah, B. W. 1985. No past: no present: no future – anthropological education and African revolution. Inaugural Lecture delivered on 19 December 1985, University of Ibadan, Ibadan.

Corbishley, M. & P. G. Stone 1994. The teaching of the past in formal school curricula in England. In *The Presented Past: heritage, museums and education*, Stone, P. G. & B. L. Molyneaux (eds), 383–97. London: Routledge.

Mbunwe-Samba, P. 1990. Archaeology and education in anglophone Cameroon. *Archaeology and Education Newsletter* 1, 5–9.

Ndambi, I. A. 1987. Archaeological research in anglophone Cameroon: a historical perspective. Unpublished BA (Hons) degree project, University of Ibadan.

Ndumbi, P. A. 1982. The prospective role of the museum in the cultural and socio-economic life of Cameroon. Unpublished thesis, University of Leicester.

Shaw, T. 1975. *Lectures on Nigerian Prehistory and Archaeology*. Ibadan: Ibadan University Press.

Ucko, P. J. 1994. Museums and sites: cultures of the past within education – Zimbabwe, some ten years on. In *The Presented Past: heritage, museums and education*, Stone, P. G. & B. L. Molyneaux (eds), 237–82. London: Routledge.

Wilding, R. 1986. Archaeological practice, education and development: making connections. In Final Papers vol. 4 (mimeo). World Archaeological Congress.

Appendix

Questionnaire for history teachers in our school system

This is a short questionnaire to find out some facts about the way our past is being taught in our educational system. The information will be used for a research paper for an international conference. Please answer as sincerely as possible. Use the back page to make any comments you think will be useful. You may fill out all or only part of the information in Section A if you so wish so that we can call on you for more details should the need arise. Answer questions 10, 11, 17, 22, 23 in some detail. Thank you very much for your patience and help.

1 Your name
2 Your school or institution
3 Your department

4 How long is your total teaching experience?
5 Your highest qualification: Teacher Grade II, I, A/L, DipEd, Post Grad Dip, MA/MSc, PhD
6 How long you have been teaching history?
7 What aspects of the history you teach do children/students enjoy? Mention two most important ones.
8 What topics about the past do you enjoy teaching? Mention two.
9 What comment(s) could you make about learners' understanding and/or enjoyment of ancient history *vis-à-vis* world affairs and modern history?
10 State briefly one main aim and objective of teaching history in our school system.
11 Mention some available teaching aids and visual aids that you use besides text books and maps.
12 Have you every been to a museum? Yes? No? Where? How many times?
13 Have you ever visited a historic site, e.g. monument, old building or old grave site for purposes of studies? Yes? No? Where? How many times?
14 Have you ever taken your students to see the things in a museum or to a historical site? Yes? No? How many times? Where?
15 How would you explain the meaning of archaeology to a learner?
16 How do you think an understanding and knowledge of archaeology can be useful?
17 Have you read any books on archaeology? Yes? No? Mention two.
18 Have you ever been to an archaeology site? Yes? No?
19 Have you ever been to a site excavated for archaeological finds? Yes? No? Where?
20 Have you every excavated a site yourself? Yes? No? Which site(s)? List three things you found.
21 Do you think that archaeology should be taught in our schools? Yes? No? Why and what aspects? Where?
22 What possibilities exist in your school or institution for the teaching of archaeology as a subject? Cite only three examples.
23 Have you had any formal training in archaeology? Yes? No?
24 Have you ever found any archaeology objects or artefacts in your environment? Yes? No? If yes, name the types:
25 Any additional comments or remarks should be entered here.

23 Prehistory, archaeology and education in Zimbabwe

GILBERT PWITI

Colonial Zimbabwe

Zimbabwe is one of those countries in southern Africa which has enjoyed a long and active tradition of archaeological research into virtually all periods of prehistory. Although great emphasis has been placed on the Iron Age, the basic culture history of the country is now fairly clear. Much more research needs to be done, however, to fill in gaps in our knowledge and to take account of changes in archaeological theories and methods. Equally important is the need to redirect research orientation in keeping with the changed political and cultural aspirations of the new nation, given that most of the existing research was conducted in a colonial context and some of the interpretation was framed within a settler colonialist paradigm (Garlake 1983). As Hall (1984, 1990) has shown in a similar case, South Africa, a colonialist regime may control the results of archaeological research and interpretation, particularly as it pertains to early farming communities in southern Africa (also see Witz & Hamilton 1994; Mazel & Ritchie 1994).

Despite this long tradition, and the presence of monumental sites such as Great Zimbabwe, it was, significantly, not until recently that a conscious attempt was made to publicize archaeology and the results of archaeological projects. This was done mainly through the education system.

The reasons for this delay are to be sought in the political history of the country. Zimbabwe provides a classic example of the link between archaeology and politics, particularly in the case of the interpretation of Great Zimbabwe (Garlake 1983; Hall 1990). The presence of this monumental site in a country occupied by the largely British white settler population in the late nineteenth century provoked considerable controversy as to the identity of its builders, its age and function. The site represented a considerable human achievement, reflecting a stable and flourishing civilization in the past. For the white settler population, the possibility of an indigenous identity for the builders of Great Zimbabwe was unacceptable. This would have contradicted part of the foundation of colonial imperial policy, i.e. the claim that they rescued Africans from a long history of barbarity and backwardness. When research commenced at Great Zimbabwe and related sites in the early part of this century, therefore, it immediately became a victim of the racial theories of the time. For most of the white settler population, Great Zimbabwe could only have been built in the distant past by a race, preferably white, superior to the country's indigenous populations. Phoenicians, Greeks and other foreign peoples were invoked as the creators of this monumental site deep in the African interior. To support this view, very early dates were put forward for the building and occupation of the site; a recent date would have made it a product of the black populations, at a time when it was argued that they were recent immigrants into southern Africa.

Early research as far back as 1906 had failed to support any exotic origins for the site, and subsequent work from the 1920s confirmed its indigenous origin, as well as suggesting occupation around the middle of the second millennium AD. Indeed, although Caton-Thompson (1931) was brought into the country by the colonial government in the late 1920s to try and 'prove' a non-indigenous origin for Great Zimbabwe, she found no evidence for extraneous origins – and so her work was rejected. The advent of radiocarbon dating and further research in the 1950s only confirmed the results of earlier work. By the 1960s, therefore, no serious scientist could question the local origin of Great Zimbabwe and related sites in the country (Garlake 1983).

Science and politics, however, failed to become reconciled, especially in the political climate of what was then Southern Rhodesia. The true facts of Great Zimbabwe were confirmed at a time when black nationalists were becoming increasingly vocal in the quest for self-rule as opposed to white settler political and economic dominance. As part of their campaign, black leaders sought to use the past to legitimize modern claims. The site of Great Zimbabwe, as a visible expression of a successful indigenous culture in the past, became the focus of such aspirations. The reaction of the settler government was to attempt to suppress the results of archaeological research findings and their publication, especially research at Great Zimbabwe. Archaeology in general, and at Great Zimbabwe in particular, became the subject of parliamentary debates and press coverage on a number of occasions, with the settlers still claiming a non-black origin for the culture.

It is against this kind of background that the question of archaeology, prehistory and education in Zimbabwe must be viewed. Prior to independence in 1980 and shortly after, it is not surprising that little of the country's prehistory was taught in schools. That which was taught was and still is within the context of the history syllabus. Emphasis in the teaching of the past was placed on the more recent history of Africa and the history of Europe or the history of the British Empire and the Commonwealth. The general impression given was that Africa had no history worth studying before the colonial era. School textbooks discouraged black pupils from reflecting on their past, but did include information about other peoples. This reveals a very similar picture to the treatment by colonial regimes of the past of the indigenous peoples in several parts of the world (see Trigger 1989; several studies in Stone & MacKenzie 1990; as well as Hall 1990 and Holl 1990). The common denominator in all these cases appears to be the desire by the colonialists to deny any past to the colonized of which they might be able to be proud.

Such a situation lasted to the 1970s, to the extent that P. S. Garlake, an archaeologist employed by the Rhodesian Government as Senior Inspector of Monuments, was forced to resign his post and leave the country in 1971. His resignation was prompted by his unwillingness to interpret Great Zimbabwe to the satisfaction of the white settler population of the day.

Postcolonial Zimbabwe

In an independence eve message to the nation, the newly elected Prime Minister of Zimbabwe, now President, announced to the new nation: 'Independence will bestow on us . . . a new future and perspective and indeed a new history . . . a new past', and in an introduction to a booklet on Great Zimbabwe by P. S. Garlake after his return from exile (Garlake 1982), the then Minister responsible for National Monuments and Museums said about prehistory and archaeology in former times:

> That cultureless regime started to interfere with the progress of archaeological research in an attempt to turn our history into a tool of their propaganda. . . . archaeologists were told what they should write for us to read. Censors moved into our museums and school libraries.

In the same introduction, he went on to appeal:

> technical experts must write guide books and other material primarily for Zimbabweans and recreate museums for Zimbabweans. All our museum displays must explain in clear precise unambiguous terms, comprehensible to every schoolchild, all that the experts can tell us of our past. Once their consciousness is stimulated and interest aroused, the people will respond. They will form a team with the technicians and together, will recover even more of our past.

These quotations demonstrate two points: the recognition at government level of the importance of prehistory and archaeology to Zimbabweans within the context of the aspirations of a newly born nation; and Government's recognition of the need to make the results of archaeological research accessible to school-children and to the general public (also see Stone 1994; Ucko 1994).

In order to investigate what the response of the education system has been to these calls, and to what extent government aspirations have been met, I have examined the content of some of the school textbooks and current syllabuses in history at O-level (high school for ages 15–17).

There is no formal teaching of archaeology in schools below university level and prehistory is taught only within history courses. Archaeology was introduced in 1986 into the university system as a subject within history. This degree programme offered an almost balanced coverage of prehistory and archaeology in three parts, with courses on the prehistory, social and economic history of Africa, method and theory in archaeology, practical and laboratory courses and a fieldwork project.

In an effort to improve the quality of the graduate by providing wider and deeper coverage of both prehistory and archaeology, the programme was revised in 1990. In Part I, for example, the introduction to African prehistory was replaced by an introduction to archaeology and world prehistory; the method and theory course in Part II was split into two courses, with the theory being taught in Part II and the methods in Part III; and a new course was initiated in Part III on cultural resources management. Another major change was the introduction of an Honours in Archaeology degree programme. This programme enables General graduates to pursue higher degree programmes in archaeology by taking an additional year of study after the General degree. Students take courses on archaeological methods, cultural resources management, elementary surveying, bioarchaeology and produce a dissertation. Apart from facilitating postgraduate study, the programme equips graduates to take up employment in archaeology without additional basic training. So far, four students have gone through this programme and two of them are already employed by the National Museums.

From the General degree programme, a number of students with archaeology in combination with one other subject in the humanities have so far graduated. Of the initial intake of twenty in the first year in 1986, five have joined the National Museums while one has joined the Ministry of Education and Culture as a Cultural Officer. The majority have gone into high-school teaching. In this context, what the introduction of archaeology at university is achieving has been to raise the level of awareness of the country's prehistory as more and more such graduates go into teaching. Prior to this, the very existence of archaeology as a discipline was largely unknown. Besides, such graduate teachers are better equipped to teach the prehistory components of their history courses.

In high school, the African history syllabuses that have been used to date cover the history of Africa and the rest of the world, with what seems to be a deliberate bias in favour of southern Africa. The temporal coverage is from the Iron Age (c. AD 300), with brief introductory sections on the Stone Age of southern Africa through to the colonial period and right up to modern times. Given this wide spatial and temporal coverage, it is perhaps not surprising that prehistory comprises only a small part of the syllabus – and that school textbooks have a similar superficial coverage.

A recently introduced new syllabus for O-level reflects a certain emphasis on materialist approaches to history, presumably in keeping with the socialist aspirations of the political party in power. Among the stated aims of the syllabus are: 'to enable the pupil to acquire a broad understanding of the different and common experiences of the peoples of Africa' and 'to acquire an understanding of the development of societies and the forces which interact to produce change' (Barnes, Mutwira, Mvenge, Pape, Prew & Pwiti 1992).

Prehistory still occupies about a tenth of the proposed course, which is divided into what has been termed pre-capitalist modes of production, proceeding to the development of complex state systems in central and southern Africa and the introduction of merchant capitalism. Most of the new textbooks for this new syllabus are still under preparation and therefore not yet available for assessment. The only one published so far is discussed below.

In the textbooks of the now changed syllabus, however, archaeology is the main (or even sole) source of data for the early periods of African history that they cover, and so introductory sections with some brief explanations of how archaeologists work are provided. Explanatory notes on the importance of, for example, radiocarbon dating are also included. Activity tasks of an archaeological nature are also encouraged. For example, pupils are asked to look in the area around their schools for archaeological sites and to try and think about what such sites can tell about the people who used them. This acts as an introduction to the discussion of the prehistory sections of the textbooks.

The one published textbook for the new syllabus is the first textbook for this level to include an archaeologist and an anthropologist among its authors, along with historians (Barnes, Mutwira, Mvenge, Pape, Prew & Pwiti 1992). Out of a total of sixteen chapters, three are entirely devoted to the prehistory and archaeology of Zimbabwe and southern Africa from the Iron Age to the period of state formation (c. AD 300–1700). One of its most commendable elements is the attempt by the authors to bring the past to life by the inclusion of lively illustrations, class activities and tasks. In addition, it attempts to show that a study of the past is not simply about great men and women, kingdoms, states or chiefdoms, but about the ordinary people who represent the vast majority of the society. This marks a significant departure from the traditional way of writing history. More importantly, the book also tries to show the relevance to pupils of studying the past. The introduction states: 'Only through a clear understanding of the past can we plan for the present and the future.'

In addition to the formal teaching, schools are also encouraged to visit museums. All major museums have Education Officers attached to them. Apart from giving guided tours and lectures on different subjects, the Education Officers also occasionally organize school outreach programmes whereby they visit schools of all levels from primary to secondary, bringing artefacts and other museum materials in a 'mobile museum'. These visits are a post-independence initiative aimed at 'taking museums to the people' and so raising archaeological heritage awareness. The Education Officers also occasionally organize workshops for school-teachers. At such workshops, teachers are made aware of the importance of the cultural/archaeological heritage around their schools and the need for preservation. In some areas, this

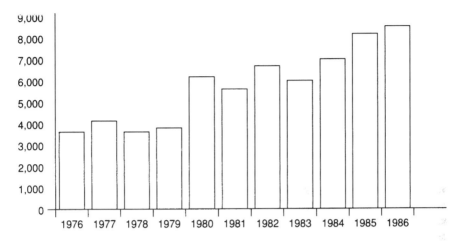

Figure 23.1 School visitor numbers to all Zimbabwean museums.

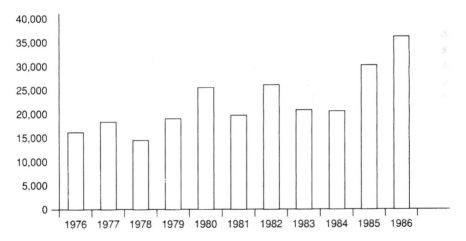

Figure 23.2 School visitor numbers to Queen Victoria Museum.

has gone some way towards curbing the vandalism of sites by school-children, once the teachers have passed on the message. This is especially so at rock art sites which are prone to vandalism (Matereke pers. comm.). Such activities complement what is actually taught within the formal education system.

It is important to recognize that the number of school parties making visits to major museums has increased considerably over the past ten years (Mabvadya 1990). Figures 23.1–5 show annual figures of visits to four of the five main museums in the country by school pupils. This provides some idea of the trends for the period immediately before Independence and after. What is fairly clear is that, despite fluctuations, there is a general upward trend in the

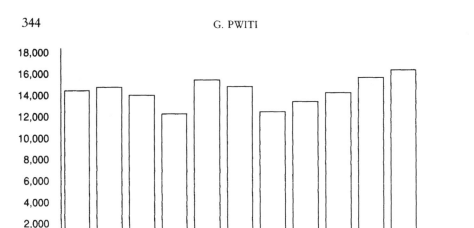

Figure 23.3   School visitor numbers to Bulawayo Museum.

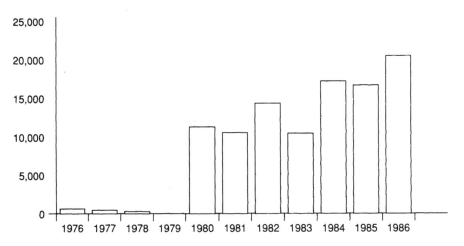

Figure 23.4   School visitor numbers to the Great Zimbabwe site and museum.
NB: The site and museum were both closed to members of the public because of the
security risk during Zimbabwe's Liberation War.

numbers of school pupils visiting museums; this suggests that the level of
awareness of and interest in the past is increasing.

  Given this description of the state of archaeology in colonial and postcolonial Zimbabwe in relation to general awareness and the teaching of
prehistory in schools, it may be tempting to paint an optimistic picture of the
future. This is especially so with the introduction of archaeology in the
University, as this can only contribute further awareness and may eventually

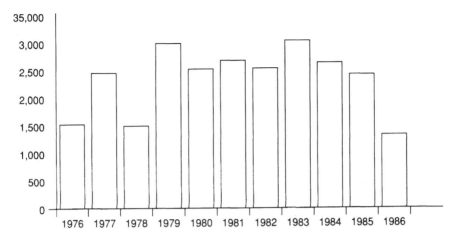

Figure 23.5   School visitor numbers to Gweru Museum.

lead to its teaching at lower levels. Problems that still exist, however, suggest that the desirable level of archaeological awareness is still a long way away.

Archaeology in a Third World context is usually ranked very low in terms of funding, since economic planners regard it as a luxury which can be sacrificed in favour of the so-called 'developmental areas' whose benefits to Third World populations are seen as more tangible. This is despite the significant role of archaeological research and its provision of data on the prehistoric past in enhancing modern development – a role clearly recognized in the Zimbabwean context, as discussed above.

Another problem concerns the dissemination of archaeological information to the general public. Even though the statistics on museum visits reflect an increase, the breakdown of the figures suggests that it is the urban schools and members of the public who account for the majority of the visitors (Mabvadya 1990). Most rural areas are not really part of the picture. This is further compounded by the fact that even though the Education Officers have been doing a commendable job, they do not have any formal training in archaeology or in how to sell the discipline to the public. A recent study (Mabvadya 1990) and interviews conducted with the Museum Education Officers themselves have revealed that the museums school outreach programmes do not always reach very far. For one thing, this particular department of Zimbabwe's Museums Service is seriously understaffed. The single officer stationed at each of the five main museums is expected to cover literally hundreds of schools from primary to secondary level within each of the five regions of the National Museums and Monuments system. Despite commendable efforts, and despite what has been reported by the Officers to be growing popularity and increased demand for mobile museums in the rural areas, this is a mammoth task, made even more difficult by constant transport problems and poor roads which make access to schools difficult. And the absence of the officer from the museum during an outreach programme causes its own problems: schools visiting the museum then have no Education Officer to attend to them, and arrangements have to be made for curators to take up this responsibility. This arrangement, while useful, does not always work for the best (Matereke pers. comm.), and so there is a clear need for increasing personnel in this service. One alternative currently being explored as a long-term solution is for Education Officers to train teachers in ways of raising archaeological heritage awareness, but this is still some way away.

These problems suggest that, even though Zimbabweans possess pride in their archaeological heritage, there is still a general lack of awareness, especially in rural areas, and this lack of knowledge sometimes results in the destruction of valuable archaeological sites.

There are difficulties as well in the formal education sector, as the study by Mabvadya (1990) reveals. Pursuing a career in archaeology at university level, as elsewhere in Africa (see Wandibba 1990, 1994, for example), is not regarded as potentially rewarding, given the limited number of jobs in archaeology after university. The anticipated expansion of the National Museums and Monuments system in Zimbabwe, the potential consumer of archaeology graduates, has not taken place at the expected pace because of financial and other constraints. It is possible, however, that the state of affairs could improve. Recently, in August 1992, National Museums and Monuments and the Government of Zimbabwe, with Unesco and the UNDP (United Nations Development Programme) produced a Master Plan and organized a Donors' Conference entitled 'Archaeological Heritage Resource Management and Development' (Collett 1992). This conference was aimed at raising funds locally and from international sources in order to develop the local awareness of the country's rich archaeological heritage, among other things. The Master Plan has a fairly detailed education component which includes a plan to develop archaeological sites as education resource centres through the construction of site museums, improve access to the sites, and provide relevant literature about the archaeological heritage suitable for young people (also see Ucko 1994). As a result of the conference the Education Service of the National Museums and Monuments has recently been the subject of an external report (Stone 1994). The report, written in conjunction with the existing Education Officers and senior Museums and Monuments staff, outlines a five-year Development Programme for the Education Service. This includes a specially developed one-year training course in heritage education and presentation for all staff involved in education. Central to this programme is a move from the Education Officers teaching children to their teaching and providing resources for teachers and student teachers. It is hoped that by the end of the first period of the Development Programme the Education Service will be in a far better position to encourage the better educational use of Zimbabwe's historic environment.

This programme can be judged as an affirmation of Zimbabwe's commitment to the goal of educating the young about the past for the benefit of the present and the future. Should these objectives be met, a sound infrastructure for the education of the past will have been created, and our optimism in the future of archaeology will have been justified.

Acknowledgements

I am grateful to Peter Ucko for his comments and suggestions on an earlier draft of this chapter and to the various participants at WAC 2 in Barquisimeto for their comments.

References

Barnes, T., R. Mutwira, G. Mvenge, J. Pape, S. Prew & G. Pwiti 1992. *People Making History. Book 1.* Harare: Zimbabwe Publishing House.
Caton-Thompson, G. 1931. *The Zimbabwe Culture.* Oxford: Clarendon Press.
Collett, D. P. 1992. *The Archaeological Heritage of Zimbabwe: a masterplan for resource conservation and development.* UNDP & Unesco Project Report (Zim 88/028).
Garlake, P. 1982. *Great Zimbabwe Described and Explained.* Harare: Zimbabwe Publishing House.
Garlake, P. 1983. Prehistory and ideology in Zimbabwe. In *Past and Present in Zimbabwe,* Peel, J. D. & T. O. Ranger (eds), 1–19. Manchester: Manchester University Press.
Hall, M. 1984. The burden of tribalism: the social context of southern African iron age studies. *American Antiquity* 49, 456–67.
Hall, M. 1990. Hidden history: iron age archaeology in southern Africa. In *A History of African Archaeology,* Robertshaw, P. (ed.), 59–77. London: James Currey.
Holl, A. 1990. West African archaeology: colonialism and nationalism. In *A History of African Archaeology,* Robertshaw, P. (ed.), 296–308. London: James Currey.
Mabvadya, E. 1990. Cultural resource management: an investigation into public attitudes towards museums and monuments in Zimbabwe. Unpublished BA final-year dissertation, Department of History, University of Zimbabwe.
Mazel, A. & G. Ritchie 1994. Museums and their messages: the display of the pre- and early colonial past in the museums of South Africa, Botswana and Zimbabwe. In *The Presented Past: heritage, museums and education,* Stone, P. G. & B. L. Molyneaux (eds), 225–36. London: Routledge.
Stone, P. G. 1994. Report on the development of the Education Service of the National Museums and Monuments of Zimbabwe. Unpublished MS.
Stone, P. & R. Mackenzie (eds) 1990. *The Excluded Past.* London: Unwin Hyman; Routledge pbk 1994.
Trigger, B. 1989. Alternative archaeologies: nationalist, colonialist, imperialist. *Man* 19, 355–70.
Ucko, P. J. 1994. Museums and sites: cultures of the past within education – Zimbabwe, some ten years on. In *The Presented Past: heritage, museums and education,* Stone, P. G. & B. L. Molyneaux (eds), 237–82. London: Routledge.
Wandibba, S. 1990. Archaeology and education in Kenya. In *The Excluded Past,* Stone, P. & R. Mackenzie (eds), 43–9. London: Unwin Hyman; Routledge pbk 1994.
Wandibba, S. 1994. Archaeology and education in Kenya: the present and the future. In *The Presented Past: heritage, museums and education,* Stone, P. G. & B. L. Molyneaux (eds), 349–58. London: Routledge.

Witz, L. & C. Hamilton 1994. Reaping the whirlwind: the Reader's Digest *Illustrated History of South Africa* and changing popular perceptions of history. In *The Presented Past: heritage, museums and education*, Stone, P. G. & B. L. Molyneaux (eds), 29–45. London: Routledge.

24 Archaeology and education in Kenya: the present and the future

SIMIYU WANDIBBA

Introduction

The role of education in archaeology cannot be overemphasized. It aims to teach people the value of their heritage and its fundamental impact on their lives and their future. In Kenya, however, archaeology has played a peripheral role in professional and academic circles for a long time. In fact, archaeology is not a subject of study at either the primary or secondary-school levels in this country. Not until university can students learn something about this discipline, but even then, archaeology is usually treated as an adjunct of history. Archaeology is considered as simply a means of extending the human historical record beyond the realms of the written record (Wandibba 1990; also see Mbunwe-Samba, Niba & Akenji 1994; Pwiti 1994).

Historians sometimes appear to have taken advantage of this situation, almost overwhelming the very few professional archaeologists in the country. However, Karega-Munene (1992) has argued that the archaeologists are also to blame for their situation since they tend to keep to themselves and do little to popularize their profession. As Karega-Munene also acknowledges, however, there are very few archaeologists in the whole of east Africa. The problem, therefore, cannot simply have arisen from the actions of the archaeologists. It is absolutely clear that in Kenya archaeologists have few resources and almost no opportunity to create the kind of interest, in public and institutional spheres, that would alleviate their situation.

The current state of archaeology education

The success of archaeology education in any country depends on how well it is represented in both formal and informal educational systems. The informal means available in Kenya for the dissemination of information about archaeology include the mass media, adult education programmes and the National Museums of Kenya. Formal education is in the hands of schools, colleges and universities. If archaeology is an established part of such systems, the public will become more and more aware of their cultural heritage and this, in turn, will create the right conditions for the proper management of the cultural heritage. What follows is a review of these various channels, as they exist in Kenya today.

Informal education

The mass media

Archaeology is insignificant in the programming of both the electronic and the print media in Kenya. Radio, television and the press do not engage in any regular or systematic transmission of information on archaeology. For example, the national television network has carried only two programmes on archaeology in the last decade or so, both of them in a single series, 'Professional View'. As for radio, the national radio station has never felt the need to include archaeology in its programmes. This would have been a sure way of reaching most Kenyans and thereby popularizing archaeology in the country.

The print media are no better at informing the Kenyan public about archaeology. The three daily papers are too preoccupied with political and world news to bother about archaeology education. In the last decade or so, two of them have carried interviews with this author about some aspects of archaeology, but the emphasis has been on the author's academic and professional interests. Magazines have mushroomed over the last five years or so but they are all devoted to other topics, such as parenting, feminism and other social issues, politics and other professions.

In general, it appears that in Kenya, only controversy, trouble or calamity is newsworthy (Sarah Elderkin, *Weekly Review*, 11 September 1992). Indeed, almost the only aspect of prehistory that catches the eye of journalists in this country is discoveries of hominid fossils. The Lake Turkana region of arid northern Kenya has, since the beginning of the 1970s, yielded a remarkable number of fossils, and they have contributed immensely to our understanding of the origins and evolution of humankind. The discoveries of these fossils are normally announced at international press conferences at the National Museum in Nairobi, and obviously they get full coverage in the following day's dailies. Such discoveries even find room in Kenya's tourist magazine, *Safari*. In the June 1985 issue, for example, fossil explorations and finds at Lake Turkana were given generous coverage: six out of twenty-nine feature pages!

Adult education programmes

Adult education programmes appear to be the best way of popularizing archaeology, since adult learners live mostly in rural areas and, as they interact with one another more often than the educated elite and the urban-dwellers, they can disseminate information more easily. Adult education programmes are run by the Department of Adult Education in the Ministry of Culture and Social Services, and by the University of Nairobi.

The main aim of the programme run by the Department of Adult Education is to teach reading, writing and basic numeracy. After literacy, the two most important adult education programmes concern agricultural and animal husbandry methods, and health and hygiene (Republic of Kenya 1983, p. 186). Adult education here is therefore basically utilitarian in nature and so archaeology does not feature anywhere in its curricula.

The University of Nairobi runs its adult education programmes through the College of Education and External Studies. Currently, the College has two programmes in adult education through the Faculty of External Studies. One of the programmes offers a degree whilst the other one is an extramural programme. Students in the degree programme may be introduced to a little archaeology as part of the course 'An Introduction to African History up to AD 1885' – depending on who teaches that course. The course 'Prehistory of Africa', available in Part II of the programme, obviously covers more archaeology. Unfortunately, as this is only one course from a selection of history courses from which students choose, it is usually the case that they take something else, as the archaeology course is seen as more difficult than some of the other offerings. The Extra-Mural Studies Programme covers continuing education, leadership and management training, community education, information and public relations programmes, and cultural programmes, but archaeology does not figure in any of these subject areas.

The National Museums of Kenya

The present museum system in Kenya dates to 1929 when construction of the Coryndon Memorial Museum began on the present site of the National Museum in Nairobi. The museum was opened officially on 22 September 1930. In December 1964, this museum was renamed the National Museum, Nairobi.

The National Museum system now consists of the headquarters in Nairobi, five regional museums, some field museums, prehistoric sites, and historical sites and monuments. The regional museums include Fort Jesus in Mombasa, Lamu Museum, Kitale Museum, Maru Museum and Kisumu Museum. Both Fort Jesus and Lamu museums are on the coast while Kitale and Kisumu are in western Kenya, and Meru in central Kenya. The regional museums are headed by curators whilst field museums and some of the prehistoric sites, and historical sites and monuments are under caretakers. As the museum system was not implemented as a national structure from the beginning, the regional museums have not been developed in a systematic way, and so they are not evenly distributed within the country. In addition, all decisions regarding the management of the museum system are controlled from the headquarters in Nairobi.

Both the headquarters in Nairobi and the regional museums have active departments of education. The present education system dates to February

1968 when the Government made its first grant to the National Museum to support its educational programmes. As originally conceived, the National Museum's education service was to teach school-children and their teachers how to understand and appreciate their natural heritage. This service has expanded over time, resulting in the creation of a fully-fledged Department of Education within the National Museum system. The headquarters has several professionally qualified teachers who are employed as Education Officers, whilst the regional museums each have one such officer.

The education services provided by the Nairobi Museum are at two levels (Muchimuti 1987). Schools that visit once in a year are not given any attention by the Education Officers, and both teachers and children have to fend for themselves. On the other hand, schools may arrange in advance for a special programme prepared by the Education Officers, such as a film show, lecture or guided tour of the galleries.

Most of the programmes offered to schools by the Nairobi Museum are based on the exhibits in the galleries and most of these programmes are tailored for the primary-school child.

Apart from these educational services, the museum has also become the centre of visual aid materials (Muchimuti 1987). Schools within easy reach of the museum can borrow teaching aids, including actual specimens of insects, birds, fossils, mammals and stone artefacts, for use in the classroom. In addition, the Department of Education has a permanent audio-visual aids office to support museum educationalists by making these aids available as and when the situation demands (Cheruiyot 1987).

The regional museums are community museums since they are run with the help of a committee formed by the local community in their respective areas. Their exhibits consist mainly of material culture artefacts obtained from the local area. Their educational programmes, however, tend to follow the model of the programmes in Nairobi, although they also mount programmes which are uniquely local in content in order to benefit the local people.

Unfortunately, there is very little room in museum educational services for archaeology education. By and large, school groups that come for the museum education services do so in order to supplement their own classroom work, and so schools will usually ask for a lecture or a film on some topic in the school syllabus. And topics outside school curricula are devoted to conservation or natural history.

The little archaeology that is taught is normally taught by people who may never have learnt anything about the subject when they were in school. Indeed, the training of museum Education Officers is a problem. According to Muchimuti (1987, p. 83), the on-the-job training given to the museum Education Officers has not been adequate for the amount of work and the educational level of various groups that are offered museum educational programmes. This lack of training makes the Education Officers less effective than they could otherwise be.

With regard to museum interpretation programmes, the museums system has been accused of catering for only two groups of visitors, namely, school-children and the specialist (Mbuvi 1991). In some programmes children are allowed to handle specimens. And specialists tend to have free access to the galleries. The ordinary visitor, however, is not catered for, as Mbuvi (1991) quite justifiably argues. He goes on to state that participatory exhibits should be for all and that the present practice, of isolating children and adults in separate programmes, should be ended, as the child of today will become the adult of tomorrow (Mbuvi 1991, p. 16).

Given these problems, especially the general neglect of learners outside the school system, it must be concluded that the National Museums system is not an effective channel through which archaeology education can be developed.

Evidence of a malaise in the National Museum in Nairobi is suggested by statistics concerning visits by secondary schools. School visits have gone down drastically since the late 1970s. For example, Muchimuti found that the number of students visiting the museum dropped from 7205 in 1976 to 2265 in 1986, that is, a drop of about 70 per cent. As suggested above, poor or uninformed interpretation may be one cause; Muchimuti also cites a lack of adequate publicity by the museum and the fact that exhibits stay up for a long time without being changed. In a study carried out in 1979, for example, Maikweki (1979) reports that the insect, fish and bird exhibits had been set up thirty years ago. The author also suggests that the exhibits in the Nairobi Museum are below contemporary standards. The observations made by the two researchers remain as valid today as they were at the time they were made.

Formal education

Primary and secondary schools

The formal school system in Kenya is largely modelled on the English system. Thus, children start off in nursery schools and end up in various post-secondary institutions, including university. Just as in the informal education system, archaeology does not fare well here. Archaeology is not a teaching subject at either the primary or secondary-school level, at which most of the school-age children actually attend school. In primary schools archaeology appears only incidentally, as part of geography, history or civics in the fifth and eighth classes (about 11- and 14-year-olds). And where it does appear, it is normally taught as part of the 'evolution of man', by teachers who, in most cases, have not received instruction in archaeology. In addition, even the resource materials have been written by people who hardly know anything about the discipline.

A more or less similar scenario exists at the secondary-school level. Although many secondary-school teachers of history now have a little knowledge of archaeology, the resource materials available to them are either miserably inadequate or out of date – again because such materials have been written by non-archaeologists. For example, in one such book published by the Government and therefore highly recommended, the hominid 'Lucy' from Ethiopia, assigned to *Australopithecus afarensis*, is given as an example of *Homo erectus*, a much later hominid. In the same book the divisions and duration of the Stone Age are given as: Old Stone Age, 3,000,000–50,000; Middle Stone Age, 50,000–10,000; and New Stone Age, 20,000–1500. This scheme gives an erroneous impression of the nature of the overlap between the New Stone Age and the Middle Stone Age. And archaeological deductions are, in this book, given as hard facts. For example, one statement reads that people in the Old Stone Age hunted by chasing animals and throwing stones at them!

When this author noticed these mistakes and numerous others, he promptly pointed them out in a letter addressed to the Director of Education with a copy to the Permanent Secretary in the Ministry. Three years later, he has not yet received any reply and the book is still in circulation.

Universities

Even at university, archaeology is only taught systematically at the University of Nairobi. However, as I have argued elsewhere (Wandibba 1990), even here students pursuing a first degree in archaeology still have to do rather too many courses in history. In fact, the archaeology programme is still being taught in the Department of History, where it has been for the last twelve years without making any significant progress towards autonomy.

The University of Nairobi also offers a course leading to a Master's degree in archaeology. This is a two-year programme and the first year is devoted to coursework and examination whilst in the second year candidates carry out research and then present the results in the form of a thesis. Candidates take four courses which include: 'History and Theory in Archaeology'; 'Archaeological Methods and Research Design'; 'Topics in African Archaeology'; and 'Quantitative Methods and Computer Processing'.

At the other three public universities, archaeology is simply regarded as one of the courses for history students. Of these universities, Kenyatta University offers three courses, all of which are optional courses. It is also worth pointing out that two of these courses are actually subdivisions of the 'Archaeology of Africa', which is taught as one unit at the University of Nairobi. The third course covers developments during the Early Iron Age in eastern Africa. At Moi University, students wishing to know something about archaeology have to opt for the 'Archaeology of Africa' in their second year of study. Finally, at Egerton University, the 'Archaeology of Africa' is compulsory for second-year history students.

In all the four universities, the facilities for the teaching of archaeology generally remain very rudimentary. Basic texts are hard to come by and laboratory equipment mostly non-existent. Moreover, fieldwork is not provided for in the curriculum, even at the University of Nairobi. At the latter university, this aspect of training used to be compulsory until about seven years ago. Since then, students wishing to participate in fieldwork have to do so by joining projects run by people outside the University. I see these as some of the factors that have hampered the development of archaeology into a viable university discipline.

Planned changes in the 1990s

The new system of education in Kenya (see Wandibba 1990) is popularly referred to as the 8:4:4 system: students take eight years in primary school, four years in secondary school and four years at the university. The pioneers of this system entered university in the 1990/1 academic year. Since these students had followed completely different curricula from those in earlier years, the four public universities had to draw up new curricula for them. In this restructuring, archaeology has, in the main, been given a chance to become an independent university discipline. Departments of Archaeology are planned for Nairobi and Egerton Universities, whilst Kenyatta University intends to establish a Department of Archaeology and Anthropology.

Ideally, the University of Nairobi should give a lead in the establishment of a Department of Archaeology. However, this will largely depend on how the Department of History handles the delicate issues of staff recruitment and the development of the necessary infrastructure. In its new curriculum, the Archaeology Sub-Department plans to teach courses on the 'Archaeology of the World' and 'African Archaeology', as well as the archaeology of specific regions of Africa. In addition, students will also have to choose archaeological topics in two areas outside Africa, from the following options: Europe, mainland Asia, Oceania and Australia, North America, Central and South America, and the Mediterranean world. Moreover, there will be courses in archaeological method and theory, spread over the four years, as well as courses in physical anthropology, bioarchaeology and geoarchaeology. Similar programmes are planned for the proposed Sub-Department of Archaeology at Egerton University.

Prospects and problems in archaeology education

Under the 8:4:4 system, a first degree is, in general, not meant to prepare a student for life. In other words, university education is not going to be an end in itself. This means that, for most university students, the first degree will cease to be the guarantee of a job. Coupled with this is the increasingly large number of students graduating every year. In this scenario, students will eventually stop asking the question, 'What does one do with a university degree in archaeology?', as the numbers opting for courses in archaeology will increase.

Another factor likely to work in favour of expansion in archaeology education is the availability of trained personnel. Lack of qualified Kenyan archaeologists has been one of the main problems militating against the development of archaeology as a viable university discipline (Wandibba 1990). At the moment there are ten students at various stages in studies leading to PhD degrees in archaeology. Most of these students, however, are in the United States of America. This phenomenon is due to the fact that, for a long time now, most of the archaeological fieldwork in Kenya has been in the hands of American scholars.

In addition, facilities are also likely to be improved, especially at the University of Nairobi. Developments in this regard will most probably affect mainly library facilities. At the moment, the University Library is very busy acquiring books, thanks to financial assistance from the World Bank. A grant from the Swedish Agency for Research Cooperation with Developing Countries (SAREC), channelled through the Central Board of National Antiquities in Stockholm, was also used for a time to improve archaeology collections in the library of the National Museum in Nairobi and the Archaeology Sub-Department Library at the University of Nairobi.

SAREC has also been trying to improve the laboratory equipment, both at the University of Nairobi and in the National Museums of Kenya.

Finally, during the period under review, public awareness is likely to increase, as more people are exposed to archaeology in the universities. Also, an increased number of trained archaeologists is likely to lead to increased research activity. Such a development is likely to bring archaeology closer to many more people than has been possible in the past.

On the other side of the coin, a number of factors are likely to hamper the development of archaeology education. First, there is the perennial problem of employment opportunities for graduates in archaeology. Many students are put off reading archaeology because of the difficulty of finding employment. One way out of this problem would be to incorporate archaeology into some of the anthropology degrees on offer in the country, a move that should make graduates more widely and more easily employable.

The other factor that is likely to hamper the development of archaeology is that, because of lack of facilities, postgraduate training will continue to be taken overseas. This tends to restrict the number of people who can train in Kenya at any one time.

Research funding

The main reason that archaeological research in Kenya is dominated by foreign scholars is, I think, that funds for local archaeologists are rarely available. At the moment, the Government does not allocate any funds for archaeological research. The National Museums of Kenya, a research institution, has never seen fit to include such funds in their annual budgets. This means that even its own archaeologists have to look for funding elsewhere – no easy task, for there are hardly any locally based funding agencies for this kind of research.

A Kenyan archaeologist interested in research has, therefore, to rely on foreign foundations for funding. In the past, this author has received funds from two American foundations: the LSB Foundation and the Ford

Foundation. The author has also received some of the funds donated by SAREC to the Kenyan team investigating the origins of the urban phenomenon in Kenya. However, raising funds for archaeological research is increasingly difficult.

What all this boils down to is that the Kenyan archaeologist is at a real disadvantage when it comes to carrying out research. In fact, most of the archaeological research is carried out by American scholars, who have access to many funding organizations in their country, and at present, Japanese and French archaeologists are also active here. In all cases, however, the selection of the research site and problem is done by the foreign scholars themselves.

The Kenya Government does attempt to support the interests of Kenyan archaeologists in such cases, however, if a long-term project is involved: the foreign scholar has to provide training opportunities for a Kenyan student at a postgraduate level. This problem of research funding is likely to become worse with the passage of time, especially as foreign granting agencies and institutions seem to be cutting down their financial assistance to foreign students. By the end of this decade we might in fact witness a dramatic decline in the number of Kenyan students studying for a PhD degree in the United States. In any case, funding for postgraduate training by foreign governments and their agencies is heavily biased towards projects concerned with economic development. This trend is unlikely to change, either during this decade or in the next century.

Conclusion

In this chapter I have tried to look at what is likely to happen to archaeology education in Kenya as we prepare to enter the twenty-first century. The main argument is that archaeology stands a chance of developing into a viable university discipline, mainly as a result of changes which have been made in our national education system. However, at the same time, archaeology is unlikely to become a teaching subject in primary and secondary schools. It is also unlikely that the discipline will become important in informal education. The mass media will continue to concentrate on political and sensational reporting and are unlikely to start popularizing archaeology education. Adult education programmes are also unlikely to incorporate archaeology education into their curricula. Finally, the National Museums system does not appear to be set to improve on its dissemination of archaeological information in educational programmes. The Division of Archaeology does not have a single Kenyan archaeologist at the moment, and unless something drastic is done, archaeology education at the museum will literally die.

I have also argued that even at university the status of archaeology is unlikely to improve dramatically. A main reason for this is lack of a clear policy concerning employment opportunities for archaeology graduates. At the moment, archaeologists can only be absorbed into a few sections of the public sector. Unlike in the developed world, there are no opportunities for archaeologists to engage in self-employment. Also there are no employment chances in local government or in the Ministries of Culture and Social Services, Environment and National Resources, Regional Development and Tourism and Wildlife, when in fact these institutions need archaeologists. The other problem has to do with training facilities in the country. The facilities are so rudimentary that they are not appropriate for training students at the PhD level.

Finally, the question of research funds will most probably remain unresolved. Since the National Museum does not budget for archaeological research, funds cannot be reasonably expected from it; and it will become increasingly difficult for Kenyan archaeologists to get funding from outside institutions.

These problems will continue to haunt archaeology education into the next century.

References

Cheruiyot, J. L. 1987. The education services of the National Museums of Kenya: a case study of the Nairobi museums. Unpublished dissertation, Diploma in Adult Education, Institute of Adult Education, University of Nairobi.

Karega-Munene 1992. Dissemination of archaeological information: the east African experience. In *Archaeology and the Information Age: a global perspective*, Reilly, P. & S. Rahtz (eds), 41–6. London: Routledge.

Maikweki, J. N. 1979. A study of museum visitors and their reactions to exhibits. Unpublished dissertation, Diploma in Adult Education, Institute of Adult Education, University of Nairobi.

Mbunwe-Samba, P., M. L. Niba & N. I. Akenji 1994. Archaeology in the schools and museums of Cameroon. In *The Presented Past: heritage, museums and education*, Stone, P. G. & B. L. Molyneaux (eds), 326–37. London: Routledge.

Mbuvi, M. M. 1991. A study on the museum as an educational facility: case studies on Kitale, Kisumu, Nairobi and Ontario museums. Unpublished BArch dissertation, Department of Architecture, University of Nairobi.

Muchimuti, R. N. 1987. Evaluation of Nairobi Museum education programmes offered to secondary school students between 1980–1986. Unpublished dissertation, Diploma in Adult Education, Institute of Adult Education, University of Nairobi.

Pwiti, G. 1994. Prehistory, archaeology and education in Zimbabwe. In *The Presented Past: heritage, museums and education*, Stone, P. G. & B. L. Molyneaux (eds), 338–48. London: Routledge.

Republic of Kenya 1983. *Kenya: official handbook*. Nairobi: Government Printer.

Wandibba, S. 1990. Archaeology and education in Kenya. In *The Excluded Past: archaeology in education*, Stone, P. & R. Mackenzie (eds), 43–9. London: Unwin Hyman, Routledge pbk 1994.

25 Listening to the teachers: warnings about the use of archaeological agendas in classrooms in the United States

LARRY J. ZIMMERMAN, STEVE DASOVICH,
MARY ENGSTROM & LAWRENCE E. BRADLEY

Introduction

In the United States, archaeology is generally regarded by the public as having little practical utility. For most who pay any attention to it, archaeology is simply an exotic hobby, a branch of history that provides little more than an interesting perspective and perhaps a bit of intrigue. Still, the exotic has appeal, and many elementary-school children fantasize a future as an archaeologist as one of their first career choices.

When archaeology is incorporated into the curriculum, however, it is usually presented as a quaint diversion for students (cf. Selig 1991, p. 3). Essentially, archaeology becomes entertainment, 'a treasure-hunting, collecting, object oriented entertainment' (Blanchard 1991, p. 1). Teachers may use the 'romance' of archaeology to teach some lessons, but few have done more with it.

Those who have studied classroom archaeology carefully, however, have recognized a greater potential: archaeology can be used to widen the range of behaviours incorporated in the learning process (cf. Blanchard 1991, p. 3). A most important aspect of this use of archaeology is 'co-curricular' study, whereby several aspects of education are linked by some outside activity. As an interdisciplinary field, archaeology can be used to lure students into the 'exotic' realms of culture and at the same time learn how their science, mathematics, writing and other courses like music and art have application in the 'real' world.

The great potential for co-curricular study to broaden the education of young people in the United States led to the development of a long-term project for the University of South Dakota and a local middle school in Vermillion, South Dakota. For the past six years, the University has sponsored Archaeology Days for sixth-grade (age 11) students in the middle school. The original goal of Archaeology Days was to promote a more realistic understanding of archaeology beyond that presented in the media; as it developed, it quickly, and unintentionally, became an effort to develop a co-curricular programme.

Archaeology Days, including the history of the project, activities we chose and carried out with the students, and some of our observations about its successes and failures are discussed in this chapter, but within a particular context and with a specific goal in mind. A plethora of excellent case studies documenting archaeology in the classroom already exists, and on one level this chapter is simply another case study of what can be done. At the same time, we hope this programme will be more than that. Frankly, those who developed Archaeology Days did so in something of a contextual, theoretical and philosophical vacuum, as the many case studies in the literature have little reference to broader questions of effectiveness and interface with broader educational concerns, strategies and goals. Archaeology Days, like many similar projects in the United States, therefore developed and grew haphazardly. But our experience has taught us a critical lesson about the relation between our educational goals and those of the teachers and students we are supposedly helping: that the archaeological agenda is not the only way to understand and use the past, that the learning process is a negotiation, not a simple transfer, of knowledge and experience across disciplines.

Archaeology Days: accidental beginnings

Archaeology Days had their origins in 1980 with a grant provided by the South Dakota Historical Preservation Center. The grant was intended to provide teaching materials for junior high school teachers in the State for use in their required units on South Dakota history. The concern of archaeologists in the University of South Dakota Archaeology Laboratory (USDAL) was to provide audio-visual and printed materials at a level both students *and* teachers could understand – the materials had to be nearly jargon-free and easy to use.

With this in mind, USDAL developed a series of four film-strips and audio-cassettes about the prehistory of South Dakota and surrounding regions, with two of the strips concentrating on two important archaeological sites in the State. An illustrated pamphlet-length *Young People's Guide to South Dakota Archaeology* (Zimmerman 1982) and several teachers' guides accompanied the package, which we called 'Ancient Peoples and Places of South Dakota'. The package was distributed free of charge to elementary schools and public libraries across the State.

We discovered that distribution of the series placed the USDAL staff and other archaeologists in the region in high demand as grade-school speakers around the State. The pamphlet was very successful, with over 7000 distributed, and comments on the audio-visual materials were quite good. Teachers continually asked what more they could do, and wanted to know whether the students could actually visit and perhaps dig at an archaeological site.

Under ordinary circumstances, such requests would have been impossible because of time, distance and costs, but the discovery of an archaeological site on the edge of the city of Vermillion (the Bliss Hill Site (39CL9)) made such a project feasible. The idea of introducing students to archaeology through excavation emerged in 1988 when members of the University of South Dakota's anthropology club, APES (Anthropology Program Enthusiasts' Society) proposed to conduct test excavations at the newly discovered site so that university students could get extra field experience. Some suggested that opening the excavation to the public might be a good promotional scheme for the Anthropology Department, the club and the University: if the public could actually dig at the site under close supervision, they would be even more interested in the subject. Unfortunately, APES began the excavations at weekends during the early autumn, but never involved the general public because of time constraints.

At the same time, however, USDAL was asked about the possibility of giving a talk on archaeology to the local sixth grade. The sixth-grade teachers also asked whether they could take students to see any nearby archaeological sites. APES had just finished working on the Bliss Hill Site (39CL9) and thought that this site was well suited for a tour. They arranged for more than 100 students and their teachers to visit our archaeology laboratory and the Bliss Hill site.

The laboratory tour showed the students most of what archaeologists do in the lab. APES built displays of topographical maps, aerial photos (normal, infra-red), site maps, a hand-made example of stratigraphy, and artefacts. They showed a film-strip on South Dakota archaeology from the 'Ancient Peoples and Places' series as well giving a tour of the artefact storage room. Finally, they showed how artefacts are catalogued and demonstrated pottery-making and decorating.

The tour of Bliss Hill was the sixth-graders' favourite part of the day. First, they walked around the perimeter of the site and were given reasons why the site was located at this particular place. After a brief discussion about safety and proper on-site behaviour, they had a short 'field school' on proper excavation techniques. Finally, each had a chance to excavate under the supervision of APES members and university faculty. Contrary to what many thought would happen, the sixth-graders did an excellent job and for the most part were patient and well behaved. An extra bonus that made this portion of the day so popular was the demonstration of an atl-atl (spearthrower) and fire-making.

The project was an overwhelming success. The whole sixth grade (about 120 students) wrote thank-you letters. Not one had a negative comment. One reason for this success was that all the students actually got to use, with their own hands, the atl-atl, or try to make a fire or a pottery vessel, or had a chance to dig in a real excavation. Teachers were also receptive. They got a reprieve from the daily classroom activity and had others take charge of their students for a day. The general conclusion was that teachers, students and the USDAL staff and APES had all learned a great deal, and the teachers invited us to do the same programme the next year.

For USDAL and APES, the day was successful in other ways, with regional media attention bringing requests from other schools in the area for us to conduct the same activity for their students. Indeed, there was an unexpectedly large amount of media coverage. Four local newspapers and four local television stations did news stories on the project and there were newspaper articles in three towns and television coverage in the four States around us. We managed to bring one other school from nearby Volin, South Dakota, to the site before cold weather came.

Archaeology Days 1989

From the successes of our 1988 Archaeology Day, we realized that the potential for our project was nearly unlimited. As the start of the academic year came, we decided that we should try the project again but expand it, demonstrating as many aspects of archaeology as was possible and in a more integrated way than in 1988. The sixth-grade teachers had recently attended a conference which discussed co-curricular approaches to teaching. They decided that archaeology was particularly suitable as a means of cross-curricular teaching because it involves so many different subjects and methods of analysis. A major problem was to decide just what areas to cover and how to do it.

USDAL staff, APES and the teachers met in both USDAL and the middle school to plan the project. Eventually, these meetings also included representatives from the University's School of Education, the State Historic Preservation Center, the W. H. Over Museum, and the Shrine to Music Museum. Together we decided on a general approach to the week and on specific activities for the students, seeking a blend of in-school and out-of-school projects.

Pre-tests and post-tests

Early in our meetings, we realized that one thing we did not know was exactly what the students had learned the year before. They seemed to have had a great time, if their exuberant letters of thanks were any indication, but what did they actually learn about archaeology? Were they just happy to be out of the regular classroom for a day or did they really absorb something about archaeology? We decided to find out by developing a set of tests that would measure pre-existing knowledge about archaeology and what students learned from the sessions – a pre-test and post-test structure. Pre- and post-tests contained the same questions, with seventeen of them multiple-choice and thirteen 'True or False' with all questions geared towards selected activities from the Archaeology Week.

Lecture activities

The one-day site/lab tour was extended to one full week to accommodate all the new activities. Nearly all academic areas involved in archaeology played a role in our new programme; they were divided into talks and presentations which had minimal amounts of hands-on activity and ones that had heavy amounts of student participation.

The build-up

Archaeology Days actually began about two weeks ahead of this intensive week in order to build interest and anticipation. Teachers gave students their first taste of archaeology by asking them to read four brief narratives in a unit called 'Understanding the Past' from their readings book *Celebrations* (Durr 1989). One narrative is a story about a stone age boy who learns to make stone tools and helps his tribe survive; another is a short poem, 'Who Am I?', that looks at a child as an integral part of the environment; the third is an article directly discussing archaeological methods; and the fourth describes what a necklace found in a site can tell. All are well written, enticing in style and reasonably accurate in archaeological content. After these readings were completed, the sixth-grade teachers discussed them with their students, administered the pre-test and announced the activities of Archaeology Week.

At the start of the next week students had a presentation by the Shrine to Music Museum on what ancient music might have sounded like and about early musical instruments. APES placed a colourful exhibit about archaeology in exhibit cases in the school commons area.

A week of archaeology

Archaeology Days began in earnest the following week with a photographic slide programme given by the South Dakota Historical Preservation Center about what it is that archaeologists actually do. This talk was a good general introduction to the week's activities. Following the talk, the first group of presentations, those with minimal student participation, began, with students rotating through them.

We selected five different areas for these presentations: bones, stratigraphy and dating, ecology, artefact classification, and a slide show on different archaeological sites from around the world. The students were divided into groups moving from one station to the next so that each group could see each station. This session was split into two days, Monday and Wednesday. On Wednesday afternoon, all students visited the W. H. Over State Museum and saw the museum exhibits, exhibit preparation, and learned about curation and the history of South Dakota archaeology.

The bones presentation showed the students different bones from many kinds of animals, including human. We explained how people's diets and the environment of the sites could be ascertained from bones. The students were also shown some bone tools and asked the function of each.

The stratigraphy and dating presentation described many methods for dating sites or artefacts using both relative and absolute methods. We discussed the use of artefact styles as time markers, but we also introduced students to more complex techniques such as radiocarbon analysis, dendrochronology and stratigraphic interpretation.

The ecology section focused on food chains and what things in a landscape would influence people to settle in a particular location. Students participated in a role-playing simulation where they 'became' different parts of the environment.

In our artefact classification unit, we used two groups of 'artefacts', one a series of items taken from a faculty member's desk and the other, a series of wooden board-game pieces. Divided into two groups, students sorted the 'artefacts'. After they had finished, the students switched places and tried to figure out how the other group had classified their 'artefacts'. We hoped this activity would show the sixth-graders the processes involved when an archaeologist classifies real artefacts found in an excavation.

The slide presentation showed the variety of types of archaeological sites to be found around the world. Some slides pictured the kind of locale where certain sites were found. The students were then asked why, just by looking at the slide, a site was located where it was. Several slides also documented the process of finding and excavating sites showing aerial photographs, maps, walking surveys, shovel tests, excavation equipment and excavation techniques.

Technology and hands-on activities

Tuesday was technology day, with 'experimental' archaeology demonstrations. We set up five stations involving the following activities: pottery-making, the building of structures, the making of prehistoric art, flint-knapping, and the use of the atl-atl and fire-making. Each of these activities showed how prehistoric peoples used the technologies. Again, the students were in five groups, moving in turn through each station.

The structures station and flint-knapping presentations were not hands-on projects. In the structures presentation, slides showed real or reconstructed shelters or buildings. We incorporated as much variety in both dwelling type and geographical area as possible.

A local expert showed the students flint-knapping techniques. He used thick glass rather than stone because of its uniform quality and ready availability. He explained how glass was like the stone used in prehistory, how glass/stone was worked and he made different kinds of chipped artefacts. He also demonstrated how ground stone tools like axes were made.

The pottery, art, atl-atl and fire-making presentations were hands-on. The pottery presentation began with a short talk and demonstration about several methods of making and decorating pottery. Students then used modelling clay (plasticine) to try some of the techniques. Plasticine is easier than potter's clay for unskilled hands to use (and is less expensive!). Cord-wrapped hand-paddles and bone and wood instruments were used to show various methods of decorating and shaping pottery common in the prehistoric sites of this region.

The prehistoric art presentation talked about cave art. Poster board was taped up on the outside wall of the school building, then covered with a thin coating of shortening to hold the colours on the paper. Cow hooves and mollusc shells were used to hold the charcoal sticks and finely crushed coloured pigments. Small hide-covered rocks and a large blow-pipe were used to demonstrate some of the ways pictures might have been made on cave walls.

For the atl-atl and fire-making presentation, spears, one atl-atl and a bow-drill for fire-making were prepared beforehand by APES. A mammoth silhouette made of styrofoam was the target for the spears. Each student had one or two chances to throw the spear using the atl-atl. Several had a try at using the bowdrill to make a fire.

Laboratory and field activities

Thursday and Friday were reserved for the archaeology lab, an archaeology computer simulation game, and activities at the Bliss Hill site. All these activities required more careful supervision than the others. They also presented greater logistical difficulties because they were at three separate locations in the city.

The computer game, 'Adventures in Fugawiland' (Price & Gebauer 1989), simulates an ongoing archaeological study of an actual archaeological zone near the Great Lakes of North America. In the game, the user can choose many sites to excavate. The results of the excavation are shown for each site. The user analyses the data and forms conclusions about the culture that has been studied. A self-test about the culture whose sites have been excavated concludes the program. As an aside, Fugawiland was written for college students but turned out to be an excellent program for children. We discovered that the sixth-graders were adept at using the program, excited by it, and almost as good as the college students who used it in university courses.

The field and laboratory exercises were conducted in much the same way as in 1988 but with a few changes. On the site, we had several more excavation squares open and had fewer students on the site. This allowed each student to receive better instruction, to have more time at the site, and both excavate and use the shaker screen. The lab tour was structured in such a way as to allow students more hands-on experiences than in 1988. We used teaching collection artefacts and old equipment to allow them to use stereo-zoom microscopes, calipers and balances, much as an archaeologist might use for analysis.

Analysis of Archaeology Days' activities

In 1989 we examined more carefully how students responded to the activities in which they became involved. We knew ahead of time that they liked the active, hands-on activities best.

Favourite presentations

After Archaeology Days, some of the sixth-graders wrote thank-you notes to their favourite presenter and others were asked to write down five things they had learned, their three favourite presentations and two things that they did not like. For the most part, the students did not like lectures. On the other hand, none said that they disliked throwing the atl-atl. Those few who said they did not like the excavation at the Bliss Hill site noted that it was only because 'digging was too dirty'. Nothing stands out about the other activities, with many of the same activities liked best or least by many students.

Test results

The pre-test and post-test results give an indication of what the students learned. Students showed improvement on 27 of 30 questions. Of these, 16 improved 10 per cent or more. Of the 11 presentations covered in the test (Table 25.1), students showed an increase in knowledge in all of them. Seven areas showed major change (10 per cent or more). It was also interesting that not only the intensive hands-on areas showed improvement; students answered more questions correctly about the slide and lecture presentations on the post-test as well.

Problems

Many of the weaknesses in our programme were apparent at the time we tried to implement each activity. Some of the presentation group sizes were simply too large to manage. When we had more than 25 sixth-graders in a lecture, there was a great deal of talking and whispering. Large group size also prevented easy questioning by students. Having their questions answered, we discovered quite by accident, proved to be extremely important to students. In one case a group got out of their rotation and we filled in the time by allowing them to ask questions of an archaeologist. That session turned out to be one of that group's favourites. We discovered that they wanted answers from the 'authorities' and were not always satisfied with answers from their regular teachers.

Another problem was that a whole week was simply too long. Teachers felt that it was a bit disruptive to their regular teaching schedule and to the other middle-school grades. From our own perspective, we felt that all our time that week was devoted to the middle school and that our own university classes suffered because of it. The sixth-grade teachers also expressed a feeling that they wanted to be more involved as instructors and do more in their own

Table 25.1 Pre-test/post-test results of Archaeology Days' presentations

Presentation	Questions	Pre-test correct	%	Post-test correct	%	% change
Primitive musical instruments	0	0	0	0	0	0
Historic preservation talk	3	219	62	255	75	13
Slide show	3	157	44	196	58	13
Structures presentation	2	118	50	132	58	8
Bones	0	0	0	0	0	0
Stratigraphy and dating	4	249	53	314	69	17
Classification	3	203	57	199	59	1
W. H. Over Museum	1	27	23	50	44	21
Flint-knapping	1	19	16	41	36	20
Atl-atl and fire-making	1	36	31	75	66	36
Prehistoric art methods	0	0	0	0	0	0
Ceramics	2	182	77	186	82	5
Ecology	1	88	75	95	84	9
Fugawiland	1	72	61	94	83	22
Archaeology laboratory	0	0	0	0	0	0
Bliss Hill site	0	0	0	0	0	0
Total students taking the test		118		113		
Total number of correct answers		1370	50	1637	63	

classes instead of depending on us. The teachers were very diplomatic about this and we suspected there were deeper, unspoken issues.

Finally, we realized after we gave the pre-test that the students already knew a great deal about archaeology. We had no idea where this came from until we studied their *Celebrations* readings carefully. The article on excavation techniques is excellent and gave them a great deal of information that was tested in the pre-test. Although the improvement on the pre/post-tests was impressive, we felt it would have been even greater had we given the pre-test before the readings.

To deal with these problems, we resolved to move to three instead of five days. To teach the same amount of material, we planned to develop units that the teachers could do in their regular classes. For instance, the art section would be made a part of the regular art instruction for the sixth grade and the industrial arts/woodworking teacher would help students make spearthrowers and bow-drills. We could do little to reduce group size in some cases, but the in-class instruction should help. We also planned to allow more time for questions by the students in *every* unit. We planned to give the pre-test before the readings.

Conclusions from 1989

From our perspective and that of the sixth-grade teachers, the 1989 Archaeology Days were a huge success except for relatively minor problems. The sixth-graders learned a great deal about archaeology and for the most part they had fun doing it. The material presented to them was not crudely simplistic; rather it was presented to them in a manner they could understand and enjoy. This is an important idea when it comes to teaching difficult scientific ideas to younger students. Choosing the proper presentation level is critical if they are not to lose interest. Popularizing science is no new idea, but it is rarely done to allow elementary students to see how virtually all fields of knowledge are related within their education. Archaeology makes an excellent mechanism for co-curricular instruction. Frankly, we were sceptical about the impact Archaeology Days would have until we saw the test results. We have also recognized that there is carryover beyond the school year. In the summer a student who had been in the class found a number of bison bones eroding from the banks of the Missouri river, contacted us and came to USDAL to find out what she should do. We can think of no better demonstration of the effectiveness of Archaeology Days.

Epilogue and lessons from 1990–2: some warnings

As we prepared for the 1990 Archaeology Day we were full of enthusiasm for what we assumed to be a very successful programme. But we simply had not heeded some warning signs, for the next three years saw a decline in the programme.

In 1990, the middle-school teachers seemed relatively enthusiastic, but the bulk of the work of organizing the structure fell to two teachers. The programme was reduced to two days with some in-class teaching. The highlight of the year was a videotape of the programme made by some of the students. No testing was done at all.

The 1991 programme remained at two days, but very much curtailed from earlier years. The technology segment was reduced to a technology 'fair' with an afternoon spent in the school with student groups rotating around eight stations with art, bones, and some of the other popular presentations. Student groups had about 15 minutes at each station. The day at the site was reduced to half a day with the students spending about a half-hour at the site in several groups. Groups not at the site went to the W. H. Over Museum.

The 1992 programme was essentially the same as the year before.

Interest was clearly declining. By the time the 1992 programme was complete, only one of the teachers was still enthusiastic about it, although a new principal at the school came to the excavation, and was impressed, giving hope that Archaeology Days would continue at some level. On the other hand,

another teacher who had strongly supported the programme in its early years
was now only mildly interested.

Whose educational agenda?

The reasons for this loss of interest among teachers, and the rapid decline in
Archaeology Days as a whole, were not clear at first. However, in the process
of developing an archaeological field school, as part of a funded programme to
develop an archaeology education initiative for the State, important factors
that contributed to the decline became apparent – factors that may be found in
many other archaeology education programmes. What we discovered was that
in our planning for Archaeology Days we failed to consider that there might
be more than one agenda for archaeology education.

In late 1992, as we began to plan a new archaeology teacher education
course, we followed the usual approach of outlining our objectives for the
course and our strategies for teaching teachers. Each of the professional
archaeologists selected an objective and outlined methods for accomplishing it.
We then met several times to clarify our goals. Finally, we met the middle-
school teacher who had maintained her enthusiasm to show her the proposed
class. Though she was interested, she seemed overwhelmed and our impression was that she was lukewarm about it. As we probed the reasons, we
discovered that the agenda of archaeologists for archaeological education is not
necessarily the same as the agenda of teachers for it.

This critical difference emerged when we examined what had been written
about why archaeology education should be done. We discovered that archaeologists had spent a great deal of time outlining what they could provide for
teachers, but they paid little attention to the needs or concerns of teachers
themselves. Indeed, there are many archaeological goals beyond those of the
professional. A handout from a 1990 workshop for teachers entitled 'Everything We Know about Archaeology for You to Use in the Classroom',
sponsored by the Archaeology Assistance Division of the United States
National Park Service, says the following: 'Recognition of the need for more,
and better, public education about archaeology is dawning throughout the
United States.'

Many American archaeologists believe that better public understanding
about archaeology will lead to more preservation of sites and data, less site
looting and vandalism, greater support for the curation of archaeological
collections and records, and a demand for yet more archaeological interpretation and participation for the public. Public outreach was identified in a
survey by the Society for American Archaeology members as one of the
highest priorities for the Society. The importance of public education has been
further emphasized by the results of the Society's 'Save the Past for the Future'
project.

Other archaeologists and agencies have professed similar goals (see Brook &

Tisdale 1992 and several papers in Butler 1992 for examples; also see McManamon 1994).

Though many of us pay lip service to such broader educational goals, and although we also advocate understanding environment, culture change and the like, few of us look beyond the goals of professional archaeology: preserving sites, preventing looting, and more public support for our efforts. At the risk of seeming overly critical, our agenda all seems very self-protective.

The point is not that our own goals are unreasonable, but rather that imposing them on students and their teachers might be. Are we attempting through our educational endeavours to bring the public into line with our goals? Is this reasonable? Teachers have different goals from archaeologists. They are concerned with a variety of issues ranging from entertaining students to maintaining discipline, from teaching critical thinking or mathematical skills to teaching factual content in subject areas. Few archaeologists go beyond simply mentioning the broader educational goals or issues (see McNutt n.d., pp. 3–6; Higgins & Holm 1986 for examples of those who do so).

Teachers are therefore forced to try to adapt our aims to their own, with little help from us. For example, our goals for both Archaeology Days and for our planned teacher course are so specifically archaeological that teachers had, and will continue to have, a difficult time implementing what they learn from us. Certainly we teach teachers how to teach stratigraphy, lithic technology, and settlement pattern analysis, but do we teach them how these aspects of archaeology can help them achieve their own educational goals in the classroom? Certainly we teach them the importance of site preservation, but do we give teachers a rationale for conveying this idea to students in a framework that is suitable to their own classroom agendas?

We discovered in talking to the middle-school teachers that it took them some time to realize the problem themselves. They and their students are interested in archaeology. Teachers do see the potential for co-curricular and other approaches to education. But they have a difficult time translating our agendas to theirs.

The whole experience of Archaeology Days has therefore taught us a significant lesson. We have learned that in any archaeology education project in the future – such as our planned teacher course – we must engage teachers as professional equals and that the first goal of our programme must be to set an agenda that is mutual and negotiated. That done, the separate agendas for archaeology education may actually be more easily accomplished.

References

Blanchard, C. 1991. Education and/or entertainment: archaeology and prehistory in the public schools. *Archaeology and Public Education* 2, 1–3.
Brook, R. & M. Tisdale 1992. Can a Federal agency educate the public about its heritage? *Archaeology and Public Education* 2, 1–4.

Butler, W. (ed.) 1992. State archeological education programs. Denver: Rocky Mountain Region, Interagency Archeological Services, National Park Service.

Durr, W. 1989. *Celebrations*. Boston: Houghton Mifflin.

Higgins, P. & K. Holm 1986. Archaeology and precollege education: a literature review. *Practicing Anthropology* 8, 24–8.

McManamon, F. P. 1994. Presenting archaeology to the public in the USA. In *The Presented Past: heritage, museums and education*, Stone, P. G. & B. L. Molyneaux (eds), 61–81. London: Routledge.

McNutt, N. n.d. *Project Archaeology: saving traditions*. Longmont, Colo.: Sopris EST, Inc.

Price, T. D. & G. Gebauer 1989. Adventures in Fugawiland. Mountain View, Calif.: Mayfield Publishing Co.

Selig, R. 1991. Teacher training programs in archeology: the multiplier effect in the classroom. In *Archeology and Education: the classroom and beyond*, Smith, K. & F. McManamon (eds), 3–7. Archaeological Assistance Study no. 2. Washington: National Park Service, Archaeological Assistance Division.

Zimmerman, K. 1982. *Young People's Guide to South Dakota Archaeology*. Vermillion: University of South Dakota Archaeology Laboratory.

372   L. J. ZIMMERMAN *et al.*

Appendix

Archaeology Week pre/post-test

A: *Multiple choice*

1 An example of an artefact is:
   (a) a tree
   (b) an arrowhead
   (c) a river
   (d) a buffalo
   (e) all of the above are artefacts

2 Stratigraphy (stratum) means:
   (a) deep
   (b) layers
   (c) soil
   (d) age

3 Which of the following is *not* an archaeological site?
   (a) burial mound
   (b) village
   (c) stone quarry
   (d) all of the above *are* archaeological sites

4 People have lived in South Dakota for at least:
   (a) only 200 years
   (b) about 1000 years
   (c) at least 10,000 years
   (d) 1 million years

5 The atl-atl:
   (a) was not used once the bow and arrow were invented;
   (b) was used to throw spears farther and with more force;
   (c) was used by early Pioneer settlers.

6 Stone tools:
   (a) are difficult to make and hard to use;
   (b) could only be used to cut things;
   (c) are the sharpest tools known, but dull easily;
   (d) cannot be made today because people have forgotten how.

7 These things can show us where early people in South Dakota lived:
   (a) a circle of stones
   (b) hearths
   (c) a circle or line of posts in the ground
   (d) all of the above

8 Which of the following things can be used to tell how old a site is?
   (a) pottery
   (b) stone tools
   (c) burned wood
   (d) remains of houses

(e) all of these things can tell how old a site is
9 Bones from archaeological sites can tell us:
(a) what the ancient environment was like;
(b) what the people who lived on the site ate;
(c) what animals lived at the same time the people on the site did;
(d) all of the above
10 Daub-and-wattle construction means:
(a) using bricks made out of mud and straw;
(b) covering a woven stick wall with mud;
(c) covering a stick frame with skins.
11 When ancient people chose a place to live, which of the following did they *not* think about?
(a) distance to water
(b) the kinds of plants and animals around the place
(c) defense
(d) weather
(e) all of the above

B: *True or false*
12 Pottery can be made from either wood or stone.
(a) true   (b) false
13 Archaeology can only tell us about life in the distant past.
(a) true   (b) false
14 The first people in South Dakota not only hunted and ate mammoth, but they also hunted other animals and used lots of different plants for food.
(a) true   (b) false
15 For archaeology, the relationship of one artefact to another is as important as the artefact itself.
(a) true   (b) false
16 Because archaeologists study the ancient past, they do not need to know maths or how to use computers.
(a) true   (b) false
17 Ancient peoples never lived in the Vermillion area.
(a) true   (b) false
18 Prehistoric peoples did not disturb or change their environment in any way.
(a) true   (b) false
19 Archaeologists study dinosaurs.
(a) true   (b) false
20 The Oneota people lived in eastern South Dakota between about 400 and 800 years ago.
(a) true   (b) false
21 Culture is the way of life of a people.
(a) true   (b) false

22 The size and shape of arrowheads can tell us about how old a site is.
   (a) true   (b) false

23 Animals, plants, weather and other natural things are part of ecological systems, but people are not.
   (a) true   (b) false

24 Fire can be made in many ways such as matches, rubbing two sticks together, or using a bow–drill.
   (a) true   (b) false

25 Archaeologists make lots of money selling the treasures they dig up.
   (a) true   (b) false

26 An archaeologist uses scientific equipment like microscopes to see small objects or scales to weigh artefacts.
   (a) true   (b) false

27 Archaeologists excavate or dig in squares to make it easier to measure where artefacts are found in the ground.
   (a) true   (b) false

28 The remains you leave behind today might become an archaeological site in the future.
   (a) true   (b) false

29 All people tell stories to teach about their history and their beliefs.
   (a) true   (b) false

30 To be an artefact, an object has to be more than 100 years old.
   (a) true   (b) false

26 Archaeo-fiction with upper primary-school children 1988–1989

PIERRE MASSON & HÉLÈNE GUILLOT

(translated by Philippe Planel)*

Introduction

At the beginning of the 1988 school year, we took over a class of twenty-nine 10-year-old pupils from the Ecole Experimentale Gambetta de Vanves; throughout the school year we attempted to introduce them to archaeology. To avoid disturbing the normal curriculum, this programme was divided into two parts:

1 a series of classroom sessions with the objective of presenting archaeological methodology and analysis; and
2 a number of visits to the Musée des Antiquités Nationales de Saint Germain en Laye with the objective of understanding the evolution of man and society.

This joint approach combined knowledge with techniques and resulted in a varied teaching strategy. The children involved themselves totally in the project: they were active at all levels including funding, as they helped with the sale of thematically linked calendars. Consent was sought from parents who, within the time they had available, helped solve the practical problems of travel and food.

The course was rounded off with a three-week trip to the Ariège, during which the children visited caves, natural and inhabited, and a number of museums. In this way they were able to compare what they had learnt with what they found in the field, confirming their knowledge by observation.

Since the involvement of parents and children was increasing steadily, it was decided to end the course with an on-site archaeological learning experience. With the approval of the Centre de Documentation Archéologique de Pincevent (Seine et Marne), it was suggested that the class participate in an excavation.

---

* Le Village, Marignac-en-Diois, Die, France.

The simulated excavation

The class was divided into two groups of fifteen pupils, each of whom spent four days on-site, accompanied by an archaeologist, an anthropologist, a teacher and three helpers. A small museum, the excavation, the atmosphere of the site and the team of archaeologists provided an excellent context for a learning experience that was at once specific to each group and yet offered some continuity. The first group had the responsibility of recreating the tomb of an individual in the cultural context of their choice, whilst the second group would excavate this tomb and interpret it. With these aims in mind, two precautionary steps were taken: the parents gave their permission and promised to say nothing to their children, who would be unaware of the exact nature of the part they would play in the unfolding activity; and the teacher taught a specific theme on burial traditions in the course of the year. At school several sessions were devoted to the study of a skeleton with an anthropologist; various artefacts had been collected to provide stimulus for the children (most of a skeleton, casts of bronze and iron objects, various flint implements, bone tools, bone beads, jewellery, etc.).

Those involved in the first group thought up a number of scenarios. By common accord the following story-line was decided upon:

> Melati was a bronze-age warrior. He was born in 2592 BC and died at the age of 41 from wounds. Melati had been entrusted with watching over the ford across the Seine; he died in 2551 BC with a flint arrowhead in the heart, during a fight with a warrior from a people living on the other side of the river. He was finally buried 11 months later, since it was the custom of his people to practice funerary rites only in the spring. On 14 June 2550 BC, Melati, wrapped in a winding sheet, was laid on his back, his head facing the rising sun, in a tomb oriented on an east/west axis, rounded off to the east and squared off to the west.

He was wearing his usual apparel: a bronze torc around his neck and a bone and horn bracelet on each wrist. The torc denoted that he was married and the two bracelets that he had two children. Various goods were to accompany the deceased on his last journey:

- his favourite weapon, a long bronze sword which he held in his right hand;
- a bronze-tipped spear placed to his left;
- his aggressor's sword, not in the same style as his own weapon; this weapon had been retrieved by Melati's family before being bent as an act of vengeance and to prevent it being used for other deeds;
- a bronze ingot, which Melati would use to forge new weapons in the after-life;
- two fired-clay statuettes. This people had a religion based on the mysteries of birth; they worshipped fertility goddesses represented by clay statuettes with prominent feminine characteristics.

Surrounded by all these artefacts, the deceased was covered over first with a layer of earth, then by a number of planks kept in position by stones arranged along the inner face of the tomb. A second layer of earth was put on top. Custom dictated that a fire be lit on top of the tomb; in this way Melati's people believed the fire would allow the passing into the after-life. Next, the tomb was backfilled, then abandoned to its destiny.

Our role was confined to guiding the imagination of the children within known historical and archaeological parameters.

The archaeological constraints of the scenario dictated that only non-perishable elements be buried (though material which would have decayed was taken into account). Evidence was left to permit the conclusion that the body was buried several months after death. The absence of certain bones from the skeleton and the distal portion of the bronze fastening pin, together with certain anatomical anomalies, such as the bent position of the feet, all acted as clues.

Once the idea had taken shape, the creation of an 'archaeological' grave took place according to plan. The grave was dug out by the children. They deposited successively:

the skeleton lying on its back;
the flint arrowhead between the ribs, on a level with the heart;
the pinhead near the sternum;
the torc and bracelets in the normal position;
the sword at the right hand with the phalanges of the thumb over the hilt;
the two fired clay statuettes, made by the children, on either side of the skull;
the tip of the lance at the left shoulder;
the bent sword at the feet;
the bronze ingot by the feet to the right of the skeleton.

Once the grave had been created, the children covered this level with a primary layer of earth so that nothing showed through; a line of stones was placed along the inside of the trench. A fire was lit, ritual dances marked this stage, and the ashes were left in place. Finally the grave was backfilled.

The fiction created by the first group was now completed; nothing showed above the ground. The secret was closely guarded by the first group, despite a brief encounter at school; thus the second group arrived on site with no prior knowledge.

The second episode took the form of a normal archaeological excavation. Our only contribution was to indicate the area which should be excavated, and then, during the excavation, to help the children use a rigorous and scientific methodology. Following the discovery of the site, the first task was to install a grid covering an area substantially larger than the grave itself. The mathematical knowledge of the children did not extend to triangulation so we used a tape and plumb-line, pointing out the deficiencies of this method. The excavation began and the edges of the feature rapidly began to appear; some children suggested at once that it must be a grave. The plan of the trench was

plotted square metre by square metre, which allowed all concerned to understand the importance of the grid and become accustomed to plotting positions.
The excavation continued and the discovery of stone and ashes, a sample of the
latter being collected for analysis, resulted in more plotting, but this time on a
large site plan; at this juncture, the work had to be completed with a level to
record the height of the different features. The stones were then removed; the
excavators continued to remove the filling of the trench and the skull began to
appear. So far most of the children were convinced they were conducting a
'real' excavation; the exposure of the skull prompted cries of astonishment,
justified to the extent that the skull had numbers on it (our skeleton came from
a comparative collection!). It was time to come clean and we were very much
afraid of disappointing them. However, after our explanations in which,
finally, we transformed their role as archaeologists into a game to recover what
had been created by the first group, their motivation redoubled in its intensity.
The excavation resumed its normal course to reach the bottom of the trench:
soil samples were taken for archaeobotanical analysis. This was the most
delicate part of the excavation since the skeleton and the associated artefacts
had to be cleaned as carefully as possible without moving anything. We were
amazed at the concentration displayed during this delicate work. The result
was perfect and, when the excavation was completed, no observable difference
existed from the invented version by the first group.

It was now time for the young archaeologists to interpret the results of their
finds; the work was divided up and each pupil considered a separate element.
The dates secured were 4350 BP ± 200 years, and pollen analysis revealed a
high percentage of daisies.

The interpretation of the second group can be summed up as follows:

> We found a tomb. The grave was rectangular to the west and
> rounded off to the east and measured 2.6 m by 1.1 m, with an
> average depth of 30 cm. At the bottom lay a skeleton, the head
> facing east, lying on its back with the arms along the body.
> Analysis of the skull indicates that this person was between 35 and
> 50 years old at the time of death; the skull allows us to state that it
> was a man. The absence of most of the teeth after death, as well as
> some of the bones of the right hand, the right foot, and several ribs
> could not be attributed to animal disturbance; in addition the ends
> of the feet were bent back on themselves: we do not have a
> hypothesis to explain these anomalies. We believe that this man
> was buried in the spring or at the beginning of the summer between
> 2150 and 2550 BC, in accordance with the results of specialist
> analysis. He was killed by a mortal wound at the level of his heart
> by an arrow, whose flint arrowhead we found between his ribs. We
> believe he was either a smith or a bronze age warrior – a smith
> because he has a bronze ingot to manufacture other weapons and a
> bent sword which he did not have time to finish, or a warrior

because he was buried with his weapons (sword and spear), the ingot representing a stock of bronze, the bent sword being purely decorative.

He held the sword in his right hand because we found the phalanges of the thumb over the hilt. The pinhead on the right ribs showed that he had clothes on the top half, at least, of his body.

He wore as decoration a torc around his neck and a bracelet on each wrist made of bone and antler beads. We found two female statuettes against each side of the skull. We noted that they were naked with pronounced abdomens; one was pregnant, the other maybe not. These objects show that the man (and his people) had very specific beliefs about reproduction.

Once the men from his people had deposited everything in the grave, the dead man was covered with earth. Stones were placed along the side of the tomb all the way round; we believe that this was to support a wooden structure which protected the tomb. Another layer of earth was placed on top and on this we found the remains of a small hearth situated in the middle of the tomb; we supposed that this was a ritual hearth. Perhaps this people believed that the soul of the departed left with the smoke towards another land. A final layer of earth fully covered the tomb and subsequently the river Seine, in flood, deposited a layer of sand on the tomb.

The experiment concluded with the meeting of the two groups at the school, in which the 'creators' and 'finders' compared their results.

Archaeology as a teaching aid

It is possible to teach many of the fundamental concepts in archaeology to CM1/CM2 children throughout the school year. They can be exposed to alternative notions of time by opposing 'closed' clock time with an open-ended continuum and, more precisely, by seeing the diversity in the evolution of humans and societies. They can learn to appreciate differences between societies, our own and others from the present and the past, through the study of economy, activities and traditions. They can develop a different view of objects, by looking further than function or sentimental value to consider objects as carrying messages about a period or a culture ('people'). They can also study the past through human skeletons; this research involves the use of different methods of study and can include other disciplines and methodologies (scientific dating methods, pollen analysis, ecology, anthropology). It is during out-of-school activities, such as archaeological excavation, however, that archaeology comes into its own.

Why a tomb? The tomb was a conceptual tool that was suited to the various aspects of the learning situation. It was initially compelling because it involved a human presence through the skeleton (a person from a specific period in a specific region) and so background information could be incorporated in a variety of subjects taught during the year. And as a burial is a definable activity with a clear focal point, the children can develop and carry out a scenario around it in a limited period of time (in this instance, four days for conception and carrying out the work and four days for excavation and interpretation).

A useful way of increasing archaeological knowledge

In the preparation of the scenario, the artefacts chosen were selected from a collection with a very long timescale. In order to carry out this selection the children had to think about what each artefact was made from, how it was made, its provenance and its period. An artefact not only has a function but is created by a technique. It becomes diagnostic of a culture, of a period, and is perhaps evidence of exchanges between cultural groups; it can also indicate social or religious ideas. Similarly, during the excavation, the identification of objects or the sex and age of the skeleton from morphological observations showed the children how an artefact is a source of information. The creation of a realistic and homogeneous assemblage was as important as finding out about the conditions in which this man lived and met his death.

These two phases in the project showed that the artefacts held information within themselves and within an assemblage, and also that their position relative to each other when they were discovered was significant (the flint arrowhead at heart level, for example). The children also appreciated the need to excavate in a painstaking manner and refrain from treasure-hunting.

Discussion of their respective roles in the project allowed them to discover and state that archaeological analysis often led to the creation of a range of hypotheses, showing that recreations of the past were always selective.

The limitations of the project

Although we did not interfere in their work directly, the children had to be guided, as their imaginations could not be given free rein. There were at least two reasons for this: to encourage full use of knowledge imparted throughout the year and to provide a framework common to both groups and common ground for discussions.

The children found it difficult to accept, before the project started, that archaeologists could not explain everything, and we had to submit to the most insistent questioning to maintain interest in the project. In the course of this we suggested solutions which were sometimes very difficult to explain (the feet bent backwards and the hand holding the sword). These artificial problems reminded us that we were carrying out an educational experience rather than an archaeological recreation.

Conclusion

What conclusions did we draw?

Absolute dating is put into context. Children have a better understanding of a chronology based on events rather than on a timescale. Consequently we retained an early date for the Bronze Age (a date chosen by the children) because it shows the difficulty of understanding the timescale, despite the year's work and the timescales displayed at the site museum.

The children no longer consider objects as things in themselves and see them in context; archaeology can thus appear as the search for meaning in the past and not a quest for objects.

We can better acknowledge and better comprehend other cultures.

The past can be questioned.

Hypotheses and arguments can be formulated.

Ideas learnt in school can be applied in an archaeological context.

Archaeology helps give meaning to our heritage.

Children find prehistory interesting. The project demonstrated that this period held specific attractions for children: there were no books, no writing, no reading and so no school.

The richness of this learning experience was at all times reinforced by the mutual support of those involved (the school, archaeologists, helpers, parents) and the enthusiasm of the children. During the project a video was made, without professional help: a 25-minute VHS film – *Melati 1989* – which received a prize in the Festival International du Film Archéologique 1989.

It is clear from this experiment, therefore, that archaeological heritage is a powerful educational force not only for considering the human past through artefactual evidence but also, through archaeological practice, allowing the practical application of skills learnt in school (from maths to writing skills). This relationship between school and archaeology is reciprocal and creative, as it encourages a modification of learning programmes and questioning about the interpretive organization of sites. And archaeology can also have social benefits at a time when there has never been such a melting-pot of peoples and cultures, for through learning experiences of the kind we have attempted, it will be possible for young people to identify with their own regional culture and, at the same time, understand young people of different cultures.

> This need to delve into our roots is so strong that it must stem from more than curiosity. . . . Archaeological riches evoke a sense of the past in nearly everybody and few, on first impulse, resist the temptation to dismantle the earth, in the same way as a child takes a toy to pieces.
>
> (André Leroi-Gourhan, 'Le geste et la parole')

Acknowledgements

This project, created and directed by P. Masson, has been recognized and supported by:

Ministère de l'Education Nationale
Ministère de la Culture (DRAC, Ile de France)
Conseil Régional d'Ile de France
Centre National de la Recherche Scientifique
Musée des Antiquités Nationales de Saint Germain en Laye
Ecole Expérimentale Gambetta de Vanves (Hauts de Seine)
Commune de Vanves.

The following persons participated in the project: P. Masson, H. Guillot, C. Pellecuer, P. Marinval, E. Boeda, the helpers from the Musée des Antiquités, the CNRS team from Pincevent, and the helpers from the Maison de Marc (Ariège).

We also especially thank N. Coulane (teacher), A. Broulis (video), E. Durand (photos), F. Chauvineau, P. Glabeck from SAMARA (loan of moulds), and finally, the parents and, of course, the children.

27 The teaching of the past in formal school curricula in England

MIKE CORBISHLEY & PETER G. STONE

Introduction

This chapter outlines the development of teaching about archaeology and prehistory within schools in England and uses the English Heritage Education Service as a contemporary example of the support offered to those teaching these subjects. At the outset it must be noted that the curriculum within which the teaching of archaeology and prehistory takes place has been written, since its first appearance in the mid-nineteenth century, by those predominantly interested only in *documentary* history (Stone 1991, pp. 63–108). The result has been an overall lack of success in introducing archaeology and prehistory into the curriculum (Alexander 1989).

Historical review

Within archaeology

One of the first archaeological commitments to the wide-ranging teaching of the past came in 1943 when Grahame Clark argued that, despite the fact that 'up to the present, educationalists as a body have ignored the story of men as completely as did the scientists of the pre-evolutionary era', education after the Second World War would have to be 'nothing less than the universal experience of man' (Clark 1943, p. 115). For Clark, the essential role of post-war education would be to stop further war by creating 'an overriding sense of human solidarity such as can come only from consciousness of common origins' (Clark 1943, p. 113) and he argued that once such 'consciousness' had been aroused 'there seems no limit to the possibilities of human betterment' (Clark 1943, p. 113).

This call for a new role for archaeology and prehistory within education went largely unnoticed, as it remained hidden away in the archaeological literature, but public interest in archaeology did increase after the war and into the 1950s, in part because post-war urban reconstruction brought the practice of archaeology to the notice of developers and 'officialdom' (Cleere 1989, p. 2) and in part because of the success of the television programme 'Animal, Vegetable, Mineral?' (see Frost 1983, pp. 4–6; Hoare 1983, pp. 7–8; Cleere 1984, p. 61). This interest coincided with the 1950s movement in curriculum reform that encouraged schools 'to look at the interaction between man and his habitat – to understand how his habitat has influenced man, but also to see how man has affected his habitat' (Harris 1976, p. 95).

By the end of the 1950s, however, fundamental differences had already emerged between the attitudes of archaeologists and those of educators about the educational role of the subjects. In 1956 a conference on schools and archaeology, jointly organized by the Council for British Archaeology (CBA) and the London Institute of Education, had been called because of 'the growing interest of school children in archaeology' (CBA 1956, p. 1). Educators wanted to make children 'aware that they were living in a time sequence, a conception best illustrated through the teaching of history and prehistory' (CBA 1956, p. 1); archaeologists were more concerned with how schoolchildren could help within the existing framework of amateur archaeology, rather than how they, as archaeologists, could help to increase awareness of the subject within the education system (CBA 1956, pp. 1–3; and see Zimmerman, Dasovich, Engstrom & Bradley 1994, for a current discussion of this attitude).

The conference discussed whether archaeology should aim to become a subject in its own right within the school curriculum – but the only reported contributions from this part of the meeting came from educators who stressed problems such as overcrowded curricula, lack of suitable resource materials, and, especially, lack of trained teachers with a background in archaeology (CBA 1956, pp. 1–3; and see MacKenzie & Stone 1990 where these same points have been identified as factors contributing to an 'excluded past' from school curricula around the world).

Since the 1956 conference, discussion of this issue within archaeology has been limited to brief articles reporting successful classroom-based projects (see, for example, the CBA's *Schools' Bulletin*, renamed *Education Bulletin* in 1986, *Popular Archaeology* and *Archaeology Today*) as well as the almost passing reference to school education in a number of professorial inaugural lectures (e.g. Alcock 1975; Evans 1975; Dimbleby 1977; Renfrew 1982). Even the occasional conferences organized specifically to discuss aspects of archaeology and education have been essentially descriptive (e.g. Richardson 1989; Southworth 1993, although see Ucko 1989).

A number of practical initiatives have, however, taken place within archaeology. In the 1970s the CBA appointed its first Education Officer to promote the wider use of archaeology in schools (Steane 1986; CBA 1991, pp. 11–12). The post has been seen as both (i) pro-active – for example, editing the *Education Bulletin*, writing and producing resources for teachers (for example, Corbishley 1982a, 1982b; Halkon, Corbishley & Binns 1992) and co-ordinating archaeological comment on national educational polices (CBA

1989) – and (ii) as re-active, acting as a source of information both for those involved in education and interested in using archaeology in their teaching and for archaeologists interested in education. Through its education committees the CBA has been central in the development of a number of examination syllabuses in archaeology (Corbishley 1983, pp. 57–63), most recently developing a new A-level archaeology examination (for 16-year-olds) (Halkon, Corbishley & Binns 1992, pp. 11–19).

Two university departments of archaeology have also supported the teaching of archaeology in schools. The 'Archaeology in Education' project at the University of Sheffield still produces a newsletter, information packs, slide sets and replicas, all aimed at assisting teachers to introduce archaeology into their teaching. The project also hosts an annual conference when the University departmental staff update teachers on recent developments within archaeology and provide the opportunity for hands-on experience in archaeological laboratories. The Department of Archaeology at the University of Southampton sponsored a three-year government-funded 'Archaeology and Education' project between 1985 and 1988. The project's aim was to assess the presentation of prehistory and archaeology in schools and to the general public and, in response to local demand, to prepare, provide and test support materials (Stone 1990). A number of archaeological field units have also developed strong links with local schools as part of the wider presentation of their work, and some produce cheap, easily readable publications about the prehistory and archaeology of their area (Johnson & Rose 1990) while a few provide a full education service (for example, Shaw 1993). In addition, there now exists the Education Service at English Heritage, the national organization with statutory responsibility for the preservation and presentation of the cultural heritage, which was created in 1984.

Despite the positive nature of the above initiatives (and with the exception of the English Heritage Service), all are – to some extent at least – condemned only to reach those educationalists and teachers who have already expressed an interest in teaching about archaeology and prehistory. Those responsible for education in England appear to remain oblivious to the reasons for widening the teaching of the past in formal curricula to include teaching about prehistory and, to a lesser extent, archaeology (Harris 1976; Slevin 1984; Stone 1991).

Within education

The existing lack of curriculum space allocated to prehistory and archaeology is in direct conflict with the expressed views of John Dewey, often referred to as one of the founders of primary education theory (see for example, Birchenough 1927; Dworkin 1959; Delaney 1986; Blenkin & Kelly 1987). Dewey argued strongly for the *inclusion* of prehistory within the primary-school curriculum and himself included it in his experimental Laboratory School on the campus of the University of Chicago around the turn of the century (Dewey 1899a; and see Stone 1991). Dewey believed that children should be educated through their own experience (Dewey 1896, p. 251). His philosophy was at odds with the contemporary teaching practice that relied primarily on 'drill and other devices which secure automatic skill at the expense of personal perception' (Dewey 1916, p. 79).

Dewey initially based his belief in the importance of teaching about prehistory on 'Recapitulation Theory', in which a young child is believed to relive the prehistoric periods of human development (Dewey 1896, pp. 247–9; 1911, p. 241). However, even after he had rejected the basis of Recapitulation Theory (Dewey 1899b, 1916, pp. 85–6), he nevertheless continued to maintain that prehistory was a suitable subject to be taught to young children and he persevered with a chronological approach to the teaching of the past.

Dewey believed that the contemporary world was too complex – with too much available detail – for it to be easily understood by young children (Dewey 1899a, pp. 151–7). Instead, he argued that young children should be taught about prehistory, which would introduce them to everything in its 'simplest elements . . . the problem of society in its lowest and fewest terms, and therefore in a way most easily grasped' (Dewey 1899b, p. 263). For Dewey, therefore, the study of prehistory was 'indirect sociology' through which a child would begin to be able to 'unlock the meanings of his present complicated social life' (Mayhew & Edwards 1966, p. 313). Indeed, because of Dewey's belief that a child's education should be based on an understanding of society, the study of prehistory became the central focus of the whole curriculum (for children between 4 and 11) at his Laboratory School (see Stone 1991 for a full description of the course and its content). Its study was cross-curricula (Dewey 1900, pp. 29–30) and social-centred, with children learning by 'doing' (Mayhew & Edwards 1966, p. 313).

The Laboratory School closed down as the result of administrative and financial pressures and there is no evidence that the specifics of Dewey's experimental curriculum were taken up again and Dewey's belief in the centrality of prehistory to the primary curriculum has been ignored ever since. At most, a few curriculum developers have accepted that the study of prehistory should retain a restricted role serving only to situate the place of documentary history:

> Children . . . should be taught that history is concerned with man only after he has succeeded in creating a highly organized society, and after he has become conscious of himself, so that he records his achievements. The historian is interested only in events that lead somewhere and are the beginnings of greater things. Brief explanations of prehistoric remains . . . will serve to emphasise the time when history began.
>
> (Bourne 1902, pp. 193–4)

A few others (e.g. Archer, Owen & Chapman 1916) have stressed other reasons for the retention of some elements of prehistory within the syllabus: 'just mention the period of prehistoric man, since some teachers may consider that the idea of progress will be best brought out if vivid impressions of the most primitive conditions are created at an early stage' (Archer, Owen & Chapman 1916, p. 108).

Indeed, the 1931 government-appointed Hadow Committee saw the distant past as being of little real historical value – other than for keeping children's interest alive: 'we would refer to the almost universal interest in the recent Egyptian and Babylonian discoveries as an illustration of the romantic appeal which the past makes and will continue to make irrespective of its significance to the present' (Hadow 1931, p. 169).

It is a remarkable fact that Dewey's convictions about the importance of teaching about prehistory live on only in a curriculum pamphlet by the Historical Association (Dobson 1928, reprinted 1950), whose author seemingly still believed in recapitulation. Despite its unique position as the only educational publication specifically to emphasize the value of prehistory and archaeology for primary-school teaching to be published in the first half of the twentieth century, Dobson's pamphlet is not referred to in any of the basic references to the teaching of the past (Stone 1991, Ch. 3).

In England, therefore, at least until the 1960s, teaching about the past has been mainly concerned with the passing on of historical 'facts'. Where few 'facts' are available – as in the study of prehistory – the value of teaching about the past has been assumed to be limited (e.g. Unstead 1956).

Since the 1960s and 1970s, there has been a reaction against the fact dominated curriculum. This 'new' history encourages children to learn the concepts and skills of the historian rather than any preordained set of 'facts' (e.g. Coltham & Fines 1971; Slater 1984). One of the leading educationalists in this new movement suggested that prehistory is a better topic than documentary history to be taught to young children because it is not cluttered with the excessive detail of later history and because it was the 'behavioral sciences and their generality with respect to variations in the human condition that must be central to our presentation of man, not the peculiarities of his history' (Bruner 1966, pp. 36, 73–101). Bruner's upper primary and lower secondary course 'Man, A Course of Study' has been taught in a few English schools (Alexander 1984, p. 29).

In 1971, the Schools Council, a teacher-dominated curriculum development group formed several years earlier, produced the 'Time, Place and Society Project' (for students aged 8–13), which introduced the concept of archaeological enquiry into history teaching in primary education (see Blyth, Cooper, Derricott, Elliott, Sumner & Waplington 1976; Standen 1981). In this course children learn through experimentation in lessons based on archaeological excavations and by playing 'the dustbin game' in which they begin to see what can be learnt about groups by looking at what they have thrown away (Thompson 1982, p. 21).

At about the same time, in the early 1970s, some publications began to argue in favour of archaeologically based experimentation and fieldwork within primary education (Salt 1970; Preston 1971; Bowen 1972; Fairley 1977). Nevertheless, a survey of the journal *Teaching History* reveals that only six out of a total of 528 articles were concerned with prehistory and only five others were concerned with archaeology (Stone 1991; and see Hodgkinson & Thomas 1979).

Just as the educational literature has largely ignored prehistory, so have the official 'Guidelines' on teaching about the past, issued by most Local Education Authorities in England in the 1970s and 1980s. Here, 'the past' is usually assumed to begin in earnest with the Romans (e.g. Cleveland County Council 1981, p. 12). Indeed, some authors have explicitly attacked the idea of teaching prehistory: the 'effort of imagination' required to make anything of a visit to a prehistoric monument is 'something beyond the capacity of Junior School children' and is an activity that 'destroys our [the teachers] pupils' belief in us – maybe for life' (Pollard 1973, p. 5).

Ten years later, the picture is one of neglecting prehistory altogether. Thus, although Low-Beer & Blyth do suggest that 'teaching at least one distant period of history is useful', they only cite ancient Egypt and the Roman Empire as examples (Low-Beer & Blyth 1983, p. 9) and they actually define prehistory as 'the evolution of the earth before the arrival of man' (Low-Beer & Blyth 1983, p. 17), in spite of the fact that both the practical syllabuses they reference as good practice have topics on neolithic society (Low-Beer & Blyth 1983, pp. 50–9).

The peripheral position of prehistory was reaffirmed in 1986 by the Historical Association's submission to the Secretary of State for Education of 'Thirty British history topics from the earliest times to c. AD 1890' and 'Thirty world history topics from the earliest times to c. AD 1890'. These topics were all to be completed by children between the ages of 7 and 14 (Historical Association 1986). In effect, the Historical Association's suggestions confined the teaching of prehistory to one-third of one-thirtieth (i.e. 1.1 per cent) of their proposed entire history course.

Much the same result emerged from a listing by the Government Inspectorate of Schools that put 'Early civilization: hunter-gatherer societies, the discovery of fire and the development of agriculture' as the first of eighteen 'outcomes' that 'children should know of' by age 16 (HMI 1988, p. 12). All other 'outcomes' derived from documentary history (HMI 1988, pp. 12–13).

In apparent contrast to such quasi-official and official advice, there is some evidence of considerable interest in teaching about prehistory from classroom teachers (see Harris 1976; Slevin 1984; Stone 1991). For example, a survey in 1982 of 369 primary schools in one English county showed that 73 per cent of them would have been interested in using prehistory in their teaching had there been available support materials and guidance (Stone 1991).

England now has a National Curriculum (DES 1989, 1991). While its prescribed history content encourages the use of sites and buildings, and while it emphasizes the study of history as including the study of the whole of the human past (DES 1990), not one of its compulsory History Study Units (that make up the majority of the course) covers prehistory (DES 1991). Although there is limited scope for teaching about prehistory within some of its thematic options – such as 'Food and Farming' and 'Houses and Places of Worship' (and see Stone 1992) – no readily available teachers' support material exists. This situation is compounded by the fact that prehistory is not covered within any of the history courses available in teacher-training colleges in the country.

It is in this historical context that the creation, in 1984, of the English Heritage Education Service must be viewed and assessed.

English Heritage

The historic environment

The role of English Heritage is to bring about the long-term conservation and widespread understanding and enjoyment of the historic environment for the benefit of present and future generations. Some of its responsibility towards the historic environment is fulfilled by giving grants – for example, to owners of historic buildings which are protected by law. Another is the provision of specialist advice, to the general public and to professionals such as archaeologists, architects and engineers. Annual grants are also given towards rescuing evidence from archaeological sites under threat.

English Heritage directly manages, and presents to the public, and to schools, over 350 sites, monuments and historic buildings which are of national importance. In 1992 nearly 5 million people visited English Heritage sites, of whom nearly 450,000 were school and college students. Educational visits to English Heritage sites are free. Among the sites in its care are most of those places which feature as landmarks in England's history: Maiden Castle in Dorset, for example, where future Roman Emperor Vespasian drove out the native tribes; Battle, near Hastings, where the history of England from 1066 was shaped; and the iron bridge in Coalbrookdale, the first of its kind in the world.

Education Service

The specific task of the English Heritage Education Service is to carry out projects, organize teachers' courses and publish materials to encourage the use of the historic environment in formal teaching for all ages, from the youngest pupils to adults. This work is carried out by a team of education specialists that consists of a Head of Education and four Regional Education Officers who are responsible for helping teachers make the best use of the historic environment in their regions. The team also has a national responsibility to comment on the teaching of the past and has been closely involved in monitoring, offering advice on and criticizing the proposed new syllabuses in the National Curriculum especially, but not exclusively, in the subjects of history and geography. English Heritage has worked closely with others in attempting to secure the inclusion of prehistory – as well as the last twenty years of the past – in the history study units (see, for example, CBA 1989; Corbishley 1989b; Stone 1992).

The Education Service believes that people need to discover that the historic environment belongs to everyone and that the past is an inheritance for future generations. Private or sectional interests must not be allowed to prevent general access to the historic environment nor must this environment be allowed to be destroyed. It is irreplaceable. The aim of the Education Service is, through education in schools and in the community, to create new generations of citizens who will understand the value of the historic environment much better than society does today and will, as a result, take better care of it.

Since the Service's policy depends on this belief that visits to sites are the most important element in learning from the historic environment, much effort is devoted to making sure that information about sites, and how to visit them, is available to teachers. This is accomplished by providing both free materials and publications for sale. Free publications include *Information for Teachers*, which gives practical help to teachers planning a visit; a tri-annual journal, *Remnants*, that is written almost entirely by and for teachers giving examples of good practice; and 'Information Leaflets' on specific sites and topics. Publications for sale include site-specific handbooks for teachers, guides to topic or project work in class, and videos.

Making a site visit

> First of all, decide why you want to take a site visit. Write down your aims. What are your educational objectives? Do you intend your pupils to develop skills or ideas or to acquire information or do you have a combination of those in mind?
>
> (English Heritage 1992, p. 2)

Courses organized by the Education Service for teachers stress that teachers should view site visits as a part of a larger programme of study. The teachers, therefore, need to:

(a) plan their visit in advance, as part of a longer programme of curriculum work and decide whether more than one visit is essential;
(b) make practical plans for the visit by going to the site in advance;
(c) work out exactly what they are going to do on site during the visit;
(d) devise classroom work to follow up the visit to make full use of the time spent out of school; and
(e) evaluate their own as well as their children's work and decide whether to repeat the project in the following year.

Resources for the National Curriculum

As has been seen above, the National Curriculum has revealed many deficiencies in the provision of resources, especially for pupil-based project work. In addition, teachers and pupils have often had to use textbooks with incorrect information about the archaeological past (Planel 1990, pp. 273–4).

The Education Service has therefore commissioned two new book lists, one of which includes titles such as *A Teacher's Guide to Using Abbeys* (Cooksey

1992), which provides information and ideas for using particular parts of the historic environment in curriculum teaching in various subjects. For example, the architectural properties of abbey arches are used to illustrate mathematical and technological problems relating to forces and stresses; the tranquillity of many ruined abbey sites is developed as a stimulus for descriptive and imaginative writing in prose and verse as part of the English curriculum; and topics on location, weathering and pollution are linked to geography and science. The other list includes titles such as *Maths and the Historic Environment* (Copeland 1992), which take as their basic 'text' the published National Curriculum instructions in English, geography and maths and apply them to parts of the historic environment which students can visit. English Heritage videos (e.g. Corbishley 1992) examine ways of using the historic environment in relation to the specific requirements of the National Curriculum. Each video deals with two subjects (e.g. history and geography), and follows classes of pupils in their preparation work in school, through site visits, and in their follow-up work back at school. The videos also contain interviews with experienced teachers who identify the strengths of the various approaches discussed in the video as an encouragement for those less experienced teachers towards whom the videos are particularly aimed.

Using all curricular subjects

Teachers are encouraged to make use of the historic environment for all subjects taught in the school curriculum. A Roman project (Jeffries 1990, p. 3), for example, involved every part of a primary-school curriculum. One class took the theme of 'communication' – how the archaeological site and modern village communicated to the children and how they could communicate their findings and understanding to others. This involved the children in working with word processors, compiling questionnaires for local residents and finally helping to put all of their results together in an exhibition. Other children looked at similarities between the ruined site and the modern buildings which they saw and used everyday, while another group studied 'water' and compared modern water provision and use with the evidence for the provision and use of water from the site. All the children used their studies as the basis for all of their school work that term – not only in history but in mathematics, science, technology, art, geography, music and English. Another project involved Chiswick House, a villa built about 1725 in London, as the resource for an expressive arts project for multi-ethnic classes that included music, dance and art (Blandford 1990, pp. 4–5). In this project children developed their understanding of arts subjects by relating their theoretical artwork to the architectural features of the house (Fig. 27.1). Each child produced a costume based on the classical designs and shapes seen in the architecture of the house. Some children then co-operated to develop a dance that took its steps and form from the house while others produced a historic play set in the house. By being introduced to a multi-ethnic group of children through their artwork, the historic house became a stimulus for ideas and appreciation rather than an

Figure 27.1 Children are taught the importance of interpreting apparently mundane items such as household rubbish. This photograph shows a section through a common dustbin. Photo: Mike Corbishley.

element of the past of only one minority group of children (Blandford 1990, pp.4–5). At Kirby Hall, a sixteenth-century house, a 'living history' project was organized for children with special educational needs, including some with severe learning difficulties. This project (Corbishley 1988a, pp. 5–8; 1988b) involved the children in a wide range of subjects over a whole school year and culminated in children living for a day 'in the past' on site – wearing period costumes, taking part in period activities and using the site as if they were there during its heyday. The value of such 'living history' events has been much debated (e.g. *Journal of Education in Museums* 9, 1988), but if they form part of a well-prepared project that is central to the historical curriculum being followed such days provide an additional way of getting children involved and interested in the past. While the particular event mentioned above involved working with special schools, the Education Service organizes such work across the age range and with all types of educational establishments.

Figure 27.2 Children using the stimulus of the historic environment in their artwork.
Photo: English Heritage.

Problem-solving and a detective approach

Problem-solving and a detective approach are methods often used to encourage teachers to help children to look closely at the remains of the past. Essentially the approach encourages children to look and think for themselves rather than to wait to be told what 'really happened' or what an artefact can tell them about the past (Fig. 27.2) (Phillips & Bryant 1988, pp. 1–2; Aston 1990; Durbin, Morris & Wilkinson 1990).

As part of the problem-solving approach teachers are encouraged to introduce the idea of a detective approach to their children by explaining: 'An archaeologist's job is to hunt for clues to help find out what happened in the past. They work a bit like police detectives investigating a crime' (Corbishley 1990b). This approach (Corbishley 1986a, pp. 1–2; 1986b, pp. 3–8; 1986c, pp. 1–4) can be further developed in games (Corbishley 1989a, p. 15; 1990a, pp. 8–9); in exercises, for example based on street observation where evidence for iron railings, and other iron street furniture, removed during the Second World War for making into armaments, is identified and explained (Durbin 1990, p. 9); and in videos. 'The Archaeological Detectives' video follows two primary-school children as they explore two very different sites (a Roman archaeological site and a medieval castle) looking for evidence to show what the sites had been and how they functioned, while the 'Clues Challenge' video, which also follows two children, explores three different modern buildings – a furnished house, an empty house and the foundations of a new house on a building site. At each site the children look for clues to show who lives/lived in the houses and for clues to indicate the functions of individual rooms. Together the videos try to link the modern and historic environments, suggesting to children and teachers that they do not have to live next to an impressive historic site to begin to learn the skills and approaches of archaeology (Corbishley 1990b, 1990c).

Conclusion

The above has only sketched attempts to extend the teaching of the past from an over-concentration on documentary history to a more balanced curriculum incorporating all aspects of the study of the past. However, despite the initiatives mentioned above, archaeology and prehistory still exist on the edge of what is perceived – by those with responsibility for the curriculum – as the real stuff of history. Until such time as these decision-makers can be influenced, the subjects will continue to be marginalized and children will continue to receive a restricted view of the past. The influencing of these decision-makers must be the real goal for those involved in attempts to broaden the teaching of the past.

References

Alcock, L. 1975. The discipline of archaeology. Glasgow: *College Courant* June, 8–14.
Alexander, J. 1989. Threnody for a generation. In *Education Bulletin 6*, Richardson, W. (ed.), 5–11. London: Council for British Archaeology.
Alexander, R. 1984. *Primary Teaching*. Eastbourne: Holt.
Archer, R, L. V. D. Owen & A. E. Chapman. 1916. *The Teaching of History in Elementary Schools*. London: Black.
Aston, O. 1990. *Primary History: problem solving*. Shrewsbury: Shropshire Education Department.
Birchenough, C. 1927. *History of Elementary Education*. London: University Tutorial Press.
Blandford, S. 1990. Arts and the environment at Chiswick House. *Remnants* 10, 4–5.
Blenkin, G. M. & A. V. Kelly 1987. *The Primary Curriculum*. London: Harper & Row.
Blyth, W., K. R. Cooper, R. Derricott, G. Elliott, H. Sumner, H. & A. Waplington 1976. *Place, Time and Society 8–13: curriculum planning in history, geography and social science*. Bristol: Collins for the Schools Council.
Bourne, H. E. 1902. *The Teaching of History and Civics in the Elementary and the Secondary School*. London: Longman.
Bowen, M. 1972. Another approach to history for young children. *Teaching History* 7, 253–5.
Bruner, J. 1966. *Toward a Theory of Instruction*. Cambridge, Mass.: Harvard University Press.
Clark, G. 1943. Education and the study of man. *Antiquity* 17, 113–21.
Cleere, H. F. (ed.) 1984. *Approaches to the Archaeological Heritage*. Cambridge: Cambridge University Press.
Cleere, H. F. (ed.) 1989. *Archaeological Heritage Management in the Modern World*. London: Unwin Hyman.
Cleveland County Council 1981. *Curriculum Review: environmental studies – primary*. Cleveland: County Council.
Coltham, J. & J. Fines 1971. *Educational Objectives for the Study of History*. London: Historical Association.
Cooksey, C. 1992. *A Teacher's Guide to Using Abbeys*. London: English Heritage.
Copeland, T. 1992. *Maths and the Historic Environment*. London: English Heritage.
Corbishley, M. 1982a. *Archaeology in the Classroom*. London: Council for British Archaeology.
Corbishley, M. 1982b. *Archaeology in the Town*. London: Council for British Archaeology.
Corbishley, M. (ed.) 1983. *Archaeological Resources Handbook for Teachers*. London: Council for British Archaeology.
Corbishley, M. 1986a. Not much to look at? *Remnants* 1, 1–2.
Corbishley, M. 1986b. Archaeology, monuments and education. In *Presenting Archaeology to Young People*, Cracknell, S. & M. Corbishley (eds), 3–8. London: Council for British Archaeology.
Corbishley, M. 1986c. The case of the blocked window. *Remnants* 2, 1–4.
Corbishley, M. 1988a. The past replayed. *Remnants* 5, 5–8.
Corbishley, M. 1988b. The past replayed: Kirby Hall. Video. London: English Heritage.
Corbishley, M. 1989a. *Prehistoric Britain: activity book*. London: British Museum Publications.
Corbishley, M. 1989b. History and the National Curriculum. *Remnants* 9, 1–3.
Corbishley, M. 1990a. The layer game. *Remnants* 10, 8–9.
Corbishley, M. 1990b. The Archaeological Detectives. Video. London: English Heritage.

Corbishley, M. 1990c. Clues Challenge. Video. London: English Heritage.

Corbishley, M. 1992. Teaching on Site. Video. London: English Heritage.

Council for British Archaeology 1956. Unpublished report on the conference on schools and archaeology.

Council for British Archaeology (CBA) 1989. Archaeology for Ages 5–16. London: Council for British Archaeology.

Council for British Archaeology (CBA) 1991. Report of the Structure and Policy Working Party. London: Council for British Archaeology.

Delaney, L. 1986. HCC Guidelines for Teaching Art. Winchester: Hampshire County Council.

Department for Education and Science 1989. From Policy into Practice. London: Her Majesty's Stationery Office.

Department for Education and Science 1990. Final Report of the History Working Group. London: Her Majesty's Stationery Office.

Department for Education and Science 1991. History in the National Curriculum (England). London: Her Majesty's Stationery Office.

Dewey, J. 1896. Interpretation of the culture-epoch theory. In Psychology: the early works of John Dewey 1882–1898, vol. 2, J. A. Boydston (ed.), 247–53. Carbondale: Southern Illinois University Press.

Dewey, J. 1899a (1956). The school and society. In The Child and the Curriculum and the School and Society, 6–159. Chicago: University of Chicago Press.

Dewey, J. 1899b (1966). Lecture XXVI on history. In Lectures in the Philosophy of Education 1899 by John Dewey, R. D. Archambault (ed.), 256–64. New York: Random House.

Dewey, J, 1900. The Elementary School Record. Chicago: University of Chicago Press.

Dewey, J. 1911. Culture epoch theory. In A Cyclopidia of Education, vol. 2, P. Monroe (ed.) 230–42. New York: Macmillan.

Dewey, J. 1916 (1968). Democracy in education. In Selected Readings in the Philosophy of Education, J. Park (ed.), 94–135. New York: Macmillan.

Dimbleby, G. 1977. Training the environmental archaeologist. Bulletin of the Institute of Archaeology 14, 1–12.

Dobson, D. 1928 (1950). The Teaching of Prehistory. London: Historical Association.

Durbin, G. 1990. Streetwise: the case of the missing railings. Remnants 11, 9.

Durbin, G., S. Morris & S. Wilkinson 1990. A Teacher's Guide to Learning from Objects. London: English Heritage.

Dworkin, M. 1959. Dewey on Education. New York: Teachers College Press.

English Heritage 1992. Information for Teachers. London: English Heritage.

Evans, J. 1975. Archaeology as Education and Profession. London: University of London.

Fairley, J. 1977. History Teaching through Museums. London: Longman.

Frost, J. 1983. Archaeology and the media. Unpublished BA dissertation. Department of Roman Studies, Institute of Archaeology, London.

Hadow, W. H. 1931. The Primary School: Report of the Consultative Committee. London: Her Majesty's Stationery Office.

Halkon, P., M. Corbishley & G. Binns (eds) 1992. The Archaeological Resource Book. London: Council for British Archaeology.

Harris, E. 1976. Is archaeology viable as a school subject? Unpublished MEd dissertation, Division of Education, University of Sheffield.

Her Majesty's Inspectorate (HMI) 1988. History from 5 to 16. London: Her Majesty's Stationery Office.

Historical Association 1986. History in the Compulsory Years of Schooling. London: Historical Association.

Hoare, R. 1983. Archaeology, the public and the media. Unpublished MA dissertation, Department of Archaeology, University of Edinburgh.

Hodgkinson, K. & J. Thomas 1979. Teaching history: a content analysis of numbers 1 to 20. *Teaching History* 23, 3–7.

Jeffries, P. 1990. Roman Wroxeter – just a pile of stones? *Remnants* 10, 1–3.

Johnson, N. & P. Rose 1990. *Cornwall's Archaeological Heritage*. Truro: Twelveheads Press.

Journal of Education in Museums 1988. Issue dedicated to discussing living history and role play. London: Group for Education in Museums.

Low-Beer, A. & J. Blyth 1983. *Teaching History to Younger Children*. London: Historical Association.

Mackenzie, R. & P. Stone 1990. Introduction. In *The Excluded Past: archaeology in education*, Stone, P. & R. MacKenzie (eds), 1–12. London: Unwin Hyman; Routledge pbk 1994.

Mayhew, K. & A. Edwards 1966 (1936). *The Dewey School*. New York: Atherton Press.

Phillips, M. & A. Bryant 1988. Problem solving at historic sites. *Remnants* 5, 1–2.

Planel, P. 1990. New Archaeology, New History – when will they meet? Archaeology in English secondary schools. In *The Excluded Past: archaeology in education*, Stone, P. & R. MacKenzie (eds), 271–81. London: Unwin Hyman; Routledge pbk 1994.

Pollard, M. 1973. *History with Juniors*. London: Evans Bros.

Preston, M. 1971. A primary school project on the Stone Age. *Teaching History* 6, 132–5.

Renfrew, C. 1982. *Towards an Archaeology of Mind*. Cambridge: Cambridge University Press.

Richardson, W. (ed.) 1989. Papers from Archaeology meets Education conference. *CBA Educational Bulletin* 6.

Salt, J. 1970. Approaches to field work in history in the primary school. *Teaching History* 3, 174–9.

Shaw, R. 1993. *Northamptonshire Archaeology Unit Education Service*. Northampton: County Council.

Slater, J. 1984. The case for history in school. *The Historian* 2, 13–17.

Slevin, S. 1984. The potential use of archaeological evidence in the teaching of history to school children. Unpublished MPhil dissertation, School of Education, New University of Ulster.

Southworth, E. (ed.) 1993. *'Ready for the New Millennium?' – futures for museum archaeology*. Liverpool: Society of Museum Archaeologists.

Standen, J. 1981. Place, time and society 8–13 with top juniors. *Teaching History* 31, 18–20.

Steane, J. 1986. The Schools Committee of the Council for British Archaeology. In *Presenting Archaeology to Young People*, Cracknell, S. & M. Corbishley (eds), 49–50. London: Council for British Archaeology.

Stone, P. G. 1990. Introduction. In *The First Farmers*. Southampton: Department of Archaeology, University of Southampton.

Stone, P. G. 1991. The teaching of the past with special reference to prehistory in English primary education. Unpublished PhD thesis, University of Southampton.

Stone, P. G. 1992 The Magnificent Seven: reasons for teaching about prehistory. *Teaching History* October 1992, 13–18.

Thompson, F. 1982. Place, time and society 8–13: the project's view of the meaning of history today. *Teaching History* 32, 20–2.

Ucko, P. J. 1989. In conclusion: some problems and questions. In *Education Bulletin 6*, Richardson, W. (ed.), 40–4. London: Council for British Archaeology.

Unstead, R. J. 1956. *Teaching History in the Junior School*. London: Black.

Zimmerman, L. J., S. Dasovich, M. Engstrom & L. E. Bradley 1994. Listening to the teachers: warnings about the use of archaeological agendas in US classrooms. In *The Presented Past: heritage, museums and education*, Stone, P. G. & B. L. Molyneaux (eds), 359–74. London: Routledge.

28 Ethnic representation in Colombian textbooks

HONORIO RIVERA REYES

Introduction

One of the main functions of education is the reproduction of society. As a result, the educational system tends to legitimize the ways of knowledge, the values, the language and the behaviours of the dominant culture (Sáenz 1988, p. 15). Schools and their syllabuses are therefore neither neutral nor passive; quite the contrary; both attempt to guide the behaviour of students by developing a conscience, a moral sense, and ultimately empowering them to reproduce received knowledge as a means of influencing others (Delpiano & Madgenzo 1988, p. 5; also see Podgorny 1994).

Social and cultural reproduction may be seen in several dimensions. The imprint of 'dominant and legitimate' culture is present in the whole of school practice: in official language, in school rules, in the social relationships within classrooms, in the presentation of knowledge, and in the exclusion of the contribution of subordinated groups to the society. All of these are elements which constitute what Sáenz (1988) called the 'hidden syllabus'. Among the components of this phenomenon are textbooks.

Textbooks are indispensable in the educational process, but their contents represent a 'selection' of the available social knowledge of a culture. The question of what to select when presenting an outline of a society is especially important when it concerns those outside the dominant group; the values and interests of other groups, such as indigenous communities, may be neglected in favour of the presentation of a national identity or society.

In Colombia, ethnocentric judgements conveyed in textbooks about the nature of society, such as the legitimation of 'wild, lower races' existing in opposition to 'civilized, higher races', have helped speed up the process of homogeneity in Colombian culture, without taking into account the cultural and biological diversity of the country's population.

The following discussion outlines how the texts utilized by Colombian teachers and students in primary and secondary schools show fanciful images of the indigenous people of Colombia, negating their past, their creativity and achievements, and, in several instances, their existence. It questions the ideals of 'progress' and 'perfection' as taken for granted by key persons in national public life, and how they have subsequently influenced the authors of textbooks, contributing in this way to discrimination against and the diminishment of black and indigenous people (also see Wade 1994).

Forty textbooks from the primary- and secondary-school system, that present information relating to ethnic groups, were selected for the purpose of this study. The sample covers a wide variety of textbooks published between 1970 and 1988 by different publishing houses. Up-to-date works were preferred, but older texts, which were important during some periods, were also taken into account. All the texts follow the official syllabus of the Ministry of Education.

Racial determinism, intellectuals, politicians and texts

The myth of racial superiority emerges when society is divided into several social groups, and when one of them – the privileged one – tries to 'justify' the current situation according to its own interests. The creation of a hierarchy engenders contempt for the so-called 'lower races', causing – in the Colombian case – black and indigenous people to become segregated and discriminated against.

The particular form of racism found among the Colombian intelligentsia emerged with the Darwinian and Spencerian schools of thought in the late nineteenth century. Spencer's interpretation of the notion of the survival of the fittest and hereditary determinism in a social context influenced the social theory of American states at a time of rapid development (see Wade 1994). The labour force needed to meet the demand for the raw materials required for social necessities to be able to function adequately could only be provided with the proper social controls. Such controls were not to be explicitly imposed, however, but would be transmitted through education and other implicit forms of indoctrination, moving people to assimilate a common body of beliefs, with the legitimacy of the social order legislated by governing institutions.

The social theory that developed from these ideas in Colombia justified the slavery of black people by interpreting it as a result of natural selection, which had already assigned them their proper place. Any kind of abolitionism would result in an attempt to change the natural state of things, threatening to diminish the 'higher race' in favour of the 'lower people'. In this scheme, 'white people' were the best adapted to survive. Their aggressiveness against other 'races' was justified as a way of putting the weakest people in the place they deserved, in accord with the faculties they had inherited (Arocha & Friedemann 1984, p. 37). Upon this premiss, the 'white people' were able to rationalize their privileged position, becoming 'redeemers' and 'civilizers', given the acceptance of 'progress' as an universal necessity.

During this century, and until the present, there have been intellectuals and politicians in Colombia, across the major political parties and institutions, who have shown their debt to – and acceptance of – this racial determinism in their views of the indigenous people.

The conservative politician Luis López de Meza, for example, stated that the Indian could not produce culture. He held that the technology, the organization of production and the moral codes of the Indian showed limitations as a result of the influence of the tropical environment, where the chemical characteristics inhibited the development of superior beings. He also insisted that genes were the main determinant of human behaviour (López de Meza 1949, pp. 39–45; 1955, pp. 79–81; and see Arocha 1988).

This biological reductionism has found its way into school texts. For example, a geography text for grade 9 students reflects López de Meza's thought when referring to the '*cundinamarques*' (a mixture of Chibcha Indian and Spaniard): 'When the Chibcha race is predominant, he is short statured, taciturn, hard working, reserved and malicious. When the Hispanic blood predominates he is tall, communicative, with lively eyes and white and rosy skin' (Soler 1979, p. 50).

Another text invites the students to read López de Meza, in particular where he exalts the 'Spanish race' and a supposed national unity:

> The Spanish race is the second link which articulates the national entity. It is a democratic race, with a great, hospitable hearth, suffering during adversity and generous during times of plenty. It knew, and may have been the only race that could know, how to mix its blood with the blood of the defeated [i.e. the Indians] and communicate to them the essentials of aspiring to do something, and something always better.
>
> (Sánchez 1979, p. 189)

The previous quotations are crude examples of racism, where the ignorance of other ethnic groups, different from the Spaniards, is presented in a way that attempts to erase them, legitimizing at the same time the system of racial castes, and pretending to create 'only one strong nationality'.

Such racism also shows up in the book *Revolution in America* by Alvaro Gómez Hurtado, who ran for president of Colombia on a number of occasions. Gómez (1978, p. 15) neglects aboriginal history, stating that the indigenous past is 'non-historic' and that social illumination comes from the progress of civilization. For Gómez, history started with the Spanish Conquest and with the christianization of the Indians. He regards the indigenous people as fatalists, sensing their lack of future. A paragraph from a school textbook follows his thoughts: 'The Indians failed not because of their primitive weapons, but due to their fatalist and defeated psychological state of mind' (Montenegro 1984, p. 79).

Gómez also stated that Indians are never the subject of history; in this he clearly does not take into account their own past. For him, the dynamic force of history is always external, generated in a non-Indian world. Related to what Gómez has said, a classic text for secondary schools proposes: 'In the Colombian territory there are still some wild tribes and others which have not assimilated the lessons from the missionaries; these tribes have not broken with their primitive customs or they have returned to them' (García 1971, p. 171).

For Gómez, therefore, the native past has been shameful; America is a continent which has aspired to be 'white', with the ideal being to become like the European. Gómez believes the indigenous people have contributed nothing to national culture, not even cultivation or fishing techniques, because the tools and techniques of the Spanish were more efficient. Similarly, he characterizes indigenous religion as a sign of primitivism, typical of a barbarian people (Gómez 1978, p. 209).

School textbooks point out something similar when they refer to the indigenous people, stating that Indians must change their style of life, that they have to adjust to progress and assume the white way of life. Indeed, when they refer to the Indian contribution, it tends to be in the past tense:

> The Colombian Indians belong to three main branches: the Andean – or inhabitants of mountains and plateaus – had a more developed culture; the Caribes, who inhabited the sea coast, were warriors and even cannibalistic; and the Pampean from the eastern plains, were very wild and primitive. Among Indian virtues, his resignation in the face of pain, his warrior spirit and his haughtiness, were outstanding, among his defects a great shyness and hypocrisy.
> (Sánchez 1975, p. 77)

These texts ignored the contribution of indigenous people to the majority society in managing the environment and in utilizing natural resources without destroying them; and they did not take into account a diverse and complex social fabric, where values and institutions positively recognized in the dominant culture could be found: solidarity, respect, honesty, love, justice, mythology, communal work, traditional medicine, arts, language richness and so on. All of these qualities remained undiscussed; it was more important to denigrate Indians, as in the following quotation:

> For sowing, the Indians from different tribes get together in 'mingas' [voluntary communal labour] or 'convites', attracted by the lavish expenditure of 'chicha' [an alcoholic beverage] which is ritual in these collective tasks, more than due to cooperative spirit.
> (García 1971, p. 223)

All of the aspects of society discussed by Gómez look towards a cultural homogeneity, which is – for him – the ideal situation. Ethnocide is seen to be a necessary step, one to be actively encouraged (Gómez 1978). The same conclusion was reached by Lucena: 'The Indian issue must be faced soon. The only possible solution is scientifically planning his acculturation, his incorporation in the national culture' (Lucena 1982, p. 35).

The folklorist and journalist Miguel Angel Martín, also former press chief of DAINCO (a state institution which administers a large area of the country with a dense indigenous population), also follows this view. He classifies the inhabitants of the eastern 'Llanos' into two main groups: the whites or rationals and the Indians (Martín 1978, p. 22). He classifies the latter as: peaceful Indians, semi-civilized Indians and aggressive Indians. The peaceful ones are those sedentary groups that have always maintained relationships with the white people. The semi-civilized Indians are those which are not completely sedentary. Finally, the aggressive ones are the indigenous groups that mainly hunt and fish; they are thieves and harmful, and even ambush white people, often using poisoned darts with curare. Of course, says Martín, white people take reprisal, without discriminating among the different groups (Martín 1978, pp. 23–4).

Thanks to this evolutionist view, societies are judged according to their position on the scale from primitive to civilized, with indigenous peoples sharing only the remote past of their 'civilized' cohabitants.

Several clear examples show how the indigenous Caribes Indians are considered as 'cannibals and wild', groups with a rudimentary economy who are characterized by aggressiveness, ferocity and cruelty. Indeed, it seems that all the textbook authors had this image of the Caribes:

> The Caribes: these peoples were very dangerous. They practised cranial deformation and deformed their calves and arms; they also broke their noses to make them aquiline. They were cannibalistic, fighting against other peoples to capture and eat the prisoners and later on to use their heads as trophies.
>
> (Mora & Peña 1985, pp. 30–1)

> In comparison with the Chibchas, the Caribes were much more barbarian and warlike; they ate human beings, which was rarely done by the Chibchas. They were well-built and muscular.
>
> (Pinilla 1986, p. 524)

None of the cited authors took the time to see the Caribes as active traders, participating in the high prestige 'Llanos' intertribal exchange in the Orinoquia region. The Caribes had also established a slave-trading network, which included the indigenous groups as agents, integrating them into the commercial chain of European products (Friedemann & Arocha 1985, p. 94). As Pineda Camacho (1987) suggests, cannibal practices did exist among the Caribes, but were associated with major ceremonial events during times of instability and conflict.

Julio Cesar García, a former member of the Academía de Historia and founder of the University La Gran Colombia, is the author of 'The Primitives', from which several extracts have been quoted above. During the

1960s and 1970s this was one of the most popular reference texts among professors and secondary students in the country (by 1971, thirteen editions had been published). García saw the Caribes in the same way as the chroniclers did four centuries before: not only were the Caribes cannibals, but almost all the Colombian Indians merited this description. 'A large proportion of the Colombian Indians practised cannibalism, sometimes as food, at other times as a manifestation of their cruelty and wildness . . . . The skulls were used like glasses to drink "chicha" ' (García 1971, p. 224).

But cannibalism was not only directed against enemies, according to García. He went further, stating that even close family kin among the Panches, a Colombian Indian group, ate each other (García 1971, p. 176).

In recently published school textbooks the cannibal stereotype is still present:

> In the immense jungles and in the plains, where the great rivers Amazon, Orinoco and Paraná flow, thousands of Indians lived and still live. They are characterized by being naked, using hammocks, cultivating special plants, and by cannibalism. All of them received the name 'Tupis' during the Conquest days, but nowadays they are known as Amazonian people.
>
> (Montenegro 1984, p. 42)

> . . . in this region – Amazonia – Indian tribes dispersed in the forest have survived. Some of them are cannibals. Among the main tribes are the 'Coreguajes', the 'Ticunas', the 'Sibundoyes' and the 'Huitotos'.
>
> (Sánchez 1986, p. 494)

Despite numerous well-researched books on the indigenous groups of the savanna and tropical rainforest, the previously cited authors continue to degrade the image of not only those Indians who faced the Spaniards during the Conquest, but also of contemporary Indian groups.

Their false image derives from an ethnocentrism that regards the violence against indigenous people as legitimate, as part of a civilizing process. Indeed, 'cruelty' was only practised by the indigenous groups that resisted the Spanish Conquest. For example, when García refers to the Pijaos, he says: 'They were the cruelest among the Colombian indigenes' (1971, p. 237).

In order to explain the extinction of indigenous peoples, these authors have rigidly adhered to a Eurocentric and ethnocentric view. For them, the causes of such extinctions should be looked for within the indigenous population:

> The disappearance of indigenous population can not be attributed to systematic destruction by the Spanish. The causes, among others, are the climatic changes . . . and due to illness. . . .
> [Referring to Quimbaya cannibalism it] is easy to understand

that the alkaloids and germs from dead bodies contributed to a great extent to the decimation of the indigenous population.

(García 1971, pp. 176, 224)

This bio-social interpretation is common in school textbooks. Social process is put on the same level as biological process, relegating human actions to biological laws of nature, and so justifying social absolutism, in which the 'civilized' European way of life is taken as a positive universal paradigm (Arocha & Friedemann 1984, p. 515). For example, when textbook authors compare the 'Cundiboyacence' (from Cundinamarca and Boyacá) with the 'Santandereano' (from Santander) and with the 'Antioqueño' (from Antioquía), they associate their assumed social characteristics with the relative degree of their Spanish ancestry:

> The 'Santandereano' type: their ancestors are of Spanish origin, constituting one of the few population groups in which the Indian blood was minimal. In the history of the country, they have been characterized as being enterprising and haughty. The 'Antioqueño' type: as in the 'Santandereano' type, are enterprising, communicative and dynamic, which led them to achieve a wide variety of economic developments.
>
> (Charris de la Hoz & Tejada 1986, pp. 172–3)

These racist ideas are included in a self-teaching programme called 'New School', from the National Ministry of Education, intended by the Government to standardize primary education among the rural population. In some texts, 'alternatives' which look for the 'ideal man' capable of facing the challenge of American development, are presented.

> The 'Triple-ethnic': this name designates the racial type which has contributions, in similar proportions, from the three main races [white, Indian and black]. Some sociologists and anthropologists say that this type would be the ideal one for the complete dominance of the Tropics, and the very creator of the future tropical civilization.
>
> (Sánchez 1975, p. 100)

These ideas implicitly undermine the significance of contemporary indigenous groups who, in contrast, are viewed as either passive or primitive and fixed on the past:

> The Indoamerican generally was short, with olive coloured skin, [lank] hair, strong build, slightly oblique and dark eyes, melancholy, attached to land and race, keeper of the customs inherited from his ancestors, patient, sober, resistant to penalties, superstitious and vindictive. Some of them had a peaceful spirit like the Muiscas, other were haughty warriors like the Pijaos.
>
> (Soler 1979, p. 49)

And yet these defenceless groups have also served as scapegoats for the current political indifference in the country:

> A great part of the current political situation can be explained by the Muisca ancestry: Their attitude in relation to the civic organiz-ation, the indifference, the unconcern, the incredulity, and the mistrust in public accounts.
>
> (Grupo de Educación Creativa 1975)

It is clear from these contemporary quotations that the attitudes about Indians of some of our most influential writers, many of whom influence the children in our schools, have scarcely moved beyond the outmoded ninteenth-century theories from which they emerged. These writers, by *their* indiffer-ence, do nothing but undervalue and therefore undermine the social position of indigenous people:

> The indigenous male is malice incarnate when he does not work his small land. He is selfish and lazy at home. He drives his woman towards the rudest tasks. The Indian is rude, cruel, distrustful, revengeful and rancorous; the dirt invades him like it does in his hut. His skin is a condenser of dust and dirt, kneaded with sweat.
>
> (Franco & Franco 1981, pp. 72–4)

Conclusion

In the idealized National Society, the multi-ethnic and multicultural character of the Indian communities is hidden. Diversity amongst indigenous groups is reduced to a contemptuous caricature of Indian values, traditions and skills. This caricature is re-emphasized in literature about the indigenous population – by ideologues and the authors of textbooks and the syllabuses of the National Ministry of Education. Such texts present distorted and fanciful images of indigenous people, and in some cases are secure in the belief that Indians are not human beings. These attitudes are the expression of a dominant class that uses information to homogenize human behaviour and so maintain social continuity and inequality, with the result that they decry alternative ways of life, of feeling and thought.

These attitudes are therefore politically motivated, and contribute to a general sense that indigenous peoples are an obstacle to progress. The domi-nant society supports the idea that the Indian territory will be transformed into 'habitable' land, oblivious of the fact that Indians have inhabited these lands, without destroying them, for thousands of years. The ruination and loss of the land not only means the loss of resources and subsistence but also the dis-appearance of traditional ways of life, bringing, as a result, the disintegration and disappearance of the indigenous communities. The destruction of these styles of life and the incorporation of the people into the national society is justified by the notion that everything that Indians do is an obstacle to progress.

What can be done to alter this misrepresentation of indigenous cultures? The trouble is that the Ministry of Education does not control the quality of the textbooks, and publishing companies are similarly uninterested, and yet both are responsible for these and many other damaging mistakes and misconceptions about Colombian ethnic groups. There was a recent controversy between the Academia Colombiana de Historia and the Sociedad Colombiana de Historiadores, the so-called 'textbooks battle', about a well-known high-school textbook called *Historia de Colombia*, but it was over the introduction of social and economic issues in textbooks, and in the creation of a more dynamic analysis of history – a debate, in other words, between 'old' and 'new' history. The controversy did not touch on the ethnic issue.

If we are to provide justice for the whole of Colombia, then we must recognize in our literature the contribution of the indigenous peoples to the very core of our society. Unfortunately, the authors discussed above have written in a very tendentious way in support of a national culture that has significance only for the privileged groups of society. We therefore need to cast aside the nineteenth-century attitudes at the basis of our interpretation of indigenous society and create a new literature, based on consultation with the representatives of indigenous communities, the Ministry of Education and all the other institutions and associations involved in the defence of the right of autonomy and respect for ethnic minorities.

References

Arocha, J. R. 1988. *El proceso de paz en Colombia: reiteración del orden señorial?* Bogotá: Sociedad Antropológica de Colombia.
Arocha, J. & N. de Friedemann (eds) 1984. *Un siglo de investigación social: antropología en Colombia*. Bogotá: Etno.
Charris de la Hoz, A. & A. Tejada 1986. *Geografía general de Colombia: serie el hombre y su medio*. Barranquilla: El Cid.
Delpiano, A. & A. Madgenzo 1988. La escuela formal, el curriculum escolar y los derechos humanos. *Educación y Cultura* 16, 5–8.
Franco, R. & F. Franco 1981. *Geografía Económica de Colombia*. Bogotá: Voluntad.
Friedemann, N. S. de & J. R. Arocha 1985. *Herederos del jaguar y la anaconda*. Bogotá: Carlos Valencia.
García, J. C. 1971. *Los primitivos: prehistoria general de América y de Colombia*. Bogotá: Voluntad.
Gómez, A. 1978. *La revolución en América*. Bogotá: Plaza y Janés.
Grupo de Educación Creativa 1975. *Historia 1: manual*. Bogotá: Voluntad.
López de Meza, L. 1949. *Perspectivas culturales*. Bogotá: Universidad de Colombia.
Lucena, M. 1982. *Historia de América 2*. Bogotá: Ed. Culturales.
Martín, M. A. 1978. *Del folclor llanero*. Villavicencio: Gráficas Juan XXIII.
Montenegro, A. 1984. *Historia de América*. Bogotá: Norma.
Mora, C. A. & M. Peña 1985. *Historia socioeconómica de Colombia*. Bogotá: Norma.
Pineda Camacho, R. 1987. Malocas de terror y jaguares españoles. *Revistas de Antropología* 3, 83–114.

Pinilla, L. M. 1986. *Enciclopedia Nueva Escuela: cuarto grado de nivel básico primario.* Medellín: Susaeta.

Podgorny, I. 1994. Choosing ancestors: the primary education syllabuses in Buenos Aires, Argentina, between 1975 and 1990. In *The Presented Past: heritage, museums and education*, Stone, P. G. & B. L. Molyneaux (eds), 408–17. London: Routledge.

Sáenz, J. 1988. El currículo oculto: democracia y formación moral en la escuela. *Educación y Cultura* 16, 14–20.

Sánchez, H. 1975. *Geografía física y general de Colombia: curso 1 de enseñanza media.* Medellín: Bedout.

Sánchez, E. H. 1979. *Historia documental 6.* Bogotá: Voluntad.

Soler, F. 1979. *Geografía económica de Colombia.* Bogotá: Ed. Culturales.

Wade, P. 1994. Blacks, Indians and the state in Colombia. In *The Presented Past: heritage, museums and education*, Stone, P. G & B. L. Molyneaux (eds), 418–37. London: Routledge.

29 Choosing ancestors: the primary education syllabuses in Buenos Aires, Argentina, between 1975 and 1990

IRINA PODGORNY

Argentinos? – Hasta donde
ydesde cuando, bueno es
darse cuenta de ello.
(Sarmiento [1882] 1915, p. 63)

Introduction

As many authors (e.g. Rockwell 1982) have pointed out, everyday life in schools is not a literal translation from the curriculum; classes do not follow faithfully its subjects and goals. But no one can deny the relevance of the syllabus for understanding school policies. From an archaeological point of view, curricula can be seen as monuments or artefacts of the ideals which schools attempt to impose. In Argentina, this means three systems of ideas from three different political groups – the first in 1975 by the 'justicialist' democratic government; the second in 1980 by the military dictatorship; and the last in 1985/6 by the 'radical' democratic government. My goal is to analyse the inner logic of these schemes through their documents and to compare the system of ideas which each of them establishes.

My case study for the first section of this chapter is the primary education system of the Province of Buenos Aires; it is the largest in the country, with 1,298,079 children from 6 to 12 years (Tedesco & Carciofi 1987, plate 18; data from the 1980 National Census), i.e. 50 per cent of school-children in the country, and it has a high degree of bureaucratic complexity and a teaching body in much disarray (Podgorny 1990). The educational syllabuses were written in the Ministry of Education of the Province of Buenos Aires by a curricular department.

In the second part of this chapter I present the results of ethnographic research conducted in primary schools in two municipalities of Gran Buenos Aires (see Podgorny 1990; Podgorny & Perez n.d.) after the introduction of the latest syllabus. These data were obtained through quantitative and qualitative techniques (surveys, interviews, participant and ethnographic observation of school class situations) between 1987 and 1989.

Social studies/sciences

The 1975 curriculum

In the 1975 curriculum, social studies, taught as one of the natural sciences starting in grade 4 (i.e., when children are 9), has two main themes: (a) a geographical determinism, linking the particular development and character of society with its natural surroundings; and (b) a concept of nationalism that was suggested was actually inherent in the land and its people before the nation of Argentina was created as a political entity.

The geographical determinism first appears in a study of 'ways of living to show the *constant* relationship between man and environment' (Ediciones 'La Obra' 1975, p. 3, emphasis added). The 'Native people' are the first group examined in the study of this relationship. In the fifth grade, the text states that 'the ways of living of the aboriginal tribes are a consequence of their interaction with the environment' (Ediciones 'La Obra' 1975, p. 7).

Aboriginal people are not mentioned again, but in the sixth grade this geographical vision is broadened to include a new category: the 'American Man', who is said to be 'influenced by the geographical environment through time' (Ediciones 'La Obra' 1975, p. 12). In the seventh grade such determinism is extended to other countries, establishing a sort of implicit law which operates in all past and present societies, i.e., that their origin and function are determined by nature and environment.

It is clear from this programme that the teaching of history is strongly connected to geography, and indeed, the natural roots of nationalism is a significant leitmotiv of the curriculum. In this syllabus the Argentinian nation is an entity that has always existed, rooted in nature and common origins. Unfortunately, however, aboriginal people have only a temporary place in this nation. European conquest was 'occupation' and the territories not yet occupied by white Europeans were 'empty spaces' (Ediciones 'La Obra' 1975, p. 8). Native people were treated as living here only temporarily at the eve of the conquest.

The minor place of aborigines is further emphasized in the treatment of world history. In the seventh grade (12-year-olds), Europe and Asia are considered as the source of the first cultures, i.e. the Greek–Latin European heritage and Christendom, and the successors of this legacy are Spain and its descendants, the Hispanic-American countries. In this scheme, the conquest of America is studied in terms of its Christian mission.

One can therefore conclude from reading this syllabus that: (a) the first humans and cultures were in Asia and Europe; (b) the conquest of America, Africa and the Pacific islands by Europeans was a natural movement of people to new spaces; (c) these spaces were regarded as 'empty' (previous inhabitants of these regions are ignored here, although they are quoted in other parts of the curriculum). The real world is limited in space and time to this chain of development.

The 1980 curriculum

In 1980 the social sciences curriculum changed the contents of each grade. The curriculum established that children under 12 'are not capable of understanding time and space', but it does not deny the teaching of the 'historic sense' for the shaping of the 'national sense and consciousness' (Ediciones Siemens Ocampo 1980, p. 1) for the later understanding of history.

This curriculum explicitly criticizes the environmental determinism so important in the previous syllabus as an 'erroneous point of view . . . the intelligence and will of man are the true guides of the development of society'. At the same time it denies the utility of 'geohistoric problems', i.e. the way that the 1975 curriculum structured the teaching of subjects. On the contrary, history is defined as the people's collective memory, needed for understanding the present and for moving into the future, as well as for preserving society as a national culture (Ediciones Siemens Ocampo 1980, p. 2). The cultural values which are supported are those of the Hispanic heritage and so historic description is based on great men, great events and meaningful places, with an assumption that the nation existed previous to its constitution.

Because of this concept of nation and history, the time period within which aborigines are studied is brief. A long history is only recognized for Europe. For America the time starts with the contact between Natives and conquerors, as a sort of a spark which opened the doors of history to the Native peoples of this continent. As a result, Native people are treated as supporting players in the beginning of the national drama. In the fourth grade, Native peoples of Buenos Aires Province are mentioned in the history of its settlement, and the coverage in the fifth grade includes the struggles between the conquerors and the Indians, the cultures and peoples who inhabited the plains of Buenos Aires when the Spaniards arrived and the main indigenous peoples of the Argentinian population. From the sixth grade on, however, they are treated only in the introduction to historical topics. The assumption throughout the curriculum is of a sort of 'national fate' which guides the course of the country despite obstacles and impediments and of one culture and one national tradition, of which both are uniform and homogeneous units. The children are taught that nationalism grows firm and in the right direction thanks to the action of great men who capture this national essence in their works.

Hence, in the seventh grade, the founding of Argentina is seen as a European phenomenon:

> the European culture spread out in America, establishing morals, traditions and ways of living, which involve conceiving Man as a spiritual and transcendent being and the World as humanist and Christian. The result of this is the grandeur of being Argentinian

assuming as the basis of society freedom, democracy, labour and
property, and the preservation of national security.

(Ediciones Siemens Ocamp 1980, p. 14)

In summary, the 1980 syllabus treats historical studies as distinct from
geography. Mankind is conceived in terms of its human essence and with a
teleology that is bound up with great men and nationalism. The Native
peoples are given a place simply to introduce the Conquest.

The 1985/6 syllabuses

In November 1985 the new democratic government of the Province of Buenos
Aires published the draft of the new educational syllabus and the definitive
version was published a year later. This final version has been in use since 1987
(Dirección General de Escuelas 1986).

The main goals of the social science and natural science areas are the same: to
'apply spatial, temporal, and causal concepts in cultural and natural processes'
(Dirección General de Escuelas 1985, 1986), assuming that in both nature and
society the same kind of relationships exist, and that the differences between
social and natural sciences are only in their object of study.

But a comparison of the two documents (draft and definitive version) reveal
that some changes were made in the short time between them. The general
structure and goals of the syllabus remain as they had been conceived in 1985,
but the *whole* of the social science area was changed.

In 1985, the social-historic diversity of the world is emphasized, as shown
by subjects conceived as the 'great themes' of American history: the origins of
man in the Americas, the culture of Native people in prehispanic times, the
contact situation and the European possession of the land. In 1986, however,
the understanding of human essence, as it appears in national culture, is the
point of departure to knowledge of other times and peoples (Podgorny In
Press).

In spite of this shift to an ahistorical approach, consistent with the original
(1975) curricula, anthropological and archaeological 'organisational structures', are subjects defined in terms of social entities. These subjects are set out
in the following order: family, school, town, local communities, locality,
province, regional configurations, aboriginal communities, Argentinian
society, and Latin American societies.

The structure 'aboriginal communities' is defined as follows: 'Native or
original groups, bearers of different cultures, now very few, marginalized and
without real integration in the national society' (Dirección General de Escuelas
1986, p. 122).

Although it is not made explicit, the order in which such structures are
presented is the order in which they are taught. They progress from local to
general levels, the last section being concerned with the history and the
territory of America. This sense of order is violated, however, by the treatment of 'aboriginal communities' – and this break in the logic betrays the fact

that this subject is regarded as different from the others in the social panorama. By its position, this subject should be more comprehensive than 'regional configurations' and less so than 'Argentinian society' – but whereas the others are progressive steps to the building of an 'us' (the Latin American peoples), the 'aboriginal communities' are part of an 'other'.

This presentation of 'aboriginal communities' is accomplished in two ways: (1) as a descriptive feature of other subjects, and (2) as an isolated subject. In the first instance, the presence or absence of aborigines is one of the features used in describing the specific 'province' or 'locality' (as in the 1975 and 1980 curricula). In the second, 'aboriginal communities' are presented as an autonomous entity, part of the historical development of Argentinian society – in contrast to other groups, which are described in terms of *how they function* and *their present traits*. The 'aboriginal communities' history is for the period 'peopling of the Americas to our present days'; archaeology is presented as the way of recovering this past (Podgorny 1990, p. 187).

Native peoples are therefore *not presented* in the totality of facts of the national history. They only participate in events related to the consolidation of boundaries (Dirección General de Escuelas 1986, pp. 128–36).

The curriculum was supported by several information brochures about Native peoples; these brochures reveal clearly how they were conceived in Argentinian society. In the brochure about aboriginal inhabitants of the Province of Buenos Aires (Dirección de Ensernanza Primaria 1986), for example, addressed to educationalists from Superintendents to schoolteachers, refers to 'rethinking possible ways of going back to the ways of living *different from our own*, considering *the others*, . . . *coming near to* the peoples whose descendants still inhabit *our land*' (Dirección General de Escuelas, circular no. 74). It is clear to whom the underlined terms refer.

The treatment of Native peoples in this curriculum is therefore an advance on previous ones in that aboriginal people are treated as the original inhabitants, but, as in the earlier curricula, they are isolated from 'national history'. The prehispanic past is regarded as self-evident and is treated as a novelty. As a result of the exclusion of Native peoples from participating in the national history discourse and from the logic of the organizational structure, they are marginalized, placed in the same category as their prehispanic ancestors (Podgorny in Press).

As to the historical vision of Argentina as a Latin American and multicultural/multilingual country, this curriculum establishes clear co-descent relationships with the other American countries since their common origins at least 12,000 years ago. The descent is linked in the first place with the indigenous roots and secondarily with the Spanish and Europeans. The children of the primary schools of Buenos Aires finish their courses with a world whose boundaries are the Atlantic and Pacific Ocean and the Bravo river of Mexico.

Discussion of results

Although there are clear differences between the curricula, there are several common traits. First, aboriginal communities are presented as a sort of 'national prehistory' from a non-indigenous point of view, and Native people are not included in discussions of 'national history'. Second, history is conceived as the search for antecedents that are rooted in the very nature of the land and its people.

In the 1975 curriculum, nationalism is an assumption and each historic event is an indication of its existence. It assumes that there is such a thing as 'Argentinian-ness' which persists although the population has changed historically (from the Hispano-American to the workers). It also assumes that the spirit of the nation existed prior to its constitution. Given that this curriculum considers each nation as having a single culture, the logic that results is one in which aboriginal peoples are placed together as a unit contemporary with the European conquest, following which they disappear, subsumed under the national tradition: the aboriginals become Argentinian.

In 1980, a uniform national culture or consciousness is also an assumption. National culture is an essence which appears in the work of the 'great men', and that, like the country itself, pre-dates the constitution of the Argentinian nation. A Spanish legacy is overestimated and Christian values are among the more frequent topics of the syllabus. Native peoples are considered in the same way as in 1975, although care is taken to emphasize the positive attitude of the Spanish missionaries and conquerors towards them.

Finally, in 1985/6, the nation is presented as a multicultural entity including aboriginal and Negro slave communities. The Argentinian lineage is an Indo-American one, although contemporary Argentina is also presented as inherent, in seminal form, in the past.

Current ideas about the past among Argentinian teachers

In attempting to develop a teaching programme that contains a more realistic treatment of the social diversity of the nation, it is important to know what relationship exists between the received knowledge promulgated through the curricula and the attitudes and practices of teachers employed to pass this knowledge on to the younger generations. The relatively rapid shifts in the focus and content of Argentinian curricula provide an interesting comparison between what a curriculum idealizes and what is actually taught in schools.

In 1989 we (Podgorny & Pérez n.d.) interviewed primary-school teachers in order to survey the current perspective of their teaching. Our assumption was that they would not have uniform points of view. The interviews focused on the teaching of history and the teaching of social sciences, as well as on the presentation of aboriginal societies in the new curriculum. Their comments were analysed taking into consideration the main themes and contradictions which occurred in the answers.

The results of these interviews revealed two ways of considering reality in the 'social sciences': the first excludes the children from active participation in the educational process, whereas the second takes the wishes of the children into account.

The teachers who exclude children

The first group considers that history and social sciences are located in museums and libraries – part of a cultural network from which they believe their pupils are socially excluded. Unfortunately, social science discourse never takes this 'reality' into consideration – the subject of social research is abstract, unobtainable, subjective and impossible to test. In contrast, this group finds the natural sciences easy to teach and experience – even outside an educational context. One of the teachers states:

> Perhaps I prefer natural sciences because there you don't find contradictions, you don't ask yourself whether you exist or not. In natural sciences, things are as they are. In social sciences I ask myself 'What am I teaching?' My own child reads a lot and he tells me things at odds with what I have always thought.

This group of teachers assumes that their world is different from that of their pupils and, in consequence, the problems of the teaching of history are rooted in a world of conflicting codes and a lack of mutual understanding. Indeed, the gulf between teacher and pupil is regarded as inevitable, as history is conceived of as a discourse of changing subjects, which can only be understood by those who know how to sort out the different versions, i.e. those in elite cultural networks who study books. In contrast, the teachers do not regard the natural world as a problematic subject because they think that it is perceived in the same way by all social classes.

The teachers who include children

The second group of teachers teach from the same world as the child. Their identification with the children is not based on common origins, however, but on the common goals they share for the future. Unlike the first group, they do not regard history and social sciences as particularly problematic fields of teaching.

One teacher refers to history as follows:

> I am very interested in history. I think there are two mankinds, one of the oppressed and the other of the oppressors. The first wants life, the second power, and history is a mirror of this. I like so much that song by nebbia . . . 'Si la historia la escriben los que ganan eso quiere decir que hay otra historia, la verdadera historia, quien quiera oir que oiga' [If history is written by winners, that

means there is another history, the true history; you who want to listen, please hear this song].

(Teacher of fifth B grade)

These teachers believe that the aim of education is not to fix a single version of history in the minds of children, but to teach children how to analyse different points of view in order to find out which is the best. Neither mentioned the 'national' past, however, although one did disagree with the idea of a national folklore. They consider family and mankind, with special reference to the oppressed, as the appropriate levels of analysis – and social structures – within which children have to recognize themselves.

Teaching about the past: an unfortunate convergence of attitudes

When it comes to interpreting the past, however, the differences between these groups dissolve. Both groups mentioned the same resources: research guides, time lines (chronological structures), and handbooks. These kinds of resources are promoted through teachers' meetings and they are widely accepted, at least publicly. And both groups agreed that the 'time line', a method of representing history in a chronological chart, was the best way of solving the problems involved in the teaching of temporal succession. They concurred in the belief that it is not possible to understand time and to teach it without reference to a geometric representation.

This conception of time reflects a fundamental problem with teaching about the past that can be directly connected to the conceptions of time and history present in the various Argentinian curricula. The use of the 'time line' portrays time as space, with the facts of the past following one another in a linear and progressive fashion. This suggests a lack of historicity, evident not only in the presentation of the indigenous past but also in the tendency to transform history into a closed system of certain facts with a persistent relation to two associated ideals: an immanent sense of nation and its inevitable progress, bound up in the character of the landscape. Indeed, the temporality mainly mentioned at school is that of the school almanac, i.e. patriotic and liturgical dates connected with the cycle of school rituals. Other times, such as those of the past and present of the aboriginal peoples, are far away from primary education – history reduced to geography: 'They [the Indians] are still close to their origins, and we can not deny that they provide an easy way of teaching geography' (Teacher of fifth B grade).

Conclusion

This chapter has considered one of the most difficult problems facing contemporary education about archaeology and the past in Argentina. Since the nineteenth century it has been widely believed that the behaviour of a whole society can easily be shaped and controlled through education and other means of ideological reinforcement. The teaching of history and the other aspects of the past have been important in this process in order to promote the concept of 'national identity', which is seen as an important ideological tool. As this chapter has shown, however, the past in Argentina is anything but unified, as it has been shaped according to the ideological and social aims of the government in power. Each military and democratic government has had its own economic and political projects and it has implemented them, as a matter of routine, in the field of education. Argentinian educational policies have therefore been preoccupied with overturning policies promoted by previous governments. Indeed, 'national identity' has changed its roots as often as the Head of the Ministry of Education has changed: a 'national identity' focused on workers and the Third World was first replaced by the notion of a closed Argentinian society without any ancestors beyond those connected with the Christian essence and then, finally, transformed into a more broadly focused concept, linking Argentina with other Latin American countries and, for the first time, presenting Native peoples' history in its own temporal framework.

Unfortunately, each attempt at creating a unified, 'national' culture has largely failed to consider what is so obvious in the present, the social and economic diversity – and inequalities – of Argentinian society. These ideological changes have therefore had a considerable impact on individual teachers, as they are confronted with the problem of translating abstract ideals into realities for students who may not, for social or economic reasons, fit into the scope of the national vision. After seeing how the Ministry of Education has spent time and money in continually modifying the ways of presenting history, some teachers react against these impositions, developing their own social position and ideological stance. All that this individual action accomplishes, however, is the dilution of constructive criticism of the curriculum and, hence, the perpetuation of the historical legacy of the system as a whole, with its outdated means of representing the complexity of the past. If we want an educational system that better reflects our cultural heritage and provides hope for the future, we must look beneath idealized national identities and cultures to people in their actual social, political and historical contexts and create educational curricula that are more in keeping with the daily lives of teachers and their students.

Acknowledgements

I would like to thank my advisors Lic. Marfa Rosa Neufeld and Drs Gustavo Politis and Guillermo Ranea for their constant help, as well as Marta Colombo, Melida Dalla Valle and Beatriz Simonchini for their help in finding a copy of the 1980 curriculum. I also thank Pablo Ben for his comments with regard to the translation of the Spanish and original version of this paper.

References

Dirección de Ensenanza Primaria 1986. *Circular general technica no. 74, nuestros primeros habitantes*. La Plata.

Dirección General de Escuelas 1985. *Anteproyecto de lineamientos curriculares de educación basica*. Buenos Aires: Ediciones Siemens Ocampo.

Dirección General de Escuelas 1986. *Lineamientos curriculares de educacion basica: primaria*. La Plata.

Ediciones 'La Obra' 1975. *Planeamientos curriculares bonaerenses: ciencias naturales y estudios sociales, 40 a 70 grados*. Buenos Aires: Ediciones 'La Obra'.

Ediciones Siemens Ocampo 1980. *Planeamientos curriculares bonaerenses: estudios sociales, 40 a 70 grados*. Buenos Aires: Ediciones Siemens Ocampo.

Podgorny, I. 1990. The excluded present: archaeology and education in Argentina. In *The Excluded Past: archaeology in education*, Stone, P. & R. MacKenzie (eds), 183–9. London: Unwin Hyman; Routledge pbk 1994.

Podgorny, I. In Press. Los indios comain dinosaurios: la presentación del pasado indifena en las escuelas primarias del Gran Buenos Aires, Argentina. *Relaciones de la Sociedad Argentina de Antropología* 18.

Podgorny, I. & C. Perez. n.d. El pasado indifena en los lineamientos curriculares de educación basica de la Republica Argentina. Unpublished manuscript.

Rockwell, E. 1982. De huellas, bardas y veredas: una historia cotidiana en la escuela. *Cuadernos de Investigaciones Educativas* 4.

Sarmiento, D. F. [1882] 1915. *Conflicto y armonias de las razas en America*. Buenos Aires: La Cultura Argentina.

Tedesco, J. & B. Carciofi 1987. *El provecto educativo autoritario: Argentina 1976–1982*. Buenos Aires: Mino & Davila.

PETER WADE

Introduction

Archaeology and anthropology in Colombia, in common with many other
Latin American countries, have largely ignored the black population which
makes up a sizeable proportion of the country's citizens. The national Gold
Museum of the state Bank of the Republic in Bogotá, and its various branches
around the country, are concerned almost exclusively with Indian society and
culture, displaying a huge testament to the rich pre-Columbian past of the
nation's modern indigenous peoples. Despite its name, which should be an
invitation to examine the crucial role of blacks in gold-mining in Colombia or
indeed traditions of gold-working in Africa, the remit of the museum is
explicitly related to the pre-Columbian era; the idea of presenting information
to the public on the history of parts of Africa which provided the millions of
slaves who were forcibly brought to the Americas or on black history in
Colombia does not figure in this kind of enterprise. Similarly, the notion of
doing archaeological research on old black communities scarcely exists.
Naturally, this kind of bias transmits itself to the educational curricula, and
black history and culture hardly make an impact on the average school
student.

   To be more specific, nowhere in Colombia is there a museum display about
black people, African history, slavery, or the role that blacks have played in
the nation. The Bank of the Republic has a branch in Quibdó, the capital of the
Chocó, the so-called black province of Colombia where 90 per cent of the
population is black because their regional history has been dominated by
colonial gold-mining based on regimented slave labour. This branch has a
Cultural Centre with a library and an auditorium where lectures and talks are
arranged. The library, used primarily by local school-children, is filled with
standard books to help them with classroom assignments; there is no special
collection of texts about black people, nor about the region itself. This task is
fulfilled to some extent by the private collection of a priest who publishes a
local newspaper and has built up a databank about the Chocó, but this is more

specialized regional information and is rarely used as a classroom resource. The talks arranged by the Cultural Centre's director during 1992 focused mainly on Indian cultures and societies, or more general themes.

In school curricula, there is virtually no coverage of issues connected with the long-standing presence in Colombia of a large population of black people. History textbooks tend to have a brief section on slavery in which this blot on the nation's history is consigned to the 'bad old days'. Geography textbooks may acknowledge the existence of blacks, but generally only in passing, since the emphasis is principally on Colombia as a mixed nation (Wade 1991).

There are, however, a few indications that things are beginning to change. For example, in 1989, I was asked by the director of the Cultural Centre of the Medellín branch of the Bank of the Republic to prepare an outline for an exhibition about black culture in Colombia. The current national director of the Bank's Gold Museum has been acquainted with my work for some ten years now and is well aware of the biases characteristic of anthropology and museums in Colombia: she was partly instrumental in this initiative. I submitted the outline, but have heard nothing since, and recently learned that the Medellín director's time had been occupied with a complex exhibition about stamp-collecting. It remains to be seen whether the planned exhibition ever materializes, but anyway the possibility of mounting it during 1992, the quincentenary of Columbus's encounter with the Americas, has now been lost.

A further more significant development is the new constitution of 1991 in which 'the state recognizes and protects the ethnic and cultural diversity of the nation'. This is partly a token gesture and, in keeping with the Indian bias of the state, actually recognizes and protects Indians much more than blacks (see next page); but it is a move in the right direction. As an example of the practical results of this change, the Colombian Institute of Culture, as part of a recent series called 'Children of Colombia', produced a volume entitled *Niños de Colombia negra* (Children of Black Colombia) (Van Vliet 1990), aimed at a school audience. This large-format, highly illustrated book runs through some basic history about blacks and slavery, including a page on slave resistance, interspersed with extracts from poems by Jorge Artel, a black Colombian, and Nicolás Guillén, an Afro-Cuban. It then gives a regional description of modern black populations, with brief details of economic practices, some traditional tales, and with much emphasis on the music and dance that blacks are best known for in Colombia. There are hints of folklorization and there is no mention of current inequalities or racial discrimination (which would controvert the still powerful official image of Colombia as a racial democracy), but the book is certainly an improvement on the unstudied silence about blacks that reigned before. As another example of the recent change in emphasis, in April 1992 the Cultural Centre in Quibdó, mentioned above, did actually host a three-day event on black people in Colombia, with talks from researchers at a university in Bogotá which has a recently created team specializing in

Afro-Colombian themes; this team also produces a new journal, *América Negra*, although this is a specialist periodical, not a classroom resource.

There are indications, then, that the state is beginning to complicate simple notions of a progressively more homogeneous mixedness as the principal image for Colombian nationhood. These are small changes and arguably tokenist in character, but, more to the point here, they are still highly biased towards the Indian population. Of course, this is not to say that the indigenous population, simply because it receives more attention from the state and the intellectual community than the blacks, has a better material position. Arguably, the position of the Indians in Colombia has been worse in many respects than that of the blacks. The interesting point is to understand, first, why the difference exists and second, what its significance is. This chapter looks at some of the reasons why blacks and Indians have a different status in modern Colombia, going back to the beginning of the colonial era. The significance of the difference is perhaps more problematic, but the different ways Indians and blacks related to the recent process of constitutional reform is indicative of the issues involved.

Under the government of Virgilio Barco (1986–90), the notion of constitutional reform was tabled with a view to altering relations between the traditional Liberal and Conservative parties, and to open up a political arena for negotiating peace in a country torn by guerrilla and drug wars. During 1990, a Constituent Assembly was convened, leading to national elections for delegates to the Assembly in December of that year. The traditional political forces, plus candidates from recently disarmed guerrilla movements, dominated the delegates, but the Indian movement also managed to get two representatives elected. There were a number of black candidates, speaking from very different platforms and with little unified organization, but none received sufficient electoral support. In fact, many blacks in rural communities in the black-dominated Pacific coastal region voted for a local Emberá Indian delegate, who spoke from a regionalist platform for local blacks and Indians alike. Although blacks continued to lobby the Assembly, they managed to get little in the way of concessions in the new Constitution, ratified on 5 July 1991. The Indians negotiated a number of articles in their favour, including rights to their native languages, rights to land, and the right to elect two indigenous senators. At the last moment the blacks managed to push through a 'transitory article' giving potential collective land rights to rural riverine black communities traditionally occupying 'state-owned' land. The transitory nature of the article means that its actual content has to be worked out and presented to Congress for ratification by 5 July 1993, or it effectively lapses. The Government stalled for a year in convening the special commission needed to negotiate the article, and finally installed it on 11 August 1992, with representatives of the Government and the black communities of the Pacific coastal region.

The issues raised by these events are complex. The Indians clearly worked from a more solid organizational base, with a longer history of mobilization, more national and international financial and advisory support, and with a clearer public image at many different levels of their identity and purpose. This paid off in concrete constitutional rights and the presence of indigenous senators in Congress. The blacks worked from a much more fragmented and weaker organizational foundation, with little support from non-blacks, and a less well-defined public image of who they were, what they were fighting for, and on what basis they were claiming special treatment. In this sense, the Indians clearly had the advantage. Yet it would be hard to argue that in general material terms they were actually any better off, or suffered less discrimination in everyday life.

In sum, then, there are clearly important differences between the positions of blacks and Indians in the Colombian social order, and in what follows, I explore the historical reasons behind these differences. The real significance of those differences can cut two ways, and it remains to be seen whether the political rights won by Indians will translate into effective action on their behalf, and whether the blacks will succeed in creating an ethnic identity for themselves that looks increasingly 'Indian-like'.

Perspectives on blacks and Indians

The history of European settlement in what is now Latin America has two major strands. It is story full of cruelty and tragedy: the massacre and oppression of Native people and Africans, their rebellion and resistance. But there is also a parallel narrative which is about the adaptation of some of both populations to the culture of the dominant stratum of colonial society, in large part through processes of *mestizaje*, mixture, understood in both sexual and cultural senses, which created new cultural identities.

The recognition of this duality of oppression and discrimination balanced with adaptation and mixture has shaped a certain academic perspective on Latin American society that, while recognizing the differences between black and indigenous populations, sees them as occupying basically analogous positions in the socio-racial order. Both are in the lowest strata of societies, colonial and postcolonial, but both are also involved, to a greater or lesser extent, in the processes of *mestizaje* on which many Latin American countries, among them Colombia, have founded their ideologies of national identity. This perspective on the modern era is represented, for example, in the work of Whitten on Ecuador (Whitten 1981, 1985) and Córdoba (1983) on Colombia. My own work on Colombia is also partly based on this view. Its symbol is a triangle, representing the social structure, of which the two lower corners are the Indian and black populations and the uppermost point is the dominant white minority. The middle ground represents the mixed majority to which all three poles contribute, although in a context of unequal power relations.

A second perspective, while not opposed to the first, emphasizes a slightly different aspect of the situation. It focuses on the differences in the positions of the blacks and the Indians, historically and today, even if in general terms there are broad similarities between them. In Colombia, this perspective is associated with the idea of the 'invisibility' of the blacks, a slogan made famous by the anthropologist Nina de Friedemann (e.g. 1984). While the vast majority of both the Native American and the black populations are found at the lowest levels of the society, the plight of the blacks is commonly ignored, and they are marginalized by the state, by educational institutions, and by the academic and literary worlds. The symbol of this perspective is the image of Colombian anthropology itself which, in a country with many more blacks than Indians, dedicates the vast majority of its efforts to the study of indigenous society and culture.

It is not a question of privileging one perspective over the other, since both are valid and neither opposes the other. Whitten and Friedemann, for example, have done collaborative work (Whitten & Friedemann 1974). The point is to grasp both the similarities and the differences between the location of the category 'Indian' and the category 'black' in society, both colonial and modern. In broad terms, the similarity lies in the fact that both categories of people have been considered as Other, above all in the colonial context, but also today; while the principal difference consists in the way each category has fitted into the structures of alterity. Despite temporal and regional variation, the condition of *alter* for the Indians has always been and continues to be much more sharply defined, partly because the category 'Indian' has been juridically constituted.

The alterity of the blacks is more ambiguous. Although in the fifteenth century Africans were considered by most Europeans to be barbarians and infidels – that is Other with little room for doubt – once within colonial society their status took on a different aspect. The identity of the blacks was not as institutionalized as that of the Indians, partly because the social condition of being black soon ceased to correspond in an automatic fashion to the status of slave, because of processes of manumission and also *cimarronaje*, slave flight. This ambiguity is also characteristic of the modern era. The particularity of the category 'black', as it has been historically constituted in Latin America, consists in the possibility for non-black people of seeing blacks as ordinary citizens with no right to claim some kind of special status (as Indians have done) and, at the same time, to exclude blacks because they are blacks, and as such, Other and inferior (although also, of course, potentially in possession of mysterious and dangerous powers). In contrast, the otherness of the Native Americans has been the object of a great deal of reflection and manipulation by colonial and postcolonial elites and this has sharpened its definition and raised its profile.

The colonial era

From the beginning of the conquest, Indians and the New World took on in the minds of Europeans an aspect very distinct from that of blacks and Africa. Perhaps the clearest indication of this was the different legal and moral status accorded to Indian and black slavery. Laws did not, of course, dictate social reality, but the fact that Indians and blacks had very different legal positions is indicative of a difference in their places in the racial order.

Roman and canon law agreed that slavery was contrary to natural law (Davis 1970, p. 113), but it was also permitted by both legal traditions (not to mention the Bible and Aristotelian philosophy) under certain conditions, such as for the captives of a 'just' war (usually meaning a war against infidels) or as a punishment for criminal acts. When the Spanish encountered American Indians, the initial tendency was to fit them into existing categories, classing them as 'barbarians', an Aristotelian category of 'uncivilized' people, that is without cities, political organization or the use of reason. In the Christian view, these characteristics were closely linked to paganism (Pagden 1982, pp. 18–22). Paganism and barbarism were strong grounds for justifying slavery. Indians were also initially classified as 'natural slaves', another Aristotelian category of people who, lacking the full range of human faculties, were naturally destined for slavery (Pagden 1982, Ch. 3).

But early on, both classifications became a major bone of contention. The Native Americans were clearly pagans, but the authority of the Pope over people who had never heard the Word of God was open to doubt. Could a war against such people be a 'just' one? Equally, the concept of a natural slave went against the idea of the unity and equality of humanity before God, because it presupposed a class of people who were not fully human. And by the 1520s and 1530s, the information available about Native society clearly showed that the Indians were humans and had the use of reason.

Some Spanish theologians, particularly from the School of Salamanca, began to propose less deterministic theories. Indians were said to be inferior to the European in terms of their level of civilization, and because of various practices that were contrary to 'natural law', specifically human sacrifice and cannibalism (both supposedly widespread in the Americas). But they were not *natural* slaves; they were more accurately comparable to children.

This point of view had its opponents, but it became widely accepted in Iberian Church and state circles, and Indian slavery was formally abolished in 1542 in Spanish America and in 1570 in Brazil. Of course, reality was a rather different matter, and in some peripheral regions and in Brazil Indian slavery persisted into the eighteenth century.

It would be unrealistic to suppose that the ponderings of a group of Spanish theologians were the only, or even the principal, cause of the abolition of Indian slavery. Other factors also played an important role. First, the Iberians had taken political and administrative control of the American territories and the inhabitants were vassals of the Crown. It was difficult to justify a just war against them on these grounds alone. The act of enslavement had to be done by the colonists themselves, and while they might have been quite willing, the legitimacy of the act provoked serious doubts. Second, the presence of the Iberians, and especially the clergy, in the conquered territories meant that the terrible impact of the conquest was openly visible. It was this that spurred the priest Antonio de Montesinos to protest in 1511 against colonist abuse in Hispaniola. It was widely thought (somewhat mistakenly) that the abolition of slavery would improve material conditions for the indigenous population. Third, the Crown wanted to control the burgeoning power of the colonists by limiting their access to Native labour power; while the Church, mindful of the speedy decline in the numbers of recent and potential converts, also opposed slavery on more self-interested grounds (Harris 1974). The abolition of Indian slavery thus obeyed a number of material and political, as well as moral, imperatives. The point is that the nature of the Indian as a type of human being had occasioned a great deal of theological reflection which eventually weighed in against slavery. These scholarly ponderings shaped actual laws that may only have been effective in the measure that they encountered little opposition from colonists: where the latter found the prohibition on Indian slavery burdensome due to lack of alternative forms of labour, they carried on enslaving the Native Americans. Nevertheless, the mere fact of reflection, discussion, and the promulgation of relevant legislation indicates that the Indians already occupied a particular place in the colonial order.

For blacks, however, the situation was quite distinct. Despite a few clerical critics (Davis 1970, pp. 210–20), slavery was never seriously questioned as a legitimate status for blacks. Manumission from slavery was enshrined both in law derived from the thirteenth-century Siete Partidas and constituted in the colonies by piecemeal legislation, and in slave-owners' practice, but the idea of black slavery was legally and socially accepted, and was only questioned when the legitimacy of the entire institution was cast into doubt. Protest at indigenous slavery had only questioned its appropriateness for Indians. As Davis observes, there was a clear 'double standard in judging Negroes and Indians' (Davis 1970, p. 24).

The causes of this difference are several. First, Africa was already known and classified in contemporary notions about the world and its peoples. It was a region of barbarians like the New World, but more important it was a continent of infidels, where some of the inhabitants had actively rejected the Christian faith, a rejection which branded the rest of the population with the same taint of infidel. Various papal bulls had conceded to the Portuguese the right to make just war against all Africans and to enslave them as the captives of such a war. Indeed, one of the most common justifications of African slavery was that it was the best way of converting them to Christianity (Saunders 1982, pp. 36–8). Second, as in the case of the Indians, it was difficult in the long term to sustain the idea that the Africans were natural slaves, once the Portuguese began to have contact with the more complex societies of west Africa. However, many writers and thinkers followed the biblical tradition in which the descendants of Canaan, son of Ham, had been cursed by Noah, condemning them to perpetual slavery. Making the connection between Canaan's offspring and black people, the argument maintained that the slavery of Africans was legitimate. Third, both Davis (1970) and Jordan (1977) argue that the mere fact of dark skin prejudiced Europeans against the Africans, since blackness was associated with evil, dirtiness, danger, and the devil himself. It is, however, difficult to know to what extent these undoubted associations actually legitimated slavery, especially in the minds of those theologians for whom the unity of humankind was a basic principle. Fourth, African slavery was already well established in Europe before the conquest of the New World: African slaves, for example, worked in Lisbon, and by the middle of the sixteenth century about 10 per cent of the city's population was African (Saunders 1982). African slavery in the New World was an easy continuation of patterns already established. Finally, a crucial factor was the virtual absence of real colonization of African territory: the whole process of enslavement was almost entirely in the hands of Africans and a few *lançados* (Afro-Portuguese people who lived in Africa). The question of the legitimacy of slavery was easily avoided, just as the social and demographic impact of the slave trade could go almost unnoticed.

In sum, the reasons why blacks were legally enslaved while Indians escaped this status, at least in theory, are based on a complex of moral and political factors. It was not that Indians were seen in some simple sense as 'superior' beings. Both Indians and Africans were considered to be barbarians and uncivilized; moreover, the practice of cannibalism was believed to be very widespread among the Native Americans, and 'the theme of anthropophagy . . . was inextricably linked to the iconography of the continent' (Mason 1990, p. 6; also see Reyes 1994). But the Indians were not Muslims, there existed no long tradition of enslaving them as the captives of a just war, and they were vassals of the Crown. Thus in the minds of many European thinkers the Africans were very different from the Indians, and this difference shaped laws and in some degree the social life of the Iberian-American world. This is not to claim that the material conditions of the indigenous population were superior to those of the black slaves, but the Indians were the object of the intellectual, administrative and juridical attention of the Spanish and the Portuguese and this could not but affect their historical trajectory.

The results of this attention can be seen in a number of areas of colonial social life. For example, among the colonists it was a common belief that 'a black is worth three Indians' in terms of work output. This depended partly on region, since black slaves were scarce at high-altitude locations like the Potosí mines. But it is difficult to believe that this widespread perception stemmed from a simple difference in physical strength and endurance. The exploitability of the black slaves was also much greater as a result of the very fact of their slavery. Slavery – and this is also true of Indian slavery where it occurred – almost always implies an uprooting: in order to control a slave force it is necessary to uproot the slaves from their families, their communities and their familiar surroundings (Lockhart & Schwartz 1983, p. 72). With the abolition of Indian slavery, the majority of the indigenous population had the possibility of maintaining some kind of link with their communities, and this meant less colonist control of their labour power. In contrast, the black slaves, uprooted from their communities, could be exploited more intensively, despite their multiple forms of resistance, from sabotage to *cimarronaje*.

A second example is the shaping of the definition of the very category 'Indian' by the authorities' view of the indigenous population. Although concepts such as 'blood' and 'parentage' clearly played a major role in the daily classification of a person, in many senses 'Indian' was a bureaucratic, or even fiscal, category. That is, for the colonial Spanish authorities an Indian was typically someone who paid tribute. In their attempt to maintain the distinction, always under threat, between the 'republic of Indians' and the 'republic of Spaniards', the authorities attempted to homogenize the category 'Indian'. In reality, of course, the category was becoming progressively more heterogeneous as some *caciques*, or Indian leaders, accumulated wealth, and spoke and dressed like whites, as many 'Indians' moved to urban areas, and as many *mestizos* began to invade the lands of Indian villages. Nevertheless, the end result of this mode of definition was the creation of a strong link between the social identity of 'Indian' and an administrative category which implied a set of specific rights and obligations. 'Indian' was an institutionalized identity.

In contrast, while 'slave' was an administrative category that, ideally for the authorities, would have remained equivalent to the category 'black', in practice 'black' as an identity did not have a strong institutional basis. It was used as a description of some individuals in parish registers and in some censuses. Frequently, however, broader, more ambiguous categories were used, such as *gente de color*, *gente libre de color*, *pardos* or *mulatos*, terms which included all those who were not slaves, but who had an indeterminate degree of putative African ancestry (see Martínez-Alier 1974; Seed 1982; McCaa 1984; Alden 1987, p. 290). The line between these and the *mestizos* (people of putative Indian–white descent) must have been very difficult to draw and sometimes was ignored: the censuses carried out in colonial New Granada at the end of the eighteenth century used the category *libre* to include all those who were not classified as whites, Indians or slaves (Silvestre 1950; Pérez Ayala 1951). Thus the simple category 'black' did not have much bureaucratic support. The *castas*, a colonial term used to refer to a variable group of mixed people which often corresponded broadly to 'free people of colour', did constitute an object of administrative attention and control. The payment of tribute was imposed on them, from which *mestizos* were exempt, and there were numerous decrees pertaining to their form of dress and their place of residence (Bowser 1972, p. 38; Rout 1976, p. 150). Even so, administrative categories such as 'free people of colour' were a great deal more heterogeneous and ambiguous than the category 'Indian' which, in spite of its own ambiguities, maintained a relatively clear administrative status during the entire colonial era.

Whatever the differences between 'Indian' and 'black' in terms of the institutionalization of social identity, the contempt shown towards black people and black heritage remained marked, exceeding at times that heaped on the indigenous population. For example, in 1514, the marriage of Spaniards and Indians was permitted (although rarely encouraged), while black–white intermarriage was frowned upon more heavily. Regulations decreed in 1778, which betrayed the elite's preoccupation with defending its social position from encroachment by mixed-bloods, obliged whites under 25 years of age to seek parental permission for marriage, the aim being to limit mixed marriages. But the Council of the Indies agreed that white intermarriage with Indians should not be opposed, 'as their origin is not vile like that of the other *castas*'. By 1805, viceregal (or in Cuba, provincial authority) permission was needed for whites of any age to marry persons of black or mulatto origin (Mörner 1967, pp. 37–9; Martínez-Alier 1974).

Not only were Indians and blacks in different positions in colonial society, but so also were their mixed descendants. The Audiencia of Mexico, clarifying the 1778 regulations, observed that *mestizos* and *castizos* (of putative Indian–white descent) 'deserved to be set apart from the other *castas* as was already done in some respects both in law and public esteem' (Mörner 1967, p. 39). 'Other *castas*' here would refer to people of putative white–black and Indian–black descent. The Council of the Indies approved the change in the regulations. The Mexican Audiencia also commented on the marriage between Indians and blacks or mulattos recommending that parish priests be ordered to warn the Indian and his parents of the serious harm that 'such unions will cause to themselves and their families and villages, besides making the descendants incapable of obtaining municipal positions of honour in which only pure Indians are allowed to serve' (cited in Mörner 1967, p. 39). Although in practice differentiating between *mestizos* and other mixed-bloods would prove increasingly impossible, both the law and social attitudes in Latin America viewed Indian descent as preferable to black descent.

Summarizing thus far, it is possible to glimpse the pattern which underlies both the colonial and the modern eras, albeit in different forms. While both Indians and blacks suffered discrimination and contempt in daily life – although in some senses black blood was considered inferior to Indian – blacks were denied, relative to the Indians, an institutional position in the official structures of the society and in the intellectual thought of the age.

This does not mean that Native Americans enjoyed then, or enjoy now, better material conditions of life: evidence could be adduced to show exactly the opposite in many cases and a lot would depend on local and temporal factors. My argument is that, while they were similar in many respects, the positions of the Indians and the blacks during the colonial era were distinct at a given institutional level which both influenced and reflected everyday social life and that this difference then shaped succeeding social structures.

The republican era

With Independence, the legal and administrative regime altered. By 1850, slavery had been abolished in most countries, although it remained in force in Cuba and Brazil. Legal discriminations against the *castas* began to be dismantled. At the same time, many governments took measures against the special status of the Indians. In the liberalizing philosophical climate of nineteenth-century Latin American nations struggling to define their identities, the idea of communal land ownership and a separate ethnic category was inimical. Indian tribute was generally abolished, and legislation was promulgated to undermine the legal basis of the Indian community, although in practice this was frequently ineffective in the absence of actual territorial and economic integration, or in the face of concerted Indian resistance (Halperín Donghi 1987). Thus the Lerdo Law (1856) and the 1857 Constitution in Mexico attacked communal land ownership, while in Colombia, 1861 legislation continued to undermine Indian *resguardos* (reserves) that had been under attack since the colonial Bourbon regime.

However, towards the end of the nineteenth century, this attack on Indian community and identity slowed somewhat and took a rather different course, although with variations in different countries. The context of this change was the development of national ideologies of identity. Between 1850 and 1880, the majority of Latin American nations began to resolve their internal conflicts over federalism and centralism, to improve their communications infrastructure and to consolidate their national bourgeoisies. One of the problems that faced national elites was how to define and represent their national identities in a world already dominated by North American and European nations. Latin American elites wanted their countries to emulate the progress and modernity of European countries, but at the same time there was a need to define a distinctive national, or Latin American, identity. Positivist liberal European thought which espoused values such as liberty, progress, science, education, industry and reason gained widespread acceptance among Latin American intellectual and political elites. But one aspect of the science then developing in Europe was biology, and this discipline was coming up with theories about heredity which argued for the innate and biological inferiority of blacks, Indians and, most threateningly, of mixed-bloods. More broadly, and lending apparent weight to these theories, there was the fact that the countries which were achieving the modernity and progress so desired by the new nations either did not have black or Indian populations, or had them strictly segregated from the white population. In contrast, all the Latin American countries had highly mixed populations and, if their elites accepted at face value this determinist biology and the apparent link between progress, racial purity and whiteness, then they would be condemning themselves to perpetual backwardness.

These themes formed the subject of intense debate in Latin America around the turn of the century and indeed until the Second World War (Zea 1963, pp. 187–8; Skidmore 1974; Jaramillo Uribe 1989, pp. 168–72; Graham 1990; Wright 1990; Stepan 1991). The outcomes of these debates varied from one country to the next, but a central feature was the attempt to compromise between the evidently mixed nature of much of the population, and the apparent link between whiteness and progress towards modernity, a link also expressed in scientific theories of biological determinism.

The compromise consisted partly in an adaptation of these scientific theories which avoided the racial determinism of the European and North American versions, and which insisted on the possibility of improving the characteristics of the population by means of education and public health programmes. European eugenics envisaged (and to some extent even practised) encouraging the reproduction of the 'fittest' individuals, and restricting the reproduction of the least fit. In the intellectual climate of Latin America, this was transformed into policies closer to social hygiene than to eugenics in the strict sense, although the emphasis on biological determination varied according to the ideas of particular medics and thinkers (Stepan 1991). At the same time, doubt was cast on the idea that miscegenation was equivalent to racial degeneration. Instead, the *mestizo* often came to be the very symbol of Latin American identity, and positive reference might be made to the Indian, or even the black, roots of national culture.

This fulfilled the need to outline a distinctive, independent Latin American identity. The other half of the compromise – the need to encompass modernity – consisted in representing *mestizaje* itself as a form of progress. Bit by bit, blacks and Indians would be integrated into the *mestizo* majority of the population, which would gradually begin to approximate the white racial type, without necessarily ever arriving at this point. Sometimes, the white type was attributed greater 'racial' potency, which gave it natural dominance over black and Indian blood, and enabled mixture to be seen as progress. At other times, white immigration was recommended (and indeed received state backing in many countries) in order to help the process of 'whitening' along (Skidmore 1974; Helg 1990; Wright 1990).

In short, for Latin American political and intellectual elites, this compromise allowed the combination of, on the one hand, democratic affirmations that everyone was 'mestizo' together, converting blacks, Indians and *mestizos* into citizens of the nations they governed, and uniting them beneath a national flag which would be distinctive in the global arena and, on the other hand, daily discrimination against blacks and Indians as the representatives of the backward past, behaviour which glorified the pretensions of the elites themselves to be white, or nearly white (Wade 1991).

I have presented this compromise in rather schematic terms to clarify its nature. In fact, the situation was more complex. Countries such as Argentina and Uruguay, which had small black and Indian populations and which had managed to attract large numbers of European immigrants, tended to emphasize their proximity to the European image, giving less room to affirmations of mixedness (Helg 1990; Stepan 1991). Countries such as Mexico or Peru, with large indigenous populations, tended rather to glorify their Native American pasts, although this indigenist ideology had many different variants, and, at least in its 'official' version in Mexico (Brading 1988), exalted the *mestizos*, which the Indians were destined to become, more than the Indians themselves (Hewitt de Alcántara 1984; Knight 1990).

Within a single country there was also variety of opinion. This has been documented, for example, in the case of Venezuela (Wright 1990), or for Brazil (Skidmore 1974). Here, for illustrative purposes, I present two examples from the Colombian material (see Wade 1993).

Laureano Gómez, President between 1949 and 1953, supporter of Franco and arch-conservative, spoke pessimistically in 1928 on the theme of Colombia's progress as a nation. Territory and race were the fundamental elements of nationality and Colombia was badly endowed on both fronts. Its broken territory was cursed with an abundance of tropical jungle, refractory to development. Racially, it had an uninspiring heritage:

> Our race comes from the mixture of Spaniards, Indians and blacks. The latter two flows of heritage are marks of complete inferiority. It is in whatever we have been able to inherit from the Spanish spirit that we must look for the guiding lines of the contemporary Colombian character.
>
> (Gómez 1970, p. 44)

Blacks he saw as living in a state of 'perpetual infantility', with a 'rudimentary and unformed' spirit, and wrapped up in 'the fog of an eternal illusion'. The other 'savage race', the Indians, were a 'barbarous element', resigned to 'misery and insignificance'. Even the Spanish were ecstatic, ignorant and fanatical and, to cap it all, race mixture held out no hopes since 'the psychic aberrations of the parent races become more acute in the mestizo' (Gómez 1970, pp. 44–7).

In this vision, the process of *mestizaje* is viewed with pessimism and the tendency is to base images of nationality only on Europeanness. However, this speech was strongly criticized for its pessimism, its environmental determinism, and its representation of the Spanish and Indian heritage. In a second speech, Gómez defended himself by lauding some features of Spanish and of Aztec and Inca cultures. Colombia was not doomed, he said, but simply in need of a firm hand to guide it out of the dire straits in which it found itself (Gómez 1970, pp. 67–140). Apparently, no one attacked his views on blacks, since he saw no need to defend himself on that score.

Luis López de Mesa, a contemporary thinker, took a rather different approach. Philosopher and essayist, he published in 1934 a small volume on the Colombian nation. He identifies in blacks and mulattos the traits of 'fantasy, sensuality and laziness' (López de Mesa 1970, p. 97), but he is equally critical of the endogamic white elite of Popayán. White immigration would tend to 'enrich the qualities of our racial fusion', but the emphasis is as much on the social input of skills and habits as on the 'enrichment of [Colombia's] good stock' (López de Mesa 1970, pp. 122–3). In this vision, then, while blacks and Indians are not seen as an ideal heritage, transmitting certain traits of laziness (López de Mesa 1970, p. 19), neither are they roundly castigated for contaminating the Colombian nation: 'creole laziness is conditioned by elements which can be dominated', such as ill health and undisciplined habits (López de Mesa 1970, pp. 20–1). Here is precisely the idea of social hygiene which Stepan (1991) notes as characterizing Latin American versions of eugenics. Mixedness is valued as encouraging democracy and lack of social distinction. 'We are Africa, America, Asia and Europe all at once, without grave spiritual perturbation,' and this becomes not 'the old democracy of equality of citizenship only for the conquering minority, but an integral [democracy] without distinctions of class or breed' (López de Mesa 1970, pp. 14, 13). This affirmation of democratic mixedness diverges from the outspoken condemnation of blacks and Indians characteristic of other perspectives, but with the emphasis on mixed populations, blacks and Indians as such tend to vanish into peripherality, appearing occasionally, like the Cauca valley blacks, who are 'constantly lazy, almost vegetative' (López de Mesa 1970, p. 108).

In these representations of national identity, it is clear that recourse is much more readily made for symbols of nationhood and its roots to images of Native American than to blacks or Africa. The attempt, noted above, to dissolve the institutional identity of the Indian began to slow down, partly due to the recognition of the negative impacts of this process (Safford 1987, p. 89), and partly because the image of the Indian began to form an element in representations of national identity. In Peru, the *comunidad indígena* was recognized as a juridical category in the 1920 Constitution under the Leguía administration, which also created a department for indigenous affairs and the national Día del Indio. In Mexico, a Departamento de Asuntos Indígenas was created in 1936, an Instituto Indígena Interamericano in 1940, and an Instituto Indígena Nacional in 1948. In Peru and to an even greater extent in Mexico, Indians also became a positive element in an indigenist discourse about nationality, although *indigenismo* had, and has, different variants and so a single exponent like Manuel Gamio, director of the Instituto Indígena Interamericano, could mix romantic glorification of Indian culture with more positivist notions of education and incorporation into a single *mestizo* nation (Brading 1988). While 'official *indigenismo*' was ultimately strongly incorporationist and relied on ideas about Indian backwardness and a future of *mestizo* homogeneity, the point is that Indians were also given a symbolic role as emblems of national identity, or perhaps the roots of national identity, even while they were exploited and disparaged in practice. A glorious Indian past could be useful as a badge of Latin American originality.

All this may not be surprising in societies with large Indian populations. In Colombia, too, with under half a million 'Indians' at current estimates, a similar situation exists (also see Reyes 1994). There, legislation passed in 1890 braked slightly the movement to divide up Indian *resguardos*, or reservations, and also legalized Indian councils. This was with the express intention of 'governing' and 'civilizing' the Indians. Although much subsequent legislation continued to undermine Indian land rights, *resguardos* still exist today under the terms of the 1890 decree (Valencia y Valencia 1972; García 1978). In the 1920s and 1930s, the radical thought of José Mariátegui and Víctor Raúl Haya de la Torre in Peru, and the work of Moises Saénz and Manuel Gamio in Mexico, impinged upon an intellectual circle which in 1942 created the Instituto Indígena de Colombia as an unofficial entity. These beginnings were to define the scope of Colombian anthropology (and ethnohistory) from then on. Seminal writers all concentrated overwhelmingly on Indian themes. Only three early anthropologists focused on blacks (Friedemann & Arocha 1979). This bias transmitted itself to the departments of anthropology set up in the 1960s and 1970s, often under the direct aegis of these researchers, and these departments again designed their curricula principally around the study of Indians (Friedemann 1984; Pineda Camacho 1984).

The state was also concerned with the 'Indian problem' and, although it devolved a good deal of control to the churches, it also founded in 1941 the Instituto Etnológico Nacional, to become the current Instituto Colombiano de Antropología in 1961. In 1960, the state created a División de Asuntos Indígenas, which effectively monopolized all development initiatives which affected Indians.

Indians in Colombia, then, as in other Latin American countries, have been a category of special interest for intellectuals and the state – which is not to say that their objective conditions of livelihood have therefore been improving. Although Indianness as a symbol of national identity does not have the same power as in Mexico or Peru, the concern with Indians among the intellectual elite gives them some of this status (and in any case the *mestizo* is always a preferable image of mixedness in Colombian nationalist discourse to that of the mulatto).

Blacks, while sharing in many respects the contempt heaped upon Indians in daily life, take a rather different place in Latin American racial orders. Simply put, blacks have been of much less interest to the states, intellectual elites and the *mestizo* populations of Latin America. In literary circles, especially from the 1930s, and particularly in Cuba, there did emerge important currents of prose and poetry that unearthed themes related to blackness and addressed them directly (Jackson 1976; Mullen 1988; see also Friedemann 1984, pp. 520–38), but this did not generally manage to cast blacks in the same mould as Indians. In Brazil, with its very large black population and clearly differentiated traits of black culture, there has been a tendency to do for blacks what other countries had done for Indians. There in the 1930s, writers like Arthur Ramos, and especially Gilberto Freyre and Edison Carneiro, attempted to recast the negative evaluations cast on blackness and African heritage, reassessing their role in the definition of Brazilian national identity. Parallel to some currents of *indigenismo*, the perspective was essentially integrationist (Skidmore 1974, pp. 184–92). More recently, blackness has become increasingly politicized

(Fontaine 1985) and at the national government level there is now an Assessoria para Asuntos Afro-Brasileiros, attached to the Ministry of Culture.

In Cuba, too, with a large black population and little chance of appealing to Indian origins, the attempts to valorize blackness and Africanness had some basis. Writers like Fernando Ortiz and Alejo Carpentier were important here (although the early work of the former is overtly racist and recommends erasing black culture from Cuban society). However, there was also powerful repression of blackness as a defining element of Cuban nationality: for example, during the so-called Guerrita del 12 (the Little War of 1912), when members of the Independent Coloured Party, along with many other Afro-Cubans, were massacred by members of the armed forces and groups of vigilantes (Helg 1990, p. 55). After the 1959 Revolution, while racial discrimination was soon officially deemed to have been superseded, Castro gave some recognition to the idea of Cuba as a Latin-African state, especially as a justification for making links with African nations. This view, however, gave little space to black identity within the country; it was directed more at the African ancestry of Cubans in general (Taylor 1988).

Venezuelans, on the other hand, 'showed no inclination to idealize the African contribution to their culture' (Wright 1990, p. 113). In the 1940s, several authors did address the theme of blackness and black culture in a positive fashion, although generally from an assimilationist standpoint (Wright 1990, p. 119). But these writers formed a minority voice.

In Colombia, very few people among the political and intellectual classes have had much interest in romanticizing or glorifying the African or black heritage of the nation's culture (for some exceptions see Jackson 1976 and Friedemann 1984). Very few academics are concerned with black communities, past or present, with most work being concentrated on the institution of slavery, rather than on blacks as such (e.g. Jaramillo Uribe 1968, pp. 7–84). And no institutes were set up – except recently by the blacks themselves – to study blacks, and certainly not by the state, which only in 1986 helped to finance a congress on blacks (Cifuentes 1986). Friedemann calculates that, between 1936 and 1978, 271 people became professional anthropologists; only five have focused on blacks.

In summary, the image of the black and of the Indian have played very different roles in the representation of Latin American national identity. This is not simply due to the discrimination suffered by blacks, since Indians also suffer discrimination. Rather, it is connected to the fact that, since the beginning of the colonial era, Indian identity has been the object of intellectual reflection and administrative institutionalization, while black identity has not, or at least not in the same form.

Conclusion

I began by illustrating the differences between the status of blacks and Indians in some aspects of contemporary Colombia, and by outlining two complementary perspectives on the place of these two populations in the social order. One was symbolized by a triangle, representing the racial structure of the country, in which blacks and Indians were located in the lower strata, whence the process of osmosis into the middle strata was accompanied by *mestizaje*, both sexual and cultural. The other perspective emphasized the 'invisibility' of the blacks compared to the Indians.

I have tried to show how black identity is different from Indian identity in certain respects – a difference which tends to get lost in the first perspective – and to show too how the invisibility of blacks is not due simply to racism or discrimination, understood as homogeneous phenomena. Rather, invisibility is the result of the conjuncture of two factors. On the one hand, black identity has not received the same institutional support from the Government, colonial and postcolonial, or from the intellectual elite. Instead, blacks have been seen (by non-blacks) as *part of* the growing mixedness which forms the backbone of Colombian nationhood: as such, blacks are citizens like any others. But on the other hand, black heritage, both cultural and consanguineal, has been considered by national elites and by large sectors of the non-black population as a mark of inferiority, even more stigmatized in some respects than Indian heritage. The visibility of blacks is lost between ideologies of whitening which scorn blackness (and Indianness), and affirmations of national *mestizo* homogeneity which rhetorically include blacks as citizens, but by the same token deny them any specific status as the targets of racial discrimination. It is in the possibility of both *including* blacks (as citizens) and *excluding* them (as inferior) that the particularity of their position lies.

This is what differentiates the blacks from the Indians in Colombian social structure. Although Indian political organizations claim rights as citizens, it is much more likely that they will be seen by non-Indians as groups culturally outside national society. One aspect of their identity consists precisely in having different languages and cultures, and indeed part of their claims as citizens is the right to maintain these differences within the Colombian nation (a right officially conceded by the new Constitution). For anthropology, Indians can thus constitute an image of the Other much more easily than can blacks – at least in Colombia, if not perhaps in Brazil. This condition is, of course, a double-edged weapon. Indians can be the object of study and special measures; but they can also be the object of a particularly violent and xenophobic racism. This difference between blacks and Indians can get lost in the first perspective outlined above. Whitten, for example, argues that the dominant society in Ecuador classifies blacks, like Indians, as 'non-nationals' (Whitten 1985, p. 42). For Colombia, too, it is common in academic and planning circles to hear black regions like the Pacific coast contrasted with so-called 'national society', referring to the *mestizo* and white majority of the more central, more developed regions of the country. But it is precisely because black people can be considered in certain contexts as 'nationals' – as indeed in my experience they would classify themselves – that the discrimination that they suffer appears to lose its specifically racial character.

Even more caution is needed with the approach taken by Stutzman (1981), who has suggested that black ethnicity in Ecuador is a conscious volitional idiom of disengagement from national culture and values. By maintaining a degree of cultural and ethnic integrity, blacks are making a statement of dissent from the whole ideology of whitening and the particular concept of nationhood which accompanies it. While some blacks do implicitly or explicitly reject the idea that blackness is inferior and thus contest the idea of *mestizaje* understood as a progressive lightening and erasing of blackness from the national panorama, it would be wrong to envisage this as a 'disengagement' from the Colombian nation as a whole. In my experience, to suggest to any blacks that they were other than Colombian would be nothing less than an affront. Other non-black people may regard some blacks as not fully representative of the Colombian nation, but it would be wrong to suppose that blacks themselves withdraw from Colombian culture and nationhood. Rather, they pose a challenge to the way these are conceived by the non-black majority.

In conclusion, both blacks and Indians have constituted the Other for different sectors of Latin American society and at different times. The nature of this image has varied, but there has been a persistent difference in the way blacks and Indians have fitted into the structures of alterity. In understanding this difference, we can understand why blacks, although in many ways in a position analogous to that of the Indians, have been much less 'visible'. Within black communities there has always been a process of self-definition in independent terms which has contested the construction of the category of 'black' by colonial and national elites: the black as free, not slave; as citizen, not vagrant; as a *sui generis* element of the nation, not as a candidate for *mestizaje*. But this process of self-definition has been difficult, and the problems of black political organization outlined at the beginning of this chapter are a testament to this. The reasons for these difficulties are many (Wade 1993), and here I have analysed just one aspect of the problem: the way black identity has fitted into visions of society that have been controlled over time by various political and intellectual elites.

References

Alden, D. 1987. Late colonial Brazil, 1750–1808. In *Colonial Brazil*, Bethell, L. (ed.), 284–343. Cambridge: Cambridge University Press.
Bowser, F. 1972. Colonial Spanish America. In *Neither Slave nor Free: freedmen of African descent in the slave societies of the New World*, Cohen, D. & J. Greene (eds), 19–58. Baltimore: Johns Hopkins University Press.
Brading, D. 1988. Manuel Gamio and offical indigenismo. *Bulletin of Latin American Research* 7, 75–90.

436   P. WADE

Cifuentes, A. 1986. Introducción. In *La participación del negro en la formación de las sociedades latinoamericanas*, Cifuentes, A. (ed.), 13–42. Bogotá: Instituto Colombiano de Cultura & Instituto Colombiano de Antropología.

Córdoba, J. T. 1983. *Etnicidad y estructura social en el Chocó*. Medellín: Lealón.

Davis, D. B. 1970. *The Problem of Slavery in Western Culture*. Harmondsworth: Penguin Books.

Fontaine, P.-M. (ed.) 1985. *Race, Class and Power in Brazil*. Los Angeles: Centre of Afro-American Studies, University of California.

Friedemann, N. de 1984. Estudios de negros en la antropología colombiana. In *Un siglo de investigación social: antropología en Colombia*, Arocha, J. & N. de Friedemann (eds), 507–72. Bogotá: Etno.

Friedemann, N. de & J. Arocha 1979. *Bibliografía anotada y directorio de antropólogos colombianos*. Bogotá: Sociedad Antropológica de Colombia.

García, A. 1978. Legislación indígena y la política del estado. In *Indigenismo. Enfoques Colombianos*, Temas Latinoamericanos, Monograph no. 11. Bogotá: Fundación Freidrich Neumann.

Gómez, L. 1970. *Interrogantes sobre el progreso de Colombia*. Bogotá: Colección Populibro.

Graham, R. (ed.) 1990. *The Idea of Race in Latin America, 1870–1940*. Austin: University of Texas Press.

Halperín Donghi, T. 1987. Economy and society. In *Spanish America after Independence*, c.1820–c.1870, Bethell, L. (ed.), 37–69. Cambridge: Cambridge University Press.

Harris, M. 1974. *Patterns of Race in the Americas*. New York: Norton Library.

Helg, A. 1990. Race in Argentina and Cuba, 1880–1930. In *The Idea of Race in Latin America, 1870–1940*, Graham, R. (ed.), 37–69. Austin: University of Texas Press.

Hewitt de Alcántara, C. 1984. *Anthropological Perspectives on Rural Mexico*. London: Routledge & Kegan Paul.

Jackson, R. 1976. *The Black Image in Latin American Literature*. Albuquerque: University of New Mexico Press.

Jaramillo Uribe, J. 1968. *Ensayos sobre historia social colombiana, vol. 1: La sociedad neogranadina*. Bogotá: Universidad Nacional.

Jaramillo Uribe, J. 1989. *Ensayos sobre la historia social colombiana, vol. 2: Temas americanos y otros ensayos*. Bogotá: Tercer Mundo.

Jordan, W. 1977. *White over Black: American attitudes toward the Negro, 1550–1812*. New York: Norton.

Knight, A. 1990. Racism, revolution and indigenismo: Mexico, 1910–1940. In *The Idea of Race in Latin America*, Graham, R. (ed.), 70–113. Austin: University of Texas Press.

Lockhart, J. & S. Schwartz 1983. *Early Latin America: a history of colonial Spanish America and Brazil*. Cambridge: Cambridge University Press.

López de Mesa, L. 1970. *De cómo se ha formado la nación colombiana*. Medellín: Ed. Bedout.

McCaa, R. 1984. Calidad, clase and marriage in colonial Mexico: the case of Parral, 1788–90. *Hispanic American Historical Review* 64, 477–501.

Martínez-Alier, V. 1974. *Marriage, Colour and Class in Nineteenth-Century Cuba*. Cambridge: Cambridge University Press.

Mason, P. 1990. *Deconstructing America: representations of the other*. London: Routledge.

Mörner, M. 1967. *Race Mixture in the History of Latin America*. Boston: Little Brown.

Mullen, E. 1988. The emergence of Afro-Hispanic poetry: some notes on canon formation. *Hispanic Review* 56, 435–53.

Pagden, A. 1982. *The Fall of Natural Man: the American Indian and the origins of comparative ethnology*. Cambridge: Cambridge University Press.

Pérez Ayala, J. M. 1951. *Antonio Caballero y Góngora, virrey y arzobispo de Santa Fe, 1723–1796*. Bogotá: Imprenta Municipal.

Pineda Camacho, R. 1984. La reivindicación del indio en el pensamiento social colombiano, 1850–1950. In *Un siglo de investigación social: la antropología colombiana*, Arocha, J. & N. de Friedemann (eds), 197–251. Bogotá: Etno.
Reyes, H. R. 1994. Ethnic representation in Colombian textbooks. In *The Presented Past: heritage, museums and education*, Stone, P. G. & B. L. Molyneaux (eds), 398–407. London: Routledge.
Rout, L. 1976. *The African Experience in Spanish America: 1502 to the present day*. Cambridge: Cambridge University Press.
Safford, F. 1987. Politics, ideology and society. In *Spanish America after Independence, c.1820–c.1870*, Bethell, L. (ed.), 48–122. Cambridge: Cambridge University Press.
Saunders, A. C. de C. M. 1982. *A Social History of Black Slaves and Freedmen in Portugal, 1441–1555*. Cambridge: Cambridge University Press.
Seed, P. 1982. Social dimensions of race: Mexico City, 1753. *Hispanic American Historical Review* 62, 569–606.
Silvestre, F. 1950 [1789]. *Descripción del Reino de Santa Fe de Bogotá, 1789*. Bogotá: Biblioteca Popular de Cultura Colombiana.
Skidmore, T. 1974. *Black into White: race and nationality in Brazilian thought*. New York: Oxford University Press.
Stepan, N. L. 1991. *'The Hour of Eugenics': race, gender and nation in Latin America*. Ithaca: Cornell University Press.
Stutzman, R. 1981. *El mestizaje*: an all-inclusive ideology of exclusion. In *Cultural Transformations and Ethnicity in Modern Ecuador*, Whitten, N. E. (ed.), 45–94. Urbana: University of Illinois Press.
Taylor, F. 1988. Revolution, race and some aspects of foreign relations in Cuba since 1959. *Cuban Studies* 18, 19–44.
Valencia y Valencia, J. 1972. Consideraciones generales sobre la política indigenista de Colombia. *América Indígena* 32, 1285–93.
Van Vliet, E. 1990. *Niños de Colombia negra*. Bogotá: Colcultura & Instituto Colombiano de Antropología.
Wade, P. 1991. The language of race, place and nation in Colombia. *América Negra* 2, 41–66.
Wade, P. 1993. *Blackness and Race Mixture: the dynamics of racial identity in Colombia*. Baltimore: Johns Hopkins University Press.
Whitten, N. 1981. Introduction. In *Cultural Transformations and Ethnicity in Modern Ecuador*, Whitten, N. E. (ed.), 1–41. Urbana: University of Illinois Press.
Whitten, N. 1985. *Sicuanga Runa: the other side of development in Amazonian Ecuador*. Urbana: University of Illinois Press.
Whitten, N. & N. de Friedemann 1974. La cultura negra del litoral ecuatoriano y colombiano: un modelo de adaptación étnica. *Revista Colombiana de Antropología* 17, 75–115.
Wright, W. 1990. *Café con Leche: race, class and national image in Venezuela*. Austin: University of Texas Press.
Zea, L. 1963. *The Latin American Mind*. Norman: University of Oklahoma Press.

31 Traditional American Indian education as a palliative to western education

SHIRLEY BLANCKE & CJIGKITOONUPPA JOHN
PETERS SLOW TURTLE

Introduction: introducing a Native American method into the traditional Euro-American approach to education

It is apparent from the problems which increasingly affect United States youth that the traditional Euro-American approach to education is no longer serving its social purpose in our complex society (also see Ahler 1994; Belgarde 1994). Alternative 'multicultural' forms of education have been widely discussed in educational literature since the 1960s, concerned with what multiculturalism means, what it should mean, and how it might be implemented. As multicultural education usually means teaching Euro-American children about other cultures, however, it cannot provide real understanding of the contemporary social milieu. Such knowledge can only be gained through the mutual experience and interaction of different social groups.

As the United States is a multicultural society, how best may it be made to 'work' in a way that is beneficial to all members of that society? What is the best way to educate children whose origins are in different cultures but whose lives will be intertwined because they live in the same place? A truly multicultural society should have traits of its constituent cultures that are shared for the benefit of all. Deeper understanding may then be developed through fostering relationships on different levels between children of differing cultures (Gunsky 1979). In order to show how such relationships could be encouraged, and how valuable this approach might be in an educational context, the potential contribution of contemporary Native American 'traditional' education to the general educational system in the United States will be considered.

Native American control of education: an illusion

The idea of multiculturalism is that all cultures within the United States be on an equal footing. Euro-American culture has always been dominant and Euro-American society has adopted the 'melting-pot' philosophy: assimilation of people from other cultures through intensive exposure to the values of the dominant culture (also see Ahler 1994; Belgarde 1994). This philosophy is actually a kind of social control, through which one group maintains power over others in the same territory.

The relation between this exercise of power and education has been demonstrated recently in work by archaeologists, anthropologists and educators from around the world (see, for example, the various authors in *The Excluded Past: archaeology in education* (Stone & MacKenzie 1990)). Ucko's (1990) foreword to this book underscores the consensus among its contributors that dominant societies in many nations mould the image of the nation to the exclusion of the histories and cultural understandings of minority peoples within them. Such peoples experience the suppression of their history as dictatorial, imperialist, or even racist (Ucko 1990, p. xv). Native Americans have suffered all these experiences.

Control by Native Americans of their education has therefore been an illusion – an issue that has been of utmost concern to them, as it affects the future of their people. Nearly 90 per cent of Native American youth is now in US public schools scattered all over the country. Even when Native American communities gain some control by contracting out schools from the Federal Government, or by being a majority in the public-school system, what they are controlling is not a Native American educational system, but a system handed to them by the dominant society.

This partial control has its risks. Gerald Wilkinson, a Cherokee and Native American youth leader, pointed out that for the Federal Government of the US, the transfer of control over at least part of the Native educational system to Native Americans has the advantage that if that education fails, the Government no longer has responsibility for it, and if it succeeds, the Government may claim credit for making it possible for the Tribes to triumph (Wilkinson 1981).

Even if Indian culture and history (including archaeology) are added to school curricula, however, such changes can be seen as merely papering over a crack, hiding a much deeper deficiency in the system. Unless a radically different and Native approach is taken, Native American youth will continue to suffer from the social disjunction that is common in schools. Indeed, the troubled character of Native youth is evident in their suicide and drop-out rates: in 1981, for example, the suicide rate was from four to seven times the national average and the drop-out rate two to three times higher (Wilkinson 1981).

Only in those areas of the country where Native Americans are in the majority, mainly in the area of the western reservations, does the possibility for Native control even exist. Although some special cultural programmes created by Native Americans are available to Native youth through the 1972 Indian Education Act, and some locally developed Native American curricula have been instituted, Native children's main exposure in schools is to simplistic cultural stereotypes and a lack of information about their heritage. There are not enough Native teachers, or others sufficiently knowledgeable about Native ways, and so Native American children must be taught by non-Natives who frequently know little about Native culture and history, and may, at worst, have racist attitudes. And standard textbooks provide little support, as they tend to perpetuate traditional stereotypes and misinformation (Blancke & Cjigkitoonuppa 1990).

Native American criticism of Euro-American education

In order to resolve some of these problems, educationalists concerned with Native American education have widely discussed the development and intro-duction of curricula and teaching methods relevant to Native American chil-dren, and how Native parents may make an impact on the schools their children attend (Christensen & Demmert 1978; Locke 1978; Christensen 1990). Some Native Americans in fact advocate not just the institution of special Native programmes, but an overhaul of the whole educational system, with its essentially Euro-American philosophy and goals, maintaining that while the failures of Native youth and those of other US minorities are particularly visible, the system is also failing white youth.

Traditional Native education is seen by many Native Americans as having a more human face than its Euro-American counterpart, since its ideals empha-size the value of the individual human personality over what Natives see as an objective body of knowledge which must be 'consumed'. The dominant system has been accused, for example, of creating mere functionaries for the businesses and bureaucracies of capitalist society (Wilkinson 1981, p. 49). What is certain is that western education has frequently appeared to Indians overly abstract and utterly impractical for their particular needs (Deloria 1981, pp. 59–60).

In two recent papers, Vine Deloria, a Standing Rock Lakota (Sioux), has made many cogent comments on these differences between traditional Native American and modern American (Euro-American) educational styles (Deloria 1990a, 1990b). In his view, the aims of the two approaches are strikingly different: modern American culture has divided knowledge into two separate categories of professional expertise and personal growth and so education has focused on the development of professionalism and expertise without concern-ing itself with the growth of the individual in relation to society. This latter function is considered more appropriate to the family or church but, with the modern decline of these institutions, such values and relations may not be taught at all. Modern American education may therefore help cause indi-viduals to confuse what they do with who they are, or gain no sense of who they are apart from what they do.

Deloria suggests that traditional Native American education, on the other hand, was oriented towards developing the growth of people with strong individual personalities who were also responsible members of the Tribal community (also see Belgarde 1994). Expertise in a particular field was a secondary requirement. This approach not only created people who knew who they were in the social context of relationships: origin stories also expanded their connection to the wider world by giving them relationships with all living beings, with nature and earth and sky, so that they understood their responsibilities to the creation at large. Teaching was through the examples of Elders, who were accorded particular respect (Deloria 1990a, 1990b).

It is no surprise, therefore, that children, Native or non-Native, raised in an environment where co-operation and interconnectedness are emphasized may have problems in a public school system where competition in preparation for the competitiveness of modern western society is emphasized. And similarly, the growth of Native traditionalism may be connected in part to this fundamental threat to their social integrity. Manitonquat, a Wampanoag medicine man, for example, advocates the adoption of traditional Native values including child-raising methods as a way to alleviate many of the problems of American society (Manitonquat 1991).

Native American criticism of western education is hardly a recent phenomenon. A much-quoted passage from a letter of Benjamin Franklin (9 May 1753) indicates why members of the Hodenosaunee (Iroquois) Six Nations politely, but firmly, refused an English offer to educate their children (Sparks 1856, vol. 7, p. 70; Deloria 1981, p. 55):

Several of our young people were formerly brought up at the colleges of the Northern Provinces; they were instructed in all your science; but when they came back to us, they were bad runners; ignorant of every means of living in the woods; unable to bear either cold or hunger; knew neither how to build a cabin, take a deer, or kill an enemy; spoke our language imperfectly; were therefore neither fit for hunters, warriors, or counselors; they were totally good for nothing. We are however not the less obliged by your kind offer, though we decline accepting it: And to show our grateful sense of it, if the gentlemen of Virginia will send us a dozen of their sons, we will take great care of their education, instruct them in all we know, and make men of them.

Because of this relation between education and society, many Native Americans think that it is tragic when Natives who have succeeded in the general educational system pass out of Native society – an outcome often seen by non-Natives as successful assimilation (Wilkinson 1981, p. 47). Alternatively, western-trained Native Americans are sometimes spurned by their communities when they try to return. Similar phenomena have been described for Australia (Barlow 1990; Watson 1990).

Alternative educational approaches

Native Americans are not the only critics of the established education system, of course. It is continually the focus of debate among educationalists as it attempts to adapt to our diverse society. Indeed, some critics share the view of Native educationalists that the system is one-sided, devoted primarily to intellectual learning and rationality at the expense of other areas of ability.

The USA is not without alternative educational systems, created to respond to perceived deficiencies in majority education, and supported by Euro-American parents whose children have not thrived in the regular schools. Among these are Montessori and Waldorf schools whose origins are in Europe. The Waldorf schools in particular, based on Rudolf Steiner's anthroposophy, consider the spiritual, emotional and motivational development of children to be equally as important as their intellectual development, and in that respect bear a resemblance to traditional Native American schooling.

Indeed, if there is to be any real prospect of furthering a goal of genuine multicultural education, different cultural approaches to learning need to be brought together. For example, Rosemary Christensen, an Anishinabe (Ojibwe) and former director of the Indian Education Department in the Minneapolis public-school system, would like to see four basic 'competences' drawn from the values of traditional Native culture taught to all teachers of Native American children. These competences would address the independence (sovereignty) of the individual, age-related respect, a connection with all living things, and discipline administered through indirect communication (Christensen 1990). These values could also benefit non-Indian children.

An important aspect of any change in the system is the development of a theoretical construct to help guide the integration of the different approaches to knowledge implied by multicultural education. Gardner (1985), for example, has examined the forms of cognition that are favoured by different educational systems, in response to what he sees as a defect in the US system: the fact that standardized tests in the USA measure only linguistic and logical abilities (Gardner 1985, p. 24). Gardner identifies seven different forms of intelligence: linguistic, logical-mathematical, spatial, musical, bodily-kinesthetic, interpersonal and intrapersonal. He suggests that non-literate education employs the greatest number of forms of intelligence: linguistic, musical, spatial, bodily-kinesthetic and interpersonal. In contrast, he maintains that modern secular schooling develops only logical-mathematical, intrapersonal (but not interpersonal) and linguistic intelligences (Gardner 1985, p. 339).

It is probably true to say that the cognitive content which is taught in non-literate or native societies tends to have a direct relevance to that society, whether it is Gardner's example of the teaching of intricate star patterns to Puluwat youths in the Caroline islands so that they may become expert sailors, the complex social relationships transmitted through Australian Aboriginal kinship systems, or the models of social theory and practice communicated through oral histories in every culture. In a rapidly changing industrial society, such as that of the United States, however, it is difficult to see how a cultural consensus, and hence, a 'universal' education system can be developed. While it is not easy to determine exactly what is relevant learning as a preparation for life in modern society, the youthful perception that something is missing is demonstrated in particular by the experience of minority youth. Perhaps the wisdom and experience of Native teachings may help to ease the problems that many people have of adapting to such a complex cultural milieu.

Concepts of traditional Native education

A good example of the ideals behind the approach to education of contemporary Native American traditionalists is found in a talk given by Cjigkitoonuppa, a Wampanoag medicine man, to foreign scholars in Concord, Massachusetts (quoted in Weeks 1986). According to Cjigkitoonuppa:

> From the very beginning Man was made clear that his task in the new world was to preserve the land for those to come. We speak of seven generations. Each Indian understood that his and her responsibility was to care for the land for seven generations to come. We all know that the earth sustains us, and that there must be a continuation of life. We learn that by watching nature. The muskrat still possesses the knowledge he had in the beginning. The Indians built their homes the same way. Today people would call such a story a legend. It may be; but legends are pictures that contain deep truths. My people understood, as do the wise ones today, that the Spirit itself works through nature, and that, by reading her script, we can form our lives in harmony with the creator.

The potential contribution of Native American education to US schools

What is the best contribution that Indian traditional education can make to the dominant culture? As interpersonal relations appear to be much more important within Native education than its Euro-American counterpart, as Gardner (1985) suggests, this area might be ideal for an infusion of Native ideas and practices. There is certainly a need for change in interpersonal relations in the modern United States. With a divorce rate approaching 50 per cent in the United States, family life is under great stress, with adverse effects on American youth, and family disintegration is particularly severe among minorities. With a lack of cohesion and support at home, and a school environment which can easily foster division as it encourages competitiveness, many American children are alienated and so fail to learn. Interpersonal training which fosters co-operative values could make an important contribution to education and to the society as a whole.

The experience of Cjikitoonuppa may be taken as a case history. Together with Manitonquat, he has developed successful programmes in several prisons in Connecticut and Massachusetts to create community feeling and cohesion among inmates. Significantly, very few of these men were Native. Cjikitoonuppa considers that his experience in prisons could be used to foster a more co-operative atmosphere in schools.

Cjikitoonuppa's approach relies on a simple Native device used in pow-wows (Native festivals) and other meetings, the talking-stick. As Cjikitoonuppa relates (quoted in Weeks 1986):

> we put the issue that is being discussed in the center of a circle of people. The person who speaks has a talking-stick. As long as he or she holds it, they are not interrupted. Everybody who speaks to the issue, speaks to how they see it. That is understood, as it is understood that when one speaks, one speaks the truth. Thus the others listen. In such meetings, we realize that the issue isn't merely solved by a majority vote. If 51 people want one thing and 49 another, we understand that there is something right as well in the 49. The principle is not abstract, it comes from recognition of that truth which each person carries.

Being able to speak for as long as they like without interruption is for many inmates the first time they have ever been listened to at all when they speak. In addition, as the group communicates respect to the speaker by listening, the speaker is encouraged to return that respect, by not speaking too long. Cjigkitoonuppa and Manitonquat have watched men who are the most alienated and hostile in society make a complete emotional about-face and give each other support, and they have found it a profoundly moving experience.

Unfortunately, many children in school are in the same predicament as the inmates with respect to having no one to listen to them. In an educational environment where many children are failing intellectually, it is suggested that such a technique practised on occasion could create an emotionally supportive environment where children might learn to express themselves without fear. Indeed, Cjigkitoonuppa has also had some experience in communicating successfully with children who have behavioural problems by getting them to speak what was on their minds. In the ordinary classroom it sometimes happens that only one or two children feel secure enough to answer the teacher's questions on a regular basis, and this pattern continues into the university. Cjigkitoonuppa considers that this fear is often caused when a teacher has inadequate respect for the student. Too often communication is a one-way street where a teacher's view is imposed, and the students do not learn to express themselves.

Recently an experiment with the talking-stick method was tested in a local

Massachusetts school system. Two groups of children were formed (one of forty and one of seventy children, the whole grade level of 12-year-olds in the school system), and each sat in assembly for about an hour. Normally the class size is between twenty and thirty children. The pupils were predominantly Euro-American, with a small number of African-Americans and some children of Asian background. There were roughly equal numbers of boys and girls.

Cjigkitoonuppa had the children sit in two or three concentric circles. The ideal is one circle so that everyone can see everyone else's face, but with large numbers, concentric circles are necessary. Cjigkitoonuppa started out with a brief introduction about who he was and how his people used the talking-stick, and then gave simple instructions about how to use it. The stick was a decorated ceremonial one belonging to Cjigkitoonuppa, but any stick could have been used. It would be passed around the circle, with respect being given to each person holding it to say whatever he or she liked without interruption, or it could be passed on without comment if so desired. He stressed that the purpose of the exercise was to speak from the heart about something of real concern to each individual, and that it was particularly important to speak the truth because otherwise it was a waste of everyone's time to listen.

In the first assembly (40 children) considerable shyness was evident. Many students stood and gave only their name and where they lived, hastily passing the stick on to avoid having to say anything more. It seemed as if just giving a name and address was a challenge. By contrast, a girl of Chinese background, who had come relatively recently to the United States, spoke fluently and eloquently about her concerns and feelings, and seemed entirely at ease with the exercise. This ease may have been a personal gift, but it is also possible that she was raised in an environment where interpersonal skills were strongly encouraged. She really stood out in the group.

In the second assembly (70 children) the first few pupils who spoke happened to be boys. Near the beginning one boy made a comment about how he liked a particular professional sports team and hoped they would win their next game. Thereafter each boy made exactly the same comment until Cjigkitoonuppa stepped in to stop it. He reiterated that the purpose of the exercise was to speak individually on matters of deep personal concern with respect to other people or the world at large. Although asking 12-year-olds to speak about worlds larger than their own experience was giving them a difficult challenge, the comments after that were more varied.

On the whole in these particular groups, the girls seemed to find it easier to express themselves than the boys, often mentioning relationships with friends or parents. Many of them also showed concern for the destruction of the South American rain-forest, something which at that time was appearing in the news, and had probably been raised in current affairs discussions in school.

While the stilted nature of many of the responses might make an observer question the value of the exercise, it should be remembered that this was the first time these children had been asked to talk about things of intimate concern to themselves in public. To see a change it would be necessary to continue to use the method for some time. The children themselves recognized this. In thank-you notes written to Cjigkitoonuppa afterwards, many thought it had been a valuable experience and some said they wished they could have more sessions, so that they could learn how to express themselves better. The children also thought that the sessions had ended too soon. This was dramatically demonstrated at the end of the second session when no one moved at the sound of the lunch bell. The teachers said they had never seen the children remain in place before at that time.

The Native viewpoint in Native American-run museums

A major difference, and that probably most difficult to bridge, between traditional Native American education and the dominant culture is the difference in attitude to history. A traditional form of western secular history perceives its approach as both rational and objective, emerging from its reliance on documentation, as opposed to hearsay. Native oral histories, on the other hand, express their past and the values of society within a metaphorical context that commonly incorporates what we recognize as spirituality. Indeed, the mythological material used in such histories is often rejected by outsiders, who judge it to be untrue because it is not a 'scientific' explanation of what really happened. And yet, mythology (in the sense of something that is untrue) in Euro-American history is often obscured because people presume that their history has been objectively recorded (although the subjective bias is readily perceived by Native Americans).

This difference is especially important when it comes to education about the past through archaeology and the display of cultural material in museums. It is important to recognize that archaeology exists in close association with its related fields of ethnography, anthropology and history, and also with art. While archaeology is often distinguished from these other subjects, a failure to take their ideas and information into account in analysis may create the kind of interpretive bias towards the past that is evident in general education.

Most children in the United States have contact with archaeology through museum programmes, but the Native viewpoint is not commonly given, as the museum world is dominated by non-Natives. The number of Native American organizations creating exhibits to portray their peoples' cultures is steadily increasing, however. The example of two such museums, created and controlled by Native Americans, shows how they convey distinctive and personal views of their own culture (also see Ucko 1994).

In upper New York State, two museums run by Hodenosaunee (Iroquois) create very different impacts.

The Turtle is a large museum in Niagara Falls, New York State. This Native American Center for the Living Arts is under Hodenosaunee management, and was built by Native Americans on modern lines. It is of concrete, with a geodesic dome for a roof, and is designed in the shape of a turtle, a

Native American symbol of the earth, Turtle Island. Directly under the dome (the turtle's back) is a dance floor for pow-wows, and higher up are circular concrete balconies which are reminiscent of the Guggenheim art museum in New York City. The balconies hold exhibit cases and displays are also in the 'limbs' and 'head' of the turtle.

In addition to the symbolic design of the museum, the exhibits themselves deal with certain Native symbols such as the circle, the eagle and the four directions. There is also some treatment of Hodenosaunee history, together with Native artwork and archaeological material from different parts of the country. The overall concept of the Turtle is clearly imaginative, therefore, and it conveys Native culture within a very modern, multicultural context.

In contrast, the Six Nations Museum in Onchiota, New York (the name refers to the six nations of the Hodenosaunee confederacy), is a small wooden museum with an old-fashioned approach to exhibition. There is a very large quantity of material in a small space, to the extent that the visitor is surrounded by objects not only on all sides but also hanging from the roof. The material is all Hodenosaunee, and although the effect at first is overwhelming, there is a sense of total immersion in another culture. The Mohawk curator may tell children and their parents a story from one of numerous examples of Hodenosaunee pictorial story belts, or explain the different kinds of *gustoweh* (hat) which each Hodenosaunee nation wore, with the different numbers and arrangements of feathers identifying each individual nation. There are wampum belts (belts made out of shell beads) and copies of such belts which relate in their patterns the laws of the Hodenosaunee confederacy, an indigenous democratic government which was used by Benjamin Franklin in his development of a model for the government of the United States (Johansen 1982). There are also many pieces of modern artwork by Hodenosaunee people.

For those interested in archaeology, artefacts from the precontact past before the arrival of Europeans are on view but without the archaeologist's attempts to reconstruct history through them. An eye-catching display made entirely out of stone projectile points represents a picture of the Hodenosaunee tree of peace with the hatchet buried beneath its roots, an episode from the foundation stories of the Hodenosaunee confederacy. While the non-Native archaeologist's first reaction might be to cringe, this is a creative way to use undocumented artefacts of little use in a 'western' scientific approach to archaeology: the creation of a symbolic picture about the Hodenosaunee past.

To anyone with any background in Hodenosaunee history, the Six Nations Museum is a fascinating place, but even for those without such a background it makes a powerful impact. The museum is not organized in an analytical western fashion to tell a particular story as museums usually now try to do, but is rather an artistic experience of cultural immersion which the curator draws on to tell whatever part of the story he chooses to his visitors (also see Ucko 1994). As such, this is a typical Native American approach: to adjust what is said to the moment and to the people, and not to pre-programme a message.

A label from this museum also demonstrated the Native sense of closeness to nature, a key concept in conveying the Native point of view:

> The Hodenosaunee believe that the animals are our brothers having equal status in the Creation.

> The birds, the animals and the fishes can teach us how to live in harmony with the earth. In earlier times, the animals taught the Hodenosaunee many things about using and protecting the natural resources.

> The passenger pigeon taught us how to give thanks each morning and evening, enjoying each day.

> The heron taught us how to use fish as fertilizer for our crops.

> The wolves taught us how to hunt in groups, for the benefit of the family.

> Animal symbols are used in traditional art to pay tribute to our animal brothers and to show our family identity.

A new museum in Warner, New Hampshire, the Mount Kearsage Indian Museum, to which Cjigkitoonuppa is advisor, also uses quotes from Native authors to particular advantage. Their identification with the natural world enhances the exhibited materials.

The creation of exhibits which convey multiple levels of information and meaning

The essence of creating an exhibit from an indigenous perspective may lie in an attempt to portray indigenous ways of thinking through the display of related symbols. The symbolic exhibits described above could have been taken further in the direction of what one might call a Lévi-Straussian technique. In *The Raw and the Cooked* (Lévi-Strauss 1969), this anthropologist analysed the symbols portrayed in some South American legends of animals, colours, directions and other aspects of the natural world, and traced them through multiple stories in an ever-widening geographic circle extending as far as North America. Through this technique he constructed patterns of meaning and association among related indigenous societies and cultures (Lévi-Strauss 1969). A similar method might be used to organize and display artefacts and ethnographic materials, in order to convey the multiple levels of thought processes and patterns of meaning that are invested in material culture – a totally different approach from the temporal and spatial forms of organization most commonly used by archaeologists to construct past cultural sequences.

Lest it be thought that such a process is applicable only to non-western indigenous cultures, the Gundestrup cauldron, as discussed in a recent paper

(Taylor 1992), may be used to show how this could be applied in Europe. Taylor traces the iconographic and symbolic associations of the representations on the cauldron across Europe and ultimately relates them to Asian Indian deities. He also suggests shamanic meanings of some of the symbols. An exhibit of the cauldron could demonstrate all of these associations through the display of related artefacts or relevant drawings with it, thus making a visual representation of the multiple levels of information and their possible meanings. An exhibit such as this would be very different from the kind of historical reconstruction regularly seen in European museums, since it would be an attempt to represent non-analytical European thinking.

The value of indigenous views of archaeology

Is it possible for western-trained archaeologists to incorporate indigenous views of archaeology into their methodologies? This seems at first impossible as it would appear to require a departure from scientific standards of proof in the direction of what has been called 'fantastic archaeology' (Williams 1991). On the other hand, while maintaining a standard scientific approach as a kind of control, the archaeologist could take an anthropological excursion into indigenous understandings of the past and derive a totally different way of seeing an archaeological site. Indigenous and archaeological understandings of the past are not necessarily contradictory, but address very different kinds of information. Indigenous views are likely to provide information about contemporary and historically derived values which can rarely be obtained through archaeological techniques.

By way of example one might consider the interpretation of Mayan ceremonial sites in the Yucatán peninsula. A modern Mayan spiritual leader or Knowledge Keeper, Hunbatz Men, is currently engaged in reviving traditional Mayan teachings in a committed indigenous community founded for that purpose and in the rededication of ancient ceremonial sites, the same sites where archaeologists work (McFadden 1991). In workshops on Mayan philosophy and spirituality which Hunbatz Men is giving in the United States, he strongly criticizes the conclusions of archaeologists about why these sites were abandoned, saying that much of what has been written is entirely misleading (Workshop in Epping, New Hampshire, August 1992). Archaeologists' understandings infer ecological, economic and political collapse of Classic Mayan culture, perhaps caused by failure of leadership, interpretations backed up by translations in the past decade of Ancient Mayan inscriptions on stele and other monuments.

Hunbatz Men looks at the abandonment of sacred sites from the standpoint of his Mayan spiritual teachings, which revolve around the concept of energy derived from the sun (Hunbatz Men 1990, 1991). In his view the Mayan pyramids were, and are once again, places to focus the sun's power for the assistance of humanity, and he thinks the reason for their abandonment in the past was that something went wrong with the energy in each of these places which could not be overcome. This problem caused the shift from one site to another, leading to the use at the time of the Spanish arrival of Izamal (Itzmal). If one were to put this view together with those of the archaeologists, one might be inclined to say that the failure of spiritual power and the other failures were related: the difference lies in where the primary emphasis is placed or what is considered the primary cause of cultural collapse. Hunbatz Men, however, denies that there was a cultural collapse, and maintains rather that Mayan teachings became secret with the arrival of the Spaniards, to be revealed now in accordance with prophecies based on the Mayan calendar. While agreement between Hunbatz Men and other Mayan traditionalists and archaeologists on this matter will never be reached, as each group uses different understandings and standards of proof, for the archaeologist the views of a Mayan leader should add an aspect to the interpretation of the past which archaeology by itself cannot achieve.

The issue of the disturbance and desecration of Native burials shows how indigenous people and those of a dominant culture may reach accommodation from an initial confrontation. In recent years Native Americans have become very distressed by the treatment of their burials at the hands of archaeologists, and by the display and storage of bones in museums (see, for example, Blancke & Cjigkitoonuppa 1990). Through the activism of many Native groups, legislation has been enacted to protect burials at both the Federal and State levels, and museums are engaged in assessing their bone collections, in some instances returning them for reburial. Some cultural materials are also being returned.

For example, the Massachusetts Historical Commission, under State law, controls archaeological excavations and the treatment of unmarked burials in Massachusetts. If a Native American grave is encountered, the Commission on Indian Affairs monitors the archaeological investigation to ensure that the remains are treated respectfully (Massachusetts Historical Commission 1992). Archaeologists are then given time to study but the bones are eventually reburied.

In some instances Native American groups have even extended their values to the protection not just of their own graves but to those of non-Natives lying in the path of development. A few years ago a Nipmuck group in central Massachusetts fought to protect a non-Native cemetery.

Conclusion

The problem of ethnocentrism, which affects all cultures, is especially severe in the traditional orientation of western education, especially as it concerns the representation of the lives of other cultural groups and, in the United States in particular, of its shared history with the indigenous people. If some of the insights and creative methods of teaching of the indigenous peoples and the many other minority cultures that make up our complex modern society were brought into the education system, our children might be exposed to the multicultural reality that exists, rather than being further bound by the ideas and goals of a dominating majority (also see Ahler 1994). This in turn would be reflected in less ethnocentric and one-sided educational methods, materials and cultural exhibits, and this would surely contribute to better relationships between peoples.

There is an intuitive wisdom in my people, a wisdom that has its source in the heart. The white people have another sort of wisdom; one might call it reason. It has light, with which it analyzes and divides, but, if that division is not going to lead to disintegration, it needs the warmth that unifies again, that has been and is still offered in this land.

(Cjigkitoonuppa, quoted in Weeks 1986)

References

Ahler, J. G. 1994. The benefits of multicultural education for American Indian schools: an anthropological perspective. In *The Presented Past: heritage, museums and education*, Stone, P. G. & B. L. Molyneaux (eds), 453–9. London: Routledge.

Barlow, A. 1990. Still civilizing? Aborigines in Australian education. In *The Excluded Past: archaeology in education*, Stone, P. & R. MacKenzie (eds), 68–87. London: Unwin Hyman; Routledge pbk 1994.

Belgarde, M. J. 1994. The transfer of American Indian and other minority community college students. In *The Presented Past: heritage, museums and education*, Stone, P. G. & B. L. Molyneaux (eds), 460–77. London: Routledge.

Blancke, S. & Cjigkitoonuppa (John Peters Slow Turtle) 1990. The teaching of the past of the Native peoples of North America in U.S. schools. In *The Excluded Past: archaeology in education*, Stone, P. & R. MacKenzie (eds), 109–31. London: Unwin Hyman; Routledge pbk 1994.

Christensen, R. 1990. Tribal peoples of Turtle Island in their struggle with the education system of the United States: a focus on Tribal people of the Midwestern Woodlands. Paper presented to the Education and Archaeology session, WAC 2, Barquisimeto, Venezuela.

Christensen, R. & W. Demmert 1978. The education of Indians and the mandate of history. In *The Schooling of Native America*, Thompson, T. (ed.), 138–52. Washington, D.C.: American Association of Colleges for Teacher Education and Teacher Corps, US Office of Education.

Deloria, V. Jr 1981. Education and imperialism. *Integrateducation* 19, 58–63.

Deloria, V. Jr 1990a. Knowing and understanding: traditional education in the modern world. *Winds of Change* 5 (1), 12–18.

Deloria, V. Jr 1990b. Traditional technology. *Winds of Change* 5 (2), 12–17.

Gardner, H. 1985. *Frames of Mind: the theory of multiple intelligences*. New York: Basic Books.

Gunsky, F. R. 1979. Multicultural education: implications for American Indian people. In *Multicultural Education and the American Indian*, 69–75. Los Angeles: The Regents of the University of California.

Hunbatz Men 1990. *Secrets of Mayan Science/Religion*. Santa Fe, N. Mex.: Bear & Company.

Hunbatz Men 1991. *Solar Meditation*. Merida, Mexico: Comunidad Indigena Maya.

Johansen, B. E. 1982. *Forgotten Founders*. Boston: Harvard Common Press.

Lévi-Strauss, C. 1969. *The Raw and the Cooked*. New York: Harper & Row.

Locke, P. 1978. An ideal school system for American Indians – a theoretical construct. In *The Schooling of Native America*, Thompson, T. (ed.), 118–36. Washington, D.C.: American Association of Colleges for Teacher Education and Teacher Corps, US Office of Education.

McFadden, S. 1991. *Profiles in Wisdom*. Santa Fe: Bear & Company.

Manitonquat 1991. *Return to Creation*. Spokane: Bear Tribe.

Massachusetts Historical Commission 1992. *KnowHow* 4. Boston: State of Massachusetts.

Sparks, J. 1856. *The Works of Benjamin Franklin*, 10 vols. Boston.

Taylor, T. 1992. The Gundestrup cauldron. *Scientific American* 266, 84–90.

Ucko, P. J. 1990. Foreword. In *The Excluded Past: archaeology in education*, Stone, P. & R. MacKenzie (eds), ix–xxiii. London: Unwin Hyman; Routledge pbk 1994.

Ucko, P. J. 1994. Museums and sites: cultures of the past within education – Zimbabwe, some ten years on. In *The Presented Past: heritage, museums and education*, Stone P. G. & B. L. Molyneaux (eds), 237–82. London: Routledge.

Watson, L. 1990. The affirmation of indigenous values in a colonial education system. In *The Excluded Past: archaeology in education*, Stone, P. & R. MacKenzie (eds), 88–97. London: Unwin Hyman; Routledge pbk 1994.

Weeks, S. 1986. Native American offers perspective on nation's beginning. *The Concord Journal* 5 June, 2.

Wilkinson, G. 1981. Educational problems in the Indian community, a comment on learning as colonialism. *Integrateducation* 19, 42–50.

Williams, S. 1991. *Fantastic Archaeology*. Philadelphia: University of Pennsylvania Press.

32 The benefits of multicultural education for American Indian schools: an anthropological perspective

Multicultural education is a philosophy for formal schooling which has been promoted among educators for nearly two decades. The old assimilation policy, the 'Melting-Pot', still an aim of American schools, came under attack as the political and social consciousness of the relatively powerless minorities was raised during the Civil Rights Movement of the 1960s; an alternative, multicultural education was demanded, one which reflected and responded to the cultural diversity of the United States. Multicultural programmes are still in the early stages of development, but their curricula are expected to incorporate ideas and methods that are sensitive to the needs and views of all the cultural and ethnic groups in the USA, not simply those of the American mainstream. For this reason, anthropology has contributed not only most of the basic concepts in multicultural education but much of the content as well. This chapter addresses the question of how anthropology through a multicultural curriculum can benefit American Indian schools.

Among several educational anthropologists and multicultural educators, Gibson (1976, pp. 7–15) and Gunsky (1979, p. 70) have outlined at least four approaches to multicultural education: benevolent multicultural education, cultural understanding, cultural pluralism, and bicultural/bilingual education. While these approaches are intended for different situations, different populations, and have a variety of goals, they have two major goals that cover most circumstances in multicultural education.

The first is concerned with meeting the educational needs of culturally diverse students by recognizing that they bring worthwhile cultural knowledge with them to school. In the classroom, this knowledge is to be reinforced and expanded so that the force of assimilation can be resisted. This approach recognizes that students who are not members of the American mainstream have equally complex and accomplished cultures. This goal is a direct response to the demands by American minority groups for educational opportunities historically denied them.

The other, more encompassing, goal is to promote cultural awareness and sensitivity among all students so that they will begin to understand and respect both their own culture and those of others. This awareness is achieved by reducing stereotyping, bigotry and other elements of ethnocentrism that cause racism and result in discrimination. At first, this initiative was designed for American mainstream students, with the idea that, if they learned to appreciate minority cultures, equity in education would be realized. However, this perpetuated the domination of the majority and also failed to recognize that ethnocentrism is a condition of all societies. Consequently, this goal is now seen as appropriate for all cultural groups of students, including Native Americans.

Commitments towards achieving these two goals through multicultural education in teacher training stem from a variety of sources. Most national professional education organizations have encouraged the implementation of multicultural education, and the National Council for Accreditation of Teacher Education (NCATE) which evaluates teacher education institutions has required the inclusion of multicultural education in teacher training since 1980. In addition, the teacher certification regulations in many States require new teachers to take multicultural education or Indian studies courses. The rationale for the Indian studies requirements is to ensure that new teachers in reservation schools and teachers of Native American students in other schools will be familiar enough with Native American knowledge resources to be able to meet the educational needs of those students. Many college and university multicultural education courses address both these requirements by teaching concepts and processes applicable to elementary and secondary students in all schools including those on reservations.

What does multicultural education mean for Native Americans, especially in reservation schools? Francis McKenna of Pennsylvania State University has alleged that:

> multiculturalism, with its presumed liberal, humane acceptance, even sponsorship, of cultural difference is for the Indian a Potemkin village – a façade – to mask the real agenda for American Indians. That agenda is the acceleration of domestic dependency or internal colonialism, the major features of which are political destabilization, economic exploitation, cultural annihilation, and the destruction of the spirits and persons of Indian nations.
> (McKenna 1981, p. 2)

In other words, McKenna views multicultural education as an extension of the centuries-long assimilationist 'Melting-Pot' policies of the US Government towards Native peoples. Indeed, some ill-informed and misguided educators and policy-makers may well want to see the assimilation of Indian students under the guise of multicultural education, but that is certainly a subversion and misuse of its expressed purpose. For that matter, any education programme has the potential for hidden agendas. Most multicultural educators strive to ensure that individual choice in cultural affiliation is protected. Forced assimilation, whether it is overt or covert, is condemned.

Teachers and parents on a North Dakota reservation were recently surveyed about their attitudes to multicultural education by Swisher (1984), a Native of the reservation. While she found that teachers' attitudes were more positive than parents', there were some interesting results within specific groups of parents and teachers. Parents who had lived away from the reservation for more than ten years had a more positive attitude than those who had lived away less than ten years or who had lived all their lives on the reservation. The more educated the parents were, the more positive their attitudes. Conversely, parents who were designated as 'full-bloods' and parents who were enrolled members of that reservation expressed less positive attitudes than others. With regard to teachers, younger ones and those with fewer years of teaching on the reservation had more positive attitudes towards multicultural education (Swisher 1984, pp. 5–8).

Because this study is descriptive, the reasons for those attitudes are speculative. Nevertheless, those parents who have less positive attitudes may possibly share McKenna's (1981) scepticism, whereas older, more experienced reservation teachers may well expect assimilation for their Native American students.

Despite misgivings on the part of some educators and reservation residents, multicultural education is becoming a reality in many reservation schools. Although implementation varies, the most common approach is to introduce Native American content, often representing the traditional aspects of the dominant reservation culture, in the form of arts and crafts, music, traditional stories and histories, and native language vocabulary. Much of this information is an addition to the regular curriculum, which remains representative of the American mainstream culture. The emphasis on reinforcing Native American culture, as opposed to a more multicultural approach, has several justifications. Learning more about one's own culture in school allows for the development of more positive self-concepts among these students, a prerequisite for broader cultural awareness. It is also appropriate in view of the historical exclusion of Native American cultural content in reservation schools as part of the attempted assimilation process. And meeting this goal would serve to protect and preserve the cultural integrity of reservation cultures. The result, however, is a bilingual/bicultural exposure, not a truly multicultural curriculum.

Some educators argue that the current form of multicultural education in reservation schools is only 'tokenism' – and might eventually conform to McKenna's (1981) assessments. I prefer to believe that it is an auspicious beginning but that the role of Native culture in reservation schools still needs to be expanded and deepened. Basic values and practices of the reservation cultures should be added to the present content. Native language should be treated as a serious aspect of language learning to include conversation, grammar, syntax and structure. Anthropological linguistics can contribute to this language curriculum.

The goal of meeting American Indian students' needs will never be achieved, however, as long as American mainstream standards, using such means as standardized testing, remain paramount and as long as the Native cultural content is a minor addition to the core curriculum rather than an integral part of it. Reservation school standards should represent the cultural values, experience and aspirations of the populations being served. American mainstream cultural content could be minimized in the core curriculum in favour of Native American cultural content without sacrificing commitments to teaching 'basic skills'. Indeed, the definition of 'basic skills' might be subject to revision by the population served.

Multicultural education for Native Americans also needs to be examined in terms of the other major goal, to increase cultural awareness and sensitivity in all students. First, it should be pointed out that the assessments and recommendations that follow are intended to concentrate on the Native Americans only because that is the purpose of this chapter, not because Native Americans especially need to address these issues. The goal of multicultural education is aimed at everyone from all cultural groups.

Increasing cultural awareness is possible because there is cultural diversity and pluralism in this society. Platero, in writing about cultural pluralism with regard to Indian education in 1973, made the following statement:

> Cultural pluralism and its implications for teaching in the nation's public and private schools is a phenomenon which has become almost a fad. To members of other clearly defined cultural groups, such as many American Indians, there is more than a touch of irony in observing the nonculturally differentiated mass clamor about the desirability of multicultural facility.
>
> (Platero 1973, p. 39)

Platero would probably now admit twenty years later that this issue is more than a mere fad. More important is the need to recognize that the group to whom he refers as the 'nonculturally differentiated mass' is a diverse group in many respects. Indeed, it is a common tendency to ignore cultural diversity among those of European descent. In fact, few of our mostly Euro-American university students so strongly identify with the American mainstream culture that they have no ties to a specific European culture or a combination of European cultures. A Norwegian–American may be as different from a Polish–American as an Arikara is from an Ojibway.

Cultural diversity within a reservation population must also be recognized. In addition to national or Tribal and band group differences, there are varying degrees of affiliation with traditional cultures and modern reservation cultures.

Anthropological expertise is essential in guiding educators in the development of curricular materials for use in accomplishing both goals of multicultural education, but especially that of promoting cultural awareness and sensitivity. Reaching this goal demands an understanding of basic concepts, attitudes and processes associated with anthropology. For instance, some reservation schools continue to reinforce the confusion between the concepts 'culture' and 'race' by using them interchangeably; Native American students, as much as all other students, should therefore be engaged in learning the complexities of the concept 'culture' as well as the reasons for the rejection by most anthropologists of the notion that racial differences indicate fundamental biological differences. Indeed, attitudes of prejudice such as ethnocentrism and racism should be examined as an integral part of multicultural education in reservation schools.

Ethnocentric barriers between and among Native American groups must also be recognized and minimized. Achieving this would help create an understanding of mutual circumstances, needs and goals; and such understanding might in turn reverse some of the divisiveness which exists among various nations and reservations and which is fostered by some government officials and agencies in order to maintain a powerlessness among Native Americans.

Ethnocentrism between Native Americans and Euro-Americans and other American ethnic groups impedes constructive communication. Too often, superficial and stereotypical differences are stressed, when understanding basic differences and exploring similarities might serve to reduce ethnocentrism and promote a better appreciation of cultural diversity.

Native American students should be told explicitly of the racism implicit in the American racial classification system, and of the need to reject it for the sake of their own group status. In reservation schools with mixed student populations, there is often a specific denial of racism, but still there are observable patterns of in-school segregation. This tension exists not only between Native Americans and Euro-Americans but also between the so-called 'full-bloods' and 'mixed-bloods'. Tensions based upon racial categories will not disappear by being ignored or denied them. Reservation schools have a responsibility to acknowledge racial discord and to solve the problem.

The understanding of 'culture' by Native Americans can be augmented not only by studying Native American and other ethnographies produced by cultural anthropologists but also by expanding their familiarity with prehistoric cultural reconstructions offered by archaeologists. Archaeology and archaeologists have in the past been largely insensitive to the attitudes of Native Americans about the past, in part because of the emphasis throughout this century on empirical methods of analysis. More recently, however, archaeologists have realized that their research places a social construction on the past, and so is not as objective as was once thought. Modern archaeologists therefore recognize more clearly why it is necessary to consider the perceptions and ideas of, for example, contemporary aboriginal populations in their study of ancient peoples. The negative characteristics associated with 'pothunters' such as the destruction of Native American sites and the exploitation of Native American artefacts for gain are still commonly applied to professional archaeologists, however. Native Americans can learn that there is value for their own cultural heritage in studying the work of archaeologists, that most archaeologists treat with respect Native American sites and artefacts, and that the purpose of archaeology is to understand, not denigrate, prehistoric human conditions and behaviour.

Archaeology can play an even more direct role in an American Indian school curriculum. Reservation schools can encourage Native American students to work at archaeological excavations on or near their reservations. Archaeologists can work with Native American students in museum training for the preservation of their own material culture. Archaeologists and students can work together in comparing the archaeological evidence with the oral traditions of its people. Archaeology can also be promoted as a career choice for Native American students.

A modest programme at the University of North Dakota may serve as an example of the way that archaeologists and American Indian schools can co-operate. University archaeologists were conducting excavations at a prehistoric site on a nearby reservation. The reservation school was contacted and invited to bring students to tour the site. Prior to scheduling visits, an archaeologist and an educational anthropologist jointly prepared and distributed to the school a paper describing and explaining archaeology in general and the reservation site specifically (Ahler & Gregg 1991). Because this 'primer' provided background for teachers and students before they visited the site, student interest was stimulated and their questions to the archaeologists were more informed.

With more administrative and financial support from educational and research institutions, such programmes could be developed into intensive, on-going studies that would contribute to cultural continuity in American Indian schools.

Borrowing anthropological insights into cultural transmission processes – particularly the influence of formal and informal methods of education – is vital for education in reservation schools. An understanding of acculturation, for example, would help Native American students see the importance of the historical practice by reservation schools of denying Native Americans access to information about their cultural heritage. Acculturation, and more specifically, assimilation, affects Native Americans so profoundly that understanding these processes may be fundamental for cultural survival. Although Native Americans are certainly familiar with the experience, multicultural education can provide for greater awareness of the processes and effects of acculturation by exposing students to the experiences of other indigenous cultures of the world that have been colonized – the San (Bushmen) of southern Africa, the Australian Aborigines, or the Maori of New Zealand, for example. It would also be valuable to point out that the colonialists themselves had been conquered and colonized in the distant past. This type of cross-cultural knowledge will therefore enhance, not detract from, cultural self-understanding for Native Americans, because they will see their lives within the context of a larger world.

In spite of McKenna's (1981) dire assertions concerning the insidious intentions of multicultural education to assimilate Native Americans further, this programme has numerous benefits that are already being seen in reservation schools. But a shift to multicultural education, with its goal of incorporating formal enculturation processes in the school, is only possible if the community desires it, if it can make decisions regarding what is appropriate, and if it will participate in that process. The use of awareness workshops may convince those reservation teachers and parents with negative attitudes of those benefits. For the future, an anthropological foundation for multicultural education which is well integrated into the reservation school curriculum will promote the attainment of the two goals of cultural self-awareness and sensitivity to the culture of others. As suggested by Goodenough (1976, p. 6), cultural knowledge is associated with power relationships. With community support and control of multicultural education, it will be impossible for assimilating elements in the schools or Government to subvert its goals. Multicultural education in reservation schools can therefore offer knowledge of the kind that represents power for those who experience powerlessness.

References

Ahler, J. & M. Gregg 1991. A primer on archaeology. Manuscript, University of North Dakota, Grand Rapids, North Dakota.

Gibson, A. 1976. Approaches to multicultural education in the United States: some concepts and assumptions. *Anthropology and Education Quarterly* 7, 7–18.

Goodenough, W. 1976. Multiculturalism as the normal human experience. *Anthropology and Education Quarterly* 7, 4–6.

Gunsky, F. R. 1979. Multicultural education: implications for American Indian people. In *Multicultural Education and the American Indian*, 69–75. Los Angeles: The Regents of the University of California.

McKenna, F. 1981. The myth of multiculturalism and the reality of the American Indian in contemporary America. *Journal of American Indian Education* 21, 1–9.

Platero, D. 1973. Cultural pluralism in education: a mandate for change. In *Cultural Pluralism*, Stent, M. D., W. R. Hazard & H. N. Rivlin (eds), 39–42. New York: Appleton-Century-Crofts.

Swisher, K. 1984. Comparison of attitudes of reservation parents and teachers toward multicultural education. *Journal of American Indian Education* 23, 1–10.

33 The transfer of American Indian and other minority community college students

MARY JIRON BELGARDE

Introduction

Many American Indian students complete associate degrees from accredited American Indian tribally controlled community colleges. After graduation, they transfer to four-year institutions and fail to complete baccalaureate degree programmes (Jeanotte 1988). Research demonstrates that this is not an unusual phenomenon. Clark (1960), Olivas (1979), Eckland (1981), Cohen & Chacon (1982), Astin (1985), Cohen & Brawer (1987) and McNamara (1982) have concluded that community college transfer students do not graduate from four-year colleges at the same rates as students who initially enrolled at four-year institutions. Clark (1960), Lamberts (1977), McNamara (1982) and Astin (1985) found that students who transfer from community colleges to four-year institutions experience a drop in grade point averages in the year after transfer and many drop out of school subsequent to the time of transfer. The Texas Coordinating Board found that only 19.3 per cent of the students enrolling in community college transfer programmes in the autumn of 1981 had transferred to senior institutions by the spring of 1985 (Mingle 1987). Given these statistics, Astin (1985) recommends that students go directly to four-year institutions if they want to complete a baccalaureate degree.

This chapter explores how students of different ethnic and social groups and communities adapt to formal educational institutions in the United States. Its main concern is to describe the barriers of educational attainment for American Indian students in higher education – in particular, how tribally controlled community colleges fit into the context of the problem.

Community college education

Junior and community colleges offer foundation courses in arts and sciences that are intended to lead to Bachelor degree programmes in four-year institutions. Unlike junior colleges, which tend to attract recent high-school graduates, community colleges were developed (in 1900) to be the bridge between high school and four-year institutions by offering programmes to the adult population. Differing slightly from standard junior colleges, community colleges offer accredited high-school equivalency degrees, general education, vocational and transfer programmes. Operating as commuter campuses, these institutions allow students to attend college close to home, maintain support from family and friends, and save on living expenses. Early administrators intended to serve a small population of students in the transfer programmes, but because students demonstrated strong interest in transfer education, the programmes blossomed (Clark 1960). In California, for example, between 60,000 and 70,000 community college students transferred to various four-year institutions during the 1983–4 academic year: 5300 to the University of California system (UC); 45,400 to the California State University system (CSU); and more than 5200 to independent colleges and universities (California Community Colleges Chancellor's Office 1984).

Unfortunately, students who transfer from community colleges have less chance of acquiring their Bachelor degrees than students who begin their studies in four-year colleges, as shown by the National Longitudinal Study (NLS) of the High School Class of 1972. NLS research (National Center for Education Statistics 1977) revealed that transfer students tended to come from families of low socio-economic status and had lower ability, achievement and aspiration levels than students who started out at four-year institutions. They were less likely than four-year college students to have graduated from high-school academic programmes and received fewer scholarships, fellowships or grants.

The lack of success of students who transfer from community colleges to universities is especially serious where Hispanics and other minority ethnic groups – including American Indians – are concerned, for these groups tend to enrol in two-year college and so will graduate at much lower rates than other ethnic groups and will remain at lower levels of economic and status attainment.

The numbers of transfer students among minorities is substantial. In the autumn enrolment in institutes of higher learning in the United States for 1986–7, 54.4% of the Hispanic college students and 54.2% of the American Indian students were enrolled in two-year institutions while 45.6% of Hispanics and 45.8% of American Indians were enrolled in four-year institutions. In contrast, 35.9% whites, 42.7% blacks, 43.2% Asians and 15.7% non-resident aliens were enrolled in two-year institutions (Mingle 1987). In California, this contrast is even greater: community colleges enrol 40% of all California high-school graduates but 80% of all the minority high-school students pursuing college (California Community Colleges Chancellor's Office 1984).

Many students from ethnic minorities enrol in two-year colleges because of the restrictive admission policies of the various higher institutions. The universities limit enrolment according to scholastic achievement: the UC system limits enrolment to the students scoring in the top 12.5% on academic achievement and scholastic achievement test scores and the CSU system enrols students from the top 33.3%. In contrast, the community college must accept all applicants who are 18 and/or have a high-school diploma (Turner 1988). Since mean academic achievement for minority students falls below that of white students, this disproportionately tracks them away from the CSU and UC systems. Over 75% of the total ethnic minority enrolment in public higher education are enrolled in community colleges; 82% of blacks and 88% of Hispanics who acquire post-secondary education attend community colleges (California Legislative Assembly 1984).

The reasons for the lack of academic success of community-college transfer students are partly due to cultural and economic factors, but it is important to consider as well the influence of the educational system itself. Using the NLS data, Eckland (1981) studied the progress of individual students four and a half years after high school and concluded that, independent of social class, race or ability, students who entered two-year colleges were substantially more likely to leave college without receiving a baccalaureate degree by 1976 than students who had been at four-year colleges.

Cohen & Chacon (1982) obtained a similar result in a study of Chicana women (i.e. of mixed Spanish and Indian heritage) in community colleges and private institutions. Socio-economic and academic differences aside, students attending private universities made better progress than students attending community colleges. Community-college students faced a number of social obstacles: they tended to be older, work longer hours, and have heavier domestic burdens, and they reported the lowest use of support services, the smallest number of friends on campus, and the smallest amount of financial support from the college. But the greatest problem was that the community colleges studied had no structures designed to prevent students from continuing a pattern of partial commitment to higher education indefinitely. The average number of units taken per semester was only six, often representing only one course per semester taken in the evening, and Cohen & Chacon found in previous studies that dropping out temporarily or taking few units increased the chance of failure to complete a programme. The record of producing students who transferred to and graduated from four-year colleges was therefore poor.

A variety of institutional and social factors that may affect academic success are revealed in Lamberts's (1977) study of students who transferred from one community college to a particular four-year institution. The problems are evident in the students' suggestions to community-college personnel for the improvement of student services:

1 prepare transfer students more adequately for the problems of institutional size, impersonal treatment, academic expectations and social life which they may face at the university;
2 improve the counselling services, as the community-college counsellors

need to be better informed about the university requirements and course sequences and should work more closely with the university counsellors and advisors;
3 increase the number of social gatherings for students;
4 increase emphasis for transfer students in the following instructional areas: writing and composition, English grammar, speech, study habits and typing;
5 make the academic expectation in community-college classes 'tougher' in the areas of examinations, grading, and course content;
6 improve information available to students concerning the specific requirements of the university and establish a well-defined, easily identifiable sequence of basic transfer courses; and
7 give more 'realistic' and personal guidance and counselling.

As Turner (1988) has shown in a study of how individual and organizational factors affect the transfer of Hispanic and non-Hispanic students from three community colleges to four-year institutions in California, efforts to accommodate the cultural diversity of students can lead to positive results. In one college with a high transfer rate of Hispanic students, Turner found that the presence of a Hispanic faculty to teach a targeted (remedial) English course favourably assisted the academic progress of Hispanic students. Being placed in remedial English may have acted as an 'opportunities equalizer' and provided the close mentor relations for Hispanic students whose parents do not have strong connections with college. The college also provided means of social integration that another college with a low transfer rate did not: it had a new student orientation programme, a student newspaper and a Mexican-American club.

Turner concluded that structural characteristics of the community colleges may affect the entire student body and that negative effects in this aspect may compound the social disadvantages faced by Hispanic students in their minority position in the larger community. It may be concluded from all this evidence, therefore, that it is an accumulation of many cultural, economic and organizational factors rather than a single set of factors that hinders the progress of minority students in higher education.

American Indian students

Most American Indian community college students attend tribally controlled community colleges because mainstream colleges and universities have failed to serve their needs. American Indian students are therefore affected by many of the same factors that influence the performance and persistence of other ethnic minority and majority students transferring from community colleges to four-year institutions.

Most empirical literature about American Indians in four-year institutions pertains to students who initially enrolled in four-year colleges and universities. Researchers have typically used grade point averages and credits completed to measure performance and graduation to measure persistence. Many have found that socio-economic status, type of high school, high-school grade point average, parental educational level, parental attitudes and support and financial aid are the most reliable clues to future college performance and completion. Study habits and attitudes, achievement motivation, career maturity, social and cultural factors also yield positive outcomes (Havighurst 1978; Sawyer 1981; Huffman, Sill & Brokenleg 1986; Rindone 1988; West 1988; Belgarde, M. 1992). Still other researchers find structural and normative characteristics within institutions to be mediating variables. Support programmes, such as tutoring, counselling and culturally based programmes (e.g. Native American studies, Native American advisory, pre-college preparatory and orientation programmes), are found to enhance student performance and persistence (Fuchs & Havighurst 1972; Patton & Edington 1973; Kleinfeld & Kohout 1974; Wright 1985).

In some studies, findings suggest that students socialized to the Indian tradition appear to have a better chance of achievement in college than their non-traditional counterparts (Jaimes 1981; Huffman, Sill & Brokenleg 1986; Rindone 1988). These studies conclude that the strength students receive from their cultural heritage and families seems to matter. For example, since college completion in some Indian communities is unusual, traditional students receive respect, encouragement and emotional support from extended family, clan and Tribal members.

As these latter studies suggest that American Indian culture, values and belief systems influence how the more traditional Indian students experience their educational environment, it is important that such ideas are considered in the design and implementation of the educational system as a whole.

Indian culture, cultural values and belief systems

Defining American Indian culture, cultural values and belief systems is complicated because of the number of Tribes and diversity among Tribes and within tribes that exist. The Federal Government recognizes approximately 478 Tribes living within the United States. Moreover, approximately 52 identifiable groups or Tribes claim to be Indian but are not recognized by the United States Federal Government (Trimble 1976, 1981). Each Tribe considers itself distinctly different from the others even if in name only (Trimble 1976); and some researchers have in fact found greater differences between Tribal groups than between Indians and Caucasians (Trimble 1988). Hence, defining Indian culture, cultural values and belief systems is also problematic because people mistakenly overgeneralize and stereotype Indian people (Trimble 1988).

Nevertheless, Trimble (1981) states that Indians are very quick to point out that the values and cultural ways of Indians as a group are quite dissimilar to those of any other culture, and they will list those values that they believe set them apart from non-Indians. A close examination of these general values finds that they are not radically different from those of other culutres but are simply different in terms of the emphasis placed upon different aspects of what are shared values. Trimble (1981) cited Bryde (1972), who suggested the following cultural differences between Indians and non-Indians:

Present-oriented versus future-oriented:
The Indian lives in the present, enjoying life today, unconcerned about tomorrow. The non-Indian lives for tomorrow, constantly looking to and planning for the future.

Generosity and sharing versus personal acquisitiveness and material achievement:
Indians who are generous and thoughtful are respected. The non-Indians are assessed by the material wealth that they have accumulated and for their interest in being socially mobile.

Lack of time consciousness versus time consciousness:
Indians take time to accomplish things without hurrying. The non-Indians are more consciously aware of time and completing tasks within time limits. Non-Indians are rewarded (respected) for their promptness. [However, Lewis & Keung Ho (1975) argue that many Native people are time conscious and that they deal with broad natural constructs, such as mornings, days, nights, months (moons) and seasons. When cultural values such as sharing, listening and social support are involved, a conversation with a friend is more important than being punctual at meetings.]

Respect for age versus respect for youth:
The Indians respect the older Indians who have lived a long time because they have acquired knowledge and wisdom. The non-Indians respect the young, particularly if they have demonstrated some knowledge or skill.

Co-operation versus competition:
The Indians emphasize getting along with others and conforming with the group. The non-Indian emphasizes competition with others. A lack of progress is synonymous with lack of competition.

Harmony with nature versus conquest over nature:
Indians are a part of nature and do not try to control or change the course of nature. Non-Indians attempt to control and master the physical world. If the non-Indian could control the course of nature, the world would be a better place to live.

Trimble (1988) also cited Zintz's (1963) research on the Pueblo Indians, which described similar values/belief systems.

Explanation of natural phenomena versus scientific explanation for everything:
The Indian believes that there is a reason for everything and accepts reasons
retold through allegories and fables (Duchene 1982). The non-Indian looks
for scientific explanations.

Win once, but let others win also versus winning all the time:
The Indians will share their wealth. The non-Indians desire to win all the
time since they perceive it to reflect their talents or skill.

Following the old ways versus climbing the career ladder of success:
The Indian believes in following traditions although many are directed
away from self and towards the extended family and the livelihood of the
community. The non-Indian's focus is on a career, not in following the
older traditions. The non-Indian's career reward may also be shared with
the immediate family but not with the community.

Anonymity versus individuality:
The Indian values anonymity within a group. The non-Indian values individuality within a group.

Submission versus aggression:
The Indians accept a submissive, passive role in meeting their own needs and
are likely to accept positive and negative situations as a part of nature. The
non-Indians are more aggressive in resolving various negative situations.

Humility versus winning first prize if at all possible:
The Indians recognize modesty and accept their own shortcomings. The
non-Indians focus on their personal attributes, downplay any shortcomings, and attempt to win and receive highest recognition.

The conflict of values in higher education

Although these widely recognized values may bolster the confidence of Indian
students with regard to their own communities, there are still significant
barriers to American Indian student performance and persistence in higher
education. McNamara (1982) and Wright (1992) identified four broad categories as barriers to educational progress and attainment for American Indian
students enrolled in all higher education institutions: (1) nature and quality of
past education; (2) finances; (3) lack of role models; and (4) culture conflicts
related to the college environment.

Past education
In general, American Indian students who enter college are less prepared
academically and appear to be less knowledgeable about the academic demands
and requirements of college than their majority peers (McNamara 1982). The
quality of their precollegiate education is related to their academic performance

in college. Duchene (1982) claims that American Indian students experience loss of contact with one environment, language and culture while trying to integrate into another environment, language and culture. Often, Indian students born and raised on the reservation have some knowledge of their Tribal language and history. They also have limited knowledge of English, mathematics, science, American history and American art and cultural forms.

Finances

Indian college students are eligible for Federal and State financial aid programmes, some of which are specially designed to serve them (McNamara 1982). In some cases they can receive scholarships or loans from their Tribes or other Indian organizations. However, the eligibility and receipt of funding does not prevent students from having financial difficulties. Most students receive barely enough money to cover their educational and living expenses. They also suffer as they do not receive financial support from their parents, a traditional source of support for most college students. Many students feel like outsiders on college campuses. Their financial situation provides a not-so-subtle reminder that they don't really belong there and certainly cannot afford many of the amenities of college life enjoyed by their majority peers (McNamara 1982; Gritts 1991).

Lack of role models

Familiarity with role models, others who have achieved educational and career goals, could expand the aspirations and strengthen the motivation of American Indian students. Lack of role models in home and college communities is a barrier to educational achievement (McNamara 1982). Many Indians do not come from homes where higher education is considered to be an inevitable phase in preparation for entering the adult and work world. They cannot turn to their families or friends for information about college institutions or for advice about career alternatives and training.

Culture conflicts

American Indian students encounter difficulties related to the 'fit' between their history, culture and values and those of the dominant culture. Many of their educational experiences are characterized by a sense of not belonging, confusion and failure. Historically, education has been used to assimilate Indians into the larger society and to relieve the Federal Government of treaty responsibilities and obligations.

Some families are sceptical about encouraging their children to attend educational institutions controlled by whites. Students who participate in education can be seen as lost to the community and as deserting it for 'white man ways'. Many times, American Indians will take care of their cultural responsibilities first; only then, if they can fit it in, will they seek an education (McNamara 1982). Wright (1992) stated that Native students leave their communities, in which Native life ways are still meaningful; they enter alien, intimidating and overwhelming environments where opposing social and structural systems are hostile, alienating and isolating.

M. Belgarde (1989, 1992) has examined the significance of cultural values and belief systems in the negative experiences that many American Indian students have in college classrooms. The more traditional students enrolled in private, elite institutions find that the institutional climate, assumptions within texts and lectures, and lack of cultural understanding by their professors are stressful for them. For example, Beverly, a mixed-blood (half-white and half-Indian) who was raised in both reservation and urban areas, had two difficult encounters with faculty members in a required two-course sequence. She said:

> I shopped around and finally came up with a class I thought I would like [because the course title implied an emphasis on cultural differences]. So I went ahead and took the class. But me and the instructor had conflict after conflict. The instructor who was Asian-American and very assimilated felt that the points that I was trying to make in class were alienating people and that he wanted his class to be comfortable. And [the students were] largely White people – there were two other people-of-colour. Everything we said he toned down – he used to cut me off a lot. And that was a very bad experience even though I ended up getting a B+.
>
> (M. J. Belgarde 1992, p. 98)

In the second course, the instructor assigned a research paper on 'our' immigrant relations coming to America as the major assignment. Beverly related the following:

> I raised my hand and said that I was an American Indian and that I didn't think I could do this adequately. She actually seemed offended and said that this had never happened before and was very flustered. As the course went on I asked her if I could pick another research topic. She said, 'Maybe you can write on how your people got put on reservations.' I didn't like the way that came across and said I wouldn't like to write on that either. After class I said, 'I'm dropping this class; I just don't feel good about this class.' But she said, 'Oh stay, stay.' So I did. I went to about four more sessions but she kept doing little things [that I found offensive] more and more and I dropped it.
>
> (M. J. Belgarde 1992, p. 98)

Students also have trouble participating in class discussions unless they have something significant to add to the discussion. Cecilia and John explain. As Cecilia relates (pers. comm.):

> In the Indian way you are taught to be quiet – not seen and not heard – but you are taught to be respectful and quiet to other

people. Here, the people who excel are people who talk the most, are willing to interrupt you.

(Belgarde In Press)

John, who is a full-blooded Indian of two Tribes, and a person who grew up on a reservation, describes his initial and later reaction to white student verbal behaviour in the classroom:

> White students were so cocky and confident in themselves. They can sit there and go on and on about a book and sometimes they didn't make sense . . . . But I thought, oh they must be gods, they know all this stuff. I didn't do that. I was scared, I didn't want to sound stupid and I didn't want to sound like I didn't know anything so I never said anything in that discussion class . . . . It was culturally inappropriate because they weren't contributing to our learning anything. They were saying or spouting off what they knew so it was like bragging on themselves about what they knew. We don't do that in the Indian way, you don't talk like you know this or that. So I would be embarrassed for them actually. . . . Some would interrupt people and they call that aggressiveness. . . . I thought it was odd that they would go on talking about themselves and not help us in any way.
>
> (M. J. Belgarde 1992, p. 144)

> Any time we talk about issues or anything it seems that a lot of times other students generalize and say 'Most of America is like this.' And it's always in the cities – like New York or San Francisco, maybe Chicago. They generalize about poverty and social issues for those places, and say, 'This is America.' And I'm jumping up and down saying, 'No! This is not America; this is a part of America. A lot of the people who are affected by what you are talking about [Indians] don't even live in the city, but in rural areas.' Being invisible, being unnoticed can be very frustrating. Especially when you're jumping up and down, trying to get their attention and they don't acknowledge it at all.
>
> (M. J. Belgarde 1992, p. 114)

> . . .my comments are always way off the wall to people because they think that I am totally strange. Something that is incredibly relevant to me is not relevant to them. We were discussing having English as a national language in one of my classes in the Classics department. . . . They were talking about [whether] people coming to the States should learn the language of the States because they will need it and because this isn't their country – they are moving into a host country. You bring up a simply, totally clear thing like the Native Americans were here first, there are still indigenous languages spoken every day, and they shouldn't be

forced to speak English either if they don't want to. They note it
for half a second and go on with their argument disregarding it.
(M. J. Belgarde 1992, p. 114)

Four-year colleges and universities are therefore alien environments for
American Indian students who identify with Indian culture, values and traditional belief systems. These mainstream institutions are fraught with institutional structures (courses, pedagogical approaches, dormitory placements and
so on) that address majority student needs and overlook the needs of students
who enrol in smaller numbers.

The Tribal community college

Twenty-four tribally controlled community colleges have been created in
response to the lack of success of Indian students in the mainstream system. As
W. L. Belgarde has stated: 'Most [American Indian students] were finding
mainstream colleges uncongenial, stopping out and returning to their Indian
communities to regroup – convinced that higher education was useful, but
questioning whether the alien culture of mainstream campuses was worth
enduring' (W. L. Belgarde 1992, pp. 32–3).

Initiated by American Indian communities in the 1970s, following civil
rights legislation, the colleges purported to offer relevant and culturally based
education, taught and administered by American Indian people (Duchene
1982; Oppelt 1982; Bordeaux 1991; Boyer 1991; W. L. Belgarde 1992).

The tribally controlled community college enrolment varies depending on
the reservation size, location of the college and the length of time it has been in
existence. Student enrolments range from 50 to 1500 students. The ages of
students range from 16 to 67 years of age. A high proportion of students are
working parents. The average student at a Tribal college is a 30-year-old
woman with two or more children. Often the sole support of her dependants,
she has poor academic preparation, and survives on an annual income well
below the poverty level. Students include those who have not had previous
access to higher education and those who have primarily attended off-
reservation colleges and dropped out.

The students attending tribally controlled colleges characteristically survive
in difficult and hostile environments. They are generally mature, highly
motivated, and resourceful. The moral support of an extended family group is
often the major source of motivation to initiate and persist in a two-year
programme that may require six years to complete (Duchene 1982; Oppelt
1982; Carnegie Foundation for the Advancement of Teaching 1989; Bordeaux
1991; Boyer 1991; W. L. Belgarde 1992).

The Tribal community college curricula vary according to the institution's
commitment to meeting the needs of the Tribe. Tribal needs differ with
respect to the social, economic, cultural and historical circumstances of each

reservation (W. L. Belgarde 1992; Houser 1992). Most colleges offer a general studies degree at the associate level, as preparation for entry into baccalaureate programmes. In response to employment needs on most reservations, many institutions offer degrees in human services or social work, business and management, and certificates or degrees in alcoholism and drug abuse training. Some colleges offer upper division teacher education curricula in an effort to prepare Native teachers for local classrooms. Two of the colleges, Sinte Gleska and Oglala Lakota (South Dakota), offer baccalaureate degrees in education, and Sinte Gleska offers a Master's degree programme in education (Houser 1992). Many Tribal colleges also offer vocational and occupational training programmes, such as data processing, computer application, media communications, management/entrepreneurship, nursing, dental assistant training, as well. Some programmes build upon their social, economic and natural environments, such as: aquaculture on the Lummi reservation (Washington); forestry at Salish Kootenai (Montana), Stonechild (Montana) and Sinte Gleska (South Dakota); game and fisheries management at Little Hoop (North Dakota); and agricultural and natural resource management at Sisseton (South Dakota). Many Tribal colleges also offer General Equivalency Diplomas (GEDs) (Houser 1992).

The Carnegie Foundation for the Advancement of Teaching (1989) report reveals that most Tribal colleges incorporate Indian culture into the curriculum. The report states:

These institutions have demonstrated eloquently that the traditional Indian cultures, rather than being disruptive or irrelevant, are supportive and nurturing influences on Indian students . . .

Beyond the differences, all tribal colleges share common goals. They seek to strengthen respect for their cultural heritage, create greater social and economic opportunities for the tribe and its members, and create links to the larger American society. The watchword at Indian colleges is not simply education, but empowerment . . . . All tribal colleges seek first to rebuild, among students, an understanding of their heritage, and in some settings this has been a particularly challenging task. On many reservations, native beliefs, language, and traditional areas were not strong. Values once shared through a rich tradition of storytelling were not being preserved – traditional culture existed to a large degree only in textbooks, while Anglo values [i.e. of people of Anglo-Saxon descent, or English-speaking] remained alien and unaccepted.

(Carnegie Foundation for the Advancement of
Teaching 1989, pp. 25, 53)

Lac Courte Oreilles Ojibwas Community College in Wisconsin offers Native studies courses in traditional clothing styles, music and dance. Oglala Lakota Community College (South Dakota) offers a continuing education course in 'How to set up a tipi', quillwork and preparation of traditional foods.

Northwest Indian College (Washington) offers classes in canoe-carving, woodwork and Indian knitting – skills unique to their tribal culture (Carnegie Foundation for the Advancement of Teaching 1989).

At Turtle Mountain Community College (North Dakota) the Indian culture is incorporated in how courses are taught. Elma Wilkie, one of Turtle Mountain's senior instructors, makes a deliberate effort to incorporate an Indian viewpoint in her sociology classes. She uses texts that treat Native Americans with respect and supplements them with additional books and articles that explain the Native American experience. For example, she uses family trees and oral histories to study the Indian family's distinctive structure, rather than simply describing family life in terms of Anglo social structures (Carnegie Foundation for the Advancement of Teaching 1989, p. 57).

The success of tribally controlled community college transfer students

Current research about tribally controlled community colleges is limited to institutional self-studies, reports and a few published articles and dissertations (see Wright & WeaselHead 1990). The research findings on Tribal college transfer students are limited to descriptive reports revealing the numbers and percentages of students who have completed baccalaureate, Master's, doctoral and law degree programmes at four-year institutions, without identifying personal and institutional factors which may inhibit their successful transition and completion of degree programmes. Most Tribal colleges lack the research personnel and financial resources needed to complete these types of studies. Nevertheless, they have been in existence for less than twenty years and have educational goals that extend beyond granting associate degrees. Many of the personnel have not yet worked out articulation agreements between Tribal colleges and four-year institutions (C. S. Kidwell, pers. comm.). However, there is some evidence to demonstrate that students who transfer have benefited from the strong cultural and academic programmes offered at Tribal colleges (Houser 1992).

American Indian students are transferring to and completing programmes at four-year institutions in higher numbers annually. Houser (1992) states that in 1990 the American Indian Higher Education Consortium (AIHEC) assessed the effectiveness of six accredited institutions during the period between 1983 and 1989: Oglala Lakota, Sinte Gleska, Standing Rock, Turtle Mountain, Salish Kootenai and Blackfeet.

During these years, 1575 Indians graduated from the six colleges. Of these graduates, 210 earned one-year vocational certificates, 1198 earned associate degrees, 158 earned Bachelor's degrees, and 9 earned Master's degrees in education. About one-third of these graduates, primarily those with vocational certificates and associate degrees, continued their education after graduation (Houser 1992, p. 9).

Wright & WeaselHead (1990) report that over 50 per cent of those who complete a two-year degree programme at Dull Knife Memorial College (Montana) and Sisseton-Wahpeton (South Dakota) pursue further study.

A preliminary student outcomes study completed by the Center for Native American Studies at Montana State University (Wright & WeaselHead 1990) examined the extent to which Tribal college graduates continued their education, the extent to which Tribal colleges prepared graduates for education, and the degree of student satisfaction with the quality of educational services among 222 students who were awarded associate degrees from Montana's seven Tribal colleges between 1976 and 1987. The researchers found that among the 222 respondents, 87 (37%) were continuing their education at four-year institutions or Tribal colleges. Of the transfer students, 84% were enrolled in courses of study related to their initial Tribal college training. Of those who were attending other institutions, only 13% encountered problems transferring from the Tribal college, although the report was not specific in identifying the types of problems that students encountered. In this study, 16% of the students continued their education at the Tribal college, with 61% pursuing career fields related to their initial training programmes.

Houser (1992) also reports that the initial evidence of another study still in progress of Montana Tribal colleges reveals that the Tribal college students who transferred to three state institutions and remained until their senior year are doing as well as or better than the students who started out in those institutions. Given these results, Houser asserts that:

> if former tribal college students terminated their educations before graduating from the four-year institutions to which they had transferred, they left for non-academic reasons – family responsibilities, finances, employment opportunities, etc. This statistical evidence reinforces narrative evidence from each institution; tribal colleges are providing education of quality to whole groups of students who had previously been excluded, for a variety of reasons, from colleges and universities.
>
> (Houser 1992, p. 10)

Future problems and prospects

Although much of the research on transfer students has focused on the individual, recent work has suggested more fundamental structural issues that organize or arrange the effect of these person-level factors for students of other ethnic groups. For example, Turner's (1988) work on Hispanic students suggests the vital role the alignment between the curriculum and programme at sending community colleges and receiving four-year institutions plays in the possibility for successful transition. In other words, the effects of such considerations as motivation and aspiration may be contingent on contextualizing factors – structural considerations, systematized underpreparation, and the combination of work and family arrangements that are the properties of a class of persons, not of particular individuals.

Such a focus enables us to pose new kinds of questions for research into how different groups and communities of students experience the formal organizational characteristics within colleges, how these arrangements and informational/support networks vary across groups, and the like. For the questions about persistence among those who do make it into four-year institutions after preparatory work in community colleges, similar and other questions emerge. For example, in the case of the Tribal colleges, quite distinct issues of cultural conflict between majority and minority/traditional ways of knowing and interacting may be significant.

Policy-makers need to be concerned about how to increase the likelihood of transfer and persistence of tribally controlled community college students. Here, issues include the means to improve (possibly accelerate) academic preparation, financial aid information, guidance, and organizational factors within community colleges and articulation agreements between institutions.

Further research can and should inform these issues and concerns. Systematic descriptive work on the characteristics of students (such as sociodemographic background, academic preparation, other work and family responsibilities) and on Tribal community college linkages with four-year institutions would be the first step. Some of this has been done, much of it in the form of case studies, but previous research has done little beyond constructing simple profiles of students. More analysis needs to be done on the strength of the relationships between the common characteristics of students and the common characteristics of the institutions they are likely to attend (as well as any interactive effects) paying particular attention to relationships suggested in the literature. The questions could include:

What are the structural characteristics within mainstream four-year institutions that may compound the disadvantages of American Indian students?

To what extent can four-year institutions meet the cultural values and needs of American Indian students transferring from tribally controlled colleges? What kinds of courses, pedagogical approaches and social environments at tribal colleges can be replicated at mainstream four-year institutions?

What is the effect of individual or group characteristics on transfer and persistence of Tribal college students?

What are the characteristics and circumstances of community colleges with successful transfer processes (see, for example, Turner 1988) and what can be learned from them?

What are the effects of broader or extended family/support networks on transfer and persistence? Much recent literature on relations between social networks and schooling attainment for minorities suggests that these networks can be vital for positive outcomes, but may also suggest responsibilities or cultural traditions that work against attainment. What is the nature of these networks among students who do and do not make successful transfers and who do and do not persist?

Although such research can contribute to a lessening of the tension experienced by American Indian transfer students, the best solution may be to expand the role of tribally controlled community colleges. These colleges have goals, missions, curricula and interaction patterns that are aligned with the American Indian students' cultural values. However, most only provide the first two years towards a Bachelor's degree. Although many of the tribally controlled community colleges intend to become baccalaureate-granting institutions, many of them lack the resources to do so at this time. Until Tribal colleges become four-year institutions, American Indian community-college transfer students will continue to endure cultural clashes in the classroom and face other academic difficulties in order to obtain the certification only available to them from mainstream higher education institutions.

References

Astin, A. 1975. *Preventing Students from Dropping Out*. San Francisco: Jossey-Bass.
Astin, A. 1985. *Minorities in Higher Education*. San Francisco: Jossey-Bass.
Belgarde, M. J. 1989. The performance and persistence of American Indian students at Stanford – a qualitative pilot study. Unpublished MS.
Belgarde, M. J. 1992. The performance and persistence of American Indian students at Stanford University. Unpublished PhD dissertation, Stanford University.
Belgarde, W. L. 1992. Indian control and interdependency: a study of the relationship between the holders of critical resources and the structure of American Indian community colleges. Unpublished PhD dissertation, Stanford University.
Bordeaux, L. 1991. Higher education from the Tribal college perspective. In *Opening the Montana Pipeline: American Indian higher education in the nineties*, LaCounte, D. W., W. Stein & P. WeaselHead (eds), 11–18. Sacramento, Calif.: Tribal College Press.
Boyer, P. 1991. Tribal colleges: creating a new partnership in higher education. In *Opening the Montana Pipeline: American Indian higher education in the nineties*, LaCounte, D. W., W. Stein & P. WeaselHead (eds), 114–25. Sacramento, Calif.: Tribal College Press.
Bryde, J. F. 1972. *Indian Students in Guidance*. Boston: Houghton & Mifflin.
California Community Colleges Chancellor's Office 1984. *Transfer Education, California Community Colleges*. Sacramento, Calif.: Analytical Studies Unit.
California Legislative Assembly 1984. *Report of the Special Committee on Community College*. Sacramento: California State Assembly.
Carnegie Foundation for the Advancement of Teaching 1989. *Tribal Colleges: shaping the future of Native America*. Lawrenceville, N.J.: Princeton University Press.
Clark, B. 1960. *The Open Door College: a case study*. San Francisco: Jossey-Bass.
Cohen, A. M. & F. B. Brawer 1987. *The Collegiate Function of Community Colleges*. San Francisco: Jossey-Bass.
Cohen, E. & M. Chacon 1982. *Chicanas in Post-secondary Education*. Stanford: Center for Research on Women, Stanford University.
Duchene, M. 1982. A profile of Indian community colleges. *American Indian Education* 19, 23–7.

Eckland, B. K. 1981. *College Attainment Four Years after High School*. Center for Educational Research and Evaluation, National Center for Education Statistics.

Fuchs, E. & R. Havighurst 1972. *To Live on This Earth*. New York: Doubleday.

Gritts, J. 1991. Financial aid and the Indian college student. In *Opening the Montana Pipeline: American Indian higher education in the nineties*, LaCounte, D. W., W. Stein & P. WeaselHead (eds), 54–62. Sacramento, Calif.: Tribal College Press.

Havighurst, R. J. 1978. Indian education since 1960. *Annals of the American Academy of Political and Social Science* 436, 13–26.

Houser, S. 1992. Underfunded miracles: Tribal colleges. In *Indian Nations at Risk: commissioned papers*, Indian Nations at Risk Task Force (eds), 1–17. Washington, D.C.: US Department of Education.

Huffman, T. E., M. L. Sill & M. Brokenleg 1986. College achievement among Sioux and white South Dakota students. *Journal of American Indian Education* 25, 32–8.

Jaimes, A. 1981. Higher educational needs of Indian students. *Integrated Education: American Indian Education* 19, 7–12.

Jeannotte, L. D. 1988. Graduation completion of tribally controlled community college transfer students. Personal conversations, Native American Studies Office, University of North Dakota, Grand Forks, North Dakota, August–December 1988.

Kleinfeld, J. S. & K. L. Kohout 1974. Increasing the college success of Alaska Natives. *Journal of American Indian Education* 13, 27–31.

Lamberts, J. A. 1977. College transfer students: Who are they? What happens to them? What are their unique needs? Paper presented at the Annual Meeting to the Washington Educational Research Association, Seattle, Washington, 26–27 May 1977.

Lewis, R. G. & M. Keung Ho 1975. Social work with Native Americans. *Social Work*, September, 379–82.

McNamara, P. O. 1982. Americans in higher education: a longitudinal study of progress and attainment. Unpublished PhD dissertation, University of California, Los Angeles.

Mingle, J. R. 1987. *Focus on Minorities: trends in higher education participation and success.* Denver: Education Commission of the States & the State Higher Education Executive Officers.

National Center for Education Statistics 1977. *Transfer Students in Institutions of Higher Education: national longitudinal study of high school seniors*. Washington, D.C.: US Government Printing Office.

Olivas, M. A. 1979. *The Dilemma of Access: minorities in two year colleges*. Washington: Howard University Press.

Oppelt, N. T. 1982. The tribally controlled colleges in the 1980s: higher education's best kept secret. *American Indian Culture and Research Journal*, 27–45.

Patton, W. & E. D. Edington 1973. Factors related to persistence of Indian students at college level. *Journal of American Indian Education* 12, 19–23.

Rindone, P. 1988. Achievement motivation and academic achievement of Native American students. *Journal of American Indian Education* 28, 1–8.

Sawyer, T. M. 1981. Indian students' study habits and attitudes. *Journal of American Indian Education* 20, 13–17.

Trimble, J. E. 1976. Value differences among American Indians: concerns for the concerned counselor. In *Counseling across Cultures*, 2nd edn, Pedersen, P., J. Draguns & W. Lonner (eds), 65–81. Honolulu: University Press of Hawaii.

Trimble, J. E. 1981. Value differentials and their importance in counseling American Indians. In *Counseling across Cultures*, 2nd edn, Pedersen, P., J. Draguns & W. Lonner (eds), 203–26. Honolulu: University Press of Hawaii.

Trimble, J. E. 1988. Stereotypic images, American Indians and prejudice. In *Eliminating Racism and Prejudice*, Katz, P. & D. Taylor (eds), 210–36. New York: Pergamon Press.

Turner, C. S. V. 1988. Organizational determinants of the transfer of hispanic students from two- to four-year colleges. Unpublished PhD dissertation, Stanford University.

West, D. K. 1988. Comparisons of career maturity and its relationship with academic performance. *Journal of American Indian Education* 27, 1–7.

Wright, B. 1985. Programming success: special student services and the American Indian college student. *Journal of American Indian Education*, 24, 1–7.

Wright, B. 1992. American Indian and Alaska Native Higher Education: toward a new century of academic achievement and cultural integrity. In *Indian Nations at Risk: Task Force commissioned papers*, Indian Nations at Risk Task Force (eds), 1–16. Washington, D.C.: US Department of Education.

Wright, B. & P. WeaselHead 1990. Tribal controlled community colleges: a student outcomes assessment of associate degree recipients. *Community College Review*, 18, 28–33.

Zintz, M. V. 1963. *Education across Culture*. Dubuque, Iowa: William C. Brown.

34 Archaeology, prehistory and the Native Learning Resources project: Alberta, Canada

HEATHER DEVINE

Introduction

In November 1984 the Native Education Project Team was established by the Alberta Department of Education. Its mandate was to develop a Native Education Policy to guide the development and delivery of education to aboriginal students (Alberta Education, Native Education Project 1985a). The project team was responsible for evaluating all learning resources dealing with Native topics intended for use in the classroom. Under the auspices of the Native Learning Resources Project, the team was given the task of co-ordinating the development of learning resources that would reflect indigenous history and culture from the Native perspective.

In early 1985, while doing research into archaeology in education for the Archaeological Survey of Alberta, I learned of the existence of the Native Education Team and its mandate to produce school textbooks. It was clear that this committee would have a profound influence over the production of any instructional materials concerned with Native peoples, including those dealing with prehistory and prehistoric archaeology. Any materials prepared by the Archaeological Survey of Alberta for school audiences might well fall under the scrutiny of this committee at some point or other. If such materials did not satisfy the evaluation criteria established by this committee, the material might not be recommended for use in Alberta classrooms, no matter how archaeologically sound or culturally sensitive it might be from the perspective of archaeologists. Therefore, the Archaeological Survey established a formal working relationship with the Native Education Team in early 1985, in the context of the Native Learning Resources Project.

Developmental framework

In cross-cultural curriculum design programmes, it can be argued that the development process is more important pedagogically than the development outcome (i.e. completed texts). A primary objective of the Native Education Project was to encourage a disenfranchised Native population to participate in the educational system (Alberta Education, Native Education Project 1985a, pp. 22–5). The first step in this process was the putting into place of a curriculum policy that would address concerns voiced by Alberta's First Nations communities. An important second step was to assert Native control – 'ownership', if you like – over the way Native culture and history were presented and interpreted in Alberta classrooms, through direct involvement in the creation of culturally sensitive learning resources.

In order to achieve this goal, an organizational framework (see Aoki, Werner, Dahlie & Conners 1984, pp. 282–7) was adopted that kept significant control over style and content in Native hands. Individual Native sponsoring organizations (e.g. Metis organizations, band councils) would join with local school boards to produce textbooks on specific topics identified in the Alberta Social Studies Program. Each team would include representatives of the sponsoring Native organization, classroom teachers, subject-matter experts (primarily Native) and curriculum specialists from Alberta Education. Final approval of content would be given by validation committees from the Native communities sponsoring each text. Each team would also work with a publisher, to bring the materials to a finished form.

Some guiding principles were established to influence the development process (Alberta Education, Native Education Project 1985b, p. 2):

1 The appropriate Native community must be involved in an active role.
2 The determination of content is a joint responsibility of the Native community and professional teachers, who will be guided by the Alberta Social Studies Program, and their interaction with students.
3 The wants and perspectives of the Native community must be respected.
4 The resulting learning resources will be a result of the ongoing interaction of the participants in the development process.

Freire (1972) has spoken eloquently of the need to produce learning materials that reflect the experiences and the world-view of the people who use them. In particular, he speaks of the influential role that such materials can play in giving oppressed peoples their own voice. According to Freire, the creation of curriculum materials should serve to bring about *praxis* – a state of action and reflection which results in what he calls *conscientization*.

> Conscientization refers to the process in which men, not as recipients, but as knowing subjects, achieve a deepening awareness both of the sociocultural reality which shapes their lives and of their capacity to transform that reality.
>
> (Freire 1972, p. 51)

Curriculum materials produced from this point of view are designed to empower, and bring about a state of critical consciousness in, the creators and the users. Therefore it is extremely important that those who traditionally control the development of curriculum materials (e.g. politicians, educators, subject-matter experts) be prepared instead to work as partners in this process.

Content validation

In the Native Learning Resources Project, it was made clear from the outset that the members from Native communities would be viewed as the primary subject-matter experts, and that the wants and perspectives of the Native community would determine the content of the texts. This meant that if any difference of opinion occurred *vis-à-vis* historical or ethnocultural information, the Native perspective would be reflected in the finished materials. Any information supplied by outside parties would be used or discarded at the discretion of the steering committees.

The Archaeological Survey of Alberta did not anticipate any conflicts over content because it would be giving information about the prehistoric past, and not more recent data that might somehow clash with oral historical accounts. The Education Officer of the Archaeological Survey agreed to assist a number of curriculum development teams where archaeological information pertaining to Native history or prehistory might be requested.

The development plan of the Native Learning Resources Project is one which most concerned persons would embrace eagerly. First of all, a multi-disciplinary team approach ensures that all interested parties participate from the outset, thus enhancing the credibility of the textbooks. Development within the school system ensures that adequate time and resources may be devoted to the field testing and revision of instructional prototypes. More importantly, the involvement of, and support by, Government, school, and special interest groups provide such a project with a wide base of support. It is unlikely that materials produced outside such an infrastructure would ever make it into the classroom. These considerations prompted both publishers, and the Archaeological Survey of Alberta, to forgo unilateral materials development and ally themselves with the Native Learning Resources Project.

This partnership approach was unacceptable, however, to a few subject-matter experts peripheral to the project. In one instance, a subject-matter expert claimed that the members of the steering committees were conducting ethnographic research and, as educators, were unqualified to do so. An unauthorized critique of a textbook in the draft stages also drew criticism because of perceived historical and ethnographic errors. This claim was unfounded, however, because some steering committees chose to interpret historical and cultural information from the aboriginal perspective – which, in some instances, was quite different from the standard ethnohistorical perspective.

Unfortunately, problems with subject-matter experts are not uncommon in curriculum development settings (Sabey 1973, p. 9). Specialists often assume a position of superiority because they think that their advanced training gives them that prerogative. In doing so, they implicitly denigrate the abilities of educators, who are the best equipped to create appropriate learning experiences for students. This behaviour by subject-matter experts can have an even more insidious effect on group dynamics in sensitive curriculum development initiatives like the Native Learning Resources Project. When subject-matter experts – anthropologists, historians or whatever – attempt to 'validate' curriculum content by contradicting and repudiating the folk knowledge of the Native subject-matter expert, it destroys the possibility of an ideological consensus, something that is absolutely necessary in cross-cultural curriculum development.

Academics do, however, express legitimate concerns. Subject-matter experts might well question the merit of a project where some of the information is at odds with generally accepted fact. They could argue convincingly that curriculum materials produced about Natives by Natives may serve to promote the kind of revisionism that perpetuates a whole new set of negative stereotypes, this time from the aboriginal perspective.

While this concern may have some validity, it still does not justify the entrenchment of power and control over Native curriculum content in the hands of non-Native educators and subject-matter experts. Clearly the 'experts' have not done a satisfactory job of presenting aboriginal heritage to school-children thus far. The appalling treatment of Native history and culture in mainstream curriculum materials is well documented (McDiarmid & Pratt 1971; Manitoba Indian Brotherhood 1979; Decore, Carney, Urion, Alexander & Runte 1981 and see for example Ahler 1994; Blancke and Slow Turtle 1994; Jamieson 1994; Wade 1994). The only way that aboriginal children will be encouraged to remain in the school system is if the Native history and culture presented to them in school textbooks reflects the understanding of their own societies. The best way to achieve this is by ensuring that Native people can contribute directly in curriculum development projects in which partnership is an operational reality rather than a politically expedient or 'correct' buzzword.

Establishing cross-cultural partnerships, however, can be a difficult process, as the progress of certain steering committees during the course of curriculum development illustrates.

Committee interaction

I worked with a number of steering committees and was able to experience first-hand how useful the cross-cultural approach was. This partnership, or 'mutualistic' approach to curriculum development, proved to be fulfilling and educational in a truly holistic sense, but it was not without its difficulties.

A variety of internal conflicts affected the work of some steering committees. Some of these disputes were rooted in the cultural differences of the participants, particularly when the discussions concerned project planning and resolution of issues. Non-Native participants tended to approach a project from a linear perspective and were sometimes preoccupied with curricular requirements and scheduling, and they held conventional understandings of issues and events. Native participants were inclined to approach the topics from a more holistic, community-centred perspective. These divergent approaches were actually complementary and productive – in the committees where the participants worked well together. In some groups, however, these differences drove people further apart, particularly when issues over content and point of view had to be resolved. The silence of Native participants was sometimes misinterpreted by non-Native colleagues as approval, or anger, or lack of interest, depending on the issue being discussed. The assertive style of some non-Native participants was viewed by some aboriginal participants as disrespectful at best and aggressive at worst. In one steering committee in which the author participated, the implicit tensions within the group resulted in the breakup of the committee, with the result that the textbook project was abandoned.

Happily, however, most of the committee dynamics were positive and productive. Some committees began their development sessions with sweet-grass ceremonies or Elders' prayers which served to ritually cleanse the participants and bless the activities of the day. Based on such positive beginnings, there were few development issues which were too sensitive to be resolved through lively debate. In rare situations where differences of opinion over content were insurmountable, the committee in question would remove the offending details from the draft text. Although excluding content might seem to be an unsatisfactory conclusion, it did not necessarily detract from the quality of the completed texts.

Despite isolated concerns about the validation of content, the committees were generally successful in producing textbooks that presented Native heritage in a balanced, accurate way. The groups that were most successful in completing their book drafts were those which had developed effective working relationships between the committee members based on mutual understanding, respect and diplomacy. It is unrealistic to expect Natives and non-Natives, educators and subject-matter experts, suddenly to gel into a cohesive, productive group when members of these highly disparate communities have never had the opportunity or inclination to work together before, and are unfamiliar with curriculum development or committee work. It is also unrealistic to expect rapport to develop quickly on the basis of one or two meetings a month. Those groups that were successful in maintaining a common direction had a realistic timetable for completing their texts and also gave themselves the time to gel as teams. By allowing themselves the time to get to know and respect each other as individuals, they were able to debate frankly to resolve sensitive issues which might otherwise have caused dissent and, ultimately, the failure of the project.

I was fortunate to be involved with a successful committee for over two years. Though the process was time-consuming, the finished product reflected the input and consensus of all members concerned.

The politics of archaeology

After almost three years of involvement in this project, how did Alberta archaeology fare in terms of its treatment in the Native Learning Resources Project? The degree to which regional archaeological content appeared in the textbooks varied according to the curriculum topics addressed, the amount of space available, and the whims of the committee in question.

While archaeology and prehistory topics had been included in some of the texts (see Pard 1985; Quilty, Fox & Eaglechild 1986; Cardinal & Ripley 1987; Rempel & Anderson 1987; Hodgins 1987), they were not discussed in significant detail. Teachers and students would have learned very little about indigenous prehistory if they were forced to rely on the contents of these textbooks for their information. And they would not have learned how archaeological research techniques contribute to our understanding of the prehistoric past. This rather cursory treatment was partly because of space and curriculum topic constraints, particularly as Alberta Education changed grade 6 topics to emphasize ancient civilizations in foreign countries, rather than the cultural developments in our own land. The project's heavy reliance on aboriginal subject-matter experts, who confined their input largely to ethno-historical, as opposed to archaeological, information could also explain the limited archaeology/prehistory content.

One other reason why archaeology is not given emphasis in these texts has less to do with curricular content and more to do with the deep-seated ambivalence of many Native people towards archaeologists and archaeological research.

Most archaeology professionals possess, not surprisingly, a firm belief in the inherent 'goodness' of archaeology. Those archaeologists who are trained as anthropologists tend to view themselves as cultural relativists, and therefore see themselves as well-equipped to approach Native cultural and historical topics with sensitivity and understanding.

It is becoming increasingly obvious, however, that these perceptions are not shared by indigenous people. A century of interaction between archaeology professionals and North American Native people indicates that in fact the opposite is closer to the truth, that archaeological research has done little to enhance the understanding and preservation of the Native cultural past (Arden 1989, pp. 376–93). This perception is shared by aboriginal activists elsewhere (see Barlow 1990, p. 79).

Indigenous people are justified in their mistrust of anthropologists and archaeologists because it is based on bitter past experience. Archaeologists doing research in the late nineteenth and early twentieth centuries were often antiquarians preoccupied with the treasures of ancient civilizations. In the New

484	H. DEVINE

World, they first concentrated on Mesoamerican civilization, and then on North American Indian culture. Archaeological research into Native prehistory generally consisted of burrowing into the numerous prehistoric graves and habitation sites, collecting information for the writing of cultural histories and artefacts for display in museums. Many more sites were threatened by pot-hunters who were interested in the artefacts alone. These practices continued well into the twentieth century, until antiquities laws were finally enacted to curb such destruction (Fagan 1985, pp. 143–8).

Unfortunately, the existence of antiquities laws has not necessarily resulted in ethical research practices. Irresponsible researchers show disrespect for Native spiritual practices by recording, photographing and publishing culturally sensitive information without the knowledge or consent of the groups involved (Adams 1984, p. 236). Indigenous burial sites have been, and still are, subject to archaeological investigation in the search for scientific data in North America and elsewhere. Unfortunately, many of the human remains used in research have found their way into the locked cupboards of museum collections. In more distressing instances, human remains have been placed on public display in exhibits (Cheek & Keel 1984; Ford 1984; Meighan 1984; Watson 1990, p. 92).

Despite the implementation in recent years of stringent ethical guidelines governing anthropological and archaeological research procedures (Price 1978, p. 277), and despite the legislation governing the disposition of aboriginal skeletal remains that clearly reflects the concerns of indigenous people, the perception still remains amongst Native people that archaeologists and anthropologists are looters and desecrators.[1]

Many aboriginal people think that by supporting archaeological research they are also supporting the archaeological theories that contradict spiritual beliefs. One theory that has caused considerable dissension amongst Native peoples and archaeologists is the Bering land bridge migration theory (see McGhee 1989, pp. 13–20). Some scientists believe that there is still no convincing evidence to indicate the presence of human beings in this region of North America prior to about 11,000 years ago. It is also believed that the first inhabitants of this region came from Siberia over a land bridge that once stretched between Siberia and Alaska, a piece of land known as Beringia. This hypothesis directly contradicts the traditional spiritual beliefs of most aboriginal people, who believe that their ancestors have been here since time began. Despite the fact that the ancestors of modern Native peoples are indisputably the first peoples to inhabit this region, aboriginal people are unwilling to entertain the idea that they too may have arrived here from somewhere else. While these beliefs have a spiritual basis, there is, nevertheless, a purely pragmatic reason for contradicting archaeological data. As long as Natives continue to struggle for a land base in Canada, there will always be resistance to any argument that might in some way undermine their assertion that, as the original aboriginal inhabitants of the region, they are entitled to fair and just land claims settlements. The increasing frequency with which archaeological regulatory bodies are involved, albeit reluctantly, in land claims disputes and land development issues does little to detract from this argument. Too often aboriginal people have seen archaeological information used in support of government policies that some consider to be counter to their interests. Consequently all employees of these agencies, including education personnel, are immediately suspect (see McGhee 1989, regarding the Bering land bridge controversy).

Although many archaeologists think that archaeology is value-free because it relies so heavily on the quantitative, rather than the qualitative, analysis of data, North American Natives are unconvinced of the 'purity' of archaeology as a science. Because archaeology is practised for the most part by non-Natives, because it is non-Natives who are drawing inferences from the raw data, there is a suggestion that archaeological conclusions are as value-laden, as ideologically loaded, as the historical records they are designed to supplement and validate (Trigger 1980; University of California 1983).

Native peoples do have justifiable concerns about the lack of input into projects dealing with their culture and history. Their lack of participation in archaeological research projects at a meaningful level (i.e. in a directorial role) has not only been noted by aboriginal peoples; the Education Committee of the Canadian Archaeological Association, having collected data nation-wide regarding the participation of Native peoples in archaeology as employees and volunteers, concluded:

> Native people do not appear to be in positions that direct the discipline. None is reported to be a permanent employee, none is reported to hold an academic or resource management position; only 0.5% are reported as being supervisors. Native peoples' participation in archaeology appears to be episodic (project-related?). Most participate as field labourers and consultants. Many of the latter positions are to provide information regarding Native culture.
>
> (Froese 1987, p. 15)

This state of affairs is not likely to change unless archaeological subject-matter is included in pre-college school curricula. If we hope to see Native history and archaeology interpreted from an indigenous point of view, then Native involvement is essential. This involvement must not limit aboriginal people to the fieldwork roles they have traditionally held, but should also include supervisory roles in planning and executing research plans. Unfortunately, this is unlikely to occur until more aboriginal people are formally trained in the fields of archaeology, cultural anthropology and history. Unless we expose Native students to these topics in primary and secondary schools, they are not likely to consider social sciences and humanities as career alternatives, particularly as there may be considerable peer and family pressure placed on Native university students to avoid taking archaeology or anthropology classes, or to resist the kinds of reality espoused by these disciplines. Indeed, exposure to, and subsequent interest in, these and other new ideas may even precipitate an identity crisis which compels the Native student to drop out of university (Porter 1988).

Merely including anthropology content in school programmes, however, will not convince Native youth of the validity of archaeology. More thought must be given to the role archaeological information can play in contributing to a deeper understanding of the aboriginal past. Will archaeological data provide a counterpoint to Native stereotypes, or will it reinforce negative perceptions that already exist? How will the information be presented?

Many of the conventional approaches used to organize the study of ethnic groups are implicitly biased and may negatively influence the development of student attitudes towards minority groups and issues. The 'museum approach' used in the elementary grades, where students are presented with a smorgasbord of hands-on activities and facts about a culture, may result in the study of isolated bits and pieces of cultural information far removed from any context which might make them meaningful. This problem of decontextualization is particularly apparent when indigenous myths and legends are presented to children with little or no regard for the historical and ceremonial role of the oral tradition in aboriginal culture, and the protocol and taboos associated with the mastery and transmission of oral stories (see Muriaki 1990, pp. 178–81).

The 'discipline' approach, which employs social science and history to study culture, may cause the student to analyse and classify cultural groups within the narrow confines of each discipline's conceptual and analytical framework without arriving at a holistic understanding of the evolution of cultural practices (Aoki, Werner, Dahlie & Conners 1984, p. 277).

These concerns are especially pertinent when one looks at how archaeological research has traditionally interpreted Native history, particularly as most archaeology educators seem to employ aspects of both the 'museum' and 'discipline' approaches. The common emphasis in archaeological research on the distant past may reinforce the notion that indigenous peoples and cultures are long extinct – a common complaint expressed by aboriginal people around the world (see Arenas & Obediente 1990, pp. 53 and 57; Blancke & Cjigkitoonuppa 1990, pp. 121, 125 and 127). More than once I have heard Native people say 'We don't want to be museum pieces!'. An archaeological preoccupation with the past also ignores the vital Native cultures of the present, and such concentration on prehistoric lifeways may encourage classroom teachers to gloss over the larger issues affecting Native peoples today. Dissatisfaction also exists over non-Natives' preoccupation with the clichés that characterize indigenous cultures of the past, whether they be the seemingly innocuous images of tipis and beadwork or sensationalized depictions of hunters killing and butchering wild animals. In this region, one might suggest that the preoccupation of prehistoric archaeology with tipi rings, stone tools and ancient hunting methods has helped to set these clichés firmly in the minds of the public.

Unfortunately, schools and school-teachers often find themselves caught in the middle of the controversy over how Native culture and history should be taught in the classroom. Elementary teachers, who are subject-matter generalists, are forced to learn a number of different subject disciplines and are under increased pressure to include even more content in their already crowded timetables. Even if teachers are fortunate enough to have knowledge or interest in Native culture, system constraints, such as lack of money or opportunities for in-service training, increase the likelihood that curricula dealing with Native content will get minimal attention.

Ironically enough, Native community reaction to the poor handling of indigenous topics may, in fact, actually contribute over the long term to the decline in Native content in mainstream curricula. In recent years, many indigenous communities across the country have chosen to opt out of mainstream school systems by building their own school facilities and developing their own curricula as a means of counteracting the cultural domination and economic exploitation characteristic of 'internal colonialism' (see Barlow 1990, p. 69, for a discussion of the theory of internal colonialism as defined by Wolpe 1975).

While few would fault aboriginal communities for taking matters into their own hands rather than waiting for a hidebound system to change, there are negative aspects to the establishment of Natives-only schools that should be recognized by aboriginal and non-aboriginal alike (Watson 1990; Belgarde 1994). First of all, when Native communities take steps to segregate aboriginal students – even if it is for their own cultural good – the pressure to make the necessary changes to the mainstream curricula they have left behind decreases to the detriment of those Native groups who remain within the majority system. Such an isolationist approach also narrows the social perspective of the student, with the result that Native people may be denied the mainstream understandings of some issues, rightly or wrongly. The lack of interest of some Native educators in presenting archaeological subject-matter in classrooms is both a function and a direct result of this deliberate withdrawal from mainstream ideology.

One of the intrinsic values of the public schooling experience is its heterogeneous mix of peoples and ideas. We need places where young people of different racial, ethnic and religious backgrounds can develop the traits of tolerance and understanding, and we need the different approaches to understanding the world that different subject disciplines – and different ethno-cultural communities – can bring to the classroom.

Should archaeologists get involved in programmes like the Native Learning Resources Project? In terms of social responsibility, good public relations and the provision for continued inclusion of archaeological subject-matter in the school programme, I would say 'yes'. Native special-interest groups will continue to increase their influence over the treatment of indigenous culture in the school programme, and rightly so. This will also have an impact on the inclusion of prehistoric archaeology. Therefore, if archaeologists want to have any say on how their discipline is treated in the curriculum, they would do well to become involved in collaborative, cross-cultural curriculum projects. However, should archaeological agencies choose to become involved in programme development, it is suggested that each organization develop guidelines to govern its own involvement in the projects prior to any commitments on behalf of its agencies.

The difficulties encountered over the course of this project were quickly forgotten as the textbooks were introduced to Alberta classrooms. Teachers responsible for field-testing draft copies of the books reported an extremely positive response from both Native and non-Native students. For the first time, Metis children were approaching their teachers and proudly proclaiming their Native ancestry. Other Native children discussed the information in their texts with parents and grandparents at home. Some Native organizations originally unenthusiastic about the idea of participation in the Native Learning Resources Project asked if they, too, could develop a textbook!

Following our involvement in the Native Learning Resources Project, the Archaeological Survey of Alberta experienced a subtle, but definite, increase in requests from Native organizations for information and guest speakers. Many schools have also contacted the Survey for presentations on Native prehistory. Some schools offering Native cultural programmes sent groups of children to our building for facility tours. Letters received from Native and non-Native children after these visits indicate that they enjoyed learning about the past through archaeology and benefited from it. Although these beginnings are modest, they nevertheless represent a tentative, but forward, step towards further collaborative efforts with Native educators in the field of archaeology education.

Archaeology, museums and the world outside: a conclusion

Heritage professionals must accept that they cannot keep contemporary socio-cultural reality outside the intellectual boundaries of their disciplines or the walls of their institutions. Increasingly, debates over research related to indigenous culture and history are being played out against a backdrop of social and political turmoil as aboriginal groups struggle to establish their corporate rights.

In 1990 a series of pivotal events occurred which resulted in extensive public debate over indigenous heritage issues across Canada. The first of these events was the armed standoff at Oka, Quebec, where Mohawks of the Kanesetake Reserve moved onto municipal lands to prevent the recreational development of territory which they have long considered to be sacred, ancestral land. The government response to the crisis, which involved the mobilization of units of the Canadian Armed Forces to end the blockade by force, resulted in a wave of protests and similar blockades across Canada by aboriginal communities involved in their own land claim litigation.

The second significant event involving Canada's Native community was the failure to ratify the Meech Lake Accord, an agreement on a revised Canadian constitution which required the unanimous approval of the elected representatives in each Canadian province before passage. The Meech Lake agreement was viewed as pivotal to the future of Canada, as the constitutional revisions were designed to satisfy the cultural and economic concerns of the francophone province of Quebec, the only province which refused to agree to the terms of the Constitution which had been negotiated in the early 1980s after its repatriation to Canada from Britain. After a controversial and much-maligned negotiation process, popularly referred to as 'the Quebec round', the constitutional agreement was approved in principle by provincial leaders despite the lack of clauses in the agreement which would explicitly recognize the rights of aboriginal peoples as among the founding cultures of Canada and as distinct societies under the Canadian Charter of Rights and Freedoms (see Turpel 1991 for a discussion of aboriginal rights and their constitutional implications). As a result, the agreement was defeated at the provincial level when a lone aboriginal member of the Manitoba Provincial Government, Elijah Harper, refused to vote in support of the agreement.

A third controversy of note is the ongoing struggle of the Cree of northern Quebec to stop the development of the James Bay II project, a massive hydroelectric development which would dam several rivers and flood thousands of hectares of traditional territory. The persistent lobbying efforts of the Northern Cree and their supporters to stop the development were a contributing factor in New York State's refusal to ratify a multi-billion dollar deal to purchase hydroelectric power from Quebec. The scuttling of the contract was a significant setback for Quebec nationalists, who view the development and sale of hydroelectric power as the economic underpinning of an independent Quebec nation. The success of the anti-James Bay II lobby, compounded by the fallout from the Oka standoff and the Meech Lake debacle, has contributed to an anti-Native backlash in the province of Quebec in the face of country-wide opinion polls that overwhelmingly favour a swift and just resolution of aboriginal claims.

During the most recent round of Canada's constitutional negotiations, which took place during the summer of 1992, the provincial leaders gave provisional agreement to a constitutional package which recognized the inherent right of aboriginal people to self-government. The concept of 'self-government' has yet to be explicitly defined to the satisfaction of either aboriginal leaders or mainstream politicians. This uncertainty may have contributed to the defeat of the 1992 constitutional package in a national referendum, though it should be noted that several Non-Native issues were considered concomitantly with the self-government question. The recent election of a new federal government in 1993 has renewed discussions over Native self-government, prompted by the new government's pledge to dismantle the Indian Act, the federal legislation that currently controls the administration of Native government.

Concomitant with these political developments are country-wide investigations into allegations of widespread physical and sexual abuse of Native children in residential schools, and the admission by the religious denominations that operated these schools that they contributed to the cultural genocide of Native people. Recent Crown investigations at the provincial level concerning the treatment of Natives within the Alberta justice system have also stated conclusively that Natives are 'victims of racism, discrimination, both from within the criminal justice system and from society at large' (Savage 1991, p. 1). In the extraction document derived from the *Justice Cawsey Report* (Alberta Solicitor-General 1991), it has been noted that '30 percent of the total Aboriginal population of Alberta (approximately 40,000 people) are in jail on a yearly basis' (Alberta Solicitor-General 1991, p. 21). The extraction goes on to observe that: 'the Indian youth has a 10 percent chance of completing high school, compared to 43 percent for non-Indian. It has been suggested that an Indian youth is more likely to go to jail than finish high school' (Alberta Solicitor-General 1991, p. 46).

Given the demonstrated failure of Canada's political, legal, educational and religious institutions to deal fairly with aboriginal people, it is not surprising that the research, collection, display and interpretation of aboriginal history and culture by museums and other heritage organizations should also come under close scrutiny by Native advocates. Proposed Federal legislation concerning the ownership and repatriation of archaeological resources has come under heated debate by representatives of heritage institutions and indigenous organizations, with no clear end in sight (Dunn 1991).

Some museums have chosen to address these problems by ignoring the debate in the hope that it will go away. Other institutions, like the Provincial Museum of Alberta (PMA), have instead made the decision to make a critical evaluation of museum ideology and practice involving indigenous heritage. In partnership with Alberta's Indian and Metis communities, the PMA is setting up a long-term strategy to develop new programmes and modify or discard old approaches to the curation and interpretation of aboriginal heritage (Sciorra 1991). An important aspect of this initiative will be the provision of logistic and technical support, upon request, to First Nations communities wishing to undertake their own community-based heritage development projects.

Heritage professionals – and the institutions for which they work – must be prepared to address the long-standing concerns of aboriginal communities concerning the ideology and practice of archaeology, cultural anthropology, and history, before these disciplines will be accepted as legitimate tools for interpreting the aboriginal past in Native schools.

This process starts by revising educational approaches to the interpretation of aboriginal culture and history within the walls of the museum itself, in order to ensure that museum offerings embody a cross-cultural ethos. A preliminary step in this process involves the adoption of exhibit development and interpretive programming policies that treat museum educators as equal partners with curatorial and design staff. Too often pedagogical concerns are denigrated or ignored by museum professionals uninterested in or unfamiliar with the goals of museum education. Exhibits which do not reflect a sensitivity for contemporary social issues as discussed in school curricula will, in all likelihood, be avoided by discriminating educators.

Involvement in museum programme development should not be confined to museum educators alone, but should also include cross-cultural curriculum specialists and representatives of Native communities and organizations, particularly when exhibits and programmes involve aboriginal content. Native participation will also enhance the development – and subsequent credibility – of outreach materials and programmes, teacher in-service training sessions, and interpretive staff development.

The institutional changes required to accommodate Native involvement in museum operations will come at some cost. It will radically alter the traditional decision-making processes of the museum to reflect a more consensual, rather than hierarchical, approach to facility administration. It will require academics within the museum to acknowledge and respect expertise acquired outside formalized educational settings and epistemologies foreign to their own. In short, the development of meaningful cross-cultural partnerships in heritage institutions will result in a profound and irrevocable process of democratization which should make these places more accountable and accessible to their multi-ethnic constituents.

The task of evaluating and changing museum theory and practice will be a long and sometimes painful process. It took well over 100 years to develop the museum infrastructure that currently exists in Canada. During much of that time, Canada's museums contributed, however inadvertently, to the deterioration of the linguistic, cultural and spiritual foundations of Indian and Metis society by their appropriation of objects of cultural significance and their unilateral approaches to the curation and interpretation of this material. It is now up to the museum community to develop working partnerships that contribute to the contemporary vitality and diversity of Native heritage, while at the same time preserving, protecting and celebrating the cultures of the aboriginal past.

Acknowledgements

This paper was originally presented at the Annual Meetings of the Canadian Archaeological Association, Whistler, British Columbia, 11–14 May 1988. I would like to thank Dr David Burley, Department of Archaeology, Simon Fraser University, for his discussion and editorial comments subsequent to my presentation which contributed to the final version of the article included in the collection of education papers presented prior to, and during, the WAC 2 Conference in Barquisimeto, Venezuela, in 1990.

Note

1 Trigger's (1980) discussion of the evolution of prehistoric archaeological theory and method and its application to the study of the Native past provides a comprehensive explanation for the legacy of mistrust that now exists between North American Natives and archaeologists.

Editors' note

Immediately prior to this book going to press we received word from Heather Devine concerning the status of the Special Services Programme. It is with regret that we have learned of the elimination of the programme because of budgetary cutbacks within the Alberta Government.

References

Adams, E. C. 1984. Archaeology and the Native American: a case at Hopi. In *Ethics and Values in Archaeology*, Green, E. (ed.), 236–42. New York: The Free Press, Collier-Macmillan Publishing.

Ahler, J. G. 1994. The benefits of multicultural education for American Indian Schools: an anthropological perspective. In *The Presented Past: heritage, museums and education*, Stone, P. G & B. L. Molyneaux (eds), 453–9. London: Routledge.

Alberta Education, Native Education Project 1985a. *Native Education in Alberta's Schools*. Edmonton: Provincial Government of Alberta.

Alberta Education, Native Education Project 1985b. Guidelines for the development of learning resources. Handout from the inaugural workshop, Native Learning Resources Project, October 1985.

Alberta Solicitor-General 1991. *An Extraction of the Justice Cawsey Report: aboriginal people and the justice system*. Edmonton: Provincial Government of Alberta.

Aoki, T., W. Werner, J. Dahlie & B. Conners 1984. Ethnicity within Canadian social studies curricula. In *Cultural Diversity and Canadian Education*, Mallea, J. R. & J. C. Young (eds), 265–89. Ottawa: Carleton University Press.

Arden, H. 1989. Who owns our past? *National Geographic* March, 376–93.

Arenas, I. V. & M. S. Obediente 1990. Education and the political manipulation of history in Venezuela. In *The Excluded Past: archaeology in education*, Stone, P. & R. MacKenzie (eds), 50–60. London: Unwin Hyman; Routledge pbk 1994.

Barlow, A. 1990. Still civilizing? Aborigines in Australian education. In *The Excluded Past: archaeology in education*, Stone, P. & R. MacKenzie (eds), 68–87. London: Unwin Hyman; Routledge pbk 1994.

Belgarde, M. J. 1994. The transfer of American Indian and other minority community college students. In *The Presented Past: heritage, museums and education*, Stone, P. G & B. L. Molyneaux (eds), 460–77. London: Routledge.

Blancke, S. & Cjigkitoonuppa John Peters Slow Turtle 1990. The teaching of the past of the Native peoples of North America in U.S. schools. In *The Excluded Past: archaeology in education*, Stone, P. & R. MacKenzie (eds), 109–33. London: Unwin Hyman; Routledge pbk 1994.

Blancke, S. & Cjigkitoonuppa John Peters Slow Turtle 1994. Traditional American Indian education as a palliative to western education. In *The Presented Past: heritage, museums and education*, Stone, P. G. & B. L. Molyneaux (eds), 438–52. London: Routledge.

Cardinal, P. & D. Ripley 1987. *Canada's People: the Metis*. Edmonton: Plains Publishing.

Cheek, A. L. & B. C. Keel 1984. Value conflicts in osteoarchaeology. In *Ethics and Values in Archaeology*, Green, E. (ed.), 194–207. New York: The Free Press, Collier-Macmillan Publishing.

Decore, A. M., R. Carney, C. Urion, D. Alexander & R. Runte 1981. *Native People in the Curriculum*. Edmonton: Alberta Education, Curriculum Branch.

Dunn, M. 1991. *'My Grandfather is Not an Artifact': a report on the Aboriginal Archaeological Heritage Symposium – February 17–18*, Hull: Government of Canada, Department of Communications, Archaeology Heritage Branch.

Fagan, B. M. 1985. *The Adventure of Archaeology*. Washington: National Geographic Society.
Ford, R. I. 1984. Ethics and the museum archaeologist. In *Ethics and Values in Archaeology*, Green, E. (ed.), 138–9. New York: The Free Press, Collier-Macmillan Publishing.
Freire, P. 1972. Cultural action and conscientization. In *Cultural Action for Freedom*, Preface by Joao da Veiga Coutinho, 51–83. Harmondsworth: Penguin Books.
Froese, P. 1987. Education Committee questionnaire results. *Canadian Archaeological Association Newsletter* 7, 14–15.
Hodgins, K. 1987. *The Art of the Nehiyawak*. Edmonton: Plains Publishing.
Jamieson, J. 1994. One view of Native education in the Northwest Territories, Canda. In *The Presented Past: heritage, museums and education*, Stone, P. G. & B. L. Molyneaux (eds), 495–510. London: Routledge.
McDiarmid, G. & D. Pratt 1971. *Teaching Prejudice*. Toronto: Ontario Institute for Studies in Education.
McGhee, R. 1989. Who owns prehistory? The Bering land bridge dilemma. *Canadian Journal of Archaeology* 13, 13–20.
Manitoba Indian Brotherhood 1979. *The Shocking Truth about Indians in Textbooks*. Winnipeg: Manitoba Indian Brotherhood.
Meighan, C. W. 1984. Archaeology: science or sacrilege? In *Ethics and Values in Archaeology*, Green, E. (ed.), 208–33. New York: The Free Press, Collier-Macmillan Publishing.
Muriaki, G. 1990. The reconstruction of African history through historical, ethnographic, and oral sources. In *The Excluded Past: archaeology in education*, Stone, P. & R. MacKenzie (eds), 173–82. London: Unwin Hyman; Routledge pbk 1994.
Native Learning Resources Project 1985. Guidelines for the development of learning resources (handout). Edmonton: Native Education Project.
Pard, B. 1985. *The Piegan: a nation in transition*. Edmonton: Plains Publishing.
Porter, D. 1988. Stages, services and directions. A paper presented at the Partners in Education Native education conference, Edmonton, Alberta, Canada.
Price, J. A. 1978. *Native Studies: American and Canadian Indians*. Toronto: McGraw-Hill Ryerson.
Quilty, J., L. Fox & R. Eaglechild 1986. *The Land of the Bloods*. Edmonton: Plains Publishing.
Rempel, D. C. & L. Anderson 1987. *Annette's People: the Metis*. Edmonton: Plains Publishing.
Sabey, R. 1973. The preparation of culturally-sensitive curriculum material for Canadian schools: an overview. *Newsletter of the Council on Anthropology and Education* 4, 7–10.
Savage, B. 1991. Alberta justice on trial. *Alberta Native News* 8, 1 April.
Sciorra, A. 1991. Human remains and other heritage issues: restructuring relations between First Nations and the museum community. Unpublished monograph on file, Special Services Section, Provincial Museum of Alberta, Edmonton.
Trigger, B. 1980. Archaeology and the image of the American Indian. *American Antiquity* 45, 662–76.
Turpel, M. E. (Aki-Kwe) 1991. Aboriginal peoples and the Canadian Charter of Rights and Freedoms: contradictions and challenges. *Canadian Woman Studies* 10, 149–57.
University of California 1983. Science or sacrilege: the study of Native American remains. Videotape. Santa Barbara: Instructional Development, University of California.
Wade, P. 1994. Blacks, Indians and the state in Colombia. In *The Presented Past: heritage, museums and education*, Stone, P. G. & B. L. Molyneaux (eds), 418–37. London Routledge.
Watson, L. 1990. The affirmation of indigenous values in a colonial education system.

In *The Excluded Past: archaeology in education*, Stone, P. & R. MacKenzie (eds), 88–97. London: Unwin Hyman; Routledge pbk 1994.

Wolpe, H. 1975. The theory of internal colonialism – the South African case. In *Beyond the Sociology of Development: economy and society in Latin America and Africa*, Oxaal, I. T. Barnett & D. Booth (eds), 228–42. London: Routledge.

35 One view of Native education in the Northwest Territories, Canada

JOHN JAMIESON

Introduction

Until recently (see Devine 1994), Canadian aboriginals have been the forgotten, silent minority. Many in the public knew that small pockets of Indians existed, but believed that their culture was lost, or not worth saving. It was better to absorb them into the dominant culture. In 1991 and 1992, however, Canada gained more insight into the issues facing aboriginal people than the whole of the past 400 years had provided. There was scarcely an evening newspaper or media broadcast without discussion of changing Canada's constitution through Meech Lake or the blockade of an Indian reservation by Natives to prevent a municipal government from ploughing under an ancestral graveyard to make a golf course. The attempt by the Province of Quebec to push through a second phase of the giant James Bay Hydroelectric Project and flood hundreds of square miles of traditional hunting-grounds of Cree Indians, without any consultation of the Cree or environmental assessment, became an issue of international proportion and involvement, and is indeed a fight postponed to the future.

As the Canadian public is becoming more aware that aboriginals fiercely want to retain their roots, their exclusion from a central place in Canadian society is coming to a close. The Government of the Northwest Territories (NWT), dominated by elected aboriginal politicians, possesses some of the best opportunities to place aboriginal culture in central focus, especially through the education system.

Although aboriginals are certainly gaining more power over education, the system is, however, still dominated by white teachers, university-educated in southern Canada and mostly temporary residents in the north. The production of qualified aboriginal teachers is simply not enough to keep up with the increase in the school population.

This importation of southern teachers inhibits the development of a locally sensitive education system: such teachers are usually sent directly to their teaching communities; teacher orientations, if available, barely touch the complexity of aboriginal culture that the teachers will find in their new community; and once in the classroom, the teacher finds that integrating cultural concepts into the curriculum, advocated by all territorial boards of education, is difficult. Indeed, there is no 'cultural curriculum', no programme of studies on culture for teachers to consult.

To affirm the integral role of aboriginal cultures in Canadian society, all such cultures need a sense of pride; this can only be accomplished when the activities and interests of each community, its sciences and arts, are directly served by its schools. This need is recognized in the Baffin Divisional Board of Education, located in the eastern Arctic. It is the most progressive Board in northern Canada in advancing cultural programming, as shown by its three mandates: to develop a strong Inuit identity of pride and self-confidence; to develop a knowledge of and skills in aspects of Inuit culture; and to develop competency in the Inuktitut language.

Achieving these goals is, however, a major problem. Baffin has made major gains in producing books in the Native language, Inuktitut, and producing learning units based on Inuit cultural themes, such as the programme entitled 'Piniaqtavut'. Piniaqtavut is to form a core of learning for kindergarten through grade 9. The first units, on polar bears, and dogs and the Inuit, will integrate science, Inuktitut language and studies of Inuktitut society into one theme. Each unit is contained in a box of materials, but the production of packages is time-consuming, expensive, and such boxes may be quickly set aside as entropy takes over in the school.

A better route to success is for each community to decide on their own needs and initiatives. The development of such programmes faces some specific obstacles, however. Much of the traditional knowledge about aboriginal culture is difficult to gather for more general educational purposes. It exists in oral transmissions between individuals, within families or small communities and may have validity only for a limited geographic area. And language and concepts vary between communities, making it difficult for Inuit staff from outside a community to work with the information.

Although there is no way in which a Board of Education can extend this highly particular information to teachers over a wide area, there are means for teachers to allow the community to set the agenda for inclusion of local knowledge into the curriculum. Delving into prehistory is one method which allows activities to be extracted which spur scientific investigation, promote literacy and yet allow a cultural appreciation to be developed by the students.

Sanikiluaq: a case study

Sanikiluaq, a community of 380 Inuit in 1985, is the only community on the Belcher Islands in the southeastern corner of Hudson Bay. Until 1985 the cultural programme at Nuiyak School was minimal and uninspiring. Past administrators had allowed the local education council to set the agenda for cultural inclusion, but no one person was designated as organizer and no attempts were made to develop leadership on the council. On some occasions Inuit hunters would arrive at the school unannounced to take the boys hunting. One afternoon per week was designated for the girls to learn sewing; the girls became quite bored with the same activities week after week and behaviour became a problem. Hunting for the boys and sewing for the girls was, unfortunately, the common theme for most schools in the territories. Some schools would spend their cultural funds all at once in the spring with a picnic or one week of camping.

In 1985, the Inuit staff of Nuiyak School and I (the principal, appointed after three years as a regular classroom teacher) decided to get some hands-on cultural activities started immediately. We never knew that the end result would become a driving force which would preoccupy the school and the community and encourage it to reach out internationally to invigorate the programme yet further.

As the logo and name for the school, Nuiyak, is a throwing-board with a bird dart, hunting equipment used on the islands until the 1960s, our school seemed symbolically prepared to study prehistoric processes. The Belcher Islands have been occupied by Dorset and Thule cultures and present-day Inuit for close to 3000 years. Remnants of sodhouses are found around the islands, and a grouping of over thirty houses is within 1 km of Sanikiluaq.

We wanted to inform the community that Inuit culture and prehistory were of prime importance in the school. We wanted a large, visible symbol outside the school to serve as our organizing theme. We therefore decided to build a sodhouse behind the school, to conform as closely as possible to the real houses found around the islands. We had little information on sodhouse construction, but we used shovels, picks and wheelbarrows to dig into the soil. It seemed that the original houses were excavated to approximately 30 cm depth and were 3–4 m wide. Rocks and sod were bermed up the sides to approximately 1 m. The original roofs were probably underlaid with logs, but our source of logs was too far from the community, and so we substituted pressure-treated wood as supports for the sod. A tunnel led to the house; it was made lower than the living areas to conserve heat in the dwelling. Flat rocks formed the floor and were arranged around the circumference of the walls.

It took several months of construction using a few hours of work per day to complete the exterior. Two Royal Canadian Mounted Police constables assisted in hauling sod with the students and the hamlet manager provided a frontend loader to haul rocks. Many students returned home with muddy and wet clothing after their work, but not one of their parents complained!

Once the dwelling was intact, the students faced the problem of deciding how it was to be furnished. The Inuk cultural instructor, Mina Inuktaluk, took over and built a cooking and drying platform, and covered the sides and ceiling with seal skins. This made a considerable difference since it reflected light back into the dwelling, giving it a warmer feeling. Mina also appeared with a *qudluk* or soapstone lamp which was of unknown age. This required a source of oil and wicks.

For a short period of time in the 1980s, all new schools constructed in the NWT were supplied with skin preparation rooms. These rooms had a wash-down floor, with a drain, an exterior door allowing easy access for bringing seals and other animals into the room, and a freezer for the storage of animal products. This room was highly prized and used on a regular basis at our school to deliver cultural programmes that required the butchering of animals, or other activities that were messy. We used it to produce oil for the soapstone lamp, by rendering the fat of some beluga whales that had recently been shot. Mina considered beluga to be a much better fuel than seal oil. An Elder in the community, Lucassie Ohaytook, was brought into the school to teach the process of making a bag from an intact seal. The body of the seal was cut away from the skin from the inside of the animal and pulled through a hole in the head. This created an intact bag from the seal and a receptacle for the fat. The bag was placed in a rock cavity near the sodhouse, and covered with logs for the summer. The maggot-coated bag was removed in the autumn and the oil collected for use in the seal-oil lamps.

During the winter, the students used the sodhouse for sleeping. They were trained in the use of the soapstone lamp and discovered very quickly that establishing an efficient wick system, using moss or fluff from arctic fireweed, would allow the lamp to function for a long period of time before it had to be adjusted. Pieces of frozen, fresh seal fat were added to the lamp to replenish the oil.

The students conducted some scientific studies, estimating oil consumed per hour and comparing inside and outside temperature to determine efficiency of lamp use, and they used a psychrometer to determine relative humidity with and without lamps. In addition to the science component, the students used the experience as the basis of speculating about how life might have existed in the prehistoric past. More contemporary snowhouses, or igloos, were also constructed by Elders working with the students for a comparison with the sodhouses.

The sleeping experiences spawned a series of new skills that had to be mastered. Perhaps the most important was the creation of fire. Several Elders were asked to demonstrate how fire was created before matches. Silatik Meeko, a matriarchal figure in the community who liked to come into the school and work with the students, had observers spellbound when she took her *kamiks* (boots) off and removed some grass from between layers of duffle socks. The grass was finely ground, almost powder. She said that all women would pack grass into the *kamiks* to help insulate them, but just as importantly, it would be used for fire-making. Silatik produced some burnt cloth from a small tin box and placed it on the grass. A small piece of chert-like rock was struck against the side of an old file and sparks fell onto the cloth. Almost instantly the embers started to smoke and very quickly Silatik nested the ember and had a fire going. It was a remarkable experience.

None of the Elders could remember making friction fire with a bow-drill, a technique used in the past by the Inuit, and so that became a new technique for the sodhouse students to master. Fortunately, we were able to make contact with a loose network of specialists in the United States who practised prehistoric skills, and I learned from one, Erett Callahan of Virginia, how to make fire by friction, flint-knapping, pottery-making, bow and arrow construction, sinew-making, the preparation and use of adzes, bone needles, microblades, antler glue, and cooking techniques.

I brought the friction fire technique back to the islands and the students made a bow from caribou antler and rope from square flipper seal hide, and, using this bow with drills and soapstone handpieces made in shop class, they made a fire. There was great excitement as the brownish powder at the base of the drill slowly turned to black and wisps of smoke appeared. The fireboard was tilted back and the black heart of an ember appeared before it was nested inside dried grass. When the students started blowing through the nest, I instantly thought of ancient Dorset carvings from the Arctic which depict faces with rounded lips – almost an exact image of our fire-making.

Our programme continued to develop, looking for activities to include. Since the Belcher Island Inuit were known for their eider-duck parkas, we asked some women to come into the school and work with the senior girls to show them the skills. The first skill was turning the hide inside out and sucking the fat from the skin and spitting it out. This is a long procedure, but critical for success. The whole school was involved in the activity. Classes would take turns sucking on the skins. The kindergarten class would start the day off and we would work through the classes and end with the grade 10 students. The women supervising also did a majority of the work, and we were actually able to see them gain in weight during the three weeks of preparation.

Dr Jill Oakes of the University of Manitoba, an expert on arctic skin clothing and footwear construction, came to the islands and worked with the women to make several coats which were put on a tour of Canada and are now stored in the Canadian Museum of Civilization. Jill also prepared a video of the process which is available to schools.

As the prehistoric and contemporary cultural activities became more numerous, it became necessary to establish a conceptual framework for exploring these skills. We developed a 1–2–3–4–5–6 system for constantly reminding ourselves of the various approaches. The numbers stand for: (1) one land bridge; (2) two peoples (Dorset and Thule); (3) three ecosystems (freshwater, terrestrial, marine); (4) four seasons (summer, autumn, winter, spring); (5) five cultural universals (food, shelter, clothing, family, beliefs); and (6) six materials (bone, skin, wood, stone, clay, fibre). Although probably not an exact scientific and/or cultural interpretation, this cultural algorithm allowed us to place our programme in perspective and focus our activities on areas which would yield more information and, therefore, more pride in the past accomplishments of the culture.

The framework allowed us to use Elders' knowledge in a very specific manner, and also suggested future research. On one occasion two Elders were brought into the school to discuss the food sources in the 1920s–1950s throughout the four seasons. The first concept the Elders explained was the control of land by various families. Families would have loose control of various parts of the islands across the seasons: one springtime location for char-fishing, another location in winter for ice-fishing, and so on. The Elders explained that this mechanism prevented overharvesting of areas that resulted from the geographic separation of gathering locations. Only sea-hunting was a shared environment.

To these Elders, the issue of transportation, not included in our original framework, was one of the most significant aspects of their culture, and so information about the co-operative production of kayaks, tools, ownership of materials, the social sharing of means of hunting, and extended family camps became integrated into the discussion. They described how families moved around the islands as the seasons, and therefore available foods, changed – such as the arrival of snow and Canada geese.

The students were able to take the knowledge of camps outlined by the Elders and establish a relationship with *polynas* (permanently open patches of water in the Arctic, caused by currents) and seasonal cracks that exist around certain parts of the islands. The location of Dorset and Thule dwellings could be related to some *polynas*, but not all, suggesting that the dwellings may not have been occupied at certain times of year, or an alternative food source was available.

The Elders also translated all the names of the camps and listed the food sources on a large map which we enclosed in a plexiglass cover on the school wall. Then our cultural instructors made a list of the foods that the students were eating at home on a daily basis and compared the subsistence of families who obtained most of their food from the land and from the co-op store.

Spotted around the islands are a series of lichen-covered stone traps possibly used by Thule to trap foxes. Elders knew how to operate the traps, although no one could remember anyone ever using them. Johnny Meeko, one of the cultural instructors, built a stone trap along with the students that resembled the ones around the community. A flat slab of stone served as a door, which was secured by a rope that went over the top of the structure and was attached to a stick inside the back of the trap to which a small piece of bait was attached. The students had a great time as dogs entered the trap, grabbed the bait and had the door slide down behind them. The children spent endless hours after school playing with the trap. They would load it with meat, or potato chips, or any other food which would entice dogs. We now wonder why the local dog-catcher would ever need anything more than this!

As our successes increased, I saw the need to get all the Inuit staff working on a programme that would establish an underlying philosophy for cultural education on our island and so develop techniques which would enable the Native staff to run the cultural programme without a white administrator. It must be emphasized here that Native staff do not control the budgets in the schools. White administrators dispense the funds and the goals of southern education administrators do not always mesh with Native staff or community. It was important therefore that native staff have the skills to secure resource material and the encouragement to push their cultural programmes with administrators, without fear.

After two years of prodding, the Arctic College Teacher Education Programme gave our school permission to teach a special projects course which would involve all our Inuit staff, including the secretary. Secretaries are among the more important people in the school, since they make many contacts for bringing resource people into the school, and can establish an atmosphere in the administrator's office just by questioning school policy.

The programme expands

Our course included thirteen sections, focusing on cultural skills which we would translate into concrete school practices: goals of the Board of Education, objectives of our cultural programme, dynamics of acquiring resources, conceptualizing the cultural programme, instructional strategies, how students learn, designing activity strategies, multimedia, reconstructing aboriginal artefacts, land programmes, an idealized northern school, culture theory, and practicum.

The 1–2–3–4–5–6 framework was applied across the grades, but varied according to the cognitive level of the student. For example, the archaeological concept of a land bridge was presented to staff and discussed. An Elder was invited in and asked about how Inuit arrived on the islands and other information about previous residents along with or before the Inuit. With this knowledge in hand, the staff established a method for presenting students with the concept that people 'move'. At the grade 9/10 level (age 15–19), the students would evaluate the highest level of learning, which would encompass the idea of the original people crossing the land bridge from Asia, but this would not be used at lower grades. The grade 1/2 teacher established the concept of moving by using people entering and leaving the nursing station and co-op. Tables were made on large paper with headings of names, time in and time out. The concept of time was incorporated along with the concept that certain times are associated with more movement. The grade 3/4/5/6 students were shown how people moved in the community because they needed a larger house for a growing family, because of marriage, the renovation or building of houses, and relocation due to death. The grade 7/8/9 teacher discussed movement to and from the islands, as various families had migrated from northern Quebec, and showed how these families brought new words, hunting skills and cultural norms to the community. Movement to the south of Canada to acquire skills was also covered.

At no time, however, was an archaeological view considered better than a view generated by Elders. The staff became united on the movement concept and each staff member knew what the other teachers were doing.

During the course, the Inuit staff also translated the most important words in this programme into Inuktitut syllabics. This was a major advance: the words were placed on computer disk along with the activities and ideas they described. Stories and pictures posted on the school walls depicted experiences around the sodhouse and described them in Inuktitut.

All the Inuit staff felt some ownership and responsibility for the direction of the cultural programme in the school and this encouraged them to suggest topics that could become subjects for the school to investigate with students. The change in attitude in the school was refreshing: twenty years of teaching had left me exhausted with educational experts who fly north promulgating their new theories, trying to excite staff, then fly away with nothing left that can be translated into classroom practice. Our cultural course allowed practice to flow from theory and left a trail of success. If more schools allowed their aboriginal staff to influence the curriculum more by working towards producing relevant schooling, perhaps job satisfaction would be attained for all involved.

The important role of Elders

One of the most successful aspects of our programme was involving Elders in the school curriculum, initiated by a grant to promote literacy in the community. Since the mandate did not specifically state literacy in English, we decided to direct it towards Inuktitut and to invite the Elders to determine what the children should learn about Inuit culture. The twenty Elders who attended a meeting at the school produced a stream of ideas, of which five were agreed on: making model kayaks, eiderskin coats, and *kamiks* (boots) and recording stories and legends from the past.

Young people not enrolled in school were also asked to participate in the literacy project: many participants were young women with children who found it difficult to come to school without babysitters. We solved the problem by hiring some ladies to establish a six-week childcare service in our kindergarten room, which was empty for half the day. It was a nice feeling to have the school populated with babies and Elders – it was a true community school.

The Elders came to school and worked with a small group of writers. Elders demonstrated an activity and the young people worked on translating the activity into Inuktitut and also learned the process by participating in the craft or activity. Students enrolled in the regular school programme also formed part of the writing teams.

The grade 10 boys became very interested in the model kayak-making. The Elder, Lucassie Ohaytook, explained that in the old days fathers would make kayaks for their children. The children would walk along the shore to collect small sculpins, put them in the 39-inch kayaks, and ferry them back to camp to be cooked on the camp-fire. The writers recorded the process in Inuktitut and the boys made models and covered them with sealskin.

An unforeseen byproduct of the activity was the selling of the kayaks. The first model kayak sold for $250. Later on, equipment was added to the models, including sails of the kind used to travel between the islands and northern Quebec, weapons, sealskin bags, sinew and other artefacts. The selling price for a customized kayak was $450.

The interest in the models led naturally to an attempt to make a real, full-sized kayak. A special grant from the Baffin Divisional Board of Education permitted the hiring of Elders to build it. The community, by consensus, picked three Elders for the project, and the school picked six senior boys to work alongside the Elders. The Elders set up a tent and fireplace at the back of the school, near the sodhouse. There was tea on the fire at all times, along with lots of bannock made by the students.

Since the last kayak was made on the islands almost thirty years before, many had never seen a kayak constructed. There was constant visitation by the community to the back of the school. It was gratifying to watch our students work with the Elders and see members of the community sitting around drinking tea, laughing and commenting on the activities. Although the Elders were told that they could start at nine, tea was brewing at six in the morning.

Hunters brought fresh sealskins to the school a week before construction started. The skins were placed inside another skin and tied. The stuffed bag was placed in front of the door and the students were asked to walk on the bag as they entered into the school. This was great fun for the children, and ensured constant churning of the skins. The Elder women said that it was necessary for the skins to stretch and this could be done only by this method of fermentation.

The frame was covered with sealskins on one day. A group of eight women, mostly Elders, worked in shifts and took nine hours to complete the water-proof stitching. Only raw beluga skin, muktuk, an Inuit delicacy, could stop the activity for a few minutes of enjoyment. The community brought food to the women throughout the day. The Elder men who constructed the kayak watched all the activities and tried to direct the women, but ended by being scolded and mocked.

Lucassie Ohaytook, one of the Elders involved in building the kayak, instructed all the students in some basic kayak procedures. A shallow lake allowed the staff to monitor students and everyone got an opportunity to paddle. It was a great experience to see their faces shine with pride as they sliced through the water. The catch phrase was 'This is history!' All the students had their pictures taken in the kayak and presented to their families. The older students donned suits used in scuba-diving and used the kayak in salt water, making the experience more realistic. Lucassie described hunting and sailing techniques from his younger years.

The hunters in the village immediately wanted to use the kayak to hunt beluga whales. They said that the kayak could be manoeuvred beside the beluga without frightening them, which was much more efficient than chasing them around with a motorboat. Two hunters used the kayak on the lakes in the summertime to collect birds' eggs on small islands. The second hunter was either stowed inside the kayak, or rode on top, spread-eagle fashion.

Lucassie was brought back into the school to construct a sealskin float or *avataq* with the students. The float was used to keep freshly harpooned animals on the surface. Lucassie listed the other tools required for seal-hunting from the kayak and a new set of activities was generated, including construction of a sail the following year.

As our confidence was increasing, and students and Elders were interacting continuously, we found that there were insufficient funds in our school budget to finance new projects. In addition, the bureaucratic procedures of the Finance Department of the Board of Education frustrated our cultural programme constantly. The Board of Education wanted to be responsible for our payment of Elders; unfortunately, the Board had a two-week delay in processing cheques and being 1000 miles from their headquarters added additional time. Elders wanted to be paid for their consultations and work as soon as they had completed their efforts, and we were unable to accom-modate them. Using this form of payment would make many Elders shy away from working in the school. In addition, it was difficult to secure materials in town. The suppliers wanted to be paid for their materials im-mediately, as was their right. They did not understand purchase orders.

It is an unfortunate fact of life that there will be little or no local control of education until finance is controlled at the local level. Rhetoric abounds from the Boards of Education that communities control their education, but, while finance is controlled by the Boards, this is just not true. To get around this situaion, the Inuit staff and I formed the Tuniq Project which we labelled a community group. As a community venture the Project was able to receive charitable donations and so allowed us to solicit funding from outside the educational establishment.

One of our first projects using grant money was the construction of a two-person kayak – a new challenge for our kayak-building skills. Our grade 10 boys became quite versatile at construction during this second kayak and now have the skills to build a kayak with only supervision from Elders.

The Tuniq Project received funding to bring an archaeologist from the Prince of Wales Northern Heritage Centre to the islands. The main purpose was to have some of the students hired and learn some archaeology skills, perhaps leading to a resident becoming interested in pursuing a career in archaeology. An archaeological survey found that one site of thirty-one Thule sodhouses had been too disturbed by previous salvaging to be of use, but excavation at three other Dorset sites proved an interesting and informa-tive experience, although very few artefacts were found. The students thought it unusual to find the Dorset sites high on the hills until they under-stood the effects of isostatic rebound from glaciation. The students also discovered that field archaeology was tiring and exacting work.

Reflecting back on our 1–2–3–4–5–6 cultural framework, we found a heavy concentration on Thule culture, but a lack of information about the earlier Dorset culture. Around the islands there are several tent rings that seem to be only 1–2 m in diameter. These sites are several kilometres inland, which would be the location of old Dorset campsites. The Elders say that the people who built these were the *tunnit*, the little people who they say lived on the islands before the Inuit.

Since the Thule sodhouse had seeded various activities, we decided that building a small skin and wood-frame dwelling similar to a Dorset construction might be a way of starting to expand our knowledge of the Dorset. Driftwood was collected and lashed with hide rope. A stone platform complete with a vertical walled hearth, perfectly simulating the archaeological remains on the islands, formed the floor. Caribou hides formed the sides, with an opening for venting smoke from the inside.

The small stone rings that probably represent the Dorset dwellings were quite isolated from each other, very different from the numerous Thule sodhouses found together. It seemed that the Dorset people were not very social or perhaps did not want to start another camp too close to an earlier one. The students immediately mentioned that a similar situation exists on the islands when they are camping: a hunter must not put his tent on the same spot where there had been a tent in the past, or risk sickness befalling his family. Thus the students had the example of a contemporary practice which might have validity for a prehistoric activity.

The students learned very quickly about the living conditions that the Dorset people experienced. The inside was very cramped, perhaps explaining why Elders believed the *tunnit* slept with legs up against the sides of their tents. Tending the fire to make the smoke rise vertically and out of the tent was extremely difficult. Another discovery was the fact that the tent became covered with snow very quickly, making us excavate a tunnel down into the snow. In this way the wind formed the insulation around the shelter – serving the same purpose as the snow in Thule igloos.

There is no better way for us to depict a past culture than to make similar artefacts, but where this is not possible casts of artefacts, objects that can be handled safely, are another valuable learning resource. The Archaeological Survey of Canada (ASC), with help from the Baffin Divisonal Board of Education, allowed Luke McCarthy, their casting technician, to come to the islands to produce casts of Dorset and Thule artefacts. The grade 10 students were able to learn the complete casting procedure, embedding the original in wax, making the silicone mould, filling it with epoxy and finally painting it to resemble the original. At last count, the school had over 160 cast artefacts on permanent display in the school, giving us one of the best Dorset and Thule collections outside a few museums.

A Thule bow-drill made from ivory, found in Arctic Bay, NWT, is a remarkable artefact which we cast and used to give the students an instant snapshot of the culture. It is engraved with domestic, hunting and warring scenes, whales, caribou, kayaks, tents, perhaps bolas, and other images. Elders were also asked to interpret the designs for information that we missed.

The sodhouse gave the school a community visibility to start our programme and our attention turned to the inside of a newly constructed school. The Prince of Wales Northern Heritage Centre (PWNHC), in Yellowknife, NWT, allowed arctic archaeologist Chuck Arnold to come to the school and make preliminary sketches for constructing display cases for cast archaeological artefacts, student-made displays and prehistoric dioramas. Using the PWNHC's drawings, the school staff constructed display cases. The foyer of the school set the school objectives. Besides the display cases packed with artefacts and a prehistoric diorama depicting the history of the islands, the walls were covered with cultural artefacts: grass and willow mats and baskets, drying racks, student-made Dorset and Thule harpoons, fishing lures, kamiks, skin bags, face masks, leather drinking-cups, and an old weathered kayak frame. The hallways were dedicated to themes: one wall of photographs showed students working in cultural programmes, another was devoted to Elders, another to Robert Flaherty, the first white man to visit the island. A 30 ft timescale for the history of early hominids to the present, marking off significant events such as the making of fire, the European discovery of the New World, extended our view of prehistory and put our fire-making and flint-knapping skills in perspective. All the displays and photographs were protected by plexiglass.

Successes and failures

The Belcher Island's experience with Inuit was successful for a number of reasons. From 1982 to 1985 I was a regular classroom teacher with a burning desire to bring more relevance to the school programme, but with no influence over the curriculum and thus no ability to bring about change. From 1985 to 1989, however, I was principal and so able to control the budget and direct the funds provided for cultural study. It was therefore possible for us to hire and treat Elders who were required to teach a cultural skill in the same professional way as substitute teachers or consultants, since they were filling both roles.

Although Boards of Education are a layer of bureaucracy which can frustrate school programmes primarily through their control of school funding, the Baffin Divisional Board of Education was completely supportive of the activities and strongly encouraged integration of cultural concepts in the school. And although they did not have the human or material resources for developing our programme, they found ways of supporting it financially wherever possible.

The local education authority, composed primarily of hunters and several Elders, supported the activities and acted as conduits to bring elders into the school. The Elders felt a sense of pride in working with the children and they always commanded attention when they were demonstrating activities.

There were few white children in the school, and consequently few white families in the community. This meant that there were no complaints about cultural instruction as part of the school curriculum. Such complaints are heard, unfortunately, because most white families in the north do not want the local culture to be part of the school programme. There is a tendency for aboriginal culture to be viewed with disdain when it is incorporated into school curricula, that cultural inclusion is fine, but it should not interfere with school programmes and it should be done outside school hours, either by the families or local cultural associations (see also Ahler 1994; Belgarde 1994; Blancke & Slow Turtle 1994; Pwiti 1994; Wandibba 1994).

Ironically, the criticism of cultural programmes in most cases is correct. They are delivered without enthusiasm, depth or conceptualization. They lack proper funding and there is no attempt to build a network with the Elders and other aboriginal stakeholders in the community.

At the grade 10 level in Sanikiluaq, this did not happen because there were two white teachers strongly committed to cultural programmes, who delivered all the academic and industrial arts courses to the students. This produced a strong integration of content across the disciplines, and included the community, through its Elders, in the curriculum.

But when the system depends on the individual initiative of a culturally diverse staff with a high degree of mobility, the problem of continuity is very real, and deeply felt by Native teachers. The Inuit staff at Nuyiak School, for example, had a forum for commenting on the conduct of the school and they used it to indicate that they felt very comfortable with the new direction of the school, but also very concerned that future administrators who didn't care about cultural programmes would destroy all that they might create.

This is, unfortunately, what happened in the Belcher Islands, for in 1989 I, too, left and a series of administrators took over the school. Unfortunately, their views of cultural programmes differed significantly and although the education council tried to resist the changes, they found themselves without any control of their own school – and many of the educational and social gains, so important to the community as a whole, were lost.

A future for the north – traditional and scientific knowledge for schools

Teachers in the north derive their concepts of 'culture' and 'nature' from many perspectives, with their own, predominantly southern experience having the most influence. Yet these same teachers control the way that these critical social concepts are conveyed to students from other cultures. Aboriginals possess their own distinctive concepts of nature and society, and these should also be given at least an equal status. When an Inuit hunter kills a goose, he removes some tail feathers and sticks them into the snow as a symbol of respect for nature, and showing his involvement in the complete process that supplied him the animal.

Mechanisms must therefore be investigated for keeping education in contact with the aboriginal and scientific community. There has been very little structuring of communication between these important endeavours.

Occasionally a researcher will pass through a northern community and a chance meeting will reveal some knowledge which is applicable to the class-room. If such a relation could be formalized, it would give our students an exposure to real and exciting research, and to possible career opportunities.

Many of the scientists doing research in the north have limited resources for making their endeavours known to the general population, but many have a sensitivity to the aboriginal people of the north and desire to establish the importance of their research. The educators have a desire to make their instruction appropriate to their students, but often lack the resources found in small communities. It might be of significant importance to establish a firmer linkage between knowledge-holders in the traditional and contemporary forms of science and culture.

Indeed, there is a wealth of prehistoric, historic and contemporary aborigi-nal processes which should be part of our northern school programmes. They can be used to demonstrate a majority of our social and scientific concepts in an exciting fashion, as we have seen at Sanikiluaq, but such efforts are limited by the lack of knowledge required from both scientists and aboriginals. Many view traditional aboriginal knowledge and western scientific knowledge as mutually exclusive and therefore inappropriate to study at the same time. Unfortunately, neither of them taken in isolation will produce the quality students that we want graduating from our small communities.

It is most important, therefore, that everyone should recognize the value of aboriginal social and scientific practices to the country as a whole. In the Northwest Territories it is rare to have Elders consulted about environmental affairs. Although Elders have a reservoir of knowledge which has been handed down for generations, and they are sensitive to environmental change, they are not looked upon as very 'scientific'. Consequently, the majority of scientists cannot work with traditional knowledge as part of their research, a problem well demonstrated by the 'missing caribou' controversy in the NWT in the early 1980s.

At this time Inuit hunters were considered responsible for the decline of the caribou herds in the western Hudson's Bay barrenlands. The hunters told the Government that the herd was in fact increasing and certain environmental factors had caused the herd to move to an area beyond the area surveyed by the Government. Although temporarily displaced, the herds would be attracted back. The Government did not believe the hunters and several court cases resulted in prosecution of Inuit for exceeding the limit of caribou that they were allowed. In the following summer, however, the herd suddenly increased beyond a level which the Government could account for, using their last survey. What this showed was that the hunters were in fact correct. They had visualized a geometry of herd behaviour which was empirically deter-mined. They had the picture clearly. Disrupting one small factor could lead to a large disturbance in the herd. Government scientists had failed to take into acount the knowledge of others who had a different relationship with the herds and had therefore failed to recognize a pattern.

Cultural programmes must therefore be part of the school programme, especially since the Government has forced attendence, removing children from their families and displaced them from more traditional activities. And it is essential that the students be grounded in strong skills in mathematics, science and literacy, learned in the ways of their own communities.

Perhaps a science exam of the future might include the following questions:

1 Preparing the bottom of skin boots requires both mechanical and chemical effects on the skin. Describe the process on the skin and the end results.
2 What physical property of sinew makes it ideal for sewing?
3 Sealskins required for kayaks require a period of anaerobic fermentation and mechanical agitation for approximately five days before sewing. What properties are added to the skin? Extension: suggest a plausible hypothesis for the discovery of this unusual process of placing sealskins in a closed sealskin bag for five days in front of a tent door and having people walk over it!
4 What are the critical points involved in making friction fire? Outline one point using your knowledge of physics and/or chemistry.
5 Alaska and Canada selected two completely different ways to transport gas and oil in pipelines. List advantages and disadvantages of both systems. The environment and effects are critical.
6 When given a preference, some Inuit fishermen would select a red fishnet over a similar green net. Outline the physics of this seemingly empirically derived observation. Extension: derive an experiment, which does not involve surgery, which would determine whether fish discriminate colours.
7 Why does the medical community argue against aboriginal midwifery? What are the arguments for both sides? Extension: can people be effectively informed about midwifery?
8 Suppose that an archaeologist has unearthed human remains from an isolated area of the NWT. Outline your reasons for permitting or disallowing research to continue. Should there be a process for overviewing archaeological research in the NWT?

There must be continuing efforts to make cultural and science instruction a collaboration among Elders, teachers, aboriginals and scientists. These individuals, working together, can increase an awareness of aboriginal culture and science more efficiently than when it is taught in isolation and, ultimately, help to bring aboriginal people into their rightful place in the centre of our mutual cultural experience.

References

Ahler, J. G. 1994. The benefits of multicultural education for American Indian schools: an anthropological perspective. In *The Presented Past: heritage, museums and education*, Stone, P. G. & B. L. Molyneaux (eds), 453–9. London: Routledge.

Belgarde, M. J. 1994. The transfer of American Indian and other minority community college students. In *The Presented Past: heritage, museums and education*, Stone, P. G & B. L. Molyneaux (eds), 460–77. London: Routledge.

Blancke, S. & Cjigkitoonuppa John Peters Slow Turtle 1994. Traditional American Indian education as a palliative to western education. In *The Presented Past: heritage, museums and education*, Stone, P. G & B. L. Molyneaux (eds), 438–52. London: Routledge.

Devine, H. 1994. Archaeology, prehistory and the Native learning resources project, Canada. In *The Presented Past: heritage, museums and education*, Stone, P. G & B. L. Molyneaux (eds), 487–94. London: Routledge.

Pwiti, G. 1994. Prehistory, archaeology and education in Zimbabwe. In *The Presented Past: heritage, museums and education*, Stone, P. G & B. L. Molyneaux (eds), 338–48. London: Routledge.

Wandibba, S. 1994. Archaeology and education in Kenya: the present and the future. In *The Presented Past: heritage, museums and education*, Stone, P. G & B. L. Molyneaux (eds), 349–58. London: Routledge.

Index

adult education programmes and archaeology education in Kenya 350–1

Africa: legacy of colonial education 315, 316, 329–30: *see also* Benin, Cameroon, Kenya, Nigeria and Zimbabwe

Alberta (Canada): controversy over the teaching of native Canadian culture and history 486–7; Native Canadian role in school education 478–91; Native Learning Resources Project 478–91; Native Learning Resources Project and archaeology 483, 487–8: *see also* Canada and Native Canadians

alternative histories: in South Africa 31–6, 39, 42

anthropology: anthropological analysis of multicultural education in the USA 453–9; its role in assisting educators in the USA 456–8

Apalachicola valley public archaeology project, Florida (USA) 89–93

apartheid 30, 31, 33, 34, 35, 39–40, 41, 230, 235

apartheid history challenged 34–5, 39–40

archaeo-fiction: introduction of in French schools 375–81

archaeological information, dissemination of to the public: in Buenos Aires Province (Argentina) 113, 114; in the USA 65–9; in Zimbabwe 345

archaeology: archaeological interpretation and its political uses 270–1; attitude of history teachers to

archaeology in Cameroon 330–1; benefits of public education for archaeology in the USA 63, 65; and the challenging of social domination in Brazil 130–2; conception of the past 1–2; conflicts between archaeologists and educators 17–18; and the creation of a common heritage in India 299–300; critique of Zimbabwean archaeology 271, 272, 273; and culture resource management in the USA 64, 84–8; disciplinary bounds of, discussion 236–7; educating school teachers about archaeology in the USA 69–71; educational value of 16–17; excavations and school children in France 376–80; future of in Botswana 56–8; and history in South Africa 41; and the history syllabus in Zimbabwe 342; indigenous archaeologists, discussion of 449–50; looting of archaeological sites in the Lebanon 96–100; and museums in Cameroon 333–4; and the National Curriculum in England 388–91; and Native American museums 446–8; Native Canadian perception of 483–6; and the Native Learning Resources Project, Alberta, Canada 483–4, 487–8; its neglect in school curricula 17–18; and the neglect of blacks in Colombia 418–19, 432; and the presentation of the past 261; promotion of archaeology to the public in Benin 318, 322; the public and the destruction of archaeological

129–31; museums and social legitimation 124, 125, 128; role of education system in reproducing social hierarchy 120–1; role of museums in society 123–5: *see also* Latin America

Buenos Aires Province (Argentina): dissemination of archaeological information to the public 113, 114; elementary school education and archaeology 109, 114–15; ethnocentrism in education 114–15; history education 409–16; nationalism and education 413; primary education curriculum 409–13; primary education system 408; relationship between the public and archaeology 112; social context of recent history of Argentina 111–12; teachers' attitudes to history education 413–16: *see also* Latin America

Cameroon: archaeology education and schools 331–3; attitude of history teachers to archaeology 330–1; colonial legacy in education 329–30; education system 326–7; history syllabus in schools 328–9; museums and archaeology 333–4; public perception of archaeology 326; the place of archaeology in university education 327–8

Canada: archaeology education and Native Canadian cultural education 496–99, 501, 505; controversy over the teaching of native Canadian culture and history 486–7; Native Canadian cultural education 495–508; Native Canadian cultural education, appraisal of its achievements 506–7; Native Canadian elders, their role in cultural education 498, 499–500, 501, 502–4, 505, 506; Native Canadian perception of archaeology 483–6; Native Canadian role in school education in Alberta 478–91; Native Canadians and their defence of their heritage 488–90; Native Learning Resources Project, Alberta 478–91; Native Learning Resources Project, Alberta, and archaeology 483–4, 487–8; schools and Native Canadian

cultural education 496–508: *see also* Native Canadians

Colombia: archaeology and education 142–4; archaeology and the neglect of blacks 418–19, 432; cannibalism and the construction of racial stereotypes 402–3; denigration of indigenous cultures 400–3; differences in the social positions of blacks and Indians 420–1, 434–5; ethnocentrism in school textbooks 398–406; *mestizaje* 421, 429, 430; moves towards the greater recognition of the role of blacks in society 419–20; Museo del Oro (Gold Museum) 150–1; Museo del Oro (Gold Museum), and the construction of national identity 172–3; museums 150–1, 159–66; museums and archaeology education 172–7; museums and the neglect of blacks 418–19; museums and the use of workshops in education 174–7; museums for children 159–66; museums, achievements of 169–71; perspectives on blacks and Indians 421–2; postcolonial racial representation of blacks and Indians 430–5; postcolonial social position of blacks 432; public involvement in archaeological research in the Magdalena River region 139, 142–3, 145; racial representations in 398–406; relationship between museums and schools 150–1; social role of archaeology, discussion of 139, 142–3, 145; teaching packages and their use 153, 155–8; use of artefacts in teaching the past 153, 155–6, 163–5, 168; use of games in teaching the past 156–7; use of the past to create identity 159–60, 169: *see also* Latin America

colonial: era in Latin America 423–7; interpretation of Great Zimbabwe 338–9; legacy in education in Africa 315, 316, 329–30

community colleges (USA) 460–75: Native American controlled 470–3; Native American controlled, success of 472–3; problems with 462–3; reasons for Native American enrolment at 461–3: *see also* Native Americans

INDEX

Centennial College Libraries

Printed in the USA/Agawam, MA
January 13, 2012

563520.120